PRODUCT POLICY:
Concepts, Methods, and Strategy

Yoram J. Wind

The Wharton School
The University of Pennsylvania

PRODUCT POLICY:
Concepts, Methods, and Strategy

 ADDISON-WESLEY PUBLISHING COMPANY

Reading, Massachusetts

Menlo Park, California · London · Amsterdam · Don Mills, Ontario · Sydney

This book is in the
Addison–Wesley Series in Marketing

Library of Congress Cataloging in Publication Data

Wind, Yoram.
    Product policy.

    (Addison-Wesley marketing series)
    Bibliography: p.
    Includes index.
    1. Product management. 2. New products. I. Title.
II. Series: Addison-Wesley series in marketing.
HF5415.15.W56   658.5   80-20004
ISBN 0-201-08343-4

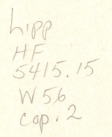

ISBN 0-201-08343-4
ABCDEFGHIJ—HA—8987654321

Preface

Product policy, despite its critical importance as a key marketing decision area, has not received the attention given to the more glamorous areas such as advertising. Yet, the product decisions of the firm are most critical for the firm's long term survival and growth. The purpose of this book is to offer a systematic coverage of the product policy area—its major concepts, methods and strategies.

Although designed as a textbook for MBA courses in product policy and as a reference book for practicing managers, the book offers a point of view which moves it away from an encyclopedic textbook toward a more personal manuscript. In particular, the unique features of the book are:

1. *Focus on all product decisions of the firm.* This requires an occasional shift in focus from that of corporate management (product portfolio decisions) to that of operating managers of new product activities or an established brand.

2. *Recognition of the importance of marketing research as input to product decisions.* Product decisions require a considerable amount of information concerning the market, competitors, and other environmental forces

—hence the heavy reliance on research. The book goes even further by advocating specific research procedures as the most appropriate for specific research needs.

3. *Managerial orientation.* The book, despite its strong reliance on research and other analytical tools for making better product decisions, is managerially oriented and nontechnical in nature.

4. *The need to tailor product policy approaches to the idiosyncratic characteristics of the decision maker and the firm.* The book does not offer a single *normative* theory of product policy. Various concepts, models, and approaches are discussed, and the need to tailor them to the unique management and corporate characteristics is recognized.

5. *An eclectic approach* to product policy. The approaches suggested in the text are eclectic and rely heavily on marketing concepts and approaches which have been found useful in real-world situations.

6. *Focus on creativity.* The traditional emphasis on evaluation procedures is augmented with continuous discussions on the need for and approaches to the generation of creative strategies and courses of action.

A final point of departure is the writing style and format which is aimed at relating the material to the reader not only in his or her role as a potential (or current) manager but also as a consumer. To this end, and to facilitate the comprehension of the material, the chapters do not end with the traditional "summary and conclusion" section (which tends to be a redundant section indicating the importance of the topics discussed in the chapter). Rather, the concluding section of each chapter includes a few assignments which, if conducted even in an intuitive way, would help evaluate the material discussed in the chapter and relate it to the reader's own experience.

The material in this book has been class-tested over the past six years in numerous product policy courses at the Wharton School. In addition, it has been field tested in a large number of executive seminars and subjected to the ultimate test of real-world applications in a number of firms. To the hundreds of students who read earlier versions of the book, the hundreds of executives who were exposed to sections of the material, and to those corporate executives who helped implement the approaches suggested here, this book owes its existence.

Given such wide exposure over a six year period, the list of people who actively contributed to the book and to whom I owe my thanks is too lengthy to be complete. I would like, therefore, to acknowledge only the few whose feedback and insight contributed most to the final form and content of the book. Professors Richard Cardozo (University of Minnesota), Charles Goodman (University of Pennsylvania), Vijay Mahajan (University of Pennsylvania), Franco Nicosia (University of California at Berkeley), and Vithala Rao (Cornell University) have all read major sections of the book and provided valuable insights and suggestions. Others, such as Neil Beckwith, Randy Batsell, and Scott Armstrong read and provided helpful comments on various chapters.

Of the numerous students who read the book in its earlier version, three have made especially significant contributions through their thoughtful comments and suggestions: Mary Seggerman, Chuck Nuel, and Roger Chiocchi.

The companies which supported most of the research reported here include Colonial Penn Group, Pfizer Pharmaceuticals, R.J. Reynolds Tobacco Company, IT&T Continental Baking, and others. The executives in these and other firms who helped design and test many of the concepts and approaches suggested here facilitated and enabled the preparation of a book which offers a mixture of the theoretical and the practical, and the building blocks for the design of conceptually defensible approaches (which utilize the latest in marketing concepts and techniques) to the solution of real world problems.

My thanks also go to Lynda Kenny, who provided invaluable support through her expert typing and thoroughness in administering the various details of preparing a book for publication, to Gwen Lipsky who helped organize the references, and to Billie Meeks for her continued cheerful and most helpful assistance. Finally, the major impact on my approach to product policy, research, and management has been that of my friend and colleague, Paul E. Green. To him, my academic mentor; my parents, my mentors in life; and to my family— Dina, John, and Lee—who provided the environment which enabled me to dedicate the time required for the completion of this book, this book is dedicated.

Philadelphia,   Y.W.
August 1981

Contents

Table of Contents

PART ONE

FOUNDATIONS

The first part of this book focuses on the foundations of product policy. An overview of the role of product policy in the management of a firm is followed by six chapters devoted to a discussion of:

- The tools available to help the manager make better product decisions (Chapter 2)
- The concept of product life cycle, its operationalization and relevance (Chapter 3)
- Classification-of-goods theories and their relationship to the concept of product positioning (Chapter 4)
- The concept of product portfolio (chapter 5)
- Product planning concepts and systems as central tools for managing new and existing products (Chapter 6)
- The changing environment and its impact on product decisions (Chapter 7)

Product Policy, Marketing, and Corporate Management____

INTRODUCTION

Place yourself in the role of a consumer and try to recall your last visit to a supermarket. How many new products did you notice in your most recent trip? Were some of the brands you like no longer on the shelves? In how many different sizes and packages were your favorite coffee and soft drinks available?

Let's continue now to a department store. Say you are considering the purchase of a new camera. Should you buy a pocket Instamatic today or should you wait for the introduction of a pocket 35 mm camera with a built-in flash or even perhaps a still camera that, like the Kodak XL 70 movie camera, needs no extra lighting? If you do buy a camera today, will a new model soon be introduced that renders yours obsolete? Whether you buy now or later, which model should you choose?

Reflecting on these and similar questions concerning almost any product and service, you may start to appreciate some of the managerial decisions which make up the realities of the marketplace.

The constant flow of new products to the market reflects one of the major efforts of modern management—the introduction of new products. Yet, how can management avoid such news headlines as "An Untimely End: How A New Product Was Brought to Market Only to Flop Miserably" (*The Wall Street Journal*, 1973). The story behind this headline was that of Brown–Forman's "Dry, White Whiskey" but it could have been about any one of the thousands of new products that have never made it to the marketplace or were withdrawn shortly after their introduction.

Since the early sixties, it has been true that:

Most new products are failures. Among the most important and effective United States companies the record shows that for every five products emerging from research and develop-

ment departments as technical successes, there is an average of only one commercial success. (Booz, Allen, and Hamilton, 1968)

This figure is even more alarming when one considers the very small percentage of R & D projects that prove successful and the even smaller percentage of new-product ideas that ever become R & D projects.

Can management improve the odds in the new-product-introduction game? How? What concepts and tools are available that can make this most crucial function of a firm more successful and prevent such failures as:

Ford's Edsel

Campbell's Red Kettle Soups

Dupont's Corfam

AT&T's Picture Phone

Colgate's Cue toothpaste

General Food's Post cereal with freeze-dried fruit

Bristol-Myer's aerosol Ipana toothpaste

Rhiengold's Gablinger Beer

Hunt's flavored catsups

Scott Paper's Babyscott diapers

Sylvania's colorslide TV viewer

Gillette's Nine Flags men's cologne

Warner–Lambert's Reef mouthwash

to mention just a few of many new product failures.

What about the sudden withdrawal of established products from the marketplace? Why did management decide to delete these products? Was it avoidable? Would it have been possible to reposition or modify the product?

In this book we attempt to answer these and other questions facing product management. More specifically, the book attempts to provide answers to four major sets of questions, corresponding to the four parts of the book. These questions are, in turn, divided into 20 specific questions which correspond to the chapters of the book and provide the framework for a better understanding of product management. These questions are:

I. What are the major concepts and tools relevant to product management?

   1. What are the interrelationships among product policy, marketing and corporate management? (Chapter 1)

   2. What can marketing, the behavioral sciences (including consumer behavior), management sciences, and marketing research contribute to product policy? (Chapter 2)

   3. What is product life cycle and how relevant is it to product policy? (Chapter 3)

   4. How can products be classified? How are "classification-of-goods" theories related to the new concept of product positioning, and what is the value of the product-positioning concept? (Chapter 4)

   5. What is the product portfolio concept, and how does it offer guidelines to the product decisions of the firm? (Chapter 5)

   6. What are the major ingredients of a product plan and how can it be put together? (Chapter 6)

   7. How do the changing economic, technological, cultural, legal, and political environments affect product management and how can management deal with the uncertainties resulting from these changing environments? (Chapter 7)

II. How can the management of new products be improved so that the chances of success for new products and services are increased?

   1. What should the new product-development system of the firm be like? (Chapter 8)

   2. How can new product ideas be generated? (Chapter 9)

   3. How can consumer reactions be used to screen and evaluate new product ideas? (Chapter 10)

   4. How can the technical, marketing, and economic feasibility of new products be evaluated? (Chapter 11)

   5. How can marketing help R&D design new products? (Chapter 12)

   6. Given a physical product, how can the entire product/marketing mix associated with it be developed and evaluated? (Chapter 13)

   7. What is the role of test market, and what is the value of various alternatives to test market? (Chapter 14)

   8. How can new product performance be forecast? (Chapter 15)

   9. How can a firm organize for new products? (Chapter 16)

III. How do managers get the most out of the firm's existing products?

   1. How do you organize for product management, and control product performance? (Chapter 17)

   2. Under what conditions and how should products be modified, repositioned, or deleted? (Chapter 18)

IV. Are the product policy concepts and approaches relevant to organizations other than manufacturers of frequently-purchased consumer goods? How can a firm move toward implementing these concepts and approaches?

1. What are the unique policy considerations of retailers, other intermediate marketing organizations, organizational (industrial) marketers, nonprofit organizations, small businesses, and firms with international operations? (Chapter 19)

2. How can the concepts and approaches discussed throughout the book be put together and implemented? (Chapter 20)

The reader of this book can follow the structure outlined above or, if one wants to begin with an overview of product planning, start with Chapter 6.

THE PRODUCT MANAGEMENT PROCESS

A marketing approach to product management can be simply defined as *generating, analyzing, organizing, planning, implementing, and controlling the organization's existing and new product efforts so as to satisfy the needs and wants of chosen customer segments, while satisfying organizational objectives.*

This definition has four major elements:

1. The management process of generation, analysis, organization, planning, implementation, and control
2. The focus on both existing and new products of the firm
3. The objectives of the firm's product efforts, which, according to the marketing concept, should be directed toward the identification and satisfaction of the needs and wants of selected market segments
4. A necessary constraint on the marketing concept in terms of the simultaneous achievement of the firm's own objectives

In making any product decisions—whether concerned with which new products to introduce, what positioning to seek, what branding policy to follow, how to modify existing products, or other issues—it might be useful to seek answers to seven key questions which constitute a framework for effective product decisions. These questions are based on the recognition that, in making product decisions:

- There are one or more objectives to be met.
- There are two or more alternative courses of action to be taken.
- There is a state of doubt as to which course of action will maximize the attainment of the objectives.
- The problem exists in an environment that affects the objectives, the admissible alternative courses of action, and the degree of uncertainty about the outcome of each course of action.
- There are one or more decision makers.

The seven questions are:

1. What decisions should be made?
2. What criteria should be used for evaluating these decisions?
3. What factors affect the decision?
4. How does each decision affect other marketing variables, and how do these variables affect the decision?
5. How does each decision affect other management functions, and how do those functions affect each decision?
6. What are the effects of the decision on the marketing system?
7. What theories, concepts, and tools are relevant and useful in improving the product decision process and its resulting product decision?

The first and most crucial step in product management is *specifying the relevant decisions*. For example, a packaging plan would involve decisions about the type of package, type of material in the package, package size, the label, the logo on the label, the color of the label and package, and others. Explicitly identifying all relevant decisions is a necessary first step in the product-decision-making process, when a product is defined in its broadest possible way as *a bundle of physical, service, and symbolic characteristics expected to yield satisfactions to the buyers and users.*

The product decisions to be specified are not limited, however, to the individual product or brand; they should take into account the firm's product line (a number of related products), product mix (combination of product lines), and product or business portfolio (assortments of product mixes). These distinctions are readily illustrated with the frequently-mentioned automotive example in which Nova is a brand of compact car; compact cars are a product, Chevrolet has a product line of compact cars (various models of Nova and other Chevy II models), and the compact car product line is part of the Chevrolet product mix, which includes the product lines of economy subcompact cars such as Chevette, luxury subcompact cars such as Monza, intermediate cars such as Chevelle, and sports cars such as Corvette.

Yet, the lines of demarcation among brands, products, product lines, product mixes, and product portfolios are quite arbitrary and depend on organizational position (that of the Chevrolet division or General Motors) as well as personal preferences in product classification systems. Product decisions are made at all corporate levels, from the president who is concerned with the corporate product portfolios to the brand manager who typically has little freedom to change the brand or add new brands but rather focuses on the development and, primarily, implementation of a marketing program to achieve the brand's performance objectives. Product decisions at the various levels are closely interdependent and require active top down *and* bottom up communications. Some examples of product decisions at various organizational levels are presented in Exhibit 1–1.

Identifying and quantifying the criteria for evaluating product decisions is the second step involved in any product decision. Profitability, sales growth, and market share are frequently used as the major criteria for evaluating brand or product performance, yet how should profitability be measured? Return on investment? Sales? Capital employed? Equity? And what is the weight of these objectives versus objectives such as market share and sales growth or the more ambiguous "social responsibility"? Given a multiplicity of objectives it is essential that before making product decisions, management should specify the criteria to be used in evaluating these decisions and the weight each criterion should be given. The criteria and their weight may vary from one company to another, from one time period to another and across products, but the explicit specification of criteria is essential.

Identifying the factors that affect the decisions. Four sets of factors should be considered with respect to the nature and magnitude of their effect on product decisions. These are:

1. *The consumer.* The anticipated consumer needs, wants, and reactions to given products are major factors in a firm's product decisions. The size of the market segment that is likely to buy and use the product; the consumer's reasons for buying or not buying it; and the demographic, socioeconomic, and psychographic characteristics of the target segments are all important to the firm's product decisions.

2. *The competitors.* Unless it is one of the few monopolistic firms, a firm must be con-

EXHIBIT 1–1

SOME ILLUSTRATIVE PRODUCT DECISIONS AT FOUR MANAGEMENT LEVELS

Management level	Typical product decision
Corporate (President, Executive Committee, . . .)	Corporate product portfolio including merger and acquisition decisions as ways of changing one's portfolio
Strategic Business Unit (SBU) (President of SBU, Division management, . . .)	SBU product portfolio (mix) including positioning of products, design of new product development process and product deletion decision
Product line (Group product manager)	Product line positioning, width and depth of product line Product modification and change Product deletion
Brand manager	Brand positioning Marketing strategy for the brand

cerned about the actions and likely reactions of their competitors. A clear picture of competitors' strengths and weaknesses (both "objectively" and as perceived by consumers) is essential to a firm's product decisions.

3. *The environmental factors.* The results of a firm's product and service decisions are constantly affected by the environment within which the firm operates, an environment determined by economic, technological, sociocultural and legal/political factors. The changes occurring in this environment, the institutions constituting it, and their activities should be taken into account in making any product/service decision. In addition, the specific marketing environment—type of distri-

bution, outlets, and promotional media available, and the nature, functions, and practice of the marketing institutions are all extremely important to a firm's product decisions.

4. *The firm's own objectives and resources.* Often ignored in explicit marketing analysis are the human, financial, and physical resources of the firm and the rules used to allocate them among products and services. No analysis of any decision is complete, however, without explicit consideration of these factors and the idiosyncratic strengths and weaknesses of the firm's marketing and other activities.

The effect of the decision on the other marketing variables. The effect of product decisions on the firm's other marketing decisions is of crucial importance to marketing management and is discussed in greater detail in the next section of this chapter.

Similarly, *the effect of the decision on the other management functions* of the firm is of utmost importance and, since it has been traditionally neglected in marketing texts, it is discussed in the last section of this chapter.

The effect of the decision on the marketing system. Whereas the effect of the entire marketing system on the product decisions of the firm has long been recognized, it is only recently that marketing managers have started to be concerned with the effect of their decisions and actions on the environment within which they operate. The growth of consumerism has no doubt led to some of this concern, but in product planning this concern with the actual and probable impact of a decision on the marketing system within which the firm operates (competitors' actions, consumer retaliation, government actions, and changes in the marketing practices of distribution outlets and media organizations, to mention just a few elements of the marketing system) should be considered explicitly.

The theories, concepts, past experience, and tools available for designing and implementing a better product decision process and marketing better product decisions. The likelihood of a product

decision's success does not lie in the financial resources of the firm. To emphasize that point, it is sufficient to mention the Edsel, Corfam, the picture phone, and RCA computers, all of which failed, despite the financial strength of Ford, Dupont, AT&T, and RCA. Increasing the likelihood of good results in the product arena lies, to a very large extent, in management's ability to utilize correctly the theories, concepts, and tools which are available to aid managers in making their product decisions. The importance of these tools, which are briefly discussed in Chapter 2, is acknowledged throughout this book, which emphasizes the use of tools for improved product decisions.

The specific decisions, criteria, and relevant determinants of the decisions depend, of course, on the decision maker's level in the organization. Product decisions of top management differ from those at the brand manager level. This book's focus is primarily, but not exclusively, on the product decisions of the operating product (brand) managers—those directly responsible for the various product decisions. Many decisions, such as positioning, require a number of approvals, and may, depending on the organizational structure, go all the way to the top. Other decisions, such as those relating to product portfolio, are however within the domain of top management.

PRODUCT DECISIONS AND OTHER MARKETING DECISIONS

Although the responsibility for the four Ps—product, price, place, and promotion—is often divided among a number of executives, the four sets of decisions are highly interrelated, and the effect of any product, price, promotion, and distribution strategy depends on its congruence (and synergistic effect) with the others. Even

under the extreme (but not unrealistic) situation when pricing is in the domain of top management, new-product responsibility is in the hands of R & D personnel, current product responsibilities are under the direction of the vice president of operations, the sales department reports to the vice president of sales, and marketing is primarily responsible only for promotion and some staff functions. It is essential to coordinate all these efforts and develop an integrated marketing program.

The *product/market* decisions of the firm—i.e., the selection of a product positioning for selected target markets—are the most central decisions a firm can make. Only after making these decisions can management decide on product features and services, set a price, decide on a communication strategy to emphasize the desired positioning, communicate it to the selected target market, and select distribution outlets most consistent with the desired positioning and purchasing pattern of the selected target market.

When taking consumers' needs and responses into account, the importance of this is quite evident. Consumers respond to the total marketing effort of the firm, not to its isolated components. In this respect, *Gestalt* psychology may provide a good description of consumers' response to the firm's marketing effort, i.e., consumers' behavior toward a product is not determined just by the product's characteristics (the individual elements), but rather by the entire marketing effort of the firm (the whole). Furthermore, the product characteristics themselves are determined by the nature of the whole.

Regardless of the organizational distribution of the various marketing responsibilities, a product/marketing plan should include all four sets of decisions: product, price, place, and promotion. It should also recognize explicitly the interrelationship among them, and include a product policy statement which explicitly states the product positioning, product features, price range, distribution policy, and the communication strategy to be used in reaching the product's intended market and in achieving the firm's objectives.

In developing such a strategy statement, managers must make a conscious choice from among a number of strategies. In evaluating such strategies, it is useful to provide answers to a set of key questions concerning each strategy's *response function*. In this context a strategy is defined as a specific level of effort (including no effort) on each of the major marketing variables. The questions pertinent to response function include:

1. What is the dollar return on investment (or performance on any other relevant criteria) of each strategy?

2. What is the market response to each marketing strategy and, in particular, the elasticity of response to changes in marketing inputs?

3. At what level of effort (on each of the major components of the marketing strategy) is the threshold of effectiveness reached?

4. What is the time lag in marketing response?

5. What is the decay rate of market response to any input?

6. What are the economies and diseconomies of scale associated with the different kinds of marketing activities?

7. What efforts can be effectively substituted for one another?

8. Which efforts tend to reinforce each other?

9. Which efforts are linked in sequence?

10. Which efforts are immune to competitive strategies?

Most introductory marketing management courses and texts focus on the four sets of marketing decisions, while their interaction and response functions are considered the domain of the more advanced marketing modeling courses and texts. Given this coverage elsewhere, we will not elaborate on it at this point and will return to it in the context of new product design and evaluation (Chapters 10 through 13) and the evaluation of the firm's current product offering (Chapter 18).

PRODUCT DECISIONS AND OTHER MANAGEMENT FUNCTIONS[1]

Peter Drucker (1973) has identified the two basic functions of the firm as *marketing* and *innovation*. Product policy can be viewed as the meeting ground of the two and as a focal point for the operations of the firm which assure the well-being of its stakeholders—labor, suppliers, stockholders, local and federal governments, and other groups with a *stake* in the future of the firm.

The interface among the various management functions and product policy takes two major avenues. First, in developing a product/marketing plan, it is essential to coordinate it with the other functions of the firm, explicitly including a financial plan, take into account production and procurement considerations, and coordinate the plan with the firm's R & D efforts and its overall personnel policy. Furthermore, such a plan should be consistent with the financial and accounting practices of the firm and be in accord with the firm's personnel and procurement procedures. Second, in developing any of the other plans (financial, production, procurement, R & D, and personnel) as well as the overall short- and long-term plans of the firm, it is essential to incorporate inputs from the product/marketing plan.

FINANCE

The *financial aspects* of the product/marketing plan include a cost and profit history for the existing brand in question (in dollars, percent of sales, or return on investment), as well as a pro forma financial statement and a budget for each product and its related product marketing plan. In addition, since the new product decisions can be viewed as investment decisions, whenever new product decisions are to be made the financial tools and criteria used to evaluate any investment (e.g., net present value) should be utilized.

Furthermore, capital allocation to new products should not be confined to the evaluation of the expected return from the product and possible deviations from this return; more sophisticated approaches, which take into account the expected uncertainty, have been developed. Van Horne (1977), for example, proposed a method, within the capital budgeting framework, for evaluating new products according to their marginal impact upon the resolution of uncertainty patterns for the firm's total product mix. This and other capital budgeting approaches, such as Bayesian decision theory, mathematical programming, and discrete optimization procedures, can and have occasionally been used in the evaluation of new product investments.

Another area to which financial analysis can and has made substantial contribution is the financial evaluation of mergers and acquisitions. Given that a firm can achieve its growth objectives either by internal product development or by product, business, and corporate acquisitions and mergers, the financial inputs to these decisions is of considerable importance (although, in many cases, such as in some of the IT&T acquisitions, financial considerations have received a lopsided emphasis leading to a situation in which marketing considerations were overlooked). Yet, in any balanced approach to mergers and acquisition, marketing and financial considerations should receive equal weight.

---

[1]For a more detailed discussion of the interrelationship between marketing and the other business functions (see Wind, 1981).

In addition, in the development of a financial plan, one should have sufficient inputs from the product/market plan concerning the planned marketing efforts and the anticipated sales and profits under a variety of possible conditions.

ACCOUNTING

Whenever the accounting practices of a firm lead to an evaluation of an alternative course of action (investment in a new product, for example) that differs from the economic evaluation of the same alternative, the discrepancy obviously has an important (negative) impact on the firm's product policy. Such a discrepancy, although undesirable, is not uncommon and should be watched for.

Managerial accounting procedures have considerable impact on the firm's product policy. Some of the more critical areas include the firm's cost-allocation procedures. Although there is a general consensus that the cause-and-effect objective should be used as a frame of reference for determining the criteria for cost allocation, the accounting "literature is replete with conflicting and not mutually exclusive criteria for choosing a cost allocation base. Among the possible criteria are physical identification, service used facilities provided, benefits received, ability to bear and fairness or equity" (Horngren, 1972). Given that each of these allocation bases and their associated allocation methods can result in different costs allocated to any given—current or planned—product (or product line) and hence affect the product profitability, it is quite crucial to understand the differences among these approaches, their "biases" and effect on the firm's product-related decisions, and the product's measures of profitability.

Of even greater importance are the differences in product profitability when fully-allocated costs are used rather than the variable costs. The justification for using the fully allocated costs as an approximation of the real, long-run, incremental cost is somewhat questionable, and the impact of each of these two procedures on the relevant product decisions should be examined explicitly in each case.

The most desirable approach to both the income statement and the problem of cost allocation seems to be the *contribution approach.* Yet, it should always be remembered that the key question in evaluating any accounting practice is: What difference does it make for the evaluation of the product performance and the firm's product decisions?

The concept of *responsibility accounting* and the use of cost centers, profit centers, or investment centers is of major importance in the evaluation of the performance of existing or planned products. It is also relevant to the firm's ability to achieve its objectives by providing the appropriate *accounting motivation* to the managers. It is well recognized that accounting practices vary in their effect on management. Hence cost, profit, and investment centers have significant implications for the design of an organization for the firm's product decisions.

Cost analysis and capital budgeting are important because managerial accounting practices and approaches are related to those of financial management, and can affect the firm's evaluation of new products. For example, the use of *residual income* instead of *ROI* as a measure of divisional performance may have considerable impact on a decision to accept or reject a new product. This and other aspects of the accounting approach to capital budgeting are critical components of any economic evaluation of new products.

PRODUCTION

The link between *production* and the product/marketing plan is also a dual link. Production capabilities determine the ability to produce the product, while an accurate sales forecast for the product line is essential to efficient production scheduling and operations.

PROCUREMENT

Procurement, and in its more general form, material management, attained, during the shortages of the early 1970s, primary importance and led many firms to devote major efforts to product changes aimed at substituting for scarce raw materials such as sugar and coffee other, more available materials, such as sugar or coffee substitutes. In addition, major new product development efforts are often initiated in response to projected resource availability and cost. Consider, for example, the move toward the design of fuel-efficient automobiles and jet planes. Efficient procurement planning, therefore, depends on close cooperation with product/market planning. Procurement plans must be based on future material requirements to meet planned new product development and product modification as well as the specific production goals of the firm.

R & D

R & D effort should be closely related to the market and product development efforts of the firm. Neglect of this maxim has led many technology-oriented firms into developing products that are the engineer's and scientist's dream but the marketing person's nightmare, since they meet no latent or overt consumer needs. The need for a strong interface between marketing, product planning, R & D, and the broader technology management area is one of the major themes of the new-product-development section of this book.

PERSONNEL

The *personnel* functions of the firm are responsible, with the marketing group, for hiring, training, and managing the personnel needed for carrying out the firm's product policy. The two chapters on the organization for new products and existing products discuss this aspect in greater depth.

TOP MANAGEMENT

Finally, *top management* is and should be involved directly in both the overall guidance of existing products and the guidance, inspiration, encouragement, and control of the firm's new product efforts. Top management plays a critical role in determining the corporate product/market portfolio as well as in the direction and approval of all other product decisions of the firm. It is not surprising, therefore, that any strategic planning at the corporate, Strategic Business Unit (SBU), or product level includes a heavy product/market component.

CONCLUDING REMARKS

Imagine that you were given the managerial responsibility for a company of your choice, such as the local supermarket, drug store, department store, discount house, home delivery route, restaurant, or any other company with which you are familiar. Reflecting on the material discussed in this chapter, try to identify the major product decisions facing the firm (be as specific as possible), assess their relationship to the other marketing decisions of this firm and to the other managerial functions.

In doing this mental exercise, make special note of all those items discussed in the chapter that you feel are irrelevant for your firm.

Upon concluding this exercise, go to your library and pick up an introductory marketing management text. Skim its contents and ask yourself the question: What are the relevant dependencies of product policy and the other marketing decisions? Completing this task, pick up your managerial accounting, financial management, production management, and management texts, review them, and identify areas covered in those texts that have direct bearing on product policy and which were not discussed in this chapter. Having gone through this literature review, evaluate your earlier answer to the situation described above and make any necessary changes.

Marketing, Marketing Research, Behavioral and Management Science Tools for Product Policy

INTRODUCTION

In making product decisions, managers in the marketing/product decision making unit (DMU) can utilize four sets of tools: marketing concepts and theories, marketing research, concepts and findings from the behavioral sciences (including the emerging discipline of consumer behavior), and the philosophy and tools of management science. Exhibit 2–1 presents, in a diagrammatic form, the relationships among these four tool areas and the marketing/product DMU.

No single chapter can do justice to these four areas. Even a cursory familiarity with these areas requires one to at least read and under-

EXHIBIT 2–1

DECISION TOOLS

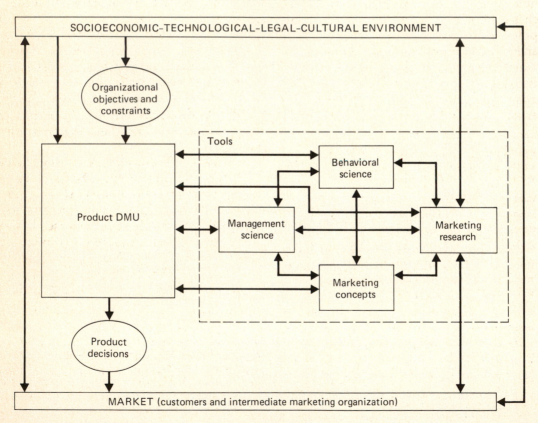

stand an introductory book in each area.[1] The purpose of this chapter, therefore, is not to provide an exhaustive review of these areas, but to highlight some of their more pertinent aspects and interrelationships as they relate to product decisions.

MARKETING CONCEPTS

The single most important marketing concept is that of the *marketing/consumer orientation* which guides the firm's integrated marketing program toward *the generation of customer satisfaction* which, in turn, helps achieve the desired organizational goals. This concept[2] has revolutionized the *approach* used in making product and other marketing decisions. It has, for example, changed the focus from technical research as the sole input to new product development to a greater reliance on marketing research. This concept has led to the development and introduction of new products, not because they suited the company's technical expertise, but because they filled a specific consumer need or want and provided consumers with a *reason* (a set of desired benefits) for buying them.

The marketing concept has led to a number of other concepts, many of which have relevance for product decisions. The more pertinent of the concepts are described below.

MARKET SEGMENTATION

Recognizing that consumers are quite heterogeneous in their responses to marketing stimuli, and accepting the logic of the economic price discrimination model,[3] marketing-oriented firms have adopted the concept of market segmentation which calls for separating a given market into homogeneous market segments.

Almost all known customer characteristics have been used at one time as bases for segmentation. Segmentation typically is based on the results of an empirical segmentation study. A variety of approaches have been used to cluster customers and establish the key discriminating characteristics of the various segments (Frank, Massy, and Wind, 1972; Wind, 1978a). In the context of product policy, the concept of seg-

---

[1] As a guide to the unfamiliar reader, the following books may be considered as providing a good introductory treatment of these four areas:

    Marketing: Kotler, 1980; Houghes, 1979
    Consumer behavior: Engel, Kollat, and Blackwell, 1978
    Management science: Kotler, 1971
    Marketing research: Green and Tull, 1978; Brown, 1980

The more advanced reader who wants to be up to date on developments in these areas is encouraged to follow the professional journals, in particular:

    Marketing: Journal of Marketing
    Consumer Behaviour: Journal of Consumer Research
    Management Science: Management Science and *Marketing Science*
    Marketing Research: Journal of Marketing Research

[2] For a discussion of the marketing concept, see Kotler (1980) and Levitt (1962, 1975).

---

[3] The price discrimination model suggests that a firm faced with heterogeneous and separable markets can maximize its profits only if it sets different prices in each market, reflecting the elasticity of demand of that market. For further discussion of this concept and its relevance to marketing segmentation, see Frank, Massy, and Wind (1972).

mentation is of crucial value in suggesting that the design of any product should be aimed at the satisfaction of the wants and needs of selected target segments, and that no product can or even should attempt to be all things to all people. Accepting this premise has major consequences for product research and strategy.

MARKETING PLANNING

Marketing as a discipline can provide few generalizations, "principles," or "laws." The major contribution of the marketing discipline is in its *approach* to problem identification and solution. The marketing approach is based on the operationalization of the marketing concept and the utilization of marketing research, management, and behavioral science concepts and methods as tools for better marketing decisions. Further discussion of the marketing-planning approach and its relevance to product planning is presented in Chapter 6.

PRODUCT DIFFERENTIATION

One of the few generally accepted "principles" of marketing is that the greater the consumers' perceived product differentiation (on dimensions important to the consumers) the higher the margins the product can command. This principle, which is the underlying rationale for product positioning (discussed in Chapter 4), is equally applicable to consumer and industrial products. Consider, for example, the following two cases: Firestone, which sells to the public and has a differentiated product, outperforms Uniroyal, which sells mostly to Detroit manufacturers. Similarly, Carpenter Technology, the specialty steelmaker which sells only one tenth of one percent of the steel industry output, is, because of its differentiated product, the most profitable steelmaker in the United States

(Forbes, 1977). Product differentiation is often a key to the differential advantage a firm can achieve over its competitors (Anderson, 1957).

MARKETING SYSTEM

Marketing decisions involve numerous participants. Even if one ignores the large number of participants and transactions preceding the manufacturing of any product or service (which include, for example, the acquisition of raw materials), there are a large number of individuals and firms involved in the transfer of a product from the manufacturer to the ultimate users or consumers. Wholesalers, retailers, other intermediate marketing organizations, transportation firms, finance companies, and others are active and important participants in the marketing system. The design of any product/marketing strategy should, therefore, take explicitly into account the needs, preferences, and behavior of all the relevant participants in the marketing process and not only the preferences of the ultimate consumers.

THE MARKETING MIX

The concept of the marketing mix is an essential aspect of marketing planning. Its relevance to product policy was highlighted in Chapter 1. It will suffice, therefore, to emphasize the recognized importance of nonprice competition and its implication for unique and differentiated product design, and the importance of establishing the congruence between the product strategy and the other marketing decisions. (Consider, for example, the situation in which a product strategy calls for a high-quality personal-care item. Would the high-quality image be achieved if the price was relatively low, or if it was distributed primarily in Woolworth's?)

MARKETING RESEARCH

Marketing research is a systematic problem definition, model building, data-gathering, data analysis and interpretation for the purpose of improved marketing decision-making and control. It provides a major set of tools for product policy. Despite the large variance in the quality of commercial marketing research and in the degree of its utilization, it is impossible to imagine how one could design, implement, and control a product strategy without having some information obtained from appropriately designed and executed marketing research studies. Many of the disappointments with marketing research, which have led some managers to a reluctance to use it, can be traced to poor-quality research. This is somewhat analogous to the case in which a car turns out to be a "lemon" and the driver stops buying and using cars.

A real understanding of the capabilities and potential value of marketing research can be gained and appreciated only through in-depth understanding of (and preferably first-hand experience with) marketing research.[4] The topics covered in this section are, therefore, only those essential to understanding the research discussed in the subsequent chapters.

THE MARKETING RESEARCH PROCESS

Marketing research should be viewed as an on-going process aimed at providing information to improve decision making. More specifically, in the context of product-related research, the expected payoff to the company is a reduction in the risk involved in product decisions. To the extent that the results of a specific research undertaking cannot improve the decision-making unit's decisions (or reduce the risk involved), there is no justification for conducting this research. Both the manager and the researcher should always consider the *cost versus the value of information* expected from any research project.[5]

The marketing research process involves a careful and detailed problem definition, which requires considerable interaction among the researcher and the members of the marketing/product decision-making unit. Given an explicit problem definition, the researcher can approach the task of developing a research design. The research design provides the blueprint for the research investigation, suggesting the population to be studied and the type of sample required, the instrument to be used, the respondents' task, whether an interview or self-administered questionnaire is to be involved, and other research elements. Following the research design stage, the data can be collected and subsequently subjected to data analyses and interpretation.

A major concept at this stage is that of the *data matrix*. The responses of each respondent to a questionnaire can be strung as a vector of responses and, when done for all respondents, a data matrix emerges. This data matrix is the basic output of the data-collection procedure and is the input to all of the data analytical procedures to be employed. Exhibit 2–2 presents illustrative data matrices for cross-sectional analysis (a single matrix for time *i*) and

---

[4]This would require, for example, familiarity and understanding of the material covered in such books as Green and Tull (1978).

[5]For a discussion of the cost and value of information, see Green and Tull (1978).

EXHIBIT 2–2

ILLUSTRATIVE DATA MATRIX FOR CONSUMER BEHAVIOR STUDIES CONCERNING
A PRODUCT DESIGN

Consumer	Sets of variables					
	Demographic socioeconomic characteristics	Personality and general life style characteristics	Attitude and other situation specific psychological characteristics concerning the product in question (including product perceptions)	Criterion for product selection (benefits sought)	Product and brand usage	Response to other marketing variables
	$1 \ldots K$	$1 \ldots K$	$1 \ldots K$	$1 \ldots K$	$1 \ldots K$	$1 \ldots K$
1	___	___	___	___	___	___
2						
3						
.						
.						
.						
N	X_{N1}					

Time 1 / Time 2 / Time N

longitudinal analysis (a number of matrices over time).

THE ART OF RESEARCH DESIGN

The most crucial part of any research undertaking is the translation of the problem into a research design. The design of a research project is, to a large extent, an art. Creative design can make the difference between an adequate research study and an insightful and potentially exciting one. Unfortunately, no guidelines can be provided to increase the creativity of the research design. A thorough understanding of research methodology is necessary but not sufficient to creativity in design.

It is important to note, however, that there is no single correct design for a given problem.

In the design of a concept test, for example, three researchers may come up with three quite different research designs. The selection of one may be influenced by personal preference, familiarity with certain designs and data analysis techniques, or other factors. The creative researcher should always question whether another design might not be better, simpler, and more efficient, while remembering that no single design (including the ones presented in this book) is "best". It is this challenge of improving a given design that should guide the researcher.

In designing research instruments for product decisions, special emphasis should be placed on *experimental designs* (e.g., Banks 1965; Green and Tull 1978; and Ramond 1974) and designs using *unobtrusive measures* (Webb, et al. 1966).

A MULTIVARIATE ORIENTATION

Most product/marketing research studies and data analysis projects are concerned with multiple dependent variables (awareness of a new brand, attitude toward it, and intention to buy it, for example) and multiple explanatory variables. Seldom, if ever, can a research problem be resolved by a single explanatory variable. It is thus essential to understand multivariate statistical procedures and to use them when they are called for. Multivariate data analysis, coupled with current computer capabilities, enables the researcher to use efficient and correct procedures on almost any aspect of product/marketing research. Exhibit 2–3 lists and classifies some commonly-used multivariate statistical techniques.[6]

CHOICE MODELS

Of special interest for product/marketing studies are the various choice models. The ability to measure and predict individuals' choice behavior is essential both to understanding consumer choices among brands, products, features, and other options, and executive

[6]For a more detailed classification of multivariate techniques and their descriptions, see Green and Tull (1978), Brown (1980), and most other recent marketing research texts.

EXHIBIT 2–3

SOME ILLUSTRATIVE MULTIVARIATE STATISTICAL TECHNIQUES

PARTITIONED DATA MATRIX

		Number of dependent variables	
		1	2
Number of independent variables	1	Correlation Regression χ^2 1	Same as cell 3 2
	2+	Multiple regression analysis 2 group discriminant analysis AID ANOVA 3	Canonical correlation 3+ group discriminant analysis Multivariate AID MANOVA 4

NONPARTITIONED DATA MATRIX

Analysis of subjects	Analysis of variables	Analysis of both subjects and variables
Cluster analysis Factor analysis	Factor analysis Hierarchical clustering Multidimensional scaling (TORSCA)	Multidimensional scaling (PREFMAP, INDSCAL, etc.) Latent structure analysis

choices among alternative courses of actions or objectives.

Numerous choice models have been proposed and applied by psychologists, mathematical psychologists, and others interested in human problem solving and cognitive processes. Yet, most studies of consumer behavior have utilized some form of an additive linear choice model. *The conjoint measurement model* is of special value in product research. The basic model assumes that consumers choose items by "trading off" one feature against another. Conjoint analysis—a recent development in mathematical psychology—is concerned with measuring the joint effect of two or more independent variables (e.g., product features) on the ordering of a dependent variable (e.g., overall liking, preference, worth, or some other evaluative measure).

The input to this procedure consists of a set of combinations of attributes (selected following an efficient experimental design) presented to the respondents, who are asked to rank (or rate) them on the desired dependent variable. The stimuli can be presented as verbal descriptions, pictorial representation, or an artist's conception.

The conjoint analysis algorithms consist of the simultaneous measurement of the joint effect and the separate independent variable contributions to that joint effect at the level of interval scales with common unit. The output is presented as utility functions, which can be estimated at the individual, segment, or total market level. (For a more complete explanation of conjoint analysis, see Appendix A and Green and Wind, 1973.)

Despite the conceptual attractiveness of conjoint analysis and its frequent mention in this book, it is just one of many multiattribute choice models. (For a review of various choice models, see Green and Wind, 1973.) Consider, for example, some alternative choice models and try to identify situations for which they might be appropriate.

Conjunctive (noncompensatory) models (e.g., Coombs, 1964 and Einhorn, 1970) assume that an alternative (e.g., a product), in order to be chosen, should have a certain minimum value on *all* relevant dimensions— i.e., high value on one dimension cannot compensate for a below-threshold value on another relevant dimension.

Whereas most compensatory (e.g., conjoint analysis) and noncompensatory models are based on *interdimensional* evaluation, there are also a number of choice models based on sequential *intradimensional* evaluation procedures. For example, the *additive difference model* (Tversky, 1969). According to this model, alternatives are compared on each dimension, a difference is determined, and the results are added to determine a choice. The original model was developed for a choice between two alternatives, but it can be extended to more alternatives in a sequential manner. Or, alternatively, the *elimination-by-aspect model* (Tversky, 1972) is based on a sequential choice process in which a dimension (aspect) is selected according to some probability, and the alternatives evaluated on it. All those alternatives that do not possess that dimension are eliminated. The procedure is repeated for the other dimensions until all but one of the alternatives is eliminated.

Identifying the correct choice model is a critical consideration in most product choice related studies (e.g., concept testing) and to the extent that this cannot be determined before the design of the study, the research design and analytical plan should allow for the identification of the correct choice rule.

ON THE EVALUATION OF MARKETING RESEARCH

Given that the results of marketing research studies can govern the destiny of many product decisions, it is essential that both researchers and managers pay more attention to the evaluation of marketing research and avoid a blind reliance on research results. Explicit evaluation of both the proposed research design and the actual research conducted does not require extraordinary expertise. Common sense and a willingness to question the authority of the researcher and his/her assumptions are the basic requirements needed to assure the relevance and value of research.

Some of the more important questions the researcher and manager should ask themselves in evaluating a research design are given below.

With respect to the constructs:

- Are the dependent and independent variables consistent with the problem to be studied? For example, what should the dependent variable in a product testing be—liking of the product? Preference for it? Intention to buy it? Plans to use it for specific occasions? Some other evaluative measure?

- Are the selected variables measured in the best way? Continuing with our previous example and assuming that preference is the desired dependent variable, how should it be measured? As preference ranking or rating? If as rating, for example, what should the scale be like—a simple dichotomy of "Prefer—Do Not Prefer," a trichotomy, based on the Sherif and Sherif (1967) distinction between regions of acceptance, rejection and indifference, a 4-, 5-, 6-, 7-point scale, or some other scale? Should each scale category be labeled or only the two extreme points? Should the scale be a bipolar scale?

Related to the specific indicators to be used are the decisions concerning the specific stimulus definition—should it be the actual product or product description? Should it be in the intended package or an unidentified package? Similarly, the researcher has to determine the associated respondent task(s). Since there is no single correct way of measuring the behavior of interest, and for different purposes (even

within the same study) one might elect to use a number of indicators and each could be measured in a number of ways, it would be helpful to adhere to the following rule for selection of correct variables and their measures: The closer the research task to the real world behavior which one intends to measure, the better the measure. This would suggest, for example, that choice is better than rating and that pictorial presentation of a stimuli is better than its verbal description.

With respect to the respondents:

- Are the respondents the correct unit of observation and analysis? If, for example, a product for family consumption is being tested, should the respondent be the housewife or should other family members also be interviewed?

- Is the sample representative of the potential market for the product?

A common tendency is to test household and food products on housewives. Yet, the increased number of working wives and single men who are heads of households suggest the need to include them in the sample design.

With respect to the research instrument:

- Can the research instrument obtain the desired information?

- Is the instrument likely to generate some response bias?

If, for example, a monadic-concept test (in which each respondent is presented only one concept) is conducted, there is considerable danger of biasing the response in favor of the test concept.

With respect to the stability of the results:

- Have cross-validation procedures been employed?

Given the danger of data massaging, most scientific journals will not accept any article with substantive findings unless the results have been cross-validated. Yet, in the commercial world, where decisions involving millions of dollars may depend on the results of a given study, cross-validation procedures are the exception rather than the rule. A cross-validation procedure, such as the Campbell and Fiske (1959) multitrait, multimethod procedure, or the simple split-sample analysis, is therefore necessary to assure the users' confidence in the results.

With respect to generalizability:

- Is the sample of respondents representative?
- Is the sample of variables representative?
- Is the sample of measurement devices appropriate?

This concern with generalizability applies not only to studies conducted by the firm, but also to syndicated services. If, for example, the Nielsen National Store Audit is being used, it is important to note the impact of such factors as: A&P is not included in the audit; audits cover a two-month time period, which may not coincide with promotional efforts of the firm; not all stores are audited on the same day; deauthorization is not reported in the distribution count if products are still available in the store; and reported dollar sales are not based on actual consumer purchase prices, but on an approximation.

Careful attention to these and similar questions is necessary if one is to get the most out of the firm's product/marketing research efforts.

BEHAVIORAL SCIENCES AND CONSUMER BEHAVIOR

One of the major outcomes of the increased acceptability of the marketing concept has been the growing attention to the study of consumer behavior. Relying heavily on theories and findings from the behavioral sciences (in particular, from psychology, sociology, cultural anthropology, economics and communication research), the new discipline of consumer behavior has emerged in the past decade.[7] The contributions of the consumer behavior discipline (and its parent disciplines) to product decisions are in the form of:

1. Providing hypotheses about consumer needs for and reactions to products and

services. These hypotheses (derived from the behavioral sciences and consumer behavior theories and findings), once tested in the context of specific marketing situations, can provide guidelines for specific product decisions.

2. Providing research methodology (e.g., econometrics, psychometrics, sociometrics) and relevant constructs applicable to the study of consumer behavior.

There are a few exceptions, but most consumer behavior and behavioral science theories and findings *cannot* be utilized directly for providing guidelines for product decisions. This is primarily due to the fact that (a) most of the behavioral science findings and theories were not developed or tested with respect to consumers' purchase and consumption behavior, (b) many of the published consumer behavior

---

[7]The "symptoms" of a discipline are the emergence of university courses and programs, the formation of a professional association (Association of Consumer Research) and the publication of a professional journal (Journal of Consumer Research).

studies and models were based on samples that were nonrepresentative of the population and variable universes of interest to most product decision makers and (c) even when a product is included in a consumer behavior study it is often of secondary concern to the researcher and offers no generalizability to other products.

One possible exception to this is found in the *diffusion-of-innovation* literature. Despite the fact that many of the original studies in this area were based on the adoption behavior of farmers in small and closed agricultural communities (as studied by rural sociologists), numerous studies have been conducted on other respondent groups (including physicians and consumers) and provide interesting hypotheses on the characteristics of those consumers most likely to "innovate" and adopt new products and services.

Some of these findings are presented below, following a brief discussion of some of the behavioral science and consumer behavior findings and concepts that may serve as useful hypotheses for researchers in the product-policy area.

SOME BEHAVIORAL SCIENCE AND CONSUMER BEHAVIOR CONCEPTS AND FINDINGS

Many behavioral science and consumer behavior concepts and findings are relevant (as hypotheses) for certain product decisions. This section sketches some of these concepts and findings and will perhaps stimulate the reader to explore others.

Product and package design In designing a product and/or a package, one should consider such factors as color, size, and shape. The behavioral sciences provide some interesting and useful hypotheses about these elements. Numerous studies have been conducted by

psychologists on the psychological meaning and impact of *color* and by cultural anthropologists on the cultural meaning of color. In a marketing context, Levy (1959) suggested that darker colors are symbolic of more traditional products, while pastel colors convey softness, youthfulness, and femininity.

Such factors as *size and shape* have also received considerable attention from psychologists and marketing researchers. Myers and Reynolds (1967), in their review of the consumer behavior literature, state the so-called square-root law, which says that attention increases as a square root of the size of the stimuli. Whether this particular ratio of size to attention exists or not is immaterial. What is important to note is that size and shape affect consumers' response to a product.

In this context, concepts relating to sensory, perceptual, and cognitive (learning) processes provide important clues for better product design. For example, the concept of *contrast* may suggest the development of unique products and packages that stand out when placed among their competitors on store shelves. At the same time, it is important not to deviate too much from consumers' experience, in order to take advantage of the consumers' association of the product with the product class and its associated benefits.

Brand name The brand name decision may also benefit from familiarity with the relevant behavioral science and consumer behavior literature. The concepts of stimulus generalization and association suggest the need for descriptive brand names that associate the brand with the desired attributes and products.

In addition, the behavioral sciences can provide the methodology for the selection and evaluation of brand names. Word-association and sentence-completion tasks are frequently-used procedures, and more sophisticated multidimensional scaling procedures have been employed for the study of the congruence of a brand name with the desired product attributes.

Product positioning   Some of the major applications of the behavioral sciences and consumer behavior to product policy relate to the product-positioning decision. Concepts such as *contrast* suggest that the greater the contrast the greater the attention generated and, therefore, the need for unique positioning. Numerous findings concerning the lack of sensory discrimination among unlabeled products, such as soft drinks, beer, cigarettes, cars, and others, suggest the need to develop both distinguishable image differences (positioning), as well as new-product dimensions that are noticeably different from those already on the market.

The Gestalt principle of *context* provides a rich theoretical justification for the study of positioning in the context of the relevant competitive setting and the study of behavior under specific situations (as opposed to generalized behavior). Other concepts, such as that of *stereotypes*, provide further insight into the possible determinants of consumers' perceptions of a product positioning.

Guidelines for the selection of potentially useful positionings are also provided by the behavioral science and consumer behavior literature. Studies focusing on the clustering of consumers based on their needs, motives, and desired benefits may suggest certain consumer typologies (segments) that can provide hypotheses for alternative positioning. Stone (1954), for example, identified four types of consumers: the economic consumer, the personalizing consumer, the ethical consumer, and the apathethic consumer. Assuming that such segments are found for the given product of interest, these consumer types can serve as guidelines for the generation of alternative positionings. Similar implications can be drawn from other consumer motivation and need

studies, such as those of Woods (1960), who identified six segments: habit determined, cognitive, price cognitive, impulse, emotional, and new. These, and most of the psychological studies focusing on personality and motivation (e.g., achievement oriented, inner-versus-other directed) can provide a rich source of hypotheses and ideas for positioning.

More general guidelines can be derived from Lasswell's (1948) concept of "triple appeal," which suggests, when applied to positioning, that positioning should appeal simultaneously to the three Freudian components of personality—the id, the ego, and the superego. Myers and Reynolds (1967), in discussing the applicability of this concept, use Cadillac advertising as an example. Since offering the status and prestige by appeal to the id—"be a big shot"—is unacceptable in our society, "you deserve a Cadillac" is used to appeal to the superego by offering the Cadillac as a reward for hard work and achievement. Finally, Cadillac ads often enlist the support of the ego by mentioning the high trade-in value of the car, its low maintenance cost, or its suprisingly good gas mileage.

Other applications   The behavioral science and consumer behavior attitude literature provides other inputs for the design of product strategies. Again, no generalized conclusions can be drawn for the design of product strategies, since attitude has to be measured with respect to *specific* products under *specific* market conditions. Yet, studying consumers' attitude formation and change (utilizing the wide range of available attitude research approaches) is, in many cases, necessary for the design of product strategy.

Other behavioral science areas of major importance to product management include *the study of problem solving*, which can be applied to a better understanding of consumer behavior, and the improvement of management decision processes. In this latter role, the study of decision-making under uncertainty is of special importance. Some of these concepts are discussed briefly in the next section and throughout the book.

A second and related area is that of the *study of creativity*. Major efforts have been devoted to the study of creativity by psychologists and design engineers, and some of the more relevant findings and approaches for overcoming the blocks to creativity and the stimulation of creativity are discussed in Chapter 9.

A third area includes the contributions of *economics* to the design of approaches to (models of) product decisions. Traditionally marketing and consumer behavior have focused on the demand side. Product policies cannot ignore, however, the supply side and economics suggest the need to focus on both the demand and supply sides. Related to this is the importance of the competitive nature of the industry structure (e.g., monopoly, monopolistic competition, competition) and its impact on decisions. In addition, the economic concept of *marginal analysis* is of critical importance in any evaluation of the economic viability of new and existing products.

CONCEPTS AND FINDINGS CONCERNING THE DIFFUSION OF INNOVATION

Given the importance of new products, a study of the diffusion-of-innovation literature is extremely important for the better understanding of consumers' adoption processes, the characteristics of early adopters, and the prediction of the diffusion pattern.

Given the availability of excellent reviews of this literature (Rogers 1976; Robertson 1971; Zaltman 1967; and others), the focus of this section is on only a few of the more pertinent concepts and findings for product decision makers.

Product adoption Numerous formulations of the adoption process have been proposed in the literature. Common to most of these models are three aspects:

- The adoption process cannot start unless the consumers are aware of the product. Hence, awareness is generally viewed as the first step in any adoption process. One seemingly major exception to this view occurs when the adoption process is seen as a problem-solving process, and the first step is therefore usually the recognition of the existence of a problem. In these models, awareness may result from one of the subsequent phases in which the problem solver is searching for a solution.

- The output of the adoption process usually encompasses two behavioral measures of *trial* and *adoption* (repeat), as well as a series of attitudinal and communication measures reflecting the adopter's experience with the product and his likelihood of communicating it to others. The distinction between trial and adoption is a major one with respect to new product-forecasting models and is discussed in Chapter 15.

- Before reaching the trial decision and after being made aware of the product, the individual, it is generally assumed, goes through a series of intermediate stages. These may include interest, comprehension (knowledge), liking (favorable attitudes), legitimization, and others. The specific stages and their sequence (which are also referred to as a hierarchy of effects) vary, however, according to the researcher's conceptualization of the process, the products or brands involved, the buying situation, and the customers' degree of involvement.

Diffusion process Following the early rural sociology studies of diffusion among farmers, the diffusion process is usually depicted as the

EXHIBIT 2–4

A "TYPICAL" DIFFUSION CURVE

Cumulative pattern

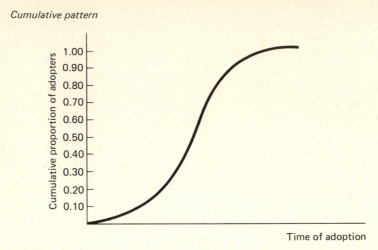

Noncumulative diffusion pattern

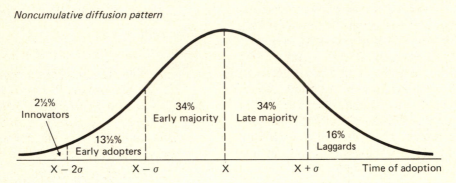

one illustrated in Exhibit 2–4. As can be seen in this exhibit, the time of adoption follows an approximately normal distribution, and adopters are classified according to their distance from the mean adoption time as innovators (the first 2.5 percent), early adopters (the next 13.5 percent), early majority (the next 34 percent), late majority (the next 34 percent), and laggards (the last 16 percent).

Innovator characteristics Many of the diffusion-of-innovation studies have focused on the discriminating characteristics of in-

novators. No conclusive generalization is possible, however, given the variability of new products and the circumstances under which they were introduced (competitive actions and structure; economic, political, and other environmental conditions; consumers' values; current inventory of products and services, etc.).

A few generalizations have been made, however. Some of the more defensible ones are those suggested by Rogers and Stanfield (1968), who, following a critical review of more than 700 diffusion studies, concluded that innovativeness is positively related to education, income and standard of living, knowledgeability, favorability toward change, aspirations for upward mobility, exposure to mass media, and exposure to interpersonal communication.

These characteristics of the innovators are based, to a large extent, on the examination of nonmarketing innovative behavior—only a few of the studies examined by Rogers and Stanfield were concerned with the adoption of new products or services.

An examination of the consumer behavior and marketing literature suggests a somewhat more ambiguous profile for innovators. The link between innovativeness and socioeconomic, demographic, and personality characteristics is quite questionable and differs from one product category to another. Massy and Morrison (1964), for example, found no discriminating socioeconomic characteristics between the early Folger coffee buyers and nonbuyers. Pessemier, Burger, and Tigert (1967), in examining the relationship between socioeconomic factors and the early adoption of a new detergent, did find (using a different research approach) some significant relationship. (For a review of some of the marketing studies on the characteristics of innovators, see Holbrook and Howard, 1976.)

As illustrative findings on the characteristics of new *product* innovators, the reader may examine the following profile of the innovator for new appliances, based on some of the more relevant studies:

- Demographic Factors
    Somewhat younger
    Higher education
    Higher income
    Higher occupational status

- Social Factors
    Greater social participation
    Higher social mobility
    Higher opinion leadership

- Personality Factors
    More venturesome (risk taking)
    Perceives less risk in new products
    Oriented toward newness

- Media Exposure
    More print readership

- Consumption Characteristics
    More likely to own many appliances.
    More likely to own *new* products

AN ILLUSTRATIVE APPLICATION: THE USE OF ATTITUDE RESEARCH IN PRODUCT DECISIONS[8]

Product decisions—with respect to both the development and marketing of new products and management of existing products—depend to a large extent on the attitude of five groups:

1. The consumers.

2. The relevant decision maker(s).

3. Top management and other organizational members who are involved directly or indirectly with the product decisions (occasionally this may include members of the advertising agency, legal or research firms working with the firm).

4. The intermediate marketing organizations (retailers, wholesalers and other distributors).

5. Members of other external organizations whose attitude can affect the organization's product decisions. These include various government agencies, labor unions, suppliers and others.

The attitudes of these publics can and should provide useful input to the design of a firm's product policy. Yet, with the exception of the

---

[8]The material in this section is based on Wind and Tyebjee (1977), which provides a more comprehensive review of the current and potential use of attitude research in product decisions.

EXHIBIT 2–5

AN ATTITUDINAL MODEL OF PRODUCT DECISIONS

Source: Reprinted from Yoram Wind and Tyzoon Tyebjee ''On the Use of Attitude Research in Product Policy'' in *Moving Ahead with Attitude Research,* American Marketing Association, 1977.

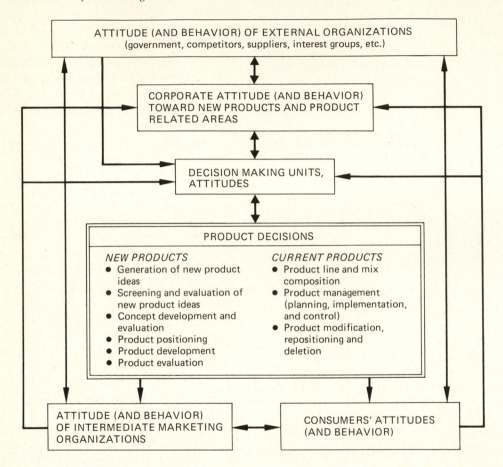

first public—the consumers—little or no effort has been made to study and understand the attitudes of these other publics and the likely impact of their attitudes on the success of the firm's product policies.

The attitudes of these publics can and do affect the firm's decisions concerning both the introduction of new products (e.g., generating new product ideas, screening and evaluating them) and the management of existing products (e.g., product modification and deletion). The relationship among some of the major product decisions and the various publics is presented schematically in Exhibit 2–5.

Given that the *attitude research* literature has included a variety of constructs from awareness to intention to purchase, one can and should explicitly consider which attitudes of which publics are required as input for each of the specific product decisions of the firm. For example, if one is considering the evaluation of a new product, attitudes such as the following should be examined.

Top management:

• Do they view the new product concept as congruent with the overall objectives of the firm?
• What is their willingness to devote the necessary resources to introduce the product?

Retailers:

• How likely will they be to carry the product and promote it?

Consumers:

• Does the new product fill an important need and how likely will consumers be to buy the product?
• How will they perceive the product's positioning?
• What is the anticipated pattern and magnitude of the product's usage?

Competitors

• What is the likelihood that various competitors will retaliate against the new product, what is their likely response and how effective will it be?

Interest groups:

• What is the likelihood that interest groups such as environmentalists or consumerists would attack or support the new product?

Government:

• What is the likelihood of legal action against the product or its marketing campaign?

The list of attitude-related questions to which the decision maker(s) would like answers before launching a new product or making any other product decision is quite lengthy and would vary according to the characteristics

of the decision-makers involved, the idiosyncratic organizational characteristics, the specific decision(s) to be made and other situational and environmental factors. To facilitate an explicit approach to the identification of the needed attitude inputs to product decisions, the decision-maker should consider developing a "public-by-attitude-by-decision" matrix. The matrix, as illustrated in Exhibit 2–6, requires the decision-maker to specify explicitly the type of decisions to be made, and for each decision the required attitudinal inputs from each of the relevant publics.

The development of such a matrix is not a trivial task. It is necessary, however, to develop it as a guideline for the determination of the nature and magnitude of the required research on those attitudes considered by management as relevant to their product decisions.

The explicit approach suggested by Exhibit 2–6 should help focus management attention on the *relevant* attitudes and guide the firm's research activities. In designing specific attitude research projects, however, the marketing researcher should supplement this matrix with the methodological considerations concerning availability of appropriate secondary sources and to the extent that primary research might be required, explicit decisions should be made concerning the research design, data collection and analysis. Exhibit 2–7 suggests a methodologically augmented "public-by-attitude-by-decision" matrix which can help in the design of appropriate attitude research studies. Completion of this matrix requires close interaction between management and research personnel to identify (a) the required product decisions (generating new product ideas, deciding whether to change the current product strategy or not and if yes in what direction), (b) the specific publics involved with each decision (customers, retailers, government) and the identification of the relevant unit of analysis (individual, husband and wife, entire family) and, (c) the specific information desired

EXHIBIT 2–6

AN ILLUSTRATIVE ATTITUDE BY PUBLIC DECISION MATRIX

Source: Reprinted from Yoram Wind and Tyzoon Tyebjee "On the Use of Attitude Research in Product Policy" in *Moving Ahead with Attitude Research*, American Marketing Association, 1977.

Public / Attitude / Product decision	Consumers				...	Government		...	Competitors	...	...
	Awareness	Motives, needs	Perception	Preference		Perception	Values		Preference		
Idea generation											
Idea screening											
.											
.											
Product design											
Brand name											
Packaging											
.											
.											
Positioning											
.											
.											
Monitoring											
Product											
Performance											
.											
.											

from each public for each decision (consumers' awareness, perception and knowledge of strategy variables or product features, the importance of these strategy variables, degree of satisfaction with current offerings, magnitude of unfulfilled needs, and the likely reactions to changes in strategy variables).

Following the completion of this part of the matrix, the researcher should complete the rows of the matrix: (a) the identification of available secondary sources, their appropriateness, reliability, validity, and cost and (b) the determination of the best primary research de-

sign to provide answers to management questions concerning the relevant attitudes of the relevant publics.

The determination of the "best" research approach for any given public/attitude/product combination is a complex task. The number of options facing the researcher is almost unlimited. Any given problem can be approached in a variety of ways. Research design is still predominantly an art, or perhaps a stylistic bias, and not an exact science. Hence, the selection of any research design depends on the researcher's skills, creativity, and personal preference. Unfortunately, there are almost no direct comparisons of alternative research approaches which could provide guidelines for the selection of the most appropriate attitude research approach. Consider for example the large number of approaches one can utilize in attitude segmentation (for a review of these approaches see Wind 1978a) or in concept testing (see for example Iuso, 1975; Wind, 1973; Tauber, 1972), and try to identify a single dominant approach. How should the attitude be defined and measured? Should the attitude study be a cross-sectional or a longitudinal design? Should it be conducted in a lab or in the real world? Who should be the respondent: individuals or the relevant buying centers? Should data be collected by mail, telephone, or personal interviews? If personal, should the interviewing be done at home or in a central location? Should an unobtrusive research approach be used? How should the data be analyzed—should the relationships among attitudes be determined using factor analysis, multidimensional scaling, or some clustering procedure? Should the relationship between attitudes and some other behavioral response be established via multiple regression analysis, AID, multiple discriminant analysis, canonical correlation, other standard multivariate procedure (for a discussion of these techniques see Green and Tull, 1978) or logit, log linear, or some other approach to the analysis of qualitative data (for a discussion of these techniques see Green, Carmone, and Wachspress, 1976).

The research problem addressed, and the scale properties involved (ordinal, nominal or interval) can help select an appropriate approach. Yet, most research questions do not have a clear-cut answer.

Designing attitude research studies following the approach suggested by the methodologically augmented attitude-by-public-by-product decision matrix (Exhibit 2–7) could help provide sharper and more operational focus to attitude research and increase the likelihood that the results of such studies will be useful.

ISSUES IN IMPLEMENTING CONSUMER BEHAVIOR STUDIES

As indicated earlier, most of the applications of behavioral science and consumer behavior theories and findings require the actual testing of a hypothesis in the context of a specifically designed consumer behavior study. The design of such studies, however, require the resolution of a number of conceptual and methodological issues. Some of the more relevant issues involve:[9]

- Development of an appropriate model that identifies and measures operationally the behavior of interest—the dependent variables (product choice, brand choice, amount purchased, usage occasions, brand loyalty), as well as the set of possible explanatory (independent) variables—and hypothesizes the nature and magnitude of relationships between the independent variables and the dependent variable or variables. In this context, it is important to note that none of the existing general consumer behavior models (such as the Nicosia, 1966a; Amstutz, 1967; Engel, Kolat, and Blackwell, 1978; Howard and Sheth, 1969; or others) can be utilized as is. Whichever model is selected, it still has to be modified to fit the unique situation facing the user of the model.

- Identification of the relevant unit of analysis—an individual respondent, a household, a subset of household members.

- Selection of the relevant time period for observation and analysis.

- Selection of the method of data collection—lab experiment, real-world experiment, survey, observation.

---

[9]For a detailed discussion of the conceptual and methodological issues involved in the study of brand choice, see Wind (1976).

EXHIBIT 2–7

THE METHODOLOGICALLY AUGMENTED ATTITUDE BY PUBLIC BY PRODUCT DECISION MATRIX

Source: Reprinted from Yoram Wind and Tyzoon Tyebjee "On the Use of Attitude Research in Product Policy" in *Moving Ahead with Attitude Research*, American Marketing Association, 1977.

	Product decision area										
	A				B				...	L	
	Public										
	a	b	...	k	a	b	...	k	...	a	...
	Attitude *l ... m*	Attitude *l ... m*			Attitude *l ... m*						
I. *Secondary data*											
Type of data											
Age of data											
Sample											
.											
.											
.											
II. *Primary research*											
Respondent's task											
Ranking											
Rating											
.											
.											
Data collection											
Personal											
Telephone											
Mail											
.											
.											
Research design											
Lab experiment											
Field											
Longitudinal study											
Cross sectional											
.											
.											
.											
Data analysis											
MDS											
Conjoint analysis											
.											
.											

MANAGEMENT SCIENCE

What is the "best" assortment of products a firm can offer? How should the marketing efforts be allocated among the firm's various products and market segments? What is the best timing of the introduction of a new product? What are the expected sales of a new product, given a variety of marketing strategies? Answers to these and similar questions are essential to successful product/marketing management.

Management science/operations research provides management with an *approach (philosophy)* that can help produce better decisions, as well as a set of *tools* that can be used as guidelines for product/marketing decisions. No attempt is made here to provide a comprehensive review of this area. The management science approach and a few of its more relevant tools are discussed. For a detailed understanding of this area, the reader is encouraged to review some of the available texts, such as Kotler (1971).

THE MANAGEMENT SCIENCE/OPERATIONS RESEARCH APPROACH

The management science/operations research approach and philosophy can best be expressed through the steps it suggests for analyzing a problem:[10]

1. Defining the real problem
2. Collecting data on the factors affecting results
3. Analyzing the data

4. Establishing a realistic criterion for measuring results
5. Developing a model (usually, but not always, a mathematical one)
6. Testing the model on sample problems to make sure that it represents the system correctly
7. Developing working tools based on the model to achieve the desired results
8. Integrating the new methods into company operations (implementation)
9. Reevaluating and revising the model as it is used.

Whether one accepts this formulation of the operations research approach to problem analysis or some other formulation is immaterial. What is important is a recognition that the solution of a management problem requires an explicit effort that centers around the development of an appropriate *model*. In many cases the major benefit of utilizing management science in the solution of marketing problems is not so much the optimal solution it suggests, but rather the discipline it requires from the management scientist *and* the manager in defining their assumptions and developing an appropriate model for the problem at hand. Such models can vary in their complexity and language (e.g., they may be verbal or mathematical), but they do present a concise and explicit definition of the relevant marketing decision variables (product positioning, packaging, promotion); the market, competitive, and environmental conditions under which they operate; and the firm's and decision-maker's goals, objectives, and constraints. In addition to specifying these variables, objectives, and constraints, the model should also include a specification of the assumed relationship among

---

[10]This sequence of steps was proposed in "The ABC's of Operations Research," *Dun's Review and Modern Industry* (September 1963).

these components, hence facilitating communication among the decision makers.[11]

An important concept (and model) of the management science approach is that of *adaptive experimentation*. Given the uncertainties of the marketplace, the adaptive experimentation approach is a decision system in which the parameters are continuously updated on the basis of changing information about sales response. The decision maker who follows this approach is not concerned with the choice of an optimal decision at time *t*, but rather with the optimization over the long run, which requires

continuous experimentation to provide updated information on the latest response function of the system.

The concept of adaptive experimentation is illustrated by the case in which the manager decides (using some optimization procedure or some decision rule) on an "optimal" level of marketing expenditures. If the manager applies this level to all markets, the sales results cannot provide any useful guidelines for the decision in the next period concerning whether to increase, decrease, or keep constant the current level of expenditures. This situation is illustrated in the upper panel of Exhibit 2–8.

To obtain *useful* information, the decision maker should vary the level of marketing expenditures in various markets in a systematic

---

[11]For further discussion of the management science/operations research approach, see Ackoff (1962).

EXHIBIT 2–8

THE CASE FOR AN ADAPTIVE EXPERIMENTATION STRATEGY:
HYPOTHETICAL EXAMPLES

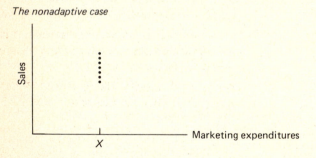

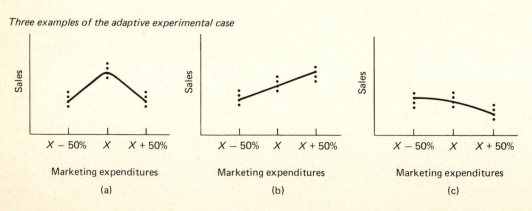

way. The minimum number of levels for a meaningful experiment is three. Let's consider the case in which the manager decided to use the optimal level and two others—plus or minus 50 percent of the optimal. Three hypothetical results for such an experiment are presented in the bottom panel of Exhibit 2–8. Case (a) is the one in which the optimal level was the correct one. Assuming no changes in the firm's offerings, consumers' behavior, and the environmental and competitive characteristics, the firm should continue at the next period with most of its efforts at the optimal level with only a few control markets above and below that level. If, on the other hand, the results were those presented in case (b), it is clear that the level X was not optimal and that the firm should consider exploring higher levels of expenditures (perhaps 2X and even higher). In case (c), the opposite situation occurs and it seems that the firm has been spending too much and should explore the possibility of cutting their expenditures even further (perhaps to ⅓X).

Undertaking the adaptive experimentation approach is costly—both in lost opportunities, as in the case of panel (a), and in the cost of gathering information on the sales results. Yet, it is an extremely important aspect of any sophisticated modern marketing management effort.[12]

Important developments in the management sciences have been the introduction and implementation of *decision calculus models* (Little, 1970). This approach is based on four major phases:

1. Verbalization by management of their implicit model of the situation to be modeled. This includes the specification of criteria variables, variables affecting them, and the relationship among them.

2. Translation of the manager's implicit model into a formal model structure. A typical model is of the form

$$Y_t = g(.) + f(x_t) + h(y_{t-1})$$

where Y_t = criterion variable (such as sales) at time t;

$g(.)$ = level of y_t in the absence of the control variable x_t;

x_t = value of control variable (such as advertising, price, etc.);

f = functional relationship between the control variable and the criterion variable (this function is typically either S-shaped or concave);

$h(y_{t-1})$ = carry-over effect.

3. Establishment of the parameters of the model. Those are typically established by using managerial judgment but to the extent that data are available they can obviously be incorporated. If management judgment is used, it typically follows the format of responses to questions such as:

• What would you expect the market share to be in the absence of advertising (or any other control variable)?

• What level of advertising would be required to maintain the current level of market share?

• What would be the next-period market share if advertising was cut to zero, increased by 25 percent, and increased to saturation level?

4. Development of an interactive computer program to operationalize the model and allow management to test for the sensitivity of the results to various levels of the control variables. This phase also tends to include tracking of results to replicate past and/or future data. This latter analysis, if conducted on past data, does not offer full validation of the model since it is possible to find a number of different parameter sets

---

[12]For a discussion of the adaptive experimentation approach, see Little (1966). For an example of its actual utilization by industry, see Ackoff and Emshoff (1975 and 1976).

that replicate past data well (Chakravarti, Mitchell, and Staelin, 1977).

SOME RELEVANT MANAGEMENT SCIENCE TOOLS

Management science tools, such as mathematical programming (linear, integer, dynamic, and target programming), queuing theory, simple and variable Markov processes, various stochastic models, simulations, and Bayesian decision theory, can and should be applied to various product/marketing decisions. This section, instead of describing these techniques, focuses on the structure of some of the major types of product decisions which are amenable to management science models and analysis.

Allocation problems Many of the product/marketing decisions are concerned with allocation of resources to activities or of activities to resources. Consider, for example, the problem of a single product and the decisions on how much to spend on its packaging versus warranties, service, price promotion, advertising, and the like. Or consider the other common situation of multiple products and the question of how to allocate resources among them. Similarly, the development of new products requires continuous reliance on allocation models: How much should be spent on new-concept generation versus testing? How much on laboratory product testing versus consumer testing? These are just a few of the more common allocation problems.

The typical allocation problem requires identification of a set of *activities* to be performed, a set of *resources* and *constraints,* and an *objective function.* The objective of the allocation problem is to allocate the activities to the resources (or vice versa) so as to maximize the total profits (or achieve any other desired objective). Whereas simple allocation problems can be solved using calculus, the most common

method for such problem is linear or other forms of mathematical programming. When the problem calls for the use of mathematical programming (many constraints), the technique provides not only an optimal allocation, but also information about the cost of imposing each resource and policy constraint. Hence, management is able to evaluate the desirability and consequences of imposing constraints.

In more typical complex problems (with considerable interactions and conflicts among activities, resources, and participating managers) it might be more advantageous to engage in heuristic modeling, or undertake the Analytic Hierarchy Process (AHP) which is discussed in Chapter 5 and Appendix A. In some of the cases, one may elect to simplify the problem and break it into more manageable parts that can be solved analytically. Yet, this is less desirable than the use of procedures (such as the Analytic Hierarchy Process) which are capable of dealing explicitly with the full complexity of most allocation problems.

Competitive problems The tendency toward problem simplification has led, in many cases, to the oversimplified assumption that the effectiveness of the decision-maker's choice is relatively independent of the actions of his competitors. Yet, a number of management science models and methods have been developed to deal with the competitive problem. The most common way of handling competitive strategy is in the context of a market simulation. As early as 1959, Cyert, March, and Feigenbaum developed a simulation of the competition between American and Continental can companies. Since then, a number of market simulations, varying in scope, complexity, and structure, have been developed and used (see, for example, Amstutz, 1967; Herniter and Cook, 1978; Kotler, 1971; Wind, Jolly, and O'Connor, 1975).

An alternative approach that can be applied in simple competitive cases is the *competitive equilibrium* approach, which takes partial derivatives of each firm's profit function, with respect to each marketing variable, setting the derivatives equal to zero, and solving them simultaneously for the optimal marketing mix for each firm (Kotler, 1971).

Markov models (Ehrenberg, 1965) and especially the *variable Markov model* (Kuehn, 1962), which describes the effect of both brand learning and the company marketing variables, can be utilized in a limited way to analyze the competitive position of a company.

Another approach for coping with competitive strategy is based on application of *game theory*. Strategies such as *minimax*, the selection of a course of action that would minimize the maximum loss associated with the game, or *minimum regret*, the minimization of post-decision regret, can be employed if the range of competitive actions and their effects are known but the specific action to be employed is unknown. Game theory, in its original formulation, has been applied primarily in military situations, although conceptually it can be applied to many marketing situations. Occasionally, competitive bidding models are structured along the lines of a game-theory approach.[13]

Decision theory Executives can absorb the uncertainty involved in marketing decisions through a variety of organizational and individual devices ranging from committee decision-making through various rules of thumb aimed at screening out high-risk decisions to heavy reliance and utilization of marketing research. Most of these and similar approaches,[14] however, do not take uncertainty explicitly into account. To overcome this shortcoming, *decision theory*, which encompasses a variety of formal methods for coping

with various levels of uncertainty, can be employed.[15]

The most common application of decision theory is based on the development of *decision trees*, coupled with the expected monetary value (EMV) criterion. As an example of the utilization of this approach in the context of a large chemical company's new product introduction decision, consider the case reported by Alderson and Green (1964). The alternatives under consideration were three pricing policies and two initial plant sizes. Given a planning horizon of thirteen years, three different forecasts of annual sales were made, representing, respectively, a pessimistic, optimistic, and most-likely outlook. A decision tree representing management judgment concerning the probability of occurrence of the three level forecasts and the resulting eighteen branches of expected present values is reproduced in Exhibit 2–9. The dollar figure at the end of each of the eighteen branches is the estimate of the present value of the expected cash flow during the thirteen-year planning period. The expected present values for each of the alternative courses of action are presented as the last column of numbers. Examination of the tree suggests that the large plant size yields the highest expected present value under all pricing policies and sales forecasts. The skimming pricing policy dominates the others under all conditions. Hence, the best decision is a large plant size and a skimming pricing policy (associated with the highest expected value of $12.03 million).

In this case, management used the EMV criterion since they had enough resources to withstand the possible loss of $30 million if it occurred. If applied consistently to all their investment decisions, the EMV criterion should

---

[13]For a comprehensive review of the game theory literature see Schotler and Schwödiaver (1980).

[14]For a discussion of uncertainty absorption devices, see Cyert and March (1963).

[15]For an excellent discussion of decision theory, see Schlaifer (1959) and Raiffa and Schlaifer (1961). For a discussion of decision theory in a marketing context, see Alderson and Green (1964).

EXHIBIT 2–9

AN ILLUSTRATIVE DECISION TREE: A NEW-PRODUCT DECISION OF A
CHEMICAL COMPANY

Source: Based on Alderson and Green, 1964.

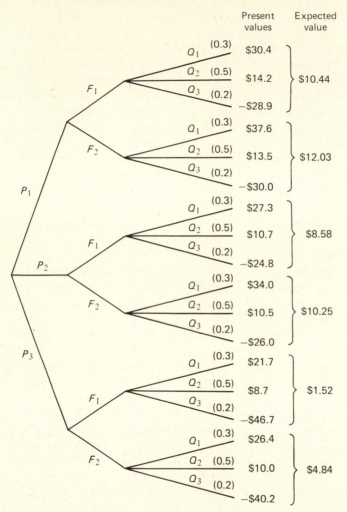

Key: P_1—skimming pricing policy; P_2—intermediate pricing policy; P_3—penetration pricing
policy; F_1—small plant; F_2—large plant; Q_1—optimistic demand forecast; Q_2—most probable
demand forecast; Q_3—pessimistic demand forecast.

yield the highest expected monetary value in the long run. Other criteria might be considered, however.[16] The expected-utility criterion is commonly used as an alternative to the EMV criterion, in recognition of the fact that different managers have different utility functions for money (Swalm, 1966). In applying both these criteria, the decision makers rely on a single number—the expected (monetary or utility) value—for each alternative. Using this single measure, the risk associated with the course of action is reflected in the expected value but is not considered explicitly by itself. An alternative approach may therefore be the utilization of two measures—the expected return (the EMV or rate of return) *and* expected risk (the variance as a measure of the dispersion among possible outcomes or, if one wants to avoid the inclusion of the opportunity side of variance, a measure of the expected value of the loss function.) Following this *risk-return criterion*, the decision-maker has to specify the decision rule for selecting alternatives (for example, based on the ratio of return to risk or the highest return providing that the risk does not exceed a certain level).

The *risk-return criterion* utilizes only two parameters, mean and variance of the expected return and risks, ignoring the possible skewness of the distributions. Given that decision-makers have different attitudes toward uncertainty (and would thus respond differently to two distributions with the same areas and variance but with different skewness), it is useful to provide them also with the information on the *probability distribution of return criterion*. Since the probability distribution of return is derived from a number of separate subjective distributions (for sales, sales growth, cost, etc.), none of which is necessarily normal, the most practical way to obtain the overall distribution is by a Monte Carlo simulation. Hertz (1964) termed this approach *risk analysis,* while others have referred to it as *venture analysis.* This approach is further discussed in Chapter 11 in the context of economic evaluation of new-product concepts.

Other problems amenable to management science Inventory problems, waiting-line problems, and replacement problems are a few of the other areas amenable to management science tools that are of some relevance as inputs and guidelines to product decisions. At this point the reader may want to review one of the basic management science/operations research texts and ask the question: Which other techniques can be appropriate to the solution of which product/marketing problems?

MARKETING INFORMATION SYSTEMS AND INTERACTIVE DECISION MODELS

The product/marketing manager needs continuous up-to-date information on consumers' behavior (awareness, attitudes, purchase, and usage behavior), the marketing environment (wholesale and retail sales, marketing efforts, and other relevant characteristics), competitive actions (prices, advertising, promotions, distribution), and other environmental conditions (government regulations, economic conditions and forecasts, technological innovations).

Information on these and relevant product performance measures (sales, market share, profits) are not available in a single well-organized document. Thousands of documents

---

[16]Note, however, that in many cases the major value of the decision tree is in the construction of the tree and the explicit identification of the relevant variables and subjective probabilities.

have to be sorted, numerous research projects undertaken, and a variety of services subscribed to in order to cover the range of required information. The gathering, processing, and analyzing of these huge amounts of data therefore require special planning and organization. To this end, companies have started developing marketing information systems. Kotler (1971), for example, has suggested the development of a *marketing information and analysis center (MIAC)*, the functions of which are outlined in Exhibit 2–10.

The experience with marketing information systems has not been very successful, however.

This has been attributed primarily to the fact that such systems were not designed to meet the information needs of their users. Recent efforts to design marketing information systems do reflect, to an increasing extent, the recognition that the system should be designed to satisfy the information needs of the decision-makers. As such marketing information systems attempt to incorporate not only a data base but also a series of models reflecting the company and its competitors' product/marketing decisions (product, price, advertising, costs), the decision models of the intermediate marketing organizations (retailers and

EXHIBIT 2–10

THE FUNCTIONS OF A MARKETING INFORMATION AND ANALYSIS CENTER
Source: Kotler, 1971, p. 570.

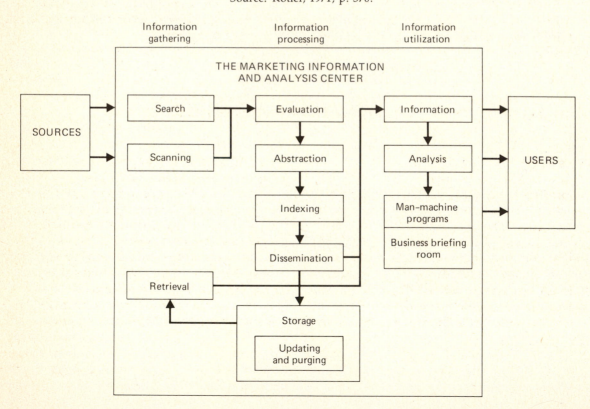

wholesalers), behavior models of consumers, and other decision models (governmental agencies), and environmental and other relevant inputs.

The data base should be updated regularly and supplemented with appropriate statistical packages with which to analyze the data and help transform them into meaningful information as inputs to the programmed and nonprogrammed decision models.

An essential part of such an information system is a set of decision models. To overcome the problem that many models are not implemented, it is helpful to follow Little's (1970) specification of a useful model. According to this approach, to be used by a manager, models should be:

- Simple to understand.
- Robust—hard to get absurd answers from.
- Easy to control—the user knows what input data would be required to produce answers.

- Adaptive—adjusted as new information is acquired.
- Complete—important phenomena will be included even if they require judgmental estimates of their effects.
- ✓ Easy to communicate with—the manager can quickly and easily change inputs and obtain and understand the outputs.

A number of on-line interactive models (consisting of a set of numerical procedures for processing data and judgments to assist in decision-making) have been developed by Little and his colleagues following these model specifications and the decision calculus principles. Some of these models are concerned with product decisions and are discussed in subsequent chapters. The development of interactive decision models is an important development in marketing and a cornerstone for better-designed and better-utilized marketing information systems.

CONCLUDING REMARKS

This chapter has provided a sketchy overview of some of the major tools that can be used to improve product decisions. Again focusing on a product or service with which you are familiar, review the marketing, marketing research, behavioral science, and management science concepts, findings, and methods and identify the key concepts and methods that you feel are relevant for the better management of your product or service. Be as specific as possible and make sure to include those items which were

not discussed in this chapter but which are relevant for your product decisions.

The tools described in this chapter are most likely to be used by professional staff personnel whose expertise is in marketing research, or the behavioral and management sciences. Yet, it is the manager's role to utilize these tools in making product decisions, requiring that the manager be familiar enough with these tools to be able to acquire the right type of tools and critically evaluate their relevance and guidance.

3

Product Life Cycle

INTRODUCTION

The concept of a *product life cycle* has occupied a prominent place in the marketing literature as both a forecasting instrument (Kovac and Dague, 1972; Chambers, Mullick, and Smith, 1971) and as a guideline for corporate marketing strategy (see, for example, Levitt, 1965; Clifford, 1964; and Patton, 1959). In its simplest form, it serves as a descriptive model of the stages of market acceptance of a product. It can thus be considered the "supply" view of the diffusion model (which was discussed in Chapter 2). The concept is borrowed from biology and sees the life of a product as analogous to the life of an organism, in that it progresses through the stages of birth, growth, maturity, decline, and death.

Biological studies have established the S-shaped logistic curve as the best representation of the process of life. This representation has been widely accepted in the study of product life cycle, with the result that product life cycles (PLC) are said to have four identifiable stages: a lag phase (introduction), an exponential phase (the growth phase), a stationary phase (the maturity and saturation phase), and a decline phase. Exhibit 3–1 illustrates this "typical" PLC.

This general pattern of product life cycle was found in a number of empirical investigations. Buzzell and Cook (1969) examined the sales histories of 192 consumer products and found that 52 percent of the products (nonfood grocery products, food products, and durables) followed the general pattern of the PLC model. Some of the products for which the PLC model was found to be representative are automobile tires (Kovac and Dague, 1972); United Kingdom sales of foods and cosmetics as well as refrigerators (Cunningham, 1969); tea and rum (Albach, 1965); certain automobiles—Hudson,

EXHIBIT 3–1

THE "TYPICAL" PRODUCT LIFE CYCLE

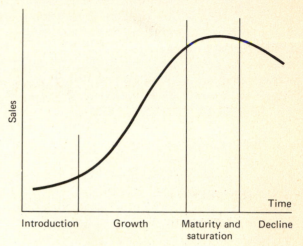

Rambler, and Nash (Brantel, 1963) and the De-Soto (May, 1961); black and white television (Patton, 1959); and four brands of "regular" cigarettes.

A number of studies were conducted on the product life cycle of industrial products. Cunningham (1969), for example, found that the United Kingdom sales trend of automobile components, chemicals, and general engineering products are represented fairly accurately by the general PLC model. Frederixson (1969) found that 41 percent of 27 new industrial chemical products followed the conventional PLC model.

In many of these and other PLC studies, the authors found either a modified S-shaped function PLC or some alternative function. Buzzell (1966), for example, found that the model is in agreement with actual trends for processed food products. New food products do pass through a period of slow growth, followed by a stage of rapid growth. Sales of "mature" products, on the other hand, did not necessarily follow the predicted stable pattern. Three patterns were observed: (1) the expected *stable maturity*, (2) a *growth maturity* due to some changes in market conditions, and (3) *innovative maturity*, which is due to some innovation by the processors. Concerning the decline stage, the empirical evidence shows that some products, such as evaporated milk, ultimately reach a stage of decline, although that has not been shown to be inevitable in the Buzzell investigation of eighteen years of product performance (1946–1964).

This empirical support for the S-shaped product life cycle is not universal, however. Polli and Cook (1969), who tested the life cycle model against sales behavior for 140 consumer nondurable products, found sales behavior consistent with the PLC model for less than half the products studied. Their conclusion, therefore, was:

> After completing the initial test of the life cycle expressed as a verifiable model of sales be-

havior, we must register strong reservations about its general validity, even stated in its weakest, most flexible form (Polli and Cook, 1969).

A few years later Dhalla and Yuspeh (1976), in a critical review of the PLC concept, concluded that with respect to *product class*, the PLC model does not hold since "many product classes (e.g., Scotch whiskey, French perfumes, automobiles, and radios, etc.) have enjoyed and will probably continue to enjoy a long and prosperous maturity stage—far more than the human life expectancy." Similarly, the PLC concept does not hold with respect to *product form*.

An examination of the PLC of the product forms of cigarettes, make-up bases, toilet tissues, and cereals suggests that "no PLC rule (indicating the movement of the product from one stage to another) can be developed" (Dhalla and Yuspech, 1976). The lack of any conclusive evidence concerning the validity of the concept requires that we examine it carefully.

THE PRODUCT LIFE CYCLE CONCEPT

Whether one accepts the S-shaped curve as a "typical" product sales pattern or only as a pattern which holds for some products (but not for others), it is useful to briefly review the conclusions which are frequently stated concerning the relationship between the various PLC stages and the various marketing forces. These generalizations should be viewed, however, only as hypotheses and not as *facts*. Only an examination of the sales pattern of a given product in a given marketing environment can lead to the acceptance or rejection of such hypotheses.

INTRODUCTORY STAGE

The introductory sales of a product are believed to be relatively slow, even after its technical problems have been ironed out, due to a number of marketing forces and consumer behavior factors. The major marketing obstacle to rapid introduction of a product is often distribution. Retail outlets are often reluctant to introduce new products, and many prefer to wait until a track record has been established before including them in their stock. Imagine, for example, that you are the marketing manager of a supermarket with an average inventory of 10,000 items. How likely would you be to buy, stock, and devote precious shelf space to a new and untested cereal?

Sequential regional introduction of a new product leads again to a slow and lengthy introductory period (when the product life cycle is developed for the entire national market) and often reflects logistical problems with physical distribution.

Consumer acceptance of new products tends to be relatively slow. The new-product-diffusion models discussed in the previous chapter have highlighted the fact that only a small percentage of consumers tend to be "innovators." The newer the product, the greater the marketing effort required to *create* the demand for it. The length of the introductory period depends on the product's complexity, its degree of newness, its fit into consumer needs, the presence of competitive substitutes of one form or another, and the nature, magnitude and effectiveness of the introductory marketing effort.

At this stage it is usually assumed that there are no competitors, and some even define the market structure at this stage as *virtual monopoly* (Schewing, 1974). Yet, although there are a very few really radical innovations with no existing substitutes, most new products and services face considerable competition from existing products.

In addition to competition from existing products, many new products face severe competitive pressure from other new products. There have been a notable number of cases in which two firms introduce similar products almost at the same time, an occurance quite possible if the two companies are working on similar technological developments. In other cases one company goes through a test market, which is noticed by a competitor, who decides, after observing the first company's test market

results, to introduce a similar product. This issue is discussed further in Chapter 14. Whatever the reasons leading to it, if two or more firms introduce products at about the same time, the result is likely to be a shorter introductory period.

The length of the introductory period is one of the most crucial aspects of the product life cycle. From a managerial point of view, the shorter the introductory period the better. The marketing strategy of subsequent stages is often based on the assumption that those who buy the product in the introductory stages are the innovators, and those who buy it in subsequent stages are the late adopters or laggards who respond differently to the firm's marketing strategy. The classification of a buyer as an innovator or laggard depending on the time that elapses between his/her purchase and the introduction of the product, may be misleading, however. Consider, for example, a buyer who hears about the product for the first time two years after its introduction. As soon as he hears about the product, he goes out and buys it. Can this individual be considered a laggard?

GROWTH STAGE

The growth stage begins when demand for the new product starts increasing rapidly. In the case of frequently-purchased products, innovators move from the trial to repeat purchase. If they are satisfied with the product, innovators may influence others by word-of-mouth, which is often considered the most effective mode of communication.[1] The product availability and visibility in distribution and in use (e.g., new cars on the roads) tend to bring

[1]If innovators have a high likelihood of engaging in positive word-of-mouth communication, an introductory strategy aimed at this market segment would have an added leverage. It could result in a faster rate of adoption.

EXHIBIT 3–2

SOME OF THE SUGGESTED MARKETING ACTION IMPLICATIONS OF THE VARIOUS PLC STAGES

Source: Reprinted by permission of the *Harvard Business Review*. Exhibit from "Forget the Product Life Cycle Concept!" by Nariman K. Dhalla and Sonia Yuspeh (January–February 1976). Copyright © 1976 by the President and Fellows of Harvard College; all rights reserved.

EXHIBIT II   HOW PLC ADVOCATES VIEW THE IMPLICATIONS OF THE CYCLE FOR MARKETING ACTION

Effects and responses	Stages of the PLC			
	Introduction	Growth	Maturity	Decline
Competition	None of importance	Some emulators	Many rivals competing for a small piece of the pie	Few in number with a rapid shakeout of weak members
Overall strategy	Market establishment; persuade early adopters to try the product	Market penetration; persuade mass market to prefer the brand	Defense of brand position; check the inroads of competition	Preparations for removal; milk the brand dry of all possible benefits
Profits	Negligible because of high production and marketing costs	Reach peak levels as a result of high prices and growing demand	Increasing competition cuts into profit margins and ultimately into total profits	Declining volume pushes costs up to levels that eliminate profits entirely
Retail prices	High, to recover some of the excessive costs of launching	High, to take advantage of heavy consumer demand	What the traffic will bear; need to avoid price wars	Low enough to permit quick liquidation of inventory
Distribution	Selective, as distribution is slowly built up	Intensive; employ small trade discounts since dealers are eager to store	Intensive; heavy trade allowances to retain shelf space	Selective; unprofitable outlets slowly phased out
Advertising strategy	Aim at the needs of early adopters	Make the mass market aware of brand benefits	Use advertising as a vehicle for differentiation among otherwise similar brands	Emphasize low price to reduce stock
Advertising emphasis	High, to generate awareness and interest among early adopters and persuade dealers to stock the brand	Moderate, to let sales rise on the sheer momentum of word-of-mouth recommendations	Moderate, since most buyers are aware of brand characteristics	Minimum expenditures required to phase out the product
Consumer sales and promotion expenditures	Heavy, to entice target groups with samples, coupons, and other inducements to try the brand	Moderate, to create brand perference (advertising is better suited to do this job)	Heavy, to encourage brand switching, hoping to convert some buyers into loyal users	Minimal, to let the brand coast by itself

new triers into the market. Of greatest importance at this stage is the entry of competitors who, through their advertising and promotional efforts, increase the total demand for the product. When Kodak entered the instant-photography market, for example, Polaroid sales increased significantly from 3.5 million cameras shipped to U.S. distributors and dealers to 4.5 million units, while Kodak sold during that period over 2 million units (Louis, 1978).

MATURITY STAGE

The maturity or saturation stage occurs when distribution has reached its planned or unplanned peak, and the percentage of total population that is ever going to buy the product has been reached. Volume (reflecting the number of customers, quantity purchased, and frequency of purchase) is stable.

This is the stage in which it becomes difficult to maintain effective distribution, and price competition is quite common.

DECLINE STAGE

Changes in competitive activities, consumer preferences, product technology, and other environmental forces tend to lead to the decline of most mature products. If the decline is for a product (as distinct from a brand), producers may delete some brands and even withdraw from the given product category. The typical reason for a product decline is the entry of new products, coupled with decreased consumer interest in the specific product. Under these conditions, one of the few options left for keeping a brand alive is price reduction and other drastic means that depress the profit margin and lead the company to consider the product's withdrawal. The conditions for product deletion are discussed further in Chapter 18.

A somewhat different case of product decline occurs when most customers no longer buy the product, but a small, loyal customer base remains. These customers continue to buy the product even if it receives no advertising or other promotional support. If this is the case, the company may decide to follow a "milking" strategy, i.e., retain the product with no marketing support as long as it generates some sales. The problem with this strategy is that it requires maintaining the distribution of the product, which becomes less and less profitable compared to other investment opportunities, as the volume of sales and margins decrease.

These and some of the other marketing implications, which are often suggested for the various PLC stages, are summarized in Exhibit 3–2.

OPERATIONALIZING THE PRODUCT LIFE CYCLE CONCEPT

The operationalization of the product life cycle concept, i.e., answering the question of how one can unambiguously determine the exact product life cycle position of a product, is necessary before the product life cycle concept can be used as a forecasting or diagnostic tool.

Operationalizing the product life cycle concept requires six major conceptual and measurement decisions.

UNIT OF ANALYSIS

What is the appropriate definition of a product? Should product life cycle cycle analysis be undertaken for a product class, product form, product line, an individual product, or a brand? A product life cycle analysis can be undertaken for each of these product levels at both the firm and industry levels. It is surprising, therefore, that little attention has been given to the identification of the most appropriate unit or units of analysis, and to the nature of the relationships among the life cycles of these various product levels. In an attempt to validate the product life cycle model, Polli and Cook (1969) concluded that the fit of the life cycle model depends heavily on the definition of product used and the relevance of product class partitioning. Attention, therefore, should be given to explicit definition of the unit of analysis.

The importance of developing an explicit definition of the unit of analysis is evident when one considers, for example, the PLC of television sets. Should one focus on all TV sets? On black and white versus color? On portables versus consoles? On battery-operated versus electricity-powered? On size of screen? With respect to size, should certain sizes be grouped together? On domestically manufactured versus imported? It is obvious that no a priori rule can be established as to the "correct" unit of analysis. Rather, management should select the unit(s) of analysis based on their needs and how they intend to use the PLC information.

RELEVANT MARKET

Implicit in most traditional approaches to the product life cycle concept is the assumption that the market is homogeneous and composed primarily of one segment with distinct subsegments that differ from each other only in their "degree of innovativeness"; i.e., the innovators are the first to buy the product, followed by the early adopters, early and late majority, and, finally, the laggards.

These traditional approaches ignore the possibility of *sequential entry* into distinctly different market segments, each of which can be further segmented according to customers' degree of innovativeness (or other relevant customer characteristics). Such sequential entry to various market segments may result in the type of a product life cycle presented in Exhibit 3-3.

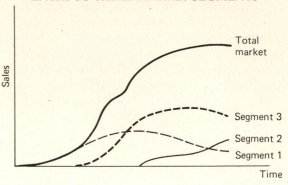

EXHIBIT 3–3

PRODUCT LIFE CYCLE WITH SEQUENTIAL ENTRY TO THREE MARKET SEGMENTS

Whereas most PLC studies have focused on product sales at the total market level, there are occasions in which it would be important to consider the PLC by type of market (e.g., domestic versus multinational), distribution outlet (e.g., discount stores versus department stores) or market segment (e.g., large versus small industrial buyers, different SIC segments).

LIFE CYCLE PATTERN AND NUMBER OF STAGES

The most common product life cycle pattern is the S-shaped logistic function with four major stages: introduction, growth, maturity, and decline. The typical *logistic function* (or the *growth function* as it is frequently referred to) is presented in Exhibit 3-4. This function, like the Gompertz curve, was developed to describe population growth over time.

The equation of the logistic curve is:

$$S = \frac{1}{1 + e^{-(a+\beta t)}}.$$

Since a is merely a location parameter, one can consider the simplified logistic function:

$$S = \frac{1}{1 + e^{-\beta t}},$$

EXHIBIT 3–4

THE S-CURVE LOGISTIC FUNCTION

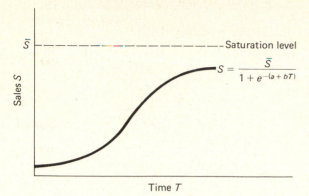

$$S = \frac{\bar{S}}{1 + e^{-(a + bT)}}$$

where $S = \frac{1}{2}$ when $t = 0$, $S = 0$ when $t = -\infty$, and $S = 1$ when $t = +\infty$.

Thus, $S = 0$ and $S = 1$ are asymtotes, and the curve is skew-symmetric about the lines $t = 0$, $S = \frac{1}{2}$.

The slope of the curve is $dS/dt = \beta S(1-S)$. This differential equation suggests that the rate of change of sales with respect to time is proportional to the sales multiplied by a factor which decreases as sales increases (here β is a rate which determines the spread of the curve along the time dimension).

This function was first popularized in the early 1920s by Pearl and Reed (1920) and was applied to a variety of biological phenomena and other growth situations such as the spread of epidemics and rumors.

This life cycle pattern, although supported by conceptual analogies from the biological life cycles (Polli and Cook, 1967) and the theory and findings concerning the diffusion and adoption of innovations (Rogers, 1976), is only one of many possible empirical life cycle patterns. Cox (1967), for example, in a study of 258 ethical drug products introduced between 1955 and 1959 found that six types of life-cycle curves were needed to describe the sales patterns of these products. These six-product life-cycle curves are presented in the upper panels of Exhibit 3–5.

It is interesting to note that only 28.3 percent of the products studied by Cox were described by the traditional S-shaped curve. The sixth life cycle pattern—polynomials of the fourth degree—was found to be the most appropriate for the drug products, with 39.1 percent of the products following this pattern. Furthermore, drugs with product life cycle patterns of Types I, II, and III, in the early stages of their developments, tend to exhibit a Type VI pattern over time.

The six life cycle patterns identified by Cox do not, however, present an exhaustive description of all possible life cycle patterns. Fad products, or products with subsequent regrowth periods, for example, are not presented in this list, and some of them are illustrated in the bottom panels of Exhibit 3–5.

Non-S-curve PLC functions were also discovered in a number of other studies. Frederixson (1969), for example, in a study of 27 industrial chemical products, found support for the S-curve in only 41 percent of the cases. Fifteen percent followed a linear model with positive slope, and 44 percent followed a rapid penetration model. Balachandran and Jain (1972) predicted the life cycle of a newly introduced industrial product by fitting a fourth degree polynomial and its derivatives to the data of a "retired" product belonging to the same family. Hinkle (1966) examined the sales trend of 275 brands of health and beauty aids, household products, and food products, and found that the majority of PLC curves consisted of a primary cycle followed by a recycle (a pattern similar to the fourth degree polynomial).

Concerning the number of product life cycle stages, it is quite evident that many of the non-S-shaped curve patterns imply other than the traditional four life cycle stages of introduction, growth, maturity, and decline.

Yet, even those who accept the S-shaped curve as the dominant pattern of product life cycle identify a varying number of stages and

EXHIBIT 3–5

ALTERNATIVE LIFE CYCLE PATTERNS

Six patterns of PLC for ethical drugs (Cox, 1967, p. 382)

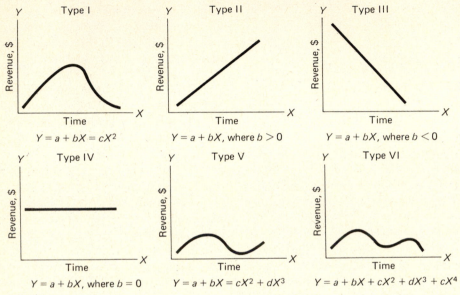

Type I $Y = a + bX = cX^2$

Type II $Y = a + bX$, where $b > 0$

Type III $Y = a + bX$, where $b < 0$

Type IV $Y = a + bX$, where $b = 0$

Type V $Y = a + bX = cX^2 + dX^3$

Type VI $Y = a + bX + cX^2 + dX^3 + cX^4$

Some other commonly found patterns

A fad product

Fad product with residual market

Specialty product

The Nielsen PLC (similar to type VI above)

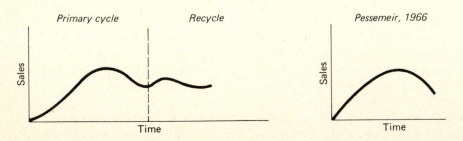

Primary cycle   Recycle

Pessemeir, 1966

labels for these stages. Booz, Allen & Hamilton, for instance, identify five stages: introduction, growth, maturity, saturation, and decline. Pessemier, on the other hand, who also identified five stages, labeled them introduction, growth, competition, obsolescence, and termination; while A.C. Nielsen identifies the product life cycle as composed of only two segments—the primary cycle and recycle.

IDENTIFYING THE PRODUCT'S STAGE IN THE PLC MODEL

Two key questions facing those who attempt to use the product life cycle concept are: (a) how to determine the PLC stage of a product, and (b) how to determine when a product moves from one PLC stage to another. Given that time-series sales data rarely obey the theoretical pattern of a smooth curve, and that the S-shaped curve is only one of a number of possible life cycle patterns, it is not at all clear whether a product's position in its life cycle pattern and its shift from one stage to another can be identified simply by observing the historical sales pattern of the product.

One of the possible operational approaches to the identification of a product's position in its life cycle pattern was proposed by Polli and Cook (1969), based on the percentage change in real sales from one year to the next. Plotting these changes as a normal distribution with mean zero, they determined that if a product has percentage changes less than -0.5σ, it is to be classified in the *decline* stage. Products with percentage change greater than 0.5σ were classified as being in the *growth* stage, and products in the range of $\pm 0.5\sigma$ were considered to be stable, corresponding to the *maturity* stage. This latter stage was further divided into decaying maturity and sustained maturity. The theoretical distribution and the corresponding four stages are presented in Exhibit 3–6.

Identifying the length of time of each PLC

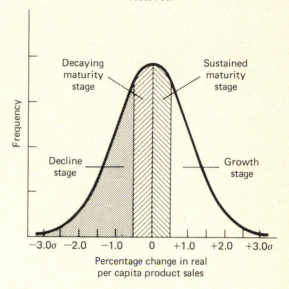

stage and the exact point at which a product shifts from one PLC stage to another is closely related to the use of the PLC model for forecasting sales. No generalized pattern can be identified, since the length of each PLC stage depends on a large number of factors such as the product's characteristics, market acceptance, and competitive actions.

DETERMINING THE UNIT OF MEASUREMENT

Whereas most product life cycle analyses are based on actual sales, there are still a number of unresolved issues. The first is whether one should use unit sales or dollar values. Second, should the analysis be based on actual sales or adjusted sales? For example, should they be adjusted to per capita sales? Corrected for strike periods, or other supply shortages? Adjusted for general economic conditions (current versus real prices), and the like?

Furthermore, should sales be the sole yardstick, or should market share figures or profits be used as well?

DETERMINING THE RELEVANT TIME UNIT

Most published product life cycle analyses are based on annual data. Yet, it is not clear why the analysis should be limited to this unit of time. In many instances, one may want to develop a product life cycle based on quarterly, monthly, or even weekly data. Given that the shorter the time period the higher the likelihood of seasonal and other fluctuations, one may use some form of a moving average. Given that most new products seem to have shorter and shorter life cycles—A.C. Nielsen (*The Nielsen Researcher*, 1968), for example, has estimated that about 50 percent of food products have a PLC of less than two years—it becomes important to use a shorter unit of measurement than the traditional annual data base.

PRODUCT LIFE CYCLE AS A FORECASTING MODEL

A natural use of the product life cycle concept is the prediction of the performance of a new product. Assuming the general S-shaped pattern of a product life cycle, with information on sales (and dollar revenues) for the first few periods and a simple predictive model, the sales in subsequent periods can be predicted. Considerable effort has been devoted to the development of PLC-based forecasting models, some of which are discussed in Chapter 15.

To illustrate the use of the product life cycle model as a predictive tool, let us consider a number of the more common diffusion-type new product forecasting models. Some of the early work in this area was done by economists. The diffusion model used by Brady and Adams (1962) is a good example of such efforts. The model proposed by them is:

$$r_t = S[1 - (1-b)^{2^{t-1}}] ,$$

where r_t = purchase rate at time t (determined as the percentage of purchases of all potential purchasers);

S = limit of purchase rate, i.e., maximum percentage of buyers or saturation level (this is determined by the researcher);

b = percent of S that buy the product (this, too, can initially be determined by the researcher and adjusted as data are generated).

In this model, the shape of the growth curve depends on the value of b. If b is small, the curve is predominantly S-shaped. For higher values of b, the curve becomes less S-shaped and eventually resembles an exponential growth pattern. Exhibit 3–7 illustrates this.

The major assumptions of this model are:

1. There is no difference in the purchase rate of users and nonusers.

2. The repurchase rate of users is 1; i.e., all first buyers would repeat their purchases.

This latter assumption is relaxed in a similar model by Fourt and Woodlock (1960) which estimates empirically and incorporates the repur-

EXHIBIT 3–7

THE SENSITIVITY OF THE BRADY–ADAM'S MODEL TO VARYING VALUES OF b

Source: "The Diffusion of New Products and Their Impact on Consumer Expenditures," by
D. Grady and F.G. Adams, *Proceedings of ASA*, 1963.

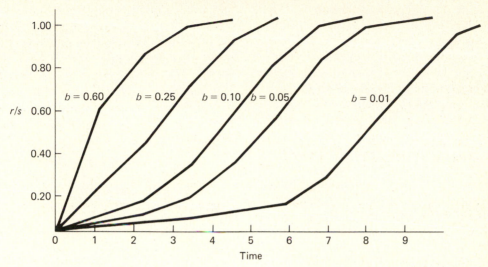

chase rates. Whereas the Fourt–Woodlock model is primarily concerned with predicting the purchase of frequently-purchased products, the Brady–Adams model includes three predictive submodels for durables, one focusing only on new purchases, a second that incorporates replacement, and a third that incorporates the *model change* phenomenon. The two basic models of Brady–Adams and Fourt–Woodlock, as well as similar diffusion models for both durables and frequently-purchased products, can generally be described in terms of four distinguishing features:

- A sales ceiling that reflects, in most cases, the researcher's belief as to the expected saturation level. Most of the models assume a constant saturation level, although they can be modified to incorporate a somewhat more realistic situation in which the level of saturation changes (at a decreasing rate) over time.

- An S-shaped diffusion curve. In a few cases, an exponential growth curve is proposed.

- An assumption of homogeneity of consumers.

- No explicit inclusion of the firm's marketing strategy or the actions of competitors.

The ceiling/saturation assumption This can be tested empirically, and evidence to date suggests that it is a reasonable assumption, especially when viewed not as a constant, but as a function of various corporate, competitive, and environmental forces.

The specific level of saturation should be established, based on all relevant information about the purchase history of similar products and an assessment of the potential impact of the firm's and competitors' actions on the market, given alternative environmental scenarios. Furthermore, in any forecasting model utilizing a saturation level, it might be useful to conduct sensitivity analysis to determine how sensitive the solution is to different assumptions concerning the saturation level.

The shape of the diffusion function As discussed earlier, the evidence to date indicates that the S-shaped curve is only one of many possible functions. Again, utilization of relevant data on the sales of related and similar products and sensitivity analysis are essential in the development of any model. The use of historical data on a related product, coupled with a few observations on the sales of a new product, was reported by Balachandran and Jain (1972), who, as mentioned earlier, predicted the sales of a new product by fitting a fourth-degree polynomial and its derivatives to the data of a "retired" product belonging to the same family. To determine the shape of the new product's life cycle, they used the Pearsonian distribution obtained from the revenues of the retired product.

The consumer homogeneity assumption One of the major developments in life cycle prediction models has been the recognition that consumers are heterogeneous. Bass (1969), for example, segmented the purchasing population into *innovators*, who buy the product because they like it, and *imitators*, whose decision to buy is influenced by the number of people who have already bought the product. The resulting sales are a function of the relationship between the two populations. The higher the imitation coefficient, the higher the peak of sales, but as found by Polli and Cook (1967) in their examination of this type model, also the more drastic the sales drop.

Another approach to dealing with population heterogeneity was proposed by Pyatt (1964), who suggested that the probability of buying a new durable product depends on the consumer's composition of owned durables,

which determines his/her purchasing *priority pattern*.

The exclusion of marketing variables New product diffusion models tend to examine the relationship between time and sales, ignoring one of the most central concepts in marketing—that of a *conditional sales forecast*, i.e., given that sales are a function of the firm's marketing strategy, the forecast should reflect alternative strategies resulting in a series of forecasted curves. This is presented graphically in Exhibit 3–8.

EXHIBIT 3–8

HYPOTHETICAL CONDITIONAL SALES FORECAST

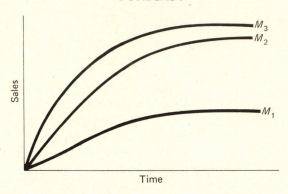

Key: M_i is a specific marketing strategy

More sophisticated approaches to new product forecasting could take into account not only the firm's marketing strategy, but also the competitors' expected actions and reactions.

How good are sales forecasts of PLC models? The proponents of various PLC models often claim high predictive accuracy. Yet, it might be useful to distinguish between (a) the ability to predict the growth and maturity phases of a new product and (b) the ability to predict the length of the maturity, saturation, and decline phases and the rate of decline. Whereas most PLC models are concerned with and able to predict the growth phase, only a few successful attempts have been made to predict the saturation and decline stages.

Among the successful efforts at forecasting the saturation and decline stages is Cooke and Edmondson's 1973 LIFER (*Life Cycle Forecaster*) model. The model is a multiplication model:

$$S(t) = c_1 t^{c_2} \exp(c_3 t + c_4 t^2) \ e(t) \ t^{c_2} \geq 0 \ ,$$

where $S(t)$ = recorded sales during period $(t-1,t)$;

$e(t)$ = multiplicative random component for period t;

c_i = parameters to be estimated from sales data.

The nonrandom component of the model is $u(t)$ = $c_1 t^{c_2} \exp(c_3 t + c_4 t^2)$, where t^{c_2} is restricted to the role of a growth component, while the function $\exp(c_3 t + c_4 t^2)$ may represent either growth or decay. This model was tested for cigarettes, beer, wine, consumer and industrial magazines, appliances, mutual fund sales, and ethical drugs, leading to the conclusion that "the predictive ability of LIFER makes it a viable forecasting tool for most product life cycle situations and, in particular, those involving extended decline phases as well as recycle."

Another approach to the forecasting of the saturation stage of PLC models is the one suggested by Wilson (1969), who focused on the discovery of leading indicators of the timing of the saturation phase. Among these indicators were declining proportion of new triers versus replacement sales, declining profits, industry overcapacity, appearance of new replacement products, decline in elasticity of advertising coupled with increased price elasticity, present users' consumption rate, and style changes.

PRODUCT LIFE CYCLE AS A GUIDELINE FOR MARKETING STRATEGY

Most of the writings concerning the product life cycle have emphasized its role in providing guidelines for strategic marketing actions (Buzzell, 1966; Smallwood, 1973; and others). In considering the possible relationship between marketing strategy and the product's life cycle, the reader should consider whether the product life cycle is an inevitable independent force to which companies must adopt their marketing efforts or whether the firm's marketing strategy can change the course of the product life cycle.

Surprisingly, most of the product life cycle literature tends to accept the first option. Only a few PLC studies have investigated empirically the marketing strategy determinants of a product's PLC. Belville (1966), for example, found seven factors which triggered the takeoff of color TV—price, volume of network color programming, public exposure to color, obsolescence of black and white sets, color quality, clarity of black and white pictures, and attitude of major set makers. It is unfortunate that, so far, most studies of the determinants of product sales are not concerned directly with the product's PLC.

Whether one accepts the independency or dependency of PLC, knowledge of the product's stage in its life cycle provides useful but only *partial* input for the design of the product's marketing strategy.

Recommendations have frequently been made concerning the type and level of advertising, pricing, distribution, and other product/ marketing activities required at each of the product life cycle stages. Typical of these recommendations is the following illustrative statement from an introductory marketing text (Buzzell, et al., 1972):

> The introductory period is characterized by heavy promotion aimed at building up primary demand; price is relatively unimportant. During the growth phase, more competition appears and there is an increasing pressure on price. Promotional expenditures decline in relation to sales; there is a shift to competition on the basis of brands and specific features. As the product enters maturity, there is increasing product brand competition, promotional expenditures and prices tend to stabilize, manufacturers begin efforts to extend life cycles, and new brands may appear. Finally, in the decline phase, further declines in price and promotional expenditures can be expected.

These rather vague recommendations are typical of those presented in many leading marketing texts (e.g., Kotler, 1971; Staudt and Taylor, 1970). Some authors have shown even more optimism by providing specific recommendations for marketing strategies at various stages of the product life cycle. Mickwitz (1959), for example, attempted to identify the changing elasticities of price, quality, service, packaging, and advertising at different stages in the product life cycle.

Such elasticities (the percentage change in sales associated with a percentage change in a decision variable), if validated, could serve as useful inputs to an optimal allocation of marketing expenditures among the various marketing decision variables at each stage in the product life cycle. Unfortunately, no conclusive empirical evidence has been provided in support of the propositions of Mickwitz and others on the elasticities of marketing policy variables at various product life cycle stages. Some initial evidence does suggest, however, that elasticities of various marketing decisions change at different stages of the PLC. Kotler (1971), for example,

reports on the experience of a packaged goods company that found a general pattern of falling advertising elasticity as products progressed through their life cycles. Similar findings were also reported by Parsons (1975), who found for a household cleaner in cake form that a time-varying elasticity formulation fit the data somewhat better than constant elasticity formulation.

Despite the exploratory nature of these and similar findings, specific recommendations are frequently made for each marketing variable. Some of the more common recommendations are discussed below but should be viewed as *hypotheses*, and not facts or normative prescriptions.

Advertising   The changing nature of advertising at each stage of the product life cycle was studied by Forrester (1961). According to him, in the introductory stage, advertising informs customers about the existence, advantages, and uses of new products. During the growth stage, advertising stresses the merits of the products compared to competing products. In the maturity phase, advertising attempts to create impressions of product differentiation. Advertising appeals to pride and noneconomic utilities. Massive advertising campaigns attempt to attract attention. And in the decline stage, the percentage of sales going into advertising decreases.

Product changes   Changes in the features, performance, design, and so forth of a product was explored by Schewing (1974), who suggested the following product changes at each stage of the product life cycle: Introduction—new product; Growth—product modification; Maturity—product modification and differentiation; Saturation—product modification, differentiation, and diversification; and Decline—product diversification.

Another view of product decisions at various stages of the PLC is presented by those who feel that a product is usually introduced in a single version (accompanied by various product problems and "bugs"). At the growth stage, the product is improved, while at the maturity stage, new versions are introduced. At the decline stage, stripped-down versions are introduced (Smallwood, 1973).

Pricing Price is usually believed to be high at the introductory period and to decline with the product life cycle stages as price becomes an increasingly important competitive weapon, especially at the late stages of growth and throughout the maturity and decline stages.

Although price cutting is quite common in many industries as the product matures (recall, for example, the radical reductions in the prices of pocket calculators and digital watches over a period of just a few years in the early seventies), many managers prefer to engage in nonprice competition. Buttler and Wyden (1965), for example, found that price cutting in the saturation stage, although common, is far less important than changes in the product, promotion, and distribution policies of the firms studied.

In determining the product's price strategy, not only the introductory price should be considered, but also what the next move might be, given alternative competitive actions. In this context, a relatively low introductory price (which is contrary to the strategy suggested by many life cycle writers) should not be ruled out automatically but should be fully examined.[2]

Distribution Initial distribution is believed to be spotty and to reach its full coverage at the growth stage, when retail outlets are seeking the product. At the maturity stage, retail outlets are the first to suffer from changes in consumer

purchase patterns, hence a manufacturer may start losing outlets. At the same time, efforts are made by manufacturers to establish new methods of distribution (bypassing the wholesalers, for instance) and new outlets (direct mail, for example).

These and similar attempts to prescribe a marketing strategy and guide the allocation of marketing resources over the stages of a product's life cycle, are to a large extent unsupported by empirical evidence and based on the erroneous assumption that the dominant determinant of a product's marketing strategy is the product's stage in its life cycle, while the differences among products, markets, and firms are ignored. Furthermore, it is implicit in such an assumption that, at any one stage of the product life cycle, the firm has only a single "reasonable" marketing strategy it can follow. This implicit assumption is not only misleading but also dangerous, since it can constrain management's creativity in generating new marketing strategies.

The correct question, therefore, is not what specific strategy the firm *should* follow at each stage of the product life cycle, but, rather, how input of the product stage in its life cycle curve can be utilized in generating, developing, and evaluating better marketing strategies. Note that accepting this view means that the preceding speculative discussion on the "typical" marketing strategies at the various stages of the product life cycle should be viewed only as possible hypotheses.

Accepting this view suggests, therefore, that the product life cycle can be utilized in two ways:

Life extension This strategy is based on the basic premise of the life cycle concept that all products do follow the life cycle of introduction, growth, maturity, and decline (regardless of the time dimension involved, the height or slope of the sales curve).

---

[2]This conclusion is consistent with the traditional marketing distinction between skimming and penetration pricing which suggests setting the introductory price based on an explicit analysis of the advantages and disadvantages of the two strategies and not the automatic acceptance of a high (skimming) price.

According to Levitt (1965), *life extension* or *market stretching* is based on the important proposition that

> When a company develops a new product or service, it should try to plan at the very outset a series of actions to be employed at various subsequent stages in the product's existence so that its sales and profit curves are constantly sustained rather than following their usual declining slope. (Levitt, 1965)

It might be difficult to follow Levitt's advice and plan for *all* subsequent product life extensions at the outset, yet the direction he suggests is most valuable. An example which is often

used to illustrate the concept of sequential actions leading to a stretched product life cycle, is the nylon industry, presented in Exhibit 3–9. The key question is obviously: What are the marketing strategies that can lead to such *life extensions*. Levitt suggests four such possible strategies and illustrates them as they apply to the case of Dupont's nylon, General Food's Jello, and 3M's Scotch tape. These strategies are:

1. Promoting *more frequent use* of the product among current users. DuPont, for example, emphasized the necessity of wearing nylon stockings at all times, while GF increased

EXHIBIT 3–9

AN EXAMPLE OF PRODUCT LIFE STRETCHING: THE CASE OF THE NYLON INDUSTRY
Innovation of new products postpones the time of total maturity

Source: Jordan P. Yale, "The Strategy of Nylon's Growth: Create New Markets," *Modern Textiles Magazine*, (February 1964,) p. 33. Copyright © 1962 by Jordan P. Yale. Reproduced by permission.

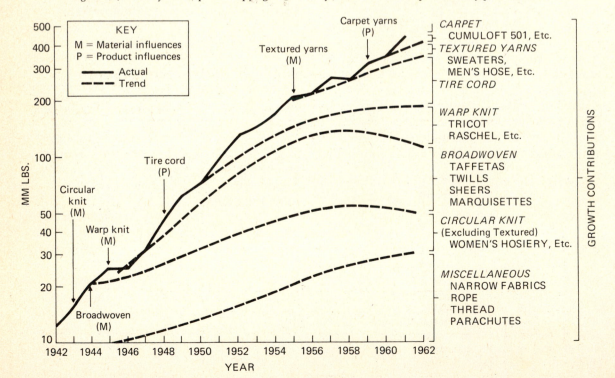

the number of available flavors, and 3M developed a variety of tape dispensers that made the product easier to use.

2. Developing *more varied use* of the product among current users. DuPont achieved this objective by offering tinted, patterned, and highly textured hosiery, converting it from a neutral accessory to a central ingredient of fashion that could be coordinated with outer garments and the occasion. GF achieved the more varied usage objective by emphasizing the use of Jello not only as a dessert but as a base for salads. 3M developed a line of colored, patterned, waterproof, invisible, and write-on Scotch tapes.

3. *Creating new users* for the product by expanding the market. To achieve this objective, according to Levitt, DuPont tried to legitimize the wearing of hosiery among early teenagers. GF presented Jello as a fashion-oriented weight-control product, and 3M developed a line of commercial cellophane tapes of various widths, lengths, and strengths.

4. *Finding new uses* for the basic material. The case of nylon is quite familiar, with nylon used in rugs, tires, and numerous other products. GF was less fortunate in discovering new uses for Jello, yet, even here, flavorless gelatin was promoted as a means of strengthening fingernails. 3M also developed new uses for the basic product, such as the double-coated tape that competes with liquid adhesives and the marker strips that compete with paint.

These strategies and examples suggest some of the ways a firm can extend the life cycle of its product or brand. At a more general level, however, Levitt's four suggested strategies can

EXHIBIT 3–10

A FRAMEWORK FOR PRODUCT LINE EXTENSION STRATEGIES

		Existing customers		New market segments	
		Given positioning	New positioning	First positioning	Subsequent positioning
Existing product	Frequency of usage				
	Amount of usage				
Add products to product line	Frequency of usage				
	Amount of usage				
Develop new products based on the same materials or technology	Frequency of usage				
	Amount of usage				

be viewed as a subset of a broader array of strategies available for management. Exhibit 3-10 suggests a more general framework for such life-extension strategies. These are based on combinations of five major dimensions.:

- The distinction between an existing product and new products in the same product line. (This would be the addition of flavors to the Jello line, for example.)

- The distinction between the extended product line and a completely new product line based on the same material or technology. (The use of nylon for tires or rugs is an example of a move from hosiery to a completely new line.)

- The distinction between attracting the current market segment and new segments. (The positioning of Jello as a diet product is an example of attracting a new segment—the diet-conscious.)

- The distinction between the usage of a product in a given positioning versus its promotion for an additional positioning in which it will compete with different products. (The example of 3M double-coated tape illustrates new additional positioning.)

- The distinction between increasing the frequency of usage and the amount of usage per occasion. (Using two packages of Jello for one dessert is an example of increased usage, while the usage of Jello every day

and not just for special occasions may suggest an increase in the frequency of usage.)

These five dimensions can result in 32 possible combinations (2^5). Exhibit 3–10 presents a simplified framework with 24 cells which does not distinguish, for the case of new product lines between a given product and additions to the product line, although this can easily be added.

It is important to note that none of these strategies (or the four Levitt strategies) suggests specific product, price, promotion, or distribution strategies, as do the strategies proposed by product life cycle writers such as Mickwitz (1959).

Incorporation with other inputs The second approach to overcoming some of the limitations of the product life cycle concept involves incorporating information on a product's position in its life cycle with other information on the product's market share (Catry and Chevalier, 1974) or market share and profitability (Wind and Claycamp, 1976). This latter, more comprehensive approach to the identification of a product's position on its relevant performance dimensions is discussed in Chapter 5. It does not suggest, however, any one action, but rather provides (a) a framework for the evaluation of the product's current and likely performance and (b) *one* of a number of diagnostic inputs to the design of marketing strategies.

EXTENSIONS OF THE PRODUCT LIFE CYCLE

As noted earlier, the product life cycle alone cannot and should not be used as the sole guideline for the design of marketing strategy. Any PLC-based normative strategy guidelines are likely to be misleading. The concept of life cycle is, however, intriguing. It recognizes the fact that any product is subject to change. It

focuses on the need to assess empirically the correct long-term pattern of sales and other key variables. It is the dynamic longitudinal focus of the concept of life cycle that can turn it into one of the major building blocks of marketing strategy. To achieve this potential, the life cycle concept must, however, be extended to at least two other areas: profitability and competitive position. The relation between profit and product life cycles is discussed next and is followed by a brief discussion of the new concept of competitive life cycle.

PRODUCT LIFE CYCLE AND PROFITABILITY

Most of the life cycle models propose a parallel profit curve, such as the one illustrated in Exhibit 3–11. This profit curve assumes very low profit margins (and negative unit profit) at the introductory stages. The profits rise substantially as volume increases until a stage in the growth phase where the profits level off and start declining.

In evaluating the profitability of a product at various stages in its life cycle, it is important to remember that profits are a function of not only the sales volume and price but also the cost associated with the product. The *marketing costs* are assumed to be the highest at the introductory stages of a product, given the need to develop the market. Similarly, the *production costs* are also assumed to be the highest at the introductory phase, since production is still at the beginning stages of the production learning curve.

A crucial factor in this respect is the allocation of costs to a product. This allocation is affected by the firm's accounting practices. It is particularly complicated by such problems as how to allocate the R & D costs and other pre-introduction development and marketing costs and how to allocate marketing costs when the marketing effort involves more than a single brand (such as in the case of advertising more than a single product in one commercial or distribution efforts that involve an entire product line).

Given these complexities in determining the cost of a product at a given time period, it is difficult to determine conclusively the profitability of a product at the various stages of its

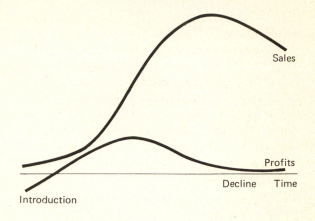

EXHIBIT 3–11

THE TYPICAL PLC AND ITS ASSOCIATED PROFIT CURVE

life cycle. The pattern suggested in Exhibit 3–11 is probably a good approximation for it but has to be examined explicitly in each case after determination of the accounting practices required to portray a realistic picture of product performance.

COMPETITIVE LIFE CYCLE

Most conventional life cycle analysis recognizes the fact that the nature and number of competitors vary at different product life cycle stages. It is often recognized that at early stages of the product life cycle the product has little or no competition and at later stages in its life cycle the competition becomes tougher. It might be beneficial, therefore, to examine explicitly the competitive environment and its changes over time. Market share can be used to measure the changing competitive structure of the market and should be supplemented by an analysis of the number of competitors and the identifiable competitive actions (such as price cutting, product modification, increased promotion) at various stages of the competitive cycle.

AN ALTERNATIVE MODEL: PRODUCT EVOLUTION

The product life cycle concept is based on the analogy of a products' birth, growth, and death to the biological life cycle. Some of the major advantages of this or any other analogy is that it might reorient thinking about an area (products) by suggesting new relationships that might not have been obvious without the analogy. It might propose relevant concepts and research approaches not utilized previously in the area of application.

The biological life cycle, unfortunately, has provided little new insight into the product policy area, and some may question whether it has provided much more than the acceptance of the premise that all products eventually die. Product life cycle forecasting models also owe very little to the biological life sciences, and the major developments in these models occurred within the marketing, management science, and econometric communities by those who have been concerned with conditional forecasting. Given the questionable benefit of the model, one may ask whether there are other, more appropriate models for describing the market behavior of products and brands. The interested reader is urged to stop reading at this point and try to suggest an appropriate analogy.

An intriguing alternative to the product life cycle model was proposed by Gross (1968), who suggested the evolution of species as described by the theory of natural selection as a model of the evolution of products in a free market economy.

The basic concepts of the Darwinian natural selection theory and marketing concepts are strikingly similar. The individual organism in the evolution theory is analogous to a product (not product class, as is often the case in the product life cycle model). The concept of *variation* of species is analogous to the differences among products and brands. The concept of *overpopulation* relates to the tremendous production capacity for most products. The *struggle for existence* and *the survival of the fittest* are quite descriptive of the product marketplace in which only a few new products ever make it.

The result of overcapacity (overpopulation) is competition among species (products). In this competition, those best suited to the *environment* (the marketplace) have the best chance for success (survival and growth). The important lessons from this analogy to *product evolution* are in some of the survival strategies proposed by the biologists:

1. "Whenever there is strong competition, specialization undoubtedly gives an advantage" (Mayer, 1964). How appropriate is this specialization as a rationale for product positioning!

2. As the environment changes, the characteristics that determine suitability also change, causing the evolutionary development we observe. This statement emphasizes, more than anything else, the need for long-range planning of product strategy.

3. Highly specialized species that are adopted for one specific set of environmental conditions are less capable of adjusting themselves to sudden or drastic changes of environment than are unspecialized forms (Mayer, 1964). This conclusion suggests the intriguing hypothesis that products aimed at narrow market segments or very specialized applications have shorter "life cycles" than more broadly based products.

4. The biological concept of *convergence*— adaptation and similarity of the structures of species with different evolutionary his-

tories, such as the porpoise and the shark, to a common mode of life. In the context of product evolution, the analogy is found in the development of functionally similar products from dissimilar technologies. For example, waxed paper comes from paper technology, aluminum foil from metal technology, and plastic wrap from chemical technology.

Are there any other insights you can gain into product evolution by considering the theory of evolution of the species? Do such concepts as "adaptation" and "protective resemblance" have product analogies? And what about the process of inheritance and mutation? What can be learned from these processes to the development of new products?

Other contributions from biology to product policy are based on some of the methodology used by biologists and, especially, the techniques of numerical taxonomy, which have great relevance to the classification of products, a topic which is discussed in the next chapter. For a comprehensive review of the PLC literature see Rink and Swan (1979).

CONCLUDING REMARKS

The product life cycle has long been considered one of the fundamental concepts of product policy. Yet, in recent years the concept has been under attack. Dhalla and Yuspeh (1976), for example, suggested that "in numerous cases a brand is discontinued, not because of irreversible changes in consumer values or tastes, but because management, on the basis of the PLC theory, believes the brand has entered a dying stage." Hence the recommendation: *Forget the product life cycle concept.*

But should management accept this conclusion? Can the product life cycle concept offer any useful insight into product management? Can it be operationalized in a way that would provide useful input to the design of marketing strategies? To answer these and similar questions it would be useful for the reader to select a product, attempt to develop its PLC, and answer the question of "what can be done with the PLC information once it has been collected?"

4

Product Classification and Positioning

Introduction

Classification-of-Goods Theories

Classification of Industrial Goods
Classification of Consumer Goods

Product Positioning

Positioning Concept
Positioning and Market Structure Analysis
Positioning and Market Partitioning
Behavioral Foundations of Positioning
Positioning Strategies

Alternative Approaches to the Measurement of Product Positioning

MDS Positioning Based on Similarity of Brands
MDS Positioning Based on the Brand's Position on the Relevant Dimensions
MDS Positioning Based on the Brand's Position on Product Attributes
MDS Positioning Based on Perceptions and Preferences
MDS Positioning Based on a Comparison of "Subjective" and "Objective"
    Evaluation
Conjoint Analysis Positioning
Research Decisions Involved in a Positioning Study

Positioning as a Guideline for Product and Marketing Strategies

Positioning by Market Segment
Positioning Over Time

INTRODUCTION

The availability of millions of diverse products and services suggests the desirability of a product *classification* scheme not unlike that used in the biological classification of species. The species-defining classification criteria of reproduction, form, and structure are somewhat analogous to the Standard Industrial Classification (SIC) system, which is based on the classification of products based on the similarity of their production technology. Yet, from a managerial point of view, the technology-based SIC classification system provides little input to the firm's product/marketing decision.

A number of attempts have been made over the years by marketing scholars to develop a *marketing-related product classification* system. The first part of this chapter discusses some of the more common classification-of-goods theories. This is followed by a discussion of the concept of *product positioning* and its relationship to the classification-of-goods theories. A major part of the chapter is devoted to the measurement of product positioning, followed by a discussion of positioning strategies. The final section of the chapter focuses on some extensions of the concept of product positioning and its measurement.

CLASSIFICATION-OF-GOODS THEORIES

The most common and widely-accepted classification of goods is the classification into *industrial* and *consumer* products and services. This distinction goes back to the early marketing writings at the beginning of the century (Copeland, 1925). Whereas one may argue against this classification on the grounds that the same products may be used by both industries and households (for example, paper clips, staples, radios, automobiles), for the time being, let us consider the classification of consumer goods and industrial goods separately.

CLASSIFICATION OF INDUSTRIAL GOODS

The Standard Industrial Classification for all industrial, commercial, financial, and service products and services (activities) was developed by the Office of Statistical Standards and has been widely accepted here and abroad for classification of industrial products and services. The SIC system defines and classifies economic activities with a seven-digit code representing (a) major groups (first two digits) such as agriculture, mining, construction, manufacturing, transportation, wholesale trade, retail trade, finance services, public administration, and nonclassifiables; (b) subgroups within each major group (third digit); (c) detailed industry categories within each subgroup (fourth digit); (d) specific product classes within each industry (fifth digit); and (e) further details on the type of product (sixth and seventh digits).

For example, corn and cotton planters are identified by the SIC code 3522320. The first two digits, 3 and 5, indicate machinery, within the manufacturing groups, except electrical. The product's association with the farm machines and equipment industry is indicated by third and fourth digits, 2 and 2. The fifth digit, 3, indicates planting, seeding, and fertilizing equipment; and the last two digits, 2 and 0, identify it as equipment designed to plant corn and cotton. A graphic example of the SIC system is presented in Exhibit 4–1.

As is evident from this example, the classification system is based on the major activity of each establishment—type of products manufactured (operating characteristics or stage of production), handled, and/or services rendered. The classification system is *not* related to the selling and use of the products.

The SIC classification system has been problematic in that there is great variation from industry to industry in the proportion of an industry's output that is accounted for by the product(s) described in the industry's SIC definition (the specialization ratio), as well as in the share of total national output of a product that is produced by firms in the SIC category (the coverage ratio), etc.[1]

Despite these and other limitations, SIC is the most widely accepted system for classification of goods. It is used by all industrial firms and is often used as a basis for industrial market segmentation. Given, however, the likely heterogeneity within any SIC category, with respect to purchase criteria, needs, and usage pattern, SIC categories (and other organizational demographic characteristics, such as company size or geographical location), can serve only as a first step in a segmentation program. It should be followed with a second, more detailed attempt to identify homogenous segments *within* each of the relevant SIC categories. (For a discussion of this two-step approach to segmentation, see Wind and Cardozo, 1974, and Choffray and Lilien, 1980).

Other than as a preliminary basis for market segmentation and an initial screening criterion for market opportunities, the SIC system, which is not based on customers' needs and behavior, is of little value as a guideline for industrial product/marketing strategy. It might be desirable, therefore, to supplement products' SIC information with marketing-research-based information on customers' (and other relevant audiences') perceptions of and preference for the products in question.

A second and somewhat less common approach to the classification of industrial products is the one based on an *Input/Output analysis*. With this approach one can cluster products based on their similarity with respect to any cells in the Input/Output matrix, resulting for example in classification of products based on the industries using or manufacturing them.

---

[1]For a further discussion of the limitations and usage of the SIC system, see Hill et al., 1975.

EXHIBIT 4–1

AN EXAMPLE OF THE SIC SYSTEM FOR INDUSTRIAL GOODS

Source: Adapted from P. Robinson, C. Hinkle, and E. Bloom, "Standard Industrial Classification for Effective Marketing Analysis," Working Paper, Marketing Science Inst., Cambridge, Mass., 1967, pp. 4–6.

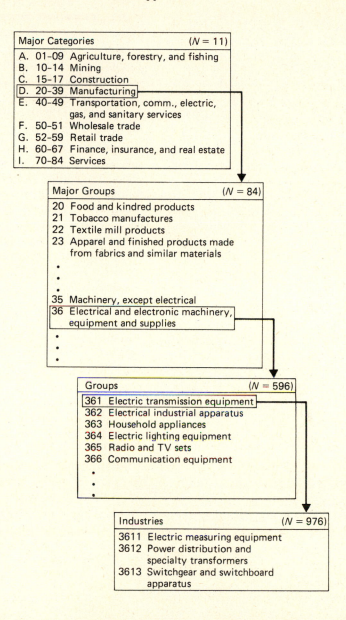

Major Categories	(N = 11)
A. 01–09 Agriculture, forestry, and fishing	
B. 10–14 Mining	
C. 15–17 Construction	
D. 20–39 Manufacturing	
E. 40–49 Transportation, comm., electric, gas, and sanitary services	
F. 50–51 Wholesale trade	
G. 52–59 Retail trade	
H. 60–67 Finance, insurance, and real estate	
I. 70–84 Services	

Major Groups	(N = 84)
20 Food and kindred products	
21 Tobacco manufactures	
22 Textile mill products	
23 Apparel and finished products made from fabrics and similar materials	
•	
•	
•	
35 Machinery, except electrical	
36 Electrical and electronic machinery, equipment and supplies	
•	
•	
•	

Groups	(N = 596)
361 Electric transmission equipment	
362 Electrical industrial apparatus	
363 Household appliances	
364 Electric lighting equipment	
365 Radio and TV sets	
366 Communication equipment	
•	
•	
•	

Industries	(N = 976)
3611 Electric measuring equipment	
3612 Power distribution and specialty transformers	
3613 Switchgear and switchboard apparatus	

In addition to classification of industrial products based on SIC or Input/Output analysis, one could consider, of course, any of the bases used in classification of consumer goods and services.

CLASSIFICATION OF CONSUMER GOODS

All classification-of-consumer-goods theories stem from the original trichotomy of *convenience, shopping,* and *specialty* goods proposed as early as 1923 by Copeland. The various classification-of-goods theories use different criteria to classify products. Yet, all theories reflect some belief about the nature of consumer decision processes. Copeland (1925) used three implicit criteria: the travel effort involved in getting to a store; the effort of comparing brands on price, quality, and style at the time of purchase; and the amount of brand attraction (which, in the case of specialty goods, according to Copeland, "induced the consumer to put forth special effort to visit the store in which they are sold and to make the purchase without shopping."

Copeland did not provide operational definitions for these criteria. This was done by Holton (1958) based on the ratio of *cost* of search to *gain* from search and the volume of demand for and supply of a certain good. Given these two dimensions, a 2 × 2 matrix can be developed, which leads to the classification illustrated in Exhibit 4–2.

Aspinwall (1962) suggested a trichotomy of red, orange, and yellow goods, the color to be assigned according to the products' marketing characteristics, length of distribution channel, and the nature of the promotion media. Miracle (1965) extended Aspinwall's marketing characteristics and developed five product categories based on characteristics such as unit value, significance of an individual purchase to the consumer, rate of technological change, technical complexity, consumer need for service, frequency of purchase, rapidity of consumption, and extent of usage.

Bucklin (1963), while maintaining the traditional distinction of convenience, shopping, and specialty goods, redefined it according to the degree to which a consumer, before his need arises, possesses a preference map that (a) indicates willingness to purchase any of a number of known substitutes (convenience goods), (b) requires a search to construct such a map (shopping), or (c) indicates a willingness to expand the effort required to purchase the most preferred items rather than a more readily accessible substitute (specialty goods). Using the criteria of preference formation, Bucklin extends the same definition to cover stores also, resulting in a nine-cell classification (three product types times three store types), which is illustrated in Exhibit 4–3.

More recently, Holbrook and Howard (1976), after a critical review of these and other approaches to the classification of goods, suggested the addition of a "preference goods" category. They base this fourfold classification

EXHIBIT 4–2

A CONSUMER GOODS MATRIX BASED ON HOLTON'S TYPOLOGY

		Volume of supply and demand	
		Both small	Both large
Ratio between cost of search and gain from search	Low	Specialty	Convenience
	High	Specialty	Shopping

EXHIBIT 4–3

A MATRIX OF CONSUMER GOODS AND STORES BASED ON BUCKLIN'S TYPOLOGY

		Stores		
		Convenience	Shopping	Specialty
Goods	Convenience	Consumers prefer to buy the most readily available brand and product at the most accessible store. 1	Consumers are indifferent to the brand or product they buy, but shop among different stores in order to secure better retail service and/or lower retail prices. 4	Consumers prefer to trade at a specific store, but are indifferent to the brand or product purchased. 7
	Shopping	Consumers select a brand from the assortment carried by the most accessible store. 2	Consumers make comparisons among both retail-controlled factors and factors associated with the product (brand). 5	Consumers prefer to trade at a certain store, but are uncertain as to which product they wish to buy and examine the store's assortment for the best purchase. 8
	Specialty	Consumers purchase their favored brand from the most accessible store that has the item in stock. 3	Consumers have strong preference with respect to the brand, but shop among a number of stores to secure the best retail service or price for this brand. 6	Consumers have both preference for a particular store and a specific brand. 9

on three sets of criteria: (a) product characteristics (magnitude of purchase and clarity of characteristics), (b) consumer characteristics (ego involvement and specific self-confidence), and (c) consumer responses (physical shopping and mental effort). Accepting these underlying considerations, they develop a 2 × 2 matrix based on two combined dimensions:

1. Magnitude of purchase, ego involvement, and physical shopping effort. When all three are low, it can result in either con-

venience or preference goods (which suggest to them a wide distribution strategy). When these factors are high, it suggests shopping or specialty goods (hence leading to a limited-distribution strategy).

2. Clarity, self-confidence, and mental effort during or prior to shopping. High clarity and self-confidence and mental effort during shopping result in either convenience or shopping goods (suggesting to the authors the need for heavy advertising effort). The opposite condition, on the other hand,

EXHIBIT 4–4

THE HOLBROOK AND HOWARD CLASSIFICATION OF CONSUMER GOODS

	High clarity, high self-confidence, mental effort during shopping via brand comparisons	Low clarity, low specific self-confidence, mental effort prior to shopping via information seeking
Low magnitude **Low ego involvement** **Low physical shopping effort**	Convenience goods	Preference goods
High magnitude **High ego involvement** **High physical shopping effort**	Shopping goods	Specialty goods

results in preference and specialty goods (suggesting to them low advertising effort). This classification is illustrated in Exhibit 4–4.

A comparison of some of the more common definitions of convenience, shopping, and specialty goods is presented in Exhibit 4–5. An examination of the various definitions highlights the diversity in the conceptualization and operationalization of the three categories.

A number of other product classification schemes have been suggested by various authors. Of some interest is the classification scheme suggested by Bourne (1957), who departed markedly from the traditional classification of convenience, shopping, and specialty products. Bourne, reporting on some of Glock's work, suggested a product classification scheme based on the degree to which products and brands (or types of products) are influenced by reference groups. An underlying dimension of his classification system was the conspicuousness (in terms of being seen, as well as standing out and being noticed) of the product, which he viewed as the most important determinant of the product's or brand's

susceptibility to reference group influence.

Another interesting product classification system is the one suggested by Nelson (1970) who classified products into *search* and *experience* products. Search products are those for which the consumer can determine the qualities prior to purchase (the style of a product). Experience products, on the other hand, are those that the consumer cannot determine the quality of prior to purchase (the taste of a canned food).

These and other classifications suffer, however, from the same limitations as the more traditional classification-of-goods theories. Most of these classifications recognize (implicitly, at least) that a product is not inherently a convenience, shopping, or specialty good, for example, but that category depends on the consumers' relationship with the product. Yet, most of the efforts toward utilizing these typologies assume that management knows the relevant (consumer behavior) characteristics of their product and could therefore classify their product correctly. Used this way, classification-of-goods theories, despite their intuitive appeal, do not provide useful guidelines for marketing strategy, since it is unlikely that all consumers will view a brand as belonging to one and only

EXHIBIT 4–5

A COMPARISON OF SOME OF THE COMMON DEFINITIONS FOR CONVENIENCE, SHOPPING, AND SPECIALTY CONSUMER GOODS

Writer	Convenience goods	Shopping goods	Specialty goods
Copeland (1925)	Those goods that are customarily purchased at easily accessible stores. The unit price for most is too small to justify going far out of the way to purchase a special brand.	Those goods for which the customer desires to compare prices, quality, and style at the time of purchase. This comparison is usually done in several stores.	Those goods that have some particular attraction for the consumer, other than price, which induces him to put forth special effort to visit the store in which they are sold and to make the purchase without shopping.
AMA Committee on Definitions (1948)	Those goods which the consumer purchases frequently, immediately, and with the minimum of effort.	Those goods which, in the process of selection and purchase, the customer characteristically compares on such bases as suitability, quality, price, and style.	Those goods for which a significant group of buyers are habitually willing to make a special purchasing effort.
Holton (1958)	Those goods for which the consumer regards the probable gain from making price and quality comparisons as small compared to the cost of making such comparisons.	Those goods for which the consumer regards the probable gain from making price and quality comparisons as large relative to the cost of making such comparisons.	Those convenience or shopping goods that have such a limited market as to require the consumer to make a special effort to purchase them.
Bucklin (1963)	Those goods for which the consumer, before his need arises, possesses a preference map that indicates a willingness to purchase any of a number of known substitutes rather than make the additional effort required to buy a particular item.	Those goods for which the consumer has not developed a complete preference map before the need arises, requiring him to undertake search to construct such a map before purchase.	Those goods for which the consumer, before his need arises, possesses a preference map that indicates a willingness to expend the additional effort required to purchase the most preferred item rather than buy a more readily accessible substitute.

one of these categories. The perception and evaluation of a brand differs from consumer to consumer and, even for a given consumer, it may vary over time or across consumption and purchase occasions.

Given the limitations of the classification systems of both industrial and consumer goods, marketing strategies frequently suggested for the products are questionable. In fact, a growing number of marketing scholars and practitioners accept the dual premise that marketing strategy (a) cannot be based only on the manufacturer's classification of products and (b) requires detailed information on how various market segments perceive the firm's brands; i.e., the brand positioning.

Positioning thus provides an *empirically-based* product/brand classification that can provide useful guidelines for marketing strategy. The "objective" classification-of-goods theories and the criteria underlying them may be helpful inputs to the design of positioning studies and the interpretation of their results, but they cannot by themselves provide useful managerial guidelines.

Given that this approach might sound quite radical, threatening one of the "sacred cows" of marketing, the reader is encouraged to refute this criticism of the classification-of-goods theories by trying to apply one to a product or service. Answering some of the following questions should be helpful in going through such an exercise:

1. What dimensions should be utilized in the development of a classification system? Which of the ones proposed by the approaches reviewed in this section are most relevant?

2. Are there any other relevant dimensions that should be incorporated? Are any of the current findings and theories of consumer behavior relevant in this respect?

3. Having classified your products into the various categories, are there any buying or usage occasions that would require a different category for the given product?

4. Are there any people who are likely to view the product as more appropriate for another category?

PRODUCT POSITIONING[2]

POSITIONING CONCEPT

The term *product (brand) positioning* refers to the place a product occupies in a given market. Conceptually, the origin of the positioning concept can be traced to the economist's work on market structure, competitive position of the firm, and the concepts of substitution and competition among products. Marketing also has been concerned with such phenomena as product differentiation (Alderson, 1957; Smith, 1956) and market position analysis, which ranges from simple market share statistics to various approaches (such as Markov processes) for forecasting changes in a firm's market position (Alderson and Green, 1964).

More recently, increasing attention has been given to product image. This suggests a new perspective on product positioning, one that focuses on *consumers' perceptions* concern-

[2]The material in this and the next section is partially based on Wind (1977b) and Wind and Robinson (1972).

ing the place a product occupies in a given market. In this context, the word positioning encompasses most of the common meanings of the word position—position as a place (what place does the product occupy in its market?), a rank (how does the product fare against its competitors in various evaluative dimensions?), and a mental attitude (what are consumer attitudes—the cognitive, affective, and action tendencies) toward the given product.

Given this view, the product (brand) positioning should be assessed by measuring consumers' or organizational buyers' *perceptions* and *preference* for the product in relation to its competitors (both branded and generic).

Product positioning and differentiation on the basis of some physical, functional, or structural characteristic (such as those used in the Standard Industrial Classification system) is not very useful unless it is consistent with consumers' perceptions of the products. Chemically, for example, two brands of aspirin can be identical, yet they might be perceived differently by different consumer segments. Conversely, two brands that are dissimilar in some physical characteristic might be perceived as similar if their differentiating characteristics are viewed by consumers as unimportant. Product differentiation, therefore, is a meaningful concept only to the extent that it is based on consumers' *perceptions* of the differences among competing products or brands.

Product positioning should not be determined, however, only on the basis of perception—perceived similarity to other products—but also on consumers' preferences for it (overall preference as well as preference under various conditions—scenarios). This is based on the premise that customer behavior is a function of *both* perception and preference and the recognition that buyers may differ with respect to both perception of and preference.

A somewhat different approach has been taken by Stefflre and his associates in their market structure analysis (Barnett, 1968, 1969, and Stefflre, 1968). In this new product development procedure, the first few research steps are concerned directly with establishing the market structure to "determine which items (products and brands) consumers see as constituting a market and the 'position' of each item in the market vis-à-vis the other items." This analysis positions the various brands based on consumers' *perceptions* (similarity) using certain multidimensional scaling programs. This positioning analysis does not utilize preference data *in conjunction with* similarities data but occasionally uses data on patterns of brand-to-brand substitution obtained from large-scale purchase panel data, when these are available.

Whether one uses perceptions, preferences,[3] or both as a basis for product positioning, operationalizing the concept of positioning requires the identification of the appropriate set of brands and products and determination of the most appropriate consumer task.

The relevant set of products and brands may include products outside the immediate product class of the brand in question and can be generated by marketing experts, based on their experience and analysis of existing information, or from unstructured depth interviews with consumers. Identifying a broad set of competing items is quite crucial, since it constitutes the stimulus set for the positioning study. In designing the stimulus set, it is sometimes desirable to include two types of products and brands—brands in the same product class and products and brands outside the physical product class that may be used by consumers as substitutes for the product in question. For example, in a study of soups, one could include a set of different soup brands, forms, types, and

---

[3]In certain empirical studies, because of cost considerations, one may elect to collect only preference data as the basis for product positioning.

flavors as the primary set, as well as homemade soup and a set of soup substitutes such as sandwich, salad, and coffee.

Given the identification of a relevant set of brands and products, the next step is to determine consumers' perceived brand positioning. This can be done by eliciting (a) consumers' perceptions using a variety of available procedures for similarity measurement, or (b) consumers' preferences—overall and under a variety of usage and purchase conditions—or (c) both perceptions and preferences.

POSITIONING AND MARKET STRUCTURE ANALYSIS

The focal point of industrial organization analysis is the market (competitive) structure. The industrial organization approach defines the competitive structure in terms of the number of buyers and sellers in a market, the relative size of these organizations, the extent of product differentiation, the shape of the function describing the economies of scale, the barriers to entry of new firms into the market, and merger activity that alters structure.

As recognized by Carman (1977) in his review of this approach, the major limitation of the industrial organization model is the approach it takes in measuring the competitive structure—i.e., the reliance, whenever hard numbers are available (such as number of firms), on "objective" measures, or the analyst's subjective judgment, as in the case of trying to determine the degree of product differentiation. One way to overcome this limitation is to use multidimensional scaling to define the market structure, using consumer perceptions. Hence, market and channel structure can be determined by an analysis of buyers' perceptions of a firm's competitive position.

Market structure can be defined as the position (strength and weakness)—as perceived by

buyers—of a firm versus its competitors in a given market. The complexity of determining market structure by positioning arises when a firm has multiple brands in multiple product lines in more than one strategic business. In this case, one can conduct the market structure (positioning) analysis at four levels—the brand level, the product class level, the business unit level (strategic business unit) or the firm level. At each level, the positioning of the brands, products, businesses, and firms is determined in the context of their natural "competitive" set—the evoked set of competing item—as perceived by the relevant publics. Such analyses provide insight into the competitive structure of the market, the key features of the brands, products, businesses, and firms, and the relevant market boundaries.

If the four positioning levels are studied, it would be useful to compare the results and see to what extent the firm's positioning is consistent in all levels of analysis and across the relevant market segments. Effective positioning analysis of market structure should consider the collection (and subsequently analysis) of the perceptual and evaluative data, not only from buyers but from other relevant publics, such as the firm's own employees, its suppliers, and even government agencies if any of those are concerned with the market structure of the given industry and the competitive position of the firm in question. Yet, it is important to note in this context that the perception of one group (e.g., government employees) cannot be used as a substitute for the perception of other groups (e.g., consumers).

POSITIONING AND MARKET PARTITIONING

The rapid diffusion of the Hendry model (Butler, 1975; Kalwani and Morrison, 1977) has led to an increasing interest in the concept of

EXHIBIT 4–6

HYPOTHETICAL MARKET PARTITIONING

Form Primary

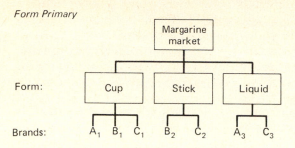

Brand Primary

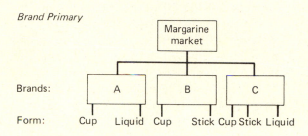

In a form primary market a consumer first selects a form and only then a brand among the set of brands offered in the given form, i.e., consumers will have a very small probability of buying a brand which does not come in the preferred form. In a brand-primary market consumers exhibit higher brand loyalty than in a form-primary market. Any introduction of a new form will lead to higher "cannibalization" than that which a firm would experience in a form-primary market.

Other types of partitioning are based on flavor, size, or a combination of product attributes. The "correct" partitioning is consistent with the various relations defined by the Hendry model and tends to be consistent over time (i.e., reliable). Yet, whether a chosen partitioning is the "true" partitioning of a market as perceived by consumers is not clear at all. In fact, in two comparisons of the Hendry's product partitioning with a *perceived* market structure as presented by a tree diagram derived from a hierarchical clustering algorithm (output similar in form to the one illustrated in Exhibit 4–9) of the products in a given market (where products were identified by brand, form, and size), the results suggested major differences between the two market structures. Furthermore, they suggested considerable heterogeneity in the market with some segments following a form, while others exhibited a brand partitioning. It would be desirable, therefore, to supplement the Hendry analysis of partitioning with the more conventional product positioning analysis which reflects consumer choice behavior.

market partitioning—the hierarchy of market structure relationship. The partition of markets into a hierarchy of product set structures is one of the major concepts underlying the Hendry model. The structure of partitioning within a product class, as illustrated for example in Exhibit 4–6, is based on analysis of actual consumer brand-switching behavior. Management judgment is used to establish a number of hypothetical partitionings, and switching patterns are examined for each structure. The partitioning which "fits" the empirical data "best" (the switching constant for each brand within a partition is identical and equal to the switching constant describing aggregate switching behavior in that partition) is selected as the one for the given market.

Three types of partitioning are often discussed: a form primary market (the top panel of Exhibit 4–6), a brand primary market (the bottom panel of Exhibit 4–6), and a mix of the two.

BEHAVIORAL FOUNDATIONS OF POSITIONING

The importance and nature of positioning is partially explained by the behavioral foundation of the concept. The concept's major reliance is on consumers' perceptual and cognitive processes. Of particular relevance are the Gestalt psychologists' concepts and findings concerning the perception and interpretation of a stimulus in relation to the organization of one's experience and the idea that the perception of the whole is greater than the sum of its parts.

A second set of behavioral concepts and findings of relevance to the concept of positioning are *image* and *symbolism*. Levy, one of the early proponents of the relevance of product image and symbolism in marketing, defined image as an interpretation, a set of inferences and reactions. Image is a symbol, since it is not the object itself but rather refers to it and stands for it. In addition to the physical reality of the product, brand, or organization, the image includes its meanings—that is, the beliefs, attitudes, and feelings that have come to be attached to it (Levy, 1959). Consider, for example, the different images of various beers (Miller Lite versus the ''luxurious'' Michelob and the one for the heavy drinker, Schaffer) and contrast it with the fact that in blind taste tests, most consumers cannot identify their most preferred beer. The concepts of image and symbolism are therefore of direct relevance to the concept of positioning, both in terms of explaining its importance and in suggesting some guidelines for its development.

Further guidance for developing a positioning strategy can be found in the concepts and findings of communication research concerning the conditions for increased communication effectiveness. Schramm (1954), for example, listed four such conditions:

• The message (positioning) must be so designed and delivered as to gain the attention of the intended destination.

• The message (positioning) must employ signs that refer to experience common to source and destination, so as to get the meaning across.

• The message (positioning) must arouse personality needs in the destination and suggest some ways to meet those needs.

• The message (positioning) must suggest a way to meet those needs that is appropriate to the group situation in which the destination finds himself at the time he is moved to make the desired response.

These and other communication research concepts and findings are especially crucial given the proliferation of competing brands in the marketplace and consumers' limited cognitive abilities (in the mid-seventies over 20 brands of soft drinks were advertised on national television) which call for ways of differentiating the given product. Communication research concepts and findings can provide useful guidelines for the design of a positioning strategy while the psychological studies of needs, motives, and personality traits and the cultural anthropology studies of values can provide hypotheses for the nature of positioning. (For further discussion of this point, see Chapter 2, Section 3.)

Numerous psychological theories, concepts, and findings emphasize individual differences and the dependency of perceptions and cognitive processes, not only on the stimulus itself, but on its interaction with the respondents' needs, personality, moods, memory, experiences, and values. Hence, one should avoid focusing on a single total market positioning but rather attempt to assess positioning as perceived by various market segments.

Many other behavioral concepts and findings can provide further insight into, and guidelines for, product or brand positioning studies. Even a cursory examination of consumer behavior concepts and findings (as summarized in any of the consumer behavior texts and articles in the *Journal of Consumer Research*) suggests a number of possible bases for positioning which could be further explored and tested. Of special interest are theories of learning and the recent distinction between low and high involvement. Given that from a strategic point of view, management is concerned with positioning over time and not only at a point in time, it is essential to have a good grasp of learning theories which can provide better insight into the process leading to changes in brand or product positioning. (For an excellent review of learning theories, see Hilgard and Bower, 1966.) The recognition that consumers differ in their degree of involvement with products and that many products can be categorized for many consumers as low-involvement products (low ego-intensity and low risk) has major implications for the way one should model the relevant consumer choice process and for the design of product positioning and marketing strategy.

POSITIONING STRATEGIES

The design of a positioning strategy involves a number of considerations:

Perceived positioning of the current products by each of the firm's relevant market segments In view of the heterogeneous nature of every market, the real value of product positioning is revealed only when the positioning is coupled with an appropriate market segmentation strategy. In many of the commercial positioning studies (see, for example, Wind and Robinson, 1972; and Wind, 1973), a segmentation analysis was included, enabling one to conduct both an overall and segmented positioning analysis. In most of these studies, the findings were quite conclusive in suggesting that differences do exist among segments and, hence, a comprehensive analysis and subsequent strategy would require positioning by segments (and not just a single positioning for the total market).

Product line considerations Since most firms have multiple products, the positioning decision of any given product cannot ignore the place the product occupies in the firm's product line as perceived by consumers and the firm's other relevant stakeholders. Conceptually, the product offering of a firm should lead to an optimal mix of product positioning by market segments, i.e., the product positioning of any given product should not be designed and evaluated in isolation from the positioning of the firm's other products and the market segments at which they are aimed. Furthermore, it should try to reduce consumers' confusion among the various products and clearly differentiate each product on some dimension relevant to the target market. A clear and distinct positioning for each product in a line could reduce product cannibalization and lead to an optimal product line for the selected target segments of the firm.

The focus of a product line positioning should not be limited only to the firm's own products but rather should take explicitly into account the product lines of its competitors. A good example of this type of positioning is the Qyx line of computerized typewriters which were introduced by Exxon in a price range between $1390 and $7750, which is just at the gap in the price line of IBM which offers less sophisticated and cheaper typewriters than the cheapest Qyx and more sophisticated and expensive models than the top of the Qyx models but no models in the middle price range. At this time, it is too early to know whether this price line positioning strategy payed off, but conceptually it does make sense.

Alternative bases for positioning In developing and communicating a positioning strategy, management can use a number of alternative bases for positioning. These include:

Positioning on specific product features. Positioning a product by its performance on specific product attributes is among the most common approaches to positioning, especially for industrial products. Price and specific performance features are often used as the basis for positioning. Product feature positioning can range from specific tangible benefits (such as the Chevette as an economy car or VW's "Think Small") to more abstract features (such as Avis' "We Try Harder").

Positioning on benefits, problem solution, or needs strongly linked to product feature positioning is benefit positioning, which is generally more effective than positioning which describes product features without their benefit to the consumer. A consistent finding in a number of studies among physicians has been the importance of specific *benefits* of a given drug (less side effects, more effectiveness, easier administration, etc.) with little concern for the chemical ingredients that lead to that benefit. A similar conclusion can also be reached with respect to consumers. Consider, for example, Crest's anticavity positioning, or TWA's on-time performance.

Positioning for specific usage occasions. Related to benefit positioning is the positioning for specific occasions. Consider, for example, the Schaffer positioning ("the one beer to have when you're having more than one"), Michelob's positioning as a weekend beer, or Campbell's positioning of soups for cooking.

Positioning for user category. A few examples of user-based product positioning are "The Pepsi Generation," "You've come a long way, baby," and "Breakfast of Champions." More detailed "user" positioning has also been used. Consider, for example, Tijuana Smalls, which was positioned as "We're not for everybody—are we for you?" and whose user was profiled as an individualist, youthful, modern, health conscious, and gregarious.

Positioning against another product. This positioning strategy can range from implicit comparison to explicit. Avis never mentions Hertz

explicitly but its positioning—"Avis is number two in rent-a-car, so why go with us? We try harder!" is an example of implicit positioning against a leader. For years many brands used an explicit comparison against "Brand X" or "the leading brand" but without naming the competition. More recently, direct comparison of named brands has become very common. Brand comparison takes two forms: the first is a comparison with a direct competitor aimed at attracting customers from the compared brand. This is the most common case of head-on positioning against a competitor (usually the category leader) which characterizes so many of the comparative advertising campaigns of the mid-seventies. Consider, for example, "The Pepsi Challenge," which declared that nationwide, more people prefer the taste of Pepsi; or GE's claim that its color TV sets required less servicing than any other domestic brand including RCA and Zenith; the Tylenol positioning; and the survey of comparative *price* ads of the Helene Curtis Suave products (e.g., Suave Protein Conditioner against Mennen's Protein 21). Head-on comparison with a competitor is also found in industrial markets. Savin Business Machine Corporation, for example, positioned its plain paper copier against both Xerox and IBM with ads which asked rhetorically: "What do Xerox and IBM copiers have most in common?" The answer: "Both are most commonly replaced by the Savin 780."

The second positioning based on brand comparison is not at the hope of attracting the customers of the compared product but rather to use the comparison as a reference point for establishing one's own positioning. Consider, for example, the positioning of Volkswagen's Dasher, which picks up speed faster than a Mercedes and has a bigger trunk than a Rolls Royce, or the Ford Granada and Mercury Monarch comparisons against Mercedes.

Product class dissociation. Such positioning is somewhat less common but one which is effective especially when introducing a new product which differs from the typical products in an established category. Lead-free gasoline and tubeless tires are new product classes positioned against leaded gasoline and non-tubeless tires. At the brand level probably the most successful anti-product class positioning is that of 7-Up with its "Un-Cola" positioning. An interesting approach of dissociation from the "natural" product class and a move toward association with a new product class is the case of *Sports Illustrated's* positioning as the "Third News Weekly."

Hybrid bases. Given the variety of possible bases for positioning, product management should not ignore the possibility of a hybrid approach incorporating elements from more than one base for positioning.

Selecting a basis for positioning Given the variety of bases which can be used to position one's products, the question is which to use. The choice depends, of course, on a number of idiosyncratic characteristics of the firm, product, market, and environmental setting. These include:

- The firm's market position. Is the product a leader, a contending Number two, or one of the smaller brands?

- The positioning used by current competitors.

- The compatibility of the desired positioning with consumers' needs, wants, and current perception of the product's positioning versus its competitors, and the given product class.

- The "newness" of the considered basis for positioning and its departure from the current practice in the market.

- The resources available to communicate the positioning effectively and the compatibility of the positioning with the firm's marketing strategy.

- The firm's desire for an innovative versus "me too" image.

- The ability to develop an effective creative execution for the chosen positioning.

- The legal environment, i.e., likely legal action against the proposed positioning.

ALTERNATIVE APPROACHES TO THE MEASUREMENT OF PRODUCT POSITIONING

The traditional approach to the *direct* measurement of the perceived positioning of a firm's products and services has been a profile chart of brands by attributes.[4] Exhibit 4–7 illustrates the output for such an analysis, which was conducted for an insurance company.

An examination of this output provides a profile of the company's and one of its competitor's perceived strengths and weaknesses. The difficulty with this output is that one can plot only a few companies per chart, and no information is provided on the relationships among

---

[4]In addition to the *direct* approaches to the measurement of a product's positioning, management can use a number of *indirect* measures to infer some aspects of product positioning. Among these indirect approaches are market share data (relative size of a product's market position), brand switching matrices (positioning with respect to the brands from which the given brand draws customers and the brands to which it loses customers), and the more recent model of brand vulnerability discussed in Chapter 6.

EXHIBIT 4–7

ILLUSTRATIVE POSITIONING BY PROFILE CHART ANALYSIS: INSURANCE COMPANY *A* VERSUS A LEADING COMPETITOR *B*

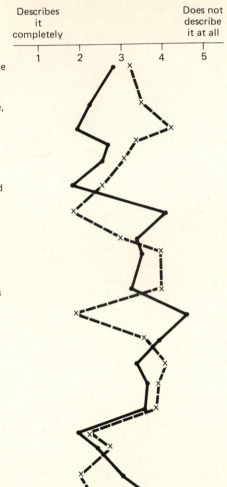

1. Company provides adequate insurance coverage for my car
2. Company will not cancel policy because of age, accident experience, or health problems
3. Friendly and considerate
4. Settles claims fairly
5. Inefficient, hard to deal with
6. Provides good advice about types and amounts of coverage to buy
7. Too big to care about individual customers
8. Explains things clearly
9. Premium rates are lower than most companies
10. Has personnel available for questions all over the country
11. Will raise premiums because of age
12. Takes a long time to settle a claim
13. Very professional/modern
14. Specialists in serving my local area
15. Quick, reliable service, easily accessible
16. A "good citizen" in community
17. Has complete line of insurance products available
18. Is widely known "name company"
19. Is very aggressive, rapidly growing company
20. Provides advice on how to avoid accidents

the attributes. Although one can overcome these limitations by first factor-analyzing[5] the attributes and then developing a series of charts

for the company against each of its competitors (or groups of competitors), a more informative approach would be to use multidimensional scaling (MDS).

Multidimensional scaling is a set of techniques developed by mathematical psycholo-

---

[5]For a brief discussion of factor analysis see Appendix A.

gists which provides a spatial (geometric) representation of relationships among brands, products, firms, or other objects of interest based on data on consumers' perceptions of and preference for these objects. These approaches are briefly described in Appendix A.

Applications of multidimensional scaling and hierarchical clustering procedures to product positioning have been reported. Wind and Robinson (1972), in discussing the concept and measurement of positioning, described a number of studies in which multidimensional scaling procedures were used to determine the product's marketing positioning. Some additional studies were described in a more recent review by Green and McMennamin (1973).

Today, the utilization of MDS in product positioning studies is widespread. It has entered the introductory marketing textbooks (Kotler, 1971), and is frequently used in commercial studies. Clustering procedures are also used in product positioning, but somewhat less frequently than MDS. Yet, it seems that neither multidimensional scaling nor clustering have been accepted by the regulatory agencies concerned with questions of market structure and competition.

Another, more recent tool for product positioning is *conjoint analysis* (which is briefly discussed in Chapter 2 and Appendix A). It can provide insight into the value of the brand name (when brands are treated as independent variables) as well as the appropriateness of various brands for providing certain types of features and benefits (when brands are the dependent variables and various combinations of product features are sorted according to their similarity to or appropriateness for various brands.) This latter case utilizes the categorical conjoint analysis procedure.

Given that both MDS and conjoint analysis procedures have been discussed in detail elsewhere, the focus of this section is on describing a number of different (although re-

lated) ways of determining a product positioning by the use of these analytical procedures.

MDS POSITIONING BASED ON SIMILARITY OF BRANDS

The simplest and most common approach to determining positioning is based on the similarity of brand i to other brands. Two types of data can be collected from the respondents: overall similarity of brands (e.g., ranking or rating of all brands according to their similarity to an anchor brand and rotation of brands until all brands have served as an anchor) or evaluation of brands—rating or ranking—on a set of relevant attributes. In the first approach—the direct measure of similarity—the $k \times k$ matrix of interbrand distance is submitted to any number of multidimensional scaling programs (e.g., TORSCA), resulting in a simple n-dimensional space.[6]

The second type of data can also be transferred into a $k \times k$ matrix of brand similarities (across attributes) and submitted to some multidimensional program. (For a discussion of the technical details involved, see Green and Rao, 1972).

This procedure results in the familiar perceptual space, presented in Exhibit 4–8, in which the position of any brand can be determined by calculating its distance from all other brands.

Examination of this exhibit identifies the positioning of each brand by its distance from the other brands. The closer two brands are (e.g., Volkswagen and Dart), the more similar they are perceived to be. The further apart two brands are (e.g., Volkswagen and Mercedes), the less similar they are perceived to be. Small distance (i.e., similarity) may also connote competition. In this case, for example, Capri

---

[6]For a brief discussion see Appendix A.

EXHIBIT 4–8

TWO-DIMENSIONAL CONFIGURATION OF BRANDS OF AUTOMOBILES
(ILLUSTRATIVE OUTPUT)

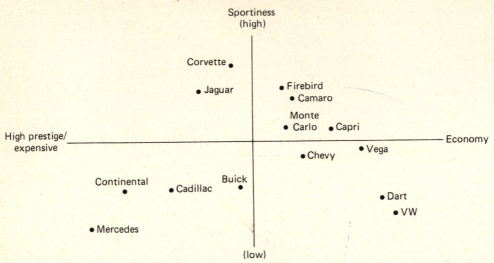

EXHIBIT 4–9

HIERARCHICAL CLUSTERING ANALYSIS OF 14 AUTOMOBILES
(ILLUSTRATIVE OUTPUT)

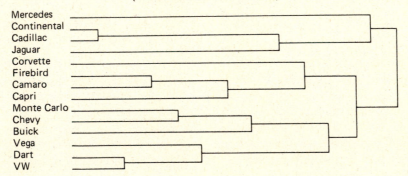

competes with Vega, Monte Carlo, Chevrolet, and Camero, but less with Buick or Dart.

For better insight into the finer structure of relations among the brands, the data can also be submitted to a hierarchical cluster analysis. The output of this analysis is presented in Exhibit 4–9 as a tree diagram.

An examination of the tree diagram of the various brands suggests that Mercedes—which in the two-dimensional perceptual space was viewed as quite similar to Continental and Cadillac—is perceived as a unique car with only slight competition from the other two luxury cars. Similarly, Corvette is also viewed as

EXHIBIT 4–10

TWO-DIMENSIONAL CONFIGURATION OF BRANDS OF AUTOMOBILES AND
THEIR CLUSTERS
(ILLUSTRATIVE OUTPUT OF SUPERIMPOSING THE RESULTS OF A HIERARCHICAL
CLUSTERING ANALYSIS OVER THE MULTIDIMENSIONAL SCALING SOLUTION)

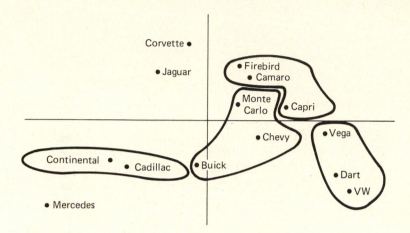

unique, but it does compete to some extent with Firebird and Camero. Interestingly, Capri is viewed as a sport car, competing more with Firebird and Camero and less with the Vega or other compact cars. To further facilitate the positioning analysis, the results of the hierarchical cluster can be superimposed on the two-dimensional map. This results in the kind of visual output presented in Exhibit 4–10.

MDS POSITIONING BASED ON THE BRAND'S POSITION ON THE RELEVANT DIMENSIONS

Further insight into the positioning of a brand can be gained by identifying the position of each brand on the major dimensions (frame of reference along which brands are compared perceptually) identified in the multidimensional space. In Exhibit 4–8, for example, the dimensions can be interpreted as economy/

prestige versus sportiness/nonsportiness, and the position of each car on these dimensions can be determined.

In conducting such analysis, the researcher can choose the desired level of analysis based on his assumption as to the homogeneity of the market's perceptual configuration. Assuming homogeneity, the researcher can conduct the analysis at the aggregate level. If, on the other hand, the researcher assumes that individuals differ in their perceptions, he (or she) can follow one of two approaches: (1) cluster the respondents based on their commonality of perceptions and conduct a separate analysis for each segment, or, alternatively (2) assume that respondents have a common perceptual dimension but that they do differ with respect to the weights they attach to the various dimensions. This latter approach seems the most attractive one and can utilize the Carroll and Chang (1969) INDSCAL model and algorithm.[7]

---

[7]For a brief discussion see Appendix A.

MDS POSITIONING BASED ON THE BRAND'S POSITION ON PRODUCT ATTRIBUTES

One of the common ways to assess consumers' evaluations of brands is to ask them to rate or rank the brands on a set of attributes. Such data (whether generated by anchoring on brands or attributes) can be submitted to a joint space analysis (e.g., MDPREF[8]), resulting in an n-dimensional space in which the brands are the points (the same ones generated from the over-all similarity data), and the attributes are vectors. In this case, the positioning of a brand can be further determined by its projections on the various attributes. An important feature of this approach is the identification of the interrelationship among the attributes (as measured by the cosine of the angle—correlation between

[8]For a brief discussion see Appendix A.

vectors). The output from this approach is illustrated in Exhibit 4–11.

Examination of Exhibit 4–11, the joint space configuration, provides information on the way the respondents evaluate the various cars (the points in the space) on a set of attributes (the vectors). In this example, consumers view Volkswagen as the most economical car, followed by Dart, Vega, Chevrolet, etc. The projection of the cars on the vectors recovers the original rank order given by the respondents (if this was the nature of the task) and provides a metric scale of the position of each car on each of the attributes (vectors). For example, whereas Mercedes and Jaguar are viewed as the worst cars on the basis of operating economy, Chevrolet is positioned midway between them and Volkswagen—the best for operating economy.

Examining the relationship between the vectors (the cosine of the angle between the vectors) suggests that, in this specific case,

EXHIBIT 4–11

JOINT SPACE CONFIGURATION OF AUTOMOBILE BRANDS (POINTS) AND
ATTRIBUTES (VECTORS) (ILLUSTRATIVE OUTPUT)

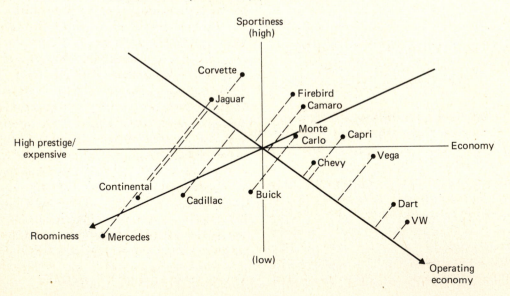

EXHIBIT 4–12

JOINT SPACE CONFIGURATION OF 12 BRANDS OF AUTOMOBILES AND
PREFERENCE PATTERN OF THREE CONSUMER SEGMENTS
(ILLUSTRATIVE OUTPUT)

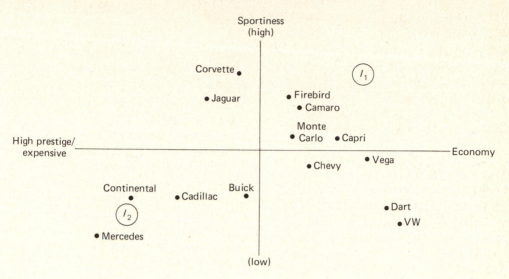

MDS POSITIONING BASED ON BOTH PERCEPTIONS AND PREFERENCES

roominess—for example—is not related positively to operating economy.

The three previous approaches were based on data on consumers' perceptions and evaluations of a set of products; ignored were consumer preferences for these products.

Further insight into brand positioning may be gained by measuring both consumers' perceptions *and* preferences for the given product in relation to its realistic competitors (both branded and generic). The data for this approach can be a simple rank order of the brands according to consumers' preferences. A joint space program (e.g., PREFMAP[9]) can be used, resulting in a joint space of the original similarity space and ideal points, each representing the locus of preference of each respondent in this space. The closer a brand to the "ideal," the more this brand is preferred. The output of this approach is illustrated in Exhibit 4–12.

Given that consumers may vary in their preference for the various automobiles, it is useful to present in the same space both the perceptual configuration of the stimuli (points in the space) *and* the respondents' preference for the cars (ideal points). The ideal point represents the point in space, which, without distorting the original perceptual configuration, satisfies the condition that the distance of all brands from it will correspond, as closely as possible, to the respondents' rank order of the brands from

---

[9]For a brief discussion see Appendix A.

most to least preferred.[10] In this illustrative map, respondent 1 prefers the sporty type cars—Camaro followed by Firebird and Capri. Respondent 2, on the other hand, prefers the luxury-type cars, such as Mercedes, followed by Continental and Cadillac.

Such analysis can be done at the individual level, enabling the researcher to segment the market according to similarities in the respondents' ideal points. Alternatively, the respondents can be clustered, based on their similarity with respect to the original preference ranking and ideal points established for each segment.

MDS POSITIONING BASED ON A COMPARISON OF "SUBJECTIVE" AND "OBJECTIVE" EVALUATION

An often-asked question concerning product positioning is: How different are consumers' perceptions of a product from the "real" objective evaluation of the product on its performance characteristics? A number of studies which compared the objective positioning of a product to its perceived positioning suggest that the two configurations may be quite distinct. A more important aspect of this comparison is not the conclusion that there are differences, but, rather, that further insight into the product positioning can be gained from an examination of the differences between the two configurations, hence suggesting more insightful and appropriate strategies.

Two such examples are discussed in this chapter. The *new diet product study*[11] was conducted in the early 1970s for one of the leading

food companies and was aimed at determining the positioning of new diet concepts. The study did provide a better understanding of product positioning of new diet products by a comparison of their objective and subjective evaluations. The respondents were women who were on a diet. Their task included grouping food items (some of which were such diet products as Metrecal and some of which were not, such as pudding, potato chips, and milkshakes) and thirteen concepts of new diet products according to their similarity.

In addition, they were asked to evaluate the products and concepts according to their overall preference and preference for serving and eating in various eating occasions (scenarios), such as for lunch, for a short crash diet to lose weight quickly, to improve appearance, at dinner, when alone. Following this task, they rated the products and concepts on a set of twelve attributes, such as calories, nutrition, taste, convenience of preparation, vitamins, cholesterol, and fillingness. This resulted in three sets of subjective data:

1. Product similarity data;
2. Product preference rankings (overall and by scenario);
3. Product evaluation on various product attributes.

These data were subjected to a variety of multidimensional scaling programs. The 40 × 40 product similarity data across subjects were submitted to the TORSCA multidimensional scaling program and to the Johnson hierarchical clustering program. The product evaluation data (both the product preference data and the evaluation of products on the set of attributes) were submitted to Carroll and Chang's joint space program (PREFMAP).

In addition to these data, a group of food technicians evaluated the various products according to their actual attributes. These data were also submitted to an appropriate set of multidimensional scaling programs, enabling

---

[10]This approach is preferred over the one which asks respondents to evaluate an explicit "ideal brand" as another brand in the competitive set. The major problem with the explicit ideal approach is that such a brand would tend to dominate all other brands and offer little diagnostic insight into the reasons for preference.

[11]This study was reported earlier in Wind and Robinson (1972).

EXHIBIT 4–13

TWO-DIMENSIONAL PERCEPTUAL CONFIGURATION OF 27 FOOD PRODUCTS
AND 13 NEW DIET CONCEPTS

Source: Reprinted from "Product Positioning: An Application of Multidimensional Scaling," by Y. Wind and P.J. Robinson, in *Attitude Research in Transition*, R.I. Haley (ed.), published by the American Marketing Association, 1972.

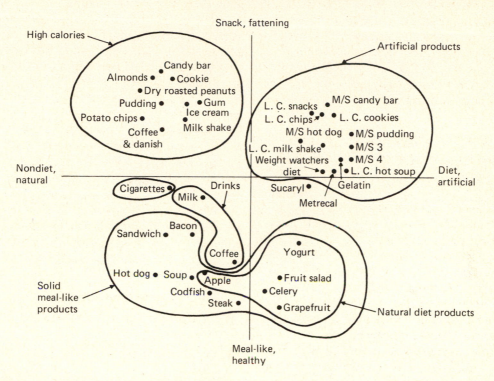

a comparison of the subjective-objective configurations.

Exhibit 4–13 presents the two-dimensional configuration of the forty items as derived from the products' similarity data. The product clusters were determined by the Johnson hierarchical clustering program and are incorporated into Exhibit 4–13. An examination of this figure suggests a number of clusters:

- A cluster of high-calorie snack/dessert products, such as cookies, candies, and milkshakes.

- A cluster of "nonnatural" diet products, such as Metrecal and all the 13 concepts of

the new diet products.

- A cluster of natural diet foods, such as yogurt, fruit salad, and celery sticks.

- A cluster of solid, meal-like items.

Examination of the new diet concepts reveals their position with respect to other products and concepts, as well as their position on the two dimensions. If one is interested in the positioning of the new diet concepts, Exhibit 4–13 suggests the following conclusions:

1. The new concepts will compete with other "artificial" diet products such as Metrecal and Weight Watchers' Complete Meal.

EXHIBIT 4–14

TWO-DIMENSIONAL PERCEPTUAL CONFIGURATION OF 40 PRODUCTS AND
THEIR "PERCEIVED" AND OBJECTIVE ATTRIBUTES

Source: Reprinted from "Product Positioning: An Application of Multidimensional Scaling," by
Y. Wind and P.J. Robinson, in *Attitude Research in Transition*, R.I. Haley (ed.), published by the
American Marketing Association, 1972.

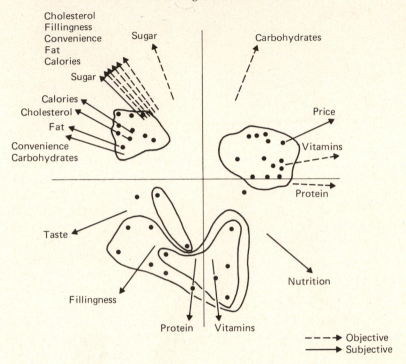

2. The concepts seem to be positioned opposite their "natural" counterparts. Hence, if dimension 2 is viewed as "fattening-healthy," it may suggest that the fattening attribute of the natural products may "rub off" on the diet concepts, leading to overestimation of the fattening attributes of concepts such as a "diet cookie."

Further insight into the position of each concept and product was gained by an examination of the joint space configuration of the products and concepts and their perceived attributes. Exhibit 4–14 presents the results of this analysis. Looking at the solid line vectors (subjective evaluations) and the relation of the vari-

ous products to them suggests:

- "Natural" diet products, such as yogurt, are perceived as being both nutritious and healthy.

- "Natural" meal items, such as steak, are perceived as filling and rich in proteins.

- High-calorie snacks and desserts, such as potato chips and candies, are perceived as being "fatty" (fat, cholesterol, and carbohydrates), sugary, and high in calories. They are, however, convenient for preparation.

- The new diet concepts are perceived as expensive, not tasty, less nutritious than

EXHIBIT 4–15

ILLUSTRATIVE CARD (ONE OUT OF 16)
FOR THE CONJOINT ANALYSIS STUDY

TYPE OF PRODUCT BOUGHT:
New truck/agricultural equipment

THE CUSTOMER'S CREDIT RATING:
Poor

LENGTH OF TERM:
18–35 months

YOUR UNFAMILIARITY WITH THE
CUSTOMER: Unfamiliar customer

DOWN PAYMENT PERCENT (INCLUDING
VALUE OF TRADE-IN): Under 10%
(i.e., 90–100% financing)

AMOUNT TO FINANCE:
Under $5,000

natural diet products, and poor on health, protein, and fillingness.

A comparison of the subjective evaluation configuration with the objective data was done in two stages. First, a two- and three-dimensional objective configuration of the forty products was derived and compared to the subjective configuration. This suggested that dieters do not perceive diet and nondiet products according to their objective attributes.

A more direct comparison was undertaken using a joint space analysis, the results of which are presented in Exhibit 4–14. A comparison of the discrepancies between the objective (broken line) and subjective (solid line) vectors (recall that the cosine of the angle between each pair of vectors measures the degree of correlation between them) suggests that the greatest discrepancy (50 percent or greater) exists with regard to fillingness, carbohydrates, proteins, and vitamins. Fairly high congruence (less than a 20 percent discrepancy) is found with respect to calories, sugar, fat, cholesterol, and conveni-

ence of preparation. This suggests that dieters are more conscious of and interested in—and, hence, knowledgeable of—this latter set of attributes.

CONJOINT ANALYSIS POSITIONING

Given the novelty of positioning via conjoint analysis, it might be useful to illustrate it by describing a study that utilized this approach.

The study in question was concerned with the positioning of a large finance company (associated with one of the automotive manufacturers) among automotive dealers. The management of the finance company wanted to get a better understanding of their competitive position as perceived by their dealers. In particular, it was concerned with its competitive position against local banks. Six factors were identified by management as constituting the major determinants of the assignment of a paper to a finance company. These included the type of product bought (new or used car), the customer's credit rating (poor or good), the length of term (18 to 36 months or more than 36 months), the dealer's familiarity with the customer (familiar or unfamiliar), the percent down payment (under 10 percent, 10 to 25 percent, or more than 25 percent), and the amount to be financed (under $5,000, $5,000 to $15,000, $15,000 to $30,000, and more than $30,000).

A fractional factorial design (Winer, 1971, and Green, 1974) was developed, which resulted in sixteen combinations (instead of the full set of 192 combinations). Each combination represented a hypothetical customer and his characteristics. Exhibit 4–15 presents one of the 16 combination cards. Each respondent was presented with all 16 cards, asked to examine them carefully, and assign each one to one of five possible finance companies.

The data from this task were submitted to the categorical conjoint analysis program and resulted in the type of output presented in

EXHIBIT 4–16

DEALERS' EVALUATION OF THE POSITIONING OF FIVE FINANCE COMPANIES:
RESULTS OF CONJOINT ANALYSIS (ILLUSTRATIVE OUTPUT)

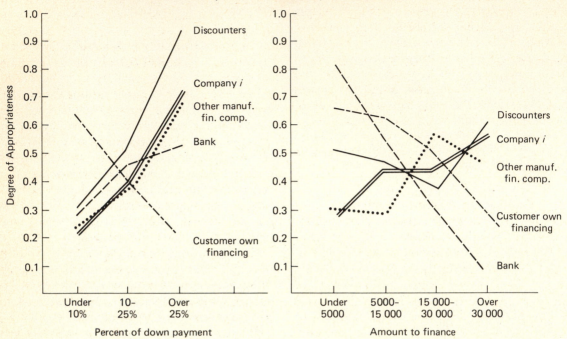

Exhibit 4–16. For illustrative purposes, the exhibit includes only two of the six factors, whereas the actual output included all six factors, of course.

Examination of this output provided answers to such questions as:

- For what type of paper is the company viewed as most appropriate? Company *i*, for example, is among the most appropriate sources for paper over $30,000 and with over 15 percent of down payment.

- For what type of paper is each of the competitors viewed as most appropriate? Banks, for example, are perceived as most appropriate for paper under $5,000 but not at all for over $30,000.

- What is the competitive position of the company on each of the various factors?

Company i seems to compete on these two factors primarily with the discounters.

- What is the relative importance of each of the factors? (This is calculated as the range of utility for a given factor as a percentage of the total ranges for all factors).

RESEARCH DECISIONS INVOLVED IN A POSITIONING STUDY

In conducting a positioning study the researcher should make three major decisions in addition to the regular decisions concerning the sampling of subjects, products and attributes, and the selection of appropriate data analysis procedure (e.g., which specific multidimensional scaling algorithm to use, for example).

Stimulus definition The brands and products selected for inclusion in the stimulus set can be defined in a number of ways and may be presented in terms of the physical objects, names of the items, verbalized profile descriptions of the items, pictorial presentations, or some other form. As might be imagined, respondent evaluations may differ depending on how the stimuli are described and semantically encoded. To select the most appropriate way of defining the stimuli, the researcher should develop stimuli which are as close as possible to those with which consumers will eventually be confronted in the real world.

Task definition Defining the respondent's task requires an explicit decision. The respondent could be asked to react to the stimuli in terms of: overall evaluation of the objects in terms of preference or their relative similarity; judgments of objects' similarity or preference (or other types of orderings) according to a set of prespecified scenarios (problem-solving conditions); or according to a set of prespecified attributes (other than overall similarity or preference). Alternatively, one can collect objective data on the characteristics of the stimuli, in which case an objective performance space rather than a subjective brand space will result. In determining an appropriate task, again,

closeness to real world behavior should be the primary criterion.

Response definition Assuming that the stimulus set and task have been defined, the researcher must still contend with specifying the nature of the subject's response. Verbal and nonverbal responses may involve ratings, judgments, ranking—including strict orderings or weak orderings (those including the possibility of ties)—constant sum procedure (e.g., allocation of 100 points among the stimuli), and assignments to prespecified classes. Even given the restriction of responses to those that represent subjective, verbalized judgments, there are numerous ways for eliciting ratings, rankings, and category assignments. The specific procedure to be employed depends on conceptual considerations (the inherent difference between ranking, rating, paired comparisons, and the like), the number of items in the stimulus set, the length of the interview, and the researcher's preferences. If one deals with a set of twenty to forty brands, sorting or rating will be a much more appropriate task than strict ranking, which is feasible only when a smaller competitive set is used. The dominant considerations in selecting a response definition are the respondent's ability to undertake the task and the validity of the measurement procedures.[12]

POSITIONING AS A GUIDELINE FOR PRODUCT AND MARKETING STRATEGIES

Positioning provides a conceptual framework for designing and evaluating marketing strategies. As such, it allows the manager to develop a number of marketing propositions, such as:

- The closer the positioning of two brands, the more likely they are to compete with each other.
- The closer a brand is to the "ideal" point of

a segment, and the farther other brands are from this ideal point, the higher the probability of purchase of the given brand.

- The more isolated a brand is on some relevant dimension, the more unique it is considered to be.

---

[12]For a comparison of 13 different attitude measurement scales, see Haley and Case (1979).

Such propositions, although still general, are essential for the development of relevant substantive market models (Dominguez and Nicosia, 1977). It is hoped that further conceptual and empirical work in this area will lead to more specific and rigorous propositions.

The discussion of positioning suggests that the concept in its current formulation and measurement approaches can provide management with answers to the key marketing questions of:

- Where am I (as perceived by relevant publics)?
- Where am I going to be if I initiate changes in my marketing strategies or if my competitors initiate some changes in their marketing strategies?

The concept and its measurement provide further flexibility since the analysis of positioning can encompass:

- brands, products, product attributes (benefits), or firms
- existing brands as well as new product concepts
- brands within or across product categories—this is especially important, given the problem of determining the "relevant" competitive setting or the exact boundaries of the market (Wind, 1977b)
- comparison of the perceived positioning with the "objective" positioning of a brand.

Two additional features of positioning analysis are of major importance as inputs for the design of the firm's marketing strategy—positioning by market segment and positioning over time.

POSITIONING BY MARKET SEGMENT

A number of published positioning studies report on the differences in perceived product and service positioning by segment (e.g., Wind and Robinson, 1972). To illustrate the importance of conducting a positioning analysis by segment, let us consider a study conducted for a computer manufacturer on the positioning of its computers.[13] The firm's and the competitors' computer models were first positioned in a performance space based on manufacturer data on performance characteristics of the various computers. This objective performance space was then compared to the perceptual positioning obtained from data gathered from two market segments—the firm's customers and matched companies that did not use the firm's computers. In addition, data were also collected from the firm's sales personnel. The subjective and objective data were submitted to a number of MDS and clustering programs, resulting in detailed positioning configurations for each segment as well as an objective performance space. The three perceptual positionings, when compared among themselves and with the objective space, revealed little congruence, suggesting a number of significant implications for the firm's marketing strategy. Exhibit 4–17 summarizes the major positioning findings of this study.

Given the strong relationship between segmentation and positioning, as clearly illustrated in this example, the two decisions should be made jointly. In fact, management can approach these decisions by focusing either on positioning or on segmentation; i.e., the question addressed by management is:

Given a target market segment, which product positioning (and its associated marketing strategy) is likely to be most effective in reaching the firm's objectives? or

Given a target product positioning, which market segment is most likely to be responsive to this positioning?

In both cases (positioning-segmentation or segmentation-positioning) the two decisions

---

[13]This study is discussed in Green and McMennamin (1974).

EXHIBIT 4–17

SUMMARY RESULTS OF THE COMPUTER PERFORMANCE POSITIONING STUDY

1. In terms of objective performance "space," RCA models compete with:
   A. Themselves, mostly
   B. XDS-6 and 7
   C. IBM 370/135; 370/145; 370/155
   D. NCR 300
   E. UNIVAC 1106

2. RCA users perceive RCA models, performancewise, as competing with:
   A. Themselves, mostly
   B. IBM 370/135; 370/145; 370/155
   C. IBM 360/20; 360/30; 360/40; 360/50

3. Nonusers of RCA CPU equipment perceive RCA models, performancewise, as competing with:
   A. Themselves, mostly
   B. To a lesser extent with UNIVAC, CDC, BURROUGHS, and XDS, but *not* with IBM

4. RCA employees perceive RCA models, performancewise, as competing with:
   A. Themselves
   B. BURROUGHS 2500; 3500; 5700;
   C. IBM 360/30; 360/40; 360/50;
   D. IBM 370/135; 370/145; 370/155

are closely related. Furthermore, regardless of which of the two approaches is followed, it is desirable to follow a complete iterative process involving both approaches.[14]

POSITIONING OVER TIME

Most product positioning studies are conducted at a *point in time* with no explicit consideration of changes in positioning over time. Yet, from a management point of view, the monitoring of *changes* in positioning is of utmost impor-

tance. To illustrate the measurement of positioning over time, let us consider a study on the changes in a retail store positioning *over time*. The study was based on the evaluation given by 200 housewives of various retail stores in a certain metropolitan area over a period of two years. The data for the first three months and the last three months were grouped separately and analyzed for the overall market and various a priori segments.

Exhibit 4–18 presents the results of matching via the Cliff Match procedure (Cliff, 1966) separate TORSCA maps of nine stores for each of the two time periods. The stores in this map have been disguised, but the configuration is derived from the actual data. The dimensions of this map could be interpreted as high prestige/relatively expensive versus low prestige/discount (the horizontal axis) and width of assortment (vertical axis).

---

[14]Some of the research approaches that allow such an iterative process are flexible segmentation componential segmentation and the POSSE system. For a brief discussion of the first two approaches, see Wind (1978a) and Chapter 13. The POSSE system is discussed in Appendix B.

EXHIBIT 4–18

TWO-DIMENSIONAL CONFIGURATION OF THE POSITIONING OF NINE STORES
OVER TIME

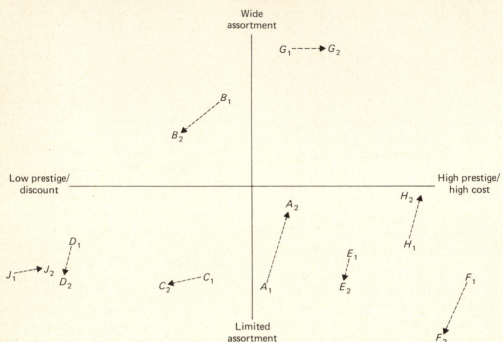

The change in the perceived position of each store is traced by the dotted line which links the store position in the two time periods. Examination of the magnitude and direction of changes in the stores' positions can provide management with considerable insight into their market position and changes in it as they occurred over the relevant study period.

As in the other positioning studies, the time series analysis can be extended to cover changes, not only in the stores, but also in the stores' position on various evaluative scales (such as good service, easy credit, best value, etc.) and/or various products for which the store may be appropriate (e.g., appliances, clothes, etc.). The analytical procedure is quite similar and the only difference is that instead of developing a "super space" (via the Cliff Match program)

based on the results of the TORSCA program, the input data to the matching program are the results of the joint space analyses of stores and evaluative scales, or stores and products.

These analyses were of diagnostic significance in revealing the positioning of the various stores in the market and the extent and direction of the change in their positioning over a known time interval. More explicit and detailed insights were derived from relating the store's policies to their positionings and shifts over time. It is important to note that changes in one's own positioning may result not only from one's own policy changes but also from the activities of competitors. Tracing the changes in positioning and relating them to the policies of the various stores may thus provide a better understanding of the market structure and consumer response functions and suggest a number of strategy implications.

POSITIONING AND MARKETING STRATEGY

The understanding of consumers' (and other relevant publics') perceptions and evaluation of the firm's products and services is an essential ingredient in the design of the firm's marketing strategy. It provides management with a clear understanding of *where they are* versus their competitors' position (by segment); it further provides some insights into *why* the company is where it is and can suggest directions for *where they may consider going*.

In the context of a joint space configuration, positioning may suggest a number of alternative strategies that management can follow:

1. Move their product closer to the "ideal point" of a target segment. This can be done by product repositioning strategies which may or may not involve actual physical product changes.

2. Introduce a new product near the target segment's ideal point, in addition to the current product.

3. Move the ideal point of a target segment closer to the positioning of the brand. This is a difficult task involving a change in the consumer belief system toward the given product category.

4. Introduce an innovative product that may change the consumers' perceptions of the market structure by changing the salient dimensions in the market. For example, when Kodak introduced its no-light movie camera, it also introduced a new dimension to the marketplace. This dimension, through promotional effort, was important in strengthening Kodak's market position.

Each of these possible strategies has its associated pros and cons, and management should carefully examine the costs, risks, and benefits associated with repositioning attempts (a position could be lost without the desired new position being captured, or "cannibalization" could occur). Given the company's unique objectives, resources, and market position, the considerations of a dominant firm may be different than those of a marginal firm in the market, especially given the differences involved in the relative strength of the firm versus that of its competitors.

Changes in positioning over time, which can be easily noticed as shifts of a brand's position in a multidimensional space, provide management with a tool to monitor, over time, the success of its and its competitors' marketing strategy.

As such, positioning—and especially positioning as monitored by multidimensional scaling—can provide a needed conceptual framework for the evaluation of the various marketing strategies of the firm. Further research is needed in this regard, however, focusing on two sets of relationships: (a) the link between changes in marketing strategy (product formulation, pricing, promotion, and distribution) of the firm and its competitors and changes in the firm's positioning (by segment) and (b) the link between changes in positioning (strategy *and* execution) and changes in sales, market share, and profitability (or any other dependent variable of interest to management).

Some progress in this direction has been made over the years. Recently, Urban (1975) developed a model—PERCEPTOR—in which he estimates the probability of purchase as a function of the squared distance between the ideal point and the new brand. Although conceptually it is desirable to include in the calculation of probability of purchase the distance of the new brand from the other brands, Urban does report satisfactory results for his simplified approach.

Having better insight into these two questions is essential for better determination of the firm's desired positioning (given alternative competitive action) and the actions—strategy generation, execution, and control—necessary to achieve such a positioning. The determination of a positioning strategy is closely linked to considerations of the firm's entire product/market portfolio which typically receives the attention of top management. In contrast, a relatively neglected aspect of positioning strategy is the *execution* phase. In too many cases creative execution is left for the copy writers, ignoring the need for strong interrelationship between strategy formulation and execution. Of considerable importance in this context is the ability to execute and communicate a positioning not only through promotional copy but also through appropriate use of the other product and marketing variables, e.g., small (7 ounce) beer cans and bottles to help position beer for women, low price to express an "economy" positioning, and distribution through specialty stores to express a high-quality service positioning.

Common to strategy formulation, execution, and eventual control is the need to rely on *positioning research*. Such research requires that *each* marketing research project that is concerned with evaluating a given marketing strategy (e.g., concept evaluation, advertising evaluation, and the like) should include an analysis of the perceived positioning of the given product or service by segment. This should provide a useful addition to most marketing studies and is essential input to the firm's positioning decisions.

REPOSITIONING

Repositioning a brand can often offer important new direction to an established brand. Consider, for example, the repositioning of Miller High Life from "the champagne of beers," a position which appeals to exclusivity, to a positioning of the brand as a reward for a job well done. The new positioning was aimed at the lower class, heavy drinker of beer, and was consistent with the findings of the earlier beer segmentation studies of the Tavistock Institute. This strategy has contributed to the spectacular growth of Miller from 7th-ranked (4.1 percent share) in 1970 to 2nd-ranked (with 15 percent share) in 1977.

Repositioning does not necessarily have to be associated with product modification (Miller did not change the product nor did DuPont, for example, who repositioned Teflon from "the new greaseless cooking discovery" to "quick and easy, no-stick, no-scour cleanup" positioning). On the other hand, product modifications are often associated with a repositioning effort.

"POOR MAN" POSITIONING

Thus far the various approaches to determine a brand's positioning were based on consumers' evaluation of a set of brands. In some instances, management does not have such information and cannot obtain it in time to provide input to a decision that requires positioning information. In this case, management may want to utilize the "poor man" solution to positioning. This entails a "quick and dirty" view of the competitive positioning. The major tool for this analysis is a simple matrix of products by "benefits." Management identifies all relevant products and brands and, through a systematic examination of their advertising and package claims, fills the matrix. An example of such a matrix for window cleaners is presented in Exhibit 4–19.

"Poor man" positioning can also be aided by available comparative data on product performance such as that which is published regularly by *Consumer Reports* and other consumer service publications. Data such as are illus-

EXHIBIT 4–19

"POOR MAN" POSITIONING: THE PRODUCT–BENEFIT MATRIX

Window cleaners (products/brands)	Benefits								
	Cleaning efficiency	No streaking	Grease cutting	Easy to use	Multiple uses	Econo-mical	Fast action	. . .	Contains ammonia
Windex	✔				✔				✔
Easy Off		✔	✔			✔			
Ajax	✔	✔							✔
Glass Plus			✔		✔				
Sparkle	✔								
.									
.									
.									

trated in Exhibit 4–20 can be helpful alone, or submitted to a hierarchical clustering or MDS program.

Note that whereas such a poor man "objective" positioning is a useful first step for any positioning analysis or an additional input to the consumer-perceived positioning of a product class, it is quite risky to base marketing decisions only on such product-benefit or product performance matrices, since it may not reflect accurately consumers' *perceptions* of the market.

SOME EXTENSIONS OF THE CONCEPT AND MEASUREMENT OF POSITIONING

A number of the basic approaches to the measurement and study of positioning were presented in this chapter. These approaches were restricted, however, to the following five conditions:

1. The basic market space is a *brand* (or product or firm) space, not an attribute (or feature) space.

2. Evaluation of brands on specific attributes requires asking the respondent to rank or rate the brands on a set of preselected attributes, anchoring either on the attributes *or* brands.

3. A brand is typically positioned against a single set of brands, i.e., most of the algorithms used in positioning force a brand to group with only one set of brands, and do not allow for overlap in cluster membership.

4. The brand space is based on the perception of individual brands and does not address the question of an *inventory* or portfolio of

EXHIBIT 4–20

ILLUSTRATIVE *CONSUMER REPORTS* DATA FOR POSITIONING OF CASSETTE TAPE DECKS

Source: Copyright 1981 by Consumers Union of United States, Inc., Mount Vernon, NY 10550.
Excerpted by permission from *Consumer Reports*, March 1981.

Listed in order of estimated overall quality as indicated by performance score with regular (iron oxide) tape; where scores are equal, listed alphabetically. Differences in score of 7 points or less were judged not very significant. Performance with metal tape noted for reference. Prices are suggested retail; * indicates price is approximate; discounts are available.

Ratings legend: Excellent ◉ · Very good ◕ · Good ○ · Fair ◑ · Poor ●

Brand and model	Price	Performance score	Height × width × depth	Midband[1] (regular tape headroom)	Treble[2] (regular tape headroom)	Meter type[3]	Meter characteristics	Comments
AKAI GXM50	$395	87	6¼×17⅜×11⅜ in.	4 to 6 dB	6 to 10 dB	F	Peak/average	A,B,C,U
HITACHI D75S	350*	87	4¼×17⅛×11½	4 to 6	0 to 5	F	Peak	E,Q,V,AA
ONKYO TA2040	370	87	4¾×16½×12¾	7 to 9	0 to 5	F	Peak	B,D,J,K,Q,R,V
JVC KDA55J	350	86	4⅝×16½×11⅛	7 to 9	0 to 5	M/5 lights	Average	F,N,P,W
TEAC A660	360	86	4¼×17×11¾	4 to 6	6 to 10	M	Peak	G,W
TECHNICS RSM51	420	85	4¼×17×10⅞	4 to 6	6 to 10	F	Peak	D,L,U
DUAL C820	420	84	5¼×17¼×14⅝	4 to 6	6 to 10	LED	Peak	C,J,Q,R,S,W,AA
AIWA M600U	390	83	4⅝×18⅛×11⅜	7 to 9	6 to 10	M/5 lights	Average	I,F,W,AA
BIC T2M	350	83	6×16¾×10⅞	4 to 6	6 to 10	M/1 light	Peak	C,O,Q,V
LUX K5A	399	82	5¼×17¼×10½	1 to 3	6 to 10	F	Peak	B,C,Q,V
SANSUI SC3300	420	81	6¼×17⅛×12	1 to 3	0 to 5	F	Peak	X,AA
YAMAHA K850	360	81	5⅛×17¾×12¾	4 to 6	0 to 5	M	Peak	E,V
FISHER DD300	350	80	5¼×17¾×10⅞	7 to 9	6 to 10	M/3 lights	Average	G,W
HARMAN KARDON HK200XM	349	80	5¼×17⅜×13¾	1 to 3	0 to 5	F	Peak	B,C,N,P,Q,Y
SONY TCK71	430	80	5⅛×17×11⅜	4 to 6	6 to 10	F	Peak	A,I,U
KENWOOD KX800	389	79	5⅛×17¾×14	4 to 6	0 to 5	M/3 lights	Average	B,D,X
SANYO RD5370	280	78	5⅛×17¼×12⅜	1 to 3	6 to 10	M/2 lights	Average	A,R,S,X
SHARP RT4488	390	77	5⅝×17×14	4 to 6	6 to 10	F	Peak	C,T,U,AA
TOSHIBA PCX60	400	77	4¾×16⅝×11	4 to 6	0 to 5	M	Peak	H,Z
PIONEER CTF750	395	71	5⅛×16½×13⅛	4 to 6	6 to 10	F	Peak/average	C,D,M,Z

Column groupings: Regular tape performance (Freedom from flutter; Dynamic range, midband; Frequency response; Dynamic range, treble; Speed accuracy); Regular tape headroom (Midband[1]; Treble[2]); Metal tape performance (Dynamic range, midband; Dynamic range, treble).

[1] Indicates number of decibels above deck's "0" reference point at which distortion is likely to occur when recording.
[2] Indicates number of decibels below deck's "0" reference point at which distortion is likely to occur when recording.
[3] F—fluorescent. M—mechanical. LED—light-emitting diode.

SPECIFICATION AND FEATURES

All have: • Noise-reduction circuitry. • Tape counter. • Provision for regular, chromium-dioxide, and metal-particle tapes. • Front-panel jack for stereo headphones. • Microphone jacks.
Except as noted, all have: • Light-touch transport controls. • Memory rewind. • Record mute switch. • Capability for timer control. • 1 tape speed (1⅞ ips). • Playback-level control. • Cassette-compartment backlight.
Except as noted, all lack: • Provision for off-tape monitoring. • Adjustable bias.

KEY TO COMMENTS

A—Has provision for off-tape monitoring.
B—Has adjustable bias.
C—Lacks light-touch transport controls.
D—Lacks memory rewind.
E—Can rewind automatically at tape's end or, on demand, to start of tape and then stop or play automatically.
F—Can rewind automatically at tape's end or, on demand, to memory point and then stop or play automatically.
G—Can rewind automatically at tape's end or, on demand, to memory point and then play automatically.
H—Can rewind on demand to memory point and then stop or play automatically.
I—Bias is adjustable, but only for normal bias tape mode.
J—Lacks playback-level control.
K—Lacks light for cassette compartment.
L—Can set recording level automatically.
M—Has auto reverse for recording and playback.
N—Has "Super ANRS" (JVC) or Dolby HX (Harman Kardon) for increasing dynamic range in treble during recording.
O—Has 3¾ ips recording speed.
P—Can scan tape automatically for gaps between recorded selections.
Q—Not controllable by timer.
R—Lacks record mute switch.
S—Has limiter for use in recording.
T—Deck has microprocessor control.
U—Tape of choice: Ampex Grandmaster I.
V—Tape of choice: TDK AD.
W—Tape of choice: Scotch Master I.
X—Tape of choice: TDK SA-X.
Y—Tape of choice: Scotch Master II.
Z—Tape of choice: BASF Professional I.
AA—According to the company, this model has been discontinued but may be available in some stores.

brands. (The mere closeness of two brands in some relevant dimensions does not indicate whether both or just one will be bought, and in what combination with other brands.)

5. The unit of analysis in most cases is the individual consumer or some segment of individual consumers, which ignores buying units composed of entire families or subset(s) of families.

Recent methodological developments enable us to relax the first three conditions. These extensions to the measurement of positioning are discussed next, followed by brief speculations on how one might approach the task of relaxing the last two conditions.

DEVELOPMENT OF FEATURE SPACE

A feature (benefit) space, as opposed to a brand space, can be of interest to management in situations such as those in which current brands do not cover or emphasize all the relevant product features desired by consumers. A feature space can be developed from consumer data on which features are likely to be associated with others. Such a space, in which the attributes are presented as points, was developed in a study of ice cream (Green, Wind, and Claycamp, 1975), which went one step further and incorporated, in the same space, the positioning of existing brands (also presented as points), based on consumers' evaluations of the brands on the various features, *and* the ideal points of each segment (defined as regular users of each brand) in the same space. Following this approach, one can make statements concerning the feature space and the relationships among the various features and the positioning of the various brands based on their relationship to other brands, all the product features and their

major dimensions, and preference of the relative segment.

UNRESTRICTED LIST OF FEATURES

Since most positioning studies present the respondents with a list of brands and a list of attributes, one may be concerned about the relevance and exhaustiveness of the attribute list. In this case, a procedure suggested by Green, Wind, and Jain (1973) for the analysis of free-response data can be employed.

Following this approach, consumers are presented with a list of brands—one at a time—and asked to say the first things that come to their minds when they hear the name of the given brand. These free-response data provide the basis for a stimulus (brands) by evoked words (attributes) matrix which is submitted to a multidimensional scaling analysis. The results of this analysis are submitted to a hierarchical clustering program, resulting in a tree structure of *both* the brands and the attributes they evoke.

Consider, for example, the following study (reported in Green, Wind, and Jain, 1973) which was concerned with the identification of the positioning of a woman's magazine among advertising agency media buyers. One of the tasks given the media buyers was to respond with the first thing that came to their minds when they thought about each of eight magazines. The results of the free-association data are presented in the upper panel of Exhibit 4–21, while the tree diagram for the stimulus and evoked words is presented in the bottom part of the exhibit. Note that magazine A, the sponsoring magazine, had a rather poor positioning—perceived as low quality and with strong competition from magazines H and C. Magazine G, on the other hand, occupied a unique and extremely strong position as a magazine with youth appeal. As a result of this

EXHIBIT 4–21

POSITIONING BASED ON FREE RESPONSE DATA (ILLUSTRATIVE STUDY)

Source: Reprinted from Paul E. Green, Yoram Wind, Awn and K. Jain, "Analyzing Free Response Data in Marketing Research," *Journal of Marketing Research*, 10, Feb. 1973, published by the American Marketing Association

Word association frequencies

Magazines (stimuli)	Evoked words														Totals
	High quality	Trustworthy	Good reproduction	Outdated	Modern	Low quality	Small page size	Good editorial	Upscale audience	Large page size	Good circulation	Efficient	Informative	Youth appeal	
A	1	1	6	6	3	16	6	6	6	1	1	2	2	2	59
B	9	3	9	1	1	1	1	9	7	15	10	1	5	1	73
C	3	2	2	1	4	2	1	2	1	2	10	7	3	2	42
D	5	21	2	6	1	2	2	10	3	2	6	10	2	1	73
E	7	2	4	4	6	1	1	13	9	19	5	3	3	2	79
F	3	1	2	5	9	1	4	15	5	3	8	5	2	1	64
G	1	1	2	1	6	1	1	6	3	1	2	1	2	52	80
H	3	1	1	1	5	2	1	1	2	2	6	5	2	2	34
Totals	32	32	28	25	35	26	17	62	36	45	48	34	21	63	504

HIERARCHICAL STRUCTURE OF EIGHT MAGAZINES AND 14 EVALUATIVE WORD ASSOCIATIONS

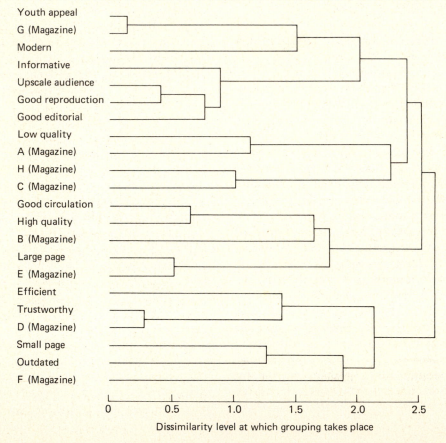

Dissimilarity level at which grouping takes place

study and other supporting evidence, attempts were made to change the editorial direction of magazine A and to acquire magazine G.

The use of free response can also be extended to the establishment of a direct brand perceptual space (not one derived from the analysis of similarities of brands across attributes). In this case, respondents can be presented with a list of stimuli brands and asked to free-associate the names of similar brands. Such data can be treated either as frequency of mention (across people) and analyzed in a similar way to the data generated from the previous task or, alternatively, the pattern of response may be analyzed treating the order of mention as rank-order data.

OVERLAPPING CLUSTERING

The development of the overlapping cluster model and algorithm (Shephard and Arabie, 1979) makes it feasible to cluster objects (brands) in a way that does not require each object to be a member of one and only one cluster, but rather allows for membership in a number of clusters.[15] This methodological development frees the researcher from the previous methodological limitation of clustering brands into mutually exclusive and exhaustive categories even when conceptually he/she knew that a brand can compete in more than one cluster of products. The graphical output of the ADCLUS overlapping cluster algorithm—when compared to the output of the more conventional multidimensional scaling/hierarchical clustering algorithms (Exhibit 4–22) illustrates the conceptual advantages of having the flexibility of clustering each brand in more than a single cluster.

---

[15] The same procedure can be applied to the clustering of subjects and has major implications for market segmentation. For a further discussion of this application of overlapping clustering, see Arabie, DeSarbo, Carroll and Wind (1979).

POSITIONING UNDER CONDITIONS OF MULTIPERSONS AND MULTIBRANDS

Whereas the attribute space, free response, and overlapping cluster approaches to positioning have been defined and tested, the other two conditions have not been studied in any rigorous way. Hence, progress in positioning research requires the development of conceptual and operational ways of determining a brand's position in the context of consumers' brand inventories and multipersons (e.g., family or any subsets of it) as the unit of analysis.

The conceptual issues involved and some of the possible research approaches to the study of multiperson, multibrand situations, are suggested elsewhere (Wind, 1975) and will require major methodological breakthroughs. Both of these problems can be partially approached by MDS. The inventory problem has some resemblance to the problem of item collection which was analyzed by Green, Wind, and Jain (1972). Yet the problem is more complex since it requires both the analysis of the fit of any product into the consumer's current assortment (inventory) of products and the positioning of assortments of products.

The change of the unit of analysis in positioning studies (from individual to multiperson) is even more complex and can be approached in a number of ways. These may include separate positioning analyses for each individual and examination of the *congruence* of the positioning among the relevant members of the unit of analysis. This can be done, for example, by matching the perceptual maps of husband and wife. Alternatively, consumers may be segmented according to the similarities of the perceptions of members of the unit of analysis and brand positioning determined separately for each of these segments. These and other approaches, however, require further development and testing.

EXHIBIT 4–22

A.COMPARISON OF BREAKFAST PRODUCTS' POSITIONING VIA TRADITIONAL AND OVERLAPPING CLUSTERING PROCEDURES
TRADITIONAL POSITIONING

Source: Green and Rao, 1972; based on a two-space configuration for TORSCA 8 analysis coupled with the results of the Johnson Hierarchical Clustering Program.

Traditional positioning

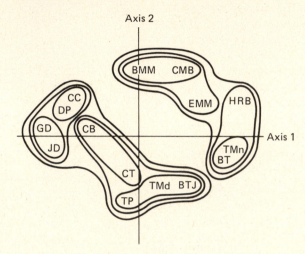

OVERLAPPING CLUSTERING POSITIONING

Source: Arabie, DeSarbo, Carroll and Wind, 1979; based on analysis of the Green and Rao data using the ADCLUS overlapping clustering algorithm.

Overlapping clustering positioning

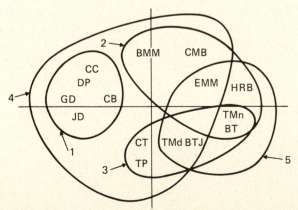

EXHIBIT 4–22 (continued)

MAPCLUS REPRESENTATION OF 15 FOOD ITEMS

Rank by weight	Items in subset	Interpretation
1	Jelly donut, glazed donut, cinnamon bun, danish pastry, coffee cake	Pastries
2	Blueberry muffin and margarine, corn muffin and margarine, English muffin and margarine, hard rolls and butter, toast and margarine, buttered toast	Foods spread with margarine or butter
3	Toast pop-up, cinnamon toast, toast and marmalade, buttered toast and jelly, buttered toast, toast and margarine	Toasted foods
4	All but hard rolls and butter, toast and margarine, buttered toast	Sweet foods (compared to those excluded)
5	English muffin and margarine, hard rolls and butter, toast and margarine, buttered toast, buttered toast and jelly, toast and marmalade	Relatively simple bread foods

CONCLUDING REMARKS

"The Positioning Era Cometh" was the title of a three-part feature article in *Advertising Age* (Trout and Ries, 1972). From both the academic interest in the topic and the large number of commercial positioning studies conducted, it seems that positioning is here to stay and is not just a marketing fad.

The importance of positioning was most clearly illustrated recently in the selection by the editors of *Fortune* of the ten business triumphs of the seventies (Fortune, 1979). A number of these triumphs are due to clever positioning. Consider, for example, Revlon's Charlie (the life-style fragrance which has become the world's best selling fragrance); Philip Morris' move into low tar cigarettes (Merit followed by Benson and Hedges Lights, Marlboro 100s, and Virginia Slims Lights); the low-calorie Miller Lite; Merill Lynch's establishment of a financial supermarket; Federal Express' positioning of "absolutely, positively overnight (delivery)", and McDonald's positioning in the fast food industry.

If firms follow a positioning strategy, it should be reflected in their marketing strategies. The next time you watch a commercial, read an advertisement, examine a package, or inquire about the price of a product, try to identify the positioning the product occupies. Consider, for example, the positioning behind these ads:

- "Alberto VO5 hair spray with Veron . . . for a hold you can't get with any other hair spray."

- ". . . twice as many doctors recommend

Fleischmann's as any other margarine and twice as many use Fleischmann's at home."

- "Ford LTD has the full size of a Cadillac but is priced like a down-sized Chevrolet."

- "CAB statistics show TWA has a better on-time performance record than American on 18 shared routes and that it tops United on 25."

- Savin ads: "Xerox is going to make you an offer you should refuse" and "The feature that works best on your present copier is the Call Key Operator button."

For further insight into positioning, select a product category and ask yourself: What is the positioning of each of the products? And, assuming that you were to introduce a new brand to this category: What positioning should you consider? And why?

Product Portfolio Analysis and Decisions

5

Introduction

The Portfolio Concept

Level of Business Analysis
Level of Market
Time Dimensions of Variables

Dimensions of Product Portfolio

Sales
Competitive Strength
Profitability
Risk
Demand on Resources
Utilization of Resources

Standardized Approaches to Product Portfolio

BCG Growth/Share Matrix
AD Little Business Profile Matrix
Directional Policy Matrix
McKinsey/GE Business Assessment Array
Risk/Return Model

Customized Approaches to Product Portfolio

Product Performance Matrix
Conjoint Analysis-Based Multistage Portfolio Approach
Analytic Hierarchy Process

Portfolio Decisions

Concentrated versus Diversified Portfolio
Resource Allocation
Competitive Portfolios
Change in Product Portfolios
Timing Changes in Product Portfolios

Concluding Remarks

INTRODUCTION

Product decisions at all corporate levels above the brand management level involve a number of products. Since most firms operate with multiproducts in multimarkets, a critical part of product policy involves the assessment of the firm's current portfolio of products and markets and deciding on the best allocation of resources among them. Without explicit attention to the entire product portfolio, the likelihood of suboptimization is high, especially in product-management-organized firms. Despite this obvious importance of the product portfolio level of analysis, most of the published work in product policy focuses on the individual product. Only recently has even scattered attention been given to the product portfolio question.

Product portfolio analysis evaluates the current products of the firm on a number of key dimensions (such as profitability, growth, and risk) and provides the input to management decisions on addition of products, modification of existing products, or deletion of products, and allocation of resources among the various products and markets. The portfolio concept, the dimensions underlying product portfolios, and the major product portfolio models and their implications for product marketing strategy are discussed. This is followed by a brief discussion of the portfolio decisions.[1]

THE PORTFOLIO CONCEPT

The product portfolio management approach has its roots and analogies in financial investment portfolio theory. The portfolio problem in financial investment management consists of determining the "optimal" portfolio of stocks and bonds. The typical steps involved in the development of a portfolio of stocks and bonds, which are also required for the development of any product portfolio, are:

- Determine the objectives of the investor/ manager, and the tradeoff between risk

---

[1]For a more detailed discussion of product portfolio analysis, see Wind and Mahajan (1982).

and return in case of the financial port-folio, and any other management objectives such as market share, or growth, in the case of a product portfolio.

- Evaluate each item in the portfolio (products in the case of a product portfolio) in terms of the objectives specified above.

- Decide on the desired portfolio and recommend that certain holdings be reduced or increased in order to give the portfolio balance and conformity with the objectives; i.e., the desired portfolio offers guidelines for the allocation of resources among products (and any other items such as markets included in the portfolio analysis).

The idea of classifying products for resource allocation purposes is not new in marketing planning. Drucker (1963), for example, suggested that products, in general, tend to group themselves into six classes—two with high contribution potential, three with low or minus contribution, and one in between. A breakdown such as the following is fairly typical:

- Tomorrow's breadwinners—new products or today's breadwinners modified and improved (rarely today's breadwinners unchanged).

- Today's breadwinners—the innovations of yesterday.

- Products capable of becoming net contributors if something drastic is done; e.g., converting a good many buyers of "special" variations of limited utility into customers of a new, massive, "regular" line. (This is the in-between category.)

- Yesterday's breadwinners—typically products with high volume, but badly fragmented into "specials," small orders, and the like, and requiring such massive support as to eat up all they earn and

plenty more. Yet this is—next to the category following—the product class to which the largest and best resources are usually allocated. ("Defensive research" is a common example.)

- The "also rans"—typically the high hopes of yesterday that, while they did not work out well, nevertheless did not become outright failures. They are always minus contributors, and practically never become successes no matter how much is poured into them. Yet there is usually far too much managerial and technical ego involved in them to drop them.

- The failures—these rarely are a real problem as they tend to liquidate themselves.

According to Drucker, the above ranking can be used to allocate corporate resources. The first two categories should be supplied the necessary resources. The lower half of the third group and groups four, five, and six either have to produce without any resources and efforts or should be allowed to die. "Yesterday's breadwinners," for example, often produce high yields for a few more years. Drucker used contribution margin as the sole criterion for measuring the performance of the product, whereas more recent portfolio models have been extended to other criteria such as market share, growth, profitability, and the like.

The first two steps of portfolio analysis—determination of the objectives (portfolio dimensions) and evaluation of the various products (both current and potential) on these objectives—are relatively easy.[2] The complex part is determining how to balance the portfolio and allocate resources among its products.

---

[2] A possible exception is when a firm does not have the necessary data on the performance of its products.

Product portfolio models offer a structured set of dimensions on which the current products of the firm can be analyzed. These dimensions include market share (as a measure of strength), growth (as a measure of attraction), as well as other dimensions such as profitability, expected return, and risk. The dimensions vary from one portfolio model to another such as the normative set of dimensions, included in the Boston Consulting Group's share/growth model (Day, 1977) or the risk/return dimensions of the financial portfolio model (Wind, 1975). In addition, as models such as the product performance matrix (Wind and Claycamp, 1976) allow management to identify the dimensions they consider relevant.

Following a classification of the existing (and occasionally, potential) products of the firm on the specific dimensions, the major and more complex managerial task is to decide on the desired target portfolio. A target portfolio should not be limited to products and would ideally include target market segments and distribution outlets. Such an extended portfolio reflects management's objectives, desired direction of growth, and the interactions among products, markets, and distribution outlets. The specification of a target portfolio should be accompanied by guidelines for allocation of resources among the components of the portfolio.

In employing the portfolio management approach to product marketing planning, the following questions may be raised:

- What dimensions should be used in constructing a product portfolio? (Section 2)

- What are the current approaches to portfolio management, and how do they differ from each other? (Sections 3 and 4)

- How can the portfolio management approach be used to develop guidelines to product marketing decisions? (Section 5)

Before moving to these three areas, it is necessary, however, to make three decisions concerning the desired level of business analysis, the level of the market, and the time dimension of analysis.

LEVEL OF BUSINESS ANALYSIS

Product portfolio analysis should be done at various levels from the product line level, through the product mix level, to the strategic business units mix level. The higher the level of business for which a portfolio analysis is conducted, the larger the range of alternative strategies that can be considered.

When portfolio analysis is conducted at a number of levels, a hierarchical structure of the various portfolios is called for; i.e., the highest level portfolio—the corporate one—should include all lower level portfolios, etc.

The customary product portfolio analysis, at all levels, involves existing products. Yet, as mentioned earlier, it might be desirable to include in a portfolio products which, although not currently on the market, can be developed to meet certain product characteristics and expected performance.

LEVEL OF MARKET

Product portfolio analysis should be conducted for each of the market segments as well as across all the markets within which the firm operates. In fact, portfolio analysis to be of value should be conducted at multilevels, i.e., undertaken first within every relevant market segment *and* at higher levels of analysis across market segments, markets, and (if the firm is involved in multinational marketing operations) across countries.

In evaluating the product portfolio within the boundaries of a market segment, the demand interrelationship among the products should be of prime concern. In fact, at this level of portfolio analysis the consumer's point of view (of perceived product positioning and perceived completeness of the portfolio) is of major importance. The perceived positioning of existing (and new) products offers the consumers' views of the relevant market boundaries. This perception by market segment is important input to management's decision on how to determine the market boundaries for the product portfolio analysis.

The consumer perception of the completeness of a product assortment is a special aspect of positioning and is consistent with recent efforts to analyze consumer product assortments rather than consumer response to a single product. This new direction takes into account the consumer's desire for variety, the consumer's inventory management activities (for example, hoarding when there are expectations for price increases), and the multiperson nature of most household consumption behavior.

Product portfolio analysis at higher levels of market segmentation tends to ignore an explicit analysis of the consumer and focuses more on the performance of each product in its relevant market segment. The two levels of analysis are thus not alternatives but rather complements.

The discussion so far has assumed a product portfolio which is evaluated at a number of market levels. Yet, conceptually, the highest level of portfolio analysis should be extended to include a second dimension: markets. This would lead to a *product/market portfolio* in which management evaluates current products/markets and decides on the most attractive combinations of products and markets. The identification of a product/market portfolio and subsequently the selection of the target products/markets is consistent with the matching of products (and product lines) with the needs of various market segments.

In certain cases in which distribution outlets are important components of the firm's marketing mix, the portfolio analysis can be further extended to include a third dimension: distribution. In this case management evaluation of its portfolio would be of its products by market segments and type of distribution outlets. In fact, acquisition or development of new distribution outlets is an often-used way of improving one's portfolio. Exhibit 5–1 illustrates schematically a three-dimensional portfolio of products/markets/distribution outlets.

TIME DIMENSIONS OF VARIABLES

In analyzing the position of various products on the selected dimensions of the product portfolio, the question is whether the dimensions, such as sales growth and profit, should be measured based on historical data or should reflect projected future positioning. Most of the product portfolio models rely on historical data. Hence, the sales growth rate, for example, is determined based on the historical rate of growth in the last *n* years.

Such an approach is satisfactory if the historical growth rate is expected to continue. If, however, there are reasons to suspect major deviation in future performance (due to entry or exit of major competitors, changes in government regulations, and the like), the historical data are not enough and should be supplemented with projected performance and, to the extent possible, *conditional forecasts* (a series of forecasts conditional on various types and levels of marketing activities) as utilized in the product performance matrix approach. The series of performance forecasts could be estimated further for various environmental and strategy scenarios.

At least three distinct scenarios should include: (1) continuation of the current trend, (2) a most optimistic scenario in which all environ-

EXHIBIT 5–1

THE PORTFOLIO OPTIONS—DIRECTIONS OF GROWTH

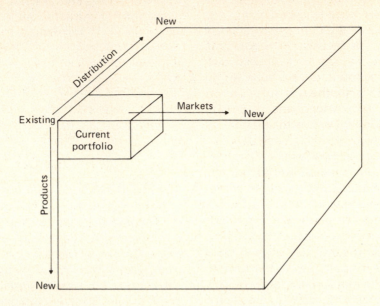

mental, market, and competitive conditions are favorable to the product, and (3) a disaster scenario. Having established these extreme scenarios (and others as seem appropriate) the sensitivity of the results to these scenarios should be determined via a series of sensitivity analyses.

DIMENSIONS OF PRODUCT PORTFOLIOS

The construction of a product portfolio requires the determination of the dimensions along which products are to be evaluated. The Boston Consulting Group's product portfolio matrix, for example, is based on the two dimensions of market share and growth (Exhibit 5–3). In contrast, the Shell International directional policy matrix is based on sector profitability and competitive position (Exhibit 5–6), while the International Harvester matrix for product portfolio analysis is based on the brand (firm) and product category (industry) sales growth, market share, and profitability (Exhibit 5–10).

Before selecting one of the existing product portfolio analysis matrices or designing a new one, it is necessary to identify and assess the value of some of the dimensions of portfolio analysis. The dimensions to be discussed are sales and stage of product life cycle, competitive position, profitability, risk, and demand on and utilization of resources.

These dimensions, although illustrative of

those that can and have been used in portfolio analysis, do not include all possibilities. In certain situations management can select different dimensions, such as relative cost advantage or others idiosyncratic to their needs and conditions. This position is in contrast to the one taken by the Boston Consulting Group and others who subscribe to a normative view that a few given dimensions are the *only* relevant set of dimensions for all products and all firms! Accepting the situational rather than the normative point of view suggests that one of management's major responsibilities is the identification of the relevant dimensions, determination of their relative importance, analysis of the performance of their products on these selected dimensions, and development of product/marketing strategies in accordance with their desired target product (and market) portfolio on the selected dimensions. This point of view suggests that the Boston Consulting Group's growth and share matrix (Exhibit 5–3) is a special case which might be more applicable to some firms than others.

SALES

Several attempts have been made to use product sales (or, more explicitly, stages in the product life cycle) as the sole guideline for marketing strategy. Recommendations for type and level of advertising, pricing, and distribution have been made (Mickwitz, 1959; Forrester, 1961; Schewing, 1974; Buzzell et al., 1972). Yet, as discussed in Chapter 3, these recommendations have usually been vague, nonoperational, not empirically supported, and conceptually questionable, since they imply that strategies can be developed with little concern for the product's profitability, market share position, and other management objectives and constraints.

Whereas sales should not be used as the sole dimension for product portfolio analysis, it is clearly one of the dimensions which should be considered as a candidate for the determination of the product portfolio framework. In this context, there are at least four distinct measures of sales:

• Absolute level of the product's sales;

• Rate of growth of product sales;

• Absolute level of industry's (product class) sales;

• Rate of growth of industry's (product class) sales.

Sales growth of both the company's product and the product class (as defined by the industry) have been used in the International Harvester product performance matrix (Exhibit 5–10) as two of the basic dimensions. In this case the focus is on two simple plots of industry and company sales against time. This is followed by the identification of the product's stage in its life cycle curve. Each product can, for example, be assigned to one of at least three product trend stages: decline, stable (which can in turn be separated into decaying and sustained maturity), and growth. The assignment of a product to one of these three or four categories can be based on the rule established by Polli and Cook (1969) or on any other explicit criterion.

As discussed in Chapter 3, the Polli and Cook approach is based on the percentage change in a product's real sales from one year to the next. Plotting these changes as a normal distribution with mean zero, they determined that if a product has a percentage change less than 0.5σ, it is to be classified in the decline stage. Products with a percentage change greater than 0.5σ are to be classified in the growth stage, and products in the range of $\pm0.5\sigma$ are to be considered stable. In contrast, the IH product performance matrix focuses on the historic sales growth levels, following the rule that:

If the annual sales trend over the past *n* years is:

- Negative, assign the product to the *decline* category;

- 0%–10% increase, assign it to the *stable* category;

- Over 10% increase, assign it to the *growth* category.

The determination of the specific criterion and number of categories is, of course, the responsibility of management, and often differs across industries, companies, and even within a company among strategic business units. It is often useful to graph the sales trend, which can be translated into a position on one of the three levels of sales, for both the company and industry.

Whatever sales measures are selected, it is necessary to establish the relevant measurement instruments in terms of units (e.g., dollar sales or unit sales), necessary adjustments (e.g., sales per capita), time (e.g., quarterly or annually), and the data sources used (e.g., company shipments versus wholesale or retail audits versus consumer purchase diaries or reports).

Various measures of sales can be viewed also in the context of the product portfolio as a surrogate for the products' stages in their respective product life cycles. This is an important conceptual point since, if accepted, it suggests that a company is not limited to product additions at the first stages of their life cycle but, rather, it can (and should) consider the development or acquisition of products at different stages of maturity. A balanced portfolio typically requires products of *all* stages of the PLC.

COMPETITIVE STRENGTH

Market share as a measure of the competitive strength of the given product has been included in most product portfolio frameworks. The Boston Consulting Group, for example, uses the concept of relative or competitive ratio. This measure is based on the product's market share divided by the share of the largest competitor, i.e., if the product's share is 40% and the nearest competitor's share is 20 percent, the competitive ratio is 2. Given that the BCG market share is measured in terms of such competitive ratios, they implicitly assume that the profitability of the product in the above example is the same as the profitability of a product with 8 percent share and a leading competitor with 4 percent share. Similarly, the performance of the products in the above example will be better than that of another product with 40 percent share but in which the leading competitor has also a 40 percent share, a competitive ratio of 1.

In contrast to this single market share definition of the BCG, other product portfolio models such as the product performance matrix recognize the multidimensionality of market share and, consequently, the need for definitional flexibility reflecting management's needs and market conditions.

A brand's market share is commonly measured as the brand's total dollar sales as a percentage of total market category sales. It is thus assumed that the correct numerator is the brand's total dollar sales, the correct denominator is total sales of all brands in the product category, and the unit of measurement is dollar sales. Yet, one could consider a number of other ways of defining a brand's market share. This requires the explication of several concepts: the unit of measurement, the product definition, the boundaries of the market and competitors; the time horizon involved, and the nature of the denominator in the share calculation. These are discussed below.

Unit of measurement Whereas the most common markt share definition is based on dollar sales, one could consider other measurement units—unit sales, units purchased, or users. Since a brand's performance might vary greatly depending on which of these measures is used, it is often advisable to compare the brand's performance on all three.

If competing products are relatively homogeneous and similarly priced, share measures in terms of dollars or units are essentially identical. Alternatively, a high-priced product will have a higher dollar share than its share of units.

The use of a dollar measure allows an aggregation across different product forms or package sizes, eliminating the necessity of defining an equivalent unit. Yet, if dollar sales are used, one must still define whether sales are based on orders, billings, retail sales or consumer purchases. In addition, depending on the accounting system in use, certain costs may be deducted from sales or counted as a marketing expense. Allowances of a temporary price reduction could therefore affect dollar sales during the period and may be subtracted from product sales or counted as a marketing expense for that period.

In a number of cases sales records (such as SAMI) do not reflect inventories held by the retailers. They do provide, however, in most cases, a good approximation of the sales data obtained from store audits (e.g., Nielsen). In addition to these two data sources, consumer purchase diaries (e.g., MRCA) and consumer surveys have also been utilized to establish share statistics. If surveys are used as the basis for the share data, care must be given to the way purchase of various brands is established since different questioning procedures (e.g., brand bought last versus brand bought most often) might lead to different results. Differences may also exist between the results obtained from survey and diary data (Wind and Learner, 1979).

If the unit of measurement is *product users,* still another dimension is added which focuses on the brand's penetration. Two brands with equal dollar or unit shares might have distinctly different shares of users. Again, it may be prudent to assess a brand's performance on all these measures since they provide different information and interpretation of the product. Share in dollars measures the proportion of consumer expenditures accounted for by the product. Share in units measures the proportion of industry volume accounted for by the product (a superior measure of size in the industry). Share of users measures the brand's penetration of users (households). Among users one can also measure the share a brand occupies as a percentage of total household purchases. (This is calculated by MRCA, for example, as the share of requirements.)

The product With the proliferation of product lines, it is quite uncommon to find a single brand in any product class. Most consumer brands come in a number of sizes and forms. The same is true for industrial products, where a plethora of minor product forms are frequently developed for different customers. Furthermore, it is not uncommon for a number of brands which constitute a product line to comprise a single promotional entity. Market share may therefore be assessed by size, form, or the entire product line. One further difficulty which is prevalent with industrial products and some consumer products (e.g., bread) and services is the lack of syndicated data. Data on individual products may be nonexistent, in which case a more practical unit of analysis would be the product line.

The market The market is the fundamental choice for both the numerator and denominator of the market share definition. It is essential, therefore, to clearly define the *market served* by a particular product. Depending on the definition of its market, any product can have a share ranging from a minute position (close to zero) to a dominant position (close to total dominance of a market). If share is to be a useful diagnostic aid, care and consistency over time are required.

Definition of the served market for a product or business is one of the key strategic decisions which must be made. The served market is defined as those customers to which the business directs its marketing effort. In any situation the market for a product is typically larger than the served market. Management selects a portion of the total market as the arena within which its product will compete and toward which it focuses its marketing effort. The business develops, manufactures, and markets products appropriate to that sector of the total market. This definition of the served market may be with respect to geography, channels, customer segments, or use occasions. A company in California may define its served market as all customers west of the Rockies. A clothing manufacturer may define his served market as all department stores. A company which makes refrigerators may define its served market as apartment dwellers and exclude the individual homeowner. A cereal manufacturer may select breakfast as the use occasion which defines his product's served market (breakfast as opposed to snack or cooking for example). An orange juice producer may advertise the appropriateness of orange juice for nonbreakfast use.

The definition of served market(s) is a critical decision because it defines the competitive arena within which the product is marketed. It also defines the product's competitors, customers, and technology. Since the served market is generally smaller than the total market, it is important to estimate its size and relate it to the total market. It also follows that the definition of served market for any two competing products may be different.

From a diagnostic point of view, the analysis of market share should be undertaken separately for *all* the relevant served markets within the four market categories (geography, channel, customer segment, and, especially, use). This is critical since it is most unlikely that a brand's share will be equally distributed among all segments.

The detailed share analysis by customer segment, usage occasion, and distribution outlet can be conducted within a single market definition (e.g., U.S. compact passenger car market), a number of geographic units (e.g., each of the 50 states or each country), and one or more product class definitions (e.g., domestic compact passenger cars, all compact passenger cars).

Such a detailed definition of the served market makes severe data demands which often go beyond the sales or purchase records and require either consumer surveys or use diaries (such as MRCA's menu census).

Time The time period over which the measurement is to be made also must be specified. If it is too short, random fluctuations will occur, making the measure difficult to use. If the period is too long, the effect of short-term tactical actions will be masked by long-term trends.

The denominator Whatever the market definition, whether the total market, a market segment, a use occasion, or a distribution outlet, one has to decide on the relevant denominator for the market share calculation. The two options which are commonly used and a third which, despite its conceptual attraction, is rarely used are:

1. All the brands in the given market (whether defined by the brand's product category or, preferably, its perceived positioning);
2. A selected number of brands, which includes at least three major alternatives:
   a) All brands within a subcategory (e.g., only national brands, excluding private brands),
   b) the leading competitor, or
   c) the leading two or three competitors;
3. All products serving the same need (or solving the same problem).

Market share can be expressed as a continuous or categorical variable. In the latter case the simplest category is low versus high. Yet, it is management's responsibility to determine the number of market share categories and the assignment criterion. For illustrative purposes, consider the following categories:

- Marginal share—If market share is less than 10 percent
- Average share—If market share is 10-24 percent
- Leading share—If market share is 25 percent or over

The market share figures that establish the three categories may, of course, vary from one strategic product area to another.

This stage assumes the availability of market share data. In many product areas, such data are available through services such as Nielsen or MRCA. In other areas, a firm may have to rely on expert estimates, or undertake commercial surveys to determine the market share of its products.

The inclusion of the market share dimension in product portfolio models reflects not only the acceptance of *share* as a measure of the

competitive strength of the product but the relationship between share and profitability and share and the market response function. The PIMS (*Profit Impact of Market Strategy*) project, for example, which examines the correlates of profitability in the modern corporation (Schoeffler, Buzzell, and Heany, 1974; Catry and Chevalier, 1974; Buzzell, Gale, and Sutton, 1975), found that businesses with large market shares are more profitable than those with small market shares. This correlation is not perfect,[3] however, and its causes not completely understood. Is it due to the benefit of the learning curve (with respect to both product and marketing economies of scale for larger-share businesses) or due to the fact that many large-share products compete on a nonprice basis and hence command higher margins and profits? Whatever the reason for the high correlation between share and profit, diagnostically it is advantageous to know the relationship between share (and its measures) and profitability.

The relation between market share and the product's market response function is even less well documented. As a general hypothesis one might expect lower-share products to require more marketing effort to achieve the same response function of a larger-share competitor. This hypothesized relationship, as illustrated in Exhibit 5–2, assumes that the low-market-share product will have lower sales at zero incremental marketing effort (assuming, of course, some existing distribution), a lower saturation level, and also probably a less effective marketing ef-

---

[3]Despite the intuitive appeal of the proposition that the higher the share of the served market the higher the product's profitability, a number of empirical studies have reported on low or negative correlation between share and profitability. For a survey of these studies and a critical evaluation of the share/profitability relationship, see Wind and Mahajan (1981b).

EXHIBIT 5–2

HYPOTHESIZED RELATIONSHIP BETWEEN MARKET SHARE AND MARKET
RESPONSE FUNCTION FOR A GIVEN BRAND

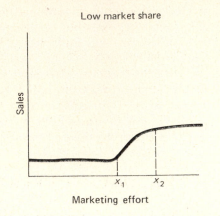

Low market share

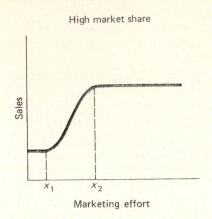

High market share

fort (not as steep a slope of the response function). The major reasons for these hypotheses are the economies of scale a larger brand can achieve and the well-known phenomenon that consumers tend to associate the marketing efforts (e.g., advertising) of a less known brand with that of a better known (and higher-share) brand.

This relationship, if true, requires greater efforts at differentiating the low-share products. It further suggests the importance of assessing the response elasticity of the various brands and to the extent that it is not highly correlated with one of the other dimensions, to consider it explicitly as one of the portfolio dimensions.

PROFITABILITY

Profitability is included explicitly as one of the major dimensions in a number of product portfolio analysis schemes. The Shell International directional policy matrix uses a profitability index as one of its two major dimensions (the competitive position being the other one). This index is based on a composite measure of market growth factors and market quality. In the product performance matrix, it is management's responsibility to establish the operational definitions of profit and determine the relevant categories. These categories, whether based on return on sales, investment, or equity, should be stated explicitly and, as with market share, can be presented as a continuous or categorical variable. In the latter case, at least three levels should be established to distinguish between *below target*, *target*, and *above target* profit performance.

RISK

Financial portfolio analysis, as discussed later in this chapter, is based on two dimensions: risk and expected return. In this context, the risk is a measure of the variability in return, and portfolios vary with respect to the degree of risk associated with them and management's willingness to accept certain levels of risk (versus expected return).

In most product portfolios it is more difficult to estimate the risk associated with the portfolio than it is in the case of a portfolio of securities. Furthermore, whenever considering the product portfolio, the *sources of risk* (and their correlation) are also of considerable importance in evaluating the product portfolio. Consider, for example, a product portfolio in which all products are subject to strong regulatory constraints. Such a portfolio is in most cases less desirable than another portfolio with similar expected return but with diverse sources of risk (e.g., government and competitors).

Another factor often complicating the estimate of risk in a portfolio is the need to focus at higher levels of analysis, not just on a portfolio of products but on a portfolio of products *and* markets, and to assess not only the performance of this portfolio in the short term but also forecast it over a relatively long time (the relevant planning horizon of the firm) and diverse scenarios.

DEMAND ON RESOURCES

A relatively neglected dimension of the standardized product portfolio frameworks is the demand the various products place on the firm's resources. This dimension is, however, one of the most critical ones, at least in the short term, for fast-growing firms for whom the real constraint on any growth is the demand on management time and, to a lesser degree, the demands on the production, marketing, and financial resources. Of particular importance in this context is the differential demand various products place on advertising and distribution. In all those cases in which this constraint is of primary importance, the product portfolio framework should include this dimension.

UTILIZATION OF RESOURCES

The level of current resource utilization and, in particular, products with seasonality and cyclical demand patterns (which represent an uneven pattern of resource utilization) are of great practical concern to the diversification efforts of the firm. Yet, most formal product portfolio analyses have ignored this dimension. To the extent that current products are subject to uneven utilization of resources, this dimension should be considered as one of the dimensions of the product portfolio framework.

STANDARDIZED APPROACHES TO PRODUCT PORTFOLIO

To date, five standardized approaches to product portfolio analysis have appeared in the literature: the Boston Consulting Group's share/growth matrix (Boston Consulting Group, 1970), the AD Little business profile matrix (Wright, 1978), the Shell International directional policy matrix (Royal Dutch Shell Co., 1975), the McKinsey/GE business assessment array (Allen, 1979), and the risk/return model (Wind, 1975). These approaches are based on the identification of two normative-type dimensions which are believed to be applicable to all products of all firms.

BCG GROWTH/SHARE MATRIX

The most widely accepted product portfolio framework is offered by the Boston Consulting Group. Their growth/share matrix is based on

EXHIBIT 5–3

BOSTON CONSULTING GROUP'S SHARE/GROWTH MATRIX

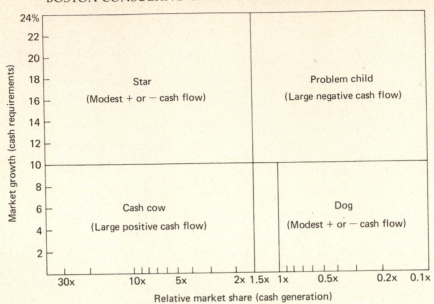

the assumption that cash flow is a measure of success and is related to the two dimensions of market share and growth rate. These dimensions are related to cash use and generation in the following way: *cash use* is a function of the growth rate of the market (a fast-growing market requires increased investment to maintain the product position in the market) and *cash generation* is a function of the market share of the product.

Given the importance of *cash management*, a firm's products (businesses) can be classified according to their relative market share and market growth and plotted in a 2 × 2 matrix as shown in Exhibit 5–3. Each cell in the matrix describes a different type of product and implies, according to the BCG, specific characteristics and required strategies.

High market share, high market growth products,—stars Stars, through their high market share, generate a substantial amount of cash

which is mostly absorbed by the need to maintain their position in a market with a high rate of growth. As growth slows, the stars will start throwing off cash, becoming cash cows. These star products and businesses represent the future of the company and hence, according to BCG strategists, call for aggressive marketing strategy and increasing or holding market share.

High market share, low market growth,—cash cows These products and businesses, due to their high market share (at least 1.5 times the size of their largest competitor)—and hence the benefit of experience curve in both manufacturing and marketing—generate more cash than is required by the low growth market in which they operate. The cash cow products provide the main source of cash and earnings to the firm, and it should be management's responsibility to generate cash, avoiding share-building strategies which tend to be too expensive (given the already high share and slow growth). The objective of these products, therefore, is the generation of short-term profits to carry the corporate load.

Low share and high market growth,—problem child Products and businesses in this category generate little cash due to low market share, but require large amounts of cash to survive due to the high growth rate of the business. The strategic option for these products and businesses is, therefore, either a drive for leadership (toward a high market share position) or a liquidation of the existing position.

Low share and low market growth,—dogs Products in this category generate little cash but do not require a lot of cash. Dogs include brands that did not make it or cash cows that drifted, and for whom, given the low rate of growth, there is little opportunity for future profits. The objective in this category should therefore be to maximize cash generation even if it involves product or business liquidation.

The concept of the BCG portfolio Given that firms might find themselves with products or businesses in all four categories, the portfolio concept would require a balance of products and supporting relationships among the various products. A balanced approach would call for transfer of cash from cash cows to problem children, while the product or business flow is from problem children to stars and from stars to cash cows. These dynamic changes in a portfolio over time are based on the premise that high growth products require cash, while low growth products should provide cash. Yet, the overall product portfolio should be balanced avoiding a situation that a portfolio has too many problem children (which require considerable amounts of cash) or too many cash cows (which generate cash but are subject to low growth).

The BCG framework, in its simplest and most common form, does not take explicitly into account the profitability of the various products, the *projected* and desired performance of the various products and the risk and cost of operation. A number of companies, as well as Day (1977), have modified the BCG framework by incorporating with it forecasted performance of the various products (Exhibit 5–4) and, in a few cases, profitability.

AD LITTLE BUSINESS PROFILE MATRIX

This portfolio scheme, as presented in Exhibit 5–5, is based on two dimensions: market position and industry maturity. The stage of industry maturity is much like the stage of product life cycle in that it has four steps beginning with "embryonic" and ending with "aging." The competitive position is broken down into five stages ranging from weak to dominant. The data used in this scheme are primarily historical and, as with the BCG, there is no explicit analysis of the correlates of the dimensions. The model is similar in most of its characteristics to the BCG and, with the exception of the definition of the two dimensions and the classification into twenty predetermined categories, offers little advantage over the BCG.

DIRECTIONAL POLICY MATRIX

The Shell International directional policy matrix (Exhibit 5–6) is based on two dimensions: *profitability* of the sector (market segment) in which the business operates and *competitive position* of the business in this market segment. These two dimensions are constructed from a number of factors which may vary from one industry to another. An important feature of the directional policy matrix is the flexibility it offers in selecting factors which are relevant to the specific industry.

EXHIBIT 5–4

MODIFIED BCG FRAMEWORK

Source: Reprinted from the *Journal of Marketing* published by the American Marketing Association. Exhibit from "Diagnosing the Product Portfolio," by George S. Day, vol. 41, August 1977, p. 34.

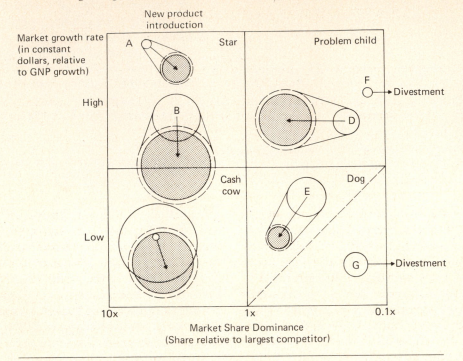

(Diameter of circle is proportional to product's contribution to total company sales volume)

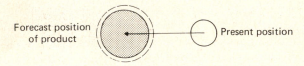

Forecast position of product — Present position

EXHIBIT 5–5

THE AD LITTLE BUSINESS PROFILE MATRIX

		Stage of industry maturity			
		Embryonic	Growth	Maturity	Aging
Competitive position	Dominant				
	Strong				
	Favorable				
	Tentative				
	Weak				

EXHIBIT 5–6

THE SHELL INTERNATIONAL DIRECTIONAL POLICY MATRIX

		Prospects for sector profitability		
		Unattractive	Average	Attractive
Company's competitive capabilities	Weak	Disinvest	Phased withdrawal Custodial	Double or quit
	Average	Phased withdrawal	Custodial Growth	Try harder
	Strong	Cash generation	Growth Leader	Leader

Profitability is determined by the market growth—the long-run growth rate of the industry category—and market quality. Market quality in turn is determined by the past profit performance of the sector and structural characteristics (which have been related empirically to profitability) such as overcapacity of the industry, likelihood of achieving product differentiation, the degree of market (supply) concentration, the degree of market (customer) fragmentation, the degree of product substitutability, the importance of the product to its customers, ease of changing suppliers, and the degree to which product and process technology represent significant barriers to entry.

Competitive position measures the relative competitive strength of the business or the product. It is composed of three factors: market position, production capability, and product research and development.

Market position is determined by both absolute market share *and* relative market share with special adjustment if a disproportional part of sales are from captive outlets. Production capability measures the firm's competitive advantage with respect to its products. Product R&D measures the firm's competitive advantage with respect to its various R&D activities.

As with the BCG's product portfolio analysis, the two dimensions of profitability and

competitive position form the matrix presented in Exhibit 5–6. The four categories of products are similar to the BCG's classifications and also provide the basis for a series of strategy recommendations not unlike those suggested by the BCG. The major difference between the directional policy matrix and the BCG share/growth matrix is in the construction of the two dimensions and the greater flexibility offered by the directional policy matrix.

McKINSEY/GE BUSINESS ASSESSMENT ARRAY

GE's portfolio strategy is designed to ensure sustained earnings in the near term while guiding the firm's investment resources to areas of growth opportunities. Rather than merely applying financial measures, such as discounted cash flow/return on investment, GE emphasizes the conditions under which a business can be successful and profitable. An important tool for this purpose is GE's "business screen," a matrix for which the two dimensions are *business strengths*, and *industry attractiveness*. This portfolio scheme, which is presented in Exhibit 5–7, is also presented occasionally in the literature as the McKinsey portfolio model (Allen, 1979). Businesses enjoying a

EXHIBIT 5–7

THE MCKINSEY/GE BUSINESS SCREEN AND MULTIFACTOR ASSESSMENT

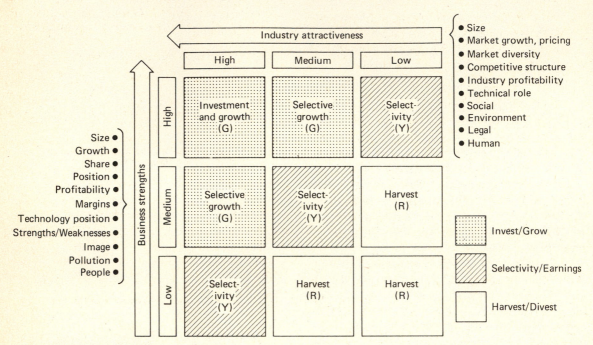

medium-to-strong position in an attractive industry fall within the "invest/grow" category (dotted area on the accompanying chart). Those engaged in industries that are less attractive or those whose position in their industry is weak, fall within the "harvest/divest" category (the dark area shown in the accompanying chart). Finally, businesses on the charted diagonal, either in a weak position in an attractive industry or a strong position in a less attractive industry, fall into an in-between category called "selectivity/earnings".

Unique to this portfolio model are the factors used to help judge the relative strengths of a business, and the relative attractiveness of the industry in which it participates. These multiple judgments—made each year, or more often if there has been change in a critical parameter—play a leading role in projecting business performance and in setting priorities for corporate investment.

RISK/RETURN MODEL

The objective of financial portfolio analysis is to determine which portfolio of stocks and bonds provides an investor with the most suitable combination of risk and return. The major assumptions of portfolio analysis are:

1. The two most relevant characteristics of a portfolio are its *expected return* and its *riskiness;*

2. Managers will choose to hold efficient portfolios which maximize expected returns for a given degree of risk, or alternatively, minimize risk for a given expected return.

The need to evaluate portfolios as opposed to single securities is evident when one considers that, although the expected returns on a portfolio are directly related to the expected returns on the individual securities, it is not possible in most cases to deduce the riskiness of a portfolio simply by knowing the riskiness of the component securities since the riskiness of a portfolio also depends on the relationships among the securities.

The notion of an efficient portfolio is illustrated in the upper panel of Exhibit 5–8. Assume that the shaded area represents all possible product portfolios that can be obtained from a given set of products. Portfolios lying on the curve AB are efficient since they offer the maximum return for any given level of risk and minimum risk for any given level of return. To illustrate, any portfolio to the right of point B, such as C', is on the boundary of the feasible set, but is not efficient since portfolio C on the curve AB offers the same expected return at a lower risk. Similarly, any portfolio on the efficiency curve AB is superior to any portfolio in the shaded area. For example, portfolio B offers, at the same level of risk as B', a considerably higher expected return.

A third major assumption of portfolio analysis is that it is theoretically and operationally possible to identify efficient portfolios by a proper analysis of information for each of *n* securities (products) on its expected return, the

EXHIBIT 5–8

THE RISK-RETURN APPROACH TO PRODUCT PORTFOLIO

Source: Reprinted from Wind, "Product Portfolio: A New Approach to the Product Mix Decision" in *1974 Combined Proceedings*, R.C. Churhan (ed.), published by the American Marketing Association, Aug. 1974.

Hypothetical efficient frontier

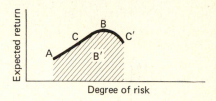

Optimum portfolio

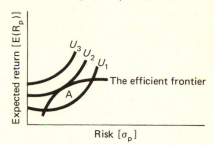

Hypothetical utility scales (derived from conjoint analysis)

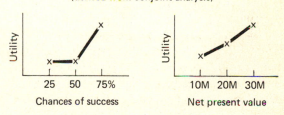

variation in that return (risk), and the relationships between the return for each security and every other security (the expected covariances).

These statistical inputs can be generated by a number of approaches ranging from projections of ex post data, through simple econometric procedures, to ex ante estimates of probability distributions. Given these inputs, the analytical approaches used in portfolio analysis range from simple graphical procedures (for up to four securities), to ones employing calculus or quadratic programming procedures. The output from these approaches provides a suggested proportion of the total securities (product) mix which should be allocated to each security (product and market) in order to achieve efficiency (i.e., maximization of return for a given degree of risk, or the minimization of risk for a given expected return).

The basic premise thus far has been that a product mix can and should be viewed as a *portfolio* of products. The similarities between the situation in which one wants to select the most efficient portfolio of securities and the selection of the most efficient product mix are striking:

Securities	Products
1. Investors' *only* objectives in buying securities: high expected return and risk reduction	1. *Primary* (but not the only) corporate objectives in offering products: high expected return and risk reduction
2. Investors differ in their needs, preferences, willingness, and ability to assume risks.	2. Managers differ in their needs, preferences, willingness, and ability to assume risks.

There are, of course, a number of differences between products and securities. The most important differences are:

1. When dealing with portfolios of securities, various combinations of returns and risk are readily available for purchase and are in most cases independent of the actions of the portfolio manager; whereas in portfolios of products, the alternatives may not be readily available and the action of the portfolio manager can affect the range of available products and their return.

2. In most product decisions, management uses more than the two objectives of expected return and risk (see, for example, the discussion on setting objectives in Chapter 6).

3. The return in financial portfolios is assumed to be a linear function of the amount invested. Yet, in product portfolios a nonlinear response function is more common.

4. The risk (variance) function in financial portfolio is assumed to be a constant. Yet, in product portfolio it is more reasonable to assume increasing variance as a factor of the distance of the new portfolio from the current portfolio (and expertise) of the firm.

These basic differences between securities and products may make it difficult to use the analytical procedures of portfolio analysis in determining an optimal product mix, but do not affect the value of the *concept* of portfolio analysis; i.e., even if one may not find products with certain risk and return characteristics, conceptually it is possible to identify the correct levels of risk and return of existing products and to specify *desired* levels of risk and return and relate other objectives to these two basic ones. Such an approach could thus provide guidelines for the firm's product development, modification, acquisition, and deletion activities.

To apply the portfolio analysis approach to the product mix decision, it is essential to have the following information:

1. Expected return of the portfolios, i.e., estimates for all n products $E(r)$;

2. Estimated risk of the portfolios, i.e., both the variance σ^2 for all n products and expected covariances (cov ij) between the n products' returns;

3. The corporate preference (trade-off) between risk and expected return (W_k, W_1).

Expected returns As indicated earlier, the return of a portfolio is simply the weighted average of the returns of its component products when the weight is the fraction of the total value of the portfolio invested in each product. Estimating the returns for the candidate products requires, however, a forecast of the market acceptance of the various products under various marketing strategies and varying competitive and environmental conditions. In this state of the analysis, management can utilize any of the forecasting procedures currently used to estimate the expected performance of its existing and new products.

Estimated risk The measure of risk most commonly used in portfolio analysis is the portfolio's variance. The variance of a portfolio, however, is not simply the weighted average of the variances of the component products. One has to take into consideration the covariances among the n products in the portfolio. Hence the variance of a product portfolio can be defined as

$$\sigma_p^2 = \sum_{i=1}^{n} \sum_{j=1}^{n} X_i X_j \text{ cov } ij \, ,$$

where σ_p^2 = variance of a portfolio p;

X_i = proportion invested in product i;

X_j = proportion invested in product j;

cov ij = covariance between i and j (i.e., the product moment correlation between i and j times the standard deviation of i times the standard deviation of j);

The estimates of the variance and covariance measures can be derived from the forecasting procedures used to estimate the expected returns of each of the n products. One should be aware, however, that estimating the expected return and risk is not a trivial job.

Management tradeoff between risk and expected return Given information on the expected return and riskiness of various portfolios, one can develop the efficient frontier (feasible set of efficient portfolios). The selection of an "optimum" portfolio on the efficient frontier requires, however, information on the decision-maker's utility function. This utility has been represented in portfolio analysis as a series of indifference curves between expected gains and risks. The selection of an optimum portfolio (the one which maximizes the expected utility) is presented graphically in the center panel of Exhibit 5–8 as portfolio A, which is the one at the point of tangency between the efficient frontier and an indifference curve.

Management preferences for and tradeoff between expected return and risk can be assessed via conjoint analysis. Following this approach, managers can be presented with a set of product portfolios which vary systematically with respect to their levels of risk and expected returns. Assuming, for example, three levels of risk and three levels of expected return, the decision-maker can be confronted with nine combinations, such as "a product mix with net present value of $10 million and 75 percent chance of success" and "a product mix with net present value of $20 million and 50 percent chance of success."

Given these nine combinations the decision makers are asked to evaluate (rank or rate) these (simulated) product mixes in terms of their relative attractiveness. The data derived from this task are then submitted to a conjoint analysis algorithm and utility functions are derived for each factor and level for each respondent. Hypothetical output from such analysis is illustrated in the lower panel of Exhibit 5–8.

An "optimal" product portfolio is achieved when a company for a given level of risk cannot improve its profits (or any other objective) by deleting, modifying or adding products.

A modified risk-return approach　Given the difficulties in fully applying the risk-return model to the product portfolio decision of the firm, a modified form has been proposed (Cardozo and Wind, 1980). This modification calls for a four-step approach for each business unit and the organization as a whole:

- Identification of the product portfolio of "investments"—the product-market combination. A simple and effective method of identifying the interrelation is to prepare a product-market matrix (products listed in one axis and markets in the other).

- Projection of the portfolio (of current and prospective product/market investments) with respect to return and resource requirements.

- Determination of managers' return/risk preferences and goals.

- Planning for portfolio modification using as a primary criterion the effect of any change on the "productivity" of the portfolio defined in terms of the return and variation of the return, i.e., the appropriate decision rule is to accept, within limits of available resources, additions that lie along or above the efficient frontier. If more of such additions are available than there are resources to fund them, priority should be

EXHIBIT 5–9

AN ILLUSTRATIVE MODIFIED FINANCIAL PORTFOLIO

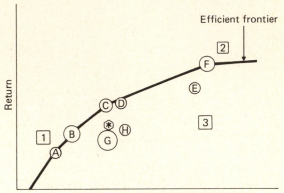

Key: Circles represent current product-market combinations for which historic and projected data were available; squares represent prospective investments for which several estimates of return were made. Risk for prospective investments is the variation among those return estimates. The size of circles and squares represents relative resource requirement for that investment. Hexagon represents weighted average return/risk of portfolio.

given to those that promise the most substantial improvements in portfolio productivity, i.e., those that will move the efficient frontier farthest up and to the left.

The modified financial portfolio analysis model thus substitutes portfolio productivity or the efficient frontier (as illustrated in Exhibit 5–9) for the hurdle rate as a criterion for accepting new investments or business units. Because productivity typically differs among business units, each business unit within an organization may have a different return/risk standard for new investments. Nevertheless, any addition that improves portfolio productivity in any business unit will improve productivity for the organization as a whole. Therefore, organizations may effectively use different standards for accepting new investments in different business units. This modified approach and its applications are further discussed in Cardozo and Wind (1980).

CUSTOMIZED APPROACHES TO PRODUCT PORTFOLIO

The basic premise of the five standardized approaches to portfolio analysis (discussed in the previous section) is that they can be applied to all products and firms. However, this premise has been challenged by a number of firms who prefer a more customized portfolio model. The first of the customized models was developed by International Harvester, which utilized a four-dimensional portfolio (Wind and Claycamp, 1976). The concepts underlying IH's product performance matrix have been adopted by other firms, and more recently two other customized approaches to portfolio analysis and decisions have been introduced by a number of companies. These involve a multistage conjoint-analysis-based approach and a unique application of the Analytic Hierarchy Process. These three approaches are discussed next.

PRODUCT PERFORMANCE MATRIX

The product performance matrix (Wind and Claycamp, 1976) requires two definitional phases which focus on the determination of the strategic product/market area under consideration and the relevant measurement instruments followed by three analytical phases:

1. Determination of current and past trends for the product line in terms of industry sales, company sales, market share, and profit (and any other relevant dimensions);

2. Integration of these four dimensions into a single analytical framework—a product performance matrix—which is presented in the upper part of Exhibit 5–10;

3. Projection of future performance with *no* changes in marketing strategy or competitive or environmental conditions and with a variety of alternative marketing strategies. This projection is illustrated in the bottom part of Exhibit 5–10.

A more advanced approach might be one in which the four dimensions are presented as continuous variables and not as categorical ones based on some arbitrary decision rule. Yet, even the simple positioning of a product within this matrix provides clear understanding of the current position of the product on those dimensions that are most relevant for management planning and control. Conducting such an analysis for each of the relevant segments of a product/market strategy area provides management with a summary auditing form that highlights the strengths and weaknesses of the firm's product line in all of its market segments.

This picture of product performance (based on "hard" data) can be supplemented by an historical trend analysis of the changes in the product's performance over time. The upper panel of Exhibit 5–10 shows a hypothetical path for two products over a three-year period. Product A has been in a growth industry for these three years. In 1973, its company sales were at a stable level, but they did increase to the growth level in 1974 and 1975. Its market share position improved considerably from a marginal share in 1973 to an average share in 1974 and 1975. The major improvement, however, occurred with respect to its profit performance, moving from below target in 1973 to above target in 1975.

Examination of the performance of hypothetical product B, however, reveals a bleak situation. The product is in a declining industry; its company sales decreased from

1973 to 1974; and while it maintained an average market share in 1973 and 1974, its share weakened to marginal in 1975. The only positive sign is that during these three years profits did not decline.

Although the product performance matrix provides a useful tool for controlling the performance of the firm's product line and answering the question "where are we?" it alone can-

EXHIBIT 5–10

A PRODUCT PERFORMANCE MATRIX (HYPOTHETICAL EXAMPLE)

TRACING TWO PRODUCTS OVER THREE YEARS

Source: Reprinted from the *Journal of Marketing*, published by the American Marketing Association. Exhibit from "Planning Product Line Strategy: A Matrix Approach," by Yoram Wind and Henry J. Claycamp, vol. 40, January 1976, pp. 5, 6.

Company sales / Industry sales / Profitability / Market share	Decline			Stable			Growth		
	Below target	Target	Above target	Below target	Target	Above target	Below target	Target	Above target
Growth Dominant									
Average								A_{74}	A_{75}
Marginal				A_{73}					
Stable Dominant									
Average									
Marginal									
Decline Dominant									
Average		B_{74}			B_{73}				
Marginal		B_{75}							

INCORPORATING SALES, MARKET SHARE, AND PROFIT FORECASTS INTO THE PRODUCT
PERFORMANCE MATRIX

Product	Current position (C)				Unconditional projection (P)				Conditional forecast (CF)			
	Industry sales	Company sales	Market share	Profitability	Industry sales	Company sales	Market share	Profitability	Industry sales	Company sales	Market share	Profitability
1	Decline	Decline	Av.	Below target	Decline	Decline	Av.	Below target	Decline	Decline	Marg.	Target
									Decline	Stable	Av.	Below target
2	Stable	Decline	Av.	Target	Stable	Stable	Av.	Target	Stable	Stable	Dom.	Target

EXHIBIT 5–10 (continued)

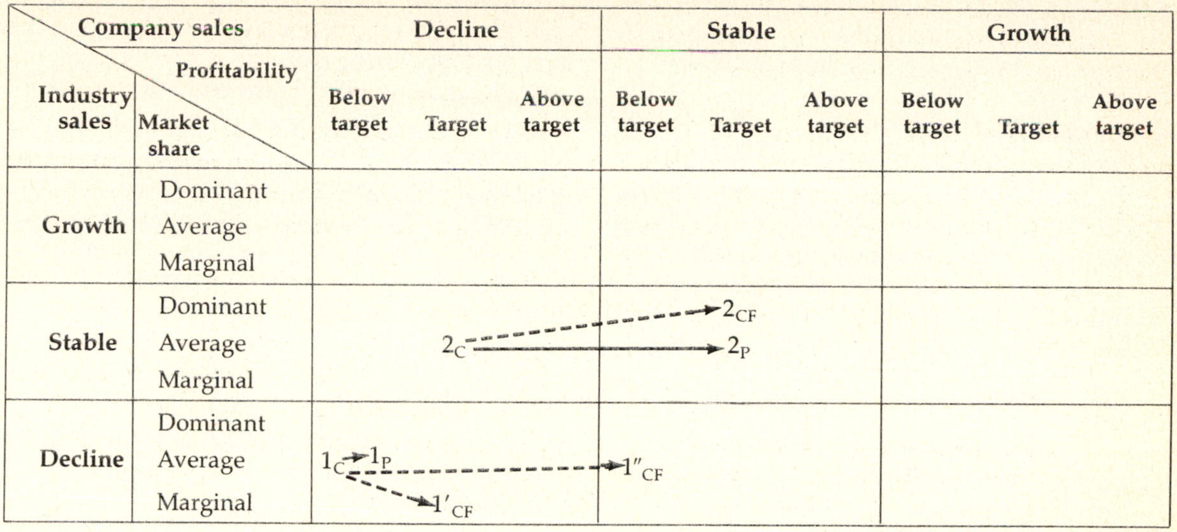

Industry sales	Company sales / Profitability / Market share	Decline: Below target	Decline: Target	Decline: Above target	Stable: Below target	Stable: Target	Stable: Above target	Growth: Below target	Growth: Target	Growth: Above target
Growth	Dominant									
	Average									
	Marginal									
Stable	Dominant					→ 2_{CF}				
	Average		2_C			→ 2_P				
	Marginal									
Decline	Dominant									
	Average	1_C → 1_P			→ $1''_{CF}$					
	Marginal		→ $1'_{CF}$							

not guide future marketing actions. To serve as a guide, the analysis must incorporate the *projected* future performance of each product and the anticipated impact of alternative corporate marketing strategies on the level of performance. These modifications are the focus of the following two steps:

1. Project the trend in sales, market share, and profitability assuming *no changes* in the firm's marketing strategies and no major changes in competitive actions and environmental conditions. This projection can be based on simple extrapolation of time series data or on any other forecasting procedure used by the firm. It should be done for each product in the strategic product/market area and should provide a range of possible results between the most pessimistic and most optimistic forecasts.

   A simplified example of the current and projected positions of two hypothetical products is presented in the first eight columns in the central panel of Exhibit 5–10. These data can then be transferred to the product evaluation matrix (the bottom part of Exhibit 5–10) to provide a clear picture of the anticipated trend in the position of each product. At this stage (even without engaging in conditional forecasting), the product performance matrix can start providing some useful guidance for the firm's product/marketing strategy for each of its products in the given strategic product/market area.

   Product 1 is clearly a poor performer. It is in a declining industry, with declining sales, average market share, and below-target profitability, and if nothing changes it is likely to stay in this situation (comparison of 1_c and 1_p). Product 2, on the other hand, is in a stable industry and is expected to increase its sales (moving from a "decline" to a "stable" level in this category), while its market share position and profitability do not change (a move from 2_c to 2_p).

2. Since the future performance of a product depends to a large extent on the firm's

marketing efforts, a *conditional forecast* should be undertaken in which the sales, market share, and profit of each product are forecast under a variety of marketing strategies. Given a number of alternative marketing strategies, a separate forecasting analysis should be conducted for each, and the results of the "best" strategy (according to the four dimensions) incorporated into the product evaluation matrix. If no dominant solution (i.e., "best" on all four dimensions) is revealed, all viable strategies are to be incorporated into the matrix, as illustrated in the lower panel of Exhibit 5–10.

Product 1 has two alternative conditional forecasts. Forecast $1'_{cf}$ suggests no change in the sales position (it remains in a declining industry with decreasing company sales), worsening of market share (from average to marginal), but an improvement in profits from below target to target. A second marketing strategy, however, may result in position $1''_{cf}$, which enables the company to maintain an average market share, increase its company sales (from "decline" to "stable" stage), but produces no improvement in its profit position, which remains below target. Assuming that only these two strategies are available, management should examine the tradeoff between maintaining market share position but being below target on profits versus losing market share but achieving profit objectives.

Product 2, on the other hand, has a single "best" conditional forecast that moves the product from 2_c to 2_{cf}. This suggests that the marketing strategy behind this forecast is likely to result in an improved market share position (from average for 2_p to dominant for 2_{cf}).

As discussed in Chapter 3, traditional product life cycle analysis provides little guid-ance for making product/marketing decisions. It ignores the competitive setting of the product, the relevant profit considerations, and the fact that product sales are a function of the marketing effort of the firm and other environmental forces. The product performance matrix provides a way of overcoming these shortcomings by taking these variables into account and providing management with the necessary information on each product's performance which, when put together, constitutes the firm's current product portfolio by each market or, if desired, across all market segments.

The results of experimentation with this approach in the International Harvester Company are encouraging, and the approach is now used on a regular basis in the preparation of all the firm's marketing plans. The suggested approach can provide a four-dimensional framework for the product portfolio, and guidelines for the strategic product/marketing decisions of industrial and consumer products companies.

This approach requires a number of levels of analysis, each with an increasing specificity of guidance, for the firm's strategic marketing decisions. The first level is based on the evaluation of the product's current position with regard to industry and company sales, market share, and profitability, and it provides the vaguest and most limited guidance. The third level, on the other hand, provides guidance based on projected product position with regard to sales, market share, and profitability under alternative marketing strategies.

Not every product/market situation requires the complete analysis of all levels. Even in its simplest form (level 1) the product performance matrix goes well beyond traditional product life cycle analysis and offers valuable guidelines for product line management. Product performance information based on hard data on sales, market share, and profitability by strategic product/market units puts into context the commonly collected consumer-based positioning/segmentation information. The approach can also be applied to competitive products, thus providing management with an ongoing performance audit of its own and competitors' products.

CONJOINT ANALYSIS-BASED MULTISTAGE PORTFOLIO ANALYSIS

The portfolio models reviewed earlier have a number of similarities. (Note, for example, the strong reliance on a *simple* framework of the order of 2 × 2 used by BCG; the common use of the market share dimension by both BCG and Shell International and the product performance matrix; profitability by both the Shell International and the product performance matrix.

Yet, these models do differ with respect to the degree to which they offer a *general* rigid (and normative) framework or a flexible framework which is subject to changes reflecting the idiosyncratic characteristics of the user. In this respect the BCG is the most rigid, followed by the risk/return model which, although rigid, allows for individual differences in the manager's tradeoff between risk and return. Both the Shell International approach and the product performance matrix recognize the need for flexibility, the Shell International in the factors determining the two dimensions, and the product performance matrix in the number and definition of the dimensions themselves.

Conceptually, the product portfolio framework *should be flexible* to reflect the idiosyncratic conditions of the decision makers, their industry, and other relevant environmental conditions. Without such flexibility in the construction of the portfolio framework, product decisions can become mechanistic (if your product is a star promote heavily, but if it is a dog consider deleting it), ignoring other important determinants of such decisions.

The more flexible the portfolio framework, the less the danger of oversimplification and neglect of important factors. Yet, this comes at the cost of losing a simple normative framework which suggests what to do when.

Given the attractiveness of a simple framework, evident from the wide acceptance of the BCG share/growth matrix, a multistage approach to the product portfolio decision is suggested. This approach combines elements of the current portfolio frameworks and suggests the following steps:

1. Management identification of the relevant dimensions;
2. Determination of the relative importance of the various dimensions;
3. To the extent that two or more dimensions are viewed as the *dominant* ones (such as the conceptually appealing risk/return dimension), construction of a matrix based on these dimensions;
4. Identification of the position of each of the firm's current products on the relevant portfolio dimensions;
5. Projection of the likely position of each product on the relevant dimensions, if no changes are expected in environmental conditions, or in competitive or the firm's activities;
6. Determination of the desired position for each existing or new product (as a basis for the development of alternative strategies that would close the gap between the current and desired portfolio).

Following this approach, the decision makers are presented with a series of factors which may be hypothesized to constitute the various components of risk (e.g., chances of success, possible negative effect on relevant publics) and asked to evaluate them in terms of their degree of risk. Similar tasks can be completed to identify the components of expected return (or any other major dimension specified by management). Given a knowledge of the components of risk and expected return, a second conjoint analysis can be undertaken to determine the trade-off and relative importance of the various levels of risk and expected returns. Here management (the respondents) provides information in the form of ranking or rating of the hypothetical profiles based on their actual trade-offs between various factors and levels. Given these data, the researcher decomposes the overall evaluation and establishes the part-worth contribution of each factor and level.

Managers' trade-offs between expected returns and risk can, in many cases, be affected by situational factors (e.g., the current corporate performance, industry and corporate expectation, and changes in government regulations). The conjoint analysis enables one to assess the managers' utilities under a variety of scenarios. Given the nine combinations of risk and return discussed earlier, the decision makers can be asked to evaluate (rank or rate) these (simulated) product mixes in terms of their relative attractiveness and repeat the task under each scenario. The data derived from this task are then submitted to a conjoint analysis algorithm, and utility functions are derived for each factor and level, by each scenario, for each respondent. Hypothetical output from such analysis is illustrated in Exhibit 5–11.

Having explicit utility values for each re-

spondent helps identify differences among the decision makers and may help them reach a desired consensus.

A different way of utilizing conjoint analysis in a multistage approach to the determination of the dimension of the firm's desired product portfolio model is illustrated in Exhibit 5–12 which includes sections from a portfolio questionnaire that has been implemented in a number of cases.

This approach (which is similar to the use of conjoint analysis to design an "optimal" product) involves four major phases:

- Determination of the relative importance of each dimension via a conjoint analysis task.

- Assessment of the current and projected position of the existing and new products on these dimensions.

- Selection of the best "mix" of current and new products based on a computer simulation aimed at maximizing the total utility of the product offering (or if cost information is available, the most favorable cost/benefit ratio.)

- Evaluation of the sensitivity of the portfolio to changes in the products' position on the various dimensions and the importance of the dimensions. This sensitivity analysis is a key diagnostic aspect of portfolio analysis.

Applying this approach for one company provided new insight into management's evaluation of the criteria for evaluating new business. It highlighted, for example, the critical importance of "demand on management time" and "government involvement." It further identified a number of interesting differences among members of top management which were not evident prior to going through this exercise. In addition, the procedure provided the framework for identifying the current position of the various products on these criteria and the desired characteristics of new products.

EXHIBIT 5–11

HYPOTHETICAL UTILITY FUNCTIONS UNDER
ALTERNATIVE SCENARIOS

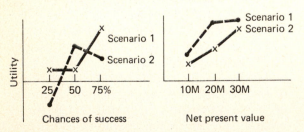

EXHIBIT 5–12

EXAMPLE OF A SECTION FROM A PORTFOLIO QUESTIONNAIRE

a) In addition to the separate evaluation of each product, management often is concerned with the overall product portfolio of the firm. To help us understand the way companies go about establishing their product portfolios, could you tell us the criteria and procedure you use in determining your most desirable product portfolio.

_____

_____

_____

b) Now, let's consider the case of the development of *new* products. One of the considerations in developing new products is, obviously, their compatibility with the current product portfolio of the firm. Considering the criteria you mentioned above and other criteria mentioned by executives, please evaluate each of your products based on the specific level below to which it best corresponds.

Factor/level	Insert your products' names					
	Product A	Product B	Product C	Product D	Product E	Product F

A. Profitability
  1. Below target
  2. Target
  3. Somewhat above target
  4. Significantly above target						

B. Market share
  1. Below average
  2. Average
  3. Slightly higher than the
     leading competitor
  4. Significantly higher than the
     next nearest competitor						

C. Product sales growth
  1. Decline
  2. No growth
  3. Slight growth
  4. Significant growth						

D. Industry sales growth
  1. Decline
  2. No growth
  3. Slight growth
  4. Significant growth						

E. Government involvement
  1. Low
  2. High						

EXHIBIT 5–12 (continued)

Factor/level	Insert your products' names					
	Product A	Product B	Product C	Product D	Product E	Product F
F. Product type						
1. Consistent with major product lines						
2. Not related to major product lines						

c) Given your current product portfolio, please consider the following 16 hypothetical products and rate each of them based on the degree to which you would like to add such a product to your portfolio.

> *Profitability:* Target
> *Market share:* Average
> *Product sales growth:* Slight growth
> *Industry sales growth:* No growth
> *Demand on management & operation:*
>   Mgmt. high, operation low
> *Government involvement:* High
> *Product type:* Not related to major product lines
> *Chance of success:* 50%

Circle one:
1 — definitely would not include in portfolio,
2 — probably would not include in portfolio,
3 — may or may not include in portfolio,
4 — probably would include in portfolio,
5 — definitely would include in portfolio.

ANALYTIC HIERARCHY PROCESS[4]

The analytic hierarchy modeling and measurement process (Saaty 1977 and 1980) is a recent addition to the various approaches used to determine the relative importance of a set of activities or criteria. The major distinction of this approach is that it structures any complex, multiperson, multicriterion and multiperiod problem hierarchically. Scaling each element in each level of a hierarchy against an element (criterion) of the next highest level, a matrix of pairwise comparisons of the activities can be constructed where the entries indicate the strength with which one element dominates another with respect to a given criterion.

This scaling formulation is translated into a largest eigenvalue problem which results in a normalized and unique vector of weights for each level of the hierarchy (always with respect to the criterion in the next level) which in turn (by a principle of hierarchical composition) via a series of multiplications results in a single composite vector of weights for the entire hierarchy. This vector measures the relative priority of all entities at the lowest level that enables the accomplishment of the highest objective of the hierarchy. These relative priority weights can provide the guidelines for the allocation of resources among the entities at the lower levels of the hierarchy. When a hierarchy is designed to reflect likely environmental scenarios, corporate objectives, and alternative product, market and distribution options, the analytic hierarchy process (AHP) can provide a framework and

[4]For a more technical discussion of this approach, see Wind and Saaty (1980) and Appendix A.

methodology for the determination of the firm's target product/market/distribution portfolio, and resource allocation among the components of the portfolio.

The major attractiveness of the AHP as a conceptual and measurement approach for the determination of the firm's target portfolio and allocation of resources within it are:

- A flexible formulation of the hierarchy reflecting management value systems;

- A flexible hierarchy which can incorporate *any* objectives (of varying units of measurement) and *any* set of environmental scenarios;

- A measurement procedure based on the relevant managers' perceived relationship among the various forces, actors, actions, and personal and organizational objectives;

- A built-in extension to incorporate the judgments of any number of decision makers and resolve conflicting views among them (Frawley and Saaty, 1978);

- A flexible *process* allowing for iteration in both the structure of the problem (e.g., alternative hierarchies) and judgments.

To illustrate the application of the AHP to the resource allocation problem, let's consider the following simplified illustration which is based on an actual application of the AHP in a large insurance company to the selection of a desired target portfolio of products/markets and distribution outlets, and allocation of resources among the portfolio's components.[5]

A hierarchy was developed jointly with the company president and is presented in a disguised form in Exhibit 5–13. This hierarchy was based on three major levels:

1. *The environmental scenarios* expressed as three summary scenarios:

---

[5]This discussion is based on Wind and Gross (1979).

- An optimistic environment (low-risk and potentially high-return environmental conditions),

- Continuation of the status quo,

- A pessimistic scenario (high-risk and potentially low-return environmental conditions);

2. *Corporate objectives*—the criteria for the evaluation of the various courses of action. Five objectives were identified:

- Profit level,

- Sales growth,

- Market share,

- Volatility,

- Demand on resources;

3. *The courses of actions*—activities. These include the three sets of products, markets and distribution outlets but went into considerably greater specificity of potential activities including various new distribution outlets not currently used by the firm, new market segments, and specific new product activities.

Given the sensitive nature of information on the firm's plans for allocation of its resources among alternative courses of action, the actual options are disguised and referred to by letters and numbers which do not correspond in any order to the items listed above.

Having selected the hierarchical structure outlined in Exhibit 5–13, the president evaluated all pairwise comparisons using the 9-point scale used in AHP applications (see Appendix A). These evaluations take the form of reciprocal matrices of the components of each level against the items in the level above. Consider, for example, the evaluation of the three major sets of activities against the objectives. This involved five pairwise matrices of the importance of products, customers, and distribution with respect to each of the five objectives. One of these five pairwise matrices is illustrated below:

Profit level	Products	Customers	Distribution
Products	1	$1/3$	$1/5$
Customers	3	1	$1/4$
Distribution	5	4	1

In this case, the president judged distribution to be of strong importance (5) over product, in leading to the achievement of the firm's target profit level, but somewhat less important when compared to customers (4). In evaluating customers versus products the president judged customers to be of greater importance

EXHIBIT 5–13

DISGUISED ANALYTIC HIERARCHY FOR THE SELECTION OF THE TARGET PRODUCT/MARKET/DISTRIBUTION PORTFOLIO FOR AN INSURANCE COMPANY

Source: Reprinted by permission from Yoram Wind and Daniel Gross, "An Analytical Hierarchy Approach to the Allocation of Resources within a Target Product/Market/Distribution Portfolio," in *Proceedings of the ORSA/TIMS Workshop on Market Measurement and Analysis,* March 26–28, 1979, © 1979 by the Institute of Management Sciences.

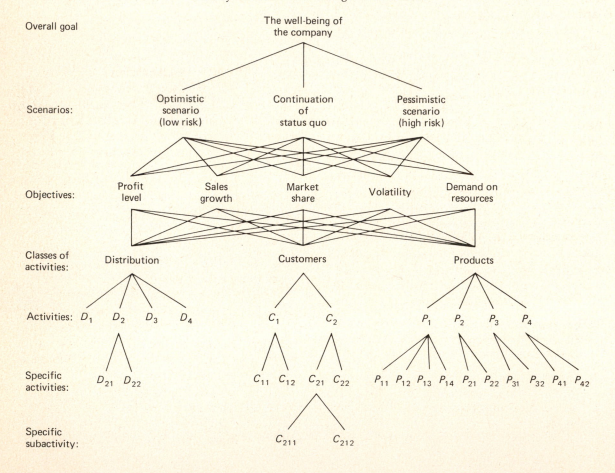

than products (3). Given the three judgments the reciprocals were added and the president continued with the pairwise comparison tasks. These tasks included the evaluation of:

- Scenarios against the overall goal of the firm,

- Objectives against each scenario,

- The class of activities (and subactivities) against each of the objectives,

- The cross-impact evaluation of the likely occurrence and impact of each component given each of the other components at the same level of the hierarchy.

These data provided the input to the eigen-value analysis (Saaty, 1977), and a resulting partial hierarchy is presented in Exhibit 5–14.

An examination of this exhibit suggests rules for allocating the firm's resources in development of products, markets and distribution vehicles under three alternative scenarios. In the disguised example presented in Exhibit 5–14, the president has a strong preference for the development of distribution outlets. In fact, the allocation of the developmental resources of the firm under this example should be 0.45 to the development of new distribution outlets, 0.32 to the development of new markets, and 0.23 to the development of new products. This allocation rule is based on allocating resources in proportion to the priorities. Other resource allocation rules, such as the ratio of priorities (benefits) to costs, can also be used. The output as presented in Exhibit 5–14 provides a significant amount of information such as:

1. The perceived likelihood of occurrence of the three scenarios is:
   - Optimistic   0.2
   - Status quo   0.3
   - Pessimistic   0.5

2. The relative importance of the five objectives are:
   - Profit level   0.2427

- Sales growth   0.1814
- Market share   0.2192
- Volatility   0.2578
- Demand on resources   0.1169

3. The relative importance of the various objectives varies considerably by the anticipated scenario. For example,

   - Sales growth is twice as important under continuation of the status quo than the other two scenarios (0.92 versus 0.046 and 0.042)

   - Market share is most important under an optimistic scenario (0.093 versus 0.068 and 0.057)

   - Profit level, volatility, and demand on resources are most important under pessimistic scenarios.

A sensitivity analysis was conducted using alternative hierarchical formulations, as well as different assumptions concerning the likely occurrence of the various scenarios. These analyses resulted in a *range of priorities*. Given that this range suggested an allocation of resources significantly different from the firm's current resource allocation pattern, it has led the president to reevaluate his firm's activities and assign task forces to those aspects of the portfolio (as suggested by the detailed priorities of Exhibit 5–14) which did not receive the attention and resources they deserve.

These task forces used the AHP to clarify their own preference structure and evaluate a larger number of alternative courses of action. The judgments of the task forces were reached in a number of group sessions, which provided the vehicle for open discussion among the members on assumptions, information, and preferences leading to the identification and resolution of a number of conflicts.

Although other procedures such as conjoint analysis can and have been used to assess the relative importance of management's objectives (Green and Wind, 1975b), conjoint

EXHIBIT 5–14

ANALYTIC HIERARCHY OF THE PRODUCT/CUSTOMER/DISTRIBUTION
PORTFOLIO OF AN INSURANCE FIRM

Source: Reprinted by permission from Yoram Wind and Daniel Gross, "An Analytical Hierarchy
Approach to the Allocation of Resources within a Target Product/Market/Distribution Portfolio," in
Proceedings of the ORSA/TIMS Workshop on Market Measurement and Analysis, March 26–28, 1979, ©
1979 by the Institute of Management Sciences.

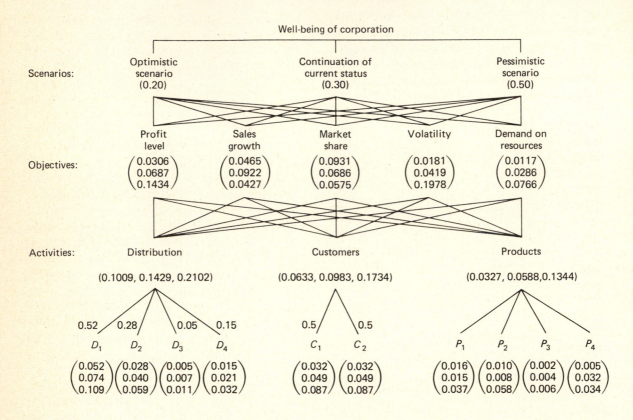

analysis, to date, has not been used on problems such as the resource allocation problem of the firm. For this class of problem, the AHP is more appropriate, given its track record, which includes: allocating transportation resources in the Sudan (Saaty, 1977), determining electricity allocations to industry in case of shortage (Saaty and Mariano, 1979), and distribution of the research funds of the Electric Power Research Institute (Saaty and Bennett, 1978).

PORTFOLIO DECISIONS

Having analyzed the current product portfolio of the firm, management's primary responsibility is to decide how to allocate resources to create the desired future portfolio. Treating product and markets as investments, much as financial portfolio analysis treats stocks and bonds, the major purpose of a product/market portfolio analysis is to guide management's product and market decisions. It involves the determination of the *desired* product/market portfolio including the balance between a concentrated and diversified portfolio. Following this decision and employing any number of possible analytical approaches (such as the AHP) to the resource allocation question and an examination of the product portfolios of competitors, management is ready to decide whether to change the current product/market portfolio or not. That is, whether to add, modify, or delete products or markets from the portfolio, and the timing of these changes. The relationship among these decisions is illustrated in Exhibit 5–15.

It is important to note that the various portfolio analysis schemes are only one of the inputs to management's portfolio decisions. GE, for example (Collins, 1978), uses the business screen matrix to help assess the relative attractiveness of the company's business units for resource allocation purposes. Central to the process are the identification and evaluation of key issues and problems, and providing early warning of a latent problem. Furthermore, within each SBU, strategic planning for individual products or product lines is conducted at GE with similar kinds of analysis. Each is treated as though it were part of an investment portfolio.

CONCENTRATED VERSUS DIVERSIFIED PORTFOLIOS

When a firm considers changes in its product portfolio and, in particular, addition of new products or deletion of products, these decisions should follow an explicit determination of the desired level of concentration within the product portfolio. New products, especially if developed internally, frequently fall within the boundaries of existing product lines. Furthermore, most of the so-called new products involve only modifications of existing products or additions of products to an existing product line. These added products tend to be similar to current products with respect to their risk and return characteristics and, hence, lead to a concentrated portfolio. In this context, the focus is on capitalizing on the current differential advantage of the firm with little effort to introduce truly innovative new products (that have higher risk). While a concentrated strategy may be consistent with the company's overall risk-averse objectives, it may lead to an unbalanced product portfolio.

On the other hand, when a firm prefers a diversified portfolio, it must develop completely *new product lines* (not directly related to the firm's current offerings), and this often calls for external (merger and acquisition) development. Yet, in cases in which management is engaged in diversification activities, most of the decisions are based on financial (or, at best, also production and marketing) considerations with little attention to the overall portfolio of products (old *plus* new ones) versus other possible portfolios. The decision of whether to have a

EXHIBIT 5–15

PRODUCT PORTFOLIO MODEL

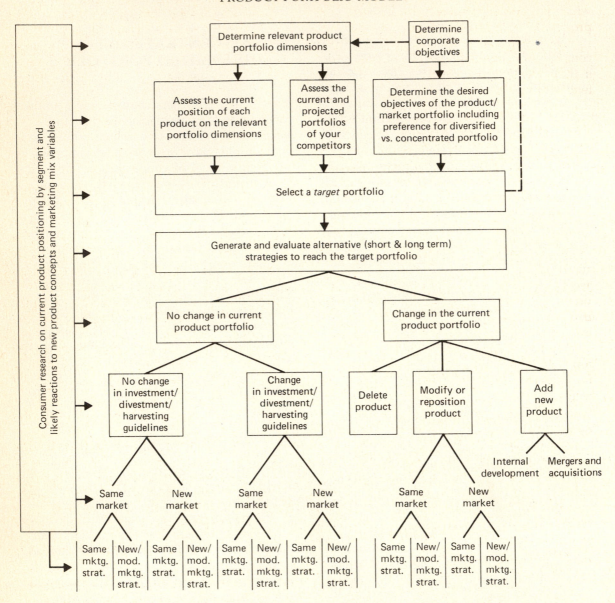

concentrated or diversified portfolio should therefore be made with an explicit attempt to optimize the *new* product/market portfolio which is now composed of the new *and* existing product lines and markets.

An explicit determination of the level of concentration/diversification of a product/market portfolio would balance the two tendencies:

a) To yield to the organizational pressures to introduce new products which are quite similar to existing offerings of the firm and

b) To add new products unrelated to existing product lines (usually via external acquisition) with no regard to their fit with and synergistic effect on the company's overall product portfolio.

To overcome these shortcomings, which may lead to a suboptimal product mix, it is necessary to encourage management to utilize a formal approach to the determination of the firm's product/market portfolio and its desired level of concentration versus diversification.

The determination of the level of concentration versus diversification is directly related to management's tradeoff between risk and expected return in both the short and long term. In general the higher the level of concentration, the higher the business (production, marketing, and management) efficiency and hence the higher the expected return, especially in the short term. Yet this is also associated with higher (long term) risks. Conversely, the higher the degree of diversification, the lower the risk but also the lower the expected short-term return. Management's tradeoff between the two factors should therefore reflect its preference and the firm's idiosyncracies.

A portfolio approach views product mix decisions as portfolio decisions. As such, it provides a framework for making product mix decisions and suggests a set of criteria for evaluating them (whether to add, modify, or delete products and product lines). Whether one accepts the objectives of expected return and risk reduction, or some other objectives such as market share and growth, the portfolio models shift the firm's point of view from a relatively narrow perspective centered around existing products to a broader perspective involving the total market/product possibilities.

RESOURCE ALLOCATION

One of the major objectives of product portfolio analysis is to provide guidelines for the firm's resource allocation decisions among (a) products and markets and (b) business (product) planning projects. Allocation of resources among products has taken one of two major approaches: factor listing or optimization. *Factor listing* takes into consideration those factors used in making decisions on the width and depth of the product mix. These include corporate objectives and resources, current marketing strengths and weaknesses, current and potential demand estimates (reflecting customer interests and purchase plans), competitive offerings and activities (the type and range of products offered by competitors and their market position), and other environmental factors.

Of special interest among the factor-listing approaches are the directions for allocation of resources suggested by Cardozo (1979). Greater marketing, technical, production, and managerial resources should be allocated to products or product lines which:

- Help achieve the corporate objectives and mission;

- Have a high level and rate of growth of primary demand for the product class;

- Have opportunities to increase market share or penetration or capitalize on competitive weaknesses;

- Have profit opportunities which generally result from favorable primary demand and competitive advantage;
- Do not require a highly disproportionate share of the corporate resources.

Yet, such guidelines should be supplemented with some explicit resource allocation rules, since regardless of the size of the firm's resources, it is most unlikely that all current and potential products could get *all* their required resources. Such allocation rules and procedures should identify the functions to be maximized and the relevant constraints.

Optimization methods have therefore been designed to help achieve an optimal allocation of resources among products and markets through the utilization of mathematical programming or simulation. The mathematical programming approach is most appropriate for static product mix optimization in which the firm has to select a set of products such that profit (or any other corporate objective, such as growth) is maximized, subject to satisfying a set of constraints. The simulation approach, on the other hand, can be utilized in those situations in which management desires to determine the "best" product mix under a variety of changes in corporate strategies, consumer demand, competitive strategies, and other environmental conditions.

Allocation of resources among planning projects   The desired product portfolio, when contrasted with the current portfolio of the firm, can also provide some useful guidelines for the allocation of resources among planning projects (and their associated marketing research activities). In this context the gap between the desired and actual product portfolio can provide insight on the relative emphasis to be placed on factors such as:

- Existing and new markets and products;
- Internal versus external growth;

- Domestic versus international operations;
- Short-term versus long-term expected performance.

A similar approach has been implemented by Corning Glass (Fogg, 1976), which specified seven criteria for evaluating projects in the context of its planning portfolio as a basis for the differences between the actual and desired distribution of resources. The seven criteria are listed in Exhibit 5–16.[6]

COMPETITIVE PORTFOLIOS

Portfolio analysis can be conducted not only for the firm's own products but also for each of the firm's major competitors. Knowing the portfolios of competitors can lead to more refined competitive strategy which takes into account the interdependencies among products and markets and the impact of allocation of resources to a specific product/market area on the availability of resources in other product/market areas. As an example, consider the case of General Foods International, which entered the United Kingdom chewing gum market partly to reduce the competitive strength of Wrigley in France. In this case, if General Foods had not entered the U.K. market, it would have left Wrigley with a much stronger competitive position, allowing them to generate resources that could be invested in other markets (such as France) in which General Foods had a strong market position. The General Foods entry into the UK market forced Wrigley to devote more competitive resources in the UK and reduced their ability to compete against General Foods in France.

The analysis of competitors' portfolios is

---

[6]These criteria are presented with the permission of C. Davis Fogg, President, Consumer Products Division, Bausch & Lomb Inc.

EXHIBIT 5–16

CORNING GLASS CRITERIA FOR ALLOCATING RESOURCES AMONG PROJECTS

Source: C. Davis Fogg, Bausch and Lomb, Inc.

Criteria	Basis	Balance	
		Desired	Actual
1. *Area of focus*	% planning time		
Materials		10	10
Components		30	37
Systems		60	53
2. *Timing of payoff*	% projects		
Short-term (1–2 years)		25	29
Medium-term (2–5 years)		35	42
Long-term (5+ years)		40	29
3. *Growth routes*	% projects		
Inside-out		50	71
Outside-in		50	29
4. *Geography*	% planning time		
Domestic		10	27*
Overseas		10	0
Worldwide		80	73
5. *Type of project*	% planning time		
Strategy		10	8
Identification of opportunities		15	10
Specific market planning		65	64
Continuing support		10	18
6. *Type of product*	% projects		
Commodity		70	71
Proprietary		30	29
7. *Expected value*	% projects		
Low ($10 MM)		33	43*
Medium ($10–20 MM)		33	14
High ($20+ MM)		34	43

*Asterisks indicate problem areas.

especially useful in estimating the likelihood that a given competitor will retaliate against the firm's actions or initiate actions (such as the introduction of new products) which might affect the firm's market position. In addition such analysis can also identify candidates for cooperative versus competitive strategies such as merger and acquisition.

CHANGE IN PRODUCT PORTFOLIO

The identification of the current product portfolio of the firm and the determination of the desired portfolio require two sets of decisions:

a) The number and type of products in the portfolio, which involves decisions concerning which new products to add to the portfolio, which ones to modify, and which to drop;

b) The amount of marketing effort and support to be given each product in the portfolio.

The number and type of desired products encompass most of the product decisions of the firm involving internal and external new product development efforts, product modification and repositioning, and product deletion. In examining these decisions (which constitute the major part of this book), it is important to take into account the following considerations:

- In adding new products or businesses, is the demand for the new products *independent* of the demand for the existing products in the portfolio? What is the expected level of cannibalization, and what is the impact of the degree of demand interdependence on the expected return and risk of the new portfolio? Similarly, when considering the deletion of existing products, what are the demand interdependency considerations and their impact on expected return and risk?

- What is the effect of adding new products or businesses on the competitive position of the firm? Similarly, what will be the competitive impact of product deletion or business divestiture?

- What is the effect of adding new products or businesses (or the deletion of products or business divestiture) on corporate resources (R&D, production, marketing,

management time) and their effective and efficient utilization?

- What is the effect of adding new products or businesses (or the deletion of products or business divestiture) on the attitude and actions of government (and other relevant stakeholders such as intermediate marketing organizations), and what is the likely impact of these actions on the portfolio's expected return and risk?

The second set of decisions concerning the marketing effort allocated to each product involves considerations about which products to promote, how much to promote them, and how. These decisions center around three major strategic options:

a) To invest (build and strengthen the product's market position and performance),

b) To hold (no major change in strategy or the resources allocated to the product),

c) To divest or harvest the product.

These strategic decisions should be derived from an analysis of the projected performance of the current portfolio versus the projected performance of a desired product portfolio (on all the relevant dimensions specified by management) and require a detailed effort to generate and evaluate alternative marketing strategies aimed at achieving the above objectives.

Of critical importance in this context is the market responsiveness to the marketing efforts for each product. Ideally, a company will have information on the response elasticity of the market(s) for each component of the marketing strategy and each product, and will allocate resources, at least in the short term, to those products with the highest return on marketing investments. Such considerations, however, are more tactical in nature and should not be the sole guide of the strategic resource allocation decision, which should take into account the broader portfolio considerations discussed earlier.

The determination of the nature of desired changes in the current product portfolio is the most critical aspect of portfolio analysis. Unfortunately, several portfolio models do *not* provide guidelines for the establishment of an optimal portfolio. Classifying, for example, the firm's products as dogs, problem children, cash cows, and stars does not suggest what the optimal mix of the four types is. The terminology used by BCG is disfunctional to a true portfolio concept. Psychologically, management would like to have as many stars as possible and delete the dogs. Yet, in many cases it is the cash cows and not the stars that provide the bread and butter for the firm. Furthermore, at times dogs might be essential as insurance against the risk of some future events. This is especially so if one considers an international product/market portfolio and the need to keep certain businesses as a hedge against currency fluctuation, likely government restrictions, or market shortages.

Development of an optimal or near-optimal mix of products (businesses) and markets is an essential task of management which should take into account the various determinants of any product/marketing strategy, mainly consumer needs and preferences, likely competitive reactions, the competitive strengths and weaknesses, the current and expected cost structure of various products and marketing actions, the likely government and other environmental constraints, etc.

TIMING CHANGES IN PRODUCT PORTFOLIO

Gaps between the current and desired product portfolios can seldom be filled in a single set of product addition, deletion, or modification activities. The *timing* of changes in a product portfolio should be planned as part of the firm's long-range strategic plan. As an example of a sequence of portfolio changes over time, consider the case of Pennwalt (as described in *Forbes*, February 20, 1978). Initially, to free the company from the commodity cycles that periodically lacerated its earnings, the company, like other chemical producers, upgraded its commodity chemicals into faster-growing, higher-profit chemical intermediates and specialties. A commodity like hydrofluoric acid, for example, was upgraded into specialties like Kynar plastics or Isotron refrigerants and aerosol propellants. The next step of development was into other areas related in some way to the chemical business—for example, Sharples centrifuges for removal of impurities from water or Stokes molding equipment used for making pharmaceutical tablets. The third move was based on further-removed acquisitions in the health-products market with acquisitons such as SS White Dental Manufacturing Co. and Wallace & Tiernan Pharmaceuticals. Between 1971 and 1976, Pennwalt's dependency on chemicals was reduced to less than 55 percent of sales, but the chemical business still contributed over 70 percent of the pretax profits of the firm.

CONCLUDING REMARKS

Product decisions should not be made in isolation from the overall desired product/market portfolio of the firm. Management should recognize that the *portfolio* approach may be of value in determining the firm's product mix. Even if initial applications lack the utilization of tools developed for selection of optimal port-folios of securities, approaching product-mix and market-segment-selection decisions (or even just the screening of new product concepts and proposed target segments) with a portfolio orientation may lead to an improved and better-balanced product/market portfolio. Such analysis should be done at various levels ranging from the simplest product line composition to the most complex corporate portfolio of strategic business units.

A number of portfolio models were discussed in this chapter. In selecting a portfolio model based on any of these approaches, the idiosyncrasies of the firm and management preferences should be taken into consideration. To get a better feel for the design and implementation of a portfolio model, select a firm or organization and try to apply the approaches discussed here to its products and markets. To the extent that you do not have first-hand experience with and/or data on a market, select an automotive company such as GM or Ford and try to develop the various portfolio frameworks, specifying the information required for each model. To the extent that none of the approaches discussed here is intuitively appropriate, ask yourself what makes the approach inappropriate, and how you would improve it.

6

The Product Planning System _____

INTRODUCTION

The management of any firm, whether a manufacturer of consumer products (such as automobiles, clothing, food, or cosmetics), a manufacturer of industrial products (such as computers or farm equipment), or even a retailer, is faced with the need to plan whether or not to add new products or services, delete any of the existing ones, or modify any of them; and if a decision for action is made, then how, when, and where to do it.

In making these decisions concerning the future product and service offerings of the firm, management is engaged in *planning*. The purpose of this chapter is not to provide a review of the considerable planning literature but, rather, to (a) briefly summarize some of the major concepts of planning and (b) propose a product-planning model which provides an operational framework for the generation, implementation, and control of product strategies.

ON THE CONCEPT OF PLANNING

In its most simplistic form planning can be viewed as a process of deciding:

- Where are we?
- Where are we headed if no changes occur in the firm's marketing strategy, the competitors' actions, or the environmental conditions?
- Where do we want to go (what are our objectives)?
- How can we get there?
- Have we achieved our objectives?

The first step in the planning process—the assessment of "where are we?"—involves a *situation analysis* to examine the current and anticipated strengths and weaknesses of the firm's offerings. Such a situation analysis calls for both an internal and external product/market audit as well as an examination of the relevant environment. The product/market audit is briefly discussed in this chapter, whereas the analysis of environmental conditions is discussed in Chapter 7.

The second step is the determination of "where are we headed?" This can be based on a simple time series projection which provides a

baseline against which to evaluate any proposed new strategy. As such it is an integral part of situation analysis or any other procedure for evaluation of product/marketing strategy.

The third step in the planning process involves the determination of the desired product objectives and their relationship to the broader marketing and corporate objectives.

The fourth step—which is the heart of the planning process—involves five separate stages:

1. *Generation* of alternative courses of action;

2. *Evaluation* of the various courses of action;

3. *Selection* of a course of action;

4. *Determination* of the size, allocation, and sources of required resources;

5. *Planning* for the implementation of the selected course of action.

The final step in the planning process involves a *control* system to provide the feedback needed to determine whether the objectives were achieved and to provide guidelines for any strategy changes.

The planning process suggested is straightforward and based on a common-sense approach to problem solving, yet it is sometimes difficult to carry it out effectively. In other words:

> The need for corporate planning is so obvious and so great that it is hard for anyone to be against it. But it is even harder to make such planning useful. Planning is one of the most complex and difficult intellectual activities in which man can engage (Ackoff, 1970).

To increase the usefulness of product planning it is advisable to consider some of the following basic concepts:

- *Don't wait for others to plan for you*. Planning is every manager's responsibility. It cannot be delegated completely to a planning unit since managing a firm's product strategy involves planning.

- *Act—don't react.* As in any competitive game (such as tennis), when playing against a good player (and there is no reason to assume that your competitor is not as qualified as your management), the only chance of success lies in planning and carrying out an offensive strategy. Leaving the initiative to the opponent and engaging in a *reactive* strategy is the fastest way to lose the game.

- *Learn*. In developing a product strategy it is important for the strategy to follow an *adaptive experimentation* approach (Little, 1966; Ackoff, 1970). The approach, when applied to product policy, is based on the premise that a firm's sales (and profits) are functions of its product (and marketing) strategies. The adaptive approach therefore requires not the selection of a single product strategy, but rather the design of a number of product strategies following an experimental design. The experimental results are used to update a sales-response model, and product strategies are chosen to maximize

expected profit in the next time period. To date, adaptive experimentation has been applied only to promotional spending. The concept, however, is equally applicable to product strategies.

- *Utilize the available concepts, methods, and findings from marketing, marketing research, management science, and the behavioral sciences.*

- *Focus on nonprogrammed areas and establish procedures for programmed areas.* Given that a firm's most scarce resource is its management time, it is useful to note the distinction proposed by Simon (1960) between programmed and nonprogrammed decisions. This would suggest that managers should devote their time (a) to the nonrepetitive, novel, unstructured, and consequential decisions and (b) to the design of procedures to handle on a regular basis all the programmed, repetitive, and routine decisions.

- *Encourage creativity.* The generation of innovative product strategies requires strong emphasis on creativity and original thinking. Without such emphasis, continuation of previous strategies or "me too" strategies is likely to happen, and better but novel approaches can be ignored.

- *Develop contingency plans.* Given the uncertainty concerning future market, competitive, and environmental conditions, planning activities should consider various future scenarios and contingency plans—not a single plan, but a set of plans, one for each major scenario. The availability of contingency plans shortens management's response time to changes in environmental conditions. In fact, the quality and quantity of contingency plans are probably the best measures of the performance of the planning function.

- *Develop a user-oriented marketing information system.* Product/marketing planning requires continuous inputs on market, competitive, and environmental conditions, as well as information on the performance of the firm's products and services. The volume of such inputs requires the design of a user-oriented information system, i.e., a system that provides only the required information, in a form which is easy to comprehend and utilize.

- *View planning as a continuous process.* Planning should not be viewed as a one-time, isolated event but as a continuous process requiring constant monitoring.

- *Integrate product planning with the planning of the other business functions.* Product decisions require inputs from most other business functions—marketing, finance, accounting, R&D, manufacturing, personnel, and top management. At the same time, product decisions affect all of these other functions. Hence, the planning of product/marketing policy requires strong and continuous coordination of the product planning function with the plans of the other business functions.

- *Avoid suboptimization.* Since product management sometimes leads to overemphasis on individual products at the expense of other products, attention should be given to avoiding such suboptimization and designing a product strategy which is coordinated at the product line and mix levels.

- *Get involvement and commitment from top management and operating management.* Product/marketing planning involves the participation of managers at various levels. To assure that a plan reflects the overall corporate objectives and strategic plan, it is important to develop an approving procedure whereby higher levels of management review and approve the critical product/marketing plans of lower levels. This is also

one of the ways to avoid suboptimization and misallocation of resources.

- *Tie the product/marketing planning to the resource allocation procedure, budgets, and corporate profit plans.* This is crucial to the effectiveness and operationalization of any product/marketing plan. The profit and resource requirements should be clearly stated and included as an integral part of any plan transmitted for corporate approval. In addition, product plans should include an explicit allocation of resources among products and markets over time.

- *Engage in both short- and long-term planning.* Short-term planning can be annual or even for two or three years. The time horizon of long-term planning varies according to the level of planning involved. At the corporate level, long-term planning may be through the year 2000; whereas long-term planning at the division or product level is usually limited to five or ten years. It is especially crucial that the planning (short or long term) of any product unit be consistent with the plans at higher levels of the organization.

- *Plan the planning process.* Given the complexity of the product/marketing planning process, it is essential to plan it, i.e., set objectives for the planning process, decide on the alternative ways to achieve the desired planning, select a planning system, allocate the resources (personnel and monetary) required for planning, set an organizational structure and procedures appropriate for the planning, and design a set of controls to assure the desired performance of the planning function. Planning the planning process and allocating sufficient resources to implement it are essential due to the pressure of daily "firefighting" management activities, which tend to divert its efforts from planning. Furthermore, since most organizational rewards are given for current performance and not long-term performance, there is little incentive for managers to engage in long-term planning which may benefit the planner's successor.

- *Design an iterative planning process that incorporates both forward and backward planning.* Most planning approaches subscribe to a forward process which, in its simplest form, can be described as stating objectives, identifying and developing alternative courses of action that will lead to the achievement of the objectives, and a final selection. A backward process, on the other hand, starts with identifying the desired state (idealized position), the problems and opportunities in reaching it, and concludes with the identification and evaluation of courses of actions which might help achieve this idealized state. Effective planning requires a continuous iterative process that starts with the forward planning (leading to the selection of a desired state) which

serves as the starting point for a backward planning process.

These and related planning concepts increase the value of the product/marketing planning process and assure its relevance. The plan itself should include the following characteristics (based on the US Army's staff officers field manual):

- Provide for accomplishing the mission;
- Be based on facts and valid assumptions;
- Provide for the use of exisiting resources;
- Provide the necessary organization;
- Provide continuity;
- Delegate authority;
- Provide direct contact;
- Be simple;
- Be flexible;
- Provide control;
- Be coordinated.

PROPOSED PRODUCT PLANNING MODEL

No single model can be proposed for the product planning process, nor is there a single best one. Product planning models should reflect the planning concepts described in the previous section as well as the idiosyncrasies of the organization and personnel involved. The marketing planning model proposed in this chapter should be viewed in this light and seen as just one model which could possibly be modified to fit the unique organizational characteristics of a given firm.

The model is presented in Exhibit 6–1 and is based on eight related phases of analysis and decisions:

1. Determination of corporate objectives, resources, and constraints;

2. Monitoring the current and anticipated environment;

3. Situation analysis;

4. Product/market portfolio analysis and decisions;

5. Analysis and implementation of changes in the current product portfolio;

6. Development of tentative product/marketing programs;

7. Evaluation of alternative programs;

8. Organization for marketing action, implementation, and control.

The second phase—monitoring the environment—is discussed in the next chapter.

EXHIBIT 6–1

PRODUCT/MARKETING PLANNING MODEL

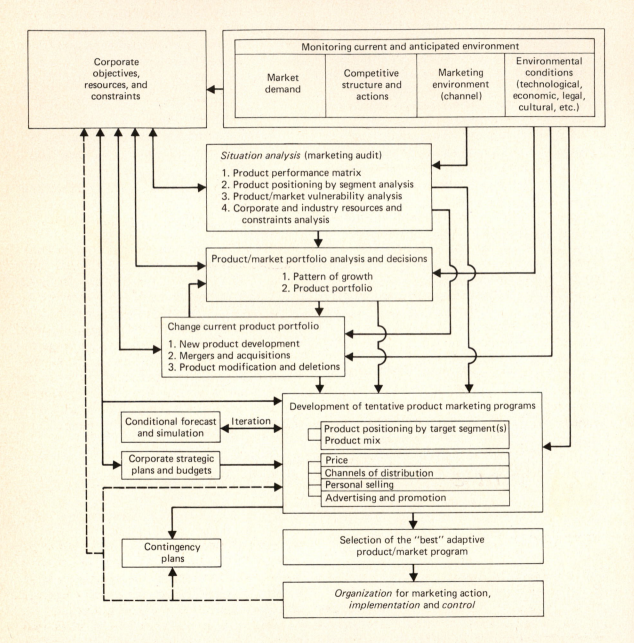

Key: The lines linking the various analysis and decision boxes are illustrative only. In reality, all phases are interrelated.

Certain aspects of the situation analysis and the product portfolio analysis and decisions were covered in Chapter 5 and the first sections of this chapter. A detailed discussion of the analysis and implementation of changes in the current product portfolio is the focus of Parts II (Adding New Products) and III (Product Modification and Deletion) of this book. The remaining phases of the model are briefly described in the next section.

Before examining the components of the proposed product/marketing planning approach, it is important to note that these related steps can be implemented in any order. The components (both concepts and approaches) of the model can be applied (obviously in varying levels of specificity and scope) to various levels of management decisions; i.e., the model can be applied to the overall strategic *corporate* product/marketing planning or, at the other extreme, to a tactical marketing plan for an individual *brand*.

At the strategic corporate level the primary concern is with setting the corporate objectives and allocating resources among businesses (product lines) and markets. At lower levels of management, the specific product/marketing decisions require a similar process. The scope of analysis and the range of variables and alternatives to be considered change, obviously, if one is concerned with the mix of strategic business units as compared to the future of a specific brand. Yet, the major steps of the analysis and the typical decisions suggested by the model do hold for all four levels of decisions:

- Top management's business/market portfolio decisions (focusing on the strategic business units);

- Divisional management's product mix decisions (the product lines within a strategic business unit);

- Group product management's product line decisions;

- Product management's brand decisions.

The lines of demarcation among these levels are arbitrary and depend on management's decisions. Consider, for example, the Maxwell House division of General Foods. Whereas coffee is recognized as a strategic business unit, should Maxwell House coffee be considered a product mix or product line? Along what dimensions should a product line or mix be determined? By product type (instant versus regular; caffeinated versus decaffeinated), size of package, distribution outlet, type of customer (household versus institution), or other?

COMPONENTS OF THE PRODUCT PLANNING MODEL

SETTING PRODUCT OBJECTIVES

The first step in the product planning process is the determination of the relevant product-related corporate objectives. The objectives provide the guidelines for the firm's decisions on its current products as well as its new product development, diversification, and divestiture activities. The objectives set the boundaries for the firm's product strategies and provide the criteria for evaluating the various product strategies. Furthermore, the specific product objectives should reflect the overall corporate objectives, resources, and constraints.

Determining the objectives requires two major steps: identification of *relevant* objectives and determination of the relative importance (weight) of each.

Identifying objectives The identification of corporate and product objectives is a relatively easy task which can be achieved in a management brainstorming session. This can be aided further by identification (through some unstructured research approaches) of the criteria used by relevant publics to evaluate the corporate performance. For example, security analysts and portfolio managers have a major impact on the price of a company's shares. Hence, identifying the criteria used by them to evaluate companies might be revealing to management. Similarly, identifying the criteria used by government officials in evaluating the performance and actions of a company is useful as input to corporate strategies aimed at avoiding confrontation with government.

Whereas traditionally, economists tended to identify a single corporate objective—maximization of profits—it is generally accepted today that most firms attempt to achieve a number of objectives. A recent study among executives of a pharmaceutical firm and 170 security analysts revealed more than 25 objectives (criteria for evaluating the corporate activities). These criteria included:

- Expected annual sales growth
- Expected annual earnings growth
- Percentage of sales generated by products launched in last five years
- Potential of new products in research
- Percentage of growth due to acquisition
- Percentage of sales spent on research
- Return on equity
- Pre-tax profit margin
- Ratio of assets to liabilities
- Long-term debt as percentage of capital
- Dividends policy
- Percent of sales and profit generated by cyclical products
- Percent of sales and profits from mature products with strong competition
- Percent of sales and profits from products outside the firm's major line of products
- Percent of sales and profits from international operations
- Patent protection, exclusivity, or other means for long lead time
- Market share of the major products

This list of criteria is not intended to be exhaustive but rather to illustrate some objectives stated by the management of one firm and some security analysts. Other criteria are, and should be, identified reflecting management preferences and values. In general, objectives tend to reflect four sets of factors:

1. *Expected performance.* This is usually the major set of criteria including both the level of performance (sales and profit levels) and growth rate.
2. *Expected risk.*
3. *Stakeholder impact.* The effect on and likely reaction of stakeholders—employees, stockholders, government.
4. *Demand on corporate resources.* The demand on both financial and human (especially management time and skills) resources is often a critical factor.

The relative importance of these four sets of objectives varies by the *level* of management involved and the *time* horizon. Objectives have to be set at all levels of management. In fact, every organization has a *hierarchy of objectives* in which lower level objectives (such as those of a brand manager) should reflect, or be means to, higher objectives.

Furthermore, at each level of management the objectives range from immediate (short-term) to long-term. The actual length of time considered long-term again differs by level of management—the higher the managerial level, the longer the time horizon. Hence, at the corporate level, long-term objectives can encompass the year 2000, whereas at the brand man-

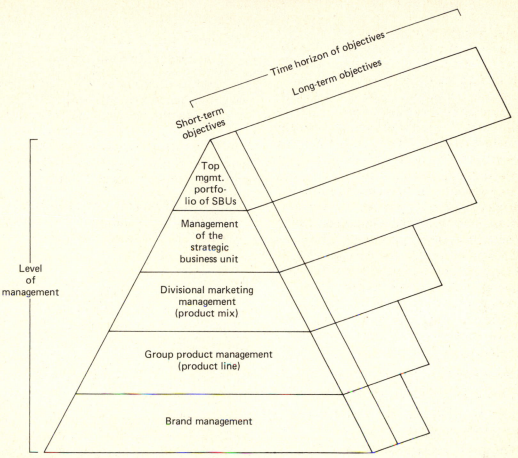

agement level, five years would be considered long-term. This level-dependent time perspective is schematically illustrated in Exhibit 6–2.

A critical consideration in the determination of objectives is the trade-off between short- and long-term objectives; i.e., should short-term profit be sacrificed for long-term competitive position? Or should, for example, long-term competitive position and growth, through investment and new products, be sacrificed for short-term profits? These and other

tradeoffs reflect management's overall business philosophy and should be made primarily at the higher levels of management, reflecting the product portfolio considerations discussed in Chapter 5.

Determining the weight of each objective Having identified a set of relevant corporate objectives and derived from them the appropriate product-related objectives (criteria), we see that the key question is how important

EXHIBIT 6–3

ILLUSTRATIVE STIMULUS CARD FOR TRANSPORTATION COMPANY STUDY

FINANCIAL ASPECTS:

  If successful:
    gross revenues reach $15 million per year
    present value over life of venture is $10 million

  If unsuccessful:
    $15 million loss is incurred

  Chances of venture's success:
    80%

EFFECT ON IMPROVING THE PHYSICAL ENVIRONMENT:

  Significant

EFFECT ON IMPROVING THE PUBLIC WELFARE:

  Significant

SUPPORT BY OTHER GROUPS:

  Neither opposed nor supported by union leaders
  Strongly supported by major stockholders

each objective is. To establish the relative importance of objectives, the relevant group of managers is asked to rate (on some importance scale), or rank (from most to least important), the objectives or to divide a constant number of importance points among the various objectives.

Recent developments in multiattribute decision-making enable one to utilize a more rigorous approach to the determination of the relative importance of objectives. Conjoint measurement (Green and Wind, 1973) has been utilized for this purpose successfully in a number of cases. To illustrate the applicability of this approach to the determination of the relative importance of the criteria to be utilized in evaluating new product ventures, let us consider the following case:

A large transportation company was interested in establishing a set of criteria for evaluating new product ventures. The top eight corporate officers participated in a brainstorming session which resulted in the identification of eight criteria. Three levels were determined for each criterion, and a fractional factorial design was developed resulting in 27 hypothetical new ventures, each described in terms of the various levels of the eight criteria. Exhibit 6–3 illustrates one of these 27 stimuli.[1]

Each of the top eight executives was presented with the set of 27 cards and asked to sort them in terms of their relative attractiveness to him. The executives' evaluations were submitted to the MONANOVA conjoint scaling program resulting in individual evaluations of the various criteria as well as a group evaluation.

---

[1]The author is indebted to Paul E. Green, S. S. Kresge Professor of Marketing at the University of Pennsylvania, and Patrick J. Robinson, President of Robinson Associates, Inc., for permission to present this case.

Each respondent received his own results as they compared to the group's average utilities. Exhibit 6–4 presents the output for one of the respondents. Having received their own utility functions and comparing them to the group's, the executives discussed the reasons for the differences in their responses. Following such discussion, the conjoint analysis task was repeated, resulting in something closer to a consensus among the executives as to the relative importance of the criteria. Even in those cases in which consensus was not reached, the procedure was useful since it identified the sources of disagreement among managers.

MONITORING THE ENVIRONMENT

Monitoring the relevant environment and projecting its trend are important to all the product marketing planning activities of the firm. Four

EXHIBIT 6–4

UTILITY FUNCTIONS FOR EIGHT NEW VENTURE CRITERIA: EXECUTIVE *A* VERSUS GROUP AVERAGE

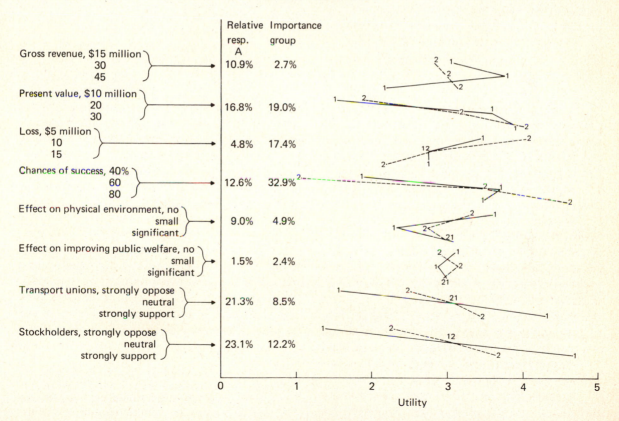

Key: Solid lines—respondent's evaluation; broken lines—average evaluation.

sets of environmental forces should be monitored and projected. These areas (discussed further in Chapter 7) are:

- The market demand
- The competitive structure and actions
- The marketing (e.g., channel) environment
- The technological, economic, social, cultural, and legal environment

It is the latter set of environmental conditions which are the most complex and difficult to monitor. Yet, a careful monitoring and projection of these environmental forces, their interrelationship (cross impact), direction and magnitude of change, and likely effect on the firm's operations are essential inputs to the planning efforts of the firm.

SITUATION ANALYSIS

Situation analysis is an essential part of any product planning procedure. The essence of situation analysis are the questions "where are we?" and "where are we going, assuming no changes in our marketing strategies, competitive actions, or environmental conditions?" To provide answers to these questions a four-fold procedure is suggested based on:

1. A product performance matrix which assesses the current and anticipated changes in the products' sales, profits, and market share positions (based on actual sales and profit data) by market segment.

2. A product/market vulnerability analysis aimed at identifying those customers most likely to switch to other products and the reasons for their vulnerability as well as the nature and magnitude of the vulnerability of customers of other firms.

3. A product positioning by market segment analysis which provides insights as to the way various consumer segments and other

relevant publics perceive and evaluate the firm's products vis-a-vis their competitors.

4. Corporate and industry resources and constraint analysis aimed at identifying the strengths and weaknesses of the company vis-a-vis its competitors with respect to available resources (material, monetary, and personnel) and constraints.

Product performance matrix As discussed in Chapter 5, the product performance matrix provides a framework for the effective organization and use of hard data on sales, market share, and profitability (or any other performance measures selected by management). The matrix is an integral part of the firm's situation analysis process and provides essential inputs to the design of a strategic marketing plan for the firm's existing product line.

Product vulnerability analysis[2] In determining the strengths and weaknesses of a product franchise, the size of its "loyal" segment has often been considered an important factor. Yet, the heterogeneity of most purchasing-based loyalty segments raises serious doubts about the viability of brand loyalty as a basis for segmentation or as a useful guideline for marketing strategy. To increase the operational value of the concepts of loyalty and switching likelihood, it has been proposed to limit the term, "loyalty," to those cases in which consumers buy the given brand on a regular basis *and* have a strong attitudinal preference for it. It is further recognized that many regular and occasional customers have varying degrees of attitudinal loyalty ("liking," etc.) toward the product in question and have different vulnerability levels. A brand vulnerability matrix is thus proposed which recognizes differences in both the magnitude and the nature of vulnerability.

The concept of vulnerability distinguishes

---

[2]The material in this section is based on Wind (1977a).

EXHIBIT 6–5

THE BASIC VULNERABILITY MATRIX

Source: Reprinted by permission of the publisher from "Brand Loyalty and Vulnerability" by
Y. Wind in *Consumer and Industrial Buying Behavior*, A.G. Woodside, J.N. Sheth, P.D. Bennett (eds.), ©
1977 by Elsevier–North Holland, Inc.

		Attitude toward brand *i*		
		Like *i*	Indifferent to *i* and others	Dislike *i*
Purchase pattern with respect to brand *i*	Buy *i* regularly	Loyal to *i* 1	Customers of brand *i* who are vulnerable to competitors 2	3
	Buy *i* occasionally	4	Customers of brand *i* who are vulnerable to competitors 5	6
	Do not buy *i*	Competitive customers who are vulnerable to brand *i* 7	8	Unlikely target for brand *i* 9

the "loyal" customers—those who both buy *and* "like" the brand—from those who buy it but "like" equally well or better other brands and hence are vulnerable to these other brands. The concept in its simplest form is presented in Exhibit 6–5.

In this oversimplified example we define "loyalty" and "vulnerability" based on the relationship between two dimensions—the purchase pattern of brand *i* and the attitude toward it. Whereas each of these dimensions can be defined and measured in numerous ways, let us first consider the basic terms used in the exhibit. Following this approach, three purchase patterns of brand *i* are identified—buy regularly, buy occasionally, and do not buy. (The last category can easily be expanded by a number of categories reflecting the buyers of other brands.) Similarly, three attitude states are identified as "like," "indifferent," and "dislike." Cross-tabulating the two dimensions results in a 3 × 3 vulnerability matrix (as pre-

sented in Exhibit 6–5). Note, that of the nine cells, only members of one cell can be defined as "loyal." Members of five cells (cells two through six) are current customers of brand *i* who are vulnerable to competitors. Members of cells seven and eight are current customers of other brands who are vulnerable to brand *i*, and members of cell nine are what one might call the "lost case"—those who don't buy and don't like the brand.

The vulnerability matrix provides some indication of the magnitude of vulnerability. In the first two rows, the higher the dislike of the brand, the greater the vulnerability. In the third row, the greater the liking of brand *i*, the more vulnerable are the customers of the competing brands to brand *i*.

The vulnerability matrix, in its simplest form, does not reveal the nature or reasons for the brand's vulnerability. To shed some light on these aspects, one has to recognize the multidimensionality of attitudes. Hence, instead of using the simplified "like—indifferent—dislike" dimensions it would be useful to identify the *reasons* for liking or disliking the brand. Such information would provide management with insights not only into the size of the loyal and vulnerable segments but also on the magnitude and nature of the customers' vulnerability. Such information is essential to the design of marketing programs aimed at reducing the customers' vulnerability and likelihood of switching to competing brands, and increasing the likelihood of attracting the vulnerable customers of competing brands.

The measurement of a brand's vulnerability is based on a two-step approach:

1. Determination of relevant purchase categories (e.g., percent of purchases of brand *i*)

2. With each purchase category, determination of the attitudinal dimension(s) of the vulnerability matrix.

The determination of the purchase categories is relatively straightforward, and most managers would most likely prefer to continue to use familiar categories such as "users versus nonusers," or "heavy versus light brand users." The difficulty arises with respect to the attitude dimension, which can be assessed using a variety of measurement approaches. The simplest approach is the one based on the utilization of a unidimensional attitude scale (based on "overall liking," "satisfaction," or some evaluative attribute such as "uniqueness," "perceived value," and the like). In this case consumers can be classified directly according to their brand rating with no need for further analysis.

It is seldom, however, that consumers' attitudes toward, and preference for, a brand can be represented by a single attitude scale. The more common situation is that a number of attitude items are developed to measure one or more of the relevant attitudinal dimensions. In these cases a number of analytical approaches

may be called for. These include:

1. Reduction of the attitude scales (concerning reactions toward the brand) to a unidimensional scale. In its simplest form this can be done by submitting the subjects by attitude data matrix to a principal component analysis. The factor scores for the first unrotated factor can serve as a unidimensional score (Green and Tull, 1978). Individuals can then be assigned to attitude groups such as "high," "medium," and "low" according to the magnitude of their factor score.

   Another approach to the establishment of a unidimensional attitude scale is based on consumers' preferences for the given brand compared to its competitors. In this case one can follow a simple assignment rule such as "most preferred," "among the most preferred but not first choice," and "among the least preferred." If a simple assignment rule is to be followed, one might as well follow the Sherif and Sherif (1967) model and ask the respondents to classify the brands into three groups—"acceptable," "indifferent," and "unacceptable."

2. Given that most attitudes can hardly be represented as a single dimension one may elect to use some multidimensional scaling or factor analysis procedure to identify the relevant attitude dimensions. In utilizing these approaches, one could conduct either a total sample analysis or, alternatively, a separate analysis for each purchase segment identifying the idiosyncratic attitude profile of each segment. In this latter case the segment profiles can be compared via some factor matching procedure. To classify the respondents into attitude segments one could submit the factor score matrix to any of a number of clustering procedures. If the INDSCAL model and algorithm (Carroll, 1969) is used individuals can be assigned to attitude segments ac-

cording to their weight on the relevant dimensions (assuming a two-dimensional solution respondents can be classified, for example, into high and low on each dimension, hence resulting in four attitude columns against the three purchase rows). Or, if more dimensions are involved the individuals can be clustered based on the commonality of their attitude weights.

3. Another approach to identifying the attitude dimension of the vulnerability matrix is to develop a measure of the strength of the favorable attitude toward the given brand.

   This measure of strength can be developed from the posterior probability output of a multiple discriminant analysis of relevant attitude statements as the predictor variables against the purchasing patterns of brand *i* (regular customers, occasional customers and infrequent customers) as the criterion variable.

   The posterior probabilities of the respondents (those belonging to the three segments) are provided as regular output of most multiple discriminant analysis programs and the respondents can be ordered from high to low and split into any number of desired categories.

4. A somewhat more direct approach to the establishment of the strength of loyalty to or vulnerability of a brand is by using conjoint analysis (Green and Wind, 1973, 1975b). Following this approach one can present the respondents with trade-off options between various brands and monetary and time costs (or any other relevant factors). The data collection procedure can follow either the combination of attributes approach (middle panel of Exhibit 6–6), when the combinations are selected following some orthogonal array design (Green, 1974), or the two-variables-at-a-time approach (top panel of Exhibit 6–6). For

further discussion of these approaches see Green and Wind (1975b).

   After using one of these approaches the respondents' data can be submitted to a conjoint algorithm analysis, and for each respondent utilities can be established for the *value* of the given brand. (The lower panel of Exhibit 6–6 presents some illustrative output). Given these data, the respondents can be categorized according to their utility scores for the given brand. The utilities are then used as the measure of the attitude dimension in the vulnerability matrix.

5. A more recent approach is the one based on multidimensional contingency table analysis. This approach when applied to the vulnerability matrix requires separate segmentation of the respondents based on their purchase and attitude patterns. Each respondent can thus belong to one purchase segment and one attitude segment in a two-way multidimensional contingency table. Having classified the respondents as belonging to various purchase and attitude segments one can utilize (a) log-linear models for the study of the mutual association among the purchase and attitude bases for segmentation and (b) logit analysis for the prediction of the probability of membership in the purchase segments given knowledge of the consumers' membership in the attitude segments. The approach was proposed in a broader context of segment congruence analysis by Green and Carmone (1976), who applied it in the segmentation of the auto insurance market utilizing four sets of variables (bases for segmentation)—the respondents' insurance companies, image of the companies, and psychographic and demographic profiles.

There are, of course, other approaches to determining attitude dimensions. In selecting a research approach one should consider, how-

EXHIBIT 6–6

A CONJOINT ANALYSIS APPROACH TO DETERMINATION OF STRENGTH
OF LOYALTY

DATA COLLECTION FOR CONJOINT ANALYSIS (TWO VARIABLES AT A TIME):
BRAND VERSUS COST AND BRAND VERSUS TIME

Brand \ Cost	10% above current price	Current price	10% below current price
i			
j			
k			

Brand \ Time	10 min search	15 min search	No search
i			
j			
k			

THREE ILLUSTRATIVE STIMULI FROM THE "COMBINATION APPROACH" TO CONJOINT
ANALYSIS COLLECTION PROCEDURE

Brand i	Brand j	Brand k
10% above current price	10% above current price	10% below current price
No search	No search	10 min search

ILLUSTRATIVE OUTPUT OF UTILITIES

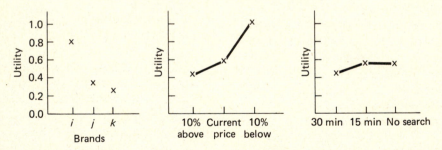

ever, some of the research complications involved in the development and implementation of the vulnerability matrix. Some of the major research considerations are:

1. What conceptual and operational definitions of purchase categories should be employed? And do these definitions take into account factors such as:

   • The probability of purchase of the given brand;

• The multiple brand purchase and usage phenomena as they relate to an inventory of brands (Wind, 1976);

• The volume of purchase (number of units bought per given period of time).

2. What conceptual and operational definition(s) of the attitude dimension(s) should be employed? And do these definitions take into account factors such as:

   • The perceived cost of switching a brand;

- The perceived value of remaining with the same brand or store;
- The reasons for temporary switching (price deal, out of stock, desirability for variety, etc.) and permanent switching (dissatisfaction with a brand, the preference for a new brand, etc.);
- The likely presence of considerable market heterogeneity with respect to the attitudinal dimension(s), requiring an attitude segmentation for each of the purchase pattern segments.

3. What is the required research design for collecting the "right" data on both the purchase and attitude dimensions. More specifically:

   - What is the relevant unit of analysis—the individual respondents, the "buying center" of the household, or the entire household?
   - What is the relevant scope of the vulnerability matrix? Should it be for the total market purchases of the given brand or should it be conducted separately for various market segments (e.g., geographical areas, demographic segments, etc.) or buying and usage occasions (e.g., purchases of food or beverage for on- versus off-premises consumption, usage of a brand for a particular occasion such as soup for lunch versus soup for a between-meal snack). Furthermore, how are the boundaries of a market to be determined? Should it include products perceived by consumers as substitutes for the given brand or should it include a broader range of competing products which might be similar in function or form (e.g., should the market share for Maxim be based only on its share of freeze-dried coffee, all instant coffee, or all coffee?)
   - What is the relevant time dimension?

Given that management's concern is with the expected future behavior, how should the data on past and present behavior and attitude be utilized? Should actual purchase behavior and current attitude data be supplemented with data on consumers expected behavior (and attitudes) under a variety of future scenarios?

- How can one assess the effect of distribution (product availability), communication effectiveness (consumers' awareness of the product) and competitive activities (the number of available brands, their market share and marketing activities) on the nature and size of the vulnerability segments?
- Can the concept of a vulnerability matrix be applied to *new* products? More specifically, can one establish the likelihood of loyalty or vulnerability at the product concept stage? At the trial stage? Only at the repeat-purchase stage?

An initial attempt to utilize the brand-vulnerability matrix was undertaken in a segmentation study for a frequently-purchased product. Preliminary results suggest that considerably more diagnostic insights into the brand's market position (and hence operational guidelines for the design of its marketing strategy) are gained by assessing the size and characteristics of the various cells in the vulnerability matrix. In this case, a number of segments were identified:

1. Those customers who are currently using the brand regularly, are satisfied with it and are likely to continue to use it;
2. Those customers who are currently using the brand on a regular basis but are likely to reduce their consumption or even change to another brand altogether. This group was further divided into three segments reflecting different reasons for and strength of dissatisfaction;

3. Two segments who are using the brand occasionally and are likely to increase their usage of it if some changes are to be introduced (reduced price for one of the segments and availability in an additional distribution outlet for members of the second segment).

4. A segment of customers who are using the brand occasionally and are likely to reduce their consumption due to greater attraction of some competing brands and products;

5. A segment of nonusers who might be inclined to try the given brand if certain features were added to the product;

6. A market segment of nonusers with strong negative attitudes toward the brand, and low likelihood of changing their attitude.

In addition to information on the size of each segment, the study provided detailed information on the product usage and demographic and attitudinal profiles of the segment members. Such detailed information can help management design reinforcement or change-oriented marketing strategies aimed at the selected target segments.

Further application of this concept, coupled with experimentation with the suggested research approaches, should be undertaken. Such experimentation should not pose serious problems since the data required for the vulnerability matrix are collected in most consumer studies. It would require, however, supplementary attitudinal data, if purchase data such as MRCA is to be utilized.

The development of a vulnerability matrix as part of the product's situation analysis provides an important supplementary insight into the product's market position.

Furthermore, changes in the vulnerability matrix measured over time could be useful for monitoring the impact of the marketing strategy of the firm and its competitors.

Product positioning by segment analysis. To provide further guidelines for the firm's marketing strategies within the strategic product/market area, management may want to supplement the product vulnerability analysis with additional diagnostic inputs. Among the more useful diagnostic analyses are those that relate to the product's competitive position—product positioning and brand switching matrices—and on the effectiveness of the firm's various promotion, distribution, and price strategies.

In the context of the product planning model, product positioning—the perceived strengths and weaknesses of the product compared to its competitors—occupies a central role. It serves as an integral part of situation analysis as well as a cornerstone of the firm's product/marketing strategy. Having discussed the concept and measurement of positioning in Chapter 4, it is necessary only to review the role of positioning in the firm's situation analysis.

A situation analysis of the current and anticipated position of the firm's products cannot be limited solely to the evaluation of the products on a number of key objective performance measures (via the product performance matrix) but should be supplemented with information on the way consumers and other relevant publics perceive the strengths and weaknesses of the product category and its various brands.

As such, product positioning by relevant market segments is an essential part of the situation analysis. If conducted on an ongoing basis, positioning information can provide useful insight into the effectiveness of the previous product/marketing strategies of the firm and how it fared in various segments compared to its competitors and their actions. Consider, for example, the battle between Datril and Tylenol. McNeil Laboratories' Tylenol was the leading nonaspirin analgesic when Bristol–Myers introduced Datril, a similar but considerably cheaper product. The initial positioning of Datril emphasized that the only difference between it and Tylenol was price. Datril was one dollar less. Tylenol retaliated by matching Datril's price. The rapid Tylenol response led Datril, less than a year after its introduction, to change its positioning to "Datril delivers more pain relief faster than Tylenol." Again Tylenol retaliated, this time by reformulating Tylenol in less-tightly-pressed tablets, which enabled Tylenol to dissolve as fast as Datril. (*Advertising Age*, April 26, 1976).

The stated position of the two brands is clear, yet the management of these brands would require information on how consumers perceive each brand. Is Datril seen as cheaper or a better buy? Has the Tylenol retaliatory campaign restored it as a favored brand, or has it lost some of its strong franchise? Is it seen as being as effective as Datril? And what were consumers' reactions to Tylenol's price-cutting? Was it welcomed or did it reduce consumers' confidence in a brand that for years charged them too much?

The Datril–Tylenol competition was accompanied by a number of new product introductions. Sterling Drug introduced nonaspirin Bayer; Miles Laboratories test marketed Actron, a nonaspirin pain reliever; Thompson Medical introduced Dantol, another product in this category; and American Home Products and Enderin increased promotion on two existing nonaspirin analgesics. The positioning of Datril and Tylenol cannot be evaluated, therefore, in a vacuum, but should take into account these other changes in the competitive environment.

Furthermore, understanding consumers' positioning of these products would not suffice. For example, until the Datril advertising campaign, Tylenol had never advertised to the consumer, limiting its advertising to physicians and pharmacists. Hence, the positioning of Datril, Tylenol, and the other products in this product category should be established for all three publics—consumers, physicians, and

pharmacists—and within each public the positioning should be considered by relevant market segments. If one were to take the point of view of Tylenol, for example, some of the relevant segments could be:

- Tylenol users who did not try Datril
- Tylenol users who are also users of Datril
- Previous users of Tylenol who switched to Datril and no longer use Tylenol
- Nonusers of Tylenol

Similarly, the physician population can be segmented within specialties into those prescribing Tylenol and those who don't.

These and other bases for segmentation can be selected by management as needed, and positioning information collected and analyzed separately for each segment.

This analysis of the relevant market segments should incorporate an explicit analysis of the current and anticipated trends in the demand of each potential segment as well as the selection of target market segments.[3]

Corporate and industry resource and constraint analysis The product performance matrix, product positioning, and brand vulnerability analyses all measure the competitive strength of a given product. If applied to competitive products as well as the firm's own products, these three analytical tools provide valuable insights into the market structure and into the performance of the firm's products and competitors. Yet, these analyses are limited to the current and anticipated performances of *existing* products. It does not reveal the potential strengths and weaknesses of the firm and its competitors. Hence, the situation analysis should be supplemented with an explicit analysis of corporate and industry resources and

---

[3]For a discussion of some of the key issues involved in market segmentation studies see Wind (1978a).

constraints aimed at assessing the firm's unique competitive advantage. Such analysis should incorporate:

- *Corporate and industry technology and production facilities.* Current technological strengths and weaknesses as well as trends in technological developments. The technological competitive advantages of the firm as well as the production (facilities, personnel, and material) resources of the firm and its competitors.

- *Corporate and industry investments and financial resources.* The cost of entry to and exit from the industry, the importance of capital investment and its sources, the rate, size, and type of assets and especially the liquid financial resources available to the firm and its competitors.

- *Corporate and industry management style and competitive profile.* The management style, capabilities, and competitive actions of the firm and its competitors.

- *Corporate and industry marketing strengths and weaknesses.* The size and type of marketing resources and activities of the firm and its competitors: the nature and strength of the firm's distribution system, corporate image, and advertising and sales promotion clout, for example.

Most important in the analysis of the marketing strength of the firm compared to its competitors is a rigorous analysis of the relative importance of each of the pertinent marketing variables for determining the firm's sales, market share, profits, and overall positioning. This analysis can take the form of a number of critical equations (for sales, market share, and profits) that, in the simplified linear case, would be of the form:

$$Y = a + b_1A - b_2P + b_3D ,$$

where Y = sales, market share or profits,

A = appropriate measure of advertising and promotion (e.g., dollars spent on advertising)

P = appropriate measure of price (e.g., actual price),

D = appropriate measure of distribution (e.g., percent of effective distribution obtained),

b_1, b_2, b_3 = parameter values estimated separately for each equation.

This linear equation, although often used, is not conceptually defensible (for most product marketing situations) beyond a relatively small range of the relevant variables. A log model is more appropriate and should therefore be considered.

PRODUCT/MARKET PORTFOLIO ANALYSIS AND DECISIONS

As discussed in Chapter 5, the analysis of the product/market portfolio is a necessary part of the firm's overall situation analysis. It also provides the basis for the major product marketing decisions of the firm with respect to the direction and nature of growth.

Having completed the situation analysis, the next step in the corporate product/market planning requires a series of decisions concerning the product/market portfolio. These decisions encompass two major areas:

1. The desired pattern of growth—the determination of the magnitude and nature of change in the target market and/or the product technology employed.

2. The desired product portfolio—the determination of an optimal portfolio of products. (This was discussed in Chapter 5.)

Pattern of growth   One of the basic product/marketing decisions of any firm is the

EXHIBIT 6–7

A SIMPLIFIED PRODUCT/MARKET MIX MATRIX

Market \ Product	Present	New
Present	Market penetration 1	Product development 3
New	Market development 2	Diversification 4

determination of the desired product/market mix. In its simplest formulation (as presented in Exhibit 6–7) the choice is between four basic strategies:

1. Further penetration of existing markets with the firm's current product line (cell 1);
2. Entry into new markets with the current product line (cell 2);
3. Development of new products for entry into the current markets of the firm (cell 3);
4. Development of new products for entry into new markets (cell 4).

The selection of any of these directions requires careful analysis of the projected sales, profits, and growth of the firm's current products in its target segments (via the product performance matrix), an assessment of the strengths and weaknesses of the firm's current products (via product positioning and vulnerability analysis) and the potential strengths and weaknesses of the firm and its competitors and the unique competitive advantages possessed by the firm (via the corporate and industry resource analysis).

Furthermore, each of these directions of growth is associated with varying degrees of risk. Obviously, the market penetration strategy (cell 1) and its associated vertical and horizontal integration strategies are associated with the lowest risk. Next in amount of risk is either the market development (cell 2) or product development (cell 3) strategy. The level of risk of these two strategies depends on the relative strength of the company's marketing versus technological skill. On the average, however, a recent survey found that 44.4 percent of 37 diversification strategies aimed at common customers and differentiated technology were successful compared to only 36.4 percent of 23 diversification efforts in which the strategy was based on common technology and different customers. The same survey also revealed that in 49 pure diversification strategy cases (cell 4)—both customers and technology were new—the success rate was only 35.4 percent.

The decision on direction of growth cannot be limited, however, to the simplistic four cells suggested in Exhibit 6–7 and should recognize various gradations of newness for both products and markets. An example of a somewhat more realistic set of alternatives based on two levels of newness is presented in Exhibit 6–8.

Yet, even this framework, which suggests eight distinct strategies, does not take into account the fact that "increasing technological newness" is not unidimensional and can be accomplished in a variety of ways ranging from

EXHIBIT 6–8

A 3 × 3 PRODUCT/MARKET MIX MATRIX

Source: Reprinted by permission of the *Harvard Business Review.* Exhibit from "How to Organize for New Products" by Samuel C. Johnson and Conrad Jones, (May–June 1957). Copyright © 1957 by the President and Fellows of Harvard College; all rights reserved.

Product objectives	Increasing technological newness		
	No technological change	**Improved technology** To utilize more fully the company's present scientific knowledge and production skills.	**New technology** To acquire scientific knowledge and production skills new to the company.
No market change		*Reformulation* To maintain an optimum balance of cost, quality, and availability in the formulas of present company products. Example: use of oxidized microcrystaline waxes in Glo-Coat (1946).	*Replacement* To seek new and better ingredients or formulation for present company products in technology not now employed by the company. Example: development of synthetic resin as a replacement for shellac in Glo-Coat (1950).
Strengthened market To exploit more fully the existing markets for the present company products.	*Remerchandising* To increase sales to consumers of types now served by the company. Example: use of dripless spout can for emulsion waxes (1955).	*Improved product* To improve present products for greater utility and merchandisability to consumers. Example: combination of auto paste wax and cleaner into one-step "J-Wax" (1956).	*Product line extension* To broaden the line of products offered to present consumers through new technology. Example: development of a general purpose floor cleaner "Emerel" in maintenance product line (1953).
New market To increase the number of types of consumers served by the company.	*New use* To find new classes of consumers that can utilize present company products. Example: sale of paste wax to furniture manufacturers for Caul Board wax (1946).	*Market extension* To reach new classes of consumers by modifying present products. Example: wax-based coolants and drawing compounds for industrial machining operations (1951).	*Diversification* To add to the classes of consumers served by developing new technical knowledge. Example: development of "Raid" — dual purpose insecticide (1955).

Increasing market newness

the utilization of new natural resources and new engineering-oriented technological processes, to new products or even new marketing technology. Similarly, the "increasing market newness" is multidimensional and depends on one's definition of a market such as the socioeconomic class reached by a retailer (Saks Fifth Avenue versus Korvettes) or the needs served (IBM's shift from computers to data processing to information handling to problem solving, IBM 1970 annual report). Hence, the product/market mix decisions should be based on an explicit definition of the relevant dimensions of the product and market, definitions which meet the firm's objectives and resources.

Having selected any new product option in the product/market mix matrix, the question is whether the firm should attempt to develop it internally or go the merger-and-acquisition route. Acquisition can be of the *technology* required to develop and manufacture the product internally or of the entire manufacturing facilities and operations of the new product. Similarly, if a new market is selected in the product/market matrix, the firm can develop its own marketing operations or acquire a marketing/distribution arm to reach the desired market.

The decision of internal development versus external acquisition of technology, marketing, or overall operations should not be treated lightly. Nor should it be assumed that internal development is the most desirable one. Management should choose between the two options. The considerations underlying the acquisition decision is further discussed in Chapter 8.

In determining the desired pattern of growth (and product portfolio), it is useful to decide on the desired level of innovativeness and leadership. To establish market leadership, it is helpful to be the innovator. This implies a high-risk strategy which, if successful, leads to high rewards. It also implies considerable technological and marketing investments. A lower-risk strategy is following the innovator. The success of such a strategy depends on the resources (especially marketing resources and strength) of the firm relative to those of the innovator, and the ability to identify "winning" products early after their introduction (ideally, even at a test-market stage). The lowest-risk strategy, often also the one with the lowest reward, is a "me too" strategy in which the firm enters an established market. Necessary conditions for success in this strategy are some differentiating characteristics (usually in the form of lower price, although other unique positioning might offer longer-term advantage).

ANALYZING AND IMPLEMENTING CHANGES IN THE CURRENT PRODUCT/MARKET PORTFOLIO

Having completed the environmental, situational, and portfolio analyses, management is in a position to determine its desired product/market portfolio. As discussed in Chapter 5, the three major portfolio decisions involve the addition of products either via internal or external (merger and acquisition activities) development, the modification of existing products, and product deletion or business divestiture. Since internal and external new product development activities are discussed in Part II of this book, and the product modification and deletion decisions in Part III, the discussion in this section will be limited to a brief outline of some of the major issues involved in analyzing, designing, and implementing changes in the current product/market portfolio. These issues include the impact of any change on:

- The perceived positioning of the remaining products and businesses;
- The organizational members and their behavior;

- The competitive action;
- The reaction of other relevant stakeholders;
- The overall objectives of the firm.

DEVELOPMENT AND EVALUATION OF A PRODUCT/MARKETING PROGRAM

Having identified the corporate objectives and resources, assessed the current and anticipated environment, completed the situation analysis, and made the basic decisions concerning the desired product/market portfolio, management is now ready to embark on the determination of the product/marketing program.

The product decisions of the firm—the desired positioning of each product in the product line and the specific product mix offered (as a result of product modifications, deletions and additions) for the selected target segments—cannot be determined in isolation from the firm's marketing decisions. Hence, the product decisions are incorporated into the firm's product/marketing program.

The program itself is based on two parts: (a) the product decisions involving the determination of the desired positioning by segment as well as the specific product mix to be offered and (b) the related marketing decisions of price, distribution, personal selling, and advertising and promotion. Since any management can easily generate a very large number of possible product/marketing programs, it is essential to quantify the expected outcome of each of these programs. This suggests the need to undertake a conditional forecast of sales, profit, and market share for each product/marketing program. The programs should be further related to the corporate strategic plans and budgets to assure their compatibility with the corporate objectives and resources. Furthermore, since the product/marketing plans are designed for the

future, they should take into account alternative scenarios, and for each one a series of contingency plans should be designed.

The selection of a plan should be in accord with our planning principles, i.e., the selection of a program which:

- Assures the achievement of the corporate and product objectives of sales, profit, and market share;
- Is compatible with corporate resources;
- Takes into account the needs and behavior patterns of all the participants in the relevant marketing system;
- Is consistent with the most likely scenario;
- Is consistent with the "adaptive experimentation" philosophy.

Having selected the "best" product/marketing program (consistent with management assessment of the most likely scenario), it is essential to select a set of other "best" programs for each of a number of possible scenarios.

Having completed the selection procedure in accordance with management objectives, an evaluation mechanism should be designed to provide continuous feedback on the performance of the product/marketing program and provide the input for continuous adjustment and changes aimed at achieving the firm's long term objectives.

The program development and evaluation procedure thus requires two distinct sets of skills: (a) creative skill to generate the best possible set of programs based on the information generated in earlier stages of the planning process and (b) managerial/evaluative skill with respect to the overall performance of the program.

The generation and evaluation processes are closely related, however. Identifying weaknesses or strengths in a strategy may lead to modified or new strategies which eliminate the weaknesses or capitalize on the strengths of any of the given strategies.

ORGANIZATION, IMPLEMENTATION, AND CONTROL OF A PRODUCT/MARKETING PROGRAM

The final stage in the product planning process is the organization for implementation and control of the product/marketing program. These activities involve both the organization, implementation, and control of the product/ marketing program and the planning (and organization) of the product/marketing planning process itself. Chapters 16 and 17 focus on the organization issues for new product development and the management of existing products, and Chapter 18 concentrates on the control aspects of product performance.

The remainder of this section, therefore, highlights some of the key issues involved in the planning of the planning process itself. These issues involve determination of:

• The *amount* of (financial, material, and personnel) resources required to implement the planning process, summarized in monetary terms over time;

• The *type* of personnel and other resources required for the implementation of the planning process. These resources should be specified beyond their monetary equivalent to assure the ability to mobilize them. If personnel have to be transferred from other parts of the corporate operations, a decision should be made whether the transfer can be made with no negative results to the overall operation of the organization;

• The *time horizon* for implementing the plan and the specific schedule involved;

• The *criteria for allocation* of the various resources to specific projects, allowing for slack time for unexpected planning needs.

As a guideline for the determination of the amount of resources required for the product planning task, one could develop various formulas based on factors such as corporate objectives, the product plan, the number of new products/businesses that would be required to achieve the corporate objectives, the timing involved between initial idea generation and market entry and the rate of return after market entry, the risks, effect, and cost involved in the development process, and number of products/markets that have to be explored before one product will be entered successfully into the target market. Fogg (1976), for example, proposed a formula for determining the number of planning analysts required for a company with stated dollar growth goals.[4] His formula as developed for Corning Glass Company is:

$$\text{Number of planners} = \frac{GPY}{\bar{P}M}\frac{1+Q}{N},$$

where G = sales gap to be filled at the end of the planning horizon (the difference between what sales are desired and what sales would be without new businesses),

P = success rate—the number of markets that must be studied before one is successfully entered,

Y = number of years during which planning and entry into new businesses must be accomplished to fill the sales gap at the end of the planning horizon,

$\bar{P}$ = expected penetration of new markets 5–7 years after entry,

---

[4]This model is presented with the permission of C. Davis Fogg, President, Consumer Products Division of Bausch and Lomb, Inc.

M = average size of new markets that will be considered,

Q = percentage of planning time (on the average) that will *not* be devoted to specific market planning but is devoted to other planning tasks, such as goal setting, opportunity identification or marketing support of existing businesses,

N = number of projects that can be handled by one analyst per year.

These and similar formulas can serve as an initial guideline for the determination of the size of the planning staff and as a rough basis for determining the budget of the planning function.

The approach used is less important than management's recognition of the importance of planning the product/marketing planning function, and appropriate control mechanisms assure the feedback needed for monitoring and evaluation of the strategies and their changes.

Whether one accepts the planning concepts and models presented in this chapter or any variant of these, a key question facing management is how to *implement* a planning process, and, in particular, strategic planning. (Note that the close link between tactical plans and budgets facilitates the implementation of a tactical plan which tends to follow a relatively tight time schedule and which, in most cases, does not depart markedly from the plans of the last year.)

Some of the major difficulties with the implementation of *strategic* (long-term) planning are:

- Lack of an incentive to undertake it. This problem is largely due to the great corporate mobility, which makes it unlikely that a successful long-range planner will see the fruits of his or her efforts.

- Management's natural tendency to focus on short-term problems and "fire-fighting" activities.

- The reluctance in many corporations, especially those with a lean management level, to "sacrifice" their key executives by removing them from line operation to strategic planning. Even "strong" managers in a strategic planning role are frequently diverted to firefighting activities.

- In contrast to the "tangible" nature of short-term planning, which usually produces results reasonably soon, long-term planning is viewed as having less tangible benefits and, hence, is assigned a lower priority.

- Lack of a clearcut criterion for evaluating and rewarding long-range planning activities.

- The interrelated nature of the planning process. Although the planning model (Exhibit 6–1) is presented as a linear system, in effect it is a complex web of relationships requiring much interaction among steps. Consider, for example, the setting of objectives. Although this is the natural starting point for a system, it is not uncommon for the objectives to be changed after a systematic review and analysis of the environmental forces and the situation analysis of the firm. Similarly, the product portfolio analysis and decisions often result in changes in objectives and especially the tradeoff between short- and long-term objectives.

Given these and similar difficulties in implementing a strategic planning model, what guidelines can be offered? Aside from the obvious "motherhood type" requirement of management recognition and participation, it seems that the most useful way of implementing a strategic planning process is by:

1. Generation of corporate-wide demands for guidelines from a strategic plan. This re-

quires the acceptance of the premise that the responsibility of every manager includes planning (even at the tactical level) and the need to link the tactical plans to the overall strategic plans of the firm.

2. Development of an incentive system for strategic planning efforts. This can be done by advancement and financial rewards as well as by increasing the *status* and social rewards associated with planning.

3. Development of, and adherence to, a strict planning schedule with deadlines, and assignment of tasks to participants.

4. Recognizing that one of the major benefits of strategic planning is management interaction throughout the planning process,

and lowering the expectation for short-term results from long-term strategic efforts. In this context, it is usually helpful to schedule, in accordance with point 3 above, periodic planning meetings for the relevant management group. Such efforts can be viewed as a "team building" process leading to better communication, interaction, and understanding among the relevant management group.

These "cues" should obviously be adjusted to the idiosyncrasies of the company and the personalities of the participants. There is no single solution to the implementation process, and a trial and error orientation would probably be the most beneficial in the long run.

CONCLUDING REMARKS

Product planning is an integral part of any corporate strategic and tactical planning. The planning concepts discussed in the first section of this chapter can help managers design and implement a better planning process. Yet, there is no single approach to planning. The planning model proposed in this chapter is one way of organizing the inputs, decisions, and activities required to design and implement the necessary product decisions of the firm. In considering the design of a product planning system, the idiosyncrasies of the firm and the personality and characteristics of management should be taken into consideration. In addition, the selected approach should not be cumbersome and a bureaucratic obstacle to management. There should be no planning for the sake of planning. Rather, a planning system should be designed so as to facilitate the natural incorporation of planning concepts and approaches in

the managerial process. Effective planning requires considerable effort in the collection and analysis of data. It is essential to avoid a situation in which an elaborate planning process is designed (with its associated time and money costs) without having a real impact on the managerial decision process.

To make planning an integral part of the managerial decision process is not a trivial task, and it requires the ability to pick out the critical elements of planning and put them together in a coherent framework which is fully accepted and implemented by management.

A complete understanding of the material discussed in this chapter would include also the ability to design a product planning process for any firm. Consider, for example, that you were given the managerial responsibility for a company of your choice, and design for it a product planning process.

7

Product Planning and the Changing Environment

Introduction

Model of Environmental Effects

Environmental Forces

Social/Cultural Environment
Political/Legal Environment

Market Forces

Consumers
Intermediate Marketing Organizations
Competition
Other Marketing and Related Organizations
Suppliers

Environmental Forecasting

Time Series Analysis
Leading Indicators and Pattern Analysis
Econometric Models
Diffusion and Envelope Curves
Morphological Analysis
Delphi Procedures

Utilization of Environmental Inputs

Concluding Remarks

INTRODUCTION

The product planning model discussed in Chapter 6 (Exhibit 6–1) suggests the importance of continuously monitoring the firm's external environment. The model singled out four aspects of the environment: (a) the market (consumers), (b) the competition, (c) the marketing environment, and (d) the external social/cultural, economic, political/legal, technological/scientific, and ecological/physical environment.

Since some of the major approaches to the study of the attitudes and behavior of consumers and competitors were discussed earlier in the context of the behavioral science/consumer behavior foundations of product policy and positioning, the discussion of these two major forces is grouped, in this chapter, with the other market forces—intermediate marketing organizations, suppliers, and other marketing and related organizations.

The nature of the environmental and market factors, their pattern of change, and their impact on the product decisions of the firm are briefly discussed in the third and fourth sections of this chapter. The conceptual relationship among these forces and the process through which they affect the product decisions of a firm are discussed in the second section. The fifth section focuses on some of the more common approaches to the assessment and forecasting of environmental changes. The final section proposes an approach to the integration of environmental inputs in product planning.

MODEL OF ENVIRONMENTAL EFFECTS

The five environmental forces—economic, political/legal, social/cultural, scientific/technological, and physical/ecological—and the four market forces—consumers, competitors, intermediate marketing organizations, and suppliers—are closely interrelated. Their major impact on the product decisions of the firm is through their influence on the organization's objectives and constraints and the decisions of the relevant decision making unit (DMU) within the firm. These influences are in terms of:

- A set of *values* which guide the preferences, choices, decisions, and actions of the DMU;
- *Constraints* on both the product decisions and the resources (natural, human, technological, and financial) available to the firm for the production and marketing of its products and services, as well as suggested *threats* to the continued product performance;
- Suggested *opportunities* for new product ideas, product positioning, and product modification or repositioning.

The set of values and the current and anticipated environmental constraints, threats, and opportunities affect the firm's product decisions, including decisions relating to the design and introduction of new products as well as the modification and even deletion of existing products and services.

The environmental factors are closely interrelated. The modern industrial society is characterized by not only rapid economic growth, but also by associated widespread education, advanced scientific and technological developments, and a psychology and behavior of affluence. Hence, the analysis of any factor has to take into account its impact on, and how it is affected by, the other factors. Such a cross-impact analysis is important if one is to understand the full scope of the effect of the environmental factors on the product decisions of the firm.

Exhibit 7–1 presents a simplified model of the environmental factors and their impact on the product decisions of a firm. The model focuses on the current and anticipated environmental conditions and actions and adds to the

more commonly-mentioned environmental forces two other factors: (a) the shareholders and other stakeholders (e.g., outside directors) who affect the organizational objectives which, in turn, can affect the corporate environment for acquisitions, the development of certain products, etc., and (b) the decision-maker's reference group(s) whose values may have a strong influence on the decision-maker's product decisions.

Viewing the stakeholders as a separate environmental force can be misleading however. Every one of the environmental (e.g., eco-

EXHIBIT 7–1

SIMPLIFIED MODEL OF ENVIRONMENTAL EFFECTS

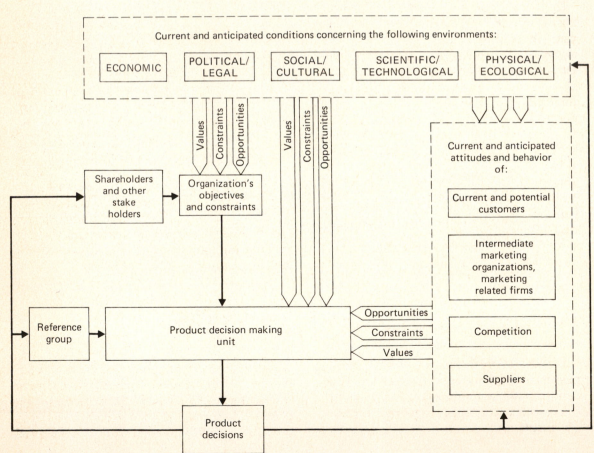

nomic, political, and others) and market forces (e.g., competitors, suppliers, and others) operate through some institutional/organizational form. Hence, most of the environmental impact on a firm's product decisions is through a continuous series of interorganizational negotiations, transactions, and influence patterns.

The relevant environment and stakeholders are a part not only of the domestic environment but also of the global environment of the firm. The growing importance of the multinational corporation and the resulting increasing dependency of a firm's operations on resources, clients, and other publics in a number of countries, make it essential to monitor not only the current and changing domestic environment but also the global environment.

This social/cultural, legal/political, technological/scientific, economic, and ecological/physical *global environment* is of great importance in shaping the firm's opportunities and constraints and in many cases has considerably greater impact than the domestic environmental forces. The tendency to include foreign governments and other multinational institutions and organizations among the important stakeholders of the multinational firms is not surprising.

Furthermore, given the multinational nature of many corporations, the organization itself and its product-decision-making unit may be divided among a number of countries. The unique characteristics of the multinational environment and its impact on the international product and service decisions are briefly discussed in Chapter 19.

An important aspect of any model of environmental effects is the recognition of interdependencies among the model components. Most of the environmental forces are related, and their interactions should be considered.

The energy versus environment battle, for example, has shown the pitfalls of a product policy which takes only one of these potent forces into account (e.g., atomic power plant construction or the gas-guzzling autos of the early 1970s), as well as the advantages of products which reconcile these apparently conflicting forces (e.g., solar energy, gas-efficient autos, recycled aluminum).

A second type of interaction is the impact the product decisions of firms may have on the environment. This two-way interaction is especially critical for the larger firms whose product decisions may have a greater and more immediate impact on the environment.

A major thrust of the model which should guide the firm's activities in collecting and analyzing information on the relevant environmental forces is the need to focus, not only on current environmental conditions, but also on expected environmental *changes*. The remainder of this chapter focuses, therefore, on the environmental forces, approaches to forecasting changes in them and a proposed approach for the design of an operational system for the monitoring and utilization of environmental inputs in product planning.

ENVIRONMENTAL FORCES

Any attempt at describing in one chapter the nature of the various environmental forces and their impact on the various product and service decisions of a firm is bound to be superficial. No single chapter can serve as a substitute for a detailed and comprehensive study of environmental forces and an analysis of their impact on the product decisions of a firm. Management should, therefore, set up two related systems: (a) as an integral part of its marketing information system, it should design a system for collecting, analyzing, and disseminating data on the current and anticipated environmental forces facing the firm, and (b) it should set up a system to analyze and evaluate this information in terms of the likely impact of various environmental forces and trends on the firm's product and service decisions.

The objective of this section is to highlight some aspects of the social/cultural, political/legal, economic, scientific/technological, and physical/ecological environments which should be monitored and examined continuously.

SOCIAL/CULTURAL ENVIRONMENT

Social/cultural forces have long intrigued researchers in multinational business and the social sciences. Both researchers and practitioners of multinational business have attempted to describe and understand the various social/cultural forces which differentiate one country from another, and examine the effect of these forces on business decisions including, of course, product-related decisions. Factors often included in these analyses are:

- Dominant cultural values (toward wealth, achievement, consumption, etc.)
- Life style patterns
- Religious and ethnic values, beliefs, and attitudes
- Class structure and social mobility
- Literary level and educational characteristics
- Attitudes toward risk taking and change

Whereas the focus of most multinational business researchers has been on the description of the relevant intra-sociocultural environment of various countries and the intercultural (international) environment, social scientists have focused primarily on the *changing* social/cultural environment. This concern with change has covered four major aspects.

The first approach involves research-based projections concerning the changing social/cultural environment. An example of such projections is the *Yankelovich Monitor* (developed by Yankelovich, Skelly, and White, Inc.) which, based on a survey of a national probability sample, provides an annual report on the changes in people's values, concerns, needs, and interests. The *Monitor* reports on the size, rate of growth, composition, and manifestation of social trends. Forty-three social values and trends were identified by the *Monitor* and changes in these reported annually. In addition, recognizing the heterogeneity in values, the *Monitor* has identified a number of value segments. In 1978, for example, they identified six segments:

The New Conformists This group represents 19 percent of the population and is the youngest segment. Members of this group are committed to economic advancement and seek personal fulfillment through self-expression and a wide variety of experiences. They exhibit a strong focus on self.

The Forerunners Representing 14 percent of the population, this group is the best educated and most affluent of the value segments. Members of this segment are committed to achievement but not at the expense of those pursuits and interests that provide a greater degree of personal fulfillment.

The Aimless Comprising 17 percent of the population, this group is relatively downscale in terms of education and income. They have little direction to life goals and exhibit a loose, unstructured life style with hedonistic overtones and little concern about the future.

The Materialists This group—15 percent of the population—holds values which are traditional in character. Personal fulfillment and self-expression are not as important to members of this segment. Yet, they do accept a less structured and rigid life style.

The Moralists Representing 19 percent of the population, this older, middle-class group of consumers is the last bastion of Protestant Ethic values. They are supporters of the work ethic, of traditional concepts of the family, and of sexual morality in general. They appear to be adopting some of the new values that relate to self-fulfillment and expression.

The Retreaters This group comprises 16 percent of the population and is the oldest, most downscale, and most resistant to new social values. The Great-Depression generation, this segment feels that the means to advancement are largely out of reach for them. They are committed ideologically to Protestant Ethic rewards, but do not actively pursue them.

Whereas most other studies of the changing sociocultural values of society stop with the reporting of the nature and magnitude of the changes, the *Yankelovich Monitor* provides an additional set of output: their assessment of the implications of the changing social trends and values on the general future business outlook, and the marketing directions for various consumer products and services. These implications vary in their specificity, validity, and insightfulness. Focusing on product categories (rather than individual brands), they do offer a useful source of hypotheses.

In addition to the *Yankelovich Monitor*, there are a number of other available data sources on consumer life style and values. These include the more recent Stanford Research Institute's VALS study; surveys done by the University of Michigan's Survey Research Center; MRCA's life style battery (which focuses on food-related life style dimensions, but is the only data base that allows for continuous monitoring of changes in life style at the individual household level); and the annual life style data collected by Needham, Harper, and Steers.

As with the *Yankelovich Monitor*, all these data sources can provide hypotheses on changes in consumer attitudes, values, and life style characteristics. The degree to which any of these data bases allows for testing of specific hypotheses depends on the specific characteristics of the data and the degree of access to the data.

The second approach to the study of social change involves speculations on the nature of the future sociocultural environment of our society. These speculations often take the format of popular presentations of the world of tomorrow and include such books as *Future Shock* (Toffler, 1970), and numerous articles in the popular press and scientific publications such as the *Futurist*, the official publication of the Society for the Study of Alternative Futures. Reading of these speculations can provide the product DMU with insights and ideas for new products and services. Consider, for example, the market implications for new products and services of some of the trends suggested by Toffler, such as the rise of disposability—the spread of the throw-away culture, the rental revolution, and as objects, things, and physical constructs are becoming increasingly transient, a greater emphasis is placed on the manufacturing and marketing of preprogrammed "experiences" (such as the experience of a vacation at a Club Mediterranee, the Esalen Institute, etc.). Whereas these and other changes are directly related to the consumption of products and services, consider the impact of some of the expected changes in the family structure leading to what Toffler calls "the fractured family" with the new concept of serial marriages and various forms of subcults, subcultures, and diverse life styles and values.

The third approach to the study of social change involves an in-depth examination of some emerging trends or movements. Traditionally, this included the study of the changes in the organization of the family, the characteristics of religious observance, etc. More recently the focus has shifted to the study of the women's liberation movement, the "drug culture," the "natural products" worshippers, the "environmentalists," and other trends. The study of these movements and trends has been conducted by both the scientific community and the popular press. Following these developments is crucial for the firm's product and service planning since the philosophy and actions of members of these movements may have major implications for their acceptance of products (consider for example the reaction of natural food enthusiasts to food products with artificial ingredients) and likely reactions to new products consistent with the philosophy of the given movement (consider for example nonpolluting products for the environmentalist, hypoallergenic cosmetics for the natural product worshipper, tailored suits for the businesswoman).

The fourth approach to the study of social change is concerned with the examination and understanding of planned and unplanned change, the forces which resist change, and strategies to induce change. The social change literature has encompassed change at the individual, group, organizational, and societal levels and has explored the correlates of a person's, group's, or society's susceptability to change. The correlates of change should be examined individually in each case in order to take into account the idiosyncrasies of the participants, the object of change, and the environmental/situational conditions. Yet, few guidelines can be drawn from the rich social-change literature. Some of the pertinent generalizations are:[1]

1. Within a society, social change is likely to occur more frequently and more readily:
   - In the material aspects of the culture
   - In the aspects close to the society's "cultural focus"
   - In the less basic, less emotionally

---

[1]Most of these generalizations are drawn from Berelson and Steiner (1964, pp. 614–618).

charged, less sacred, more instrumental aspects
   - In the nonsymbolic elements of the society
   - In periods of crisis and stress
   - In the cities
   - The more heterogeneous the society is
   - If the change is not imposed from outside
   - If the change is not imposed from outside
   - If the change does not originate in the lowest social stratum.

2. An individual is more likely to accept a change:
   - The greater his (her) willingness to take risks
   - The higher his (her) educational level
   - The more consistent the change is with his (her) values, life style, and consumption system
   - The greater the social support he (she) perceives the change will get

POLITICAL/LEGAL ENVIRONMENT

To fully appreciate the constraining power of the legal environment, consider some of the following examples and their implications for the production and marketing of existing products, their redesign or repositioning, and the development of new products:

- The Consumer Product Safety Commission has the power to prescribe *mandatory safety standards* for virtually all consumer products (except those for which specific safety legislation exists, such as tobacco, food, drugs, motor vehicles). This includes the power to recall products, such as the five million Mattel Battlestar Galactica toy missiles. Similarly, the National Highway Traffic Safety Administration, based on the Motor Vehicle Safety Act, has recalled products ranging from the 14.5 million Firestone 500 radials to 1.4 million Ford Pintos and Bobcats.

- Numerous states (for example, Oregon, Vermont, South Dakota, Minnesota, and California) have banned or imposed a tax or mandatory deposit on throwaway beer and soft drink containers.

- Various national health insurance programs have been proposed and are still under consideration.

- Labeling requirements such as the FDA's on foods with nutritional claims or foods with added nutrients, the FTC Voluntary Detergent labeling agreement, and the Agriculture Department's proposal for meat-product labeling.

- The FTC's product warranty requirements which include disclosure of written warranty terms, presale availability of warranties, and the minimum requirements for informal dispute settlement mechanisms.

- The increasing number of product liability suits and the difficulties and cost of obtaining product liability insurance. The expenditures on product liability insurance by manufacturers and retailers are increasing constantly and in 1978, according to *Business Week* (1979), they reached $2.75 billion in addition to an undisclosed amount of self-insurance.

- The supporting documents required by the FDA for a new drug, and the lengthy approval procedure.

- The FDA's tendency toward class labeling and generic drug substitution.

These examples and the illustrative legislation listed in Exhibit 7–2 are only a small sample of the current regulatory environment. The growing maze of laws and regulations has led to

EXHIBIT 7–2

ILLUSTRATIVE FEDERAL LEGISLATION OF RELEVANCE FOR PRODUCT PLANNING

INFORMATIONAL

Pure Food and Drug Act (1906) prohibits misbranding of foods and drugs.

Wheeler–Lea Act (1937) Amended FTC Act of 1914 to give jurisdiction over advertising of food, drugs, cosmetics, and therapeutic devices.

Federal Food, Drugs, and Cosmetics Act (1938) gives FTC more authority over packaging, misbranding, labeling.

Wool Products Act (1939) requires labels on wool products to indicate percent of wool, reprocessed and revised.

Fur Products Labeling Act (1951) prohibits false labeling and advertising of fur products.

Flammable Fabrics Act (1953) prohibits manufacture and sale of apparel which is dangerously flammable.

Textile Fiber Products Identification Act (1958) regulates labeling of textile products including synthetic fibers.

Hazardous Substances Labeling Act (1960) regulates proper labeling of toxic, corrosive, and irritating products.

EXHIBIT 7–2 (continued)

Fair Packaging and Labeling Act (1966) requires mandatory and accurate labeling of kitchen and bathroom products concerning content, weight (truth in packaging).

Consumer Credit Protection Act (1968) requires disclosure of credit terms, annual rates and interest, finance charges on loans and installment purchases (truth in lending).

Consumer Protection Act (1970) provides for an individual to file class action suits for damages when deceptive practices involved; but Supreme Court (1974) ruled all members of class must be notified.

Magnuson–Moss Warranty–FTC Improvement Act (1974) provides minimum disclosure standards for written product warranties.

Perishable Agricultural Commodities Act (1974) protects from misbranding of fruits and vegetables.

PRODUCT QUALITY

Pure Food and Drug Act (1906) and the Federal Food Drug & Cosmetic Act (1938). The 1906 Act forbids adulteration of foods and drugs sold in interstate commerce, while the 1938 Act extends it to cosmetics.

Meat Inspection Act (1907) requires inspection of slaughtering, packing and canning.

Poultry Products Inspection Act (1957) upgrades poultry inspection practices.

Noise Control Act (1972) directs the EPA to set noise emission standards for a range of products.

Mobile Home Construction & Safety Standards Act (1974) directs HUD to establish appropriate federal mobile home construction & safety standards.

PRODUCT PRICING

Clayton Act (1914) prohibits price discrimination.

Robinson-Patman Act (1936) prohibits discriminatory pricing and promotional allowances.

Miller-Tydings Act (1937) permits resale price maintenance.

McGuire-Neogh Act (1952) reinstated nonsigners clause of Miller-Tydings Act.

Automobile Information Disclosure Act (1958) requires sticker price and all accessories be posted on car.

PRODUCT SAFETY

National Traffic and Motor Vehicle Safety Act (1966) permits secretary of transportation to issue safety standards.

Poison Prevention Packaging Act (1970) requires safety packaging for products.

Public Health Cigarette Smoking Act (1971) requires labeling of cigarettes as harmful to health.

Consumer Product Safety Act (1972) established the Consumer Product Safety Commission. A 1976 amendment adds that the commission has the power to conduct its own civil enforcement actions.

National Traffic & Motor Vehicle Safety Amendments (1972) encourages experimentation in new safety approaches and low auto emission systems and provides certain exceptions for smaller manufacturers.

Toxic Substance Control Act (1976) regulates commerce and protects human health and the environment by requiring testing and necessary use restriction on certain chemical substances.

Medical Devices Amendment (1976) provides for safety and effectiveness of medical devices intended for human use.

a rapidly-increasing governmental power over business. The general purpose of government's regulatory efforts are allegedly to: (a) maintain competition (note for example the FTC antitrust suit against four major cereal manufacturers—Kellog, General Mills, General Foods, and Quaker Oats—aimed at reducing the number of brands and promoting more generic products and more price competition), and (b) to protect the consumer.

The numerous laws and regulations in the consumer-protection category are, to a large extent, in response to considerable lobbying by consumer groups and the growing consumer movement. The increasing influence of consumerism is clearly evident from various legislative outcomes and the establishment of offices such as the White House Special Assistant for Consumer Affairs.

The enormous complexity and rapid growth of laws and regulations with direct impact on the product decisions of the firm are evident even from a casual observation of the popular press and from a casual examination of the number of federal and state regulations. When considering product recall alone, one finds there are eight federal agencies with recall power. These are the Consumer Product Safety Commission, National Highway Traffic Safety Administration, FTC, FDA, HUD, US Coast Guard, FAA, and EPA (for a discussion of the powers of these agencies, see Guzzard, 1979). It is essential, therefore, when planning product policy, to rely heavily on the advice of the legal department of the firm.

In addition to the legal environment one should not ignore the political environment of the country. This factor, although of major importance to international product decisions, is also of considerable importance within a country. Factors of concern are, for example, the quality, efficiency, and effectiveness of the legal structure; political stability; the political organization of the country (including the distribution of powers among the federal, state, county, and city agencies); the judicial system and its powers and value system; the flexibility of the law and the nature and magnitude of legal changes; and other political factors as they relate to the governmental influence on the other environmental factors and the general business conditions in the country.

SCIENTIFIC/TECHNOLOGICAL ENVIRONMENT

The new industries of the 1970s and 1980s—the polymers and plastics, fiber optics, aerospace and communications—are all integrally science-based. The importance of science and technology to the improved production of existing products, the development of new products, and the overall growth and security of the country is one of the fundamentals of the modern "post-industrial state." In 1975 alone, US companies invested $15.1 billion of their own funds in R&D, and the federal government invested $20 billion more (*Business Week*, June 28, 1976). The link between R&D expenditures and new product activities and successful performance is clear when one examines the top 20 firms in R&D expenditures (which together accounted for more than a third of total R&D expenditures of US firms in 1975)—GM, IBM, Ford, AT&T, GE, Du Pont, United Technologies, Eastman Kodak, ITT, Chrysler, Xerox, Boeing, Exxon, Dow Chemical, Honeywell, Sperry Rand, 3M, McDonnell Douglas, IH, and Westinghouse.

The investment and continuous involvement in R&D activities are crucial not only for high technology firms. Even firms who believe in the "me too" philosophy should monitor the technological environment. Consider for example a toothpaste manufacturer who positioned his product as effective against tooth decay. Recent dental research suggests that within the next decade a vaccine against tooth decay is quite likely. Given such technological developments, what do you think would happen to the sales and profits of the current brand? What actions should the manufacturer take in this case?

Technological factors are important not only in shaping the nature of the supply of products and services (consider for example the availability of computer scientists and the nature of existing production technology) but also in determining the demand for consumer and industrial products.

An important source for technology assessment and forecast is the classified patent search files of the Patent and Trademark Office. The files contain over 22 million technological documents distributed among 100,000 subdivisions of technology. Each year about 250,000 new US patent documents and 280,000 new foreign patents are added to the files, which are restructured to accommodate new technologies and changes in existing technologies. To help disseminate the vast technological data in the files, the Office of Technology Assessment and Forecast issues periodic reports on highly active technological areas, areas experiencing a high level of patenting by foreign residents, profiles of patenting patterns of the residents of selected foreign countries and the US, and comparisons of patent activity with economic activity in selected standard industrial classification categories. In addition, the data base can be used for the production of tailormade reports.[2]

[2]For further information on the data and publications of the Patent and Trademark Office, see the 9th report of *Technology Assessment and Forecast*, U.S. Department of Commerce, Patent and Trademark Office, March 1979.

ECONOMIC ENVIRONMENT

The general economic structure and philosophy of the country (capitalistic, Marxist, or whatever), the monetary and fiscal policy, the inflation and unemployment rates, the economic stability of the country, the nature and organization of the capital markets, interest rates and availability of capital, the size and rate of growth of the country's GNP, income distribution, the rate and nature of industrial expansion, and other economic factors are all important determinants of all aspects of business decisions. Product decisions are no exception. Economic decline such as we experienced during the mid and late 1970s affects the rate of new product introduction, and corporate efforts toward product modifications and product line simplification.

The forces which shape the general business and economic conditions of the country affect the product decisions of the firm both directly (e.g., availability of capital for new product expansion, design of products which can provide the cash flow needs of the firm) and indirectly through its impact on the other environmental and market forces (e.g., on consumers' disposable income and intentions to buy, purchases and inventory levels at the various channel levels, availability of capital for R&D expenditures, the climate for mergers and acquisitions).

PHYSICAL/ECOLOGICAL ENVIRONMENT

Concern with water, air, and solid waste pollution, the protection of the physical environment, energy conservation, and other environmental forces has been among the most notable forces of our time. Ecological concerns and their lobbyists have had major impact on government legislation, business decisions, and consumer values.

Energy Of the various ecological issues, energy shortages and conservation actions have probably had the greatest impact on product decisions. The most notable impacts of the ecological forces have been on the design and positioning of new products. Consider for example the growing emphasis of the automobile industry on gas mileage economy. The shift toward better gas mileage involved major R&D efforts. Yet, even more dramatic have been the R&D and marketing efforts for solar energy. Astronauts use solar energy to generate electricity, and an increasing number of residential and industrial buildings use solar heating. Solar heating not only can help solve the energy crisis and save fuel costs, but it also offers considerable ecological advantages by preventing air pollution or the need for atomic power plants (and their radioactive waste problems). Recognizing the importance of this energy source, government has been a continuous supporter of research on solar energy (spending $300 million in 1976). Advances in solar heating technology would have considerable implications for architectural design, heating for swimming pools, remodeling of existing structures, and numerous other products which can be powered by solar energy. This is all in addition, of course, to the potential for development and marketing of solar power generators and solar based products.

Government concern with energy conservation has not been limited to solar energy. ERDA (The Energy R&D Administration), for example, supports R&D activities aimed at the development of energy-efficient appliances, lighting systems, and heating and cooling equipment. Similarly, the activities of the Office of Energy Administration can have major impact on the product decisions of the future.

Environmental protection The Federal Environmental Protection Agency has been concerned with federal legislation to conserve the environment. Throwaway beer and soft drink containers, for example, were banned from all federal property. The EPA is also actively urging voluntary waste reduction. (A program was established to focus industry efforts on product redesign that enables product reuse, requires less material and energy in manufacture, and assures longer product life expectancy.)

In addition to federal and state legislation aimed at protecting the environment, there are a number of active private environmental groups such as the Sierra Club, the Wilderness Society, and the Wildlife Federation, which have been lobbying for particular environmental protection legislation and action.

Even industry has a nonprofit environmental protection group—Keep America Beautiful, Inc.—which, among other things, has initiated an advertising campaign to combat litter.

The physical environment The product decisions of firms are and should be influenced not only by the environmentalists' efforts to preserve and improve the environment, but also by the actual physical, geographic, and climatic conditions of the environment. These features of a country have a strong impact on the consumption and usage patterns of many products and services. Consider for example the need for air conditioners in Alaska or overcoats in Florida or the product and service implications of the more casual lifestyle found in warmer climates, such as California.

The physical environment should also be considered part of the firm's relevant infrastructure. In particular, it affects the availability and cost of physical resources such as electricity, energy, and water as well as the distribution of human (managerial and labor) resources needed for production of products.

MARKET FORCES

In addition to the impact of the five environmental forces, product decisions are affected by market forces including (a) consumers, their current and anticipated demand for and response to various product and service offerings and the determinants of that demand, (b) various intermediate market organizations, (c) the current and anticipated competition, (d) other marketing and related organizations such as advertising agencies and marketing research firms, and (e) suppliers of the various material, financial, and human resources. The continuous monitoring of these forces should be done regularly and is often included as an integral part of a marketing audit—"a comprehensive, systematic, independent, and periodic examination of a company's, or business unit's marketing environment, objectives, strategies, and activities with a view of determining problem areas and opportunities and recommending a plan of action to improve the company's marketing performance" (Kotler, Gregor, and Rogers, 1977).

CONSUMERS

Input on the current and potential market for the firm's existing and planned products and services requires continuous research effort on the nature of and changes in consumers':

- Demographic characteristics
- Socioeconomic characteristics
- Values and life styles
- Needs for, perceptions of, and preference for (attitudes) existing and potential new products
- Product purchase, usage, and disposal patterns
- Response to marketing variables

Demographic characteristics Demographic characteristics are important indicators of the size and nature of the market. The *size* of the population suggests an upper boundary of market potential for products aimed at the mass market. The *rate of population growth* is an important indicator of market size and stability. The age distribution is a major demographic factor. Many products, such as baby foods, rock music records, and geriatric products are heavily dependent on the size of certain age groups. Similarly, the changes in family composition, such as the increase in the divorce rate (from 2.5 per 1000 population in 1965 to 4.8 per 1000 in 1975) provide important insights into the nature of the market. The geographical distribution and mobility of the population are also important market indicators—note for example the trend toward sunbelt states and its implication for products and services in the states within and outside the sunbelt. Related to the geographical distribution of the market are the population density and degree of urbanization.

Socioeconomic characteristics The current and anticipated socioeconomic characteristics are critical factors in determining consumers' ability to buy new products and services. Overall, two-digit inflation and soaring energy costs have recently lowered the discretionary income. A cover story in a January 1980 issue of *Business Week* focused on the shrinking standard of living. The implications of the worsening economic condition of the country means weak consumer spending with associated shifts in spending patterns and lowered economic growth. Obviously, not all market segments are affected equally, and every firm has to examine carefully the economic projections for various market segments.

One of the major changes of the 1970s has

been in the socioeconomic domain—the flood of women into the work force. This trend and its implications to two-paycheck families and households with a single, female head is predicted to continue through the 80s.

This trend has major impact on other environmental forces. (Consider, for example, the impact of working women (and the changing shopping patterns) on types of retail outlets preferred and the impact on store location and operating practices (evening and weekend hours) and merchandise mix.

Values and life styles   Dominant cultural and subcultural values are frequently important determinants of the consumption and usage pattern of various products and services. Consider, for example, the product implications of factors such as attitudes toward the role of the family, women, and children, and of various values concerning religion (and its various taboos), the role of work, the legitimacy of various leisure-time activities, and the like. Similarly, consider the implications of various life style patterns on the demand for various products and services.

As with the other market factors, values and lifestyles affect not only the demand for products and services but also the nature of the supply.

Needs for, perceptions of, and preferences for existing and new products   The importance of continuously monitoring these factors is hardly debatable and is usually undertaken as part of the monitoring of the firm's product positioning for each of its relevant "need" segments.

Product purchase, usage, and disposal patterns   Where the product or service is already sold, data pertaining to purchase, use, and disposal patterns of the product and its complements and substitutes are crucial for assessing the extent of market saturation and poten-

tial. The analysis of the purchase, use, and disposal patterns of existing products can also serve as useful input to the identification of new product and service ideas. In this latter context, consumption analysis is a frequently-used tool in consumer markets. For industrial products, the presence of certain key user industries can be a major determinant of the potential demand for a product. Input/output analysis can thus be a useful tool for assessing the demand for industrial products and services.

Response to marketing variables   Data on the response function of various market segments (e.g., price elasticities) can be of considerable value as input to the product and marketing decisions of the firm. Most firms do not have easy access to such data. It might be useful, however, to design an adaptive experimental system to collect and analyze such data.

INTERMEDIATE MARKETING ORGANIZATIONS

The distribution system facing a firm—the wholesale and retail organizations—are a critical element of its infrastructure and an integral part of the overall marketing system. Certain convenience foods are typically sold through intensive distribution channels such as supermarkets. If such channels do not exist, management has either to create its own outlets, not enter the given market, or radically alter distribution strategies. The number, size, and type of retail outlets have to be taken into consideration in determining what products or services to offer. Where the distribution structure is highly fragmented, costs of physical distribution, personal selling, and trade promotions are likely to be high. Furthermore, distributor margins are often higher, thus raising retail prices and limiting market penetration. Similarly, services offered by different types of retail outlets may differ. For example, small independent operations may offer poor servicing. Similarly, the absence of discount operations may affect ability to pursue an aggressive pricing policy. Availability of mail-order houses and other nonstore retailers may also provide a low-cost means to tap potential markets. Distribution outlets and a firm's current strength in reaching them are often considered a major constraint on the direction of new product development in the short run.

Changes in the distribution network also have to be taken into consideration. Consider, for example, the changes in the type of distribution outlets, the changes in their offerings and activities, and requirements from suppliers. Development of self-service department stores, or large-scale retail operations such as the French hypermarkets, franchising and the tremendous growth of nonstore retailing (such as telephone and mail-order operations) have changed the range of distribution outlets available for distribution of products to target market segments.

The operating characteristics and offerings of most distribution outlets also have been going through major changes. Evening and weekend hours are now common for many stores and shopping centers. Similarly, twenty-four hour shopping by phone is not uncommon. Prospects for new patterns of shopping with two-way cable TV and home computers are within our reach. Additional changes in the functions of retailers and other distribution outlets relating to discounting, promotion, and advertising activities, etc., place new demands on manufacturers.

In many parts of the world, distribution structures and functions, traditionally an area slow to change, are now evolving rapidly in response to the pressures and stimulation of multinational retail operations, and an increased tempo of social change, generally. In addition, there is an increased recognition that innova-

tive approaches to distribution are as important as product innovation in leading to growth and profitability. Consider, for example, the success of L'eggs Pantyhose, which was the first nationally branded and advertised hosiery to be distributed through food and drug outlets.

COMPETITION

The attractiveness of a given market depends not only on the potential market size, but also on the market share which the company can obtain in that market. An important determinant of this share is the degree of competition. Measures which can be used to assess this include:

Number and size of firms The number of firms selling similar products and services provides an initial indication of the strength and nature of competition in the market. Relatively few large firms may suggest intense competition and, hence, difficulties in market entry. A large number of small firms may suggest a highly fragmented market, and thus greater ease of entry.

Sales analysis Examination of sales or surrogates for sales of potential competitors may further isolate major potential competitors and indicate whether certain firms are likely to dominate the market. Detailed analysis of this type, however, may pose a number of problems in obtaining relevant and accurate data. In many industries, such as insurance, bread, consumer durables, and retail trade, it may be impossible to obtain market-share data. Similarly, in many countries companies are not required to publish sales or operating statements and do not.

Growth rate of competing firms The rate of growth of sales of competing firms may indicate future competitive patterns and major sources of competition and hence may be a useful aspect to examine.

New product activities   A major aspect of the competitive environment with potentially critical impact on the firm's operations and performance are the new product activities of competitors. Most trade publications, such as *Advertising Age*, regularly feature information on expected new products, new product entry to test markets and national or regional introduction of new products. More recently, Nielsen has introduced a weekly publication—*Preview*—which condenses into one source the new product information published in over 40 trade journals, plus information (and photos and ad copy) about new products appearing on shelves, but not in trade journals, as reported by Nielsen representatives worldwide.

Competitive analysis   is one of the most crucial aspects of any environmental and situation analysis. This analysis should be done on a regular basis and not be limited to the traditional industry boundaries. Consider, for example, the competitive environment of a bank. Limiting the examination of its competitors to other banks within the same state might be hazardous, given the increased competition the bank is likely to have from out-of-state banks, S&L institutions, credit unions, brokerage firms and an increasing number of financial consultants. The competitive array might change over time and one of the major objectives of the competitive analysis is to identify the relevant set of competitors and assess the impact of their activities.

The competitive analysis should be quite detailed and encompass all those aspects which could provide the firm with better clues on potential threats and opportunities. These would include information similar to that which is often sought by the firm itself in making product decisions. Namely, information on the competitors':

- Product market portfolio
- Product positioning and market segments
- Marketing strategies and activities
- Financial resources
- Technological capabilities
- Management style (and likely competitive reactions)

In interpreting competitive data, management should be cautious in interpreting lack of existing competition in attractive markets as necessarily implying, in the long run, desirable market conditions. Other competitors are likely to be aware of these conditions and may also attempt to take advantage of them, which may result in intensive future competition.

OTHER MARKETING AND RELATED ORGANIZATIONS

An important aspect of the relevant environment are the supportive marketing and non-marketing organizations. Advertising agencies, marketing research firms, and new product generation and development firms can and do provide useful inputs to the firm's product decisions. Furthermore, certain functions and activities can be delegated to these firms, allowing management to make a *make-buy* type decision concerning the performance of the various product development and management functions within or outside the firm.

Nonmarketing organizations such as transportation companies (rail, air, water, and road transportation), financial institutions, insurance companies, mass media organizations, and the mail, telephone, and utility firms are an important part of the relevant infrastructure within which the product decisions of the firm have to be made. These organizations and the infrastructure they constitute constrain the product decisions and at the same time may suggest interesting opportunities for new products and services. A careful analysis of the current infrastructure and its anticipated change is thus essential for the firm's operation.

SUPPLIERS

The suppliers of resources are important stakeholders of any corporation. The doomsday predictions concerning the state of the world's natural resources have focused attention on these stakeholders and their impact on the firm's ability to manufacture and market their current and new products. Although some of the predictions have been reversed and an increasing number of experts believe that the world's resources are adequate, the concern with the availability and cost of raw materials and capital and human resources is among the major concerns of management. Substitute resources are sought—coal or solar energy instead of oil—and new products which depend less on scarce resources are being developed.

The available (and potential) resources on a worldwide basis should be examined and monitored since they constitute a major constraint on the firm's ability to produce various products. At the same time, they also suggest tremendous opportunities for modification of existing products (with substitute materials) and the development of new products. In this latter case, the resources facing the firm should be considered in conjunction with technological, financial, and market considerations. Rohr Industries, for example, succeeded in shifting its emphasis from total reliance on the aerospace industry to mass transit and other energy conserving transportation systems (*Business Week*, April 14, 1975).

The importance of sources of supply and the tremendous impact suppliers may have on the survival and growth of the firm suggests the importance of interfirm negotiations and the increasing role and importance of the buying function. Research activities aimed at the discovery and purchase of better and cheaper sources of supply should, therefore, be undertaken on a regular basis. Furthermore, the desirability of backward vertical integration should be considered as one of the expansion strategies of firms with strong dependency on outside sources of supply.

ENVIRONMENTAL FORECASTING

Environmental forecasting should provide systems of analysis and data for predicting (a) future environmental changes, (b) cross-impact of changes in an environmental force (e.g., technological changes) on other environmental forces (e.g., ecological, economic, social, and legal environments), and (c) the likely impact of each environmental scenario on the firm's product decisions (e.g., the assessment of future market needs and likely response to alternative marketing strategies under alternative scenarios).

The forecasting techniques that can be employed depend on the environmental force to be examined. Exhibit 7–3 lists some of the major methods used to forecast environmental forces.[3] It is important to note that most of these approaches can be employed for the forecasting of more than a single environmental force.

Long-range environmental forecasting has

---

[3]For a detailed discussion of the various long-term forecasting techniques, see, for example, Martino (1972) or Spencer, Clark, and Hoguet (1961).

EXHIBIT 7–3

APPROACHES TO ENVIRONMENTAL FORECASTING

Forecasting methods	Environmental forces					Market forces				Overall environmental effects
	Economic	Techno-logical	Social/cultural	Political/legal	Physical/ecological	Population and market	Marketing organizations and related institutions	Compe-tition	Supplies	
Time series analysis										
Leading indicators and pattern analysis										
Economet-ric models										
Diffusion and envel-ope curves										
Morpholog-ical analysis										
Delphi pro-cedures										

spread from "think tanks" (Rand, The Hudson Institute, The Institute for the Future, and many other research and consulting firms) to corporate planning departments and government policy makers. Futurism or the study of alternative futures is becoming a recognized interdisciplinary field of study with professional organizations (The World Future Society), publications (*The Futurist, Technological Forecasting & Social Change* and *Futures*), and university programs of study. The concern and interest in the study of the future is clearly evident from the numerous books and articles on the subject. Consider for example the following books: *The Year 2000, The Next 500 Years; Inventing the Future; Beyond Despair: Directions for America's Third Century; The Next 200 Years: A Scenario for America and the World; Understanding Tomorrow; Prognostics: A Science in the Making Surveys the Future; Redesigning the Future;* and many other

explorations and predications of alternative futures.

Futurism is not only concerned with the forecasting of long-range future events, but also with the development of strategies which could help mold the future by proper allocation of current resources to areas with the greatest potential long-term impact on the achievement of the DMU's goals. In the technological forecasting area, for example, an effective forecasting system would not only identify likely technological changes, but would also assess their range of application and effect on other technologies.

TIME SERIES ANALYSIS

The most common and simplest form of forecasting is some form of extrapolation such as time series analysis. Utilized primarily in the forecasting of economic conditions, and population and climatic conditions, time series analysis provides a simple projection of future events, assuming no changes in any of the patterns that governed past events. This assumption, which underlies time series analysis of both the simple linear form (with constant amount or rate of change) and other functional forms, such as the S-shaped logistic curve, ignores any major breakthroughs in technology or other environmental discontinuities which may affect the course of future events. Yet, even in its most simplistic form, time series analysis provides a base projection against which other projections can be compared.

LEADING INDICATORS AND PATTERN ANALYSIS

Leading indicators are among the most popular approaches to the forecasting of economic events. The use of leading indicators is based on finding a data series that shows leads of fixed time periods (such as six months or a year) with substantial regularity for the economic activity of interest. The logic underlying the use of leading indicators is that various economic processes tend to move through the course of the business cycle in consistent, but different, time sequence.

Whereas the use of leading indicators has been limited primarily to economic forecasts, pattern analysis can and has been used to forecast social/cultural and political trends. The essence of this approach is the content analysis of social phenomena (such as newspaper articles, advertisements, political platforms, laws and regulations, or any other area of interest) with the purpose of identifying the major areas of concern (content categories) and their direction, rate, and pattern of change over time.

ECONOMETRIC MODELS

The major forecasting tool for economic forecasting has been the large-scale econometric models such as the Wharton econometric model, the Chase econometric model, and others. These models provide macro level projections and, to a limited extent, projections for various 2-digit SIC industry groups. Recent efforts are also aimed at the development of regional models on the one hand (e.g., the Wharton econometric model for Pennsylvania) and worldwide models on the other (e.g., Wharton's project LINK).

DIFFUSION AND ENVELOPE CURVES

An extrapolation method of special interest is the one based on the concept of "escalation" (Buckminster Fuller and Robert Ayres) which has been developed under the name of envelope curve analysis. This approach plots the best performance of the parameters of any particular invention (e.g., train) or a class of technology (e.g., high speed transportation) over a period of time. The method assumes a final fixed limit (due to intrinsic theoretical limits such as 17,000 miles an hour as the maximum speed beyond which a vehicle could be sent into atmospheric orbit) or an extrinsic stipulated level. Given the final limit, one can plot previous escalations and presumed intermediate escalations by the tangents along the backs of the individual curves. In essence, an envelope curve is a "super" S-shaped curve made up of many smaller ones, whose successive decrease in the rate of growth occurs as the curve approaches its upper limit. Exhibit 7–4 illustrates an envelope curve for a speed trend which was developed by the Hudson Institute, one of the major users of this approach.

EXHIBIT 7–4

ILLUSTRATIVE ENVELOPE CURVE

Source: S.C. Wheelwright, S. Makridakis, "Forecasting Methods for Management, 3rd ed., John Wiley & Sons, Inc., 1980, p. 272. Reprinted by permission.

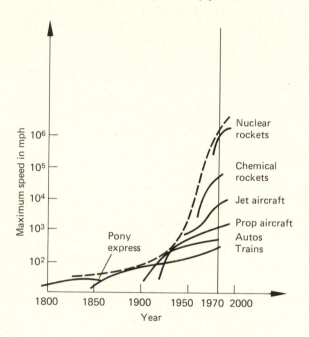

MORPHOLOGICAL ANALYSIS

Morphological analysis offers an orderly and systematic way of looking at all possible solutions to a large-scale problem. Morphological analysis was first developed by Zwicky, who also founded the Society for Morphological Research. The concept underlying morphological analysis is intuitively appealing and in widespread use. What is unique about it is the use of mathematical techniques to assign values to the different parameters of the problem.

"Relevance trees" are a form of morpho-logical analysis which is based on the concept of decision trees. Exhibit 7–5 illustrates a simple relevance tree for methods for the preservation of food nutrients.

Morphological analysis and relevance trees are in a sense systematic mapping devices. The forecasting arises in the effort to unfold the problems, new technologies, and various courses of action over five to ten years or even longer planning sequences.

DELPHI PROCEDURES

The Delphi procedure is one of the more common approaches to the collection and analysis of experts' intuitive thinking and informed opinions. The Delphi approach was developed at the Rand Corporation by Olaf Helmer and his colleagues. The approach is designed to arrive at some sort of panel consensus regarding the likely occurence of alternative events.

In its orginal format the Delphi approach avoided face-to-face contact among the experts, and a series of pollings were done by mail through a central clearinghouse. Yet, in a number of modified forms, Delphi procedures are used in conjunction with group discussions after each round of polling to discuss and air the reasons for various estimates. In addition, some Delphi-type procedures add a series of questions exploring the likely interrelationship among the events (following some format of cross impact analysis) and the likely effect of each event or group of events on the firm's area of operations. Exhibit 7–6 presents an illustrative questioning sequence from a Delphi-type study of the *Future of Retailing* (Robinson Associates, 1973), while Exhibit 7–7 shows some of the results of the study.

The Delphi approach is one of the most appropriate for forecasting political, sociocultural, and technological events.

EXHIBIT 7–5

"RELEVANCE TREE" FOR PRESERVATION OF FOOD NUTRIENTS

Source: D.M. Kiefer "The Future Business," *Chemical & Engineering News*, 47, Aug. 11, 1969, pp. 62–75. Reprinted with permission. © 1969, American Chemical Society.

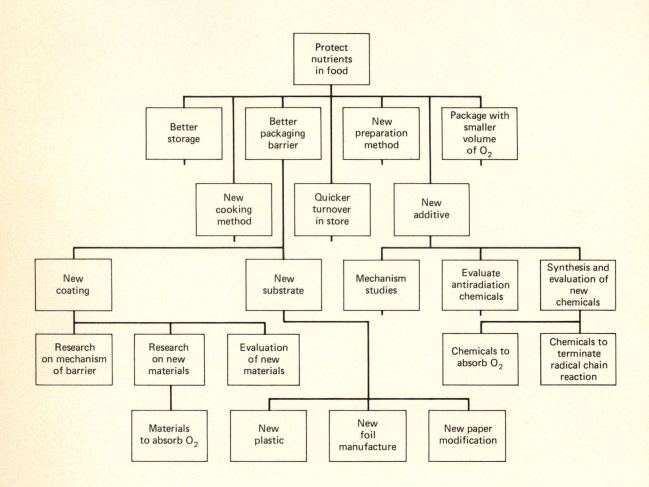

EXHIBIT 7–6

ILLUSTRATIVE QUESTIONING SEQUENCE FOR A DELPHI STUDY OF THE FUTURE
OF RETAILING

Source: *The Future of Retailing*, 1973, a DELPHMAPP® futures study to the year 2000, conducted by Robinson Associates, Inc. for the Bureau of Advertising, ANPA (since renamed the Newspaper Advertising Bureau). This study was replicated by RAI for the NAB, with minor modifications, in 1978.

---

1. The four day work week will be standard in most businesses.

a) Do you feel this event will occur by the year 2000?   Yes _____ No _____

b) If yes, when (what year) do you feel this event will occur?   Year _____

c) Now look at the following scale.

0	20%	40%	60%	80%	100%
Not at all confident	Rather unsure	As likely to be right as wrong	Rather confident	Highly confident	

Place a check mark on this scale that best represents your degree of confidence in the prediction that you have just made.

d) How would you rate the need for retailers to take immediate action (in operations or planning) in anticipation of this event? (Please circle the appropriate number.)

Virtually no changes required now	Small changes required now	Considerable changes required now	Sweeping changes required now
1	2	3	4

EXHIBIT 7–7

MEAN AND RANGE OF YEAR FORECASTED, EXTERNAL EVENTS

(FROM THE DELPHI STUDY ON THE FUTURE OF RETAILING)

Source: *The Future of Retailing*, 1973, a DELPHMAPP® futures study to the year 2000, conducted by Robinson Associates, Inc. for the Bureau of Advertising, ANPA (since renamed the Newspaper Advertising Bureau). This study was replicated by RAI for the NAB, with minor modifications, in 1978.

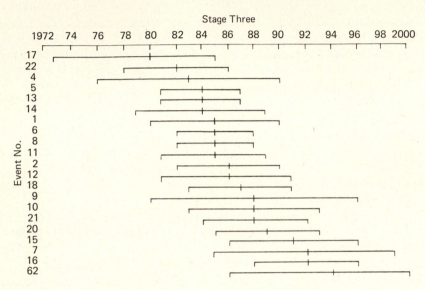

17 Government moves to desegregate schools will be abandoned.

22 Government controls over business.

4 Higher education no longer necessary.

5 A solution for teenage unemployment.

13 Government expenditures will reach 30% of total GNP.

14 Price of most goods include factors to cover cost of disposing of them.

1 Four day work week.

6 At least 25% of population will move every year.

8 Average hours worked will be 32.

11 Federal support programs or a negative income tax will have eliminated poverty.

2 Incomes of $15,000 or more.

12 Percentage of women working will be 65%.

18 Centralized credit and banking system eliminate need for individual store credit cards.

9 Labor productivity renders sustained increase.

10 Services 40% of personal consumption expenditures.

21 50% of U.S. males in 30–34 age bracket will have some college training.

20 Massive infusion of public funds.

15 Wide band cable television.

7 Massive urban reconstruction lures white middle class back to central cities.

16 Two-way communication on CATV.

62 U.S. population will stop growing in actual size.

UTILIZATION OF ENVIRONMENTAL INPUTS

The complexity and rapidity of changes in the environmental forces suggest the need for continuous monitoring of the changing environment and an ongoing analysis of the impact of the various environmental forces on the firm's product and service decisions. Undertaking the second task entails a major commitment to long-range planning and the willingness to allocate the needed resources. The assessment of the impact of the various environmental forces on the product decisions of the firm involves a six-stage process which is outlined in Exhibit 7–8. These phases are:

Phase 1   The examination of the relevant environmental forces and range (as opposed to point) projections of likely changes in them.

Phase 2   Having identified and projected individual environmental forces is not enough. The interdependencies among the environmental forces requires the undertaking of a cross impact analysis. The objective of this analysis is to identify those environmental forces and events which have the greatest impact on other environmental events in terms of increasing their joint effect on the firm's operations and the joint likelihood of occurence. Cross impact analysis should result not only in a better understanding of the interrelationship among the environmental events but also in a greater insight into the *pattern* and sequential nature and impact of the environmental forces.

Phase 3   The next step is integrating the environmental projections and speculations in a series of *scenarios*. The need for this integration is quite evident if one recalls that econometric forecasting, for example, assumes steady-state technological change and no political changes. Similarly, technological forecasts assume to a large extent a static economy. The integrated

scenarios should, therefore, reflect the planner's views of the whole range of alternative future developments for both the short- and long-range planning horizons. Scenarios have been utilized frequently by the Rand Corporation and the Hudson Institute. The scenarios usually start with "surprise-free projections" such as population growth rates, and build outward from there. "Scenarios," according to

EXHIBIT 7–8

APPROACH TO THE UTILIZATION OF
ENVIRONMENTAL ANALYSIS
AND FORECASTING

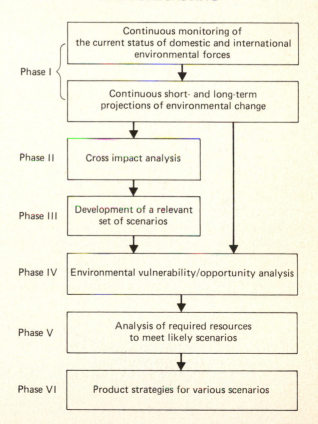

EXHIBIT 7–9

PROJECTED DEVELOPMENTS RELATED TO MEDICINE

Source: J. Maxmen, *The Post-Physician Era: Medicine in the 21st Century,*
Wiley-Interscience, New York, 1976.

Year	Communication and computer technology	Biomedicine and therapeutics	Education and occupations	Miscellaneous
By 1980	Establishment of TV network for MDs Wide use of computers for hospital record storage and data retrieval Routine use of cable TV for medical conferences	Development of useful tissue adhesives to replace sutures Development of tests for rapid diagnosis of viral diseases General availability of home diagnostic kits for urine and fecal examinations	Pharmacist's education stressing his consultant role Unrestricted medical license granted only after completion of residency Ombudsmen widely used in hospitals and clinics	Laboratory creation of protein for food by *in vitro* cellular processess Enactment of national health insurance covering 75 percent of medical costs Noncarcinogenic cigarette
By 1985	Wide use of videophones in hospitals Wide use of computers for medical history taking Portable telephone widely available	Artificial heart implantation Chemical synthesis of specific antibodies Laboratory solution of immunologic rejection problem Development of reliable chemical test for psychotic disorders	Use of teaching machines that respond to a student's answers and to his physiologic state (tension) Virtual obsolescence of the general practitioner The "classical" lecture system ended in 40 percent of medical schools by teaching machines, closed circuit TV, interactive TV, and audio-visual aids	Decriminalization of marijuana Red Cross a semi-public agency in most nations Government established standards for medical computers

Kahn and Wiener (1967), "force one to plunge into the unfamiliar and rapidly-changing world of the present and the future by dramatizing and illustrating the possibilities they focus on."

The scenario development process is lengthy and requires numerous iterations and revisions. Ultimately one should have, however, a set of scenarios which cover the entire range of future events and their interactions (as determined, for example, by appropriate cross impact analysis), almost regardless of their likelihood of occurence.

EXHIBIT 7–9 (continued)

Year	Communication and computer technology	Biomedicine and therapeutics	Education and occupations	Miscellaneous
By 1990	Frequent use of "telemedicine" Wide use of computers to prescribe medications Some people able to have daily checkups of body	Development of artificial colon Development of safe chemical means to reverse effects of arteriosclerosis Chemical cure for schizophrenias Development of anticancer vaccines Wide use of tests in children that will reliably predict their developing some major mental illnesses in adulthood	Wide use of professional nurses to deliver primary care	Failure to consult a computer considered grounds for malpractice suit Water and air pollution problems largely diminished Chemical synthesis of cheap nutritious food
By 1995	General availability of computers to conduct psychotherapy Frequent use of conference videophones for group psychotherapy Extensive use of interactive TV to monitor aged within their homes	Development of drugs that alter memory and learning *In vitro* fertilization of human ovum with implantation into host mothers Development of synthetic blood substitute General availability of physical and chemical means to modify some forms of criminal behavior First human clone	85 percent pharmacists working in hospitals and clinics rather than in drugstores	Techniques that permit useful exploitation of ocean through aquaculture farming, with the effect of producing 20 percent of the world's caloric intake

Having established the set of scenarios, one can proceed to evaluate them on their likelihood of occurence. Scenarios can be specified at different levels of abstraction and generality. In a sense, one may consider a hierarchy of scenarios ranging from the broader environmental considerations (of population, legal, and technological trends, for example) to the more specific scenarios for a given industry or firm. As an example of an industry-specific scenario, let us consider some of the projected developments in medicine (presented in Exhibit 7–9) as seen by Jerrold Maxmen in his book, *The Post-Physician Era: Medicine in the 21st Century.*

Phase 4   Each environmental force (when considered separately) and each scenario has to be evaluated on two key dimensions: (a) their likelihood of occurrence and (b) assuming they were to occur, their likely impact on the firm. These evaluations are mostly subjective and should therefore be made by a number of knowledgeable individuals (either individually or in a group setting). If a Delphi procedure were undertaken on the individual environmental forces, the results of this analysis could be used as the input to this step. Once the evaluations are complete, it is desirable to portray them graphically on the "environmental vulnerability" and "environmental opportunity" matrices presented in Exhibit 7–10.

Having placed all relevant environmental forces and scenarios on these matrices, management now has a way of ordering the environmental forces according to the urgency in attending to them. The most urgent ones are those with low likelihood of occurence and catastrophic impact. Also of high priority should be those events which have high likelihood of occurrence and can offer tremendous opportunities to the firm. Examination of the entries in these matrices also highlights those environmental forces and scenarios which can be ignored in the short run, those with low likelihood of occurrence and limited positive or negative impact.

The categories of the environmental vulnerability and opportunity matrices and the time horizon for analysis (likelihood of occurrence by next year, five years from now, or by the year 2000, for example) should be determined by management to reflect their needs.

EXHIBIT 7–10

ENVIRONMENTAL VULNERABILITY AND OPPORTUNITY ANALYSES

ENVIRONMENTAL VULNERABILITY MATRIX

Harmful impact on the business	Probability that the event/condition will occur			
	0—25%	25—50%	50—75%	75—100%
Catastrophic				
Severe				
Moderate				
Limited or none				

ENVIRONMENTAL OPPORTUNITY MATRIX

Opportunity to the business	Probability that the event/condition will occur			
	0—25%	25—50%	50—75%	75—100%
Tremendous				
Very high				
Moderate				
Limited or none				

Phase 5 Each scenario should next be evaluated carefully with respect to the question of how the firm can best prepare itself today to achieve its future objectives if the scenario were to occur.

A systematic examination of each of the scenarios could provide not only ideas for new products and a listing of existing or expected constraints on the product decisions of the firm but also a set of priorities for allocating corporate resources over the relevant planning horizon. This latter outcome is of utmost importance given that, in its absence, management can invest in projects which, although profitable today, will not help gear the company toward likely future events. The determination of priorities for resource allocation is a critical task, even when one is confronted with a single environmental scenario, since it cannot be isolated from the power struggle among the various stakeholders of the firm. Imagine undertaking this task not under the assumption of a single (let's say most likely) scenario but under the condition of a set of scenarios, each with considerable uncertainty as to its likely occurrence. To overcome this situation one might start by assuming that all scenarios are equally likely and ask what allocation of resources is required

today to keep alive all the necessary options for coping with any of the scenarios. The equal likelihood assumption can then be relaxed and sequential consideration entered. Alternatively, management can employ the Analytic Hierarchy Process (AHP), discussed in Chapter 5 and Appendix A, as a resource allocation procedure that examines the sensitivity of the various allocations to different scenarios and their likelihood of occurrence.

Phase 6 The final stage involves the identification of the most likely scenarios, the development of a set of products and their associated marketing strategies for each scenario, and undertaking a conditional forecast analysis for each strategy.

By following this procedure, management can tie together their short- and long-term marketing strategies with the likely environmental scenarios. This procedure can serve as the basis for the development of contingency plans, as suggested in Chapter 6.

Given the uncertainties involved in any futuristic projections, the scenarios and the individual projections on which they are based should be examined on a regular basis and revised as needed.

CONCLUDING REMARKS

Systematic and continuous short- and long-term environmental analysis and forecasting should be viewed as an integral part of product management. Yet, the magnitude of this task and its costs are not trivial. Successful planning in general and product planning in particular require considerable amounts of information on the environment likely to be faced by the firm. It is critical, therefore, to carefully design an environmental monitoring system. Such a system can start with the monitoring of a few key environmental forces, but even in these

cases, it is strongly recommended that the other forces are at least briefly examined (to assure that no key factor is left out) and a procedure such as the one outlined in Exhibit 7–8 followed to link the environmental information to the planning process. To fully appreciate the importance of such analysis, select a product or firm and identify the environmental forces and scenarios of greatest relevance to them and develop a procedure for integrating information about these forces and scenarios with the planning process for a product.

PART TWO

NEW PRODUCT DEVELOPMENT

One of the major activities of any firm involves the development and marketing of new products and services. Whether a radically innovative new product, a minor modification, or a line extension, successful generation, evaluation, and implementation require employment of a systematic process involving various concepts, methods, and strategies.

The nine chapters in this part encompass the new product activities of any organization. Chapter 8 outlines the philosophy underlying new product development systems and describes a specific approach which serves as a framework for organizing the remaining chapters in this part. The chapter also deals with the make/buy decision, i.e., internal new product development versus a merger and acquisition approach to the development and introduction of new products.

Chapter 9 discusses alternative approaches to generation of new product ideas; while Chapters 10 and 11 concentrate on approaches to the evaluation of new product ideas, concepts, and products. Chapter 10 focuses on consumer based approaches, and Chapter 11 highlights management's role in this evaluation and the essence of economic evaluation of new concepts.

Chapter 12 centers on the product development process itself. Chapter 13 focuses on the generation and evaluation of the marketing program needed to accompany the product. Chapter 14 discusses the test market evaluation stage and its alternatives—pretest market simulators. Chapter 15 focuses on the new product forecasting models which can be employed at any of the evaluation stages (whether one evaluates a concept, a product prototype, or a product and marketing strategy).

The final chapter in this part of the book, Chapter 16, centers on the organization for new products. Organizational design considerations are outlined and alternative approaches reviewed.

New Product Development Systems

INTRODUCTION

Between 30 percent and 40 percent of current grocery sales are in products that did not exist ten years ago. Ten years from now, at the current rate, more than 50 percent of grocery sales may come from products which do not exist today (Grocery Manufacturers Association).

In certain product categories—household waxes and cleaners, soaps, drugs, beauty preparations—products introduced in the past five years account for 13 percent to 90 percent of annual sales (Hesse, 1976).

On the average, in the period 1972–1978, over 6500 new items were introduced into supermarkets (*The Nielsen Researcher*, 1979).

The number of major new products (i.e., excluding modest line extensions and minor design changes) introduced to the market over the past five years varies enormously from one company to another. Some have launched only one or two, while a few have brought out scores or even hundreds. For industrial firms, the median number of major new products introduced during this five-year period was eight; for consumer products firms, it was six (Hopkins, 1980).

Looking at the future, two-thirds of the reporting executives (of 148 companies surveyed by the Conference Board) expect their companies to have an even greater dependence on new products over the next five years (Hopkins, 1980).

This constant stream of new products is unfortunately associated with an extremely high number of new product failures. The exact percentage of new product failures varies considerably depending on the measures used. Booz, Allen and Hamilton, for example, estimate the rate of new product failure among well-managed large companies at 30 percent to 40 percent of all products which emerge from R&D—an estimate consistent with that of a report of the Conference Board (Hopkins and Bailey, 1971); and, in turn, only a small fraction of R&D activities ever results in final products. Even a well-managed and sophisticated marketing company such as P&G had a substantial number (7 out of 16) of test market failures during the 1960s (Vanderwicken, 1974). "The penalties for misjudging the success of a new product are substantial. The expense and risk associated with new product introductions have given added urgency to companies' attempts to prevent costly mistakes" (J. Crichton, President of AAA, in his preface to the AAA *New Product Advertising* brochure). To prevent

such mistakes and reduce the risk and cost of new product introduction, management should design an efficient new product development system, a system which enables the company to achieve its objectives with respect to new products given the risks and costs involved. The system should balance the advantages and disadvantages of internal versus external (mergers and acquisitions) new product development. It should also specify the research steps required and provide guidelines for organizational design for new product development.

The chapter starts with the choice between internal and external development. It follows with a discussion of the major characteristics of external development of both the entire new product development system (mergers and acquisitions) and various stages of the new product development (e.g., licensing of technology). The third section of this chapter illustrates a few of the new product development systems proposed in the marketing literature. This brief review is followed by a discussion of the criteria for design, evaluation, and selection of a system. Following the discussion of these criteria, an internal new product development system is proposed which also serves as the organizing framework for Chapters 9 through 15. The next two sections discuss some of the tools for effective planning and control of the new product development efforts, and how to determine the new product development budget, while the final section briefly discusses the development of a system for innovative versus noninnovative products.

OVERVIEW OF INTERNAL AND EXTERNAL NEW PRODUCT DEVELOPMENT ACTIVITIES

The addition of new products to the firm's product/market portfolio can be done either by internal development or external acquisition. In its simplest form the decision facing management, therefore, is whether to design a system for internal new product development (the "make" decision) or to acquire the new product from outside sources (the "buy" decision). In reality, however, it is not a simple either/or decision since even if management decides on internal development it still can (and under certain conditions should) go outside for a number of phases of the new product development process such as licensing of technology, buying of product design, or packaging or marketing research activities.

The choice between the two major options of internal or external new product development depends on a number of factors which should be considered in making all the make/buy decisions of the firm whether involving the merger or acquisition of a new business, the acquisition of skilled personnel, or the acquisition of some minor technology. These factors include:

The compatibility of the alternative (internal or external development) with corporate objectives Of special importance in this context is the expected level of innovativeness of the resulting products. Quite often mergers and acquisitions involve a greater emphasis on the performance of the acquired firm's current products than on its potential for developing innovative new products. Acquisition of existing product(s) (versus acquisition of a potential for development of new products) is a reasonable course of action under certain conditions such as management preference for lower risk. In fact the acquisition of *potential* has, with respect to the risk involved, more similarity to internal new product development than to the acquisition of existing products.

Timing considerations In general internal new product development is a much longer process than acquisition. Yet, even with a merger or acquisition there are a number of time delays involved with the identification and selection of an acquisition candidate, the negotiation process, the integration of the acquired business with the current organization, and the undertaking of any needed additional research prior to the introduction of the new product to market. Time considerations are often among the major determinants of the make/buy decision. Whenever market conditions, expected environmental forces (such as government regulations or competitive activities), or the idiosyncratic needs of the firm call for a rapid entry into a market, the external acquisition route becomes more attractive.

Cost considerations There is a much higher uncertainty about the cost of development of internal new products than about a merger or acquisition for which the purchase amount is known.

Although the cost of a merger or acquisition theoretically should be higher than the internal costs of developing a similar product (since one pays a premium for immediate possession as compensation for the risks taken by the entrepreneur) this can vary markedly depending on the market price of the stock and idiosyncrasies of the bought firm.

All other things being equal, external new product development will be called for whenever the cost of such acquisitions is significantly lower than the cost of internal development. This simple rule is not very operational, however, since seldom is it the case that all other things are equal. Often there are quality differences between the resulting products, different technical, management and other synergistic effects involved, and the risk factors are quite different.

Many aspects of the decision can be converted into cost figures. A faster entry into market can be achieved, for example, by acquiring an existing product or increasing the efforts (and costs) of internal development. Yet, given the uncertainties involved and the constraints which cannot be easily ignored (for example, government regulations or prestige considerations of management), the make/buy decision cannot be limited to cost considerations.

Technical, management, legal and market feasibility Internal or external development is occasionally chosen not because of clear-cut advantages of one alternative over the other, but rather because one of these options is not feasible. Consider, for example, a situation in which the internal R&D capability is inappropriate for the development of new products requiring different types of technical skills.

Another typical situation is the one in which management cannot allocate the time necessary for the development of new products. Legal constraints on acquisitions might force a company into internal developments. On the other hand, certain market conditions might dictate the need for external acquisition as the only efficient way of gaining access to certain distribution outlets.

The decision to go for external development at the business, product, or technology level versus internal development should take into account the major advantages and disadvantages of the external acquisition route. The major advantages of external development are:

- It enables management to establish an immediate position in the given market without the lengthy delays involved in internal developments, which also implies a relatively immediate stream of revenues. Olympia Brewing Company, for example, to compete effectively in the most competitive beer market, acquired Lone Star of Texas and Theodore Hamm and by these acquisitions improved its industry rank from 9th position (with 2.7 percent share) to 6th position (with 4.2 percent share).

- It buys the necessary (technological, marketing, managerial) skills without the need to develop them internally (which is usually a lengthy and costly procedure).

- It reduces the uncertainties of new product development.

On the other hand, external development has a number of disadvantages:

- Difficulties in finding "right" acquisition candidates.

- Requirements for a high initial investment.

- The needed "fit" between the acquired company and the acquiring firm's product portfolios.

- Most acquisitions, with the exception of those acquired for their technological skills, offer "noninnovative" products and compete in already-established markets.

Given a decision to add new products to the firm's product/market portfolio, management has to undertake an explicit examination of the short- and long-run costs and benefits associated with internal versus external new product development. This analysis should be done at two levels:

- A conceptual level of overall desirability of one mode of operation versus the other.
- A detailed evaluation based on specific information on the expected costs and benefits of alternative internal development systems and external alternatives.

Given that the second level analysis can be performed only if detailed information is available, the decision every firm should make is whether they would at all consider internal de-

velopment or external mergers and acquisitions. If one of these options is conceptually inconsistent with management philosophy no further consideration should be given it in the short run. If both internal and external modes of new product development are acceptable, management should gear for the planning (and possibly also implementation) of two systems—one for internal development and the other for analysis and evaluation of external opportunities. It is thus not an either/or alternative, but rather two options which should be explored in detail prior to a corporate decision on the "best" mix of these modes of development. This mix cannot be determined, however, in an abstract manner since the advantages or disadvantages of merger and acquisition depend on the candidates and the likely synergistic effects between the acquired and acquiring firms. Consider, for example, an acquired company that can offer strong family branding for its products versus the company with no strong consumer franchise.

EXTERNAL APPROACHES TO NEW PRODUCT DEVELOPMENT[1]

External approaches to new product development range from the acquisition of entire businesses to the acquisition of a single component needed for the internal new product development effort of the firm. In most firms the make/buy decision covers all new product development phases of the firm (such as acquisition of a product or product line, or skilled personnel, or technology).

Surprisingly, little attention has been given in the marketing literature or by marketing

practitioners to the systematic identification and evaluation of merger and acquisition candidates. It is not uncommon, therefore, that merger and acquisition decisions, which potentially can have a tremendous impact on the firm's survival and growth, are dominated by financial considerations and top management's preferences.[2]

A marketing approach to merger and ac-

[1]The material in this section is partially based on Wind (1979a).

[2]The limited concern for marketing considerations is clearly evident if one examines the M&A literature (Wakefield, 1965; Rockwell, 1968; Scharf, 1971; Gussow, 1978) and typical M&A checklists. An illustrative checklist is presented in Exhibit 8–14.

quisition and other modes of new product/ market development, such as licensing and joint venture, is both pragmatically important and intellectually challenging.

MARKETING-ORIENTED MERGER AND ACQUISITION MODEL

Approaching the merger and acquisition (M&A) decision from a marketing perspective involves:

1. Top management recognition that the merger and acquisition decisions should not be based solely on financial considerations.

2. An explicit statement of the acquisition objectives, boundaries, and criteria. These should, of course, be consistent with the overall objectives of the firm. In this context, merger and acquisition can be extended to include other forms of *external* development and involvement such as licensing and joint ventures.

3. A continuous update of the M&A objectives and boundaries based on changes in critical environmental conditions and the conditions of the firm.

4. The identification of M&A candidates should not be limited to products but should include all possible activities, such as technology (R&D), manufacturing facilities, and market activities.

5. A sequential procedure for the identification of M&A candidates should be designed to take advantage of available data and reduce the cost of search. Given this objective a common two-step approach includes first a search at the product class level followed by a considerably more detailed evaluation of specific M&A candi-

dates (e.g., brands) within the acceptable product categories.

6. If such a two-step procedure is employed, it is important to further examine each of the rejected product categories for exceptional products; i.e., even though a product category might not meet the firm's M&A criteria, a brand within the category might have considerable potential and meet the M&A criteria of the firm.

7. In the establishment of M&A criteria, some of the *sets* of criteria which should be considered are:

   • Current and projected market (product category and brand) size and growth rate.

   • Current and projected market strength (as assessed by market share of leading brands, the brand-switching pattern and brand vulnerability, and product positioning analyses, if such data are available).

   • Current and projected profitability.

   • Compatibility with the firm's current product mix and desired product/market portfolio.

   • Compatibility with the firm's major strengths (such as promotion, distribution) and the demand it is likely to place on the firm's resources and, particularly, management's time.

   • Degree of external (e.g., governmental) control over the market, product entry, and marketing strategies.

A simplified M&A model which reflects most of these aspects is presented in Exhibit 8–1. Whether one accepts this approach or some variant of it is immaterial. What is critical is the recognition that M&A decisions should not be made only in response to the initiative of some M&A candidates or brokers, but rather be *planned.* Furthermore, there is a need for a sys-

EXHIBIT 8–1

MARKETING ORIENTED M&A MODEL

Source: Reprinted from *1979 Educator's Conference Proceedings,* edited by Neil E. Beckwith, published by the American Marketing Association. Exhibit from "A Research Program for a Marketing Guided Approach to Mergers and Acquisitions," by Yoram Wind, pp. 24–28.

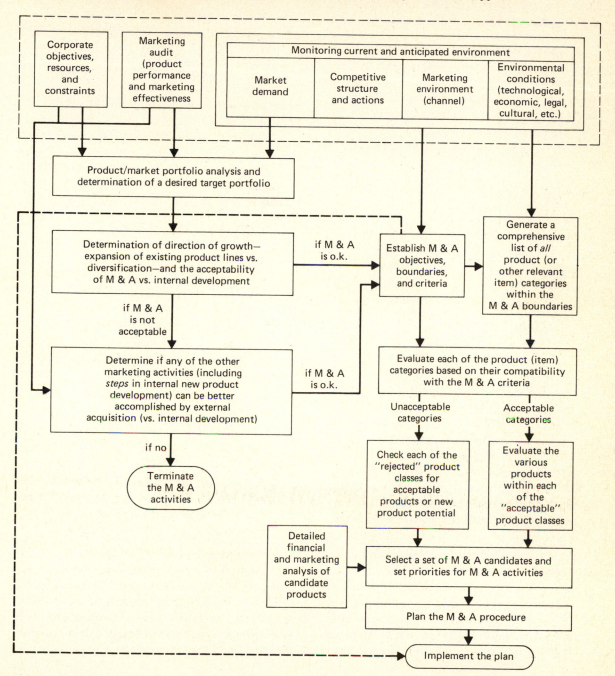

tematic, active approach to the identification and evaluation of a comprehensive set of M&A candidates. Such an approach should be based not only on financial considerations but also on marketing and other relevant inputs.

The historical experience with acquisitions suggests a relatively high failure rate (although not as high as with internal new-product development). To increase the likelihood of success in the acquisition route, detailed M&A analysis along the lines suggested in Exhibits 8–1 and 8–14 is required. Such analysis can be aided by the following conclusions as to some of the characteristics of mergers and acquisitions with high likelihood of failure:

- *Type of acquisition* In an early study on mergers and acquisitions, Kitching (1967) found that there is a high probability of failure in conglomerate-type mergers (customers and technology different from those of the buying company)—42%; a high failure rate in concentric marketing acquisitions (same customers as buying company but different technology)–26%–and concentric technology acquisitions (same technology as buying company but different customers)—21%; the lowest failure rate in horizontal acquisitions (same industry as buying company)—11%; and no failures at all (although representing only 3% of a very small sample) for vertical integration in which the acquisition is of a major supplier or customer of the buying firm. These findings were further supported in a study of international acquisitions (Kitching, 1973).

- *Size* In his 1967 study, Kitching found that in 84% of the failures, the acquired company's sales volume was less that 2% of the parent company's at the time of acquisition. This conclusion was further supported by his subsequent study of European acquisitions in 1973.

- *Market Share* Kitching's (1973) European study found that the probability of success is almost directly related to the share of market purchased. Acquisitions with market shares of less than 5% had over 50% failure rate. In contrast, acquisitions with over 50% share had only about 25% failure rate.

- *Profitability of the acquired firm* Similarly, the higher the profitability of the acquired firm, the higher the chance of success. For example, Kitching (1973) found that the success rate for highly profitable firms was 67% compared to 36% for firms with low profitability.

- *Management characteristics* In his 1967 study, Kitching identified a number of management characteristics which contribute to the success or failure of acquisitions. While he did not qualify these factors, his discussion places great emphasis on them. Consider, for example, the following illustrative conclusions:

  The quality of management talent determines the success or failure of the venture.

  Most managers feel that synergy is not inherent in a situation but rather a product or result of superior management.

  The sum of management skills must be greater than the joint management task.

  The most successful acquisitions seem to be distinguished by specific relationships between the parent company management and the subsidiary management.

Such historical analysis of successful and unsuccessful M&A is helpful in suggesting some of the characteristics that should be examined in making the M&A decision. Yet, in many situations they should be viewed only hypothetically, given the idiosyncrasies of the parties and conditions involved.

MARKETING RESEARCH PROGRAM FOR MERGER AND ACQUISITION ACTIVITIES

A necessary condition for the feasibility and success of a marketing-guided approach to M&A is the design and implementation of a marketing research program. Such a program, not unlike the research programs for new product development (discussed in Chapters 9 through 15) or product deletion (discussed in Chapter 18) can vary markedly from one company to another, reflecting the idiosyncrasies of the company, the individuals involved, their preferences, and the situational variables operating at the time the system was designed. No single, "ideal" approach can, or even should, be advocated. Rather a research program should be designed that incorporates those research approaches and designs which can provide the necessary information at the desired quality—level of detail, reliability and timing—at an acceptable cost (based on cost versus value of information considerations) while being acceptable to management and implementable by the marketing research function of the firm.

The proposed research program for the M&A activities of the firm is in the final implementation stage in a large packaged-goods firm. It is operational and is presented here as an illustrative approach. This research program is based on two major sets of research activities. The first involves four general marketing research phases which, although critical to the M&A decisions, are general in nature and serve as useful and critical input to other decisions of the firm. The second set of research phases is specifically designed for the M&A decision. The general marketing research phase includes a system for monitoring changes in the environment, marketing audit procedures, determination of corporate objectives, resources and con-

straints, and a product/market/distribution portfolio analysis. These procedures were discussed earlier in this book; the thrust of this section is, therefore, on the second set of research procedures.

These involve projects and programs which are designed to provide inputs to the M&A decisions. The impetus for the development of such a research program is management recognition that M&A is one of the accepted ways of (a) adding products to the product portfolio of the firm and (b) acquiring outside resources (such as technology, marketing, and distribution outlets). These M&A research programs involve four major research phases:

Establishment of the M&A Objectives and Boundaries Not unlike the establishment of the corporate and marketing objectives and the process of identifying the dimensions of the product portfolio, this phase is based on a series of studies with management. Typically, this phase requires a two-step marketing research approach:

1. Identification of the relevant M&A objectives. This is typically done with some unstructured interactive research approach (e.g., brainstorming) among the relevant group of managers.

2. Assessment of the relative importance of the criteria. In determining the relative importance of the various criteria, conjoint analysis (Green and Wind, 1975b) and the Analytic Hierarchy Process (Saaty, 1977; Wind and Saaty, 1980) have been found to be useful approaches to assessing management trade-offs among the various criteria. The output from such analyses can serve as a basis for discussion among the relevant management team of the merits of the criteria, and not unlike a Delphi procedure, the data collection task can be repeated a number of times until some con-

sensus is reached or clear points of disagreement identified.

In addition to establishing the M&A criteria and
their relative importance, the research task at
this initial phase should include identification
of the M&A boundaries, i.e., which product,
market, and distribution options are clearly unacceptable to the firm. As with the identification
of the M&A criteria, the relevant research approaches involve some unstructured brainstorming-type session with the relevant management team.

**Generation of a comprehensive list of product
(item) categories** Having established the
M&A criteria and boundary definition in the
phase above, the next research task is to identify as complete a list as possible of the products
which fall within the boundaries. (If the M&A
boundaries include technologies or marketing
functions, the research task is similarly the generation of a comprehensive list of types of
technologies and marketing functions.

This stage relies heavily on secondary
sources and involves not only the development
of a list of product (item) categories, but also the
collection of available information about these
categories on the criteria established in the first
phase. Library type research (including search
of sources such as brokerage firm reports, government publications and documents—which
can be obtained under the Freedom of Information Act—and published reports by research
firms) constitutes the major thrust of this research phase. Yet, it must be supplemented
with a number of personal interviews with relevant respondents. These interviews are aimed
at:

• Getting help in isolating sources of information.

• Assessing the relevant characteristics of the
  various product classes on the qualitative

criteria. To the extent that the evaluation of
the product (item) categories requires a
number of qualitative criteria, it is important to use at least two judges and establish
the degree of interjudge consensus.

This stage is the most demanding in terms
of resources and time. To overcome this limitation (especially if the set of items considered is
large and a large number of criteria are used) a
sequential screening procedure can be employed. In this case, the initial data collection
will be only on the few critical variables which if
not met will lead to a rejection of the given item.
Following such initial screening, a full-scale
data collection (on *all* relevant criteria) is conducted for the items which survived the initial
(limited) screen.

Evaluation of the product categories The
second research phase should result in a data
matrix of the n product categories by the k
criteria. This matrix by itself provides useful
information and should be examined carefully
by the relevant management group. If a programmed evaluation is desired, this matrix
should be supplemented by a vector of weights
for the k criteria. Such an evaluation requires,
however, the conversion of the various evaluative items which are orginally expressed in a
number of different units (e.g., dollar sales,
percent growth, number of competitors) into a
common scale. The conversion to such a scale is
essential if the evaluation is to be programmed.
A convenient method of standardizing the data
is by calculating the mean and standard deviations for each variable (across a sample of
products) and converting these data into a
five-point scale in which the mean is 3, one
standard deviation takes the values of 2 and 4,
and two or more standard deviations take the
values of 1 and 5. Following such a conversion
rule one can now consider the calculation of a
score for each product based on its rating on the

five-point scale and the weight of the specific criterion.

In a number of cases, it might be desirable, prior to the calculation of a product class score, to undertake (a) a factor analysis of the criteria and (b) explore the sensitivity of the results to different weighting schemes. In a recent application of this approach, it was found that equal weighting resulted in virtually the same rank order of candidate product classes as the rank order obtained from weighting the criteria by the subjective weights of three judges (rank order correlation of over 0.75).

The evaluated product classes can be classified as acceptable for consideration or unacceptable based on their summary scores. Even if management prefers a ranking of all product classes according to their attraction score (as an indication of the priority of examining each product class), it is still useful to classify the product classes into the two categories of acceptable and unacceptable.

Evaluation of M&A candidates within the product classes   Having classified the product classes into two major categories—"for further consideration" and "for rejection"—the next task is a detailed evaluation of all products (and firms) within each of the accepted product (item) classes. This examination involves additional variables not included in the initial evaluation and a considerably greater amount of qualitative evaluations. These evaluations require further collection and analysis of secondary sources and interviews with both relevant members of management (who are familiar with the various products) as well as informed outsiders.

The result of this phase of the analysis is a sorting of the products within each product class into three categories: (a) for immediate consideration, (b) for possible future examination (keep tracking their performance), and (c) for

of no interest (rejection).

In addition to this detailed analysis, which should be undertaken for all products within each of the accepted product classes, additional analysis could also be conducted on each of the rejected product classes to briefly scan (in a programmed manner) all products within each category to assure that there are no outstanding products hiding in poor-product categories. Such products, if identified, should then be subjected to the same detailed analysis that products within the acceptable product classes receive.

Detailed financial and marketing analysis of the M&A candidates   The preceding procedure can result in a large number of M&A candidates. These candidate products still have to go through a detailed financial, marketing, and legal analysis. Such analysis requires considerable information and, in particular, detailed projections of likely future performance under alternative marketing strategies and levels of effort. In addition, the possible synergistic effects (with respect to marketing, production, and other managerial domains) of adding the product (items) to the current portfolio should be examined. At this stage the nature of the required marketing research activities and outcomes (a set of conditional forecasts) is not unlike the type of information required for the go/no go decision of any new product considered by the firm.

Unlike new products which are developed internally, the analysis of the M&A candidates is hampered in most cases by limited ability to undertake the necessary studies and experiments (especially if the analysis is done without the knowledge of the candidate firm). In fact, the economic analysis is often based on available secondary sources and limited market surveys and experiments. Such procedures, therefore, tend to rely much more on subjective management judgment and rigorous analysis of secondary sources. Despite this inherent limitation of most M&A procedures, positioning studies can offer extremely valuable information on the perceived strengths and weaknesses of candidate products if they are included in the competitive set of products studied.

SOME ILLUSTRATIVE NEW PRODUCT DEVELOPMENT SYSTEMS

New product development systems vary markedly from one company to another. Even within an industry, some companies may have extremely formal and elaborate procedures while others follow sketchy, intuitive, and largely informal new product development systems. Exhibits 8–2 and 8–3 illustrate two new product development systems, one for a consumer firm and one for an industrial firm.

An examination of these two systems suggests a much greater emphasis in the industrial case on R&D activities. Yet, it is important to note that these are just illustrative systems and that the variance among firms within any industry is huge.

This diversity is further illustrated if one examines the new product development system proposed by Gerlach & Wainwright (1968) and presented in Exhibit 8–4.

These and other new product development systems[3] vary in their complexity and specificity and involve a relatively large set of activities which require a considerable amount of human and capital resources.

An informal examination of new product development systems employed by various consumer and industrial firms suggests that many firms do not have a formal comprehensive new product development system, and that most systems, when available, evolved over the years and were not the results of systematic planning. The commonly found new product development processes, not unlike the ones illustrated in the preceding exhibits, have a number of weaknesses:

- The processes tend to start with some form of idea generation with no concern for setting explicit new product objectives.

- The process tends to have one or two stages in which formal economic evaluation is undertaken instead of developing a system in which the economic viability of the new idea/concept/product is examined at each stage in the process.

- Little concern for the design of continuous evaluation systems of the product's performance after its introduction.

- A mix of activities and actors. Given the likely variety in the nature of the actors over organizations and time and the variance in individuals' inclination to undertake various new product development activities, it is desirable to separate the two and propose a new product development only in terms of the necessary activities.

The complexity of new product development activities is rarely captured in simplified flow charts such as those presented in Exhibits 8–2 and 8–3. It might be useful, therefore, to

---

[3]The reader who is interested in examining other new product development systems is referred to: Hopkins (1974); Pessemier (1977); Boyd and Massy (1972); Andrews (1975); Kollat, Blackwell, and Robeson (1972); Urban and Hauser (1980), and most introductory marketing management texts.

EXHIBIT 8–2

ILLUSTRATIVE NEW PRODUCT DEVELOPMENT SYSTEM FOR CONSUMER
PRODUCT (COSMETICS) FIRM

Source: "Evaluating New Product Proposals," *The Conference Board,* 1973, p.2. Reprinted by
permission.

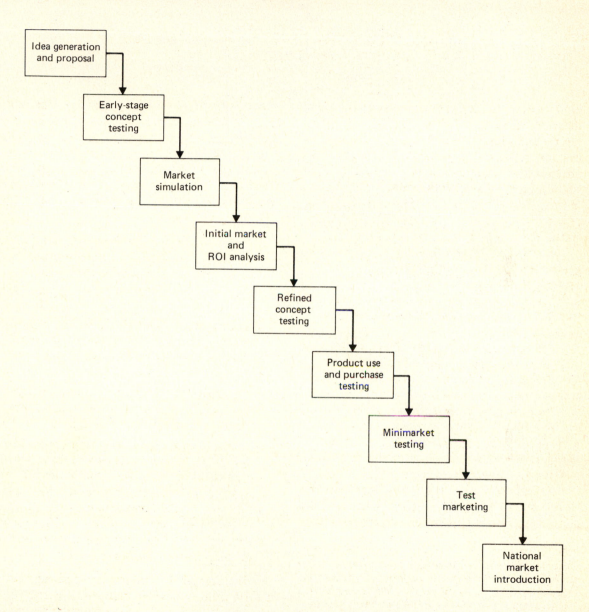

EXHIBIT 8–3

ILLUSTRATIVE NEW PRODUCT DEVELOPMENT SYSTEM FOR INDUSTRIAL FIRM

Source: R.M. Hill, R.S. Alexander, J.S. Cross, *Industrial Marketing*, 4th ed., 1975, p. 208. Reprinted by permission of Olin Corporation.

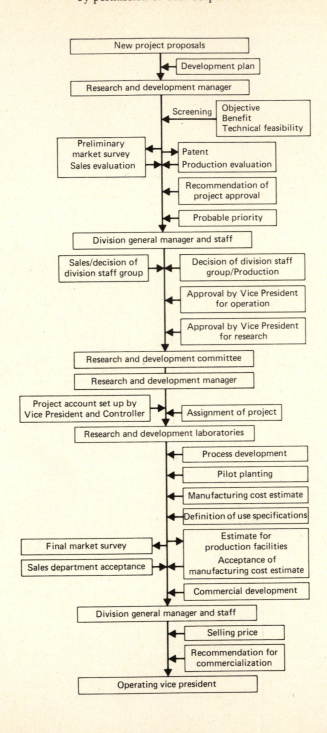

EXHIBIT 8-4

ILLUSTRATIVE NEW PRODUCT DEVELOPMENT SYSTEM

Source: C.A. Wainwright and J.T. Gerlach, "Successful Management of New Products,"
Hastings House, New York, 1968. Reprinted by permission.

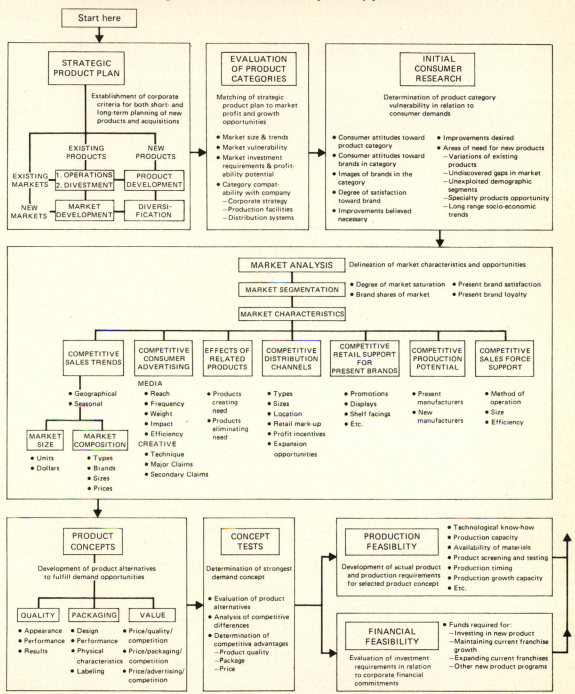

briefly examine the list of activities suggested by Oxenfeldt (1966) and summarized in Exhibit 8–5.

Even though this list is not exhaustive and certainly not the only way of formulating the

process,[4] it starts conveying the range of activities involved and the need for a systematic approach to the design of a new product development system.

The next step toward a better understanding of new product development processes and their management is a specification of the criteria for design, evaluation, and selection of a new product development system.

---

[4]For alternative formulations of the new product development activities see, for example, Harris (1965) and Pessemier (1966, 1977).

EXHIBIT 8–5

PROCEDURES FOR DEVELOPING AND INTRODUCING NEW PRODUCTS

Source: From A. Oxenfeldt, *Executive Action in Marketing* (Belmont, CA: Wadsworth, Inc., 1966), pp. 364–67. © 1966 by Wadsworth, Inc. Reprinted by permission of Kent Publishing Company, a Division of Wadsworth, Inc., 20 Providence Street, Boston, MA 02116.

A. Exploration
1. Determine the product fields of primary interest to the company.
   a) Analyze major company problems.
   b) Evaluate the company's principal resources.
   c) Identify external growth opportunities ready for exploitation, such as expanding markets, technological breakthroughs, or rising profit margins.
2. Establish a program for planned idea generation.
   a) Identify idea-generating groups.
   b) Give them a clear concept of the company's interest fields.
   c) Expose creative personnel to idea-generating facts.
   d) Conduct exploratory technical research.
   e) Utilize team approach.
   f) Minimize distractions from current problems.
3. Collect ideas through an organized network.
   a) Designate an idea-collection point.
   b) Establish comprehensive idea-collection procedures.
   c) Cover selected outside sources of idea.
   d) Solicit ideas actively and directly.
   e) Consider each idea first on a "can-do" basis.
   f) Treat the idea man with care.

B. Screening
1. Expand each idea into a full product concept.
   a) Translate the idea into business terms.
   b) Identify the key business implications of the product concept and its development.
   c) Prepare a written proposal of the product idea.
2. Collect facts and opinions bearing on the product idea as a business proposition.
   a) Select evaluation techniques to fit the specific idea.
   b) Identify the best sources of facts and qualified opinions.
   c) Use quick and inexpensive fact-gathering methods.
   d) Apply strictly the principle of diminishing returns to fact gathering.

EXHIBIT 8–5 (continued)

3. Appraise each idea for its potential values to the company.

   a) Estimate the magnitude of the profit opportunity.

   b) Assess the investment, time, and risk requirements.

   c) Check the idea against other selection criteria.

   d) Provide for subsequent review of ideas discarded or shelved.

C. Business Analysis

1. Appoint persons responsible for further study of each idea.

   a) Select a small product team representing major departments that would be affected by the product.

   b) Tailor team size and composition to the nature of the product.

   c) Select team members on the basis of their self-interest.

2. Determine the desirable market features for the product and its feasibility.

   a) Determine characteristics of the market and its trends.

   b) Appraise both competitors and their products — existing and potential.

   c) Conduct experimental market and technical research within budget limits established for preliminary investigation.

   d) Identify appeal characteristics that would differentiate and sell the product.

   e) Establish feasibility of developing and manufacturing a product with these features.

3. Develop specifications and establish a definite program for the product.

   a) Evaluate various business alternatives to determine desired product specifications.

   b) Establish a timetable and estimate expenditures to evolve this product through succeeding stages.

   c) Reduce the proposed idea to a specific business proposition in terms of time, costs, manpower, profits, and benefits.

   d) Get top-management approval or revision of the product idea in terms of its specifications and program before authorizing the development stage.

D. Development

1. Establish development projects for each product.

   a) Explode the product proposal into as many projects as are required for administrative control.

   b) Schedule these projects within the approved budget and timetable for the product.

   c) Maintain the product team for company-wide coordination.

   d) Pin-point responsibility of all team members and identify them in all reports and records.

   e) Establish yardsticks for measuring performance and progress.

2. Build the product to designated or revised specifications.

   a) Exhaust available information.

   b) Maintain security against outside information leaks.

   c) Continue market studies as a basis for enhancing product salability.

   d) Hold to agreed specifications or make formal revisions by repeating the specification stage.

   e) Keep top management informed; report promptly anticipated changes in objectives, schedule, or budget.

3. Complete laboratory evaluation and release for testing.

   a) Complete laboratory tests adequate to determine basic performance against specifications.

EXHIBIT 8–5 (continued)

b) Provide checks and balances through organization and procedure to assure objectivity of product appraisal.

c) Apply commercial rather than scientific standards to determine product release point.

d) Prepare a management report summarizing the product description and characteristics; report project completion.

E. Testing

1. Plan commercial experiments necessary to test and verify earlier judgments of the product.

   a) Expand the product team, if required.

   b) Outline the nature and scope of the commercialization phase.

   c) Identify the major factors that must prove out to support successful commercialization.

   d) Establish the standards by which product performance and market acceptance will be judged.

   e) Plan test methods, responsibility, schedule, and cost.

   f) Construct a testing program and recommend it to top management for approval.

2. Conduct in-use, production, and market testing.

   a) Continue laboratory testing.

   b) Design and test production facilitites.

   c) Submit products to customer use for abuse testing.

   d) Conduct test marketing programs in line with plans for commercialization.

   e) Survey company, trade, and user reactions to the product and its commercialization program.

3. Make the final product decision; freeze the design.

   a) Interpret test findings objectively; drop or

modify products that fail the tests.

b) Incorporate test findings in product design and commercialization plans.

c) Detail the program for full-scale production and sales, including schedules, budgets, and manpower.

d) Recommend the product and its commercialization program, with full supporting data, to top management for final product decision.

F. Commercialization

1. Complete final plans for production and marketing.

   a) Establish patterns for over-all direction and coordination of the product.

   b) Expand the product team to encompass all departments involved.

   c) Designate individuals responsible for each part of the commercialization program.

   d) Assure that these individuals work out all program details to fit the coordinated plan.

2. Initiate coordinated production and selling programs.

   a) Brief all participating personnel.

   b) Maintain established program sequence and schedule.

   c) Provide feed-back mechanisms for program corrections.

3. Check results. Make necessary improvements in product, manufacturing, or sales.

   a) Make design changes promptly to correct bugs.

   b) Work continuously for cost reduction and quality control.

   c) Shape the product and its program to meet competitive reaction and changing internal pressures.

   d) Maintain necessary team members until the product is a going commercial success, absorbed by the established organization.

CRITERIA FOR DESIGN, EVALUATION, AND SELECTION OF A PRODUCT DEVELOPMENT SYSTEM

The design of a new product development system should follow the steps utilized in the planning of any product/marketing program. As such, it is subject to the general planning guidelines proposed in Chapter 6. In addition, however, it should incorporate the following criteria:

Top management commitment   The success of a new product development system depends to a large extent on the commitment of top management. This commitment is operationally expressed by the allocations of the necessary resources to the firm's new product development activities, as well as the assignment of corporate priorities to new product development efforts.

Selective top mangement involvement   While top management commitment to the product development effort of the firm is critical, their involvement in the process should be quite limited. It is often dysfunctional to get their approval for the results of each phase in the process. Potentially promising ideas and concepts can easily be killed if presented without sufficient support and development for top management approval. It is thus desirable to limit top management involvement to (a) approval of the process, (b) identification of target new product development areas consistent with the desired product/market portfolio of the firm, and (c) a limited number of approval points once the system is in operation.

Development of a continuous new product development system   New product development efforts should not be undertaken on a one-shot basis, but rather as a continuous process. Only a continuous system will allow the company to reap the benefits of cumulative new

product development experience. The need to develop an ongoing *system* for new product development is evident if one considers the numerous cases in which rejected new ideas have been accepted enthusiastically a year or so later, when market conditions changed, a new manager took over, or a competitor introduced a similar product.

Multiple product development efforts   At any given point of time, a number of new products should be in each of the development stages. This follows the old dictum of not putting all one's eggs in one basket. Failing to have multiple new product candidates at each stage of development might result, in the event of a failure of the only new product candidate, in an undue pressure to continue development and even enter the market with a losing product.

Designing a new product development system which allows for a large number of projects at each of the various developmental stages is especially crucial given the high ratio of product failures at each of the developmental stages. Consider, for example, the following estimate based on the experience of a large industrial firm (Fogg, 1976) for the number of projects required to get one market success:

Stage of development	Number of projects needed to get one market success
Idea generation	40
Technical search	10
Technical feasibility	6
Prototype development	3
Pilot to confirm costs	2.5
Product launch	2
Market success	1

The experience of consumer products firms is not much better. General Foods (*Business Week*, 1973), for example, had the following experience over a 10-year period:

	Number of projects
Screening and analysis of new product ideas	600
Development	118
Test market	87
Market introduction	40
Market success	30

To improve the odds of new product success, it is critical, therefore, to have a system with multiple new product candidates at each stage of development.

A modular approach with multiple entry and termination points Any new product development system should enable entry into the system at any point. Similarly, it should facilitate termination at any stage of development if the product evaluation suggests low likelihood of success.

Continuous evaluation at each phase To be consistent with the multiple entry and termination approach, operating management should engage in explicit evaluation of each new product candidate at each stage in the development process. The specificity of the evaluation would be, of course, a function of the information available and the cost and value of a detailed evaluation at the given stage. Yet, even at the very early stages in the development process, it is imperative to evaluate the various new product candidates. This evaluation should encompass technical, legal, and economic feasibility. In fact, early evaluation is especially important since the cost of development and testing increases considerably with time of development. This relationship is clearly illustrated in Exhibit 8–6.

EXHIBIT 8–6

RELATIONSHIP BETWEEN STAGES OF NEW PRODUCT DEVELOPMENT, THE PERCENTAGES OF SURVIVING PROPOSALS, AND COST OF TESTING

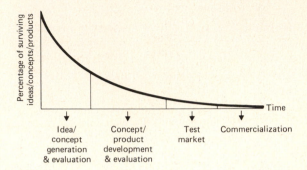

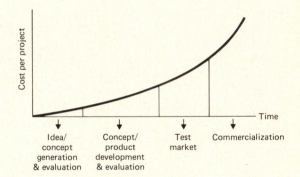

Flexibility The new product development system should be flexible, offering a framework which is adaptable to changes in company needs and environmental conditions. The structure imposed by the system should avoid putting the decision-makers in a straightjacket and restricting their ability to operate effectively within the system.

Application of a market segmentation philosophy Consistent with the marketing orientation, any new product development efforts should be geared toward the satisfaction of the needs of specific target market segments; i.e., new products should not be developed for the "total market" but rather be designed to satisfy the needs or solve the problems of specific and identifiable market segments.

Operational link between marketing, R&D, production, finance, and personnel The new product development system should provide an operational link between the relevant business functions. It should prevent the dominance of one function (whether marketing or R&D) and strive for a balanced and coordinated operation which takes into account the relevant outputs from the various functions and integrates them into a cohesive operational system.

Offer an optimal mix of internal and external development activities The system should allow for a mix of internal and external development activities. New product development can be based on internal development, acquisition, some joint venture or licensing between the firm and an outside firm, or some other mix of internal-external development, which can take place at various stages of the product evolution process. It is important, therefore, to coordinate effectively the internal and external efforts to achieve an optimal mix.

"Fit" the system to the unique firm and product characteristics No new product development system can be transferred directly from one company to another. The fact that a given system proved successful in Company X does not imply that it will be appropriate for Company Y. A new product development system should be designed to fit the idiosyncrasies of the given company—its management style, objectives, resources, and competitive advantages.

Similarly, different products might require a different new product development process. Most new product development systems are based on the decomposition of a product into specific attributes (concept, physical product features, package, name, and the like) and the

design of research projects for the generation and evaluation of these components followed by a final "total proposition" test. Yet, for many "image" products (such as perfumes and cigarettes) this procedure might not be appropriate, and an alternative procedure might be required in which "total propositions" are tested and not individual components.

In designing a new or evaluating an existing new product development system, it is desirable to assess the degree to which these criteria are adhered to. In addition, the system should offer safeguards against the typical causes of new product failure. There are a number of commonly-mentioned reasons. Crawford (1977), for example, content-analyzed eight commonly-cited studies on new product development and identified seven major reasons for new product failure. A summary of these reasons plus those which were identified in various other studies[5] follows:

1. *Lack of meaningful product uniqueness and differentiation.* This involves both cases in which the product offers no differential advantage and those cases in which the value of the differences was overestimated by management (all studies quoted by Crawford).

2. *Poor price/performance value.* Davidson (1976) in a study of 50 successful and 50 unsuccessful products reported that three-fourths of the successful products had better performance either at a higher or the same price, whereas 80 percent of all failures had the same or worse performance at the same or higher prices.

3. *Poor planning* including poor positioning,

---

[5]These studies include those by Abrams (1974), Angelus (1969), Booz, Allen and Hamilton (1968), Constandse (1971), Diehl (1972), Hopkins and Bailey (1971), MacDonald (1967), and Miles (1974). For a review of some of the other studies on new-product success and failure see Cooper (1980).

poor segmentation, and underbudgeting; lack of understanding of consumer needs and the market environment; poor research; or overenthusiasm which crowded out the facts.

4. *Wrong timing* including late entry.

5. *Defensive action by competitors* including introduction of competing products or reduction of price of competing products.

6. *Product performance* including technical problems with products, or unexpectedly high product cost.

7. *Product lacked a champion* or fell victim to company politics.

Most of these problems can be avoided if a system is used which employs the concepts and methods discussed in Chapters 9 through 16 of this book.

PROPOSED NEW PRODUCT DEVELOPMENT SYSTEM

The previous section pointed out that no single new product development model can or should be applied to all companies. Yet, identifying the major phases of a new product development system can serve as a framework for the design of new product development systems. Exhibit 8–7 suggests such a framework. The proposed model is based on four major sets of inputs:

- Corporate and marketing objectives and constraints;
- The firm's strengths and weaknesses (assessed during the corporate situation analysis);
- Information on the current and anticipated market, competitive, and other environmental conditions;
- The desired product/market portfolio.

By using these sets of inputs, management can undertake the first stage of the new product development system—the setting of objectives for new product development (the criteria for new product evaluation) and the selection of the desired mix of internal development and external acquisition activities.

As indicated earlier, the option of external development is not limited to the acquisition of a business or product. Each phase of the new product development process is subject to the make/buy decision or some mix of the two. Whenever marketing research is required (for example for generating new product ideas, concept testing and the like) most firms tend to use some outside research firm. The reliance on outsiders is not limited, however, to the marketing research function and there are companies which specialize in contracted R&D activities or even the entire range of new product development activities.

After determination of objectives (following the procedures discussed in Chapter 6), the next steps in the system are:

1. Generation of ideas
2. Idea/concept screening
3. Concept/product development
4. Concept/product evaluation
5. Development of product/marketing strategy and final product evaluation
6. Design of a system for continuous evaluation of product performance
7. Product introduction

The core of the process is the *development and evaluation of ideas/concepts/products.* These stages can be conducted a number of times be-

EXHIBIT 8–7

NEW PRODUCT DEVELOPMENT SYSTEM

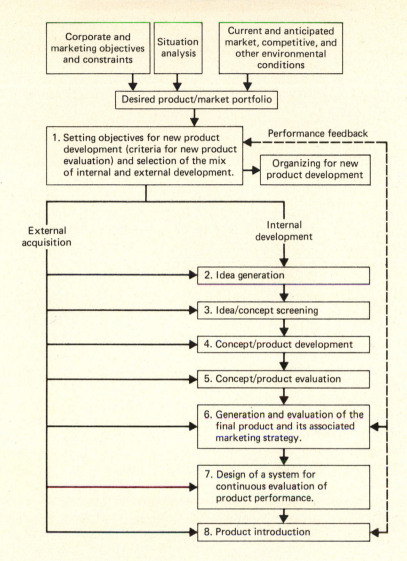

fore the final product evaluation stage and preparation of an introductory marketing campaign for the most promising products. The suggested process includes *all* major phases of a new product introduction system. Yet, in many cases management can decide to use shortcuts. Consider, for example, the routes illustrated in Exhibit 8–8.

EXHIBIT 8–8

SOME ALTERNATIVE ROUTES FOR NEW PRODUCT DEVELOPMENT

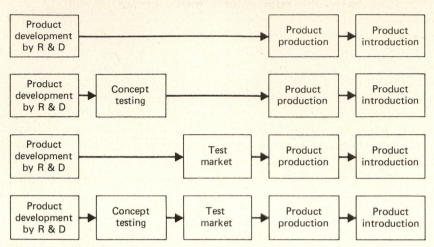

In addition, the selected new product development process should reflect the need for:

1. Detailed studies for the generation and evaluation of various components of a product, such as package or name. A number of studies for any given product candidate can be included as subphases of the concept/product development and evaluation phases.

2. Change in the order and type of studies. As mentioned earlier in the case of "image products" (products which cannot be distinguished by their physical characteristics and need a certain "image" to command a premium price), the new product development process should focus from its inception on the generation and evaluation of total propositions and not components. Such a situation might require a new product development process which skips the idea/concept screening stage and moves directly from an idea generation stage to the development of the idea in the form of an advertisement (reflecting the total proposition) and its testing. This step can be followed with a product development and testing (on the compatibility of various product formulations with the selected product image (as conveyed by the ads).

The selection of any of these or other routes depends on management confidence and willingness to take risks, the information available at the conclusion of the R&D process concerning consumer acceptance, product performance, the competitive environment and likely competitive action, etc.

The new product development process rarely follows the neat flow suggested in Exhibit 8–7. The process is interrelated; it starts at various stages and involves numerous loops and excursions. It is not uncommon to find a new product development process which involves over 20 or even 30 marketing research projects. In these cases it might be beneficial to conduct a careful analysis of the new product development process aimed at assessing the value of each of the projects undertaken and explore the possibility of eliminating some projects or modifying others. In three cases in which such evaluation was undertaken, the number of projects typically undertaken was cut considerably leading to substantial cost and time savings. This experience, which suggests that many new product systems suffer from overkill and excessively long research stages, is not surprising given that most new product development systems are not designed, but rather evolve over time by adding projects which even if necessary in one case might not be in another but which are rarely deleted and are added to

the repertoire of projects that become the "system". An audit of the new product development system should also be considered whenever the process involves very few marketing research projects, since this can be an indication of inadequate or inappropriate use of market-based input.

Any new product development process involves the participation of numerous people and organizational functions. To provide some feel for the multifunction involvement at the various stages in the new product development process, let's consider Exhibit 8–9.

EXHIBIT 8–9

INTERFUNCTIONAL INVOLVEMENT IN THE NEW PRODUCT DEVELOPMENT PROCESS

Source: Reprinted with permission from Y. Wind, "Marketing and Other Business Functions," in *Research in Marketing*, Volume V (January 1981), Greenwich, Conn.: JAI Press, Inc.

Stages in new product development process	Organizational function					
	Top management	Marketing	Finance	R&D	Manufacturing	Other (legal, procurement, personnel, etc.)
1. Setting objectives or selection of internal vs. external development	Primary responsibility	Inputs	Inputs	Inputs		
2. Idea generation		Primary responsibility	Inputs	Primary responsibility	Inputs	Inputs
3. Idea/concept screening	Approval	Primary responsibility			Inputs	Inputs
4. Concept/product development		Primary responsibility		Primary responsibility	Inputs	Inputs
5. Concept/product evaluation	Approval	Primary responsibility				Inputs
6. Final product evaluation & development of marketing strategy	Approval	Primary responsibility		Inputs	Inputs	Inputs
7. Continuous evaluation of product performance	Approval	Primary responsibility	Inputs	Inputs	Inputs	Inputs
8. Product introduction		Primary responsibility			Primary responsibility	

The functions performed by each participating group vary, of course, from one organization to another and even within the same organization from one product development effort to another. To illustrate some of the activities that can be performed by the various

EXHIBIT 8–10

ILLUSTRATIVE NEW PRODUCT DEVELOPMENT FUNCTIONS OF TECHNICAL AND MARKETING RESEARCH

Source: B.F. Bowman, "Coordinating Technical & Marketing Research," in T.L. Berg and A. Shuchman (eds.), *Product Strategy and Management*, Holt, Rinehart and Winston, Inc., New York, 1963, pp. 446–447. Reprinted by permission.

	Phase I Ideas	Phase II Investigation exploration	Phase III Research and development	Phase IV Testing	Phase V Initial sales and manufacturing
Technical Research	Experimentation Mechanical development Related technical departments Technical solution of existing problems Outside sources	Technical possibilities Scientific problems Technically practical Availability of men and facilities Fit present processes or require new equipment	Product characteristic and design Performance Formulation Basic or applied research Competitive products Stability Costs Processes	Process development Pilot plant production Preliminary plant production Process costs Control methods Ingredient specifications	Aid to production in manufacturing Product specifications for procurement Control
	Decision area / Selection for phase II	Decision area / Authorization for phase III	Decision area / Authorization for phase IV	Decision area / Authorization for phase V	Decision area / Product moves into regular operation
Market Research	Interpretation of sales, advertising, and related marketing data Outside sources	Thorough preliminary commercial evaluation	Market potential Market requirements Cost and profit aspects Share market goals Competition Selling techniques	Pilot marketing Panel tests Consumer tests Market tests Review of previous evaluations Appraisal of sales potentials and marketing plans	Thorough review with sales and advertising of: Product potentials Suggested techniques Consumer reaction Technique in approach to the actual marketing

functions involved in the new product development effort, let us examine the activities of technical and marketing research which are illustrated in Exhibit 8–10 and the multifunction activities involved in the various developmental stages of a new industrial product, which are illustrated in Exhibit 8–11.

An examination of these lists of activities suggests some of the complexity involved in the new product development process. The process itself is complex and involves a considerable number of interrelated activities which have to be performed by numerous intraorganizational units and outside individuals and groups. This complexity is further revealed in the more detailed discussions in Chapters 9 through 15 of the phases of the new product development process. This complexity and multiplicity of actors also has major implications for the way a firm should organize for its new product development activities. The organization for new products should be designed to meet the firm's specific new product objectives and fit the firm's overall objectives, organizational philosophy and structure, and resources. It is not a given, but rather an area which requires a specific set of decisions. These decisions are further discussed in Chapter 16.

EXHIBIT 8–11

INTERNAL PRODUCT DEVELOPMENT: STEPS IN THE EXECUTION PHASE

	Technical search 1	Technical feasibility 2	Prototype 3	Pilot 4	Launch 5
Overall goal of step 1	*Identify technologies* Identify one or more technologies that can potentially be developed into a product that will meet the market's technical and cost needs	*Product technology works* Prove that one or more basic technologies work and can potentially be used to make the proposed product	*Develop & test prototypes*	*Confirm costs* Confirming that product can be manufactured at forecast cost on pilot line	*Implement plans* Full scale implementation of product launch plans, with the objective of pushing product to success (or failure) as rapidly as possible
Key business disciplines involved 2	R & D Market research/planning	R & D Market research/planning Top management (first critical decision point as prototype stage usually involves investment expenditures)	R & D Market research/planning Sales (for initial market development) Mfg. (for pilot line) Product Mgmt. (for market development) Top Mgmt. (for decision to proceed)	Sales Product Mgmt. Manufacturing R & D Market resources/planning	Same as in Step 4

EXHIBIT 8–11 (continued)

	Technical search 1	Technical feasibility 2	Prototype 3	Pilot 4	Launch 5
R&D role 3	*Identify technologies* through literature search, patent search, examination of in-house technologies, internal — external peer knowledge, technical consultants, universities, government research projects, etc.	*Experiment* on laboratory equipment to see if the proposed technology works. Will probably construct a few crude devices for internal testing	*Develop & test prototypes* Build the required no. of prototypes for the product line necessary for complete internal & external (customer) testing *Design pilot line* Propose & design pilot mfg. line & make detailed capital investments & product cost estimates	*Confirm costs* by installing & debugging pilot line(s) to be used to produce product during early stages of market development. Make sufficient product under normal production conditions to confirm that product can be made at forecast cost. Continue to supply customer samples. *Document the process* so that it can be turned over to mfg. smoothly	*Further develop product line* by establishing projects to develop needed product improvement or extension *Develop advanced manufacturing processes* to improve quality or reduce cost
Marketing role: planning 4	*Provide rough product specifications* to R & D — both technical performance & cost *Provide business justification for project* Justify technical search, based on crude assessment of product fit with pre-established financial & strategic criteria for new products *Limited market research* Obtain needed product cost & market information through extremely limited market research, including survey of key potential customers, literature searches & other traditional market research technologies	*Continue support of R & D* by providing tighter product specs, including market reaction to any changes in product spec likely, due to limitation of the proposed technology *Limited market research* to provide any additional information (market size, growth, product fit, potential share, competitive advantage & fit with new product criteria) necessary to justify proceeding to next stage	*Define complete product line* needed for product launch if not done during technical feasibility stage. *More detailed market research* to gather extensive information needed to define element of product launch plan — market size, share, product positioning, i.e., competitive products, pricing strategy, sales & distribution methods, promotional approach & methods, packaging required, customer strategy, etc. *Prepare draft launch plan* including financial, marketing & strategic justification for entering the business	*Produce final launch plan* with emphasis on tactical factors such as sales training, distribution, advertising literature, pricing competitive strategy, customer targets, etc. *Complete internal preparations for launch* including literature printing, preparation of selling aids, complete creative advertising work & place in media, train sales force & distribution system, install inquiry follow up & order entry system, establish internal & field inventories. *Establish benchmarks* Agree, with top management, key sales, cost & profit goals & checkpoints for future reviews	*Tracking progress* by measuring progress vs. marketing goals & other checkpoints *Identifying product extensions*

EXHIBIT 8–11   (continued)

	Technical search 1	Technical feasibility 2	Prototype 3	Pilot 4	Launch 5
Marketing role: market dev. & product mgmt. 5	None	None	*Begin market development* by initiating product testing at key customers to insure that product will meet their needs. Retest product concept & confirm its benefits. Obtain *tentative* purchase commitments from key customers who will form base of business *Assume management responsibility* for the product line	*Continue market development and management of the product line*	*Coordinate implementation of launch plan* focusing on key customer development, pricing, implementation of promotional plans and direction & motivation of the sales force & distribution system
Mfg. role 6	None	*Aid R & D* May be involved to suggest potential methods of further developing & mfg. the product	*Aid R & D* by participating in design of pilot facility and making initial cost estimates.	*Confirm costs* as above, in conjunction with R & D *Take over mfg.* Once turnover cost goals and process quality & select goals are reached.	*Mfg. product* for sale & execute cost reduction program *Define future programs* for cost reduction, process improvement, & second generation equipment
Finance 7	If search successful, crude RV analysis to justify proceeding to technical feasibility	RV analysis	Detailed sales, cost profit, investment & ROI analysis to justify proceeding to pilot plant stage. RV>0	Reconfirm costs & that project is still financially "go."	Report on performance vs. plan
Other functions 8	None	None	*Begin sales planning* Sales, distribution, advertising, back-up engineering, service functions participate in planning their role in product launch	*Complete sales planning* Same as prototype	*Implement plans* Sales, distribution, advertising, engrg. & service execute plan & are responsible for achieving goals

EXHIBIT 8–11   (continued)

	Technical search 1	Technical feasibility 2	Prototype 3	Pilot 4	Launch 5
Output of stage 9	*Rough development plan* A technical development plan (costs, resources required, timing) for promising technologies, including concepts on material systems & mfg. processes that might be used to mfg. the product. Plan includes crude financial evaluation of the business, showing that it's worth proceeding to the next stage.	*Prototype plan* A technical plan for developing prototype product, including estimates of the probability of technical success and cost goals *Preliminary business plan* including rough financial plan over the life of the proposed marketing strategy, and justification to continue to the prototype stage	*Fully developed product line* for initial launch *Detailed launch plan* focusing on strategic elements, including financial justification to proceed to market, marketing strategy, and internal organization necessary to manage the product line	*Launch product* if all signs are "go."	
Normal reasons for failure at this stage 10	*Technical failure* Cannot find a technology that will potentially meet technical and cost goals	*Technical failure* Technology is unable to meet product specifications *Cost of materials* or manufacturing processes thought to be so high that product cannot be sold profitably *Probability* of successfully developing a prototype thought to be too low	*Technical cost failure* Product does not service extensive testing; cost to manufacture is too high to be competitive	*Cost* Mfg. process unable to produce the product at forecast cost. *Competition* Entry of a new, superior (cost or performance) competitive product or significant change in competitive strategy	*Insufficient resources* Sales, advtg., and support resources cause failure or underachievement of goals. *Unanticipated competitive moves* A new superior product or drastically lowered prices undercut demand and profit *Market fails to develop* as anticipated, due to field product failure to meet specifications, a change in the customer's basic need or poor market research and testing, resulting in inflated demand estimates

UTILIZING CPM FOR NEW PRODUCT DEVELOPMENT ACTIVITIES

Given the large number of stages and functions involved in the development of new products and the relatively long lead time involved, it is useful to design and utilize a formal time/cost planning system. PERT (*Program Evaluation and Review Technique*), PERT/Cost, or CPM (*Critical Path Method*) are all methods developed to provide management with the time and cost information required for effective and orderly planning, coordination, and control of complex projects.

CPM has been utilized by a number of companies in the planning of their new product introduction efforts. Dusenbury, in 1965, for example, reported on the experience of the Diamond Alkali Company and their use of CPM:

> . . . the use of CPM as a tool for organizing and coordinating new product introductions has been of extreme value to us. In the case described it helped us to launch our new products on the market six months to a year earlier than would otherwise have been the case, with maximum sales results.

Compared with its utilization in government-related project management and R&D operations, CPM and PERT have received relatively little attention as a tool in the planning of the new product development efforts of business firms. CPM can and should, however, be used in the planning of the firm's new product development efforts. In its simplest form, it provides a detailed and explicit listing of the activities to be performed, their distribution, the various departments, and time estimates for the completion of each activity. The activities should be arranged sequentially in a network-type diagram and the time estimates can include either the expected time or a series of optimistic (o), most likely (m), and pessimistic (p) estimates. A simplistic PERT network is presented in Exhibit 8–12.

The relationship between the expected time and the three estimates is illustrated in one of the procedures for estimating the duration of an activity and its uncertainty (Wang, 1964):

The expected duration $E(t)$ is:

$$E(t) = \frac{o + 4m + p}{6},$$

and the uncertainty of this estimate is the variance of the distribution of the time estimates:

$$\sigma^2 = \frac{(p - o)^2}{36}.$$

Given the specified times for the occurrence of key activities, the scheduled times and variances, management can estimate the probabilities of completing an activity by the specified dates.

Given that any overall time estimate depends on the accuracy of the estimate for each activity and the completeness of the network of activities, it is important to have sufficient controls on the design of the network to assure that any major time-consuming and cost-consuming activity will not be omitted.

An important dimension omitted from simplified time networks is the *cost* of undertaking the various activities. The introduction of a test market, for example, not only increases the time prior to introduction but also considerably increases the cost. Hence, the network, in order to be complete and of value as both a planning and control tool, should incorporate cost estimates. This allows management to make trade

EXHIBIT 8–12

USE OF PERT AT SERCK-JAMESBURY

Source: R. Hill, *Marketing Technological Products to Industry*, Oxford, Pergamon Press, 1973.
Reprinted by permission.

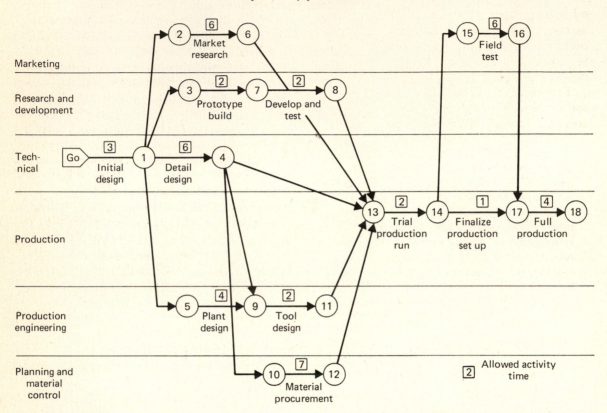

offs among the time, cost, and quality of the given activity.

A choice between test market or one of its many alternatives could be made more easily better if management compared the time involved (six months for test market versus three months for a simulated test market study), the cost involved (over $500,000 for test market versus $150,000 for simulated test market), confidence in the estimated sales forecasts, and the like.

The cost and time estimates can be combined in a CPM network to facilitate a visual inspection of the overall network and its cost and time components. Time and cost networks provide not only a useful planning tool, but also an essential control mechanism to determine whether at any time the new product development project is off schedule and budget, and by how much. Such information allows management to undertake corrective actions to bring the project under control and attempt to remain within the planned time schedule and budget.

The development of CPM networks accompanied with time and cost estimates is not a trivial task. Yet, it is an essential component of the overall new product development planning and management efforts. Such a network can also be used as an initial guideline for the allocation of resources among the individual parts of the project schedule and budget and as a continuous *control* mechanism.

The benefits of the CPM method in new product development were succinctly summarized by Wang (1964), who said:

> . . . (the CPM) provides the basics for anticipating management action. Trouble areas can be predicted. Remedial actions may be taken in sufficient time to avoid bottlenecks. Management of resources may be efficiently planned and controlled . . . supervisors may assume greater responsibility . . . Management-by-exception is a reality . . . The detailed estimates of times, costs and resource utilization, obtained from personnel responsible for the tasks, can be judged

against management objectives to determine plan feasibility. Areas of exceptional and substandard performance can be identified from actual progress.

CPM and PERT provide useful management tools for handling the complex new product development process. They assure planning that considers the interdependencies among the corporate groups involved in the process and the requirements and timing for reviews and decisions. Given that "moving new products through the total process from inception of the idea to commercialization of the product on schedule and at a satisfactory cost" presents one of the most frequently-mentioned management problems (Booz, Allen, and Hamilton, 1968) the utilization of some formal planning and control tool such as PERT, especially if coupled with some formal model for the evaluation of the progress at each stage of development, can be viewed as almost a necessary (but obviously not sufficient) condition for successful new product development efforts.

DETERMINATION OF THE NEW PRODUCT DEVELOPMENT BUDGET

One of the major questions facing any firm is how much to spend on new product development. No single answer can be offered since the amount that *should* be spent depends on a variety of corporate, market, competitive, and environmental conditions. These factors include, for example, the corporate objectives (new product as a source of growth versus defense of an existing market position), the alternatives available (acquisition of existing firms or product lines, licensing, or internal development), the available and projected resources of the firm, and its idiosyncrasies.

These and other factors affect management's initial determination of their new product development objectives (including, in addition to the conventional financial goals, the specification of *time* constraints and goals) and provide the guideline for the decision on which alternative courses of action to consider. Having determined the range of alternatives to be considered, and evaluated the various options, the total budget for new product development and its allocation should follow the regular corporate procedures for capital investment decisions—assuming, that this procedure is compatible with the acceptable financial principles of investment analysis.

Whereas the investment evaluation procedure (as discussed in Chapter 11) provides an approach to the "correct" determination of the budget for new product development, most firms seek and attempt to develop "norms" against which to compare their level of effort. The average expenditures for new product development by the industry or by the firm's direct competitors often serve as a basis for comparison. Yet, given that information on the total new product development budget of competitors is rarely available, firms tend to rely on surrogate measures which are not always appropriate. Consider for example the problems one might encounter if the basis for comparison is the number of new products introduced by a competitor.

Numerous studies on R&D expenditures and number of R&D employees have been conducted, and most of these can provide an indication of the amount spent on R&D activities by industry and size of firm. It is important to note, however, that the size of the R&D expenditures does not necessarily reflect the correct magnitude of the total cost of a firm's new product development efforts, nor is it directly related to the effectiveness of the firm's new product activities.

A complicating factor in determining the budget for new product development is the difficulty in measuring the value of various activities. How, for example, can one measure the "value" of the basic research department of a large chemical firm? A number of cost-benefit analysis procedures have been designed and utilized to help in the determination of the value of various new product development activities. Yet, given that the budget has to be determined for future activities and given the uncertainty involved in any new product development effort (especially if more innovative work is undertaken), it is difficult to establish accurate projections for the expected costs and benefits.

This uncertainty can be dealt with to some extent with Bayesian decision theory. Following this approach the cost and value of developing new products can be assessed as well as the cost and value of new product development activities. The Bayesian approach to the evaluation of new products (as briefly discussed in Chapter 2) has been applied in a few simple cases to the GO, NO GO, ON decision of a new concept/product, the timing of the decision, and the expected value of the information to be generated.[6]

DEVELOPMENT SYSTEM FOR INNOVATIVE AND NON INNOVATIVE "NEW" PRODUCTS

Innovation in the modern industrial society is often hailed as an ultimate objective and mark of achievement. Note, for example, the advertisement in Exhibit 8–13 which appeared in

---

[6]For a simple illustration of Bayesian decision to the product decision of the firm, see Green (1962).

Business Week: "Everybody has a Board of Directors. We've added a *'Board of Inventors'*".

Yet, as noted by Levitt (1966):

> In spite of the extraordinary outpouring of totally and partially new products and new ways of doing things that we are witnessing today, by far the greatest flow of newness is not innova-

EXHIBIT 8–13

FOCUSING ON INNOVATION

Source: *Business Week*, October 20, 1973. Courtesy of Gould, Inc.

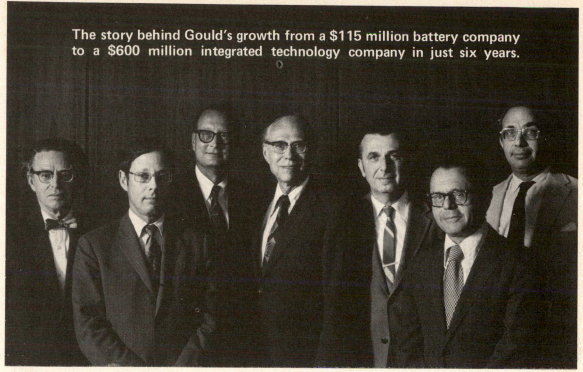

The story behind Gould's growth from a $115 million battery company to a $600 million integrated technology company in just six years.

Mr. Lynch   Dr. David   Dr. Heffner   Dr. Pierce   Professor Harmon   Dr. Fubini   Dr. Goldmuntz

Everybody has a Board of Directors. We've added a "Board of Inventors."

Our "Board of Inventors" aren't all inventors in the normal sense. But they are scientific leaders who together form our Scientific Advisory Board.

The purpose of this board is to assist our inventors by monitoring our technical activities on a continuing basis and advising us of emerging opportunities in science and technology outside Gould.

Each member has a technical background that complements our integrated technology concept. And each man adds a new and objective dimension to our advancement in technology. These scientific leaders are available as individuals for regular consulting tasks.

Our "Board of Inventors" and their fields of expertise: Chairman, Dr. Edward David, President of Gould Laboratories, former Science Advisor to President Nixon and Executive Director of Research for Bell Telephone Laboratories • Dr. Eugene G. Fubini, Director of Gould Inc. and former IBM Group VP and Asst. Sec. of Defense—electronics, computers, defense systems • Dr. Lawrence A. Goldmuntz, Chairman, Economics & Science Planning, Inc.—transportation and urban form, electro-optical systems • Leon D. Harmon, Case Western Reserve Univ.—medicine and biomedical engineering • Dr. Hubert Heffner, Stanford Univ.—electrochemistry, including fuel cells • Thomas Lynch, Group VP, Gould Inc.—physical science, acoustics, oceanography, instruments and systems • Dr. John Pierce, Calif. Institute of Technology—communications, materials, electronics.

Our Scientific Advisory Board is another way we're increasing our commitment to product development to maintain our growth record.

Gould Inc., 8550 West Bryn Mawr Avenue, Chicago, Illinois 60631

GOULD
the proud inventors

tion at all. Rather, it is *imitation*. A simple look around us will, I think, quickly show that imitation is not only more abundant than innovation, but actually a much more prevalent road to business growth and profits. IBM got into computers as an imitator; Texas Instruments, into transistors as an imitator; Holiday Inns, into motels as an imitator; RCA, into television as an imitator; Lytton, into savings and loans as an imitator; and *Playboy,* into both its major fields (publishing and entertainment) as an imitator. In addition, though on a lesser scale, we see every day that private brands are strictly imitative, as are most toys and new brands of packaged foods. In fact, imitation is endemic. Innovation is scarce.

Whether management decides to engage primarily in innovative new product development or *innovative imitation,* as suggested by Levitt, the new product development effort should be planned. Innovative imitation requires, not unlike total innovation, a series of decisions about product design and positioning which should be based on consumer reactions to the product as well as the reactions of other relevant stakeholders (e.g., retailers, competitors, regulatory agencies).

Innovative imitation requires a systematic strategy of new product development efforts, but with somewhat different allocation of resources among its various stages. For example, instead of massive investment in the research phase of the R&D process, it may require modest amounts for the development stage involving primarily product design and modifications. Also, where a similar product has already been introduced and information can be obtained on its market acceptance, the consumer acceptance research may be considerably less involved and cheaper.

What is called for is a balanced and systematic approach to new product development which encompasses the firm's efforts both in true innovation and the more mundane (but

important) imitation. The desired balance between the two depends on management style, tradeoff between short- and long-term performance, willingness to accept the higher risk of truly innovative efforts, and the resources available to take a me-too product and turn it into the market leader. In fact, many companies are noted for their creativity in identifying promising new products, duplicating them, perhaps with minor modifications, and introducing them into the market with a strong marketing campaign which overshadows the efforts of the original innovator. Consider, for example, the success of Revlon which has been based to a large extent on the marketing power of the corporation in promoting products which originally were developed by others.

The risks of introducing a me-too product are quite substantial, however, since any product has to have a *reason* for existence. To reduce risks and increase the likelihood of success it is therefore desirable to design a new product development system that can examine such "me too" product ideas, identify their potential strengths and weaknesses, and implement a formal and explicit marketing program for their introduction, consistent with the corporate overall product policy objectives and compatible with the rest of the firm's product portfolio and the positioning of its various products.

Truly innovative new products are much harder to develop than me-too products. They are usually more expensive to develop, have higher uncertainty, and longer development time. It is not surprising, therefore, that the short-term orientation of most firms leads to an overemphasis on new products in the form of line extensions and relatively minor product modifications. It is desirable, therefore, to strive for a more balanced new product development effort which includes at least some long-term projects with a high potential for generating truly innovative products.

CONCLUDING REMARKS

This chapter outlined the foundations of new product development systems and highlighted some of the strategic decisions involved in the design of such a system. These decisions involve:

- The determination of the mix between internal and external new product development;

- The development of an approach to external new product development;

- The development of an internal system for generation and evaluation of new ideas/concepts and products and their introductory marketing campaign;

- The development of a CPM for planning and controlling the new product development activities of the firm;

- The development of an approach for the determination of the budget for new product activities of the firm;

- The choice of the right mix of innovative and imitative products.

The discussion in this chapter is by necessity brief. It is designed to highlight some of the many decisions involved in the design of a new product development system, and it outlines a proposed system. This model (Exhibit 8–7) provides the organizing framework for the remaining chapters of this part of the book.

To fully appreciate the steps involved in the design of a new product development system, it would be useful for you to select a firm and attempt to design for it a new product development system. To fully appreciate the need for matching the new product development system to the idiosyncratic characteristics of the firm, upon completion of your first task, select another firm, ideally in a different industry, examine the first system you designed and assess to what extent you can use the same system for the new firm and what changes, if any, should be considered.

EXHIBIT 8–14

BUSINESS AND LEGAL INVESTIGATION CHECKLIST FOR MERGERS AND ACQUISITIONS

Source: Based on Charles A. Scharf, *Acquisitions, Mergers, Sales and Takeovers: A Handbook with Forms*, Englewood Cliffs, N.J.: Prentice Hall, 1971, pp. 84–113.

A number of checklists have been proposed as guidelines for the analysis of merger and acquisition candidates. Among the most thorough ones is the checklist developed by Charles A. Scharf in *Acquisitions, Mergers, Sales, and Takeovers: A Handbook with Forms* (Englewood Cliffs, N.J.: Prentice Hall, 1971, pp. 84–113). This checklist is divided into two lengthy lists focusing on (a) a business investigation and (b) a legal investigation.

The *business investigation form* includes 11 sections focusing on over 250 items. Yet, despite this great detail, this and many other checklists often overlook key marketing dimensions. The major categories proposed by Scharf, together with some of the areas that should be added to any checklist are identified below (in italics):

1. *Corporate background*—business description, ownership, stock performance, board minutes, etc.

2. *Basis of proposed acquisition*—highlights of agreement and formula for evaluation of shares.

3. *Financial*. This section includes a focus on financial status (including working capital, investments, etc.) and financial operations (including detailed sales, income, expense, and profit analysis over time, etc.).

EXHIBIT 8–14 (continued)

These data should be adjusted for inflationary effects and, to the extent possible, evaluated as a function of the firm's activities and objectives and compared with similar businesses.

4. *Products.* A description and evaluation of all major products overall and by market segments. The Scharf outline suggests a focus on four major product areas: product classification, analysis of major products (including their description, application, competition, market acceptance, etc.), anlysis of markets and prices (including domestic and foreign competitive practices, price policies, and market characteristics), and government business. *Noted in their absence from the list are the essential dimensions of the product's positioning by market segments, the strength of the product's market franchise, and an explicit portfolio analysis.*

5. *Sales.* Five sections are included in the Scharf sales analysis: distribution, sales organization, sales policies, sales planning, and advertising and promotion. *Excluded from the analysis of the 24 items in this section of the Scharf checklist is the critical concern with the effectiveness (market response function) of the various marketing strategies.*

6. *Management and industrial relations.* This part of the Scharf checklist includes four sections: general organization characteristics (including type and number of employees), management and office personnel, shop labor (including union contracts), and personnel policies and practices.

7. *Facilities.* This category includes land and buildings, equipment, services and utilities, and adequacy of and future needs for facilities.

8. *Production methods and processes.* Twelve sections are included in this part of Scharf's checklist: parts fabrication methods, assembly methods, processing operations, quality control and inspection, salvage control, material handling, methods and operation sheets, tool design, procurement, and repair, storage and warehousing, safety, efficiency of production operations, and adequacy of facilities.

9. *Engineering and research.* Scharf's engineering and research list includes seven sections: engineering personnel, facilities, importance to product, adequacy of product engineering, research and development, relations with manufacturing and sales, and patents. *Ignored in this section are the extremely important technological ability of the firm and the current and projected technology which is of relevance to the investigated businesses.*

10. *Controls.* Scharf breaks this list down to two major sections: financial controls (including budgets, cost systems, status of operating procedures, accounting methods, etc.) and production planning and controls (including master schedules, coordination between sales and production, material and inventory control, etc.). *Notable in their absence are controls over the marketing operation of the firm and the use of ongoing control mechanisms based on an adaptive experimentation approach.*

11. *Outlook for buyer.* The final sections of Scharf's business investigation include earnings prospects per buyer share and required return on capital to buy and operate the acquired business. *A missing component of the outlook analysis is an explicit projection of the expected performance of the joint operations under alternative scenarios and planned strategies. Such an anlysis should include explicitly any synergistic effects between the acquired and acquiring firms as they relate to marketing, production problems, technology, or any other relevant aspect of management.*

Scharf's *legal investigation* checklist consists of 10 sections:

1. *State laws.* This includes 18 detailed laws pertaining to corporation statutes, "blue sky" laws, bulk sales laws, and assumption of liabilities.

2. *Seller's corporation organization, powers, and commitment.* This includes 25 items pertaining to corporate charters, bylaws, minute books, and stock books.

EXHIBIT 8–14 (continued)

3. *Seller's and subsidiaries' assets.* Twenty-five specific items are listed classified into four areas: real properties, real property leases, personal property, and intangibles.

4. *Contracts.* This section of the checklist includes a listing of the seller's existing contracts with distributors, unions, customers, etc., and a review of each contract with respect to assignability, possible antitrust violations, enforceability, breaches or defaults, redetermination clauses, and escalation clauses.

5. *Liabilities.* This includes an examination of loan agreements, bonds, and debentures.

6. *Antitrust considerations.* A check for existing violations, status of acquisition under §7 of the Clayton and Sherman Acts, and determination of how business should be conducted after the acquisition.

7. *Taxes.* Twenty-three tax items should be investigated, including income taxes, taxable acquisition, and other taxes.

8. *Brokerage.* If applicable, all brokerage agreements should be carefully examined.

9. *Securities and Exchange Commission.* Registration of buyer's stock and related considerations.

10. *Stock Exchange requirements.*

In designing a merger and acquisition checklist, these and similar items can offer a useful starting point. They should be modified, however, to the idiosyncratic characteristics of the firm. Such modifications should reflect the considerations used in the regular planning activities of the firm (as discussed, for example, in Chapter 6) and any other relevant marketing, finance, and management concepts.

9

Generation of New Product Ideas

Introduction

Creative Process

Conceptual Blocks to Creativity
The Creative Person
Creative Output of Individuals Versus Groups

**Unstructured Consumer-Based Approaches to Generation
of New Product Ideas**

Motivation Research
Focused Group Interviews
Consumption System Analysis
Consumer Complaints

**Structured Consumer-Based Approaches to Generation
of New Product Ideas**

Need/Benefit Segmentation
Problem Detection Studies
Market Structure Analysis/Gap Analysis
Product Deficiency Analysis

**Unstructured "Expert"-Based Approaches to Generation
of New Product Ideas**

Brainstorming
Synectics
Suggestion Box
Independent Inventors and Licensors

INTRODUCTION

The probability that a new product development system will lead to a successful product entry depends to a large extent on the number of new product ideas generated at the start of the process. The fewer the ideas generated, the greater the risk that if these ideas do not meet the criteria set for subsequent screening and evaluation, management will be left without any new product entries, or even worse, it would be tempted to relax its performance requirements and introduce an inferior product. The generation of a large number of innovative new product ideas, therefore, is one of the most crucial first tasks in the new product development process.

Whereas the desirability of having a large number of innovative new product ideas is hardly debatable, the major question is: How can a company go about generating innovative new ideas? Imagine, for example, that you were given the responsibility for developing new product ideas for a manufacturer. Can you come up with 10, 20, or more new ideas?

How many ideas did you list? How different were they from each other? Were they really *new* or were they only minor modifications of some existing products or services?

If you are disappointed with the innovativeness of your ideas and the shortness of your list, can you think of any other approaches to generating new product ideas?

Most people would first approach the task of generating new product ideas for a given manufacturer (or product category) in an unstructured manner, i.e., they would write down any ideas that came to their mind. Under pressure to generate more ideas, the tendency is to move to a more structured approach based on some attempt to develop a framework and generate ideas within it. In considering the task of generating new product ideas for a beverage manufacturer, for example, this second approach might involve (a) developing a list of occasions of usage, package forms, benefits offered by beverages, and the like, and (b) the generation of new product ideas within each of these frameworks. Other structured approaches include systematic literature search, analysis of existing products, and the like.

There are numerous approaches to the generation of new product ideas and the objective of this chapter is to briefly discuss some of the more commonly-used ones. These approaches can be classified based on two major dimensions: (a) the type of approach used—structured versus unstructured and (b) the identity of the respondents—consumers or "experts". In this context "experts" are all those individuals within or outside the corporation who are not responding as consumers but rather as persons knowledgeable in the given area.

Exhibit 9–1 presents some of the more common approaches to the generation of new product ideas and categorizes them according to these two dimensions.

Before embarking on the examination of these approaches, however, it is desirable to explore the creative process involved in the generation of new product ideas and the current state of knowledge concerning how to increase creativity, reduce the blocks to creative thinking, and facilitate the task of generating new product ideas.

EXHIBIT 9–1

ALTERNATIVE APPROACHES TO THE GENERATION OF NEW PRODUCT IDEAS

Source	Research approach	
	Unstructured	**Structured**
Consumers	Motivation research Focused group interviews Consumption system analysis Consumer complaints	Need/benefit segmentation Problem detection studies Market structure analysis/Gap analysis Product deficiency analysis
"Experts"	Brainstorming "Synectics" "Suggestion box" Independent inventors	"Problem/opportunity" analysis Morphological analysis Growth opportunity analysis Environmental trends analysis Analysis of competitive products Search of patents and other sources of new ideas

The R & D Process

CREATIVE PROCESS

What is the nature of the creative process? How can the creative person be identified? Can creativity be taught or enhanced? These and similar questions have for decades interested philosophers, psychologists, novelists, and other scientists and artists. Yet, despite the wide interest in creativity, little is known about the creative process. Psychological studies have identified some distinguishing characteristics of the creative person, and it is generally agreed that creativity can to some extent be taught and the creative process enhanced by an appropriate organizational environment.

The objective of this section is not to provide an exhaustive review of the current knowledge about creativity but rather to provide some background to the discussion of approaches to the generation of new product ideas. The focus is therefore, on three aspects of creativity: (a) conceptual blocks to creativity, (b) some discriminating characteristics of the creative person, and (c) the creativity of individuals versus groups.

CONCEPTUAL BLOCKS TO CREATIVITY

The work on blocks to creativity originated at the Stanford University Design Division and was summarized in the excellent work of Adams (1974). Defined as "the mental walls which block the problem solver from correctly perceiving a problem or conceiving its solution," there are five sets of interrelated blocks—perceptual, cultural, environmental, emotional, and intellectual/expressive. These blocks vary in nature and intensity from individual to individual. Yet, it is important to recognize them and avoid them.[1]

Perceptual blocks

Perceptual blocks are obstacles which prevent the problem solver from clearly perceiving either the problem itself or the information that is necessary to solve the problem (Adams, 1974).

Adams recognizes at least six perceptual blocks which include:

- Difficulty in isolating the problem
- Tendency to delimit the problem area too narrowly
- Inability to see the problem from various viewpoints
- Seeing what you expect to see—stereotyping
- Saturation
- Failure to utilize all sensory inputs

Cultural blocks

Cultural blocks are acquired by exposure to a given set of cultural patterns (Adams, 1974).

These cultural blocks include:

- Cultural values which accept reason, logic, and practicality as good while feelings, intuition, and qualitative judgments are bad (note, however, that at least among a subculture of America, *feelings* and emotions are coming to be thought of as good).
- The preference in some cultures to preserve traditions and oppose change.
- The belief that any problem can be solved by scientific thinking and lots of money.

---

[1]Reprinted from and based on *Conceptual Blockbusting, A Pleasurable Guide to Better Problem Solving,* by James L. Adams, with the permission of W.W. Norton & Company, Inc. Copyright © 1974, by James L. Adams.

Environmental blocks

Environmental blocks are closely related to cultural blocks and are defined by Adams as those blocks "imposed by our immediate social and physical environment."

These blocks include:

- Lack of cooperation and trust among colleagues
- Autocratic boss
- Distractions—telephone, frequent intrusions
- Lack of physical, economic, or organizational support to bring ideas into action

Emotional blocks

Emotional blocks may interfere with the freedom with which we explore and manipulate ideas, with our ability to conceptualize fluently (which refers to the number of ideas), and flexibility (which refers to the diversity of ideas generated), and prevent us from communicating ideas to others in a manner which will gain them acceptance (Adams, 1974).

These blocks include:

- Fear of making a mistake, failing, and risking.
- Inability to tolerate ambiguity
- Preference for judging ideas, rather than generating them
- Inability to incubate and "sleep on an idea"
- Lack of access to areas of imagination and lack of imaginative control. These blocks were conceptualized by the psychoanalytic models which suggest that at least part of creativity occurs below the conscious level of the mind and that the conscious mind, or ego, is a control valve on creativity.

Intellectual and expressive blocks

Intellectual blocks result in an inefficient choice of mental tactics or a shortage of intellectual ammunition. Expressive blocks inhibit one's vital ability to communicate ideas—not only to others, but to oneself as well (Adams, 1974).

These blocks include:

- Using an incorrect language (verbal versus visual for example)
- Lack of correct information
- Inadequate language skill to express and record ideas
- Inflexibility or inadequate use of intellectual problem-solving strategies

THE CREATIVE PERSON

Despite numerous studies of creative people, no definite conclusions can be drawn concerning their discriminating characteristics, nor can the standard personnel tests isolate such persons and predict, with any accuracy, their level of creativity. The difficulties involved in the prediction and identification of the creative person stem, to a large extent, from the diversity in the conceptual and operational definitions of creativity, and the diverse methodologies used to study it.

Some conclusions concerning the characteristics of the creative person can, however, be suggested. These characteristics should be viewed only as general guidelines for the identification of the creative person, and deviations from this profile can be expected. Some of the major discriminating characteristics of the creative person are presented next.[2]

Intellectual characteristics Although measures of general intelligence fail to predict creativity, the creative person typically poses-

---

[2]The discussion in this section borrows heavily from Steiner (1965) and Berelson and Steiner (1964). It is interesting to note that during the late 1960s and 1970s there has been relatively little work in this area.

ses the following intellectual characteristics:

- *Conceptual fluency* measured as the number of ideas generated within a limited period of time, the number of items beginning with a specific letter that can be listed, etc.
- *Conceptual flexibility* The ability to change frame of reference and approaches as needed.
- *Originality* The ability to give unusual, atypical answers to questions, responses to situations, or interpretation of events.
- *Preference for complexity* The acceptance of complexity as a challenge.

Personality traits　Some of the major personality traits which were identified in various studies as the likely characteristics of creative persons (as reported by Steiner, 1965) are:

- Independence of judgment
- Negative attitudes toward authority—highly creative people tend to view authority as arbitrary and contingent on continued and demonstrated superiority.
- Less reliance on source credibility
- Higher likelihood of impulsive behavior[3]

The distinguishing personality traits of the creative person are perhaps best illustrated in the following profile of highly creative architects:

> Since they (the creative architects) are not preoccupied with the impression they make on others or the demands that others make on them, they are freer than others (less creative architects) to set their own standards and to achieve them in their own fashion. It is not that they are socially irresponsible, but that their behavior is guided by esthetic values and ethical standards which they have set for themselves and which have

been effectively integrated into their images of themselves and of their ideals. They are perhaps the prototype of the person of strong ego, the man of will and deed. Confident of themselves and basically self accepting, they are to an unusual degree able to recognize and give expression to most aspects of inner experience and character, and thus are able more fully to be themselves and to realize their own ideals (MacKinnon, 1965).

In addition to these common personality traits, there are some indications that creative persons share some similarities in their family backgrounds. Child (1968) summarizes some of the findings in this area stating:

> . . . (creative persons) have more frequently a history of parental values stressing independence, integrity, and self determination rather than conformity and parental dictation.

Approach to problems　Steiner (1965) in reviewing the psychological studies concerning the creative person suggests that creative persons tend to have a number of distinguishing characteristics in their approach to problems. These include:

- Creative persons are more perceptive to, and more motivated by, the interest inherent in the problem and its solution. Accordingly they get more involved in the task, and work harder and longer in the absence of external pressures or incentives. Consistent with this orientation they also show preference for and interest in novelty, complexity, and situations which require unusual resolution rather than those that are routine and cut and dried.
- Creative persons tend to be "cosmopolitans" in their orientation and aspirations as opposed to the less creative persons who tend to have a "local" orientation.
- Creative persons often spend more time in the initial stages of problem formulation, in broad scanning of alternatives. Less crea-

---

[3]Reprinted from G. Steiner, *The Creative Organization*, 1965, by permission of The Unversity of Chicago Press.

tive persons are more apt to "get on with it." In the early stages of the creative process, the creative persons tend to be more open-minded, willing to seek and accept relevant information from all sources, to suspend judgment, defer commitment, and remain aloof in the face of pressure to take a stand.

- No regular progress can be expected from creative persons since "creativity is rarely a matter of gradual, step by step progress; it is more often a pattern of large and largely unpredictable leaps after long periods of no apparent progress".

Can these and other characteristics of creative persons be measured reliably? Consider for example the following profile of 40 of the most creative architects in the country and imagine how you would approach the identification of these traits in a prospective architect (or other creative person if one could assume that these creative qualities are common to creative persons in all fields):

> . . . (the creative person has) high level of effective intelligence, openness to aesthetic sensitivity, cognitive flexibility, independence of thought and action, high level of energy, unquestioning commitment to creative endeavor, and unceasing striving for creative solutions to the ever more difficult problems which he constantly sets for himself (McKinnon, 1965).

From management point of view, the ability to measure these and similar characteristics and hence identify (and select) the creative person is of major concern. Many of these qualities can be measured. But, as indicated by Steiner, "the instruments are far from perfect and more seriously, the correlation between each of these distinguishing characteristics and on-the-job creativity is limited. The characteristics 'distinguish' highs from lows only in the sense that highs, on the average, have more of, or more often exhibit, the particular quality. And that is far from saying that all highs have more of each

than all lows." This conclusion, drawn more than ten years ago, holds today. The ability to predict creative performance is quite limited, although the utilization of some creativity tests improves the odds of selecting at least some creative persons. Understanding the characteristics of the creative person provides, however, additional insights into the creative process and can help one design an environment and processes which are more conducive to creativity. The design and selection of approaches for generation of new product ideas should take these factors into account. Similarly the design of the most effective organizational arrangements for new product development (as discussed in Chapter 16) should be based on an understanding of the characteristics of the creative person.

CREATIVE OUTPUT OF INDIVIDUALS VERSUS GROUPS

Implicit in most of the group approaches to creativity—brainstorming, focused group sessions, and the like—is the premise that the creative output of groups is better than the creative output of individuals. The rationale underlying the formation of interdisciplinary research and R&D teams is partly based on the same premise. Yet, there are a number of psychological studies which found that group interaction during the generation stage of problem solving is dysfunctional. Taylor, Berry, and Block (1958) showed that interaction among group members inhibits the generation of alternative solutions to problems. In an experiment among college students, they found that individuals generated a larger number of different solutions, a larger number of high-quality solutions, and a larger number of unique solutions than groups of similar students. Dunnette, Campbell, and Jaastad (1963) replicated this experiment using industrial employees as subjects. Their conclusions confirmed the earlier findings that interaction inhibits the creative phase of problem solving, i.e., the generation of alternative solutions to a problem. This conclusion is also supported by the results of another study that utilizes a different experimental design which was conducted by Vroom, Grant, and Cotton (1969).

On the other hand, there are numerous studies on small group behavior and actual experience with generation of new product ideas by groups, that suggest against the dismissal of groups from the creative process.

Creativity—"the combination of previously unrelated structures in a way that you get more out of the emergent whole than you have put in" (Koestler, 1967)—can be achieved by both individuals (especially those with creative abilities) *and* groups (especially those structured along the lines of a creative organization which provides the necessary enhancing environment). It is desirable, therefore, at least initially, to design procedures for generating new product ideas which utilize both individual *and* group approaches rather than relying only on one of these sources. As experience accumulates with these two approaches, it might be possible to identify the conditions under which one is better and refine the system accordingly.

UNSTRUCTURED CONSUMER-BASED APPROACHES TO GENERATION OF NEW PRODUCT IDEAS

One of the major consequences of management acceptance of the marketing orientation has been the widespread reliance on studies of consumer "needs" and "motives," and the sources of consumer dissatisfaction with existing products and services. The reliance on consumer studies for the generation of new product ideas is a common practice among large manufacturers of consumer products and services. These studies include both structured and unstructured research approaches with the latter type still playing a major role. These unstructured approaches include primarily three types of studies—individual-based motivation research, focused group interviews, and consumption system analysis—and a fourth and somewhat different source of new product ideas—the analysis of consumer complaints.

MOTIVATION RESEARCH

Motivation research—the study of the "why" of consumer behavior—has been used by many companies since the early 1950s as one of the major sources of ideas for new products and services. Motivation research is aimed at the exploration of consumers' underlying needs, motives, predispositions, sensations, feelings, and emotions. It is used either to enable consumers to say what new products and services they would like to have or, more appropriately, provide the researcher with enough insight into consumers' needs to suggest new product ideas which could fulfill some unsatisfied needs and motives.

Motivation research studies provide intriguing insights into consumer motivation. Consider for example the numerous examples presented by Dichter in his *Handbook of Consumer Motivation* (1964) in which he summarized the findings of more than 2,500 studies conducted over a 20-year period by his Institute for Motivational Research in the US and other countries. The insightful, though anecdotal, descriptions of the motivations underlying the purchase and use of food, clothing, shelter, cosmetics, drugs, toys, sports, transportation, liquor, cigarettes, and other products and services, provide a rich source of product ideas.

Translating these (anecdotal examples of) motives and needs into specific product ideas, however, is the most difficult and problematic part of motivation research. It is in this context that the creative motivation researcher is distinguished from the less creative one. Having a frame of reference for the interpretation of consumer needs and desires is helpful, but can also be restricting, since a "Freudian," for example, would almost always attempt to interpret his finding in light of the Freudian interpretation of behavior. It is here that a number of researchers—each with a different philosophical and disciplinary orientation—might be of great value.

Motivation research encompasses a large number of research methods and in recent years has emerged beyond the boundaries of clinical psychology. Many other social scientists, especially social psychologists, cultural anthropologists, family sociologists, to mention just a few, have been involved in various motivation research studies. The approach to be utilized depends primarily on the researcher's preference and philosophical orientation. In general, however, the major distinguishing characteristic of the various motivation research approaches is the use of unstructured and/or disguised research approaches.

Unstructured approaches Depth interviews, qualitative interviews, nonstructured interviews, clinical interviews, and focused interviews are all terms used to describe a set of unstructured (and mostly nondisguised) research approaches aimed at the identification of consumers' innermost motives and needs. The main advantages of these approaches were succinctly summarized by Selltiz et al. (1959), who stated:

> . . . the unstructured or partially structured interview, if properly used, helps to bring out

the affective and value-laden aspects of the subject's responses and to determine the personal significance of his attitudes . . . This type of interview achieves its purpose to the extent that the subject's responses are spontaneous rather than forced, are highly specific and concrete rather than diffuse and general, are self-revealing and personal rather than superficial.

Unstructured interviews vary in their degree of unstructuredness and the amount of direction provided by the interviewer. They also vary with respect to whether the unstructured interview is the sole research instrument used or part of a more structured interview. This latter case is the more common one today. It usually involves a number of exploratory, open-ended questions tacked on to a structured survey. In these open-ended questions, respondents are asked their likes and dislikes of certain products, suggestions for change, sources of dissatisfaction, and the like.

Disguised approaches Disguised methods, typically referred to as *projective techniques*, are often used by clinical psychologists to overcome possible respondent reluctance or inability to respond and to help discover the respondent's "real" motives and needs. Among the projective techniques which can and have been used to generate new product ideas are a set of psychological testing procedures such as word association tests, sentence and story completion tests, thematic apperception tests (T.A.T.), cartoon tests, and others. In addition to these tests which can and partially have been adapted for use in generating new product ideas, specific projective tests can be developed for the generation of new product ideas involving a series of in-depth probing of the product needs or unsatisfied needs of "friends," other stereotyped individuals ("youth," "liberated women"), or the projected future needs and desires of the respondent and others.

FOCUSED GROUP INTERVIEWS

The focused group interview (FGI) is probably the most widely-used approach to the generation of new product ideas. The FGI enables the researcher to explore consumers' underlying needs, motives, feelings, predispositions, and semantic associations within the context of a group setting. The group setting stimulates discussion and the elaboration of feelings, needs, and attitudes by contrasting one's own experience and desires with those of others. It also encourages the consumers to think aloud about their needs, goals, and current dissatisfactions as a response to the stimulation of others and the group leader. It is in such free-flowing verbal (and nonverbal) context that the new ideas can be obtained, problems with existing products and services identified, and latent desires and needs explored. Sequences of associations and the nature of the group reactions to various ideas (simultaneous discussions and excitement versus silence and embarrassment) can all provide insights into consumers' needs and motives and initial guidelines for the generation of new product ideas.

The evaluation of the results of an FGI is obviously subjective and reflects the analyst's disciplinary training and philosophical orientation. The analyst/leader should, therefore, be trained in the use of psychological principles for both enabling consumers to participate comfortably and effectively in the group discussion and interpreting the results consistent with relevant behavioral science theories. Since there is no single general theory of consumer (or human) behavior, it might be desirable, whenever FGIs are used, to employ at least two different researchers (with different orientations) to conduct and interpret the results of the FGI. Such a move does not necessarily increase the cost of the research but would most likely increase the insight one gains into consumers' needs and motivations and the number and diversity of new product ideas that can be generated.

CONSUMPTION SYSTEM ANALYSIS

A somewhat neglected source of new product ideas is the careful and systematic examination of consumer consumption patterns. Consider for example the product class of household cleaners. If one wanted to generate new product ideas in this product category, a study could be designed in which an interviewer follows consumers around the house exploring in depth, and recording, how they clean each room, what type of problems they have in cleaning various rooms, what products they use in cleaning, and other relevant aspects involved in the cleaning process. An analysis of the tapes from such on-premise interviews can lead to a better understanding of consumers' problems with existing products and desire for new products. It can thus provide useful guidelines for the generation of new household cleaning products and services.

This and similar research approaches to consumption system analysis can be utilized with respect to most product classes including food, clothing, stereo systems, and gardening products and services.

CONSUMER COMPLAINTS

A rich source of new product ideas which is rarely tapped in a systematic way is consumer complaints. A careful examination of consumer complaints might suggest a number of needed product improvements or even new product ideas. The major problem with using this source of ideas is the organizational separation found in many firms between the group responsible for new product development efforts and the group in charge of handling consumer complaints.

The examination of consumer complaints does not have to be limited to the experience of one's own company; examining public complaint files of the Better Business Bureau, consumer protection agencies and newspaper action columns, for example, may all suggest ideas for new products and services.

STRUCTURED CONSUMER-BASED APPROACHES TO GENERATION OF NEW PRODUCT IDEAS

The generation of new product ideas from consumer-based research is not limited to the unstructured approaches discussed in the previous section. A number of structured marketing research procedures have been developed and utilized in the generation of new product ideas.

NEED/BENEFIT SEGMENTATION

Motivation research procedures and focused group interviews are often used for the identification of consumer needs and desired benefits. Yet, these procedures cannot provide quantitative assessment of the size of the various need segments nor can they identify the patterns of needs and benefits. To overcome these limitations and reduce the subjectivity associated with any conclusions derived from unstructured qualitative approaches, marketing researchers have developed and utilized structured need and benefit surveys. These surveys are usually conducted on relatively large samples of respondents and are aimed at the identification of specific need or benefit segments.

A prototypical need (or benefit) survey follows five major steps: (a) identification of a list of needs (or benefits) which is usually generated from a literature review and some unstructured initial interviews with consumers, (b) the design of a questionnaire in which consumers are asked to rate (or rank) the various needs or benefits in terms of their importance, desirability, or some other evaluative scale, (c) the data generated from such a study are usually submitted to an item factor analysis aimed at identifying the major need factors, (d) utilizing some clustering procedure, the respondents are then grouped into segments based on their commonality of needs or benefits (factor scores). This phase results in the identification of need/benefit segments for which (e) the demographic and product usage profile is determined following a series of cross tabs or preferably a series of multiple discriminant analyses (which identify the key discriminating characteristics of the various need/benefit segments).

The final output of such a study is the identification and measurement of specific need or benefit segments. An examination of the profile of these segments can suggest a number of new product ideas which could meet the needs or the benefits sought by the various segments.

PROBLEM DETECTION STUDIES

Can consumers articulate and specify their needs or wants? Since a positive answer to this question is not universally accepted, researchers have proposed and utilized an alternative approach to the generation of new product ideas. This alternative approach is based not on the examination of the desired, positive characteristics but rather on exploration of the negative—the problems which bother consumers. Two major approaches have been utilized following this orientation—BBDO's problem detection studies and the. Problem Inventory Analysis proposed by Tauber (1975).

The problem detection study is aimed at the identification of frequently-occuring sources of dissatisfaction—problems—that are important to the consumers. The procedure used by BBDO involves three major phases:

1. Developing a list of problems. A long list of possible problems is developed based on FGIs and other sources. This list usually encompass problems with existing products, with the end use of the product and/or with various use situations.

2. A quantitative survey, among a sample of respondents, which includes three major tasks: evaluation of each of the problems on the frequency of its occurence (on a four-point frequency scale), evaluation of the problems with respect to their severity (on a four-point importance scale), and finally an assessment of the problems' preemptibility, i.e.: Do consumers know of any brands which claim to solve the given problem?

3. Analytically the three scores are multiplied to produce a *problem score*. The problems are in turn arrayed according to their problem scores and serve as input for the generation of new product ideas.

The procedure has been utilized in more than 100 situations resulting in some of BBD&O's more successful new products, such as "Have it your way" hamburgers for Burger King, which came in response to the problem of not having a choice to add or delete items from the standard prefabricated hamburger. Another example of the usefulness of problem

detection is a study conducted on the dog food market which identified three major problems—current dog foods smell bad, cost too much, and do not come in different sizes for different dogs. These problems served as guidelines for three successful new dog food products: (a) "dog food that smells so good it is called stew rather than dog food," (b) "a product . . . mixing chunks, which is used in conjunction with dry food, making it inexpensive," and (c) several products in different-sized cans for different-size dogs (Norris 1975).

This approach can be simplified and improved by asking consumers to evaluate the importance of only those problems which occur quite frequently. Furthermore, the analysis can be conducted not at the total market level but at the individual level enabling the segmentation of the market based on commonality of problems experienced by consumers.

The second approach to the generation of new product ideas via the identification of relevant problems is the approach suggested by Tauber (1975). The problem inventory analysis is based on presenting consumers with a set of problems and, for each one, asking what products come to mind as having that problem.

Similar to the BBDO approach, the problem inventory also requires the development of a list of problems. An illustrative list of problems in the food industry which was developed by Tauber is presented in Exhibit 9–2. Once such a list is completed, a self-administered questionnaire is designed. The questionnaire is based on a series of statements each of which mentions a problem but not a product; for example, "preparing _____ leaves so many pots to clean." The respondents are asked to fill in the blanks.

This approach can link problems with products but cannot indicate the relative importance of these problems nor how widespread they are. Yet, this approach, the BBDO problem detection study, and simple, open-ended

EXHIBIT 9–2

SOME EXAMPLES OF CONSUMER PROBLEMS RELATING TO FOOD

Source: Reprinted from "Discovering New Product Opportunities with Problem Inventory Analysis," by E.M. Tauber, *Journal of Marketing*, 39, (January) 1975, p. 69, published by the American Marketing Association.

Physiological	Sensory	Activities	Buying and usage	Psychological/ social
A. *Weight* Fattening Empty calories B. *Hunger* Filling Still hungry after eating C. *Thirst* Doesn't quench thirst Makes one thirsty D. *Health* Indigestion Bad for teeth Keeps one awake Acidity	A. *Taste* Bitter Bland Salty B. *Appearance* Color Unappetizing Shape C. *Consistency/texture* Tough Dry Greasy D. *Decomposition* Melts Spoils Separates	A. *Meal planning* Forget Get tired of it B. *Storage* Run out Package won't fit C. *Preparation* Too much trouble Too many pots/pans Never turns out D. *Cooking* Burns Sticks E. *Cleaning* Makes a mess in oven Smells in refrigerator	A. *Portability* Eat away from home Take in a carried lunch B. *Portion control* Not enough in a package Creates leftovers C. *Availability* Out of season Not in supermarket D. *Spoilage* Gets moldy Goes sour E. *Cost* Expensive Takes expensive ingredients	A. *Serve to company* Won't serve to guests Too much last-minute preparation B. *Eating alone* Effort when I cook for myself Depressing when prepared just for one C. *Self-image* Made by a lazy cook Not served by a good mother

questions about problems associated with various products (which can be added to any consumer study) can provide insights into the dissatisfactions and problems faced by consumers. These approaches can thus provide useful input to the creative process of identifying solutions to these problems.

MARKET STRUCTURE ANALYSIS/GAP ANALYSIS

Market structure maps (as discussed in Chapter 4) can reveal *gaps* which might suggest ideas for new products. In order to provide useful guidelines for new product ideas, these gaps should meet two conditions: (a) have no other brands occupying the given position on the relevant dimensions and (b) have a target market segment who would like to have products with features suggested by the unoccupied space.

These conditions encompass three distinct situations:

1. A gap in a brand space with no change in the dimensionality of the market. Consider for example the market for coffee before the introduction of freeze-dried coffee. The two major dimensions of this market seemed to be taste and convenience. Instant coffees were perceived as low on taste and high on convenience while regular percolated coffees were viewed primarily as good on taste but relatively low on convenience. A gap existed with respect to highly convenient *and* good tasting coffee. Since there was a segment who wanted this combination (and was willing to pay for it) there seemed to be a need, which the freeze dried coffees tried to fill.

2. A gap in a brand space involving the identification of a new desired dimension. Consider for example the movie camera market. Prior to the introduction of the Kodak XL movie camera with no lights, the movie camera market was characterized (in some studies) by two major dimensions—quality and convenience of operation. The new feature which enables one to take indoor pictures without light was viewed by many consumers as an important new dimension that in concept testing led to a distinct change in the market from two dimensions to three dimensions, with considerable importance placed, by a segment of the movie camera market, on the new third dimension of no movie light.

3. A gap in a feature (benefit) space. The above two cases are based on perceptual

and preference brand maps. Since brand maps, if not including new concepts (as in the example of the movie camera) can represent only the existing structure of the market, it is useful to consider utilizing a feature space for the identification of desired market gaps (i.e., desired locations in the feature space with no brands filling them). An example of a feature space is discussed in Chapter 4.

The major questions that can be addressed in the process of generating new product ideas from market structure analysis are:

- What dimensions (combinations of product features) do consumers evoke in comparing brands within some broadly-defined product class and the relevant usage occasions?

- How is each of the existing brands positioned in this product feature space?

- Which areas of the space are unoccupied by existing brands?

- What possible new product concepts/ combinations of product features by occasions of usage could be generated?

- What real brands will be close to (likely to compete with) each possible product concept?

- Is there a large enough market segment that would prefer the new product concept(s) over existing brands?

To provide rigorous answers to these and similar questions, a two-stage study is called for:

1. Identification of relevant use occasions and constructs as related to the product class of interest. (This can be done with an analysis of previous studies or an FGI.)

2. A survey among a sample of respondents in which the respondents would:
(a) Rate each brand on each product fea-

ture by each use occasion;
(b) Rate the various use occasions on their frequency of occurrence; and
(c) Rate the brands on their preference and overall appropriateness for each relevant use occasion.

These data can be submitted to appropriate multidimensional scaling and cluster analysis resulting in multidimensional representation of brands, product features, occasions, and preference for brands in a basic product feature space. Such a procedure can provide insights into the generation of new product ideas by focusing on both possible new concepts (as combinations of product features by occasion of usage) and the positioning and ideal points of various market segments. As indicated in Chapter 4, positioning is useful only if evaluated by specific segments. As such an analysis of the market structure by segment may suggest relatively ignored segments which can be addressed either with some modified or new products. Consider for example the development of cosmetics for black women and the establishment of the first women's bank in New York.

A procedure of special interest in this context is the one proposed by Shocker and Srinivasan (1974) which ties a model to predict consumers' predispositions to purchase different "brands" (represented abstractly as a set of coordinates in an attribute space) in a relevant product market with a search process to identify optimal new product ideas.

PRODUCT DEFICIENCY ANALYSIS

The rationale underlying this approach is that consumers can provide useful information on how they would like to change existing products. In its simplest form, this approach is based

on presenting consumers with their existing (or most preferred) product and asking them to indicate what product features they would like to delete from this product and what features to add, if any. This task can be done as an open-ended response or by presenting consumers with lists of product features and asking them to indicate how they would like to modify their product by adding or deleting features from the list. In its more advanced form, the product deficiency analysis can be designed following a conjoint analysis framework. In such a study, consumers are asked to complete two tasks:

• Single factor at a time evaluation of a selected set of factors versus the specific levels and factors of the respondent's current brand. Such an evaluation leads to the development of unidimensional utility functions for each factor.

• Evaluation of a set of combinations of factors (designed following an orthogonal array design) in which each factor appears either at its lowest or highest level. The respondent task is to evaluate each of the combinations (hypothetical products) on his/her likelihood of switching to it from the current brand. The data from this stage are submitted to a conjoint analysis algorithm resulting in utility values, with common unit, for each of the factors.

The results of the unidimensional evaluation of step 1 are now calibrated with the results of step 2 leading to the development of multidimensional utility functions that incorporate the utility for all levels of each of the given factors. These utility functions can be developed at the individual level and submitted to a computer simulation aimed at determining the *switching* likelihood of the customers of various brands to modified or new products. Conjoint analysis based brand switching simulations are discussed in Chapter 10.

UNSTRUCTURED "EXPERT"-BASED APPROACHES TO GENERATION OF NEW PRODUCT IDEAS

The reliance on consumer inputs for the generation of new product ideas has led a number of consumer product companies to decrease their utilization of "experts." Yet, the relevant "experts" such as R&D personnel, managers, salesmen, and others, are an extremely important source of new product ideas.

As with the consumer-based approaches, the approaches discussed in this section are both structured and unstructured, involving both experts as individuals and as members of a group. These approaches are to a large extent, but not exclusively, marketing research oriented.

BRAINSTORMING

Brainstorming by a select group of "experts" can be viewed to a large extent as analogous to FGIs with consumers. The brainstorming sessions are based on the premise that creative ideas can be generated if the atmosphere encourages creative thinking and evaluation and judgment is suspended. In its most common format a brainstorming session involves a relatively small number of participants (usually under 15). The major rules governing a brainstorming session according to Osborn (1953) are:

- No evaluation of any kind is permitted, since criticism and judgment may cause people to defend their ideas rather than generate new and creative ones;
- Participants should be encouraged to think of the wildest ideas possible;
- Encourage a large number of ideas;
- Encourage participants to build upon or modify the ideas of others "as combinations or modifications of previously suggested ideas often lead to new ideas that are superior to those that sparked them" (Adams, 1974).

Some of the major advantages of brainstorming were presented as:

- Less inhibition and defeatism.
- Contagion of enthusiasm.
- Development of competitive spirit; everyone wants to top the others' ideas.

To achieve its greatest impact it is usually a good idea to:

- Include among the participants of a brainstorming session people with diverse backgrounds and experience, and from both within the company and outside (researchers who conducted studies in the given area can be useful in such a session since they can link the session to information on consumer wants and needs);
- Conduct the session for a relatively long period of time, to enable (and force) the participants to go beyond the superficial, first, top-of-mind responses.

Whereas typical brainstorming sessions are concerned with generating ideas for solving problems, occasionally firms use "reverse brainstorming" sessions designed to uncover possible problems and flaws in a product or some proposed solution to a product's problem. General Electric for example has used this approach to identify potential weaknesses in new product prototypes and then develops solutions to these problems (McGuire, 1972).

SYNECTICS

The approach developed by Synectics, Inc., is a somewhat more structured approach (to creative problem solving in a group setting) than brainstorming. The purpose of the approach "is to provide the individual with a repeatable procedure which will increase the probability of his success and hasten his arrival at an innovative solution" (Prince, 1970). Synectics involves a complex group process based on two major psychological mechanisms of "making the

EXHIBIT 9–3

SYNECTICS FLOWCHART

Source: Adapted from G. Prince, *The Practice of Creativity*, Harper & Row, 1970. Reprinted by permission.

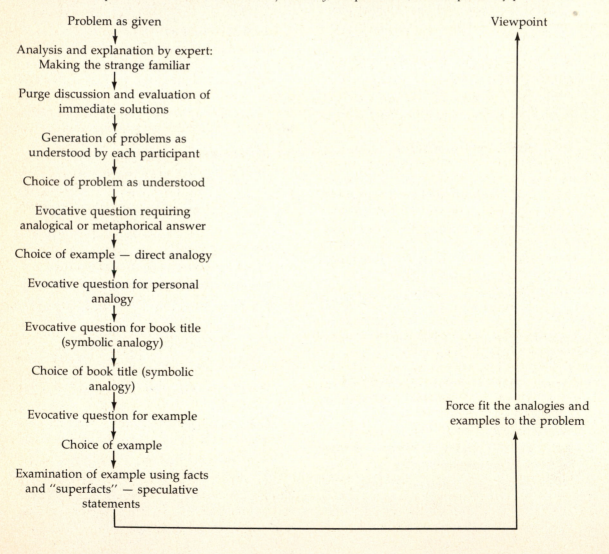

strange familiar" (via three basic procedures of analysis, generalization, and model-seeking or analogy) and "making the familiar strange" (by distorting, inverting, or transposing the everyday ways of looking and responding). The Synectics flow chart, reproduced with minor modifications in Exhibit 9–3, contains all the mechanisms of Synectics. The key to the Synectics approach seems to be the use of metaphor. Four operational mechanisms are employed:

a) *Direct analogy*—direct application of parallel facts, knowledge, or technology;

b) *Personal analogy*—personal identification with part or all of the problem and its solution. This requires the identification not only with others (role playing) but with nonhuman entities—speculating how that *thing* would "feel" and act in the problem situation;

c) *Symbolic analogy*—assessing the essence and meaning of the key words associated with the problem. The utility of the symbolic analogies ("book titles" in Synectics terminology) is related to its "strangeness." Often a symbolic analogy embraces an apparent paradox (e.g., involuntary willingness) and the effort to resolve the paradox leads to insightful solutions;

d) Fantasy analogy—the use of fantasy to solve problems.

Synectics can be viewed as a structured brainstorming group session that, following a careful examination of the problem definition, "seeks new lines of speculation, and these in turn lead to potential solutions (by means of force fit)" (Prince, 1970).

More recently Synectics has extended its approach to the generation of new product ideas conducting its three-five day sessions not only with the company personnel but also with groups of consumers who are heavy users of the product class. These consumers are trained in Synectics idea-generating methods and

"turned loose" on new products possibilities in that area (McGuire, 1972).

SUGGESTION BOX

A widely used source of new product ideas is the employee suggestion system. The National Association of Suggestion Systems includes 1200 member companies which processed in a recent year more than 3.5 million ideas, nearly one for every two employees in the member companies. About 25 percent of these ideas were used and more than $50 million were awarded to the employees submitting these ideas.

Employee suggestion systems include both regular year-round procedures for submitting new product ideas and special new product idea contests involving special incentives and awards.

A recent review of the experience with suggestion boxes by the Conference Board suggests 9 practical pointers that can increase the value of this approach in generating new product ideas. These are:

- Set tangible goals
- Enlist employee support at all levels
- Don't expect all ideas to be winners
- Maintain the continuity of the program
- Welcome all ideas
- Help employees develop their ideas
- Provide complete recognition package
- Handle all employees' new product ideas promptly
- Provide for an annual audit of the suggestion system

Also, to be successful, suggestion boxes should not be limited to the company's own employees, but should include "experts" such as the members of the firm's distribution system and advertising agency.

INDEPENDENT INVENTORS AND LICENSORS

Independent inventors and licensors are often an important source of new product ideas. The importance of the independent inventor has often been ignored. Yet, during the period 1966 to 1977 about 20 percent of all U.S. patents were granted to individuals (*Technology Assessment and Forecast*, 1979).

Licensors, on the other hand, tend to be large companies with "surplus technology" and willingness to license this technology to other firms.

The problem facing any firm with respect to these two sources of new product ideas is how to reach the relevant independent inventor or potential licensor. The utilization of these two sources tends to follow a passive route, i.e., companies respond to approaches by inventors and licensors but only seldom design and implement an active system to identify and reach these sources of new product ideas.

Patent expositions, patent listing publications (such as *US Patent Gazette*), trade shows, patent brokers and attorneys, all facilitate the identification of a prospective inventor. The identification of licensors also involves trade shows, personal contacts, licensing brokers, and various publications such as GE's bimonthly journal *New Business Opportunities*, which offers a periodic summary of GE products and technology available to licensees.

Licensing of new products and processes includes both consumer and industrial items and is marketed by GE and other major industrial firms, in both the US and other countries. In fact many large firms are developing license marketing groups aimed at promoting licensing to other firms.

New product ideas, whether from independent inventors or licensors tend to share three important features:

1. They tend to be technically feasible and in most cases require little further technical development.

2. Their market potential has rarely been established.

3. They are usually encumbered by a vast complexity of legal issues; careful legal advice should be sought prior to the design and implementation of any plan aimed at the utilization of these sources on a regular and systematic basis.

STRUCTURED "EXPERT"-BASED APPROACHES TO GENERATION OF NEW PRODUCT IDEAS

Most "expert"-based approaches to generation of new product ideas rely heavily on various structured marketing research efforts.

PROBLEM/OPPORTUNITY ANALYSIS

Similar in spirit to the product deficiency analysis and problem detection studies among con-sumers, the problem/opportunity analysis is conducted among relevant "experts" and can result in useful new product ideas.

Approaches to the identification of problems and opportunities can range from efforts to identify problems associated with a specific product or product class to a totally unconstrained "bug list." In the latter case respondents (experts, but also consumers if so desired) are asked to list all the things that "bug" them. The bug list is used, for example, at the Stanford School of Engineering's Design Division. Following the construction of bug lists the students are asked to turn the bugs into inventions and "almost invariably, an interesting invention results" (Adams, 1974).

As a similar concept one could develop a list of new uses or users for a given product or technology resulting in an explicit list of opportunities. In this latter approach one can be aided by some explicit "checklists" such as the one developed by Osborn (1953) in his book, *Applied Imagination*, and represented in modified form in the following list of questions:

- Can the product be used in any new way?
- What else is like this product and what can be learned from this comparison?
- How can the product be changed—in meaning, function, structure, use pattern?
- What can be added to the product? To make it stronger, longer, thicker, etc.?
- What to delete? What to subtract, how to make it smaller, condensed, lower, shorter, lighter, etc.?

Another approach to the generation of new product ideas based on problem/opportunity analysis is illustrated in the case of an insurance company which developed a list of all the restrictions found in current policies and used these as a stimulant to the generation of new insurance policies aimed at relaxing the limitations and restrictions of existing policies.

MORPHOLOGICAL ANALYSIS

Given that creativity is often defined as the combining of seemingly disparate parts into a functioning and useful whole, morphological analysis seems to be of great value in the generation of new product ideas. These approaches question things as they are and ask why they

can't be combined, used in new ways, modified, magnified, minified, rearranged, reversed, etc.

Of the various morphological approaches to the generation of new ideas, the following are of particular interest:

Heuristic ideation technique (HIT) This approach for generating new product ideas was proposed by Tauber (1972) and involves two major steps:

- Identification of all "relevant" factors that could be associated with a given product area (e.g., food processing);
- Generation of new ideas by undertaking all possible combinations of factors, examination of these combinations (cells in a matrix), and identification of the more interesting ones.

The example presented by Tauber for the utilization of his procedure involves a matrix of food forms by packages and is partially reproduced in the upper panel of Exhibit 9–4.

Product analogy matrix A somewhat different approach combines the concept of analogy with morphological analysis. In this approach the experts involved identify a number of diverse product classes and attempt to combine their functions with product forms in the product class of interest. If, for example, one is interested in food products, this procedure requires the following four steps:

- Identification of relevant product classes that can serve as analogies. In the case of food, for example, this could include cosmetics, medicine, etc.;
- Identification of the major functions of each of these product classes.
- Identification of the major product forms of the product class of interest;
- Development of all "relevant" combinations of the product forms (of the product

EXHIBIT 9–4

THREE APPROACHES TO MORPHOLOGICAL ANALYSIS

A. FACTOR-BY-FACTOR MATRIX (HIT)

Source: Reprinted from E.M. Tauber, "HIT: Heuristic Ideation Technique—A Systematic Procedure for New Product Search," *Journal of Marketing*, 36, p. 60, 1972, published by the American Marketing Association.

Food form	Packages							
	Aerosol	Bag	Boil 'n bag	Bottle	Box	Jar	Tube	. . .
Bisquit Bread Burger Butter Cereal Cocktail : :								

B. PRODUCT ANALOGY MATRIX

Pet food form	Functions and types of human food products					
	Baby	Diet	Gourmet	Health	Hors d'oeuvres	. . .
Dry Canned In a bag : :						

C. MORPHOLOGICAL FORCED CONNECTION

Source: Reproduced from "Conceptual Blockbusting" by J.L. Adams, by permission of W.W. Norton & Company, Inc., © 1974, 1976 by James L. Adams.

Example: Improved ball-point pen

Attributes:

Cylindrical   Plastic   Separate cap   Steel cartridge

Alternatives:

Faceted   Metal   Attached cap   No cartridge
Square   Glass   No cap   Permanent
Bladed   Wood   Retracts   Paper cartridge
Sculptured   Paper   Cleaning cap   Cartridge made of ink
:   :   :   :

class of interest) with the functions of the other products.

Utilizing this procedure has suggested the development of food items which perform some cosmetic functions (nicer and smoother skin, suntan, etc.) and other food products which provide added medication (headache remedies in a drink, antacid cookie, aspirin in a chewing gum, etc.). The middle panel of Exhibit 9–4 represents an illustrative matrix for such an approach.

Morphological forced connections This morphological approach is based on the concept proposed by Koberg and Bagnal (1974). This "foolproof invention-finding scheme," according to the authors, requires the following three steps:

- List the attributes of the situation;
- Below each attribute, place as many alternatives as you can think of;
- When completed, make many random runs through the alternatives, picking up a different one from each column and assembling the combinations into entirely new forms of the original subject.

This approach is illustrated in the lower panel of Exhibit 9–4.

Morphological procedures seem to be among the most powerful approaches to generating new product ideas. Most of them can be conducted by means of a computer, further facilitating the exploration of large numbers of possible combinations of relevant attributes.

The major attributes of these approaches are that they are:

- Systematic
- Capable of encompassing a very large number of alternative new product ideas
- Flexible with respect to the selection of relevant attributes
- Simple and relatively inexpensive to use

GROWTH OPPORTUNITY ANALYSIS

An important source of new product ideas can be an analysis of the firm's strengths and weaknesses. This analysis should include an evaluation of the firm's product line, distribution system, product usage pattern, and the competitive environment. An interesting integrated approach to the analysis of all these factors was suggested by Weber (1976) who coined the term "Growth Opportunity Analysis." This approach is best summarized in Exhibit 9–5, which illustrates the growth opportunity strategies and a set of examples.

These and similar analyses, such as the ones suggested in Chapters 6 and 7, have often resulted in interesting and useful ideas for new products, suggesting the need for continuous monitoring of the firm's performance and environment.

ENVIRONMENTAL TRENDS ANALYSIS

As indicated in Chapter 7, a careful monitoring and projection of environmental (economic, social, technological, and legal) trends can provide an extremely useful source of ideas for new products and services.

A system should therefore be designed to collect, interpret, and disseminate among the relevant new product development personnel all the *relevant* information on the changing environment and projected environmental trends.

The existence of such a system can mean the difference between being the leader with some new product entry or being a follower. Consider for example the trend in the last few years toward natural fiber. Keeping abreast of the relevant medical research could have given food companies a considerable lead in the development of natural fiber products. Yet, the

EXHIBIT 9–5

ILLUSTRATIVE STRATEGY RECOMMENDATIONS OF GROWTH OPPORTUNITY
ANALYSIS

Source: J.A. Weber, Growth Opportunity Analysis, 1976, p. 184. Reprinted by permission of
Reston Publishing Co., A. Prentice–Hall Company, 11480 Sunset Hills Road, Reston, VA 22090.

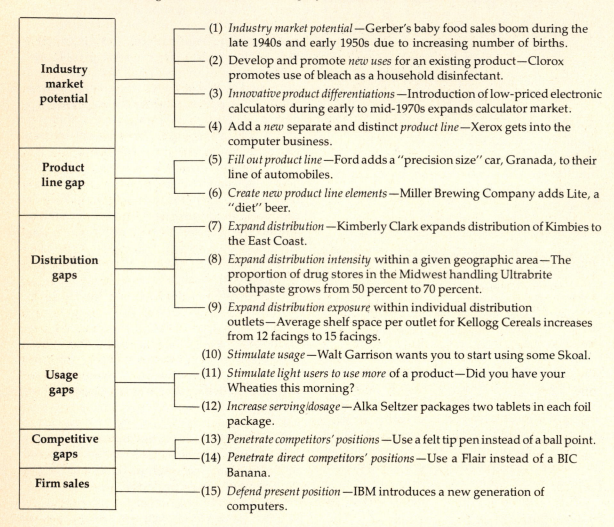

Industry market potential

(1) *Industry market potential*—Gerber's baby food sales boom during the late 1940s and early 1950s due to increasing number of births.

(2) Develop and promote *new uses* for an existing product—Clorox promotes use of bleach as a household disinfectant.

(3) *Innovative product differentiations*—Introduction of low-priced electronic calculators during early to mid-1970s expands calculator market.

(4) Add a *new* separate and distinct *product line*—Xerox gets into the computer business.

Product line gap

(5) *Fill out product line*—Ford adds a "precision size" car, Granada, to their line of automobiles.

(6) *Create new product line elements*—Miller Brewing Company adds Lite, a "diet" beer.

Distribution gaps

(7) *Expand distribution*—Kimberly Clark expands distribution of Kimbies to the East Coast.

(8) *Expand distribution intensity* within a given geographic area—The proportion of drug stores in the Midwest handling Ultrabrite toothpaste grows from 50 percent to 70 percent.

(9) *Expand distribution exposure* within individual distribution outlets—Average shelf space per outlet for Kellogg Cereals increases from 12 facings to 15 facings.

Usage gaps

(10) *Stimulate usage*—Walt Garrison wants you to start using some Skoal.

(11) *Stimulate light users to use more* of a product—Did you have your Wheaties this morning?

(12) *Increase serving/dosage*—Alka Seltzer packages two tablets in each foil package.

Competitive gaps

(13) *Penetrate competitors' positions*—Use a felt tip pen instead of a ball point.

(14) *Penetrate direct competitors' positions*—Use a Flair instead of a BIC Banana.

Firm sales

(15) *Defend present position*—IBM introduces a new generation of computers.

bread companies, for example, did lag behind other food companies.

An important part of the environmental analysis is the analysis of trends in consumer demographics, values, and needs. A number of continuous surveys on changes in consumer values are available (e.g., the social monitor discussed in Chapter 7). Examination of these social trends and other changes in society's life style, value system, and the like can provide important sources for new product ideas. Consider, for example, the change in family structure—the formation of single-person households, of communes, of persons of the same or opposite sex living together without marriage, and consider some of the implications of these trends to the products and services of tomorrow.

In examining these trends, attention should be given to the emerging trends, even if associated with small segments of the population. Waiting for major trends is safer, but might be too late if the objective is an early identification of emerging trends.

ANALYSIS OF COMPETITIVE PRODUCTS

One of the continuous sources of new product ideas can be the examination of other products in the same and related product categories. Of special interest in this area is the examination of foreign products which can be adopted to the local environment as new products.

The examination of foreign markets and the products in other product categories is often done, however, in a nonsystematic manner. Executives on a foreign vacation might bring back an idea or two. Yet, both the foreign markets and other product categories require a careful, systematic, and continuous evaluation which can lead to the generation of new product ideas.

Examination of competing products within the same product category has received considerable attention. Greater focus, however, should be placed on (a) the efforts of small firms which might be introducing a new regional product which if modified or supported by the resources of a larger firm might become a market leader and (b) related product

categories. The automatic travel check dispenser located at airports might suggest, for example, the possibility of such automatic distribution of life insurance policies and similar "products."

SEARCH OF PATENTS AND OTHER SOURCES OF NEW IDEAS

A number of publications devoted to new product ideas are available. These publications include specialized new product newsletters such as the *International New Product Newsletter* and others listed in Exhibit 9–6. These newsletters are supplemented by numerous other publications issued by high-technology or new product brokerage firms. In addition, there are specialized publications such as *Innovations*, and a number of magazines have special sections on new products such as *Advertising Age's* "Idea Marketplace." *Advertising Age* also publishes information on new products in test market and new product advertising as reported by BAR (Broadcast Advertising Report) monitor. A regular column on new market ideas appears in *Popular Science,* called "New Ideas from the Inventors," and *Newsweek* introduced a special section on new products and processes which was later expanded to a regular newsletter, followed by annual compilation which is sold separately.

Other important sources of new product ideas are the listing of domestic and international patents and patent applications, and available technology for sale or lease from government and nongovernment organizations. NASA, for example, has made considerable efforts at marketing its space technology to industry for consumer product applications. Similarly, some of the larger R&D laboratories such as GE's create and market technologies which are outside the scope of their regular operations.

EXHIBIT 9–6

ILLUSTRATIVE LIST OF NEWSLETTERS ON NEW PRODUCT IDEAS
AND INTRODUCTION

Nielsen Early Intelligence System A weekly preview of new developments in consumer products.

Marketing Focus: New Products and Trends A report for HBA, cosmetics and appliance marketers, and a separate report for grocery and household marketers. Published by A.R. Schwalb, Stamford, CT.

The Rountree Report: New products, new processes, new developments. Biweekly, published by Rountree Publishing Co., Garden City, N.J.

DFS New Product News Dancer, Fitzgerald, Sample, N.Y.

NACDS Product News Notes Published by the National Association of Chain Drugstores, Inc.

Seidman News Bulletin Published by S. Seidman, West Redding, Conn.

Inside Industry Published by Magazines for Industry, N.Y.

Brainstorming Marketing Intelligence Service, Naples, N.Y.

International New Product Newsletter Issued by the International New Product Center.

ROLE OF THE R&D PROCESS IN GENERATION OF NEW PRODUCT IDEAS

R&D expenditures in 1979 exceeded $52 billion—about 2.3 percent of the GNP. As such it represents a major activity with enormous impact on the direction and nature of new product development. About 50 percent of this amount came from the federal government, 47 percent from industry, 2 percent from universities, and 1 percent from other nonprofit institutions. The bulk of these amounts was devoted to development (64 percent), 23 percent to applied research, and only 13 percent to basic research.[4] A key dimension of the R&D activities is the generation of new ideas. In this section we will briefly address some of the issues involved in generating new product ideas with R&D personnel. Not discussed are the nature of

---

[4] R&D spending (and professional employment in R&D) has increased in real terms since 1975, primarily due to Federal energy R&D investments. For a detailed analysis of the national pattern of R&D resources, see NSF (1978).

the R&D process, its contribution to new product development, and its management. These are briefly discussed in other chapters.

DEMAND-INDUCED VERSUS SUPPLY-PUSHED INNOVATIONS

Supply-pushed innovations are typical of those firms in which "the R&D scientist/engineer is king." Supply-pushed innovations "result from the persistent, maybe even impassioned, advocacy of an inventor who sees an opportunity or latent need that he believes he can satisfy or who conceives a solution for which he seeks to demonstrate or even create a need" (Steele, 1975). These types of innovations can result in major technological breakthroughs. Yet, accomplishments of this magnitude are likely to be infrequent while the risks for failure are quite high. The demand-induced innovations, on the other hand, are much more receptive to market demands, relying on requests and suggestions from sources outside the R&D group. According to Steele (1975) in his study of innovation in big business, "Most of the innovations that occur in the US, defined not in terms of dollar value per innovations but rather in terms of numbers of changes successfully introduced, undoubtedly are of this type." These include requests for lower-cost products, elimination of a nagging field problem, design of some kind of a product to offset a competitor's product advantage, and other requests which challenge the R&D personnel to discover solutions to perceived needs of the firm. Characteristics of these "micro inventions" are that they involve lower risks, but also lower long-term payoff than the supply-pushed innovations.

This critical role of demand-induced new product ideas was recognized by Souder (1981) who concluded his study on the R&D/marketing interface by stating:

In general, ideas which originated within R&D had lower commercial success rates than those ideas which originated within the marketing functions of the firms. Many of the ideas that originated in R&D did not stimulate the interest of the marketing department, or did not fit the company's philosophy or current lines of business. New product ideas that originated from top management did not have high success rates. Most of them required more capital than could be obtained. However, if top management promoted an idea that originated elsewhere, it often succeeded."

Demand-induced innovations follow two major routes: (a) a manufacturer-initiated process in which the manufacturing firm engages in formal and informal marketing research activities aimed at discovering the needs and problems of potential users or other relevant respondents (e.g., the firm's own salesforce), and (b) a user-initiated process.

Von Hippel (1978) summarized the findings of eight empirical studies which support the hypothesis that many—and perhaps most—commercially successful new industrial products were developed in response to an idea provided to the would-be manufacturer at the initiative of a would-be customer.

The Von Hippel findings are somewhat at odds with the commonly-accepted paradigms of industrial innovations rising from a manufacturer-initiated need assessment and a manufacturer-based development of a new product idea which is responsive to customer needs. However, his findings and other studies on industrial innovations and organizational buying behavior, e.g. Von Hippel (1977, 1978), Robinson et al. (1967), Utterback (1971), and Isenson (1969), emphasize the role the buying organization has in the development of new product ideas. The buyer's role can vary from a minimal involvement in which the buyer recognizes a problem that requires a new product solution, through various stages in which the buying organization can determine the solution type, develop product design specifications, and even in extreme cases develop a product prototype.

From a corporate point of view the ideal solution, of course, is to have a "creative balance" between the two approaches. What this suggests for the generation of new product ideas is the encouragement of the R&D personnel to engage in supply-pushed innovation and at the same time participate actively, as part of the "expert" team, in generation and evaluation of demand-induced new product ideas. Furthermore, given the Von Hippel findings, any comprehensive program for generating new product ideas should incorporate mechanisms for identifying those client companies which develop their own new products. In these cases an important marketing function of the manufacturing firm is to convince the innovative client that their firm is the one to work with on the development and manufacturing of the new products.

R&D ACTIVITIES FOR NEW PRODUCT INNOVATIONS, PRODUCT IMPROVEMENTS, OR NEW PROCESSES

Although the previous discussion of approaches for the generation of new product ideas focused primarily on *new products*, two important distinctions should be made: (a) between the development of innovative new products versus some modification to an existing product. The balance between the two varies by industry, type of firm within an industry, and obviously the balance between supply-pushed and demand-induced innovations; (b) between innovations in product (whether new or modified) versus innovations in the production process. A 1970 study of the R&D process in 170 firms found only a handful of companies who directed R&D efforts toward the development of new processes (Gerstenfeld, 1970). (It is important to note, however, that the process of one company may be the product of another.)

R&D ACTIVITIES BY NON-R&D PERSONNEL

New product (and process) ideas and their research and development are not limited to the R&D personnel. Engineers in other departments, industrial designers, and scientists in various organizational functions all can generate new product ideas and occasionally even undertake the entire development process. Systematic management of new product development effort should take these individuals and groups into account, especially with respect to the first and most crucial step of the generation of new product ideas.

SYSTEM FOR THE GENERATION OF NEW PRODUCT IDEAS

Given the variety of approaches which can and have been utilized in the generation of new product ideas the question often arises as to which of these approaches should be used. The answer often is not a simple one since no single approach can assure the generation of all the relevant new product ideas. Whereas no one can assure the exhaustiveness of the list of new product ideas, the utilization of a *number* of approaches is clearly preferable to the reliance on the outcome of a single approach.

Consistent with this multiapproach philosophy, Dr. Bujake, a member of the new product development group at Coca Cola's foods division, suggested a four-step method for programmed innovation which incorporates a number of approaches to the generation of new product ideas:

Opportunity search This phase is the starting point for the new product idea generation process and is concerned with the appraisal of a given product area. Two approaches are utilized in this phase: attribute analysis—the listing and analysis in a group session of "all the uses, together with the desirable and undesirable characteristics and attributes of known products in a particular area" (the objective of this analysis is to generate combinations of desired attributes without any of the undesirable product characteristics), and systems analysis (this approach is based on an examination of all the inputs and outputs of a physical system that involve the product area of interest).

Form evolution This phase of the new product idea generation process attempts to develop a unique *form* for a product concept by using the material generated in the previous step and subjecting it to *morphological analysis*.

Concept expansion This phase involves the "generation of large numbers of alternative approaches relating to the attributes and forms." The approaches utilized in this phase are the *group ideation* technique (Osborn, 1953) and its modifications and the *trigger method* which adds the dimension of competition within the group to enhance idea generation. This procedure involves a number of cycles in which each group member develops and presents to the group a list of key words and ideas relating to the problem under investigation. The presentation of key words and ideas triggers other ideas and may lead to the generation of additional new product ideas.

Concept development This final phase of the process is based on in-depth probing of the new concept to provide innovative solutions to various aspects of the concept. The approach recommended by Bujake for this phase is the Synectics technique discussed earlier.

The integrated multiphase approach suggested by Bujake is a good illustration of how a number of approaches to the generation of new product ideas can be put together in a systematic fashion. The suggested approach, however, is somewhat rigid and should be viewed primarily as an illustrative system. The order of the specific phases is quite arbitrary, and the approaches selected reflect the preferences of one researcher and should not be viewed as an endorsement of these specific approaches as opposed to others discussed in this chapter.

An alternative to the proposed rigid, multiphase procedure for new product generation is to select a number of alternative approaches for the generation of new product ideas which complement each other and with which mangement feels comfortable. As a general guideline it is suggested to select at least one approach from each one of the four cells in Exhibit 9–1.

CONCLUDING REMARKS

The focus of this chapter has been on the generation of new product ideas. Yet, the approaches described are not limited to the generation of *new products* and can, as suggested by

Schumpeter (1961) be applied to:

- The invention and introduction of new *methods of production;*
- The creation of and entry into new *markets;*
- The creation and utilization of new sources and types of raw materials and other supplies;
- The design of new *management and organizational* systems.

Creativity, according to Webster's dictionary, involves the new, unique and original; of bringing something into existence for the first time. As such, creativity is essential in the generation of new product ideas. A number of approaches to the generation of new product ideas were suggested in this chapter. Review these approaches and select those that are most appropriate for a firm or product class of your choice. Using these approaches generate as many new ideas as possible. Upon completion of this task, examine the ideas for their variety and degree of innovativeness and assess the usefulness of the various approaches you employed.

10

Consumer-Based Concept Screening and Evaluation

INTRODUCTION

Having generated a large set of new product ideas, the next step in the new product development process should be the evaluation of these ideas. This screening and evaluation procedure is of crucial importance to the overall success of the new product development process since a failure to eliminate a poor idea may result in unnecessary costs and the diversion of resources from more promising ideas. Similarly, the deletion of a promising idea may be associated with a lost opportunity cost.

To avoid such problems and provide the necessary guidance to the allocation of resources among competing new product ideas, a variety of concept testing procedures have been developed and utilized. The objective of this chapter is not to provide an exhaustive review of the various approaches, but rather to present in some detail two approaches to consumer-based concept screening and evaluation.

To place these procedures in the right context, the chapter starts with a brief discussion of the three major steps of any concept evaluation procedure—initial management screening, consumer-based screening and evaluation, and initial economic evaluation. The remainder of the chapter is devoted to the second phase—consumer-based approaches to concept testing. The first part of this discussion is devoted to a general evaluation of qualitative versus quantitative approaches to concept testing. The superiority of quantitative approaches is suggested, and two quantitative approaches to concept testing are presented. The first is based on an a priori definition of a concept, whereas the second approach is based on a conjoint analysis design. The discussion of the various consumer-based approaches to the screening and evaluation of new concepts concludes with the specification of a number of conditions which, if followed, could help increase the value of such procedures.

CONCEPT EVALUATION PARADIGM

New product ideas, whether in their most generic and simplistic form (as a core idea) or in some more defined form (as a concept description), should be evaluated on a number of key questions:

- How congruent are they with management's objectives?
- Are they technically feasible?
- Are they legal?
- What is the expected demand for them?
- What is the expected cost of manufacturing and marketing them?

The answers to these questions involve three distinct stages:

1. An initial management screening aimed at answering the first three questions;
2. A consumer evaluation procedure to assess the expected demand;
3. An initial economic analysis of the concept's viability and profitability (combining the results of the consumer evaluation phase with the estimated impact of competitive reaction and production and marketing costs).

INITIAL MANAGEMENT SCREENING

The first evaluation of any new product idea should be based on its compatibility with management's objectives. If a food company, for example, does not consider tobacco and liquor products consistent with their family-oriented corporate image and objectives, and if regardless of the potential profitability of such products they will not change their position, there is little to be gained by pursuing any further tobacco or liquor new product ideas.

Similarly, if management decides, for example, that any new product entry should capitalize on and utilize the firm's distribution strength, any new product idea which does not meet this criterion should, at least for the time being, be screened out.

The danger in management screening is quite obvious. Truly innovative new product ideas may be screened out if they are viewed as incongruent with the current objectives or they involve a higher risk than management is willing to accept. Yet, given the importance of management acceptance and support, there is no easy substitute for this initial screening. Safeguards must be established, however, to minimize the possible negative consequences of such screening. These safeguards against the misuse of the initial concept screening stage require: (a) the inclusion of diverse and open-minded participants and, to the extent possible, outside independent consultants in the screening session, (b) exclusion of top management personnel (getting their approval at later stages), and (c) the recycling of all rejected ideas in a subsequent evaluation stage.

The second task of the first management screening stage is the initial evaluation of the technical feasibility of the various ideas. Given the generic and vague nature of most new product ideas, it is quite difficult to provide an exact evaluation of whether the idea can be implemented technically or not. Yet, an initial technical evaluation is essential even at this early stage. The objective of this technical screening is to identify those ideas that clearly cannot be implemented given the current state of technology and at the same time to identify the technological domains that if developed (or acquired) might benefit a number of new product ideas.

To assure an accurate assessment of the technological feasibility of new product ideas, it is desirable to supplement the firm's own R&D personnel with outside scientists and experts. The involvement of outsiders in the technical evaluation stage is necessary to assure that any technical judgment is based not only on the company's current technological level but on the latest developments in relevant technological areas.

The third task of the initial management screening is the evaluation of the legal appropriateness of the concepts. As the scope of government regulation continues to increase, it becomes essential to consider, even at this early stage in the new product development process, the likely legal implications. The severity of the legal restrictions differ by industry, but should be considered an integral part of most concept screening procedures. In assessing the legal evaluation, it is important to note, however, that from a legal perspective the trend is to be conservative—aiming at reducing the risk of legal problems with the new product. Strict adherence to legal requirements, therefore, might be detrimental to the innovativeness of the surviving concepts. To avoid this risk, it is often useful to view the legal screen as a way of identifying, early in the new product development process, likely areas of (legal) vulnerability that should be addressed during the development process, rather than as a "go—no go" screen.

The various management considerations at the screening stage are further discussed in Chapter 11.

CONSUMER-BASED CONCEPT SCREENING AND EVALUATION

Having survived initial management screening, the new product ideas are ready for their next test—their acceptability by consumers.

Consumer based concept evaluation is often divided into two parts: a *concept screening* phase which is designed to provide, in cases in which a large number of ideas survived the first management screening phase, an initial consumer-based screening of ideas leading to the identification of a workable number of potentially promising ideas. The surviving ideas are then developed into more detailed concepts and submitted to further evaluation in a *concept testing* phase.

Concept screening and testing should provide guidelines for two key management decisions: (a) should we continue developing the given idea/concept, modify it, or abandon it? and (b) if a "go" decision has been made, how should we proceed?

To answer these two questions, concept testing studies should provide answers to the following research questions:

1. What is consumer reaction to the concept? What is the size of the potential market? Which attributes are most important in accounting for consumer reactions to the concept?

2. How many market segments exist, and what are their characteristics (socio-economic, demographic, psychographic, and product and brand usage patterns) and reactions to the various concepts?

3. What is the relevant competitive setting of the given concept? What is the most desirable positioning for the concept, and how likely is the concept to cannibalize the current products of the firm?

Most concept screening and testing procedures focus only on certain aspects of the first question. The segmentation and positioning issues are dealt with in separate studies. Given that markets are heterogeneous, it is essential to evaluate concepts on the basis of acceptance by consumers in general *and* by specific market segments. Furthermore, the evaluation of the concepts should be conducted in the context of a realistic competitive environment (including, if appropriate, the firm's existing products). Information on the reaction of *each* relevant segment to the various concepts in their competitive setting provides the necessary guidelines for improving the concepts, the initial design of their marketing strategy, and their initial economic evaluation.

INITIAL ECONOMIC EVALUATION

Inputs on consumers' reactions to the new products can be translated into estimates of anticipated product trial. This trial estimate, if supplemented with estimates of repeat purchase reflecting likely competitive reactions and manufacturing and marketing costs, could result in tentative profit estimates. The evaluation of the likely economic performance of a concept is by necessity very crude at this early stage of concept development. Yet, it is important to have at least some general idea of anticipated performance under a variety of assumed conditions. The approaches to the economic evaluation of new product concepts are further discussed in Chapter 11.

QUALITATIVE VERSUS QUANTITATIVE APPROACHES TO CONCEPT EVALUATION

Focused group interviews (FGIs) in some form or another have often been used to evaluate consumer reaction to new product concepts. Insightful analysis of the FGI can provide useful guidelines for concept development, modifications, and wording. Most researchers and managers would, correctly, hesitate to "kill" a concept based on the perceived reaction of a few groups. Yet, the total reliance on FGIs to provide the necessary input on consumers' reactions to new product concepts is not uncommon.

Consider for example the article "Concept Testing: An Appropriate Approach" (Iuso, 1975) which criticized the common (quantitative) concept testing approaches and suggested an alternative approach in which:

> Concepts are not assessed on the basis of consumers' own self ratings, but rather on the basis of trained researchers' overall analytic judgments which result from the systematic categorizations of consumers' discursive reactions to concept stimuli.

Although Iuso's criticism of some of the common approaches to concept testing is justified, it seems that the solution suggested by him has its own limitations. It is desirable, therefore, to briefly examine some of the major limitations of both quantitative and qualitative approaches to concept testing.

LIMITATIONS OF THE COMMON QUANTITATIVE APPROACHES TO CONCEPT TESTING

The most common concept testing approach involves a consumer survey in which consumers are presented with concept descriptions and asked to rate them on intentions to buy, overall liking, and a number of other attributes as well as to indicate what they like and dislike about the concept(s).

The heart of most concept testing procedures is the assessment of consumers' likelihood of buying the concept. This assessment is most often based on a concept rating on a five-point intention-to-buy scale:

1—Definitely would buy

2—Probably would buy

3—May or may not buy

4—Probably would not buy

5—Definitely would not buy

Yet, other scales—4-, 6-, 7-, or 10-point scales—can often be found. Also utilized are constant sum procedures, in which 10 or 100 points are distributed among a set of concepts based on the relative attractiveness of each concept. An infrequently used procedure is an explicit paired comparison of a concept with a control concept, the consumers' currently most preferred brand or the market leader.

As indicated correctly by Iuso and others (Wind, 1973), the frequently used quantitative approach to concept evaluation has four major limitations:

1. Intention to buy scores may not reflect consumers' "real" reaction toward the concept. Whether top box is rated because of "courtesy endorsements" or other reasons, the major problem is that such a task is frequently associated with a monadic test in which the consumer is not placed in a choice situation (between the new concept and competing brands).

2. Most concepts are multiattribute in nature

(yet, they are frequently presented as a single statement). This may lead to the situation cited by Iuso in which "It is possible for a consumer to like various aspects of a given concept stimulus, and thus rate it highly, while at the same time remaining rather uninvolved with the basic idea from the standpoint of her own problems in the life activity addressed by the idea" or conversely: "a consumer may be genuinely involved with the core thrust of an idea, but may intensely dislike certain in particular (correctable) features, thus resulting in an overall 'poor'."

3. Most quantitative concept testing procedures do not provide the necessary diagnostic information. Iuso, for example, suggests that a concept testing procedure "should be prescriptive of 'how go' as well as 'if go'." The need for diagnostic information in terms of finding the positioning of a concept by market segments was discussed in earlier papers on concept testing (Wind, 1973) but is still not a widely-used practice.

4. Most concept testing studies rely on a single evaluative criterion. Intention to buy is frequently used as the sole criterion and even more limited than this, quite frequently management base their decision solely on the percentage of people who definitely intend to buy the concept (top box raters) ignoring the complete distribution of responses to this single criterion.

IUSO'S QUALITATIVE SOLUTION AND ITS LIMITATIONS

To overcome these limitations, Iuso suggests a "qualitative" approach to concept testing. The description provided by him is vague and nonoperational. Yet, it suggests an approach based on:

Intensive questioning to determine how well a concept dovetails with consumer frame of reference, along with professional analysis and a mediated synthesis of information drawn from both company and consumer.

This intensive questioning is further defined as

rather lengthy conversations with appropriate consumers. The consumer must be allowed to think and talk about a conceptualized product or service idea.

It is these conversations, and not enigmatic scale points which provide the most reliable and complete indications of market reactions to an idea . . .

Iuso does not specify whether these interviews are individual interviews or focused group interviews. In either case, his approach is based on interviewer judgment as to the consumers "real" reactions to the concept. This is clearly stated by him:

The analysis and syntheses of these intensive interactions with consumers should be made by skilled research analysts on the basis of a careful overall appraisal of each consumer's responses to an entire series of open ended and semi-structured questions.

He further states:

If numbers are required, it is the researcher's task to assign scale points—not the consumer's.

In abstract this might seem an "appropriate" solution. The researcher—or more appropriately "the marketing psychoanalyst"—diagnoses the verbal and nonverbal responses of the consumer and based on this in-depth diagnosis determines the score of the concept. In reality, however, this suggestion is totally inappropriate due to two major limitations:

1. Given the depth of interview required, and the scarcity of qualified marketing psychoanalysts, to try to conduct such an in-depth analysis on an adequate sample size will most likely be prohibitive from a cost point of view. Given that the results of

concept testing studies should be project-able to the entire market, small and non-representative sample size, which is implied in Iuso's approach, may lead to misleading conclusions.

2. The suggested procedure relies on interpretation by the interviewer/researcher. Iuso does give lip service to this problem by stating:

> The approach must be organized and 'depersonalized' as much as possible by providing a system of formal rules and checking for use by research analysts. This ensures that the same 'judgment' would be reached by different research analysts.

Yet, he does not suggest operational ways in which this consensus among researchers can be obtained. The field of content analysis does provide some guidelines for determining interjudge reliability (Gerbner et al., 1969; Hosti, 1968, for example), but it does not seem that Iuso or other qualitative researchers are willing to go so far. Relying on the interviewer/researcher interpretation is similar to the case of focused group interviews, in which the same consumer response can be interpreted quite differently by researchers with different orientations—the clinical psychologist versus the family sociologist versus the cultural anthropologist to mention just three. These different interpretations and recommendations are not as severe when present in focused group interviews designed to generate hypotheses but may be of serious consequences if used to *evaluate* ideas.

Current so-called qualitative concept testing studies based on simple rating of a single complex concept are subject to a number of serious limitations. The qualitative approach as suggested by Iuso does not solve these problems in a satisfactory way and adds a number of other serious limitations. Available research methods for product positioning and segmentation coupled with advances in measurement and multivariate data analysis techniques provide a number of operational and rigorous approaches to concept testing which overcome the above limitations without having to rely on the subjective interpretation of a "marketing psychoanalyst."

CONCEPT EVALUATION BY USING A PRIORI CONCEPT DEFINITIONS

Most concept testing procedures start with the definition of a number of distinct new product concepts. Consider for example the following three examples taken from actual concept-testing studies of a large food company, a bank, and a health insurance company.

- *Tear-resistant soft bread*. Tear-resistant soft bread is a loaf of soft white bread, made by a special process, which is less likely than the regular white bread to tear when spread with butter, peanut butter, and the like.

- *A professional financial counseling service offered by your bank*. This counseling service is designed to assist you in determining and developing priorities for your financial goals (such as children's college education, retirement, purchase of a home) and to aid in the selection of a program tailored to achieve these goals. Your overall financial situation would be confidentially reviewed (including insurance policies, pension benefits, savings) so that various investment alternatives could be explored. The service would provide for periodic review. Price for average yearly usage would be $100 for the initial year and $25 for each year thereafter.

- *Vision care insurance.* A plan that pays $20 for each of the following annual vision care expenses: eye examination, single lens prescription, bifocal lens prescription, trifocal lens prescription, and a set of frames.

Having developed a number of concept definitions, the most common quantitative procedure for concept evaluation involves the presentation of these concepts to a sample of respondents asking them to rate the concepts on intentions to buy, overall liking, and a number of other attributes and to indicate what they like and dislike most about the concept.

Given that such procedures cannot provide the answers to the three questions we stated earlier as the critical ones in any concept testing approach, the remainder of this section will be devoted to a discussion of a concept testing procedure which was developed in the late 1960s and employed in a number of commerical concept testing studies.[1] The major features of the procedure include the following:

1. Up to eight concepts in a given product class can be evaluated in the same study.
2. Concept evaluation is done explicitly in the context of the concepts' relevant competitive setting.
3. Rigorous multivariate statistical and multidimensional scaling techniques are used to identify the key discriminating characteristics of the various segments and to establish the concept positioning.
4. The "hard-core" potential buyers are identified by requiring a choice (including a

measure of "behavioral commitment" to try or buy the concept) between the concept and the leading competitive brands.

THE DATA

The data for the concept testing analysis are usually derived from personal interviews but can be adjusted for mail questionnaires. A sample of 200–500 female, male, adult, and/or child respondents—depending on the nature of the concept—is often used. A typical questionnaire might include the following eight parts:

1. An overall preference ranking of existing brands and concepts (including a control concept with known marketplace performance) as well as concept rating on an intention-to-buy scale. The concepts are all presented in a write-up form with or without an artist's conception, while the existing brands are presented either as names or as color photographs.
2. A set of five to ten relevant product benefits presented singly or in combinations (depending on whether one wants to use conjoint analysis procedures to identify benefit segments) to be ranked in terms of relative importance to the respondents.
3. Open-ended responses on things most liked and disliked about the concepts. Also, concept ratings are given on each of the product benefits and other prespecified constructs—such as uniqueness, believability, and informativeness—that are judged to be important in explaining the reaction to the concepts.
4. Selection and rating of concepts and control brands according to their appropriateness for various use/consumption occasions.
5. Respondent usage and brand preference data for the product class under study and evaluation of the various occasions in terms

[1]The discussion in this section is based on Wind (1973).

of their frequency of occurrence.

6. Selected general and product class-related lifestyle and attitudinal statements.

7. Standard socioeconomic and demographic questions.

8. Behavioral commitment: choosing ("buying") a brand/concept when confronted with a choice among the concepts, other leading brands, or money.

PLAN OF ANALYSIS

The data are subjected to a number of analytical procedures which range from simple cross tabulations to multivariate analysis and multidimensional scaling. The major steps of the analyses are summarized in Exhibit 10–1 and discussed briefly below.

Segmentation Of the numerous possible bases for segmentation (Frank, Massy, and Wind, 1972), three are particularly appealing: (a) consumers' reactions to the concepts (those with positive reactions versus those with negative reactions), (b) consumers' expectations (benefits sought) from the given product class, and (c) current users of a target competitive brand (against which the new concept is being positioned). Management preferences should determine the desired basis for segmentation, although benefits (Haley, 1968, 1971; Green, Wind, and Jain, 1972) are suggested as at least one of the bases for segmentation to be used.

Following the clustering of respondents into segments, the remaining analysis—concept evaluation and positioning—is done by segment. It may also be desirable to conduct the analysis on the total sample.

Concept evaluation Determining which concept is most promising for the overall sample, as well as for each market segment, involves the following calculations:

- The percentage of those with positive intentions to buy;

- The percentage of those with both positive intentions to buy and behavioral commitment to buy or try the concept (hard-core potential buyers);

- The anticipated usage of the concepts—intentions to buy for each occasion weighted by the frequency of occurrence of the given occasion;

- Interval scales (based on Thurstone's law of comparative judgment) indicating the relative preference for the concepts and control brands for each of the occasions and overall.

- Determination of which attributes are important in explaining consumer reactions to the concepts. This can be done by using multiple regression analysis for the overall sample and each market segment. This analysis enables the researcher to assess the statistical association between the set of evaluative scales—each concept's rating on the product benefit scales and message attributes such as degree of believability—and the overall concept liking score (the dependent variable).

- A *content analysis* of the open-ended questions on likes and dislikes about the concept which when coupled with the regression results provides some idea as to which aspect of the concept led to its being liked or disliked.

In assessing consumers' reactions to the various concepts, it is essential to isolate the true reaction to the concept by removing any "yes-saying" bias. This can be done by forcing the respondent to make a choice among the concepts and their likely competitors (including the brands currently used by the respondent), or if rating scales are being used (such as in the case of intentions to buy scales), it might be desirable to standardize the data.

EXHIBIT 10–1

OVERVIEW OF ANALYSIS OF CONCEPT EVALUATION USING A PRIORI CONCEPT DEFINITION

Source: Reprinted from the *Journal of Marketing* published by the American Marketing Association. Exhibit from "A New Procedure for Concept Evaluation" by Yoram Wind, vol. 37, October 1973.

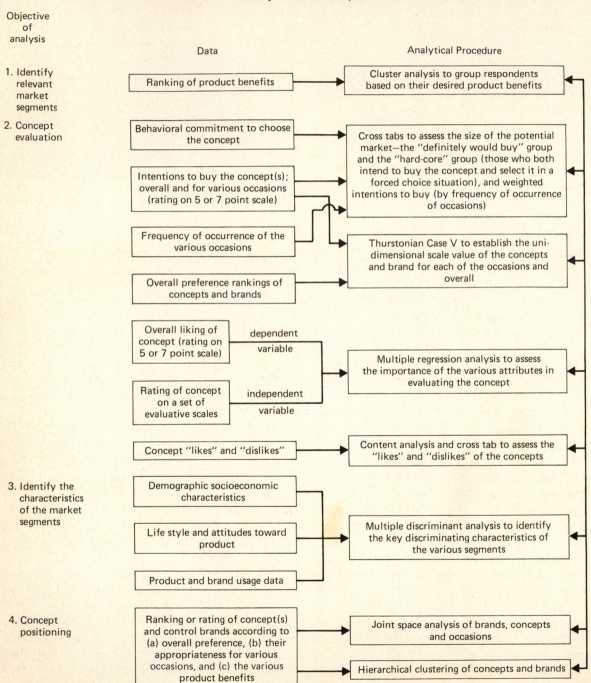

Standardization may also help provide a more realistic assessment of the consumers' reactions to the concepts aside from their possible favorable reaction to the "novelty" inherent in any new concept.

Identifying the key characteristics of the various segments   A series of multiple discriminant analyses is undertaken to establish the key discriminating characteristics and provide better insight into the nature of the segments. Since the total number of predictor variables is usually large, four separate stepwise discriminant runs are conducted for the: (1) socioeconomic-demographic characteristics, (2) product usage data, (3) general and product-specific life-style and attitude data, and (4) the key discriminating variables from the previous three runs. These runs are repeated for each set of segments, i.e., if one uses benefit segmentation and reactions to the concepts as the two bases for segmentation, two sets of the four discriminant runs will be conducted.

Depending on the researcher's preference, an alternative search procedure is to first go through factor analysis and use as the predictor variables in the multiple discriminant run either the factor scores or the key representative variables (those with the highest factor loadings on the relevant factors). Neither procedure is ideal; yet the preferred procedure of one large factor analysis for all three data sets, and one discriminant run, coupled with an appropriately designed cross-validation sample, requires a considerably larger sample which cannot always be justified.

Assessing the concept's market positioning.   The input for this analysis consists of consumer ratings of the concepts and control brands according to overall preference, appropriateness for various occasions, and degree of achievement of desired product benefits. These data are subjected to both multidimensional scaling and hierarchical clustering programs,

and the results are summarized in appropriate maps and tree diagrams of the brands, concepts, and the relevant product benefits. These results provide a clear profile of the market structure and the relative position of each concept with respect to the set of existing competitive brands and the position of both the concepts and brands on a set of product benefits.

ILLUSTRATIVE APPLICATION

Of the analytical procedures employed in the concept testing data analysis, the multidimensional scaling techniques are somewhat more novel and are, therefore, illustrated in the following example.

A rum manufacturer is interested in determining the reactions to some new rum mixed drinks. Six concepts—the new rum mixes including rum Old Fashioned, rum sour, Hathaway cocktail, Caribe cocktail, rum and iced tea, and rum gimlet—and 22 "control" drinks (six of which were rum-based) constituted the basic stimulus set. Each of the drinks was accompanied by a description of its major ingredients. The proposed procedure was followed and a questionnaire administered to 20 male graduate students. The small sample size does not permit proper use of the multivariate statistical techniques (multiple regression and discriminant analysis) described earlier, but it does illustrate use of the segmentation and concept positioning techniques previously discussed. The other components of the output are not illustrated here, but they are in the common format of multiple regression, discriminant analyses, and cross tabs.

Concept positioning   The concept positioning analysis at the aggregated (nonsegmented) level is presented in Exhibit 10–2. The exhibit illustrates a two-dimensional configuration of 22 alcoholic drinks and six new mixed-drink concepts. This map was obtained by means of

EXHIBIT 10–2

TWO-DIMENSIONAL CONFIGURATION OF 22 ALCOHOLIC DRINKS AND SIX NEW
RUM CONCEPTS

Source: Reprinted from the *Journal of Marketing* published by the American Marketing Association.
Exhibit from "A New Procedure for Concept Evaluation" by Yoram Wind, vol. 37, October 1973.

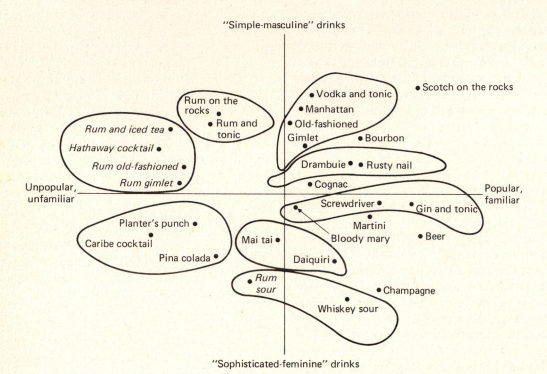

the TORSCA multidimensional scaling program (Young and Torgerson, 1967) as applied to the subjects' overall preference rating of the 28 stimuli. In this study, data were also collected on perceived similarity of the 28 drinks. A multidimensional scaling analysis of these data, via the TORSCA program, resulted in a similar configuration. Given both similarity and preference data, it is preferable to use a joint space multidimensional scaling program in which the stimulus space is based on similarity data. Yet, in practical applications one can reduce the data collection cost considerably by not collecting

direct similarity data (which lengthens the interview time) and using instead perceptions of the stimuli on a set of attributes.

The two-dimensional solution fit the original data well (stress value of 0.06). Examining the two dimensions, one might subjectively interpret the horizontal axis as a popularity or familiarity axis, enabling one to arrange the drinks from the most popular ones to the least popular and familiar of those using rum as a base. The vertical axis seems to arrange the drinks on a "simple-masculine" versus "sophisticated-feminine" dimension with scotch on the rocks and vodka tonic as examples of "simple-masculine" drinks, and whiskey sour, rum sour, and champagne as "sophisticated-feminine."

Further insight into the positioning of the six new concepts can be gained from an examination of the drink clusters. The results of the hierarchical cluster analysis were incorporated in the perceptual map. These results suggest that five out of six new concepts are viewed predominantly as rum drinks which compete with other existing rum drinks. Interestingly, most mixed rum drinks do not compete with their nonrum counterparts, rather they compete with other rum drinks. For example, rum gimlet is not viewed as a substitute for gimlet or, similarly, rum Old Fashioned is not a substitute for Old Fashioned. The only exception to this rule is the rum sour drink, which is viewed as similar to whiskey sour.

The analysis suggests that if a manufacturer is interested in expanding the usage of rum, he should consider promoting the rum sour and not the other new rum drinks. This conclusion further supported and clarified the intention-to-buy data. The concepts with the highest intention-to-buy score (when weighted by frequency of drink and when unweighted) were rum sour and rum Old Fashioned. Without the positioning information, both drinks would be viewed as equally attractive; yet, given the anticipated product positioning, the rum sour is a more promising concept.

Segmentation The analysis up to this point assumed a homogeneous market. Recognizing the possible heterogeneity of the actual market, a segmentation analysis was undertaken. This procedure calls for subjects to rank the twelve benefits of alcoholic drinks (such as "good tasting," "exotic," "easy to prepare," "prestigious") in order of their importance. The resulting 20 × 12 matrix of subjects by benefits was submitted to a clustering algorithm. Examina-

tion of the clustering results suggested two distinct benefit segments. To identify the unique benefit structure of each segment, the data were analyzed via Thurstone's law of comparative judgment (Thurstone, 1959) which provides some quantitative meaning (in the form of an interval scale) to the frequency of choices of one stimulus over another.

The results of this analysis are shown in Exhibit 10–3. Examination of these results suggests that both segments would prefer "good-tasting" drinks. However, they do differ with respect to the secondary benefits they seek. Whereas members of segment I drink to "loosen up" and look for strong stimulating drinks, members of segment II look for refreshing, social drinks which are appropriate for all occasions, easy to prepare, and prestigious.

Concept evaluation by segment Given the different benefits sought by the two segments and the scale separation among the various benefits, the question is whether they evaluate the various concepts differently. Exhibit 10–4 presents the results of PREFMAP joint space analysis (Carroll, 1972) for a subset of (new and existing) rum drinks and their evaluation by the two segments. In this case, the drinks are presented as points in the two-dimensional space, and the segments' evaluation of the drinks on various attributes (the benefits) are presented as vectors in a common metric space. For illustrative purposes, only a few of the benefits were plotted in Exhibit 10–4; but the actual output included the vectors for *all* benefits for each of the segments.

Note in Exhibit 10–4 the differences between the two benefit segments in the evaluation of the rum drinks and concepts on the various benefits. These observed differences are represented by direction and angle differences between the vectors of the two segments. For example, consider the way members of the two segments evaluate the various drinks on

EXHIBIT 10–3

INTERVAL SCALE VALUES OF PRODUCT BENEFITS FOR THE TWO BENEFIT
SEGMENTS (DERIVED BY THURSTONE'S CASE V METHOD)

Source: Reprinted from the *Journal of Marketing* published by the American Marketing Association.
Exhibit from "A New Procedure for Concept Evaluation" by Yoram Wind, vol. 37, October 1973.

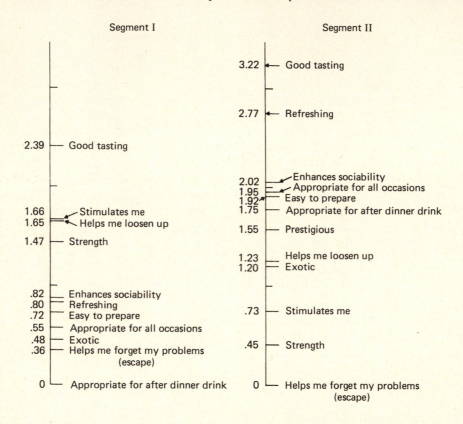

"refreshing." Members of segment I view Daiquiri as the most refreshing drink, followed by Mai Tai, Pina Colada, and Planter's Punch. Mai Tai, which was viewed as one of the two *most refreshing drinks* by segment I, is viewed as one of the least refreshing by segment II. This analysis suggests that a completely different message should be used for segment I than for segment II.

Similar analyses of the preference for the various drinks under the various benefits suggest a number of implications for promoting and positioning the drinks for each of the segments. In this case, if we were interested in promoting rum on the rocks and rum and tonic, for example, we note from Exhibit 10–4 that they are viewed by both segments as simple, man-like strong drinks. From the benefit preference profile of the two segments (Exhibit 10–3), we note that only members of segment I are interested in strength. Hence, it could be a wrong strategy to try to promote these drinks to segment II. It may be advisable, however, to promote them to members of segment I by de-

EXHIBIT 10–4

JOINT SPACE CONFIGURATION OF 12 RUM DRINKS AND CONCEPTS AND THEIR
EVALUATION BY THE TWO SEGMENTS ON SELECTED ATTRIBUTES

Source: Reprinted from the *Journal of Marketing* published by the American Marketing Association.
Exhibit from "A New Procedure for Concept Evaluation" by Yoram Wind, vol. 37, October 1973.

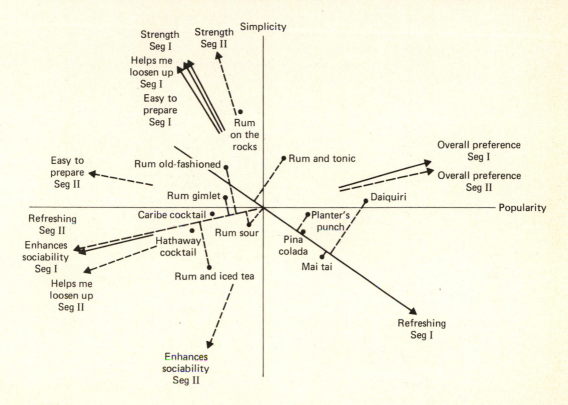

signing messages which emphasize strength, the appropriateness of the drinks for loosening up, and their ease of preparation.

Segment characteristics Further insight into the design of the promotional campaign aimed at the appropriate segment can be gained from an analysis of the life-style and background characteristics of the two segments. In this case, in view of the small number of subjects relative to a large number of background variables, univariate F tests were conducted rather than the

multiple discriminant analysis technique sugested earlier. The results of these tests indicated that only three of the mean differences, taken singly, were significant at the 0.05 level or better. These three variables led to the following group profile: (1) members of segment I are heavier drinkers (drink more often than members of segment II) and, relative to members of segment II, they (2) "almost always feel rushed and in a hurry" and (3) "get very tense and anxious when they think other people are disapproving of them." These characteristics may help understand why members of this segment prefer strong stimulating drinks that help them loosen up.

Summary   Exhibits 10–2, 10–3, and 10–4 illustrate some of the output from an integrated concept testing procedure. The utility of evaluating new concepts by segment is shown (note in Exhibit 10–3 the differences in benefits sought). The importance of concept positioning is illustrated (note the insight into the nature of the concepts gained by understanding the concept's position relative to competing brands, other concepts, the key dimensions, and the various product benefits). The significance of evaluating a concept on its overall preference as well as its various attributes or benefits is demonstrated (note in Exhibit 10–4 the similarity between the overall preference of the two segments as opposed to the differences in the segments' evaluation of the drinks on the specific benefits).

CONJOINT ANALYSIS APPROACH TO CONCEPT EVALUATION

A concept may be described in terms of its *structural* characteristics such as color, texture, ingredients, and smell for a food product. It may also be described in *functional* terms—what the food product can be used for and on what usage occasion; or in *psychological* terms—how the product characteristics agree with one's self-concept. It can further be described in *social* terms—what type of people use it; or in *economic* terms—how much it costs, and so forth.

Most concepts include some mixture of the above factors which represents the researcher's (and frequently also the advertiser's and marketer's) concept of the "best" possible composite concept. For example, it is not unlikely to find a concept such as:

A new vanilla dessert mix, high in vitamin and protein content, yet low in calories, convenient to prepare and economical.

Obtaining information on consumer reactions to this concept still raises the question of *which* of the five concept elements are liked (or disliked) by consumers. The overall reaction to the concept (which is the primary information used by most managers) does not reveal it. The diagnostic information obtained via the open-ended likes and dislikes and the evaluation of the concept on a set of prespecified attributes also tend to be of limited value, since consumers usually play back the major elements presented in the concept.

The alternative and more desirable procedure, therefore, would be to (1) design concepts in such a way as to assure the researcher's ability to "break down" the overall reaction to the concept and quantify the relative importance of each of the concept elements, and (2) obtain evaluative responses that reflect the consumers' trade-offs among conflicting concept components (for example, more vitamins at a higher price or less vitamins at a lower price?). Conjoint analysis enables one to achieve this objective. It is concerned with measuring the joint effect of two or more independent variables (concept components) on the ordering of a dependent variable (overall liking, intentions to buy, believability, worth, or some other evaluative measure). The output of this procedure consists of the simultaneous measurement of the joint effect and separate independent variable contributions to that joint effect, all at the level of interval scales with common unit.

From the standpoint of concept testing, conjoint analysis can be used to break down overall concept evaluation into specific utilities for each component of a multicomponent concept.

ILLUSTRATIVE EXAMPLE[2]

As an example of the use of conjoint analysis in concept testing, let us consider the previously-mentioned concept of a vanilla dessert mix. Given that the generic concept includes five components—high vitamin content, low calories, convenient to prepare, economical, and high protein content—and each component can be present or absent in a specific concept formulation, a number of concepts (31 to be exact—32 combinations minus the null combination of no components) can be developed. Each of the "concepts" represents a different combination of these components. A subset of these combinations based on a fractional factorial design of only fifteen combinations permits one to estimate all main effects and is all the combinations one needs.

Fractional factorial and other orthogonal array designs provide a guideline for the selection of the "concepts" (different combinations of components) to be included in the study. In this example, each respondent was presented with a set of fifteen cards and asked to imagine that he/she could purchase a packaged pudding that tasted good and, in addition, contained various combinations of the five product attributes (benefits). After examining the cards, the respondents were asked to rank them according to their likelihood of buying the specific product described by each combination.

Exhibit 10–5 shows the above experimental design as well as the data of one subject who ranked the fifteen concepts (each composed of a specific combination of components). Note that the quadruple of components "ABCE" received the highest preference, while the pair "BD" received the lowest preference.

These data were submitted to a conjoint analysis algorithm—MONANOVA—and the results are summarized in Exhibit 10–6 which shows the scale values, interval scaled with common unit, for the five concept components.

The subject's utility for component A (high vitamin content) was highest, while her utility for component D (economical) was lowest. Not surprisingly, different subjects had different utilities, leading to a segmentation according to the procedure of benefit bundle analysis (Green, Wind, and Jain, 1972).

The conjoint analysis approach to concept testing overcomes the limitations of the common concept testing approaches and avoids the pitfalls of the Iuso and other qualitative approaches. This approach has now been utilized in a large number of concept testing studies in diverse industries ranging from food and other frequently purchased household products to insurance, durable goods, travel packages, and numerous industrial products.

The specific research steps involved in the design and analysis of a conjoint analysis approach to concept testing are:

1. The identification of the relevant set of concept components—the structural, functional, psychological, social, and economic characteristics of the concept.

2. Given a set of components (factors) each at various levels, a fractional factorial (or other orthogonal array) design has to be developed, resulting in a set of hypothetical concepts. Each of the concept descriptions portrays a multi attribute concept described in terms of levels of the various factors.

3. Decide on the most appropriate stimulus execution—verbal description, pictorial presentation, ad format, etc.

[2]This example is borrowed in a somewhat modified form from Green and Wind (1973) and is also discussed in Wind (1973).

EXHIBIT 10–5

FRACTIONAL FACTORIAL DESIGN—FACTOR LEVEL PRESENT (1) OR ABSENT (0)—FOR CONCEPTS BASED ON FIVE CONCEPT COMPONENTS AND ONE SUBJECT'S RANKING OF COMBINATIONS

Source: Reprinted from the *Journal of Marketing* published by the American Marketing Association. Exhibit from "A New Procedure for Concept Evaluation" by Yoram Wind, vol. 37, October 1973.

Experimental combination*	A	B	C	D	E	Subject's ranking of each combination
AB	1	1	0	0	0	8
AC	1	0	1	0	0	11
AD	1	0	0	1	0	7
AE	1	0	0	0	1	9
BC	0	1	1	0	0	5
BD	0	1	0	1	0	1
BE	0	1	0	0	1	3
CD	0	0	1	1	0	4
CE	0	0	1	0	1	6
DE	0	0	0	1	1	2
ABCD	1	1	1	1	0	13
ABCE	1	1	1	0	1	15**
ABDE	1	1	0	1	1	12
ACDE	1	0	1	1	1	14
BCDE	0	1	1	1	1	10

*Letters refer to components: A—high vitamin content; B—low calories; C—convenient to prepare; D—economical; E—high protein content.
**Top-ranked combination.

4. Determine the criteria for evaluation, e.g., intentions to buy, intentions to switch from current brand(s), appropriateness for various consumption occasions, etc.

5. Administering the task to consumers, i.e., ask each respondent to rank or rate the various concept combinations on the desired dependent variable(s).

6. Submit these data to one of the conjoint analysis algorithms.

Following this procedure one avoids the problems associated with rating of a single complex multiattribute concept descriptor, since the researcher can "decompose" the overall concept evaluation into specific utilities for each component of a multicomponent concept. This provides the researcher with three useful results:

- The identification of the "best" *concept* (the combination of concept components with the highest utilities) among all possible combinations and not only the ones given to the consumer following the orthogonal array design (i.e., if, for example, there are eight components each at three levels, and an orthogonal array of 27 combinations is

EXHIBIT 10–6

DERIVED SCALE VALUES OF FIVE CONCEPT
COMPONENTS

Source: Reprinted from the *Journal of Marketing* published
by the American Marketing Association. Exhibit from "A
New Procedure for Concept Evaluation" by Yoram Wind,
vol. 37, October 1973.

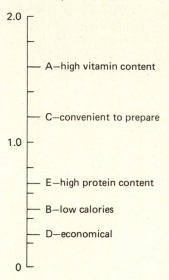

- Guidelines for concept development in terms of what will be the utility or disutility of any change in the concept characteristics. This enables a selection of the most advantageous trade-offs among concept components (based not on the researcher's subjective judgment but on consumers' utilities for each component).

- Guidelines for concept development and marketing plans in terms of information on the relative importance of each component.

The other advantages of this procedure are that the researcher can select any dependent variable(s) of his/her choice; the consumers' task is similar to the real life brand choice situation (i.e., selection of multiattribute brands from a given set of brands); and the results are obtained at the individual level enabling one to segment respondents based on the similarity of their reaction to the tested concepts.

When coupled with a computer simulation (which helps evaluate the expected market share of each concept) and MDS analysis which helps position the concept(s) against existing brands by various market segments, this concept testing approach provides management with the necessary diagnostic information for subsequent concept development and design of marketing strategy.

designed, the output in terms of utilities for each component level enables the researcher to select the best combination out of the entire set of 6,561 combinations, that is, 3^8.

HOW TO GET MORE FROM THE CONCEPT TESTING PROCEDURE

Regardless of the concept testing procedure used, there are a number of key questions which should be answered before management accepts and relies on the results of concept testing studies. Three such key questions are:

- Would the reaction to a concept vary with the definition and execution of the concept description?

- How "valid" are the results of a concept testing procedure, i.e., how can the results of a concept testing procedure be translated into expected trial rates?

- How likely is a new concept to cannibalize the sales of the firms's existing products, and can this be determined from a concept testing study?

Addressing these three questions is important if management wants to get more out of their concept testing procedure. No conclusive answers to these questions can be offered, but in designing a concept testing procedure, one should be cognizant of these questions and their implication.

CONCEPT EXECUTION

Ideally, one would like to define a concept in terms as close as possible to the ones which will be presented to the consumer in the final product. The further removed the concept description from the perceived final product, the harder it is to translate any intention to buy responses into market acceptance figures.

Accepting this idea suggests that the presentation of any concept should be in the form of an advertisement for the product. Going this route, however, suggests further difficulties due to differences in advertising executions for the same concept. This difficulty has led many firms to the reliance on a bare-bones description of a concept, a description void of any "selling" efforts. Yet, in many cases a simple concept description may lead to completely different responses than an advertising execution of the same concept. Consider for example concepts for new male or female fragrances. How can the concept of a "sexy" fragrance be communicated verbally, and would consumers react to this the same way they would to a commercial or a print advertisement which illustrates the concept or creates the right "mood"?

To illustrate this difficulty, examine the three advertisements presented in Exhibit 10–7 and consider how you would present the concepts for the advertised products (or services) without the benefit of the advertisement.

Current research on the effect of execution on the response to a concept suggests the importance of execution. Haley and Gatty (1968) demonstrated that the same concepts when executed by different copywriters produced statistically different concept test scores. Similarly, Tauber (1972), in examining the effect of the form of presentation, concluded that the same idea when presented as a simple printed statement, print advertisement, TV commercial, and prototype product, resulted in different levels of consumer interest.

VALIDATION

The major premise of any concept-testing procedure is that consumers' reactions to a concept are good indicators of their likely future behavior in the marketplace. Conceptually, this premise falls within the boundaries of the "attitude-behavior" relationship in social psychology and more recently in consumer behavior. Without getting involved with the numerous conflicting findings on this critical relationship, it is important to note that the statistical association between attitude (or intention to buy) and subsequent behavior holds at the *aggregate* level but not at the individual level.

An interesting validation study on the relationship between purchase-intention scales and subsequent trial is reported by Tauber (1980) who reinterviewed 543 consumers who were the respondents to a concept test study. The reinterview was conducted 25 weeks after the introduction of the product to the test market. His findings suggest that purchase in-

EXHIBIT 10–7

ILLUSTRATIVE ADVERTISEMENTS FOR DIFFICULT TO EXPRESS CONCEPTS

Source: House ad by Spiro and Associates, Philadelphia, advertising and public relations agency.
Reproduced by permission.

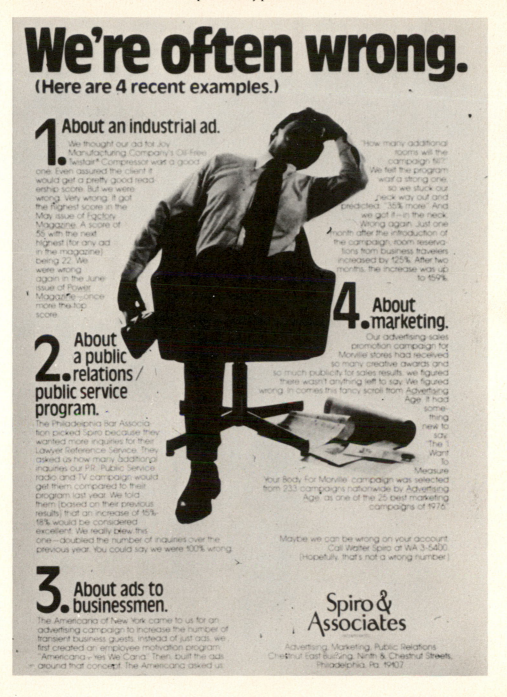

EXHIBIT 10–7 (continued)

ILLUSTRATIVE ADVERTISEMENTS FOR DIFFICULT TO EXPRESS CONCEPTS

Source: Reprinted by permission of Automatic Data Processing, Inc. Prepared by Schaefer Advertising, King of Prussia, Pa.

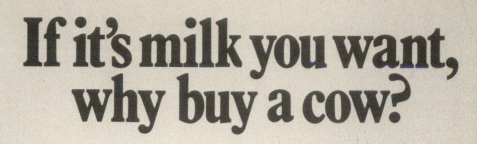

If it's milk you want, why buy a cow?

For years, we've all been hearing about what a good thing the computer is.

Small wonder, then, that when confronted by rising piles of numbers in need of crunching, the first reaction is, "Get a computer."

Don't.

Most times, you'd be better off getting *computing* instead.

From ADP. The computing company.

We don't sell computers. We sell computer solutions. To over 40,000 clients.

They get the data they need, where they need it, in the form that they need it.

Without capital investment.

Without development costs.

Without staff-building.

Without worrying about system obsolescence.

Without, in short, buying the cow. We can do the same for you.

Relieve you of bookkeeping-related chores like payroll, accounts payable, accounts receivable, general ledger and financial reporting.

Bring your inventory and invoicing under control.

Place sophisticated analytical models and data bases at your command.

Or plug you into an intercontinental remote-computing network.

There are, in fact, hundreds of ways for us to put computing to work for you—with none of the bother of owning a computer.

Our new Services Brochure will show you what we mean. For your free copy, call us at 201-472-1000, look us up in your local phone book, or write *Automatic Data Processing, Inc. 405 Route 3, Clifton, New Jersey 07015.*

ADP
The computing company.

©Automatic Data Processing, Inc. 1977

tentions had the highest correlation to subsequent behavior and that addition of other evaluative responses did not improve the correlation. The specific results he obtained were:

Purchase intent	Tried the product	
	% of total sample	% of those aware of product
Definitely would buy	22	31
Probably would buy	9	16
May or may not buy	9	17
Probably would not buy	4	8
Definitely would not buy	4	10

While the "definitely-would-buy" have greater probability of purchase than the other groups of respondents, the other categories should not be ignored. In fact, total trial relies heavily on purchases from members of these groups. Consider, for example, Tauber's findings in the above study on the percent of total trial which comes from each purchase intent group:

Definitely would buy	25%
Probably would buy	30
May or may not buy	22
Probably would not buy	8
Definitely would not buy	15

To establish the validity of concept-testing scores as predictors of market trial requires the examination of a number of concept scores and the subsequent performance of the concept in test market (or in the national introduction phase). Establishing this relationship requires a considerable number of cases for each product class in question. Without it management can have no confidence as to the meaning of a concept score in terms of trial.

A few studies along these lines conducted by food companies suggested two simple correspondence rules. One is the simplest relation-ship between the percent of top box score and market trial. Such relationships can be determined based on simple regression analysis of ITB scores (or other dependent variables) and desired dependent variables such as percent trial in test markets. Such analyses have been conducted by a number of firms for a large number of cases (20+ studies), and resulted in strong statistical association between the two. The established regression line and confidence levels around it offer the firm a simple guideline for translating the results of each concept score into expected trial. The specific regression line (both slope and intercept) can vary, however, by product class and should be conducted separately for homogeneous product lines. Exhibit 10–8 illustrates such a relationship for one product class.

The second attempt is to assign each of the given points on the intention to buy scale a probability of purchase and come up with an aggregate score based on some probability distribution such as 0.80 of the "definitely-would-buy," 0.60 of the "probably-would-buy," 0.40 of the "may-or-may-not-buy," 0.20 of the "probably-would-not-buy," and 0 for the "definitely-would-not-buy."

EXHIBIT 10–8

ILLUSTRATIVE RELATIONSHIP BETWEEN INTENTION-TO-BUY SCALE AND TRIAL

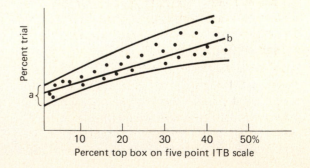

Percent trial

Percent top box on five point ITB scale

A more elegant and accurate procedure to establish the correspondence rule between ITB scores and trial was proposed by Morrison (1979) who proposed a three-step model to transform stated intentions into a purchase probability estimate. These involve:

1. Transforming stated intention (I_s) into an estimate of the true intention ($\hat{I}_t$). This is based on a "regression to the mean adjustment" which deflates the high stated intentions and inflates the low stated intentions in an effort to more accurately represent the intentions at the time of the survey. A beta binomial true intentions model is proposed for this step by Morrison.

2. Transforming the true intentions ($\hat{I}_t$) into an unadjusted purchase probability estimate ($\hat{p}_u$) by an exogeneous events model which replaces individuals who changed their purchase intentions (buy when originally they did not plan to buy due to some exogeneous reasons or conversely did not buy in cases in which they planned to buy) by randomly selecting individuals from a population with a beta distribution of I_t.

3. Transforming the unadjusted purchase probabilities ($\hat{p}_u$) into an estimated purchase probability ($\hat{p}$) by a probability adjustment model.

This three-step procedure was applied by Morrison to appliance and automobile purchase intention data resulting in useful statistical relationships between stated purchase intentions (I_s) and purchase probabilities. One of the resulting relationships for automobiles is presented in Exhibit 10–9.

Based on an actual examination of the relationship between intention to buy scores and subsequent market performance data, or frequently based on some management judgment, many companies attempt to develop action standards for concept acceptance. These

EXHIBIT 10–9

RELATIONSHIP BETWEEN STATISTICAL INTENTION TO BUY AND PURCHASE PROBABILIZATION FOR AUTOMOBILES BASED ON THE MORRISON MODEL

Source: Reprinted from the *Journal of Marketing* published by the American Marketing Association. Exhibit from "Purchase Intentions and Purchase Behavior" by Donald G. Morrison, vol. 43, Spring 1979, p. 72.

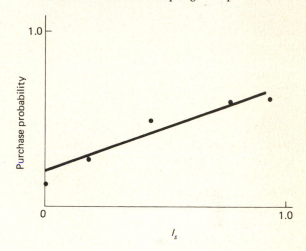

standards are stated, for example, in terms of "A concept is acceptable if it achieves at least 25 percent of top box (definitely would buy)" or alternatively "A concept is acceptable if it achieves at least a mean score of 7.5 on a one-to-ten-point intention-to-buy scale," etc. Such action rules are useful, however, only to the extent that they are based on actual data on the relationship between the intention score and subsequent trial data.

An important built-in bias in most concept testing procedures is that they tend to validate only the success or failure of the "acceptable concepts" (those that scored in the testing procedure above the threshold level of acceptance). Ignored in most cases is the other type of possible error—that of rejecting, based on the results of a concept testing study, a potentially successful and profitable product. To guard against this bias, it is desirable to select occasionally a "losing concept," continue with its development, and test its acceptability in the marketplace. Occasional tests of this nature are essential for the assurance of the long-term viability of the firm's new product concept testing procedure.

CANNIBALIZATION

An important aspect of the evaluation of concepts which could conceptually be viewed by consumers (or the trade) as a substitute to one of the existing products of the firm, is the question of the degree of accepted cannibalization. Whereas monadic concept-testing procedures ignore this issue, approaches which include an evaluation of a concept against control products (the market leaders *and* the firm's own products) do provide the data for cannibalization analysis. This analysis can be based on simple cross tabulation of the percent of current product users who would prefer (intend to buy) the new concept over (versus in addition to) their current product(s). At a somewhat more rigorous level, the analysis of cannibalization can be based on a computer simulation of consumer choices based on their individual utility functions (as developed in a conjoint analysis approach to concept testing). Such a simulation can result in estimated share of choices and brand-switching matrices showing the brands from which any of a number of new concepts can draw these customers. This approach is further discussed in Chapter 12.

The cannibalization question can also be viewed as a special case of the broader problem of *conditional preference*, i.e., the preference for and likelihood of buying a new product concept depends on the consumer's inventory of other products which satisfy the same need, and the compatibility of the new concept with the con-

sumer's desired product portfolio. For example, the reaction to a new health insurance plan depends to a large extent on the respondent's current inventory of health insurance plans. Analytically, the compatibility of a new concept with the current portfolio of products can be analyzed by appropriate segmentation schemes (evaluation of the reactions to the concept by inventory-based segments), positioning analysis, or explicit cannibalization models.

Given a satisfactory solution to the questions of concept definition, validation procedures, and estimate of cannibalization, one should still be concerned with the design and implementation of an appropriate concept-testing procedure. In developing such a procedure one should take into account the following major considerations.

I. Develop a procedure which assures the evaluation of the new concept(s) by segment. The major advantages of this are:

1. It reduces the risk of rejecting a concept which does not have a wide enough appeal to attract a substantial proportion of the market, but which does have a considerable appeal to a specific segment. Such a segment, despite its small size, may justify pursuing a product represented by the concept to which the segment members were attracted if the segment is reachable and potentially profitable;

2. It enables a more accurate evaluation of new product concepts which are designed to appeal to specific market segment(s) or occupy a specific market position;

3. It provides richer guidelines for the further development of the product as well as initial guidelines for the marketing strategy for the new product if it passes the next step in the firm's new product development process.

II. Evaluate the concept in the context of its anticipated competitive setting of existing brands and other new concepts, hence reaping all the benefits of positioning.

III. Assure a flexible procedure which can be modified to respond to specific product, market, and environmental changes, management needs, and various forms of concept definitions.

IV. To the extent that historically management did use some other concept-testing procedure, include the critical "traditional" measures which relate to the action criterion used by management (such as a five-point intention-to-buy scale) in the new procedure. Incorporating these measures would assure the continuity of, and comparison with, previous research.

V. If a concept is based on a number of components, it is desirable to consider utilizing a procedure such as conjoint analysis which enables the researcher to provide specific guidelines for concept modifications and development of new concepts.

VI. In designing a consumer-based concept-testing procedure, special care should be given to the problem of the consumer's likely familiarity with and understanding of the concepts. If totally new concepts are to be presented (the rare cases of truly innovative product concepts) the concept-testing procedure should allow for respondent education prior to the elicitation of his or her judgments. This education can be aided by video tapes or other visual instructional material which should be given the respondent before the actual concept-testing starts. In these cases the design of a respondent task should be geared to reducing the bias introduced by exposure to the educational material.

VII. Given the ambiguity of many concepts and the advantages of continuous modification and redefinition of concepts, concept-testing procedures should not be viewed as a one-time activity but rather as part of a continuous process of concept evaluation, reformulation, and reevaluation.

CONCLUDING REMARKS

One of the most striking things about concept-testing procedures is the contrast between the conceptual complexity of the problem and the oversimplistic approaches employed by most firms. To better grasp the various problems associated with the design of a concept-testing procedure, generate an idea for a new product and try to design a procedure to assess its acceptability by consumers.

In developing such a procedure, how would you avoid for your concept the problem of distinguishing between an idea and a concept? To illustrate this problem, consider the example suggested by Tauber (1972)—the idea of a powdered product that adds considerable nutrition when mixed with milk which could be presented as an instant breakfast, a snack for children, a diet meal, or a health food.

11

Management and Economic Concept/ Product Screening and Evaluation

INTRODUCTION

As discussed at the outset of Chapter 10, concept screening requires a three-tiered evaluation—management, consumer, and initial economic evaluation. Various approaches to consumer evaluation of new product concepts were discussed in the previous chapter and the objective of this chapter is to cover the other two aspects of new concept screening.

The concepts and procedures discussed are applicable, at different levels of specificity, to all levels of evaluation, i.e., from initial idea screening to final product evaluation. As such, although the term used most frequently is new *concept* unless otherwise specified, the material is applicable for *ideas, concepts,* and *products.*

The major differences in the evaluation of ideas, concepts, and products is with respect to the type and quality of available information. The more abstract the idea or concept the harder it is to translate consumers' reactions to such stimuli into likely reactions to the final product. Similarly, the further management is from a final product the less accurate their cost and production estimates. Yet, there is great value in an early assessment of economic performance. In general, the earlier in the new product development process one can assess the expected economic performance of the idea/concept/product the better. Hence as suggested in Chapter 8, economic evaluation should take place at *each* stage in the product development process. This is consistent with the typical business practice of sequential new product development efforts. Following a sequential approach, one proceeds from rough estimates of the economic viability of the idea/concept/product to successively more refined and accurate estimates. At each step in the process, more resources are committed and, in turn, it is expected that as each step is completed, more and better information will be available to improve the accuracy of the estimated economic performance of the idea, concept, or product.

The chapter starts with a discussion of management screening. This part starts with the concepts underlying management screening and follows with a number of alternative approaches to such evaluation. The second part of the chapter focuses on the economic/financial evaluation of new idea/concept/product performance. This part starts with a discussion of the components of economic evaluation—cost, revenue, profits, uncertainties, and synergistic effects—and proceeds with a discussion of various static and dynamic approaches to economic evaluation. The chapter concludes with a brief discussion of two critical aspects of idea/concept/product evaluation: evaluation of the entire portfolio of projects and implementation considerations.

MANAGEMENT SCREENING AND EVALUATION

The dimensions on which management evaluates ideas/concepts/products encompass all key management areas and in particular should reflect the corporate idiosyncrasies and unique situational factors. Of the areas often covered in management screening, the most important ones are:

Congruency with corporate objectives Among the most important aspects of idea/concept screening is the consistency of the proposed new product with corporate objectives and in particular the firm's target portfolio of products and markets. A special aspect of this consideration is the likely impact of the proposed new product on the desired corporate image (as perceived by the relevant stakeholders of the firm). This fit (with objectives and desired image) should be determined relatively early in the new product development process to avoid spending time and effort on products which even if potentially profitable will be unacceptable to management.

Technical feasibility The feasibility of developing the technology required for the new product is a crucial aspect of the evaluation process. Relevant considerations in this area are the technological skills and potential of the corporate R&D personnel versus the available or potential outside technology; the short-run versus long-run feasibility. Whereas many technologies might not be feasible in the short run there are hardly any limits on technology in the long run, given enough time and resources. In evaluating the technical feasibility and resources required for technological developments, an important consideration is the likely synergistic effect of a given technological development on related areas or as a basis for subsequent technological developments.

Legal clearance As government involvement in almost all aspects of corporate life increases, it becomes increasingly important to assure that the new idea/concept/product is legally acceptable and will be able to obtain all the necessary bureaucratic approvals. The legal clearance is especially critical in safety-sensitive areas such as food, drugs, and children's toys, but, as discussed in Chapter 7, is not limited to these areas.

Demands on corporate resources One of the relevant considerations in screening new ideas/concepts/products is the demands the new products are likely to place on the various corporate resources. This consideration is especially crucial in the short run and is of relatively little importance in the long run. Yet, for many companies the development of new products for the immediate future is constrained by the demands such products may place on various corporate resources, in particular management time, utilization of current resources, and financial and manpower requirements.

Compatibility with marketing and corporate activities and strengths An important consideration, especially in the short run, is the compatibility of the proposed new products with the firm's marketing operations and strengths (channels of distribution, advertising and promotional skills, etc.).

These and other factors should be identified by management and serve as the criteria against which to evaluate new ideas/concepts and products as well as potential acquisition candidates. These criteria are not unlike the ones used in determining the relevant dimensions of the corporate product/market portfolio, and similarly, can't be limited to identification but require determination of their relative importance. Having screened an idea/concept/product on these criteria, management is ready to assess the expected economic returns based on a more detailed evaluation of the likely sales, costs, and risks given alternative marketing strategies and environmental scenarios.

ALTERNATIVE APPROACHES

Management screening and evaluation procedures vary greatly in their degree of formalism and specificity. Conceptually, it is desirable to follow an explicit procedure reflecting management's idiosyncratic evaluation criteria. The formal approaches to screening ideas, concepts, and products include three primary approaches: factor listing, desirability index, and a special application of the Analytic Hierarchy Process (AHP).

Factor listing   The criteria identified by management for the evaluation of ideas, concepts, and products can serve as a single checklist or as the basis for a desirability index. In its simplest form the factor listing provides only a checklist against which concepts are evaluated, but no specific choice rule is established, i.e., based on the profile of the idea/concept/product on the list of factors, management decides in each case how to proceed.

Desirability index   On the other hand, a desirability index adds to the factor listing a numerical measure of idea/concept/product desirability. This desirability index is calculated by assigning the levels of each factor certain numerical values and adding the total sum of each idea/concept/product on the selected set of factors. Exhibits 11–1 and 11–2 illustrate the factors identified by the Innovation Center of the University of Oregon and by John T. O'Meara respectively. Such checklists provide a useful initial guideline for idea/concept/product evaluation. Any attempts to assign summary desirability scores to ideas/concepts/products based on their rating on the various factors should be viewed with caution since, despite the simplicity of this approach, it can be misleading. The major problems with a single desirability index are:

1. It tends to ignore factors which are necessary conditions for product development or introduction. Although this limitation can be overcome by an appropriate choice rule, most performance indexes tend to ignore this case.

2. Most performance indexes are based on an additive score on a set of variables. These variables are rarely factor analyzed, resulting in a possible overweighting of the factor which is described by a larger number of measures.

3. A unidimensional index tends to ignore qualitative differences in the way an index is computed. Consider for example the following three cases in which we assume two factors with equal weights.

	A	B	C
Potential demand	High (5)	Low (1)	Avg. (3)
Technological feasibility	Low (1)	High (5)	Avg. (3)
Total sum	6	6	6

As is clearly evident from this simplified example, all three cases, although markedly different, with distinctly different strategic implications, have the same overall score. In this case, weighting of the factors will break the tie but will not help capture the multidimensionality of new concept/product performance.

4. If more than a single "judge" is used to evaluate the profile of the new idea/concept/product, how should their responses be reported? Is an average score meaningful? Should the differential expertise of the respondents be taken into account and if so, how is it to be determined?

5. If the factors are weighted (as suggested by a number of authors) a number of questions are raised concerning the way the weights are determined, the identity of the judges, the approach used to summarize their independent evaluations, the independence of the weight from the score of a given concept/product on the various factors, and the interdependency of the factors.

Are there meaningful summary measures which can rank the various ideas/concepts/

EXHIBIT 11-1

THE OREGON NEW PRODUCT EVALUATION INSTRUMENT

Reprinted from *PIES-II Manual for Innovation Evaluation*, by Gerald E. Udell and Kenneth G. Baker, published by the University of Wisconsin System, 1980. Copyright by Gerald E. Udell and the Board of Regents of the University of Wisconsin System; used with the permission of the authors.

Project No. _____   Evaluator No. _____   Evaluator's Name _____

PIES — II
INNOVATION EVALUATION INSTRUMENT

by

Gerald G. Udell and Kenneth G. Baker

Wisconsin Innovation Service Center
College of Business and Economics
University of Wisconsin
Whitewater, WI 53190

Action to be taken: (check appropriate category)
□ SBI Program   □ MTA Program   □ Technology Transfer   □ Close File.

DIRECTIONS:

Check the response that best corresponds to your evaluation for each Criterion. Be sure you answer all questions. NOTE that "don't know" and "not applicable" responses are coded "DK" and "NA". Be SURE to use them when they are appropriate.

After each Factor group, a space is provided for your written comments relative to that section. If you have any specific information, comments or suggestions, use this space. These comments are highly useful in providing additional information and insights.

SOCIETAL FACTOR

1. LEGALITY CRITERION: In terms of applicable laws (particularly product liability), regulations, product standards, this idea/invention/new product . . .
    - ___ might not meet them, even if changed
    - ___ might require substantial revision to meet them
    - ___ might require modest revision
    - ___ might require minor changes
    - ___ will meet them without any changes
    - ___ DK
    - ___ NA

    End Statements

2. SAFETY CRITERION: Considering potential hazards and side effects, the use might be . . .
    - ___ very unsafe, even when used as intended
    - ___ unsafe under reasonably foreseeable circumstances
    - ___ relatively safe for careful, instructed users
    - ___ safe when used as intended, with no foreseeable hazards
    - ___ very safe under all conditions, including misuse
    - ___ DK
    - ___ NA

    End Statements

3. ENVIRONMENTAL IMPACT CRITERION: In terms of pollution, litter, misuse of natural resources, etc., use might . . .
    - ___ violate environmental regulations and/or have dangerous environmental consequences
    - ___ have some negative effect on the environment
    - ___ have no effect on the environment if properly used
    - ___ have no effect on the environment
    - ___ have a positive impact on the environment
    - ___ DK
    - ___ NA

    End Statements

4. SOCIETAL IMPACT CRITERION: In terms of the impact (benefit) upon the general welfare of society, use might . . .
    - ___ have substantial negative effect
    - ___ have some negative effect
    - ___ have no effect if properly used
    - ___ have no effect on society
    - ___ have a positive effect on society
    - ___ DK
    - ___ NA

    End Statements

COMMENTS:

BUSINESS RISK FACTOR:

5. FUNCTIONAL FEASIBILITY CRITERION: In terms of intended functions, will it actually do what it is intended to do?
    - ___ the concept is not sound; cannot be made to work
    - ___ it won't work now, but might be modified
    - ___ it will work but major changes might be needed
    - ___ it will work but minor changes might be needed
    - ___ it will work — no changes necessary
    - ___ DK
    - ___ NA

    End Statements

6. PRODUCTION FEASIBILITY CRITERION: With regard to technical processes or equipment required for production, this invention might . . .
    - ___ be impossible to produce now or in the foreseeable future
    - ___ be very difficult to produce
    - ___ have some problems which can be overcome
    - ___ have only minor problems
    - ___ have no problems
    - ___ DK
    - ___ NA

    End Statements

7. STAGE OF DEVELOPMENT CRITERION: Based on available information, there is . . .
    - ___ only an idea with drawings and/or description; no prototype
    - ___ a rough prototype which demonstrates the concept but is not fully developed and tested
    - ___ a rough prototype with performance and safety testing completed
    - ___ a final prototype with testing completed; however, minor changes might be needed
    - ___ a market-ready prototype
    - ___ DK
    - ___ NA

    End Statements

8. INVESTMENT COSTS CRITERION: The amount of capital and other costs necessary for development to the market-ready stage might be . . .
    - ___ greater than returns — investment will not be recoverable
    - ___ excessive — might not be recoverable
    - ___ heavy — probably recoverable
    - ___ moderate — recoverable within five years
    - ___ low — recoverable within two years
    - ___ DK
    - ___ NA

    End Statements

9. PAYBACK PERIOD CRITERION: The expected payback period (time required to recover initial investment) is likely to be . . .
    - ___ over 10 years
    - ___ 7 to 10 years
    - ___ 4 to 6 years
    - ___ 1 to 3 years
    - ___ less than one year
    - ___ DK
    - ___ NA

    End Statements

Implementation funding made available by the Wisconsin Private Sector Initiative Program, Inc. under the Comprehensive Employment and Training Act.
Copyright 1980 by Gerald G. Udell and the Board of Regents of the University of Wisconsin System
Permission to use this document is granted to the Wisconsin Private Sector Initiative Program, Balance of State — Wisconsin, and the Department of Labor.

EXHIBIT 11–1 (continued)

10. PROFITABILITY CRITERION: Profitability is defined as the extent to which anticipated revenues will cover the relevant costs (direct, indirect, and capital). Anticipated revenues...

    _____ might not cover any of the relevant costs
    _____ might cover direct costs but contribute minimally to indirect and capital costs (ROI)
    _____ might cover direct and indirect costs but might not meet capital costs (ROI)
    _____ might cover direct and indirect costs and meet minimum capital costs (ROI)
    _____ will cover direct and indirect costs and easily exceed capital cost (ROI)

_____ DK _____ NA

11. MARKETING RESEARCH CRITERION: The marketing research required to develop a market-ready product is estimated to be...

    _____ extremely difficult and complex
    _____ relatively difficult and complex
    _____ moderately difficult
    _____ relatively easy and simple
    _____ very simple and straightforward

_____ DK _____ NA

12. RESEARCH AND DEVELOPMENT CRITERION: The research and development required to reach the production-ready stage might be...

    _____ extremely difficult and complex
    _____ relatively difficult and complex
    _____ moderately difficult
    _____ relatively easy and simple
    _____ very simple and straightforward

_____ DK _____ NA

COMMENTS:

DEMAND ANALYSIS FACTOR

13. POTENTIAL MARKET CRITERION: The total market for products of this type might be...

    _____ very small — very specialized or local in nature
    _____ small — relatively specialized or regional in nature
    _____ medium — limited national market
    _____ large — broad national market
    _____ very large — extensive national and possible international market

_____ DK _____ NA

14. POTENTIAL SALES CRITERION: Expected sales of this product might be...

    _____ very small
    _____ small
    _____ medium
    _____ large
    _____ very large

_____ DK _____ NA

15. TREND OF DEMAND CRITERION: The market demand for products of this type appears to be...

    _____ rapidly declining — product might soon become obsolete
    _____ declining — potentially obsolete in near future
    _____ steady — demand expected to remain constant
    _____ growing slowly — modest growth opportunity
    _____ rapidly expanding — significant growth opportunity

_____ DK _____ NA

16. STABILITY OF DEMAND CRITERION: The fluctuation in demand is likely to be...

    _____ highly unstable — subject to severe unpredictable fluctuations
    _____ unstable — susceptible to moderate unpredictable fluctuations
    _____ predictable — variations can be foreseen with reasonable accuracy
    _____ stable — modest variations can be accurately foreseen
    _____ highly stable — not susceptible to fluctuations

_____ DK _____ NA

17. PRODUCT LIFE CYCLE CRITERION: The product life cycle is likely to be...

    _____ less than two years
    _____ two to four years
    _____ five to seven years
    _____ eight to ten years
    _____ more than ten years

_____ DK _____ NA

18. PRODUCT LINE POTENTIAL CRITERION: The potential for additional products, multiple styles, qualities, price ranges, etc., is...

    _____ very limited — single product only
    _____ limited to minor modifications only
    _____ moderate — multiple markets/use potential
    _____ high — new product spin-offs likely
    _____ very high — could be the foundation of a new industry

_____ DK _____ NA

COMMENTS:

MARKET ACCEPTANCE FACTOR

19. COMPATIBILITY CRITERION: Compatibility with existing attitudes and methods of use is...

    _____ very low — will block market acceptance
    _____ low — some conflict, will slow market acceptance
    _____ moderate — no negative effects
    _____ high — compatibility will aid marketing effort
    _____ very high — will give market acceptance a strong boost

_____ DK _____ NA

20. LEARNING CRITERION: The amount of learning required for correct use is...

    _____ very high — expensive and/or time consuming training required
    _____ high — detailed instructions required
    _____ moderate — normal instructions sufficient for most users
    _____ low — minimal instructions needed
    _____ very low — no instructions needed

_____ DK _____ NA

21. NEED CRITERION: The level of need filled or utility provided by this innovation is...

    _____ very low — gimmick soon forgotten by the owner
    _____ low — would only superficially fulfill psychological non-essential needs
    _____ moderate — fulfills both psychological and physical non-essential needs
    _____ high — fulfills either basic psychological or physical needs
    _____ very high — fulfills both psychological and physical needs

_____ DK _____ NA

22. DEPENDENCE CRITERION: The degree to which the sale or use of this product is dependent upon other products, processes or systems is...

    _____ very high — no market control: very high cost
    _____ high — little market control: high costs
    _____ moderate — reasonable market control and cost
    _____ low — strong market control: low cost
    _____ very low — complete market control: very low cost

_____ DK _____ NA

EXHIBIT 11-1 (continued)

23. VISIBILITY CRITERION: The advantages and benefits are...

    very obscure — very difficult and/or costly to communicate
    obscure — requires substantial explanation
    visible — requires some explanation
    visible — easily communicated
    very visible — advantages are obvious and easy to communicate
    —— DK   —— NA

24. PROMOTION CRITERION: The costs and effort required to promote the advantages, features, and benefits are likely to be...

    very high — prohibitive in relation to expected sales
    high relative to expected sales
    moderate — commensurate with expected sales
    low relative to expected sales
    very low relative to expected sales
    —— DK   —— NA

25. DISTRIBUTION CRITERION: The cost and difficulty of establishing distribution channels are likely to be...

    very high — prohibitive in relation to expected sales
    high relative to expected sales
    moderate — commensurate with expected sales
    low relative to expected sales
    very low relative to expected sales
    —— DK   —— NA

26. SERVICE CRITERION: The cost and difficulty associated with providing product service is likely to be...

    very high — will require frequent service and parts
    high — will need periodic service and parts
    moderate — will need occasional service and parts
    low — need for service and parts will be infrequent
    very low — will require little or no parts and service
    —— DK   —— NA

COMMENTS:

COMPETITIVE FACTOR:

27. APPEARANCE CRITERION: Relative to competition and/or substitutes, appearance is likely to be perceived as...

    very inferior — no customer appeal
    inferior — little customer appeal
    similar to competition/substitutes
    superior — has customer appeal
    very superior — has strong customer appeal
    —— DK   —— NA

28. FUNCTION CRITERION: Relative to competing and/or substitute products, services or processes, the function performed might be perceived as...

    very inferior — a significant competitive disadvantage
    inferior — some competitive disadvantage
    similar — to competition/substitutes
    superior — some competitive advantage
    very superior — a significant competitive advantage
    —— DK   —— NA

29. DURABILITY CRITERION: Relative to competition and/or substitutes, durability of this product is likely to be perceived as...

    very inferior — a definite competitive disadvantage
    inferior — might be a competitive disadvantage
    similar — to competition/substitutes
    superior — might be promoted as an improvement
    very superior — easily promoted as a major improvement
    —— DK   —— NA

30. PRICE CRITERION: Relative to competition and/or substitute products, the selling price is likely to be...

    much higher — a definite competitive disadvantage
    higher — a competitive disadvantage
    similar to competition/substitutes
    lower — a competitive advantage
    much lower — a definite competitive advantage
    —— DK   —— NA

31. EXISTING COMPETITION CRITERION: Existing competition for this innovation appears to be...

    very high — new entry might be difficult and/or relatively expensive
    high — only a small market share is likely
    moderate — market penetration can be gained with reasonable effort and expense
    low — a significant market share might be possible
    very low — entry might be easy and/or relatively inexpensive
    —— DK   —— NA

32. NEW COMPETITION CRITERION: Competition from new entrants or competitive reaction is expected to be...

    very high — product lead will be very short
    high — product lead will be relatively short
    moderate — market share can be maintained
    low — product lead will be relatively long
    very low — a strong chance to sustain large market share
    —— DK   —— NA

33. PROTECTION CRITERION: Considering patents (or copyrights), technical difficulty or secrecy, the prospects for protection appear to be...

    no legal protection or secrecy possible
    no legal protection but some secrecy might be possible
    limited legal protection but some secrecy might be possible
    might be patented, copyrighted and/or short-run secrecy possible
    can definitely be patented, copyrighted and/or long-term secrecy possible
    —— DK   —— NA

COMMENTS:

In my opinion, the likelihood of this idea, process or product being successful in the marketplace is: (Place an X at the appropriate place on the line marked A - B.)

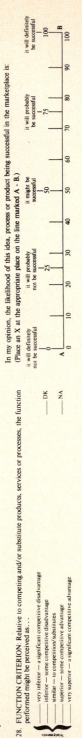

it will definitely not be successful   it will probably not be successful   it might be successful   it will probably be successful   it will definitely be successful

A   0   10   20   25   30   40   50   60   70   75   80   90   100   B
0   100

EXHIBIT 11–2

FACTOR AND SUBFACTOR RATINGS FOR A NEW PRODUCT

	Very good	Good	Average	Poor	Very poor
I. Marketability					
A. Relation to present distribution channels	Can reach major markets by distributing through present channels.	Can reach major markets by distributing mostly through present channels, partly through new channels.	Will have to distribute equally between new and present channels, in order to reach major markets.	Will have to distribute mostly through new channels in order to reach major markets.	Will have to distribute entirely through new channels in order to reach major markets.
B. Relation to present product lines	Complements a present line which needs more products to fill it.	Complements a present line that does not need, but can handle, another product.	Can be fitted into a present line.	Can be fitted in a present line but does not fit entirely.	Does not fit in with any present product line.
C. Quality/price relationship	Priced below all competing products of similar quality.	Priced below most competing products of similar quality.	Approximately the same price as competing products of similar quality.	Priced above many competing products of similar quality.	Priced above all competing products of similar quality.
D. Number of sizes and grades	Few staple sizes and grades.	Several sizes and grades, but customers will be satisfied with few staples.	Several sizes and grades, but can satisfy customer wants with small inventory of nonstaples.	Several sizes and grades, each of which will have to be stocked in equal amounts.	Many sizes and grades which will necessitate heavy inventories.
E. Merchandisability	Has product characteristics over and above those of competing products that lend themselves to the kind of promotion, advertising, and display that the given company does best.	Has promotable characteristics that will compare favorably with the characteristics of competing products.	Has promotable characteristics that are equal to those of other products.	Has a few characteristics that are promotable, but generally does not measure up to characteristics of competing products.	Has no characteristics at all that are equal to competitors, or that lend themselves to imaginative promotion.
F. Effects on sales of present products	Should aid in sales of present products.	May help sales of present products; definitely will not be harmful to present sales.	Should have no effect on present sales.	May hinder present sales some; definitely will not aid present sales.	Will reduce sales of presently profitable products.
II. Durability					
A. Stability	Basic product which can always expect to have uses.	Product which will have uses long enough to earn back initial investment, plus at least 10 years of additional profits.	Product which will have uses long enough to earn back initial investment, plus several (from 5 to 10) years of additional profits.	Product which will have uses long enough to earn back initial investment, plus 1 to 5 years of additional profits.	Product which will probably be obsolete in near future.
B. Breadth of market	A national market, a wide variety of consumers, and a potential foreign market.	A national market and a wide variety of consumers.	Either a national market or a wide variety of consumers.	A regional market and a restricted variety of consumers.	A specialized market in a small marketing area.

EXHIBIT 11-2 (continued)

	Very good	Good	Average	Poor	Very poor
C. Resistance to cyclical fluctuations	Will sell readily in inflation or depression.	Effects of cyclical changes will be *moderate,* and will be felt *after* changes in economic outlook.	Sales will rise and fall with the economy.	Effects of cyclical changes will be *heavy,* and will be felt *before* changes in economic outlook.	Cyclical changes will cause extreme fluctuations in demand.
D. Resistance to seasonal fluctuations	Steady sales throughout the year.	Steady sales — except under unusual circumstances.	Seasonal fluctuations, but inventory and personnel problems can be absorbed.	Heavy seasonal fluctuations that will cause considerable inventory and personnel problems.	Severe seasonal fluctuations that will necessitate layoffs and heavy inventories.
E. Exclusiveness of design	Can be protected by a patent with no loopholes.	Can be patented, but the patent might be circumvented.	Cannot be patented, but has certain salient characteristics that cannot be copied very well.	Cannot be patented, and can be copied by larger, more knowledgeable companies.	Cannot be patented, and can be copied by anyone.
III. *Productive ability* **A.** Equipment necessary	Can be produced with equipment that is presently idle.	Can be produced with present equipment, but production will have to be scheduled with other products.	Can be produced largely with present equipment, but the company will have to purchase some additional equipment.	Company will have to buy a good deal of new equipment, but some present equipment can be used.	Company will have to buy all new equipment.
B. Production knowledge and personnel necessary	Present knowledge and personnel will be able to produce new product.	With very few minor exceptions, present knowledge and personnel will be able to produce new product.	With some exceptions, present knowledge and personnel will be able to produce new product.	A ratio of approximately 50-50 will prevail between the needs for new knowledge and personnel and for present knowledge and personnel.	Mostly new knowledge and personnel are needed to produce the new product.
C. Raw materials availability	Company can purchase raw materials from its best supplier(s) exclusively.	Company can purchase major portion of raw materials from its best supplier(s), and remainder from any one of a number of companies.	Company can purchase approximately half of raw materials from its best supplier(s), and other half from any one of a number of companies.	Company must purchase most of raw materials from any one of a number of companies other than its best supplier(s).	Company must purchase most or all of raw materials from a certain few companies other than its best supplier(s).
IV. *Growth potential* **A.** Place in market	New type of product that will fill a need presently not being filled.	Product that will substantially improve on products presently on the market.	Product that will have certain new characteristics that will appeal to a substantial segment of the market.	Product that will have minor improvements over products presently on the market.	Product similar to those presently on the market and which adds nothing new.
B. Expected competitive situation — value added	Very high value added so as to substantially restrict number of competitors.	High enough value added so that, unless product is extremely well suited to other firms, they will not want to invest in additional facilities.	High enough value added so that, unless other companies are as strong in market as this firm, it will not be profitable for them to compete.	Lower value added so as to allow large, medium, and some smaller companies to compete.	Very low value added so that all companies can profitably enter market.
C. Expected availability of end users	Number of end users will increase substantially.	Number of end users will increase moderately.	Number of end users will increase slightly, if at all.	Number of end users will decrease moderately.	Number of end users will decrease substantially.

products? Conceptually, expected return and risk offer two such meaningful summary measures. The difficulty, however, is in management's ability to estimate accurately the expected return. Furthermore, the perceived risk varies by management's level of commitment to the project as well as a number of uncontrolled factors. It might be desirable, therefore, to follow two distinct management evaluation procedures depending on the amount (and quality) of available information. At early stages of product development, with little available information, management screening should be limited to relatively few and critical dimensions which if not satisfied would require a temporary (until next evaluation of ideas/concepts) termination of the given idea/concept. Exhibit

11–3 illustrates one such simplified screening form.

Such a screening approach does not rank ideas/concepts but rather sorts them into acceptable ideas—those which received a 'yes' to all the relevant screening questions—and those which were rejected on one or more of the critical dimensions. To further sort the initially acceptable ideas/concepts into priority categories, more information has to be collected and project interdependency considerations (especially with respect to technological development) taken into account. The rejected ideas/concepts can also be reevaluated or subjected to some additional development, especially on the dimension on which they were initially judged unacceptable.

EXHIBIT 11–3

AN ILLUSTRATIVE SIMPLIFIED FORM FOR INITIAL SCREENING OF
IDEAS/CONCEPTS

1. Is idea compatible with corporate objectives?   Yes ____ (go to 2)   No ____ (terminate)

2. Is idea legally accepted?   Yes ____ (go to 3)   No ____ (terminate)

3. Can idea be technically developed within desired time and budget constraints?   Yes ____ (go to 4)   No ____ (terminate)

4. Is there a demand for such a product?   Yes ____ (go to 5)   No ____ (terminate)

   What segment is it likely to appeal to (and why), is it large enough, and can it be reached by the firm?

   What products is the new idea/concept/product likely to compete with, and what share of the segment can it expect under the most optimistic conditions?

5. Is the idea compatible with the current and desired marketing activities and strengths of the firm?   Yes ____ (proceed with development)   No ____ (terminate)

An important consideration in the use of any profile listing approach, whether summarized on some desirability score or not, is the validity of the approach. Such validity can be determined by a two-group discriminant analysis of successful and unsuccessful concepts/products, against the various factor scores of these concepts/products. Alternatively, if one considers the degree of success (not a dichotomy of successful/unsuccessful) a multiple regression or n-group multiple discriminant analysis can be used.

The Analytic Hierarchy Process (AHP)
Ideas/concepts/products can be evaluated using the AHP. The process, which is described in Chapter 5 and Appendix A, provides management with an evaluative framework, a measurement approach, a procedure for incorporating evaluative data with management's subjective judgments, and a procedure for resolving conflicts among the relevant decision makers. In its simplest formulation, a two-step hierarchy can be developed of criteria and concepts. Yet, it can easily be extended to incorporate alternative scenarios and the likely objectives and activities of the relevant actors (e.g., consumers, distributors, competitors, government agencies, etc.).

The development of an expanded hierarchy (e.g., scenarios—actors—objectives—activities—concepts) can offer management not only a summary score for each concept (i.e., total priority score) but also considerable diagnostic insight into the likely strengths and weaknesses of each concept vis-a-vis all the relevant stakeholders. For further discussion of various applications see Wind and Saaty (1980).

In contrast to the oversimplified initial screening, more detailed concept/product evaluation requires a considerable amount of information. The dimensions of this more detailed economic evaluation and the various approaches that can be taken are discussed in the remainder of this chapter.

COMPONENTS OF ECONOMIC EVALUATION[1]

Economic evaluation of concepts/products involves at least six major components—cost, revenue, profit, tax considerations, uncertainties, and synergistic effects. Other criteria, such as expected market share, expected industry sales growth, and other factors included in portfolio analysis (Chapter 5) can also be incorporated but are frequently viewed as determinants or consequences of the firm's economic performance. The discussion in this section, therefore, is limited to these six major economic factors.

COSTS

Estimating the cost of developing, testing, producing, and marketing a new product is an essential component of every economic evaluation. Cost estimation should take into consider-

[1]For a detailed discussion of economic evaluation see any of the books on capital budgeting (e.g., Bierman and Smidt, 1960) or managerial accounting (e.g., Moore and Jaedicke, 1976).

ation the following items:

Expected development costs including the cost of technical and marketing R&D. These are the cost components with the greatest uncertainty.

Expected set-up cost Assuming successful new product development, the cost of setting up the production facilities are a major cost component. Complicating factors in estimating the setup costs are:

- The expected demand for the product and its likely fluctuation over time—the greater the expected fluctuation, the higher the set-up and operating costs.

- The expected cost interdependencies—i.e., the degree to which the new product could share the production facilities of other products.

- The geographical distribution of demand and the logistics costs (of materials and final product). These considerations coupled with the expected economies of scale in production determine whether a single plant or a number of regional plants are more economical. The number of plants and their geographical distribution are thus important components of the production set-up costs.

Operating costs A key cost factor in the determination of the product's long-term profitability is the expected operating costs. Given the effect of manufacturing learning curves, the degree of economies of scale depends directly on the expected demand which in turn is affected by the firm's marketing efforts, the nature and degree of competitive activities, and other environmental factors outside the control of the firm.

A special difficulty in estimating operating cost is the time horizon involved. If, for exam-

ple, the evaluation is at the concept evaluation stage, the estimated operating costs are for a few years ahead, when the development program is completed and the product is ready to enter the production stage. The further into the future the costs of raw materials, labor, utilities, and other production costs are estimated, the higher the uncertainty around them.

Marketing costs A major component of the operating costs are the expected marketing expenditures for the promotion and distribution of the product. These costs are subject to the same estimation difficulties as operating costs.

Management costs An often-ignored cost component is the demand a new product places on management time. Difficult to estimate and even more difficult to place a dollar figure on, management time is often viewed as free. Given the glamour associated with new product development, not accounting for management time can result in its misallocation and can lead to wrong concept/product evaluation.

Cost estimates for the development and marketing of a new product vary in their accuracy depending on the time horizon involved (planned production six months or six years ahead), the newness of the new product (a minor or programmed product change versus radical or nonprogrammed new product requiring new production and marketing technology), the extent of cost interdependencies, the stability of the economy, and relevant environmental factors (such as availability and price of raw materials, inflationary pressures, and the like). Furthermore, costs may vary markedly depending on the geographic location of the operation. In 1979 R&D costs in Israel, for example, were about one-third of their equivalent US costs. Production costs in Korea, Puerto Rico, and China are considerably lower than those in the US and other developed countries.

REVENUES

The expected direct revenues from a new product are from two major sources: the sales of the product and the sales or license of the technology developed for or generated as a by-product of the given product. The accuracy of revenue estimation from the sales of a product depends on the accuracy of the following:

- *Conditional forecast* of the market demand over the product's life cycle which requires an estimation of the market response (and lagged response) functions to price, advertising, distribution, and the overall marketing campaign of the firm and its competitors.

- *Conditional forecast* of the firm's market share.

- The selling price (which in turn depends on the price elasticity of various market segments, the discount and price structure and elasticity of selected intermediate marketing organizations) *and* the premium price the given product can command over the product's life cycle (including the lead time a new product can achieve over its competitors).

- The expected life of the product (PLC) and the prices, market share, and profitability the product is expected to achieve at each stage of its product life cycle.

- The firm's *cost of capital* (discount rate) and its likely change over time.

A second source of revenues is the licensing or sales of technology. Although often ignored in the evaluation of new concepts/products, it can be an important revenue component, especially if the new product development requires major R&D activities.

In calculating the revenues from both product sales and technology licensing or sales

agreements, it is important to assess the expected cash flows. This requires estimates of seasonal fluctuations, retail inventory practices, and other factors which affect the time distribution of revenues.

PROFITS

Given estimates of the expected revenues and costs it is a relatively simple matter to calculate the expected profitability of each concept/product. In calculating the anticipated profitability of a new concept/product break even analysis is often utilized.

Break-even analysis identifies the number of units that must be sold (or sales revenues that must be generated) if the company is to operate without a loss (break even). The calculation of break-even analysis takes into consideration the selling price, volume of sales, unit variable cost, and total fixed costs and is typically accompanied with a break-even chart:

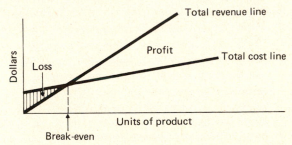

For planning and control purposes, break-even analysis is often supplemented by appropriate profitability ratios such as ROI, return on sales, return on equity, or return on assets employed. These measures often take into account the stream of expected costs and revenues via calculations of net present value.[2] These can be

---

[2]An ROI approach which does not incorporate a discounted cash flow analysis is conceptually unacceptable since it ignores the time value of money.

further supplemented by the expected payback period, although the payback criterion by itself is in most cases inappropriate for evaluating new product projects.

In calculating the discounted cash flow the most common approach is to evaluate the new product proposal against the firm's cost of capital.[3] This approach, however, has a severe limitation since the average cost of capital of the firm might not be the appropriate criterion. To overcome this limitation two approaches have been suggested—a multiple hurdle rates approach (Donaldson, 1972) and the use of a security market line (Sharpe, 1970; Weston, 1973). Following the multiple hurdle approach different products might be subject to different hurdle rates. More specifically, Donaldson proposed the following criteria for setting the hurdle rates:

• Internal strategic hurdle rate for any one division is the demonstrated return in the competing division that has the best financial track record, present and prospective (adjusted for material difference in perceived risk).

• External strategic hurdle rate is the return on the best of several alternatives that are external to the present business and capable of implementation by management through internal development or acquisition (again adjusted for risk differences).

---

[3] The *net present value* (NPV) of a project is calculated as:

$$NPV = \sum_{i=1}^{n} \frac{A_i}{(1+k)^i} ,$$

where A_i = *net* after-tax cash flows generated by the product in year i;
n = expected life of the product;
k = firm's cost of capital.

• Internal tactical hurdle rate would be a measure of the demonstrated rate of return in that decision and a realistic assessment of what is attainable in that particular product line and market.

• External tactical hurdle rate reflects the performance of the most efficient competitor in the same product and market area.

The specific criteria used should reflect management preference and the strategic versus tactical nature of the product decisions under evaluation. Whatever the criteria are, the important concept is that more than a single hurdle rate of return should be employed.

The second alternative to the use of the average cost of capital approach is the use of the market model to generate the risk-adjusted discount rate. This is calculated using Sharpe's equation for the security market line (Sharpe, 1970):

$$E(R_j) = R_f + [E(R_m) - R_f] - \beta_j ,$$

where $E(R_j)$ = expected return on security j;
R_f = risk-free rate of interest (e.g., return on US Treasury bills);
$E(R_m)$ = expected return on *all* securities in the market;
β_j = beta coefficient for security j which is estimated by

$$R_{ij} = \alpha_j + \beta_j R_{im} ,$$

where R_{ij} = return on security j in period i;
R_{im} = return on *all* market securities during period i;
α_j = intercept coefficient for security j;
β_j = beta coefficient for security j (used as a measure of systematic risk).

The estimation of beta for new product investments is not as straightforward as the estimation of the beta of securities. Yet one can use a number of surrogates such as the average beta coefficient of a group of firms operating in the market at which the new product is aimed. Alternatively, the beta coefficient of the most likely competitors can be used. Given a surrogate beta, it is relatively straightforward to determine the rate at which the expected cash flow from a new product should be discounted. Consider, for example, the following hypothetical case in which:

- The beta for the relevant competitors is 2.0;
- The firm expects the return (for the group of relevant firms) to average 10 percent;
- The risk free rate is 6.0 percent.

By using the Sharpe equation for the security market line, we can find the required return for this product as $6.0 + (10.0 - 6.0)2.0 = 14$ percent which is the rate at which the expected cash flows should be discounted in the net present value formulation.

TAX CONSIDERATIONS

To the extent that all new product alternatives are subject to the same tax rules, no special consideration should be given to this component. Tax considerations, however, are critical factors wherever the various new product alternatives differ in their tax implications or whenever a new product proposal is evaluated against investment in existing products.

Some of the major tax considerations which could markedly affect the effective return for a new product are:

- *Depreciation rules*
- *Income tax and investment tax credits* (the latter might be a major factor in determining the desirability of merger or acquisition versus initial development)
- *Tax incentives*. These are especially critical in foreign investments. Puerto Rico, for example, allows extremely attractive tax incentives to pharmaceutical companies. Such incentives can change the expected attractiveness of various projects (one which requires continental US production versus production in Puerto Rico, for example).

These and other tax considerations and the frequent changes in the tax laws of various countries suggest the need for expert counsel on the tax implications of alternative new product proposals.

UNCERTAINTIES

The economic evaluation of new concepts/products should incorporate explicitly an uncertainty component. Uncertainty confronts every business decision and is especially critical in new concept/product evaluation. All the components of economic evaluation require forecasts which in turn are subject to considerable uncertainty due to inflation, material shortages, new technological innovation, government involvement, changes in consumer's preferences, competitive actions, and other changing environmental conditions. These uncertainties surround the estimation of both the demand and cost functions. Following Kotler (1971) the uncertainties can be attributed to six sources:

1. Exogenous variable uncertainty—uncertainty surrounding the future level of exogenous variables;
2. Form of variable uncertainty—uncertainty regarding the nature of the effect one variable has on another: linear, squared, logged, etc.;
3. Coefficient uncertainty—the variance that surrounds any estimate of the response coefficient;

4. Structural form uncertainty—the uncertainty surrounding the basic structure of the equation;

5. Omitted variable uncertainty;

6. Stability uncertainty—the stability of the equational relationship over time.

The magnitude and severity of these uncertainties are often estimated using management's subjective judgment. These evaluations, when done explicitly, can be done as a single, overall measure expressed in a variety of ways and measured on various scales (such as a 100-point likelihood of success) or as a series of estimates, for each relevant variable or outcome, incorporating at the minimum an optimistic, pessimistic, and most likely estimate.

Alternatively, the assessment of uncertainty can be done, in various degrees of formalism, for each of the evaluation criteria used in the factor-listing approaches or the calculation of rate of return. These approaches can be supplemented by the evaluation of external experts via a Delphi type approach.

Another way of measuring uncertainty is via a surrogate—the variance of the expected profits of the new concept/product or, in cases in which the firm has other existing products, the differential uncertainty of adding the new concepts/products as measured by the standard deviation of the differential profit distribution. This latter procedure is used by Urban (1968) in his new product evaluation model.

Uncertainties have also been incorporated into more traditional investment analysis in a variety of ways:

- Risk-adjusted hurdle rates in which the expected rate of return for some products is increased, subjectively, to allow for different levels of perceived risk;

- Adding a subjective risk-adjustment factor to the cash flows in the NPV model.

Following this certainty equivalent approach, the NPV model is:

$$\text{NPV} = \sum_{i=1}^{n} \frac{C_i A_i}{(1 + R_f)^i} \, ,$$

where C_i = certainty-equivalent coefficient for year i (ranges between 0 and 1);

A_i = net after-tax cash flow generated by the product in year i;

R_f = risk-free rate of interest (approximated for example by the return on short-term government securities).

The advantage of this approach is that it allows management to explicitly take into account the nature of the time pattern of risk.[4]

SYNERGISTIC AND CANNIBALIZATION EFFECTS

The development and marketing of a new product is rarely undertaken in isolation from other products and services of the firm. This raises the possibility of interdependencies between the *new* product and existing ones, and between the new product and other potentially new products. Some of these interdependencies were briefly mentioned in the context of cost. Yet, the impact of technology, production, marketing, and management interdependencies goes beyond cost interdependence and is often referred to as *synergistic* effects. Whereas these effects refer to the *positive* impact a new product might have on the firm's operation, often the introduction of a new product can effect negatively the profitability of existing products. In these cases management should be concerned with the *cannibalization* effect of the new product and estimate its magnitude and timing.

---

[4]For further discussion of this approach see Robichek and Myers (1965) and Van Horne (1971).

ALTERNATIVE APPROACHES TO ECONOMIC EVALUATION

The six components of economic evaluation can be categorized into the two major dimensions of expected return (reflecting the expected costs, revenues, profits, tax considerations, and the profit impact of any synergistic or cannibalization effects) and uncertainty.

These two major dimensions (and occasionally others) have been employed in a number of alternative approaches to determine the economic viability of new ideas/concepts/products. These approaches, despite varying formulations, share a strong reliance on the financial approach to investment analysis, and the analysis of expected risk and return. The experience with the various approaches varies and each has its proponents. Since no single approach can be clearly identified as best for all products, companies and situations, the reader is encouraged to experiment with a number of approaches and adopt the one which best fits the idiosyncrasies of a given firm.

Given the strong reliance of most of the new product evaluation models on risk-return analysis we first describe this simplistic approach to new product evaluation. Following this section, a number of models are presented. These include: risk analysis (Hertz, 1964), the DEMON model (Charnes, Cooper, De Voe, and Learner, 1966), SPRINTER (Urban, 1967, 68), VENTUR (Pessemier, 1977), and RESCUE (Claycamp, 1978).

RISK-RETURN ANALYSIS

In its simplest form, knowing the expected return and risk of the idea/concept/product, and management trade off between the two criteria is all that is needed to evaluate mutually exclusive ideas/concepts/products. This simplistic

EXHIBIT 11–4

RETURN-RISK CONDITION

Source: Philip Kotler, *Marketing Decision Making: A Model Building Approach*, N.Y., Holt Rinehart and Winston, 1971, p. 265. Used with the permission of the author.

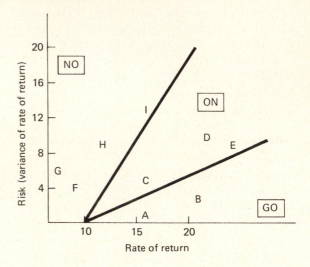

model is presented in Exhibit 11–4 as a Return-Risk Grid. Using this simple graphical device, each new concept/product can be placed in the grid based on its expected rate of return (r) and risk (σ_2—the variance of the rate of return). The return-risk space is divided into three regions based on management trade off between risk and return—the slope of the lines defining (a) the regions and (b) the threshold levels for acceptance of any new concept/product, even if riskless, that would yield less than the value of the intercept (10 percent rate of return in Exhibit 11–4). Following the construction of the three regions the evaluation of any new concept/product is relatively simple. If it falls in the GO region management should proceed, since the concept/product has favorable risk-return characteristics. If, on the other hand, a concept/product falls in the NO region it is rejected in its current form given unfavorable risk-return characteristics. The central region of ON includes those concepts/products for which management needs more information so as to be in a position to move them into either the GO or the NO region.

The classification of new concepts/products into these three categories offers both an initial screening and guidance as to which project to further examine. In addition, knowing management's risk-aversion coefficient, it is possible to rank all the new concept/products which fall within the GO region based on the following simple utility function:

$$U_i = r_i - (RA)\sigma r_i^2 \,,$$

where U_i = utility of new concept/product i;
r_i = expected rate of return on new concept/product i;
RA = management's risk-aversion coefficient (range from 0 to 1);
σr_i^2 = variance of rate of return on new concept/product i.

As an example, let's consider the two new concepts/products in the GO region of Exhibit 11–4. The expected return for these concepts is 15 percent for concept A and 20 percent for concept B. The variance for the two concepts is 1 percent and 3 percent, respectively. The choice between the two would thus depend on management risk aversion. If, for example, management has a high risk-aversion coefficient (such as 0.8), concept A would be preferred:

$$U_A = 15 - 0.8 \cdot 1^2 = 14.2 \,,$$
$$U_B = 20 - 0.8 \cdot 3^2 = 12.8 \,.$$

If on the other hand management has a lower risk aversion (such as 0.4), new concept B would be chosen:

$$U_A = 15 - 0.4 \cdot 1^2 = 14.6 \,,$$
$$U_B = 20 - 0.4 \cdot 3^2 = 16.4 \,.$$

The return-risk criteria are conceptually attractive, and consistent with the financial approach to portfolio analysis. There are, however, some questions as to the best measure of risk. The most common measure of risk—the variance—has a number of problems due to the fact that it does not distinguish between over (high pay-off) and under (risk) expectations and does not take into account the other characteristics of the distribution (such as skewness). To overcome the first limitation a number of alternatives have been suggested. These include the definition of risk as the expected value of the loss function, as the semivariance that measures the downside risk, or as the probability of losing an amount equal to or greater than the manager's perceived level of ruin. (For further discussion of these alternatives see Kotler, 1971, Chapter 10.) To overcome the second limitation of the variance a number of new concept/product evaluation models have utilized not only the variance but the probability distribution of rate of return. The importance of considering the distribution and not only the mean and variance is illustrated in Exhibit 11–5 which presents two hypothetical distributions for products A and B, which have

EXHIBIT 11–5

HYPOTHETICAL ROLE OF RETURN DISTRIBUTIONS FOR TWO NEW CONCEPTS

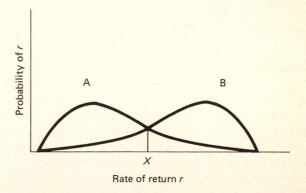

identical means and variances but opposite skewness, which leads to a clear dominance of Product B over A.

RISK ANALYSIS

Recognizing the limitations of using only the mean and variance of expected rate of return, a number of risk-analysis models have been proposed which incorporate the distribution of uncertainties surrounding each of the significant factors (such as market size, selling price, market growth rate, and share of market) into a formal model for forecasting earnings, cash flow, or any other relevant outcomes. Hertz (1964), for example, in describing the risk analysis program used by McKinsey and Company proposed a three-step approach for the design and implementation of such analysis:

1. Estimate the range of values for each of the factors and within that range the likelihood of occurrence (resulting in a probability distribution) of each value. This step assumes a preceding step in which management identifies the relevant factors such as:

- Market size
- Market growth rate
- Market share
- Selling price
- Expected life of product
- Operating and fixed costs
- Required investment
- Residual value of investment

These range and likelihood estimates are usually obtained from management following any number of procedures suggested in the decision theory literature for establishing management's subjective estimates. These estimates, to be of value, should be based on specific environmental scenarios. Specifying explicit

scenarios is important to assure that all subjective estimates and forecasts are made against a common environmental backdrop.

2. Determine the returns that will result from random cominations of the factors involved. Such estimates are derived from a relatively simple computer simulation which incorporates realistic restrictions (such as a maximum amount of change in total market size), takes into account interdependencies among the factors, and uses some form or another of a discounted cash flow analysis.

3. Repeat the process to define and evaluate the odds of the occurrence of each possible rate of return. The results of these simulation runs are the probability distribution for achieving various rates of returns including the average expectation (the average of the values of all outcomes weighted by the chances of each occurring) and the variability of outcome values from the average.

The risk analysis simulation proposed by Hertz (1964) is summarized in Exhibit 11–6. Its major value is not the generation of a specific solution but rather its usefulness in ascertaining the sensitivity of the results to each or all of the input factors. By running the simulation with changes in the distribution of an input factor, it is possible to determine the effect of these changes on the results.

DEMON

DEMON—*DE*cision *M*apping Via *O*ptimum Go-No *N*etworks—views the product evaluation process as a networking problem focused on three decisions:

- GO—introduce the new product;
- NO—reject the new product;
- ON—investigate further and continue development.

EXHIBIT 11–6

SIMULATION FOR INVESTMENT PLANNING

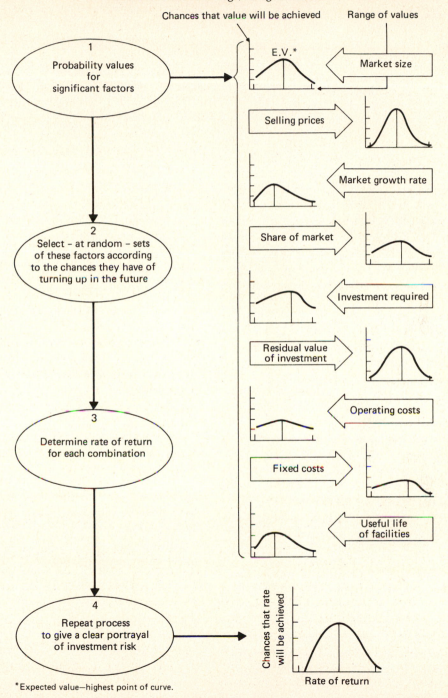

*Expected value—highest point of curve.

EXHIBIT 11–7

DEMON EVALUATION PROCESS

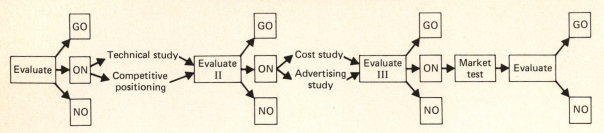

The choice between GO, NO, and ON depends on the new product's expected profit and uncertainty. More specifically, the DEMON model sets two constraints that specify the GO, NO, ON regions. These constraints reflect management's financial and risk policies toward a given product category, and are:

- For a GO decision, the probability of identifying a target discounted rate of return must exceed a specified level.

- For a NO decision, this probability must be less than a specified level.

DEMON exploits in a cumulative fashion, all the available information and provides not only a decision—a GO, NO GO or ON—but also specifies in the case of ON the marketing factors to be revised and tested. Following such additional data a new decision based upon the cumulative information is made and the procedure continues until a GO or No decision is reached. Schematically, the process suggested by the DEMON model is presented in Exhibit 11–7. The model itself is based on five steps:

1. Link all relevant performance ratios (awareness-triers; triers-users, etc.) to determine the most likely level of product acceptance. These ratios encompass all relevant marketing factors including advertising expenditures, promotion expenditures, advertising awareness, media reach and frequency, distribution levels, price, product trial, product usage, and usage rate.

2. Evaluate product acceptance in the context of profit and risk against management's stated objectives for minimum acceptable profits over the planning period.

3. On the basis of the evaluation of product acceptance, profits and risk decide GO, NO or On.

4. If the decision is ON, select the appropriate marketing factor to alter and the research required to evaluate that alteration to assess how much the marketing mix can be improved.

5. Use the new research results to revise the initial performance ratios and cycle through again until either a GO or No decision is reached.

The model itself is based on the solution of DEMON-type functional equations, which have been reduced to a solution of a separated system of equations which, for discrete distributions, can be solved by linear programming methods (Charnes et al., 1968).

SPRINTER

The new product analysis and decision model proposed by Urban (1968) is based on a sequential analysis of four submodels of demand, cost,

EXHIBIT 11–8

MAJOR COMPONENTS OF THE SPRINTER MODEL

Reprinted from Glen L. Urban, "A New Product Analysis and Decision Model," *Management Science,* Volume 14, #8, April, 1968, pp. B490–B517. Copyright 1968 by the Institute of Management Sciences.

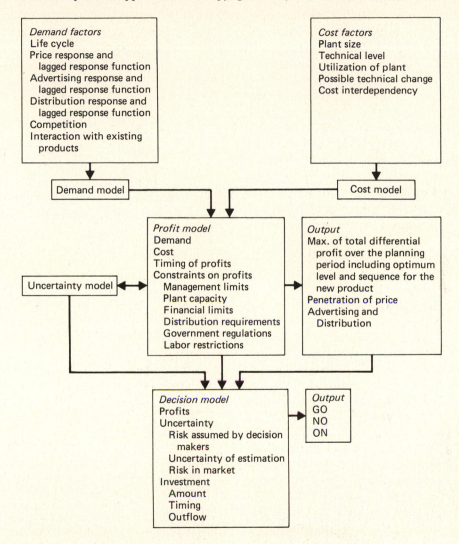

profit, and uncertainty, and their interactions. The model is used to determine whether a new product should be added (GO), rejected (NO), or should be investigated further (ON). The *demand model* is structured to consider product life cycle, marketing mix effects, industry, competitive, and product interdependency effects; admit nonlinear and discontinuous functions; and incorporate the dynamic effects of diffusion of the new product innovation and lagged responses. A *cost minimization* model is joined to the demand model to formulate a constrained profit maximization problem. The *optimization* is accomplished by the use of dynamic programming. The final decision is reached based on the decision makers' trade off between rate of return and uncertainty. The composition of the SPRINTER (*S*pecification of *PR*ofits with *IN*teraction under *T*rial and *E*rror *R*esponses) model is presented in Exhibit 11–8 which outlines the major inputs of the model and some of its outputs.

The SPRINTER model, not unlike other risk analysis models, enables the researcher to test the sensitivity of the various results to changes in the input data and constraints. It offers insights to the best marketing strategy (in terms of price, advertising, and distribution levels over the life cycle of the new product) for a GO decision. It further offers the best allocation of research funds for ON decisions.

VENTUR

Not unlike the other risk analysis simulations, VENTUR is a financial risk analysis model developed by Pessemier (1977) as one of a series of new product development models. These models start with DESIGNR—a diagnostic tool for dealing with product and communication design, pricing, and market segmentation. The model allows the testing of alternative product strategies to assess the effect, in terms of sales, market share, and profits, of a new product entry (a repositioning of a mature product) assuming that the perceptual and distribution goals have been met within each active market segment.

The ADOPTR model is designed to predict the *early* market behavior of a new (or substantially improved) product. It allows testing introductory marketing programs that vary in magnitude and character. The model can include the predictive output of DESIGNR, re-

sulting in unit sales forecasts, and supplemented by the cost of the marketing program and its associated cash flow patterns.

The cash flows generated by the new product strategy model (ADOPTR) can be formally examined using VENTUR, the full product life, financial risk analyzer. VENTUR provides the information needed for planning the investment and other financial requirements of a prospective new product.

The model inputs include three sets of data:

1. Marketing (annual) data by product type and segment
   - Unit sales*
   - Unit price*
   - Promotional expenditures (as % of sales)
2. Manufacturing-investment (annual) data
   - Capital investment*
   - Investment tax credit
   - Salvage value
   - Capacity limit (by product)
   - Variable cost per unit at each output level and period by product*
3. Financial data
   - Opportunity cost of capital
   - Tax rate
   - Annual working capital (%)
   - Annual depreciation
   - Other fixed costs
   - Other costs as % of sales (by product)
   - Minimum acceptable sales

These data are mostly generated from executives based on a common procedure for obtaining subjective estimates on the expected value and for some of the items (the starred items in the above list) also for the 10th and 90th percentile. The model is based on a simulation which utilizes the Telchrowe, Robicheck, and Montalbano (1965) discounting procedure which finds the ROI that equates the discounted sum of the net cash flows to zero. The discount factor used for the appropriate year depends on whether or not the cumulative sum of the discounted cash flows is positive or negative. If positive, then the factor used is based on the opportunity cost of capital. If the cumulative sum is negative, then the factor is based on the trial ROI.

By repeated sampling from the relevant key variable distribution a series of simulated economic results are computed. The distribution of these results represents the risk-return characteristics of adapting a given strategy under specific market conditions.

The output of the VENTUR model includes detailed financial data as well as summary product and financial data by product and total. Its primary output is annual cash flows, sales margins, and profits for each tested alternative. More specifically these outputs include the mean and variance of the simulated outcomes for the following measures:

1. Detailed financial data
   - Annual and cumulative dollar sales
   - Annual and cumulative net cash flows
   - Annual and cumulative after-tax profits
   - Rate of return on investment
   - Present worth of net cash flows
2. Summary product data (average annual data by product and total)
   - Unit sales
   - Unit price
   - Unit dollar sales
   - Unit cost of sales
   - Unit contribution profit
3. Summary financial (average annual) data
   - Investment
   - Working capital
   - After-tax profits
   - Net cash flows
   - Dollar sales

- After-tax return on sales
- Sales loss due to capacity limits
- Value of unused capacity

VENTUR, like other risk simulators, uses the summary output as the starting point for a variety of sensitivity analyses including possible reduction in uncertainty (as a result of increased confidence about input variables) and strategy reformulations.

RESCUE[5]

RESCUE, a risk analysis system, was originally developed by Henry Claycamp in 1966 as a cash flow simulator for the management of a large defense-oriented company which wished to evaluate returns and risks associated with alternative investments. The model was designed to accept single-point (deterministic) estimates or ranges of values (probabilistic) as input for any element of a cash flow equation and produce as output cumulative probability distributions for a wide variety of investment criteria.

Revised time sharing versions of RESCUE have been used in executive development programs and business schools in the US and Europe and in a large number of firms for evaluating new product alternatives. At present it is being used throughout the International Harvester Company in a wide variety of problem situations.

The structure of RESCUE is presented in Exhibit 11–9. It consists of two basic simulation models—both of which accept deterministic or probabilistic (minimum-maximum and most-likely) estimates as inputs. The *Demand Simulator* accepts estimates of market demand and market share for a single product or range of products in up to ten market segments and an estimate of product capacity. Using com-

[5]This section is based on Claycamp (1978).

EXHIBIT 11–9

RESCUE MODEL

Source: Henry J. Claycamp "New Product Investment Decisions and Management Science Techniques," unpublished manuscript, 1977. Reprinted by permission.

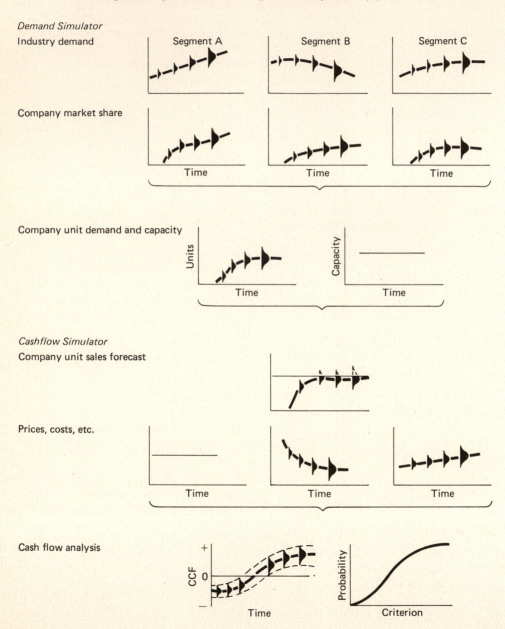

EXHIBIT 11–10

RESCUE WORKSHEET (1)

Source: Henry J. Claycamp "New Product Investment Decisions and Management Science
Techniques," unpublished manuscript, 1977. Reprinted by permission.

Periodic data		Line	No. items	Type	Min.	Most likely	Max.	Conf.
YEAR 2								
Industry demand (000)	Seg. A	200	2	3	5.4	6.5	8.2	0.90
	Seg. B	201		3	4.0	4.5	6.4	0.90
		202						
Market share	Seg. A	210	2	3	0.15	0.20	0.22	0.80
	Seg. B	211		3	0.14	0.18	0.20	0.80
		212						
Production capacity (000)		220	1	1		3.3		
		221						
		222						
Price	Seg. A	230	2	1		3.535		
	Seg. B	231		1		3.535		
		232						
Variable cost	Seg. A	240	2	1		2.582		
	Seg. B	241						
		242						
Fixed cost (000)		250	1	1		1.322		
		251						
		252						
Depreciation (000)		260	1	1		88.8		
		261						
		262						
Change in working capital (000)		270	1	1		1.571		
		271						
		272						
Other cash flows (000)		280						
		281						
		282						

puter simulation RESCUE produced confidence interval forecasts (i.e., probability distributions) of company demand, and product sales (demand constrained by capacity) for up to twelve years.

The *Cash Flow Simulator* utilizes the confidence interval forecast of unit sales produced by the Demand Simulator and user inputs for variables such as price and variable costs that affect cash flow; and generates a wide range of outputs that can be used to analyze the risk and return profile of the investment.

To illustrate the way the RESCUE model is used, Exhibits 11–10 to 11–14 present an actual case history for new industrial products reported by Claycamp (1978). In this case a number of inputs have been adjusted to avoid disclosure of proprietary information.

In using RESCUE, management has to provide, in addition to estimates of demand, share, prices, and costs, information on tax rate, derived discount rate, and the estimated product planning period. They must also specify the desired output:

- Table of industry demand, company demand, company sales and cumulative cash flows at 90 percent, mean and 10 percent levels

- Yearly mean cash flows

- Distribution of present values

- Risk-adjusted present value analysis

- Distribution of internal rates of return

- Distribution of pay-back values for the firm

- Distribution of maximum investment values

- Distribution of times to maximum investment

- Pro forma profit and loss statements

The type of data inputs provided by management is illustrated in Exhibit 11–10. In this example, forecasts of demand for the second year of the analysis for two market segments are included. "Confidence" indicates that the user has a high degree of confidence that total demand of segment A in year 2 will be between 5,400 and 8,200 units, with the "most likely value" equal to 6,500 units. Market share forecasts for the two segments are shown on lines 210–211. Planned production capacity of 3,300 units was expected to be available by the beginning of the second year—only 20 units were to be produced and sold in year 1. The input value "3" in the "Type" column instructs RESCUE to treat a variable as serially correlated over time, whereas an input value of "1" in the "Type" column indicates a point estimate.

Exhibit 11–11 shows forecasts of industry demand, company demand, unit sales and cumulative cash flow at the 90 percent, mean, and 10 percent confidence levels resulting from inputs of the type shown in Exhibit 11–10. The graph shows the time path of the cumulative cash flow distribution over the seven years of analysis.

For example, the output indicates that there is a 90 percent chance that total industry demand in year 2 will be less than 2, 615 units, a 10 percent chance it will be less than 1, 763 and the expected or mean value is 2,176. Thus, the values of 2, 615 and 1,726 describe an 80 percent confidence interval forecast for the total demand in both segments. Similar interpretations can be made of company demand, company sales, and cumulative cash flow.

In year 3 and subsequent years a discrepancy exists between the forecasts of company demand and company sales at the 90 percent level. This example illustrates the importance of distinguishing between demand and sales. It is clear that the company would run into a capacity problem early in the life of the project if optimistic conditions actually prevail in the marketplace.

Exhibit 11–12 shows a forecast of (a) the expected value of the period-by-period cash flow, (b) the cumulative probability distribution of the cash flow discounted at 10 percent and (c) the risk-adjusted present value.

Although the Present Value Cumulative Probability chart appears complex at first glance, it is easily interpreted. For example, the values at the right indicate the probability that the net present value will be less than the amount shown at the left of the chart. To make interpretation even easier, specific values are printed for key points on the chart.

The final output shown in Exhibit 11–12, titled Risk-Adjusted Present Value, is an attempt to create a single, simple measure of both return and risk that makes intuitive sense to managers. It is calculated using the forecasted present value probability distribution and an estimate of a fair market price of insuring the

EXHIBIT 11–11

Source: Henry J. Claycamp "New Product Investment Decisions and Management Science Techniques," unpublished manuscript, 1977. Reprinted by permission.

UNIT DEMAND, UNIT SALES AND CUMULATIVE CASH FLOW (000)

			INDUSTRY DEMAND	CO DEMAND	CO SALES	CUMULATIVE CASH FLOW
YEAR	1	90% LEVEL	13.453	2.029	.020	−637.16
YEAR	1	MEAN	11.967	2.176	.020	−637.16
YEAR	1	10% LEVEL	10.463	1.763	.020	−637.16
YEAR	2	90% LEVEL	14.661	2.615	2.615	−1584.01
YEAR	2	MEAN	12.119	2.172	2.172	−1793.04
YEAR	2	10% LEVEL	10.309	1.726	1.726	−2003.42
YEAR	3	90% LEVEL	14.768	4.012	3.300	−1493.77
YEAR	3	MEAN	11.996	3.266	3.106	−1777.58
YEAR	3	10% LEVEL	10.191	2.838	2.838	−2040.78
YEAR	4	90% LEVEL	12.965	3.685	3.300	−856.71
YEAR	4	MEAN	11.135	3.078	2.997	−1235.24
YEAR	4	10% LEVEL	9.420	2.562	2.562	−1602.26
YEAR	5	90% LEVEL	11.951	3.453	3.300	450.90
YEAR	5	MEAN	10.248	2.913	2.880	31.56
YEAR	5	10% LEVEL	8.761	2.455	2.455	−351.08
YEAR	6	90% LEVEL	13.058	3.991	3.300	856.07
YEAR	6	MEAN	10.902	3.187	3.055	403.55
YEAR	6	10% LEVEL	9.305	2.616	2.616	39.58
YEAR	7	90% LEVEL	13.775	4.112	3.300	1248.25
YEAR	7	MEAN	11.184	3.248	3.068	770.16
YEAR	7	10% LEVEL	9.639	2.666	2.666	457.21

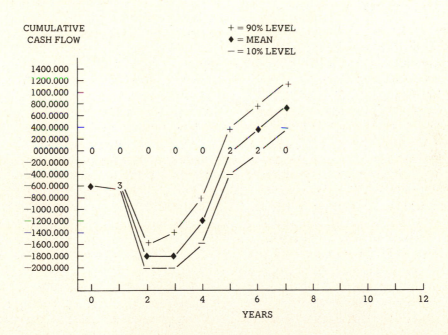

CUMULATIVE
CASH FLOW

+ = 90% LEVEL
♦ = MEAN
— = 10% LEVEL

YEARS

project against a negative outcome. For example, the present value probability distribution indicates that although the expected value is −$21,230, there is a 10 percent chance that it will be less than −$243,570, and a 10 percent chance that it will be greater than $259,360. Given the risk profile shown by the chart it is not difficult to develop a reasonable estimate of the cost of insuring the project against possible negative outcomes. This cost has been labeled the risk-adjustment cost. In this example, the risk-adjustment cost is $93,300 and the risk-adjusted present value is −$114,500. Thus, given the inputs to RESCUE, the results indi-

EXHIBIT 11–12

Source: Henry J. Claycamp "New Product Investment Decisions and Management Science Techniques," unpublished manuscript, 1977. Reprinted by permission.

EXPECTED CASH FLOW

PERIOD	UNDISCOUNTED	DISCOUNTED
0	−588	−588
1	−49	−45
2	−1156	−955
3	15	12
4	542	370
5	1267	787
6	372	210
7	367	188

PRESENT VALUE AT 10.00 PERCENT DISCOUNT

CUMULATIVE PROBABILITY CHART

VALUE	10 20 30 40 50 60 70 80 90 100	PROB
−429.40	◆	.00
−346.49	◆◆◆	.04
−263.58	◆◆◆◆	.06
−180.68	◆◆◆◆◆◆◆◆◆◆◆◆	.30
−97.77	◆◆◆◆◆◆◆◆◆◆◆◆◆◆◆◆	.40
−14.87	◆◆◆◆◆◆◆◆◆◆◆◆◆◆◆◆◆◆◆◆◆◆	.58
68.04	◆◆◆◆◆◆◆◆◆◆◆◆◆◆◆◆◆◆◆◆◆◆◆◆◆◆◆	.70
150.94	◆◆◆◆◆◆◆◆◆◆◆◆◆◆◆◆◆◆◆◆◆◆◆◆◆◆◆◆◆◆	.74
233.85	◆◆◆◆◆◆◆◆◆◆◆◆◆◆◆◆◆◆◆◆◆◆◆◆◆◆◆◆◆◆◆◆◆◆	.86
316.75	◆◆◆◆◆◆◆◆◆◆◆◆◆◆◆◆◆◆◆◆◆◆◆◆◆◆◆◆◆◆◆◆◆◆◆◆	.94
399.66	◆◆◆◆◆◆◆◆◆◆◆◆◆◆◆◆◆◆◆◆◆◆◆◆◆◆◆◆◆◆◆◆◆◆◆◆◆◆	1.00
VALUE		PROB

THE EXPECTED VALUE IS　　−21.23

THERE IS A 90 PERCENT CHANCE OF EXCEEDING　　−243.57

THERE IS A 50 PERCENT CHANCE OF EXCEEDING　　−30.53

THERE IS A 10 PERCENT CHANCE OF EXCEEDING　　259.36

RISK ADJUSTED PRESENT VALUE ANALYSIS

EXPECTED PRESENT VALUE		−21.2
STANDARD DEVIATION	206.1	
RISK ADJUSTMENT COST		93.3

RISK ADJUSTED PRESENT VALUE	−114.5

EXHIBIT 11–13

Source: Henry J. Claycamp "New Product Investment Decisions and Management Science Techniques," unpublished manuscript, 1977. Reprinted by permission.

MAXIMUM INVESTMENT EXPOSURE

CUMULATIVE PROBABILITY CHART

	10 20 30 40 50 60 70 80 90 100	
VALUE	• • • • • • • • • • •	PROB
−2187.18	◆ • •	.00
−2113.26	◆◆◆◆ •	.06
−2039.33	◆◆◆◆◆◆◆ •	.12
−1965.41	◆◆◆◆◆◆◆◆◆◆◆ •	.20
−1891.48	◆◆◆◆◆◆◆◆◆◆◆◆◆◆◆◆◆ •	.36
−1817.56	◆◆◆◆◆◆◆◆◆◆◆◆◆◆◆◆◆◆◆◆◆◆◆ •	.54
−1743.63	◆◆◆◆◆◆◆◆◆◆◆◆◆◆◆◆◆◆◆◆◆◆◆◆◆◆◆◆ •	.66
−1669.71	◆◆◆◆◆◆◆◆◆◆◆◆◆◆◆◆◆◆◆◆◆◆◆◆◆◆◆◆◆◆◆◆◆◆◆ •	.82
−1595.78	◆◆◆◆◆◆◆◆◆◆◆◆◆◆◆◆◆◆◆◆◆◆◆◆◆◆◆◆◆◆◆◆◆◆◆◆◆•	.88
−1521.86	◆◆◆◆◆◆◆◆◆◆◆◆◆◆◆◆◆◆◆◆◆◆◆◆◆◆◆◆◆◆◆◆◆◆◆◆◆◆◆	.96
−1447.93	◆◆◆	1.00
VALUE	• • • • • • • • • • •	PROB

THE EXPECTED VALUE IS   −1888.08
THERE IS A 90 PERCENT CHANCE OF EXCEEDING   −2047.04
THERE IS A 50 PERCENT CHANCE OF EXCEEDING   −1837.49
THERE IS A 10 PERCENT CHANCE OF EXCEEDING   −1589.95

TIME TO MAXIMUM INVESTMENT EXPOSURE

CUMULATIVE PROBABILITY CHART

	10 20 30 40 50 60 70 80 90 100	
VALUE	• • • • • • • • • • •	PROB
2.00	◆ • •	.00
2.20	◆◆◆◆◆◆◆◆◆◆◆◆◆◆◆◆◆◆◆◆◆◆◆◆◆◆◆◆◆ •	.60
2.40	◆◆◆◆◆◆◆◆◆◆◆◆◆◆◆◆◆◆◆◆◆◆◆◆◆◆◆◆◆ •	.60
2.60	◆◆◆◆◆◆◆◆◆◆◆◆◆◆◆◆◆◆◆◆◆◆◆◆◆◆◆◆◆ •	.60
2.80	◆◆◆◆◆◆◆◆◆◆◆◆◆◆◆◆◆◆◆◆◆◆◆◆◆◆◆◆◆ •	.60
3.00	◆◆◆	1.00
VALUE	• • • • • • • • • • •	PROB

THE EXPECTED VALUE IS   2.40
THERE IS A 50 PERCENT CHANCE OF EXCEEDING   2.00
THERE IS A 10 PERCENT CHANCE OF EXCEEDING   3.00

PROFIT, LOSS (AVERAGE VALUES) (000)

	YEAR 1	YEAR 2	YEAR 3	YEAR 4
REVENUES	71	7678	10978	10595
VARIABLE COSTS	222	5608	8019	7739
VARIABLE MARGIN	−151	2070	2960	2856
FIXED COSTS	11	1322	1719	1587
OPERATING MARGIN	−162	748	1241	1269
DEPRECIATION	0	89	151	121
BEFORE TAX PROFIT	−162	659	1089	1149
AFTER TAX PROFIT	−80	326	539	569
DEPRECIATION	0	89	151	121
WORKING CAPITAL	0	1571	675	147
OTHER FLOWS, CREDITS	31	0	0	0
TOTAL CASH FLOW	−49	−1156	15	542
CUMULATIVE CASH FLOW	−637	−1793	−1778	−1235

PROFIT, LOSS (AVERAGE VALUES) (000)

	YEAR 5	YEAR 6	YEAR 7	YEAR 8
REVENUES	10180	10800	10846	
VARIABLE COSTS	7436	7889	7922	
VARIABLE MARGIN	2745	2912	2924	
FIXED COSTS	1322	1587	1640	
OPERATING MARGIN	1423	1325	1284	
DEPRECIATION	90	60	14	
BEFORE TAX PROFIT	1332	1265	1270	
AFTER TAX PROFIT	659	626	629	
DEPRECIATION	90	60	14	
WORKING CAPITAL	517	314	276	
OTHER FLOWS, CREDITS	0	0	0	
TOTAL CASH FLOW	1267	372	367	
CUMULATIVE CASH FLOW	32	404	770	

EXHIBIT 11–14

Source: Henry J. Claycamp "New Product Investment Decisions and Management Science Techniques," unpublished manuscript, 1977. Reprinted by permission.

INTERNAL RATE OF RETURN

CUMULATIVE PROABILITY CHART

VALUE	10	20	30	40	50	60	70	80	90	100	PROB
2.21											.00
3.74											.02
5.27											.06
6.80											.30
8.33											.40
9.86											.58
11.39											.70
12.92											.74
14.45											.90
15.98											.96
17.51											1.00
VALUE											PROB

THE EXPECTED VALUE IS   9.66
THERE IS A 90 PERCENT CHANCE OF EXCEEDING   5.78
THERE IS A 50 PERCENT CHANCE OF EXCEEDING   9.46
THERE IS A 10 PERCENT CHANCE OF EXCEEDING   14.43

YEARS TO PAYBACK

CUMULATIVE PROBABILITY CHART

VALUE	10	20	30	40	50	60	70	80	90	100	PROB
4.60											.00
4.76											.20
4.91											.40
5.07											.52
5.23											.60
5.39											.66
5.55											.74
5.71											.78
5.87											.90
6.03											.94
6.19											1.00
VALUE											PROB

THE EXPECTED VALUE IS   5.19
THERE IS A 90 PERCENT CHANCE OF EXCEEDING   4.69
THERE IS A 50 PERCENT CHANCE OF EXCEEDING   5.04
THERE IS A 10 PERCENT CHANCE OF EXCEEDING   5.87

cate that the project cannot be expected to yield a return equal to the discount rate of 10 percent and if one includes a fair cost estimate for risk, the expected discounted cash flow is $114,500 less than the initial investment.

The risk-adjusted present value is highly sensitive to the amount of uncertainty in the net present value forecast and the magnitude of the negative values that might occur. And, since it involves concepts familiar to most managers, it has proven to be an effective summary measure of both risk and return.

The remaining outputs requested of RE-SCUE in this example (Exhibits 11–13 and 11–14) indicate the following:

- The expected internal rate of return is 9.55 percent with an 80 percent chance that it will be between 5.78 percent and 14.43 percent;

- The expected time to pay back is 5.2 years with a 10 percent chance that it will pay back in less than 4.7 years and a 10 percent chance it will take longer than 5.8 years;

- The maximum investment exposure (i.e., investment in plant equipment and working capital) of $1,829,000 can be expected to occur in the second year of the project.

Based upon the results shown in these exhibits, one would be forced to conclude that the project is at best marginal. However, repeated RESCUE analyses showed that the risk and return profile of the project was highly sensitive to the capacity constraint. For example, repeated runs showed that (1) an increment of 200 units of annual production capacity would result in an expected internal rate of return of 11.67 percent with 80 percent confidence that the return would be between 6.9 percent to 16.64 percent and a risk-adjusted present value of +$38,000; (2) an increment of 700 units capacity per year to 4,000 units which required an incremental investment of $300,000 would result in risk and return profiles that were nearly identical to those obtained using a 3,300 unit constraint.

These results illustrate the importance of methods that incorporate explicit estimates of uncertainty in the analytical process. For example, if this analysis is done using a single-point forecast of demand equal to the expected value shown in column 2 of Exhibit 11–10 and a capacity constraint of 3,300 units (194 units more than the highest quantity forecast for any year) the results would show an internal rate of return greater than 10 percent and a present value of approximately +$150,000. However, when it is recognized that it is impossible to predict future sales perfectly and that the 3,300-unit capacity constraint might limit the company's potential profit opportunities, the results show that the project is, in fact, a high-risk proposition.

EVALUATING THE PORTFOLIO OF PROJECTS

The economic evaluation of concepts/products has been focused primarily on the evaluation of a concept or a product at a time. In fact, the implicit assumption underlying most new product evaluation systems is that each product or concept is independent of any other concept or product in development as well as other existing products or concepts. Focus on cannibalization and synergistic effect, to some extent, has taken care of the latter assumption, i.e., the evaluation of a concept or product not only in terms of the market response it might generate but also in terms of the incremental effect it might have on the firm's performance, which reflects possible synergistic or cannibalization effects within the current product line. Ignored, however, in most cases, have been the interdependencies among various new product concepts. This neglect is partly due to the organizational arrangement for new product development wherein one individual is often assigned to a given product concept which competes for resources with other concepts in development. This setting encourages a climate for the evaluation of one concept at a time. Yet, the interdependencies among concepts at various stages of development as well as among developmental R&D projects require explicit attention to the selection of the best *portfolio of concepts or projects*, and not limiting the economic evaluation to that of a concept or a product at a time.

Evaluating the portfolio of projects is a critical component of any new product evaluation system. It allows for the explicit evaluation of the interdependencies among various R&D, production, and marketing technologies, and the identification of the best scheduling of the development efforts (e.g., if confronted with two projects, A and B, which have similar profit potential, select for initial development the one that would require the development of a technology which could provide assistance to the development of other technologies or products).

In addition, evaluating the portfolio of new product development projects increases the likelihood that the firm's new product activities are better coordinated and follow a multiple project philosophy (i.e., having at any given point a number of projects at each of the new product development stages).

In constructing a portfolio of projects, the concept of portfolio analysis (as discussed in Chapter 5) is equally applicable. Of particular interest in this context are those models used in the evaluation of a portfolio of R&D projects. Integer programming has been used, for example, in conjunction with the judgments of 17-member technical evaluation committees of the Department of Energy to select a portfolio of proposals for solar photovoltaic application experiments from among 77 proposals (Golabi, Kirkwood, and Sicherman, 1978). These and similar approaches can and should be considered in the design of an economic evaluation system for new products and development projects.

IMPLEMENTING AN ECONOMIC EVALUATION SYSTEM

In discussing his experience with implementing the RESCUE system, Claycamp (1978) identified three major barriers to acceptance of formal risk-analysis techniques for new product decisions:

1. Poor understanding of the implications of implicit methods (such as "conservative" adjustment of sales forecasts) of dealing with uncertainty;
2. Use of technical jargon to explain the benefits of formal risk-analysis methods;
3. Cumbersome and inflexible techniques.

These barriers can and have been overcome. In fact, the implementation of a risk-analysis system is relatively simple and should receive high priority in any organization involved in new product development activities. The implementation of such a system involves four major components:

- Development of an economic evaluation model which can follow any of the models presented in this chapter or some modified version which fits the firm and its new product activities.

- Development of a simple set of procedures and forecasting forms by which new product planners structure the uncertainties (in the form of probability distributions) surrounding each input to the economic evaluation model, under selected scenarios.

- Development of a simulation model (preferably on a timesharing computer) that incorporates the various probability inputs and allows the planner to determine the consequences of changes in any of the input variables or systems' constraints on the discounted cash flow and other relevant measures of product performance.

- Training the new product planners to use the system themselves.[6] Given recent advances in computer technology and languages, the use of a time sharing simulator to evaluate alternative new concept/product alternatives can be learned in a short training course and enables the new product planner to use the economic evaluation system on as routine a basis as the pocket calculator.

In considering the implementation of an economic evaluation system for new ideas/concepts/products it is important to note, however, that most current models assume independence of the new concepts/products that are being evaluated. If the proposed projects are interrelated, this increases the computational complexity of the models, but is still conceptually tractable.

Another consideration in implementing an economic evaluation system, such as the ones discussed in this chapter, is that it should be designed to coexist, for at least the first few years of operation, with the firm's current system for evaluation of new product prospects. Once management gains experience in using and confidence with the *new system* they may decide to stop using the previous approach (especially if an informal implicit approach was utilized) or continue to operate with a mixture of evaluation methods (e.g., if a break-even analysis has been utilized).

The design of an implementation system for the new product evaluation activities is no different than the design of any modeling implementation effort.[7] As such it should be based on models which are simple, robust, easy to control, adaptive, complete on important issues, and easy to communicate with (Little, 1970). In addition, new product evaluation should be structured as a *process* which continues throughout the new product development efforts (starting with rough estimates and concluding at the final stages of development with accurate forecasts of sales, share, and profit over the life of the product).

CONCLUDING REMARKS

New ideas/concepts/products require continuous evaluation to decide whether to GO, NO GO or continue development. In making these decisions, risk-analysis techniques have been used extensively in a number of simulators. In selecting the most appropriate economic evaluation procedure management should consider:

1. The available information (and its quality)

and stage in the new product development process; the earlier in the concept development stage the more general the evaluation can be.

2. The cost of rejecting a potentially "good" product versus the cost and consequences of accepting a "poor" product.

3. The need to design an economic evaluation

---

[6]An alternative approach would be the employment of staff specialists to help the planner in his/her interface with the computer.

[7]For a detailed discussion of implementation problems and approaches see Naert and Leeflang (1978).

system that not only selects the "best" idea/concept/product but also provides information on

- Possible improvement in the concepts/products and their marketing strategy;
- The sensitivity of the results to changes in the input data, management constraints, and uncertainty;
- Expected risk-return characteristics given alternative marketing strategies, and relevant environmental scenarios;
- The attractiveness of the conceptual and operational measures used to evaluate the alternative concepts/products.

To fully appreciate the scope of an economic evaluation system, its desired output and required inputs, select a new product concept and design for it an economic evaluation approach.

Product Design

Introduction

Product Design Decisions and Their Determinants

Corporate Marketing Objectives
Corporate Constraints
Environmental Constraints
Customer Profile

Physical Product Features

Product Design Decisions
Research Approaches
Illustrative Conjoint Analysis Application
Conjoint Analysis versus Other Approaches
Consumer Research and Technological R&D

Packaging

Packaging
Packaging Research

Branding

Branding Decisions
Research Approaches

Associated Services

Research Approaches
Illustrative Conjoint Analysis Application

Putting It All Together

Concluding Remarks

INTRODUCTION

The transformation of new product concepts (which survived the screening and evaluation stages) into actual products is one of the most challenging tasks in the new product development process. This transformation typically involves the conversion of verbally stated (and occasionally pictorially presented) product features into a product prototype, package, brand name, and associated services such as warranty or after-sales services.

Traditionally the responsibility of this stage of product development has been vested in R&D. Yet, in recent years, marketing research, legal, and other corporate functions have been playing a greater role in this process. Mansfield et al. (1971), for example, in analyzing the distribution of costs of innovation among the various stages of the innovation process, identified six stages, some of which are not commonly included in the R&D task definition. These stages include: applied research, specification, prototype or pilot plant, tooling and manufacturing facilities, manufacturing startup, and marketing startup. Yet, even these phases understate the role of other organizational function in the actual new product design phase since they do not include marketing research or legal clearance.

Product design decisions, their determinants, and the role of R&D and other business functions in carrying these decisions out are briefly discussed in the first section of this chapter. The next four sections are devoted to the major components of product design: the physical features of the product, the package, the brand name, and the associated services. Each of these sections focuses on two parts: (a) the relevant decisions and some of the major management considerations impinging on them, and (b) some of the research approaches which can and have been utilized to provide inputs to these decisions. Common to the research approaches discussed in these sections is the assumption that a final product is predominantly a combination of its various parts. The final section focuses on how the various components can be put together. Special attention is given to imagery-based products which do not constitute a simple combination of the various components and which require a somewhat different research approach. In addition, the section focuses on some of the more recent approaches to identifying optimal (or quasioptimal) product design.

PRODUCT DESIGN DECISIONS AND THEIR DETERMINANTS

Product design decisions encompass *all* aspects of the extended product including the actual product features, packaging, brand name, and associated services. These four sets of decisions are closely interrelated and should be integrated into a total system which is consistent with the product benefits desired by the target market segment, and is congruent with the firm's target product positioning (by segment) and the other components of the marketing program.

In making the various product design decisions four sets of factors, not unlike the factors affecting all product decisions (and discussed in Chapters 1, 6, and 7), should be considered:

CORPORATE MARKETING OBJECTIVES

The product, packaging, brand name, and associated services, which are also referred to as the "augmented product concept" (Levitt, 1965), should be consistent with corporate objectives, in particular, the desired product positioning, the current product line objectives, and the desired corporate image.

CORPORATE CONSTRAINTS

New products should be designed within specified financial boundaries and, to the extent possible, be compatible with the firm's production technology and facilities, although obviously not limited to them. Furthermore, the design efforts should take into consideration overall corporate plans and time requirements. Recognizing, however, that most constraints can be relaxed with enough resources and time, the severity of constraints is primarily in the short run.

The identification of the organizational factors which could affect the new product design decision can be aided by empirical findings on the factors which influence the R&D share of innovation costs. In one of these studies on chemical innovations Mansfield and Rappoport (1975) found empirical support ($R^2 = 0.55$) for the following hypotheses:

- The bigger, more important the innovation (as measured after the fact by its sales volume), the larger the proportion of costs that go for R&D;
- The greater the R&D experience in the relevant technological area the lower the per-

cent of total innovation costs devoted to R&D (a learning effect);

- The higher the total innovation costs the lower the percentage of costs devoted to R&D;
- If a new product plant has to be built, the lower the percentage of total costs devoted to R&D.

In general, however, R&D costs are a relatively small fraction of the total costs of innovation, the bulk of which tend to be in the commercialization stage.

ENVIRONMENTAL CONSTRAINTS

Some of the most severe constraints on new product design are environmental constraints such as legal regulations and technology. As briefly discussed in Chapter 7, legal clearance is a must in most product categories, and familiarity with current and potential technology is a critical input to any product design effort. The legal environment affects all aspects of a product's design from the ingredients/features that can be used in designing it (consider, for example, the FDA ban on saccharin), the claims that can be made, the package design which has to meet safety and labeling requirements, and the trade name and its registration requirements. Similarly, the technology available affects all aspects of product and package design.

CUSTOMER PROFILE

The demographic and psychographic profiles of the target segment(s) are obvious guidelines for product designers. These profiles should be calibrated against the anticipated *consumption system* of the new product. This requires an assessment of the likely consumer attitudes and

EXHIBIT 12–1

PRODUCT, PACKAGE, AND SERVICE DESIGN AND ITS DETERMINANTS

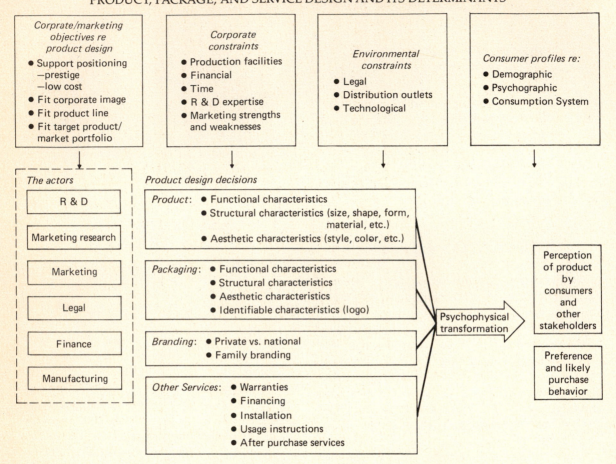

behavior with respect to consumption related activities. An illustrative set of activities for a food item bought for home consumption would include:

- Prepurchase information processing and decisions

- Shopping

- Transporting the product from the store to home

- Storing

- Preparation (e.g., cooking)

- Using (e.g., eating)

- Disposal

The consumption systems for other products, such as on-premises consumption of food items (which do not require, for example, a storing and preparation activity), or a durable product (which is likely to include maintenance and repair activities) are quite different. Yet, effective product decisions take these likely activities into consideration when designing the product, its packaging, product name, and related services.

Of special importance to the various design decisions is the assessment of the *likely response,* by consumers and other relevant stakeholders, to the various product design options. This requires a series of systematic studies aimed at the evaluation of the respondents' perceptions of and preference for the designed new product and its attributes. Such studies, not unlike some of the more advanced concept-testing studies (utilizing conjoint analysis) are aimed at identifying the product features most desired by consumers. Unique to these studies is a focus on the *matching* of the physical product (and package) characteristics with the desired product benefits. Such studies are often based on multidimensional psychophysics, conjoint analysis, multidimensional scaling and related techniques.

The interrelationships between the new product design decisions, the primary set of considerations involved in making them, and the key decision makers are summarized in Exhibit 12–1.

PHYSICAL PRODUCT FEATURES

PRODUCT DESIGN DECISIONS

Product design, even for relatively simple products, often involves a seemingly infinite number of decisions. These decisions incorporate choices among numerous functional, structural and aesthetic characteristics.

Functional characteristics   are those related to the benefits expected from the product. For example, a deodorant is supposed to provide protection without any allergic side effects or staining of clothes; soft drinks are expected to be thirst-quenchers; a raincoat must be waterproof; a watch should show the time accurately (and in recent years other functions such as date).

The development of new functional characteristics challenges technical skills, and is often the area in which R&D breakthroughs occur. Consider, for example, the development of a movie camera that does not require movie light, the development of 400 speed film, the instant photography still camera, more recently the development of an instant photography movie camera, the development of washable wool, and chewing gum with time-released flavor. Such developments are often R&D-generated, although the impetus for many of them come from consumer studies which help discover desired product benefits.

Structural characteristics   Functional product features (and the consumer benefits associated with them) can be delivered in a variety of ways, via various structural characteristics. These include factors such as size, shape, form, color, material, odor, and tactile qualities. The range of options within each structural product feature is large and the number of possible combinations almost endless.[1]

Minor structural differences often can serve as the basis for the development of a number of related products within a product line. Consider, for example, the thermos. With small design changes (such as color, pictorial design,

---

[1]Part of the range of structural and functional options for a relatively simple consumer product—a pen—is presented in Exhibit 9–5.

EXHIBIT 12–2

NEW PRODUCT DEVELOPMENT PHASES
FOR OFFICE EQUIPMENT:
THE XEROX COMPANY

Source: Zoppath, p. 27.

Develop concept proposal
Approve for feasibility phase

Breadboard designs
Define market and economics
Propose engineering approach
Approve for definition phase

Build engineering and preprototype design
Verify market, production, performance, and
　　investment estimates
Propose prototype design
Approve for design phase

Build prototype and preproduction models
Field test preproduction model
Update all production and marketing data
Approve resources for release to manufacturing

Start manufacturing
First ship
Evaluate customer experience

National launch

and minor physical changes) one can easily develop a thermos line encompassing a variety of use situations—camping, boating, skiing, jogging, work, school.

Aesthetic characteristics　involve both the actual design, shapes, and colors used and the other, less clearcut "ornamental" features which together help create an appealing, visually attractive, and distinct product.

The functional, structural, and aesthetic characteristics are closely interrelated. Miniaturization of calculators has affected the *size* (a structural factor), which has changed markedly

the *functional* features of a calculator, its use patterns and benefits. Furthermore, the small size has led to aesthetic design innovations such as watch calculators, pen calculators, and business-card-sized calculators.

Product design does not involve a single set of decisions on the combination of features, ingredients, and components to be put together. Rather, it is a *complex* process involving numerous developmental and research stages. This complexity is illustrated in Exhibit 12–2, which presents the product development phases followed by the Xerox Company.

RESEARCH APPROACHES

In addition to technology-oriented R&D research, product design requires a considerable amount of marketing research. Numerous research procedures are used to establish consumers' preferences for product features. Blind product taste tests and in-home use studies for foods and beverages, smoke tests for cigarettes, and smell tests for fragrances are common practice in most product design efforts of consumer goods companies. These and other product tests vary markedly in their design and output. The choices facing the researcher in selecting a product testing procedure are:[2]

1. Nature of the stimuli (products being tested)
   a) One or more?
   b) Designed to systematically vary on attributes or simply constitute a set of a priori selected products that "look good"?
   c) Branded or blind?
2. Environment of the test
   a) Lab or home?
   b) Response assessed after some use ex-

---

[2]For a detailed discussion of these choices, see Batsell and Wind (1980).

perience or instantaneous response after
exposure to product?

c) Repeated or single measurement?

d) Frame of reference for preference statement:

- Implicit (monadic tests—implicitly
compared with currently used product)
or explicit?

- If explicit, how many products and
which ones?

3. Nature of dependent variable

a) Definition: preference, liking, intention
to buy, product qualities, or attributes?

b) How measured: rating, ranking, constant
sum, dollarmetric, hedonic index,
categorical sorting?

c) If rating scale, should it be semantic differential, Likert; should scale position 5
be labeled; should ends be rotated?

4. Sample

a) Size?

b) Composition:

- Panel or fresh recruits?

- Random, stratified random, or quota?

- If stratified or quota, should it be with
respect to user/nonuser, heavy user/
light user, demographic characteristics,
target group?

5. Analysis of data

a) Testing for differences in reactions to test
products: differences in means, differences in proportions?

b) Fitting models for scaling products
and/or attributes?

In making these choices, the researcher
who is confronted with a huge array of possible
product testing designs should consider seven
criteria:

**Responsiveness to management information
requirements**   Conceptually the most desirable information would (a) lead to an understanding of consumers' preference structure,
which would allow for design of new products
even if not included explicitly in the study and
(b) offer diagnostic insight into the likely reaction to new product design and positioning by
selected target segments.

Appropriateness for product type   The type of
product involved—frequently versus infrequently purchased, taste-versus smell-based
product choice, low-versus high-involvement
product, major versus minor imagery factor,
etc.—has major implications as to the most appropriate testing design.

Appropriateness for market type   The characteristics of the intended market—children versus adults, consumers familiar with the product
versus those not familiar with it, etc.—should
also be taken into consideration in designing a
product test.

Validity   A critical criterion for the evaluation
of any test is its validity. Unfortunately, the
assessment of validity is one of the most complex and difficult tasks. The validity of any test
should not be taken for granted, however, and
every product test should be examined for it. In
general, the closer the test environment and
task to the real-world conditions in which
products are bought and used, the higher the
test's validity.

Test reliability   As a necessary (but not sufficient) condition for validity, the reliability of
any testing instrument should be determined.

Cost   Since the cost of testing can vary
markedly, an explicit analysis of the cost versus
value of information should be undertaken to
determine the worth of the information management can obtain from the test. The cost
analysis should not be limited to monetary
costs, but the *time requirements* and their monetary tradeoffs should also be evaluated.

Standardization Even though one might be tempted to custom-design each product test, there are some advantages to standardizing procedures and measures. Such standardization allows comparison of results across tests and can provide the foundation for accumulating generalizable information across studies.

Of the various marketing/consumer research approaches utilized for product design, conjoint analysis seems to meet these criteria best and indeed has been used for the design of a large and varied range of products and services.

ILLUSTRATIVE CONJOINT ANALYSIS APPLICATION

The use of a conjoint analysis-based approach to provide guidelines for product design is illustrated by a study of consumers' perception of and preference for bar soaps.[3] The questions which guided the study design were:

- Are consumers perceptually sensitive to different types and strengths of soap fragrances?
- How does color, type of fragrance, and intensity of fragrance influence consumers' evaluations of the *appropriateness* of the soap for various types of uses and users?
- How are color, type of fragrance, and fragrance intensity related to consumers' *preferences* for soaps under different "scenarios," or end uses?

Method The stimuli in this experiment consisted of 18 bar soaps synthesized according to a $3 \times 3 \times 2$ factorial design. Each bar of soap was of standard size, weight, and shape. The bars varied by:

- Color—gold, pink, and aqua;

[3]This study was reported in full in Green and Wind (1975a).

- Type of fragrance—floral, lemon, and "medicinal";
- Strength of fragrance—low-intensity (an amount of fragrance just sufficient to mask out other odors) and high-intensity (twice this amount).

The experiment was run on an individually-supervised basis with 120 housewives residing in the Philadelphia area. Interviews ran between 30 and 40 minutes. Four phases of the experiment were involved:

Phase I. In this phase each respondent was shown 15 pairs (all distinct pairs of type and intensity of fragrance, holding color constant). Color was rotated across respondents so that, over the total sample, each color appeared an equal number of times. The respondent was asked to examine each pair of bar soaps (pairs were randomized prior to presentation to respondent) and to indicate: (a) if their odors were the same or different and (b) if different, to rate their degree of dissimilarity on a four-point scale ranging from "almost identical" to "extremely different." This step was repeated for all 15 pairs. The respondent was then given time to relax and "clear her nose" before proceeding to phase II.

Phase II. In this phase the respondent was shown all 18 bars of soap in randomized order and a sort board specifying four use occasions:

a) Moisturizing facial soap for dry skin
b) Deep-cleaning facial soap for oily skin;
c) Woman's-type deodorant soap;
d) Man's-type deodorant soap.

Each respondent was asked to look at and smell each bar of soap and, in turn, assign it to the one category that represented the most appropriate end use for a soap of that type. No restrictions were imposed on the way the soaps were assigned to the categories. After this task, the respondents again took a short break.

Phase III. In phase III the respondents returned to the table where they had grouped the

18 bars into four end-use categories. Starting with the first category, they were asked to look at and smell each bar in that category and choose the one most preferred in that category. Then they proceeded to the second category, and so on, until first-choice preferences, conditioned by the respondent's end-use assignments, were obtained.

Phase IV. Phase IV entailed the collection of a modest amount of background data on brand use, personality profiles, and demographic characteristics of the respondents and other household members.

Results of the study The reported findings are restricted to the total sample findings (based on all 120 respondents), although a number of individual type and segment level analyses were made as well.

Phase I results. The purpose of phase I was to examine whether respondents could perceive differences in type and intensity of fragrance. Since all bars were different in at least one respect (type or intensity of fragrance), we first examined the number of "false negatives"—instances in which a respondent incorrectly called a different pair "the same." The incidence of such errors was low, averaging slightly less than one out of 25 for each respondent. That is, the type and intensity levels of fragrance were sufficiently salient to be recognized practically all of the time.[4]

Since each color was represented an equal number of times in the sample, the six combinations of type and intensity of fragrance (within color) led to a data matrix of $120 \times 6 \times 6$ of dissimilarity ratings on a five-point dissimilarity scale.[5] This matrix of judged dissimilarities was scaled by means of the INDSCAL program (Carroll and Chang, 1969), which provides both a group stimulus space and a subject "space," representing individuals' saliences for the various dimensions of the group stimulus space. Since the three "qualities" (type of fragrance) can be represented spatially in two dimensions, we hypothesized that INDSCAL would find a satisfactory solution in three dimensions—two for accommodating the qualitative variation in type of fragrance and one additional dimension to handle the intensity of fragrance.

This conjecture was borne out when the data were scaled in four, three, and two dimensions. (The variance accounted for in three dimensions was 0.70. This increased only slightly (to 0.73) in four dimensions but decreased markedly (to 0.54) in two dimensions.) Exhibit 12–3 shows a plot of selected subspaces of the three-dimensional group stimulus space. Since INDSCAL provides a unique orientation of axes, the configuration should be—and evidently is—interpretable as it stands.

The first two dimensions accommodate the class-like variation and show that respondents considered the three types of fragrances to be about equal with regard to dissimilarity. The axes of the group stimulus space of Exhibit 12–3 are differentially stretched in accordance with the relative potency of the dimensions. In this case, however, relative potencies were almost equal. The points denoting type of fragrance cluster around the vertices of a triangle that is close to being equilateral in the two-dimensional subspace of the three-dimensional solution.

The third dimension, showing variation in intensity, lines up almost perfectly with the characteristic representing physical variation.

---

[4]The same type of procedure could, of course, be used to examine discrimination thresholds. Moreover, if desired, identical pairs could be included to determine the incidence of "false positives." In this study, however, our principal emphasis was on Phases II and III rather than the question of stimulus confusability.

[5]A five-point dissimilarity scale was obtained by assigning 1 to the response category of "identical," 2 to "almost identical," and so on, up to 5, assigned to "extremely different."

EXHIBIT 12–3

INDSCAL ANALYSIS OF BAR SOAP JUDGED SIMILARITIES

Reprinted from *Attitude Research Bridges the Atlantic*, published by the American Marketing Association, edited by Philip Levine. Exhibit from ''Recent Approaches to the Modeling of Individuals' Subjective Judgements,'' by Paul E. Green and Yoram Wind, 1975.

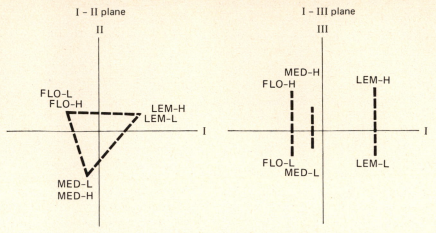

Key: FLO—floral fragrance, LEM—lemon fragrance, MED—medicinal fragrance, L—low intensity, H—high intensity.

EXHIBIT 12–4

CONJOINT ANALYSIS OF JUDGED APPROPRIATENESS OF BAR SOAPS FOR VARIOUS USES

Reprinted from *Attitude Research Bridges the Atlantic*, published by the American Marketing Association, edited by Philip Levine. Exhibit from ''Recent Approaches to the Modeling of Individuals' Subjective Judgements,'' by Paul E. Green and Yoram Wind, 1975.

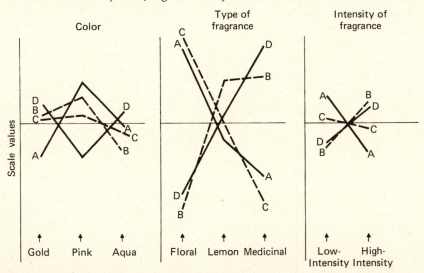

Key: A—moisturizing soap for dry skin, B—deep-cleaning soap for oily skin, C—woman's-type deodorant soap, D—man's-type deodorant soap.

However, an interesting interaction is noted between type and intensity. That is, although the physical stimuli were designed to vary equally in intensity (across type of fragrance) respondent perceptions suggest a psychological intensity interval for the medicinal fragrance that is smaller than those for floral and lemon. (This finding was also observed in subgroup analyses.) Apparently, in the case of the medicinal fragrance, one needs a larger physical change to produce a psychological separation equal to that found for the floral and lemon fragrances.

To explore the question of whether color interacted with fragrance type or intensity, we examined the mean vector of dimension saliences across the three color groups via a one-way multivariate analysis of variance. The mean vectors of all three groups did not show significant variation, indicating that color did not influence perceptions of fragrance type and intensity.

Phase II results. The analysis of phase II data entailed the application of both monotonic and categorical conjoint analysis algorithms. By tabulation of the frequency of category assignments across respondents, one can develop, at the total sample (or segment level) a ranking of incidence with which each of the 18 bars of soap was assigned to the four use occasions (to be analyzed via monotonic conjoint analysis), as well as the modal category to which each bar of soap was assigned (to be analyzed via categorical conjoint analysis).

• *Monotonic conjoint analysis.* The objective of this analysis was to find "psychophysical" functions for each factor whose additive combination would produce a rank order that was most concordant with the original ranking. This step was conducted separately for each of the four categories. Since the MONANOVA algorithm scales data to comparable sums of squares, all four scalings can be represented on the same graph. Exhibit 12–4 shows the

psychological scale values associated with each of the three factors: color, type of fragrance, and intensity of fragrance. In general, the fits of the additive conjoint analysis model were good. The rank order correlations of the fitted (main effects) model to input data were: 0.93, 0.65, 0.87, and 0.96, respectively, for categories A through D. The low value of 0.65 associated with category B was due to an interaction between color and fragrance intensity (that was determined through subsequent analysis).

When type of fragrance is examined, we first note that the effect of this factor is quite pronounced, compared to the psychological effect of color or intensity; that is, the range of scale values is considerably wider. In terms of category appropriateness, the floral fragrance is deemed most appropriate for categories A and C and viewed as least appropriate for categories B and D. Thus, although category B—deep cleaning soap for oily skin—is nominally classed as a facial soap, *psychological* appropriateness with regard to type of fragrance would place it closer to a man's-type deodorant soap (category D).

The intensity of fragrance, compared to type of fragrance, is not a prominent factor in appropriateness judgments, as noted by the range of its scale values compared to those involving fragrance type. Again we note the "similarity" of category B to category D in terms of the intensity factor. Only category C suggests little effect of intensity level on judged appropriateness. Categories B and D suggest that higher intensities are viewed as more appropriate; this is the reverse of category A.

• *ANOVA and interaction effects.* The preceding analyses all involved a main effects, additive model after allowing for a monotone rescaling of the input data. To check on the possibility that interaction effects might still be present, one can take the monotonically transformed input data (where the monotonic function is chosen so as to optimize additivity) and submit

EXHIBIT 12–5

BAR SOAP APPROPRIATENESS: TWO-FACTOR PLOTS OF POSSIBLE INTERACTION
EFFECTS (CATEGORY A—MOISTURIZING SOAP FOR DRY SKIN)

Reprinted from *Attitude Research Bridges the Atlantic*, published by the American Marketing
Association, edited by Philip Levine. Exhibit from "Recent Approaches to the Modeling of
Individuals' Subjective Judgements," by Paul E. Green and Yoram Wind, 1975.

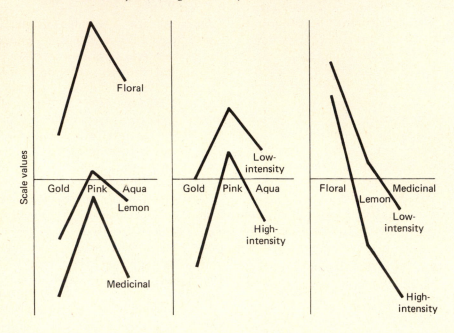

them to traditional ANOVA procedures. This was done for all four categories.

In general, main effects models (after monotone rescaling) provided good accounts of the data. This is illustrated for category A—moisturizing facial soap for dry skin—in Exhibit 12–5. Each of the three two-factor "interactions" is plotted. We note, for example, that the effect of color on judged appropriateness (left-most panel) does not vary with changes in type of fragrance. That is, the line segments are reasonably parallel. The strongest hint of an interaction effect is noted in the right-most panel where we observe that the effect of type of fragrance is somewhat conditioned by fragrance intensity. That is, the interest in low-intensity versus high-intensity is greater for the medicinal fragrance than it is

for the floral fragrance. This interaction was not statistically "significant," however.[6]

• *Categorical conjoint analysis.* As indicated earlier, categorical conjoint analysis (Carroll, 1969) was also used to analyze the appropriateness data. This can be done at the total sample level by using the modal response category (across respondents) as the appropriate "assignment"

---

[6]No "significant" interaction effects were found with the exception of Category B, as pointed out in the preceding discussion. Even at that, the contribution of the color-fragrance intensity interaction to total variance (at 7 percent) was not high. As indicated, however, the significance tests and statements about variance accounted for should be taken with a large grain of salt, in view of the monotonic transformation.

EXHIBIT 12–6

CATEGORICAL CONJOINT ANALYSIS OF BAR SOAP END USE ASSIGNMENTS

Reprinted from *Attitude Research Bridges the Atlantic*, published by the American Marketing Association, edited by Philip Levine. Exhibit from "Recent Approaches to the Modeling of Individuals' Subjective Judgements," by Paul E. Green and Yoram Wind, 1975.

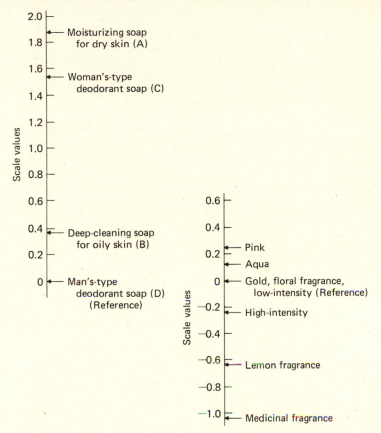

for each of the 18 bars of soap. Categorical conjoint analysis then finds scale values for categories and factor levels such that the category values are most highly correlated with appropriate additive combinations of the factor levels.

Exhibit 12–6 shows the results of this part of the analysis.[7] If we examine the left-hand scale

first, we note that the soaps are separated into two groups, categories A and C and categories B and D. This result is consistent with the findings summarized in Exhibit 12–4 and indicates that factor levels combine in rather similar ways for categories A and C but that these combinations differ from those related to categories B and D.

The right-hand panel indicates that the scale value spread among levels of fragrance type considerably exceeds the range noted for color or fragrance intensity. Again this is in accordance with the findings of Exhibit 12–4.

---

[7] The canonical correlation associated with the first pair of variates—the pair described here—was 0.81 and was "significant" at the 0.05 level.

EXHIBIT 12–7

CONJOINT ANALYSIS OF BAR SOAP *PREFERENCES* (CONDITIONAL UPON END
USE APPROPRIATENESS)

Reprinted from *Attitude Research Bridges the Atlantic*, published by the American Marketing
Association, edited by Philip Levine. Exhibit from "Recent Approaches to the Modeling of
Individuals' Subjective Judgements," by Paul E. Green and Yoram Wind, 1975.

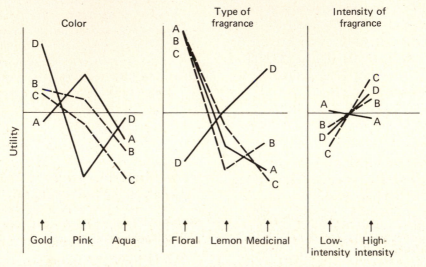

Key: A—moisturizing soap for dry skin, B—deep-cleaning soap for oily skin, C—woman's-type
deodorant soap, D—man's-type deodorant soap.

The results of the categorical conjoint analysis provide a type of summary statement regarding the contributions of factor levels to all four sets of category assignment and, hence, are complementary to the separate-category results of Exhibit 12–4.[8]

Phase III results. In phase III, first-choice preferences were obtained, conditioned by appropriateness assignments to categories A, B, C, and D. At the total sample level, one can develop a ranking of the 18 bars of soap in terms of preference, conditioned by end use. Hence,

monotonic conjoint analysis can be employed here in a manner analogous to that summarized in Exhibit 12–4.

Exhibit 12–7 shows the results of these analyses. The rank correlations between the additive, main effects model and input data were: 0.64, 0.70, 0.81, and 0.75 for categories A through D, respectively. In general these were lower than their "appropriateness" counterparts. With respect to color, pink is most preferred for category A—moisturizing facial soap for dry skin. As a matter of fact, the preferred levels of type of fragrance (floral) and intensity of fragrance (low) are the same as observed in Exhibit 12–4. Insofar as category B is concerned, we note differences, however, with respect to most preferred color and, in particular, most preferred type of fragrance (floral in this case).

---

[8]Although not shown here, one could also submit the scaled category values to a standard ANOVA-type analysis for the purpose of "testing" the significance of main effects or the possibility of examining "residual" interaction effects.

Categories C and D do not show marked differences between appropriateness and preference. The major difference in this part of the analysis concerns the preference for floral fragrance in category B, although lemon or medicinal fragrances were deemed as more appropriate for this category.

Perhaps the most significant result is the finding that type of fragrance continues to be the most important factor influencing preferences (in addition to end-use appropriateness). While color becomes a more important factor, relatively, in preference judgments, it is still less influential than type of fragrance. (Intensity of fragrance plays a relatively minor role in both sets of judgments.)

Phase IV results. Background data were also obtained on personality trait ratings, usage, and demographics. One could, therefore, find out whether differences in judged appropriateness and preferences are associated with either personality or demographic characteristics. Because of the large number of variables involved, preliminary factor analyses were conducted prior to examining respondent similarities (via canonical correlation) across the three sets of factor scores. In this study, this step produced nothing of value. Neither canonical correlation was significant. That is, while individual differences in phase II category assignments were observed, these were not highly associated with personality trait ratings, usage, or demographic variables. Despite these results, given the small sample size involved, future studies should continue to collect and analyze such data.

The above procedure and study are one illustration of a rigorous marketing research approach to the determination of consumers' perceptions of and preferences for various product formulations. This approach has a number of unique characteristics:

- While multidimensional scaling of similarity and/or preference judgments can still be profitably undertaken, primary emphasis is on the psychological transformations of these perceptual or evaluative spaces to the researcher-designed *objective* space.

- Conjoint analysis procedures—monotonic or categorical—provide a methodological framework for the development of appropriate "psychophysical" transformations that can be used to ascertain the importance of classes of variables (e.g., color versus type of fragrance) and scale values for various factor "levels" (e.g., floral, lemon, medicinal) *within* the factor—type of fragrance.

- If interaction effects are hypothesized, either the conjoint analysis models (typically main effects, additive) can be modified to handle interactions or, if desired, standard ANOVA procedures can be used (descriptively) to examine "residual" interactions after a preliminary transformation is made to "optimize" additivity.

- The results of such a research approach can be used to predict preferences or other kinds of psychological responses to changes in various objective variables of interest to the marketing practitioner.

CONJOINT ANALYSIS VERSUS OTHER APPROACHES

The bar soap example, even in its oversimplistic formulation (limited number of factors, excluding (controlling for) other factors such as level of sudsiness, shape, weight, and texture, and a limited number of levels for the included factors (ignoring the possibility of other colors and fragrances, for example) illustrates the value of using the full-profile conjoint analysis approach. This allows for the construction of physical stimuli that enable the researcher to establish an objective space exploring optimal (or near-optimal) product designs. This is similar in spirit to the steepest ascent or similar

EXHIBIT 12–8

ILLUSTRATIVE PRODUCT AND SERVICE CATEGORIES IN WHICH PRODUCT
DESIGN STUDIES UTILIZING CONJOINT ANALYSIS HAVE BEEN CONDUCTED

Industrial products
Copying machines, printing equipment
Data transmission
Diagnostic x-ray equipment
Other medical equipment
Automotive styling
Information retrieval services
Ethical drugs
Freight train operations
Air travel

Consumer durable products
Automobiles
Small household appliances
Clothing
Lawn mowing equipment

Consumer services
Financial services
Insurance (auto, health, life, etc.)
Credit cards
Travel and entertainment packages
Car rental services
Telephone services
Airline services
HMO

Frequently purchased consumer products
Food products
Cigarettes
Toiletries (bar soaps, shampoos)
Carpet cleaners
Gasoline
Facial tissues

designs used in the optimization of manufacturing processes.

Conjoint analysis designs (although most frequently based on verbal or pictorial representation of the stimuli and not the actual physical prototype as in the bar soap study) have been the major thrust in over 1000 commercial studies aimed at the design of new products and services. Exhibit 12–8 lists some of the products and services in which conjoint analysis studies were undertaken as input to new product/service design or as a way of evaluating new product/service alternatives.

Two important features of conjoint analysis-based product tests are the use of experimental designs and the identification of optimal product designs.

The use of efficient experimental designs (such as fractional factorial designs)[9] enable one

to deal with large numbers of factors, each at various levels (including both qualitative and quantitative factors). This has the dual advantage of requiring only a limited number of prototypes (while allowing the evaluation of all possible combinations of features included in the design) and reducing the respondent task (hence increasing the reliability of the data). To further this latter aim, occasionally the orthogonal array design is supplemented with a BIB (Balanced Incomplete Block) design which reduces even further the number of stimuli given to each respondent. At the extreme, in a few POSSE (Product Optimization and Selected Segment Evaluation) type studies (Green et al., 1981 and Appendix B), each respondent is asked to evaluate only one or two new product prototypes.

The identification of optimal or near-optimal product designs is of great importance and can follow two approaches: simulation and optimization procedures. Most conjoint analysis

---

[9]For a discussion of such designs, see Green (1974) and Addelman (1962).

studies to date have included a computer simulation to estimate market share of new "products"—any interpolated combination of factor levels (that can be related to the calibration set). Moreover, as discussed in Chapter 10, since individual or subgroup predictions can be maintained, the market share estimates for any new product can be examined in terms of respondent background characteristics. Simulation models also have included interactive-type evaluation models, when the main effects additive model proved to be inappropriate, and share estimates were conditioned upon scenarios of end use, marketing strategy, competitive activities, and environmental conditions. More recently a number of optimization procedures have been employed in conjoint analysis studies to determine the optimal or near-optimal new product design. Parker and Srinivasan (1976), for example, used a set of heuristic search procedures to determine a set of rural primary health care facilities that yielded near-optimal total incremental benefit, subject to the constraint that its total incremental cost did not exceed a prespecified budget. An alternative optimization procedure using quadratic programming was developed by Green as part of the POSSE procedure. This is further discussed in the last section of this chapter and in Appendix B.

Even with the advantages of these new advances in conjoint analysis (which identify the optimal region of product features for any given market segment or the market segment most likely to accept any given product design), the research needed for new product design cannot be limited to conjoint analysis type studies. Often the new product design stage requires a series of studies covering various aspects of prospective new products. Blind taste tests are often conducted to assess variation in product formulation and to offer a head-to-head comparison with the leading competitive brands. Labeled taste tests can follow, and use tests (usually of the in-home type) are frequently

required before the final new product formulation.

Even for the purposes for which a conjoint analysis approach is proposed (especially when complemented with a simulation or some optimization procedure such as the one proposed by the POSSE procedure), other approaches can and have been used. Among these procedures, two of the few which have been used extensively, published, and validated are consumer preference distribution analysis (Kuehn and Day, 1962) and the ECLIPSE system developed primarily for the formulation of new food products by MPI Sensory Testing Inc. (Moskowitz, 1978 and Moskowitz et al., 1977).[10]

Consumer preference distribution analysis is based on the following procedure:

- Determine the physical characteristics of a product that appears to be significant to consumers;

- Establish a scale of values, in equal increments, from a minimum level up to a maximum level for each characteristic;

- Test consumer preferences for products located at approximately equal incremental levels on the scale in a series of paired comparison tests, using representative samples of consumers;

- Analyze the results of all the tests for each product characteristic simultaneously, so as to estimate the percentages of consumers who prefer each level and the ability of consumers to recognize their true preferences;

- Relate preference levels to patterns of end use or other significant actions of consumers;

- Locate the value of the preference scale

---

[10]For a description of other approaches, the interested reader is referred to Eastlack (1964), Benson (1965), Stefflre (1971), Pessemier (1977), and Batsell and Wind (1980).

possessed by each product already on the market;

- Estimate the preference shares of existing products and evaluate opportunities for product changes and new product entries in all "neglected" segments of the market.

The ECLIPSE methodology is based on the Stevens (1975) magnitude estimation procedure [11] and includes a series of three product optimization procedures:

- ECLIPSE I converts concepts into an actual product recipe (of specific ingredients levels) that satisfies the concept-generated expectations.

- ECLIPSE II selects the perceptual attributes that are minimally redundant in a given market or closest to the respondent's ideal product and develops a nonlinear equation of attributes related to consumers' purchase interest. ECLIPSE II optimizes the equation to generate maximum purchase interest given feasible sensory attributes. The "optimal" design can be plugged into ECLIPSE I to identify the needed ingredients and their levels.

- ECLIPSE III integrates the previous steps and generates a product which is maximally liked, subject to higher purchase interest in the optimal product than in the consumers' current product, feasible physical ingredients, acceptable sensory profile of the optimized product, and acceptable cost.

The ECLIPSE method has been used by a number of companies including RJ Reynolds, Campbell Soup Company, Cheeseborough-Pond, and Pepsi.

Of the various approaches to the design of "optimal" product features the POSSE model is conceptually the most attractive one. Yet, at this stage of its development it has not yet been tested as widely as some of the more conventional conjoint analysis approaches or models of the ECLIPSE type. The selection of a specific approach is a complex decision which requires detailed examination of the criteria suggested earlier, in particular, the expected output, reliability, validity, and monetary and time costs of the alternative approaches. Whatever the selected procedure, it should allow the assessment of the "best" product features at the market segment level avoiding the "majority fallacy" which seeks a product acceptable to the majority of consumers (and hence potentially less acceptable to most consumers) (Kuehn and Day, 1962).[12]

---

[12] The majority fallacy can be demonstrated clearly in the following example in which four new products, A, B, C, and D, were evaluated by six respondents. Four products were ranked in terms of their performance as:

Respondent	Most preferred (1st ranked)	Second most preferred	Third ranked	Fourth ranked
1	A	D	B	C
2	A	D	C	B
3	B	D	A	C
4	B	D	C	A
5	C	D	B	A
6	C	D	A	B

In this case, if the choice is based on the mean score (the lower the score, the more preferred the product), the score of the four products is: 2.67 for products A, B, and C and a clear win of 2.00 for product D even though it is clearly less preferred by the three segments (those preferring A, B, and C).

---

[11] Stevens, one of the founders of psychophysics, measured "perceptual magnitudes" by ratio scaling methods and cross-modality comparisons and established the Steven's law, which states that perceptual magnitudes are a power function of their physical correlates. A critical evaluation of Steven's work and the earlier psychophysics work of Fechner and his law (which states that sensations are a logarithmic function of the stimuli that produces them) is presented in Savage (1970).

CONSUMER RESEARCH AND TECHNOLOGICAL R&D

The focus in this section on research approaches for new product design has been on consumer-based research. Such research should be supplemented, however, with technological research which is often the primary source of truly innovative new products. Consumer research can identify product opportunities and offer an invaluable way of evaluating alternative product features and designs, but it is up to the R&D scientists and engineers to innovate and develop the new products. Furthermore, most of the major innovative products of our time—television, instant photography, automobiles, drugs, "run-flat tires" (a tire which runs for 40 miles at 40 miles an hour after it has been punctured and hence might eliminate the need for a spare tire), transistors, computers, microprocessors, bubble memories, and numerous other innovations—emerged from R&D labs.

Bell Laboratories, for example, since its establishment in 1925, has received over 19,000 patents—an average of nearly two per working day. Yet, these and similar technological innovations by scores of firms of all sizes, all industries, and all types, still require some consumer input on the best way of translating the technological innovation into a consumer product offering the most desired benefits to its potential users.

Any new product development program should allow, therefore, for the needed collaboration and cooperation between technological and consumer research.

PACKAGING

Packaging is an integral part of most products. Can a perfume be separated from its package? Are a purse-size atomizer, spray bottle, and regular bottle of the same perfume the same product or three distinct products? Are different size, color, and design packages of identical facial tissues interchangeable products or different products? Is a seven-ounce can of beer perceived by consumers and retailers as the same product as a 12-ounce can? Are stick margarine, margarine in a tub and liquid margarine in a squeeze bottle the same product? Is an aerosol hair spray or deodorant the same hair spray or deodorant with identical physical features but in a different product form and packaging (liquid or cream)?

In these and numerous other cases the medium (package) is, in effect, the message. "Packaging has proved as effective as advertising in building sales in markets where products differ little" concludes a special *Business Week* (1965) report on packaging. New product design should therefore recognize the role played by packaging, the factors determining the desired package, and the research methods used for package design and evaluation.

ROLE OF PACKAGING

Packaging plays a number of diverse and interrelated roles. These roles include:

Promotional (communication) components The package is often the final "salesperson." In self-service outlets the consumer is in direct and immediate contact with the package, which supposedly should answer any questions the consumer might have about the product. Even more important, the package should attract the consumer's attention. Not unlike the situation with mass media in which a commercial or ad is designed to "stand out" in the crowd, a successful package should distinguish its product and make it stand out and attract its customer's attention.

The promotional merchandising role of a package parallels in fact the role of advertising—it is supposed to generate awareness and recognition for the brand as a member of a given product class and as distinct from its competitors, create or reinforce favorable attitudes toward the brand, increase the likelihood of its being bought, and occasionally increase the amount bought.

In designing the package from a promotional point of view it is the shape, size, color, materials, and design (logos, etc.) which provide the major ingredients for effective package design.

The promotional aspects of packaging are not limited to the package itself but extend to the shipping containers (cartons) which can be used not only to protect the product in shipment but also as promotional devices in the retail store. Sylvania, for example, designed a shipping carton that converted to a display—a departmentalized selling rack—of light bulb trays that saved the retailer the time of arranging the light bulbs in a display and in addition offered a more attractive point-of-purchase display for the product. The display racks and packages were also color coded according to wattage for ease of identification by the retailer in the stockroom and by the consumers in selecting the right bulbs.

Information component   Three informational components are typically found on packages:

How-to-use-it copy which provides use instructions. This can also be supplemented by more detailed package inserts.

Legal requirements for information disclosure. This can range from a brief usage warning such as in the case of cigarettes or open dating information on farm and other perishable products (such as film), to detailed listings of product ingredients as is the case with an increasing number of food and drug products (e.g., the FDA's requirements for nutrition labeling). In this latter case it is interesting to note that the FDA labeling and information-disclosure requirements are not necessarily consistent with the FTC requirements and standards with respect to the product's other advertising activities. Labeling and information disclosure requirements may lead to a situation of information overload on consumers' cognitive capabilities which might affect the degree to which consumers use the information in their purchase decisions.

Seals, emblems, and other symbols. These include both mandatory seals and symbols such as the meat and poultry quality seals and UPC numbers, and nonmandatory symbols such as the Good Housekeeping, *Parents* magazine, and other seals of approval.

Functional features   In addition to the information and promotion function of packaging there are a large number of functional roles packages can and should provide. These include primarily convenience (due to size, shape, and new materials), protection, disposability, preunitizing, shelf-life, and the performance of new functions (such as a package which serves also as cookware).

Convenience is one of the major functions of packages. Special spouts or other functional designs facilitate the use of the product, ease of opening, ease and quality of the resealing possibilities, ease of handling, carrying and storage, etc.

Size and shape are important determinants of convenience. The addition of new package sizes is often viewed as analogous to the introduction of a new product (or legitimate line extensions). Note, for example, the addition of "soup for one," the seven-ounce beer can, the giant or family-size detergent box. In addition, there are multiple packs—six- and eight-pack soft drink packages and variety packs such as the one common in cereal. Similarly, new materials and shapes (which often are associated with new sizes) also tend to be viewed as new products, can facilitate display, and add to the convenience of storage and handling.

Convenience in storage, display, and handling in the store and in storage and handling by the customer is often increased by the use of new packaging material. Consider, for example, the packaging of milk in plastic bags instead of the traditional paper or plastic bottles.

Protection. One of the most basic functions of packaging is the protection of the product from damage in shipping and handling. The protection feature is relevant both for consumer *and* industrial products. Consider, for example, the case of Frank Lumber Company which shipped its lumber wrapped in especially coated and reinforced color-coded paper wrapping. This wrapping kept the lumber dry, increased the ease of handling and storage, and facilitated inventory management (*Business Week*, 1965).

Disposability. Environmental concern has led to numerous legislative rules concerning disposability of products. Among the alternatives considered are bans or taxes on one-way disposable containers, mandatory bottle deposits, and other incentives to encourage returns, prohibition of certain materials (such as polyvinylchloride) in packaging, etc.[13]

Preunitizing of the packaged product into predetermined units (six-packs, one-pound packages, etc.) is one of the major functional roles of packaging. The increased use of the preunitized packages has also increased the number of "products" offered to consumers (aspirin in packages of 2, 12, 24, 100, and 500 can be viewed, for example, as five distinct products) and can simplify the purchase decision process.

Shelf life. A functional factor of great importance to both the intermediary marketing organizations (wholesalers and retailers) as well as consumers is the expected shelf life of the product, which to a large extent is affected by the product's packaging and form (e.g., frozen versus refrigerated, or with no need for either).

New functional use. Packaging often offers major product use benefits by performing functions which in the past were performed by other products. As such packaging requires as much innovative design work as any other feature of a new product. Consider, for example, boil-in-the-bag foods, and more recent developmental work in "spray-on foods" and in "ovenable paperboard". Ovenable paperboard is a thin cardboard container in which the food product can be warmed in both microwave ovens and conventional ovens up to 400 degrees. Such developments could replace foil disposables and reduce the use of traditional cooking pots and pans. This development is not an isolated incident. Rather it is illustrative of numerous new developments, especially in materials—new plastics, new metal applications, new paper, and new combinations of new materials.

Secondary use. In addition to the primary functions of packaging, packages are often designed to offer consumers a secondary use. The use of glassware to package sour cream, designer storage containers as packages for jams, spices, or coffee, and wine bottles in the shape of a carafe, are only a few examples of packages which can be used for other purposes.

These functions and their relations to the major stakeholders involved in packaging are summarized in Exhibit 12–9.

This variety of packaging roles and the great potential for packaging innovations

---

[13]For a discussion of environmental concerns in packaging see Gunn (1972).

EXHIBIT 12–9

SOME OF THE MAJOR ROLES OF PACKAGING

Stakeholder and function	Promotion Aesthetic & physical features	Information Aesthetic & physical features	Functional features					
			Conve-nience	Pro-tection	Dispos-ability	Shelf life	New functional use	Secondary uses
Consumers								
In store:								
Selection of product	X	X	X	X	X	X	X	X
Handling of product				X				
In transit:								
Handling			X	X				
In home:								
Storage			X	X		X		X
Handling		X	X			X	X	X
Disposal					X			X
Retailers/wholesalers								
Storage				X		X		
Display	X		X					X
Handling				X		X		
Government and Environmental groups								
Safety		X	X					
Deceptive promotion	X						X	
Environmental protection					X			
Consumer information	X	X						

which can enhance the value of the product, cut the total cost of production, increase usage, help promote the product, and comply with government regulations, have led to an increased level of packaging research, to the establishment of an organizational function responsible for packaging development, and to greater top-management involvement in planning the packaging progress. General Foods Corporation, for example, instituted a function of packaging development and procurement services, and National Biscuit Company established the office of vice president of packaging. (*Printer's Ink*, 1965). These and other companies have started emphasizing the role of top management in setting policies and maintaining active and effective direction of packaging programs (Lippincott and Margulies, 1956).

Packaging management in its more sophisticated form follows the 5M's—management, marketing, material, machinery, and money—proposed by Arthur D. Little (1961) as the key to good consumer packaging. Management of packaging involves basic sound management and make-buy decisions. Marketing calls for the marketing approach to packaging management. Material and machinery involve considerations not unlike those involved with the design of new products. Money is both the means to and the end of an integrated packaging program. The determination of a packaging budget is therefore essential and should take into consideration costs such as time and the facilities required to determine the packaging requirements of a product and gather and evaluate the characteristics and costs of alternative packaging systems and materials, time and supplies spent on machinery development, physical and performance-testing facilities, money spent for design services, and management's time for supervising and evaluating the packaging development program. To these development costs it is necessary to add production and marketing costs. Whereas relatively accurate packaging cost estimates can be obtained, the *value* of packaging changes or a new package is difficult to estimate since it is often impossible to separate the packaging effect from that of the product and the other components of the marketing mix.

PACKAGING RESEARCH

Given the multiple objectives of packaging, no single test can assess the effectiveness of package design. Rather, a *packaging research program* should be developed and its components coordinated with the product and branding research needs of the firm.

Packaging research can include three types of studies:

Visibility and distinctiveness tests Not unlike the advertising recall measures which assess the ability of an ad to penetrate the advertising clutter of the media, this type of packaging research is designed to assess the ability of a package to "stand out" in the crowd of other packages, and to register the brand name and any other desired messages.

This type of information can be obtained using a variety of procedures varying primarily in their degree of realism. A "pure" lab test is often constructed with the help of a Tachistoscope, which controls the length of exposure time to a package (and its competitors) and measures the respondents' response time.

More realistic lab tests involve simulated shopping environments (e.g., simulated supermarket) in which the respondent is asked to go through a simulated shopping trip and a camera monitors the time he or she spends in front of the test package versus alternative packages. Such tests usually require more elaborate settings and prototypical package designs, whereas the Tachistoscope-type studies require only slides of the test packages.

Most tests in this category are conducted with relatively small sample sizes (often less than 100 respondents per test cell). Although monadic tests are often conducted, comparative tests (of the test alternatives versus some existing packages) are conceptually better.

Functional packaging tests Ease of handling, opening, resealing, and storing often require inputs from consumers. To obtain such information (especially as compared to the anticipated competitive packages) small-scale studies can be administered with prospective consumers. Such studies can be based either on individual interviews or focused group-type sessions. A likely problem with these lab-type tests is the *validity* of the findings. In a test in which the respondents know that the focus is on packaging, they are more likely to read the instructions for operating and handling the package than in real-world usage. It might be helpful, therefore, to conceal the real purpose of the test and get the necessary packaging information as a by-product of product information provided by the respondents. In this context, examination of the used packages after an

EXHIBIT 12–10

PRODUCT BENEFIT VALUES FOR THE THREE BENEFIT SEGMENTS

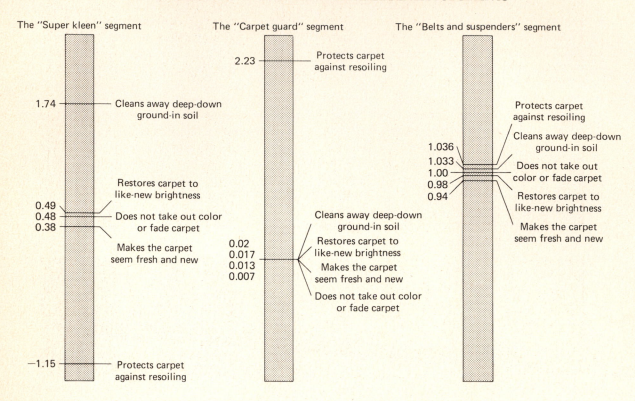

in-home use test might be of considerable value in revealing how the consumers actually used the package. In addition to this concern with validity, given the relatively small sample size of most packaging studies, care should be given to the respondents' selection and their representativeness to assure the generalizability of results.

Perceptions of and preferences for various packaging features Not unlike product design studies, final packaging decisions require input on two major items: (a) the perceived compatibility of package components with the desired product positioning and (b) the preference for specific package features.

As with product designs, a variety of attitude measurement approaches have been used to assess consumers' perceptions of and preference for various package designs. Many of these studies followed a modified advertising testing research design. But as with product testing, availability of a large number of possible packaging features, and the limitations of self-explicated attitude measurement approaches, suggest the advisability of a conjoint analysis-based packaging study.

This approach is briefly illustrated in the following example of a packaging study conducted for a carpet cleaner. In this case management identified five possible benefits, and the first part of the study was designed to assess

EXHIBIT 12–11
EXPERIMENTAL PACKAGES (BASED ON A GRECO-LATIN SQUARE DESIGN)

EXHIBIT 12–12

SCALE VALUES FOR VARIOUS COMPONENTS OF PACKAGE DESIGN (THE SUPER CLEAN SEGMENT)

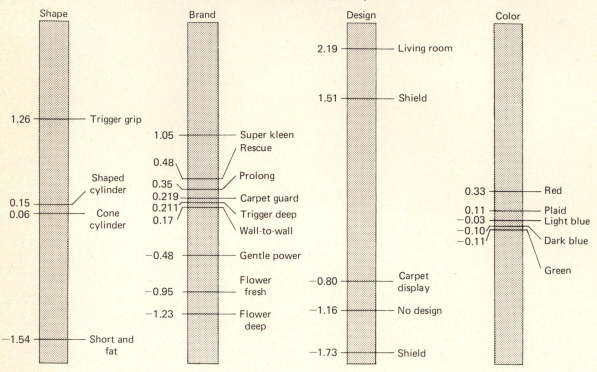

consumers' preferences for various benefit bundles. A conjoint analysis task was conducted and the analysis of these data suggested the presence of three benefit segments. Exhibit 12–10 summarizes the benefit preference pattern of these segments.

The second phase of this study involved an evaluation of 25 alternative package designs based on their compatibility with the respondents' most-preferred benefit or benefit combination. The 25 packages as illustrated in Exhibit 12–11 were selected following a Greco-Latin square design composed of the following factors: shape of the package (trigger grip, cylinder, shaped cylinder, cone, short and fat), color (light blue, green, red, plaid, and dark blue), package design (living room design, shag car-

pet, shield, carpet display, and no design), and brand name (nine brand names were tested: Rescue, Super Kleen, Prolong, Trigger Deep, Gentle Power, Carpet Guard, Flower Deep, Wall-to-Wall, and Flower Fresh). Yet to achieve efficiency in design (via use of a Greco-Latin square design), the sample was split into two parts and two identical Greco-Latin square designs were used with the only difference being the brand names used. One brand name was used in both.[14]

---

[14]In the analysis stage the data from the two designs were tested for similarity. Given no significant differences in any of the results from the two subsamples, the data were combined and the final results were presented for nine brand names.

EXHIBIT 12–13

SCALE VALUES FOR VARIOUS COMPONENTS OF PACKAGE DESIGN (THE CARPET GUARD SEGMENT)

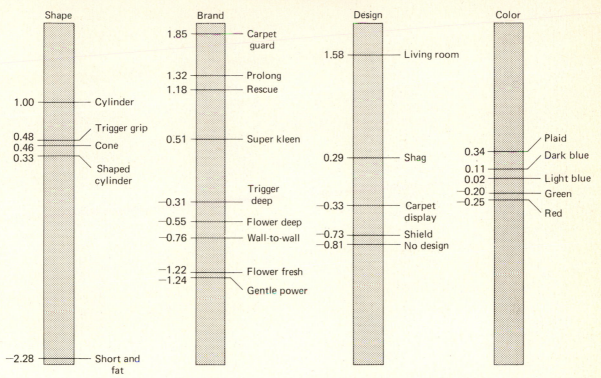

The appropriateness and preference data were submitted to a conjoint analysis algorithm, and the data were analyzed at the benefit segment level. Exhibits 12–12 through 12–14 present the most preferred package design features for the three benefit segments identified in the earlier phase of the analysis. Given these results, management selected both the most desirable package features and the target benefit segment to go after. Two benefit segments—the "super clean" and the "belt and suspenders" segments—were selected, and it was decided to appeal to them with the single product featuring a trigger grip-type package, with the Super Kleen name, a living room design, and light blue color—a package design most preferred by both segments.

This study illustrates the use of conjoint analysis in the evaluation of alternative package designs. In this respect it is not dissimilar to the use of conjoint analysis in product design. The study also illustrates a way in which a final selection and evaluation of brand names can be made. Note that the selection of both product features and brand name should correspond to the benefits sought by consumers, avoiding a situation in which the most-desired product features are not congruent with the benefits consumers' desire.

As with design of product features, a package test using conjoint analysis or a similar procedure is best performed with a physical product/package prototype, or if this is not feasible, with a picture of it. Verbal descriptions

EXHIBIT 12–14

SCALE VALUES FOR VARIOUS COMPONENTS OF PACKAGE DESIGN (THE BELT
AND SUSPENDERS SEGMENT)

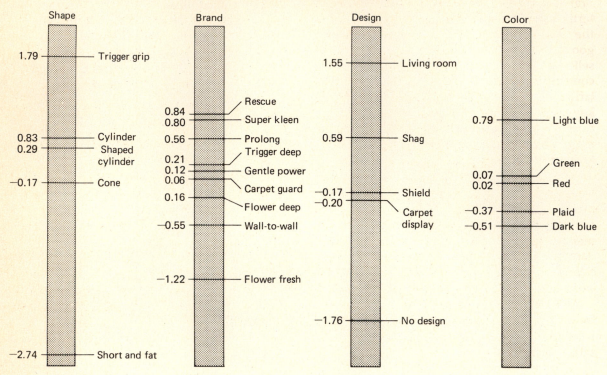

are not very helpful in this context. This also implies that if conjoint analysis is used for product/packaging tests it should be the full-profile approach, and not the two-factor-at-a-time, since the latter approach does not lend itself to the construction of actual product prototypes.

Despite the attractiveness of conjoint analysis to the generation and evaluation of alternative package feature designs, it is important to note that not all cases require this level of detailed analysis. If management is considering only a limited número of options (which is common in the modification of existing packages in which only a few minor changes are

under consideration) other approaches can be used.

The packaging research discussed so far involves primarily consumer-based research. Another important component of package research is basic packaging R&D, particularly in new packaging materials, designs, and related processes (such as research on electrostatic and three-dimensional printing which allows printing on almost any kind of surface). These research and development activities are not unlike the basic product R&D activities for which successful completion requires close interface between technical and marketing research.

BRANDING

Branding refers to the use of a brand name, a term, a symbol, a design, any combination of the above, or any other means used to identify goods and services of one seller or a group of sellers and to distinguish them from those of competitors.[15] The branding decision, particularly the selection of a brand name, is one of the key new product decisions of the firm and is closely related to the desired product positioning and overall marketing program for the given product or service.

The selection of a brand name and other ways of branding a product, not unlike the product and package decisions, involve a number of considerations and requires a systematic effort at generating alternative brand names, screening them (primarily for legal clearance,[16] consumer and trade acceptability) and selecting the best alternative.

The range of possible brand names and trademarks is clearly illustrated if one considers some of the options on the following, non-exhaustive, list.[17]

- A word with no meaning at all (Kodak, Ipana, Decca);
- An ordinary word that has no meaning in connection with the product on which it is used (Camel, Arrow, Eagle);
- A word whose meaning suggests some quality or function of the product (Whirl-pool, Mustang, Aspergum);
- A word suggesting what the product is or does (Kleenex, Jell-O, Tintex);
- A foreign word whose English meaning may or may not have some significance for the product (Lux, Carioca, Femme);
- A name of an owner or founder of the company (Ford, Singer, Gillette);
- A name of some famous person selected arbitrarily (Lincoln, Raleigh);
- A name from mythology or literature (Venus, Ajax, Peter Pan);
- Initials (RCA, BVD);
- Numerals (No. 5);
- Combinations of letters and numbers (V–8, A–1);
- A pictorial mark with or without explanation (Four Roses, The White Rock Girl, Elsie the Cow).

BRANDING DECISIONS

Some of the questions which management has to address in making branding decisions are as follows:

1. Should the name communicate the desired consumer benefits offered by the product (Kool, Easy-Off)?
2. How closely should the name be associated with the product class?
3. How closely should the name be associated with the firm and should it be part of a "family brand" (a member of "Heinz 57," Sears' Kenmore appliances)?
4. How different should the name be from the brand's competitors? (It is not al-

---

[15]This definition is based on McCarthy (1975, p. 255).

[16]For a detailed discussion of legal problems with trademarks and their implications, see Diamond (1973).

[17]This list is reprinted with permission from *Trademark Problems and How to Avoid them,* by S.A. Diamond, Crain Communications, Inc., 1973. Copyright © 1973 by Sidney A. Diamond.

ways desirable to differentiate the brand from competing brands. In cases in which a "me too" poistioning is sought a name similar to that of the target brand might be appropriate).

5. Is a brand name strategy preferable to a private or generic brand strategy, or mixed strategy?

6. How can the firm avoid developing a brand name (trademark) that is likely to become a common descriptive term for that type of product, and become public property. Names such as cellophane, cola, aspirin, trampoline, yo-yo, shredded wheat, kerosene, and brassiere, once brand names, have been stripped from their holders as generic. Furthermore, in May 1978 the FTC announced its intention to challenge other trademarks that have become generic (*Advertising Age,* 1978).[18] Xerox, for example, to prevent their name from becoming generic, has been advertising that you don't "xerox" things, you photocopy them with a Xerox copier made by Xerox.

7. Should a name connote a foreign origin, or should the "made in country X" be mentioned explicitly; and if yes, which country should be used (assuming that the firm has a choice in terms of country of manufacturing)?

8. How important are the following characteristics which are often prescribed for a "good brand name"?[19]

- Short, simple, and easy to spell and read
- Easy to recognize and remember
- Pleasing when read and easy to pronounce
- Not disagreeable sounding
- Pronounceable in only one way
- Always timely (does not get out of date)
- Adaptable to packaging or labelling requirements
- Available for use (not in use by another firm)
- Pronounceable in all languages
- Not offensive, obscene, or negative
- A selling suggestion
- Adaptable to any advertising medium (especially billboards and TV)

The evidence concerning the "correct" answers to these questions is inconclusive. Some of these areas have been studied systematically, while others are still subject to myth and diverse other (and often conflicting) considerations. Consider, for example, the degree of association between the brand name and the product class and its benefits. From a legal point of view it is desirable not to have direct association with the product class. Yet, from the consumer's recall and attitude perspective, close association is desired. Miller, Mazis, and Wright (1971), for example, found that an extremely ambiguous and novel brand name can negatively influence a consumer's response to information about characteristics of the branded product. This finding is consistent with the general findings of Berlyne (1963) that extreme ambiguity of a stimulus inhibits respondents' curiosity about it.

---

[18] Section 14 of the Lanham Trademark Act provides that status as a common descriptive name, or "genericness" is one of the six grounds for trademark cancellation. This provided the basis for an FTC petition to the Trademark Trial and Appeal Board to cancel "Formica" as Generic (CCH 50,372, June, 1978; BNA ATRR, No. 867, June 8, 1978, A–2). In this case the FTC alledges that "Formica" became the common descriptive name for decorative plastic laminates used on counter tops, table tops, and the like and is used to describe a class of products rather than identify a particular brand or manufacturer.

[19] This list is based on McCarthy (1975, p. 254).

Given the questionable generalizability of some of these and similar findings and their dependency on consumers' perceptions of the nature of the stimuli (for example, degree of ambiguity of the brand name), the desired brand name characteristics should be determined empirically in each case.

This empirical orientation is further supported by the interdependency of many of these decisions on other product and marketing decisions. The effect of family branding, for example, was found to be determined by shelf arrangement, price changes, and product class (Neuhaus and Taylor, 1972). Similarly, the decision on whether to offer private brands or not, even though it has been studied (see, for example, Cook and Schutte, 1967) requires in-depth consideration of a number of idiosyncratic characteristics of the firm, the product class, its distribution structure, the level and nature of competitive activities, and the general consumer and environmental climate.

RESEARCH APPROACHES

Branding research involves two major phases: the generation of new brand names and the evaluation of those names which survived legal clearance and management preference.[20]

Generation of brand names can be done with consumer research, solicitation of "expert" opinions, or brute-force computer analysis.

Consumer approaches to the generation of name brands are based primarily on the concept of associations in language and thought.[21]

Free-response and sentence-completion tasks are often used to identify consumers' semantic association with desired product benefits. Occasionally other motivation research approaches (such as focused group interviews or individual depth interviews) have been used to generate brand names. Yet, the most useful approach to generation of brand names seems to be the one based on some form or another of free-association task (either in an individual or group context).

An *expert's* role in generating new brand names is not unlike the expert's role in new-product generation (as discussed in Chapter 9). In fact, given the emotional involvement with brand names it is almost impossible to prevent management and other involved personnel from suggesting names. A systematic way of collecting such ideas and procedures to encourage the generation and submission of names is thus required.

Computer-based approaches are quite common today and are based primarily on random or systematic combinations of syllables. The name Exxon, for example, was generated by a computer, and the use of simple computer programs to generate names is increasing.

Evaluation of brand names involves more complex research procedures, not unlike the research approaches to the screening (of a large number) and evaluation (of a more limited number) of concepts.

The key factor in evaluative brand name research is the question of the dependent variable. Should it be recall, association with a product class, association with a certain benefit, association with a firm, association/disassociation with a likely competitor, or some other evaluative measure?

Once a dependent variable is selected, the research approach can vary from simple tasks such as free associations or rating or ranking of names based on the degree to which they are

---

[20]The legal screening of brand names can be viewed as another research step, one involving legal research and opinions.

[21]For a discussion of the structure of associations in language and thought, see Deese, 1965.

perceived to be associated with an anchor stimulus, to conjoint analysis studies in which brand names are included as one of the factors, such as in the package design study referred to earlier in the chapter. Given this likely diversity in data collection procedures, the data analysis approaches can range from simple cross tabulations (of evoked words by brand names for the free-association task) through multidimensional scaling and clustering of such data, as discussed in Chapter 4, to conjoint analysis algorithms.

Most of the research which focuses on the generation and evaluation of branding alternatives has focused on brand names. Other symbols which can be used to brand a product often have been left to the designer with little research inputs. This gap in most new product research programs should be closed since some empirical research in the area of visual perceptions suggests the value of other components in stimulating recall and favorable attitude toward a message. Consider, for example, the results of a study by Mackworth (1963) who found that in terms of recall the rank order of the effectiveness of message components is digits, letters, colors, and shapes. Some of his results are presented in Exhibit 12–15. These and numerous other findings from the visual perception area (see, for example, Haber 1969) suggest the need for greater attention to the examination of the various components of branding.

EXHIBIT 12–15

RECALL OF DIFFERENT MESSAGE COMPONENTS

Reprinted from the *Journal of Verbal Learning and Verbal Behavior,* published by Academic Press, Inc. Exhibit from "The Relation between the Visual Image and Post-Perceptual Immediate Memory," by J.F. Mackworth, Volume 2, 1963, pp.75–85.

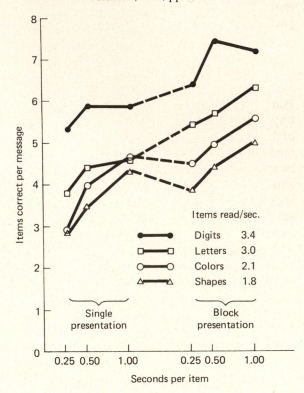

ASSOCIATED SERVICES

Product design cannot stop with the determination of the most desirable bundle of product, packaging, and branding features but should also consider other associated services such as warranties, money-back guarantees, credit and financing, maintenance contracts, and other features which can constitute an important, integral or optional part of the product bundle consumers buy. Many of these decisions require coordination with other business functions, and are not within the sole domain of the new product management team. Yet, these associated services can in many cases determine the success of the new product. In fact, at times it is difficult to separate the associated services from the product features. How, for example, would you consider the software packages for computer hardware?

RANGE OF DECISIONS

Warranty For many products warranty is an important feature sought by at least a segment of the market. Most durable products offer warranties which occasionally are supplemented by an additional implicit warranty of the store in which the product is purchased. If warranties are given by all manufacturers, little differential advantage is gained by it and it further increases the cost of marketing the product. Warranties are especially crucial for lesser-known brands, and as a way of increasing the credibility of "quality" positioning. Consider, for example, the introduction of a distinctly-shaped, two-year warranted light bulb by Westinghouse which stressed the length of warranty as its major product positioning feature (Peterson, 1978).

Whereas in many cases manufacturers have been reluctant to offer extended warranties for obvious cost reasons, recent legal developments concerning manufacturer responsibility and product liability have changed this situation, since manufacturers are likely to be forced to correct product malfunctions. Product recall and free repairs in cases of product malfunction are common remedies by the courts. (Consider, for example, the numerous car recalls and arrangements such as the one agreed to in 1978 by the Zenith Radio Corporation to replace defected components in color TV sets produced in 1974 and 1975.) Hence, instead of suffering the costs of such corrective actions and the negative publicity associated with recall, manufacturers should consider offering extended warranties which might not be much more expensive than the recall costs and which would offer the product a distinct advantage.

Installation, training, maintenance, and service Product installation and training are often important considerations in the purchase decision of complex durable products. Similarly, maintenance and service contracts play an important role in the purchase decision of certain products (such as industrial products and certain types of consumer durables).

Money-back guarantees The extreme warranty is a money-back guarantee. The attractiveness of such an offer is its psychological impact on reducing the perceived risk associated with the purchase. In a number of studies on household appliances and products such as carpet cleaners, a money-back guarantee was viewed by at least one market segment as an extremely important feature.

Credit and financing Credit terms and financing arrangements for expensive items such as durable products are also an important determinant of the purchase decision of some market segments. Credit terms and financing arrangements have long been recognized as important components of the firm's offering. Yet, they have often been excluded from consideration at the new product design stage. Given, however, the importance of price and other financial considerations, credit and financing arrangements should be incorporated explicitly in any new product offering.

RESEARCH APPROACHES

Given the likely importance of associated product services, new product research should include research efforts aimed at the generation and evaluation of various alternative offerings. These research efforts should be coordinated and incorporated with the research on product features, packaging characteristics, and branding. As with these other areas of study a variety of marketing research approaches can and have been utilized.

The selection of a research approach for generating and evaluating alternative associated product services is not unlike the process and consideration used in the selection of any research approach. The various approaches to the generation of new product ideas discussed in Chapter 9 are as applicable to this area as they are for the generation of new product ideas. The evaluation stage can benefit from a conjoint analysis type study. In fact in the example used for packaging research earlier in this chapter, one could easily add to the set of factors examined product features (such as the nature of the chemicals used, degree of foaminess, etc.) and a number of associated services (such as money-back guarantee). In fact a number of commercial new product evaluation studies which were based on a conjoint analysis model and algorithm did include not only product features but also a number of the associated services discussed here. A carpet cleaner study included, for example, variables such as package design, price, brand name, money-back guarantee, and a Good Housekeeping seal of approval (Green and Wind, 1975b). A study of toasters included, in addition to the more conventional product features, the nature of the warranty (extent and length of coverage). A study of major appliances included, besides product features and price, the financing arrangement. A series of auto insurance policies included a guaranteed issue for life and guaranteed level of premiums for a given number of years (an "inflation fighter" concept).

Experience to date with these and other studies which incorporated product features with a set of associated services, suggests that conjoint analysis is a powerful and useful approach to the evaluation of the "best" offering for selected market segments, the relative importance of each of the studied factors, and the consumers' trade offs among the various controllable product, package, and service features.

PUTTING IT ALL TOGETHER

Even though conjoint analysis-type studies allow for the simultaneous evaluation of the relevant product, package, and service characteristics, as well as brand name and even price, most new product design programs are built as a sequential process, typically involving a large number of studies for each component. It is thus quite common to find new product development processes which involve a number of product feature tests, a number of independent packaging tests, and a number of brand name tests. The implicit premise of such a system is that the "best" components when put together would result in the "best" product offering. This premise, if accompanied by appropriate research designs which assure an explicit link among the various components of the product offering, is acceptable for the class of nonimagery products. Imagery products—perfumes, cigarettes, and other products whose primary position is based on image—cannot be built effectively by a sequential step-by-step approach which starts with each component and culminates in a "total proposition" study of the best surviving items from each preceding step. The more conceptually appealing approach for imagery products is a reversed and shorter process. Such a process starts with a positioning concept which is developed, executed (as an ad or commercial), and tested. Each execution incorporates components such as a name, a package, a positioning, all of which are designed to communicate a desired image. This phase can be designed as a conjoint analysis type study which incorporates image components as factors and levels, and the stimuli are executed pictorially as ads. As a result of this phase a positioning/concept ad can be selected and the remaining new product development program is simply aimed at selecting a product (combination of physical attributes) which best *matches* the desired product image/positioning.

Such a process requires a greater and earlier involvement of the creative advertising personnel. It is a conceptually appealing process for the development of new imagery products and has been at the time of this writing in the final stages of implementation by a large consumer goods manufacturer.

This reverse procedure is appropriate for the extreme cases of *imagery-dominated* products. Most products, however, have only some imagery component. In those cases research approaches that focus on objective-type spaces are based on the ability of synthesized representations to capture the "totality" of the object. One way to assess the incremental contribution of image is to compare the results of "blind product tests" with those of similar tests with identified products and with products which are presented together with an advertising execution. In some cases the product "iden-

tification" can be handled as a type of covariate. In principle, this would introduce no major complexities of analysis and could allow one to measure image effects as the change in utility between the various experimental cells. Given that this issue can be dealt with, it is important to incorporate such a test as a standard part of product design studies in which the question of representation arises.

The most comprehensive and constructive way of putting together all the product features is with the aid of a computer simulation and/or an optimization procedure. One of the most comprehensive product optimization programs is the POSSE procedure (Green et al., 1981). It is based on conjoint analysis-type input data (in terms of respondents' preference for either pictorial (or verbal) product descriptions or for actual test products that can be used in either a controlled or natural setting). The particular optimization program used involves a modified gradient method. A quadratic function is maximized allowing for versatility inasmuch as it can include ideal point phenomena (where some intermediate level of an attribute is preferred to either extreme) or diminishing or increasing returns to changes in an attribute. The program also allows for the introduction of linear constraints to restrict the range of each attribute to technologically and economically feasible levels.

This quadratic optimization is thus designed to answer questions such as:

- What is the optimal product configuration?
- What is the optimal product, conditioned on holding certain attributes at a priori selected levels?
- What is the optimal product, conditioned on a particular target segment?
- What is the optimal target segment, conditioned on the optimal product?
- How sensitive is expected return to depar-

tures of various attributes from the optimal level?

The latter question is especially important since it allows examination of the nature of the objective function surface in the vicinity of the optimum by providing "tolerance" contours that show for any single variable or pair of variables and segment characteristics (specified in terms of either product features or market segment characteristics) how sensitive the objective function is to departures from the optimal setting of these variables. This unique feature provides the product designer a larger set of (near optimal) options to choose from and not just a single "optimal" alternative. (For a more detailed discussion of POSSE, see Appendix B).

POSSE and other large-scale optimization procedures or simulations offer a useful way of "integrating" and pulling together the various outputs of various product tests and integrating them in an operational decision support system that can help the product designer construct products which have a higher likelihood of meeting consumers' needs and achieving the corporate objectives.

CONCLUDING REMARKS

Product design as illustrated in this chapter involves a large set of decisions concerning product features, packaging characteristics, branding components, and associated services. These decisions are too important to be left to R&D personnel. Marketing thinking and marketing research inputs are essential ingredients of successful product design activities. In fact, most "innovative" firms are incorporating their R&D and new product marketing (and particularly marketing research) activities. Yet, technical and scientific sophistication (in marketing and technical research and in management approaches) are no guarantees of successful products. The creative genius is still required

and the planning of a new product design system should take this individualistic, creative, artistic component into consideration (by means of personnel recruiting and organizational arrangement).

To fully appreciate the scope and complexity of new product design, select a new product of your choice and try to identify the number of decisions made by its designers. Having completed it, generate for each component a number of options (i.e., different color, brand name, package design, product features, etc.) and design a research approach to test and select from them the "best" combination of features.

INTRODUCTION

As indicated in Chapter 12, product design involves more than the selection of physical product features. It involves a considerable number of interrelated marketing decisions. Whereas packaging, branding, and related services were discussed in the previous chapter, there are still a number of key marketing decisions involving pricing, promotion, advertising, and distribution which have to be determined prior to the introduction of a new product to the market. The design of a marketing strategy for the introduction of a new product is an integral part of the new product development activities and should receive explicit attention prior to the final assessment of the new product's market acceptability and consistency with corporate objectives.

The design of a marketing program for a new product involves the entire range of marketing decisions and entails both short- and long-term marketing plans. It is not the intention of this chapter to summarize or even review in detail the domain of marketing strategy.[1] Rather, the intention of this chapter is to provide a brief overview of some of the major considerations that should be taken into account in planning the new product marketing introduction or in assessing any necessary product changes to meet the requirements of a specific marketing plan.

The generation and evaluation of alternative marketing strategies require taking into account the corporate objectives, the characteristics of the target market segment(s), the intended positioning of the product, the likely competitive and environmental conditions, and the other factors discussed in Chapters 6 and 7.

GENERATION AND EVALUATION OF MARKETING STRATEGIES

In determining the price, promotion, advertising, and distribution strategies of a new product, the two key components are the need to develop procedures that stimulate the generation of creative alternatives, and procedures for systematic and thorough evaluation of the generated alternatives. Both of these procedures are not unlike the ones used in the generation and evaluation of ideas/concepts/products. The importance of generating new creative strategies can never be overemphasized. Most of the marketing literature has focused on evaluation procedures. Yet, evaluation of a set of poorly-conceived and noninnovative strategies might offer little benefit to the company. The development of creative marketing strategies is an important ingredient in a successful new product introduction. The generation of marketing strategies should therefore entail, as should the generation of new product ideas, a variety of approaches and participants.

Relevant inputs for the generation of marketing strategies are:

- Characteristics of the new product, its intended positioning, and target segments

---

[1]For a good introductory marketing management text, see Kotler (1980) or Hughes (1978).

Generating and Evaluating the Product/Marketing Strategy

- Past experience of the firm
- Expected competitive activities
- Strategies used successfully in other product categories

An examination of new product marketing campaigns suggests that most campaigns are not very creative. How many truly innovative marketing campaigns can you remember? Yet, note the tremendous success associated with the few truly innovative marketing programs—the supermarket distribution of L'eggs, the first time cash rebates were used by Chrysler, and the pricing of calculators by Texas Instruments, for example. The generation of creative strategies and the design of an organizational climate and procedure conducive to the generation of creative, non-"me too" strategies are among the major challenges facing management. The obstacles to creative strategies are many:

- Human tendency to get satisfaction, i.e., go ahead with the first strategy that seems to be acceptable;
- Risk reduction climate which dominates most firms, and the perceived high risk of truly innovative strategies;
- Managerial reward for short-term performance, which tends to enhance the risk-reduction tendencies;
- The bureaucratic barriers for the design and implementation of strategies which differ from old, established, and proven methods of operation.

The removal of these and other barriers for the generation of *creative* new marketing strategies are among the major responsibilities of top management. Yet, it is often top management itself that attempts to reduce the risk of new strategies. Top management can thus be one of the major barriers for the development and implementation of creative and "different" marketing strategies.

The evaluation of new marketing strategies is quite similar to the procedures used to evaluate new ideas, concepts, and products. The evaluation entails environmental analysis, primarily to obtain legal clearance, and assessment of consumers' and other relevant stakeholders' reactions to the new marketing strategies. This evaluation requires a series of research inputs which, when supplemented by internal corporate data, culminate in an economic evaluation of the proposed new marketing strategy. Research designs for the evaluation of alternative marketing strategies encompass most of the research approaches utilized in assessing reactions to new products, as well as lab and field experiments. In designing an evaluation mechanism to evaluate alternative marketing strategies, consideration should be given to:

- Likely response functions to the proposed marketing strategies. This can be checked against historical response functions of similar products.
- Likely synergistic effect of the marketing strategy.
- Likely cannibalization.
- Likely competitive retaliation and reaction to the firm's competitive activities.
- Likely government reaction.

MANAGEMENT SCIENCE APPROACHES

In addition to the research inputs that can help management generate and evaluate alternative marketing strategies, there are numerous management science models that have been used to help management formulate and evaluate alternative marketing strategies. Most of these decision support models are quite similar to one another. One of the early and widely-used models is BRANDAID, which was developed by John Little (1975a and b). The major charac-

EXHIBIT 13–1

THE BRANDAID MODEL STRUCTURE

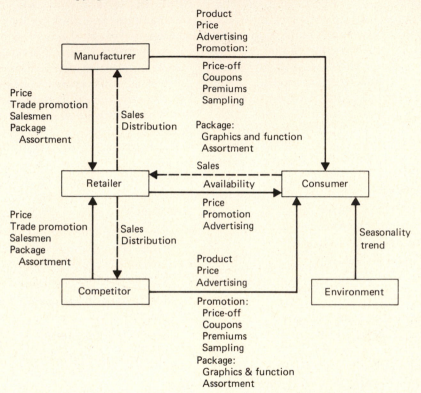

teristics of the BRANDAID marketing mix model are:

1. A flexible, online modular series of models aimed at evaluating alternative marketing strategies.

2. An aggregate response-type model which relates decision variables (e.g., advertising, pricing, etc.) to sales, share, and profit as the performance measures of the firm.

3. The model includes a number of major submodels including:

   a) Advertising submodel which employs a long-run (nonlinear) sales response to advertising rate and a linear lag process. Advertising rate is in turn modeled as a function of copy effectiveness × media efficiency × spending rate.

   b) The promotional submodel covers a wide variety of promotional strategies such as premiums, temporary price reductions, and sampling. This submodel is built up from a characteristic time pattern of response for the type of promotion.

   c) The sales force submodel is similar in

nature to the advertising submodel.

d) The price submodel does not include temporary price changes, which are considered in the promotion submodel. The response to wholesale price changes is assumed to occur in the same time period of the price change. The price model also takes into account the retail price ending effect on consumers (i.e., a change from 49 cents to 51 cents may have a bigger reduction in sales than a change from 51 cents to 53 cents.

4. In addition to these submodels, BRAND-AID incorporates both retail distribution (availability) and competition, which enters in a modular, symmetric way through a matrix of competitive coefficients that determines the sources of sales for each brand.

The overall relationship among the submodels and the overall structure of the models is summarized in Exhibit 13–1.

Common to the BRANDAID and other management science models for the generation and evaluation of marketing strategies are the following characteristics:

1. The need to estimate empirically and vali-date the market response function to the different marketing variables. Without accurate response functions these models cannot serve as useful decision aids. Although the sensitivity of the results to changes in the response function can be tested, it is critical for its long-run use to update regularly the market response function based on results of empirical market research studies. Furthermore, to be of greater value, the market response function should be assessed at the market segment level, not only at the total market level.

2. An important input to most of the models is management's subjective evaluation of likely events and responses to activities. The development and implementation of such models calls for procedures for dealing with judgments of a number of managers and the resolution of conflicts among them, if any.

3. The development of marketing strategy for many new products entails a long-term orientation. Proposed strategies which are sensitive to likely changes in market conditions require, therefore, an explicit examination of marketing strategies under alternative environmental scenarios.

MARKETING STRATEGIES FOR A NEW PRODUCT

The marketing program for a new product involves explicit decisions concerning the various components of the marketing mix—pricing, promotion, advertising, and distribution. The next four sections briefly discuss the key decisions involved in determining the most appropriate strategy, some of their idiosyncratic determinants, and a few of the research approaches that can be used to select the most desirable strategy.

PRICING DECISIONS[2]

In many respects price can be viewed as an integral part of the product offering. The price

---

[2]For a more detailed discussion of pricing, see the pricing section of any introductory marketing text and the more specialized pricing books such as Palda (1971) and Monroe (1979).

of a product isn't just a way to establish the product's positioning; it also determines the available resources for the development and acquisition of the product features and is a prime determinant of the firm's profitability. From a consumer's point of view, price is not only the cost of obtaining a given set of product benefits but also a measure of the product's quality. This price-quality relationship is a well-established finding in consumer research, and is of major implication to the pricing decision of the firm.

The determination of the price of a new product is an extremely important component of the introductory marketing program. The pricing decision is especially complex given the wide range of pricing options and the numerous actors involved. The importance of the pricing decision has led a number of firms to remove it from marketing and keep it as a top management decision.

The pricing decision of the firm should not include only the actual price for the new product but also the price structure, taking into account the distribution outlets that are going to be used, the quantities expected to be sold and their timing. In addition, pricing decisions should not be limited to determining the introductory price, but rather should include a planned long-term pricing strategy incorporating price changes over the product life cycle. As discussed in Chapter 3, there are a number of scholars who argue that pricing objectives and policy should vary at different stages of the product life cycle.

To fully appreciate the complexity of the pricing decisions, their relationship to other product and marketing decisions, the key actors involved, the information required, and the various theoretical inputs to the pricing decision, let's examine Exhibit 13–2.

This exhibit suggests a number of pricing decisions:

Skimming versus penetration price   The high (skimming) versus low (penetration) introductory price alternatives have long been considered the two major choices for the pricing of a new product.

Premium versus commodity price   A related decision is the degree to which the firm wants to position the product as a commodity ("me too") product in the given category or get a premium price for it due to some unique positioning (benefits for the buyer/user).

Product line pricing   The determination of the range of prices for a product line and the price position of each product within the line versus the pricing of a single product (consider, for example, the pricing of the Kodak line of pocket instamatic cameras).

Price structure   The pricing structure involves two major decisions:

- A single comprehensive price versus a base price plus options;
- A unified price for all or discriminatory prices associated with minor product differences (within the boundaries of the price discrimination laws) allowing for price segmentation.

Promotional pricing   Retail deals and consumer coupons and cents off. Temporary price changes via these and similar means are an extremely important marketing mix strategy and are discussed separately under the promotion section.

Planned price changes   In contrast to temporary price changes, an important part of the long-term pricing plans of the firm is planned price changes. The planning of long-term price changes is one of the most difficult planning activities due to the large number of actors involved and factors affecting it. It is of special importance in inflationary periods.

EXHIBIT 13–2

PRICING MODEL

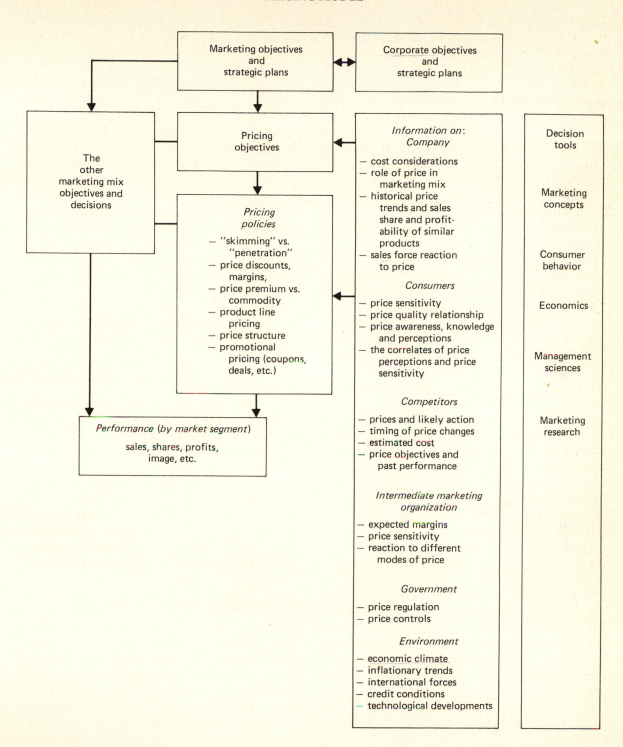

Marketing objectives and strategic plans ↔ Corporate objectives and strategic plans

The other marketing mix objectives and decisions

Pricing objectives

Pricing policies

— "skimming" vs. "penetration"
— price discounts, margins,
— price premium vs. commodity
— product line pricing
— price structure
— promotional pricing (coupons, deals, etc.)

Performance (*by market segment*)

sales, shares, profits, image, etc.

Information on:
Company

— cost considerations
— role of price in marketing mix
— historical price trends and sales share and profitability of similar products
— sales force reaction to price

Consumers

— price sensitivity
— price quality relationship
— price awareness, knowledge and perceptions
— the correlates of price perceptions and price sensitivity

Competitors

— prices and likely action
— timing of price changes
— estimated cost
— price objectives and past performance

Intermediate marketing organization

— expected margins
— price sensitivity
— reaction to different modes of price

Government

— price regulation
— price controls

Environment

— economic climate
— inflationary trends
— international forces
— credit conditions
— technological developments

Decision tools

Marketing concepts

Consumer behavior

Economics

Management sciences

Marketing research

Price discounts and margins Given the large number of participants in most marketing transactions, the price policies of a manufacturing firm should take into consideration the expected distribution structure and the expected margins of wholesalers and retailers. In addition, to the extent that special discounts are to be allowed either for quantity bought, early payment or other reasons, a discount structure should be determined.

These pricing decisions should reflect the pricing objectives of the firm, which in turn should be consistent with the marketing and corporate objectives and plans. In addition, the pricing decisions should take into consideration the other marketing decisions. This interrelationship between pricing and the other marketing decisions is illustrated in Exhibit 13–3.

In determining the pricing objectives and policies, six sets of information are required: information on the company (its cost considerations, production technology, etc.), consumers (their price sensitivity, price perceptions, etc.), competitors (their cost structure, likely pricing objectives and policies, etc.), intermediate marketing organizations (their price sensitivity, expected margins, etc.), government (price regulations, likely price controls, etc.) and the environment (the economic climate, inflationary trends, likely developments in related technological areas, etc.).

This information requires a considerable amount of research in terms of the organization and collection of the firm's own data, the search of secondary information sources (for government regulations, for example), the use of management's (and other experts) subjective judgment of likely events (such as competitor's likely pricing activities) and the undertaking of primary research activities.

Pricing research approaches vary in their accuracy of estimating price elasticity and their data requirements and cost. The "best" approach is field experimentation in which a firm follows an experimental design that allows the testing of a number of alternative prices and price strategies in a number of markets (or retail stores within a limited number of markets). Such experimentation can determine the "true" consumer price elasticity of a given product under real world conditions. An alternative approach for estimating price elasticity is ruled out for most new products, since it relies on econometric analysis of historical price and market response data. Occasionally this approach can be used on other products perceived by managers (or consumers) as being similar to the new product. If historical data on price, other marketing variables, and sales (and other performance measures) are available for an analogous product, managers can use the results of econometric analysis to measure the likely price sensitivity of the new product. The problem which is often encountered in this type of approach is that in many situations it is almost impossible to obtain *clean* price data. If managers believe that their product is sensitive to price, they are likely, whenever increasing the price, to accompany it with some compensating activity such as increased advertising, trade, or consumer premiums. Thus, the multicolinearity between price and the other compensating variables would preclude any conclusions concerning the relative importance of price (the price elasticity). A third approach to estimating price elasticity of a new product is via lab experiment. Lab experiments of the simulated test market variety (as discussed in Chapter 14) can often serve as a vehicle for estimating the price elasticity of a new product.

A problem associated with these approaches is the relatively limited number of price alternatives that can be evaluated. To overcome this limitation, conjoint analysis-based designs are often used to estimate the relative importance of various price options (levels and types) versus other product components. This use of conjoint analysis has been widely accepted for both consumer and indus-

EXHIBIT 13–3

HYPOTHESIZED RELATIONSHIP BETWEEN PRICING AND OTHER MARKETING
MIX VARIABLES

	Low (penetration) Price	High (skimming) Price
Product		
Type	Commodity	Noncommodity
Positioning	Me-too	Unique (commanding premium price)
Usage versatility	Limited	High
Importance of "quality" positioning	Low	High
Likely obsolescence	Low	High
Distribution		
Desired coverage	Intensive	Selective
Channel length	Short	Long
Expected inventory turnover	Fast	Slow
Advertising		
Expected level	Low	High
Uniqueness of message	Low	High
Promotion		
Expected level of retail and consumer promotion	Low	High

trial products. Some of the examples used in the previous chapters illustrate the type of output one can get from such studies.

PROMOTION

Promotion is an important component which, although often ignored in the marketing literature, is of great importance to marketing managers. In fact, many companies have a higher promotional budget than advertising budget. Promotions include a variety of incentives to purchase for both retailers (e.g., trade allowances) and consumers (e.g., coupons, cents-off, and premiums attached to a given product). Most of the conceptual work on marketing incentives has focused on the role of advertising, and to a limited extent on the role of price changes. Little attention has been given to the area of promotion. It is essential, therefore, to develop an understanding of how promotion works, the response functions for various types and levels of promotions, and the relationship between promotion's effectiveness and other marketing components, market and competitive conditions. The effectiveness of various promotional approaches has been established in a number of studies. A recent small-scale (and unpublished) study on a frequently-purchased product found that the response to a list price of 99 cents and 25 cents coupon was considerably higher than the response to the same product with the same positioning at 74 cents.

Promotion research should focus on assessing the likely response function to one promotional approach versus another as well as the relative effectiveness of the promotions in the context of the entire marketing mix. This latter criterion calls for both an analysis of the compatibility of a given promotion with the desired positioning and the distribution of the product, as well as the likely results of changes in the promotional mix of a new product.

Promotional response functions can often be viewed as having a short-term effect. In fact, it is often assumed that the primary effect of promotional efforts is to change the *timing* of sales—borrow future sales without an increase in the total sales of the product and increase temporarily the amount purchased. The upper panel of Exhibit 13–4 illustrates this case. There are, however, situations in which the promotional effort leads to a small increase in the total sales of the product (primarily in frequently-purchased products in which increased product usage is due to the product's availability). This case is illustrated in the central panel of Exhibit 13–4. Occasionally, a promotion can lead to an increase in sales due to both increased usage and the attraction of new customers. This situation is illustrated in the bottom panel of Exhibit 13–4 and is likely to occur only if the nature of the promotion succeeds in attracting a new market segment. An example for this can be a price promotion that attracts price-conscious customers who have not bought the product in the past or a segment responsive to a specific premium (pictures of baseball players as a "collection type" premium for kids). Such premiums can provide an incentive for continued use of the product (at least for the duration of the premium) attracting customers who are interested in the (free or self-liquidating) premium itself. Premiums are especially important for a brand with no other differential advantage over its competitors.

As with other marketing variables, such as pricing or advertising, the planning for a new

EXHIBIT 13–4

THREE HYPOTHETICAL PROMOTIONAL
RESPONSE FUNCTIONS

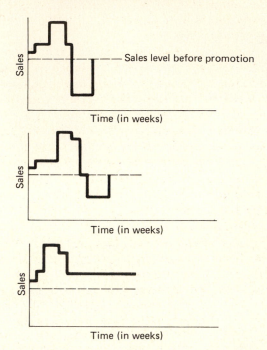

product promotion mix should not be limited to the initial promotional effort but rather should, at least in broad terms, encompass an entire promotional plan for the first few years after introduction. In many respects the promotional plan cannot be isolated from the pricing and advertising strategies of the firm and should be viewed as supplementary to them.

Consider, for example, the use of *samples* as an introductory marketing campaign. In most frequently-purchased products, the first and foremost objective of the introductory campaign is the generation of *trial*. Some of the most effective ways of generating trial are advertising campaigns, in-store promotions (product demonstrations and sampling, point-of-purchase displays and coupons), and consumer sampling. Although a combination of these and other marketing strategies is often called for, there are a number of firms which place most of their introductory efforts on one of these. In this respect samples, whether home delivered, introduced in stores, or offered via coupons, is considered an effective way of generating trial.

The use of samples is not limited to the introductory marketing campaign. Pharmaceutical companies often use sampling to physicians (either distributed by detailpersons or mail) as an effective ongoing promotional tool to stimulate prescriptions of their products. For certain products it was found, however, that an increase in samples lead to a decrease in the number of new prescriptions. This can be attributed to cases in which the physician, instead of prescribing the drug, gives the patient a full supply of samples.

The variety of promotional alternatives that can be used as part of the introductory marketing campaign of the firm is illustrated in the following partial list of promotional strategies:

Consumer promotions
- Product "discounts"—cents-off, coupons;
- Free product samples—miniature package, regular package, coupon for regular package;
- Premiums—self-liquidating (the consumer pays for them, a nominal price which covers their cost to the manufacturer) versus free, inserted in the package or obtained separately;
- Bonus packs.

Trade promotions
- Product discounts—trade discounts, promotional allowance, etc.;
- Free products—free demonstration products;
- Point-of-purchase promotional displays;
- Factory salespersons and demonstrators.

The range of promotion options (how large a discount, which premiums, when to offer it and for how long, etc.) suggests the need for a systematic approach to the generation and evaluation of the various options and selection of the most appropriate promotional mix. In selecting a promotional mix, the manager should take into consideration the same inputs discussed in the overall product/marketing planning model (Exhibit 6–1) and the considerations governing the pricing decisions (outlined in Exhibit 13–1).

ADVERTISING

Advertising has long been the thrust of the communication effort in the introduction of new consumer products and services. The introductory advertising effort is often viewed as the most critical marketing activity and it is not uncommon that a firm spends on its first-year advertising more than it can expect in total sales for the same period. In the cigarette market, for example, an introductory advertising and promotion campaign of over $100 million dollars is not an uncommon level of expenditure aimed at achieving a one-percent share.

The advertising mix for a new product includes a large number of decisions, subject to the same set of determinants as all advertising decisions.[3]

Advertising objectives   Determination of specific *advertising objectives* involves such questions as should the advertising campaign for the new product generate awareness, interest, favorable attitude toward the product, a unique image or trial? Or should it be aimed directly at the generation of repeat purchase (relying predominantly on sampling to generate the initial trial of the product)?

---

[3]For a discussion of the major advertising decisions and their determinants, see any advertising text such as Aaker and Myers (1975) or Longman (1971).

Advertising budget   The determination of the advertising budget is not an easy decision, and a number of approaches have been suggested in the literature for its determination (Longman, 1971). The task approach coupled with some intuitive guidelines as to the range of expenditures for the new product is often followed. These intuitive guidelines have often been based on industry experience (the levels spent by competitors) or in the case of more sophisticated companies, on an econometric analysis of the relationship between advertising levels and awareness, preference, and trial of similar products. Exhibit 13–5 illustrates some of these possible relationships.

EXHIBIT 13–5

ILLUSTRATIVE ADVERTISING RESPONSE FUNCTION

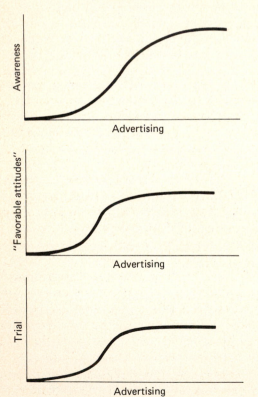

Advertising strategy   The third set of decisions requires the determination of an *advertising strategy*. This set of decisions is closely related to the positioning decision by market segment and is designed to establish the communication components. Strategy research can provide guidelines to the positioning by segment decision and also some initial guidelines for the development of copy executions. In fact, in many new product development systems prior strategy research provides most of the necessary information on positioning and the characteristics of the market segment most responsive to this positioning. In these cases no additional research is required at this stage and the advertising research can be limited to the generation and evaluation of copy alternatives.

Message design[4]   A given positioning can be presented in a variety of ways and the effectiveness of alternative executions has to be determined. The generation of a number of advertising messages (commericals and ads) has now been instituted as almost a regular procedure in the development of most new product advertising campaigns. The messages generated, however, are in most cases quite similar to each other. Minor variations rather than dramatically distinct approaches are often tested. This should be changed! In a number of cases in which drastically different executions (for a given positioning) were tested the range of results was very large. In one case, for a frequently-purchased product, the results obtained from three commercials in terms of a choice of the new product versus the brand currently bought were 12 percent, 19 percent, and 27 percent.

Similarly, in a recent direct-response mailing for a financial service, one ad execution

_____

[4]For an insightful discussion of message design considerations, see McGuire (1977), or Roman and Maas (1976).

pulled almost three times as many responses as another. These and similar findings suggest the importance of generating and testing truly distinct communication executions.

Message research involves consumer testing aimed at assessing the congruence of the message with the intended positioning, its communication ability, and its impact on likely consumer purchase behavior. Message evaluation can take a variety of approaches in a lab or real-world setting. In either case, it is important to determine the characteristics on which the advertising copy is to be evaluated—recall, attitude toward, intention to buy, or actual purchase of the product as well as the recall, attitude toward, and believability of the ad.

Media selection —The media mix should be designed to reach effectively and efficiently the target market segment(s) and enhance the advertising message via the media's editorial content. A variety of media selection models are available and have been used.[5]

A related decision which is often incorporated in the media selection decision is media scheduling. The media schedule should take into account the time response function to the introductory advertising, the time it takes to achieve the threshold and desired level of penetration among the selected distribution outlets, as well as the likely competitive reactions.

Advertising campaign Following the selection of the most appropriate components of the advertising program (i.e., best message, media, and scheduling), a capaign orientation should be taken to evaluate the entire *advertising campaign*. The design of an advertising campaign takes into account the likely interactions and synergistic effects among the various advertising components. As with the message or media decisions, this phase requires an explicit effort to generate a number of alternative campaigns, and a *systematic* approach for evaluating them. This evaluation is closely related to the overall evaluation of the effectiveness of the introductory marketing mix effort and can follow similar research approaches.

Most of these approaches require some form of real world experimentation (either test market or a market introduction following an adaptive experimentation scheme). Such experimentation allows for the testing of different advertising weights, scheduling, media mixes and the best mix of advertising and promotions (various types and levels of sampling, couponing, and point-of-purchase promotions, for example, versus different advertising mixes).

DISTRIBUTION

The extent and nature of distribution for a new product are among the major determinants of the product's acceptance and success. Distribution affects not only the availability of the product to prospective customers, but also the product's positioning.

Availability is often measured as the percentage of outlets (of a given type) that carry the new product. Yet, this is too simplistic a measure since it ignores the place the product occupies in the given outlet. Not all locations within a store are equal in their ability to attract customers. For frequently-purchased products, for example, a number of studies found that the end-of-aisle displays are considerably better (holding everything else constant) than regular shelf positions. Similarly, eye level shelf position is better than the bottom or highest shelf.

The type of store and the service associated with it—Saks Fifth Avenue versus Korvettes—

---

[5]For additional discussion of the media decisions, see Gensch (1973), Little & Lodish (1969), Aaker (1975).

is an important determinant of perceived image and positioning of the new product. The effect of distribution on brand positioning goes beyond the store identity and its services. The location of a product within a store can also determine its perception. In one experiment placing a new meat tenderizer in the supermarket section devoted to sauces led to one-third of the sales the same product enjoyed when placed adjoining the meat counter. Placing a dress in the basement of a department store, in the junior department, or in the better dress section might change the perception of the product, its acceptability, and its sales performance. These considerations are critical to the success of the new product's introductory effort and require careful attention to the distribution a new product is likely to achieve. In this context, it is important to remember that the distribution decisions, in most cases, are not totally in the hands of the manufacturer, but rather in the hands of a number of independent organizations. Distributors should therefore be treated as organizational buyers whose needs, attitudes, perceptions, preferences, and in particular, the criteria they use in making purchase decisions, are important inputs to the introductory marketing plan. In fact, the initial marketing effort should be directed at the desired retail outlets. It is not uncommon therefore to find manufacturers who have as one of their major objectives to increase the likelihood of product acceptance by distributors. Test market, undertaken under such circumstances, can be used to *demonstrate* the successful acceptance of the market rather than to *test* the "true" consumer reactions to the new product. The important role of the intermediate marketing organizations (IMOs) in determining the success of a new product is clearly illustrated in the hypothetical response function in Exhibit 13–6. It further requires the undertaking of two specifically designed research programs aimed at:

1. Members of the IMOs, to establish their perceptions and likely acceptance of and

EXHIBIT 13–6

ILLUSTRATIVE EFFECT OF EXTENT OF DISTRIBUTION ON THE RESPONSE TO A NEW PRODUCT

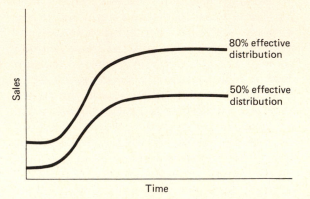

willingness to support and promote the new product;

2. Consumers, to establish the distribution outlets most compatible with the product's intended positioning, and most likely to be patronized by them for the purchase of the product.

In planning such studies, the research procedures employed are not unlike the ones used in product research discussed in other parts of the book. Research on retail buyers entails the same problems encountered in all organizational buying research—the identification of the organizational members involved in making the buying decision, and the assessment of the "organizational" responses when the members of the organizational buying center have conflicting preferences.[6] The measurement of the criteria used in making the purchase decisions, the perception of the new product, and the support likely to be given the new product are key aspects of research on IMOs requiring research

---

[6]For a discussion of the problems associated with organizational buying research see Wind and Thomas (1980).

methods such as conjoint analysis, MDS, and various multivariate statistical procedures. These methods have been used effectively to provide information and predict the IMO's likely response to a new product.

Similarly, when focusing on consumer research aimed at establishing the perception and acceptability of alternative distribution outlets for the purchase of a given product, the same research methods used for concept testing and positioning can be utilized. These studies (especially when based on conjoint analysis approaches) can establish not only the positioning of the stores but also the level of service desired for various product offerings.[7]

Distribution research is unfortunately one of the most neglected areas in marketing and whenever expansion decisions have been addressed, the traditional approach has been a focus on the product-market matrix. However, it is important to consider distribution as a third dimension since by developing new (store and nonstore) distribution outlets management can expand the market penetration of their product. Consider for example the case of an insurance company which traditionally sold only by direct mail. By expanding the distribution domain to include telephone solicitation and service, the scope of the marketing effort of the company increased and they achieved increased growth by attracting a new market segment which was not attracted to the (same) product when offered by mail but were responsive to it when offered in a different distribution outlet.

PRODUCT LINE CONSIDERATIONS

Rarely is a product introduced as a single product or as unrelated to the firm's existing product lines. Most commonly, new product introductions involve a product which is added to an existing product line or introduced as part of an entirely new product line. In both of these cases questions of cannibalization and synergistic effect should be addressed.

The cannibalization question is especially crucial if the new product has lower profitability than the established products. The likely magnitude and nature of cannibalization should be assessed and the positioning of the new product changed, if necessary, to minimize cannibalization. In fact, any product/market mix decision should take the likely cannibalization of a new product (or product line) into account, developing a new product (or product line) that will help maximize the *total* sales profit or share of the entire product mix (current and new products) and not just performance of the new entry.

Cannibalization by itself is not necessarily bad. In fact it might be planned to preempt a market positioning which otherwise might be the target for a competitor. The nature and degree of cannibalization should therefore be determined and evaluated in the context of the product/market portfolio of the firm.

A product line introduction has a number of important implications as to pricing, positioning, promotion, and distribution. Should the entire product line be available in each distribution outlet, or should the product line be divided among different distribution outlets? What should the price differential among items within the line be? Is each product in the line designed to meet the needs of a specific market segment? What is the positioning of the entire line and how are the individual products within

---

[7]For an example of this type of research, see Cacchione, Gross, and Wind (1977).

the line distinguished from each other? Etc.

Underlying these and similar decisions is the concern for minimizing the negative effect of cannibalization and maximizing the synergistic effects of the various products in the line. The key difficulty with this decision is the estimation of the likely cannibalization and synergistic effects. To provide management with accurate estimations of these effects there is no substitute for positioning information by segment which could reveal the perceived substitutability of the various products by use occasion and user type. Accurate positioning information could also reveal the likely market partitioning and consumers' response to a new product or product line entry.

MARKET SHARE CONSIDERATIONS

One of the major determinants of the marketing program, which has not received appropriate attention in the literature, is the market share position of the firm and, in particular, the unique needs of small-share businesses.

Market share, even though it has long been recognized as one of the important dimensions of a firm's product portfolio analysis, has not been considered explicitly in most of the marketing strategy literature. Yet, the strategy of a market leader should vary considerably from that of the number two brand or other small share brands.

The dependency of strategy on share position is evident if one examines, for example, the BCG portfolio model and the different implications offered by this model to low-share versus high-share products. The difficulties with the measurement of share, discussed at the beginning of Chapter 5, suggest, however, that the simplistic approach of relative share used by BCG does not offer the necessary insight and richness required for market strategy determination by share. The importance of share to the accuracy of a marketing strategy is clearly illustrated in Exhibit 13–7. In a large share position, the target area for the firm's activities is fairly large and any marketing effort, as long as it's delivered to the segment, cannot be considerably off the mark. On the other hand, in low-share products, the marketing strategy, in order to have any impact, should be extremely accurate and targeted at the bull's eye—the relatively small market for the given product. The importance of adjusting the marketing strategy to the share position of a product has increased markedly in recent years with the proliferation of brands within most product categories. There are very few product categories in which one dominant brand occupies over 50 percent of the market, such as Campbell's soup or Jell-o gelatin. Most product categories are going through a situation in which the average share of a product is less than five percent. Brand proliferation, which has been common in the cigarette market is now apparent in an increasing number of product categories. Shampoo, for example, has proliferated to the extent that

EXHIBIT 13–7

SHARE AS A TARGET

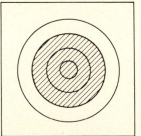 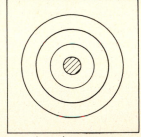

Large share target   Low share target

EXHIBIT 13–8

ILLUSTRATIVE MARKET SHARE DISTRIBUTIONS IN A NUMBER OF PRODUCT
CATEGORIES

Source: 1979 Simmons Market Research Bureau, *The Study of Media and Markets*

Deodorants & antiperspirants (female)

Almay	0.3%
Aramis	0.1
Arm 'N Arm	0.7
Arm 'N Hammer Spray	0.7
Arrid Double XX Aerosol	1.9
Arrid Double XX Roll-on	2.1
Arrid Extra Dry Aerosol	7.2
Arrid Extra Dry Pump Spray	1.7
Arrid Extra Dry Roll-on	6.6
Arrid Extra Dry Cream	2.0
Avon Dri 'N Delicate	3.3
Avon Feeling Fresh	2.8
Avon on Duty 24	4.4
Other Avon	2.5
Ban Basic	3.0
Ban Roll-on	19.1
Ban Spray	1.9
Ultra Ban Roll-on	4.3
Ultra Ban Super Dry	1.2
Ultra Ban 5000	0.8
Ultra Ban II	1.5
Body All	0.5
British Sterling	0.3
Brut	1.3
Calm	0.1
Dial Roll-on	3.0
Dial Very Dry	2.7
Other Dial	1.7
English Leather	0.5
Five Day Aerosol	0.1
Five Day Pads	1.3
Five Day Pump Spray	0.3
Five Day Roll-on	1.6
Fresh	0.7
Hour After Hour	0.5
Mennen Speed Stick	3.7
Other Mennen	0.6
Mitchum Aerosol	0.6
Mitchum Pump Spray	0.6
Mitchum Roll-on	3.1
Mum	2.5
Old Spice	2.6

Right Guard Aerosol	9.4
Right Guard Pump Spray	2.5
Right Guard Roll-on	3.8
Secret Pump Spray	5.6
Secret Roll-on	13.6
Soft & Dri Roll-on	3.5
Soft & Dri Spray	4.9
Sure Roll-on	6.4
Sure Spray	6.6
Tickle	6.1
Tussy	2.4
Others	8.1

Deodorants & antiperspirants (male)

Almay	0.1%
Aramis	1.1
Arm 'N Arm	0.5
Arm 'N Hammer Spray	0.7
Arrid Double XX Aerosol	1.5
Arrid Double XX Roll-on	2.5
Arrid Extra Dry Aerosol	6.6
Arrid Extra Dry Pump Spray	1.5
Arrid Extra Dry Roll-on	2.5
Arrid Extra Dry Cream	2.5
Avon Dri 'N Delicate	0.6
Avon Feeling Fresh	0.4
Avon On Duty 24	2.1
Other Avon	1.9
Ban Basic	1.6
Ban Roll-on	12.9
Ban Spray	1.9
Ultra Ban Roll-on	2.2
Ultra Ban Super Dry	0.6
Ultra Ban 5000	0.9
Ultra Ban II	0.8
Body All	0.2
British Sterling	0.9
Brut	6.8
Calm	0.1
Dial Roll-on	1.8
Dial Very Dry	2.0
Other Dial	1.3

EXHIBIT 13–8 (continued)

English Leather	2.5	Meister Brau	0.2
Five Day Aerosol	0.2	Michelob	13.3
Five Day Pads	0.5	Miller High Life	14.5
Five Day Pump Spray	0.2	Narragansett	0.2
Five Day Roll-on	0.4	National Bohemian	0.1
Fresh	0.3	Old Milwaukee	4.4
Hour After Hour	0.2	Old Style	1.3
Mennen Speed Stick	15.3	Olympia	4.8
Other Mennen	1.9	Pabst	7.9
Mitchum Aerosol	0.4	Pearl	0.3
Mitchum Pump Spray	0.3	Pfeiffer	0.2
Mitchum Roll-on	1.8	Piels Draft	0.5
Mum	0.8	Piels Regular	0.4
Old Spice	14.2	Rainier	0.8
Right Guard Aerosol	18.5	Red, White & Blue	0.3
Right Guard Pump Spray	3.1	Rheingold	0.9
Right Guard Roll-on	5.8	Rolling Rock	1.4
Secret Pump Spray	1.9	Schaefer	1.7
Secret Roll-on	2.9	Schlitz	8.5
Soft & Dri Roll-on	0.6	Schmidts	2.3
Soft & Dri Spray	1.0	Strohs	4.5
Sure Roll-on	2.9	Tuborg	1.7
Sure Spray	5.2	Utica Club	0.6
Tickle	1.3	Wiedemann	0.4
Tussy	1.4	Others	2.1
Others	4.3		

Domestic beer (in cans or bottles)		**Imported beer (in cans or bottles)**	
		Alt Heidelburg	0.3%
Altes	0.1%	Becks	2.2
Andeker	0.6	Carlsberg	0.9
Ballantine	0.8	Carta Blanca	1.5
Blatz	1.4	Harp	0.3
Budweiser	18.4	Heineken	11.6
Busch Bavarian	2.2	Holsten Lager	0.1
Carling Black Lable	0.9	Kirin	0.3
Coors	10.5	Labatt's Blue	1.1
Dixie	0.2	Molson Canadian	2.8
Falls City	0.3	Ringnes Special	0.2
Falstaff	1.4	Watney's	0.2
Genesee	2.2	Wurzburger	0.4
Grain Belt	0.4	X Beer	0.5
Hamms	1.6	Others	2.1
Heileman	0.6		
Iron City	0.4	**Ground coffee**	
Jax	0.1	A&P (Decaffeinated)	0.5%
Lone Star	0.5	A&P (Regular)	2.8
Lowenbrau	4.8	Brim	4.7

EXHIBIT 13–8 (continued)

Butternut	3.1	Heartland	1.9
Chase &Sanborn	3.0	Kelloggs All Bran	10.6
Chock Full O' Nuts (Decaf.)	0.9	Kelloggs Apple Jacks	8.0
Chock Full O'Nuts (Reg.)	3.5	Kelloggs Bran Buds	3.3
Edwards	1.5	Kelloggs Cocoa Krispies	4.3
Folgers Flaked	7.5	Kelloggs Corn Flakes	37.7
Other Folgers	21.1	Kelloggs Corny Snaps	1.0
Happy Medium	0.1	Kelloggs Country Morning	1.3
Hill Bros.	10.2	Kelloggs Cracklin' Bran	3.8
Luzianne	1.3	Kelloggs Froot Loops	13.7
Martinson	1.0	Kelloggs Frosted Flakes	18.4
Maryland Club	1.8	Kelloggs Frosted Mini Wheats	6.9
Max-Pax	1.0	Kelloggs Fr. Rice Krispies	5.4
Maxwell House ADC	13.2	Kelloggs Product 19	7.3
Maxwell House Mellow Roast	2.7	Kelloggs Raisin Bran	24.0
Other Maxwell House	13.1	Kelloggs Rice Krispies	27.7
Mr. Automatic	0.2	Kelloggs Special K	18.1
MJB	3.8	Kelloggs Sugar Pops	8.5
Sabro	0.1	Kelloggs Sugar Snacks	7.6
Sanka	9.9	Kelloggs Toasted Mini-Wheats	2.8
Savarin (Decaffeinated)	0.4	Kelloggs 40% Bran Flakes	7.6
Savarin (Regular)	1.7		
Yuban	3.4	**Toothpaste**	
Others	6.0	A&P	0.8%
		Aim	17.0
Breakfast cereals (cold)		Aqua-Fresh	3.1
Alpen	0.4%	Avon Smoker's Toothpaste	1.6
Boo Berry	1.4	Other Avon	0.4
Bucwheats	3.0	Close-Up Red	11.3
Cheerios	29.4	Close-Up Green Mint	3.2
Chocolate Cows	1.7	Colgate MFP	28.1
Cookie Crisp	6.1	Crest Regular	36.7
Corn Chex	9.7	Crest Mint	18.8
Rice Chex	11.9	Gleem II	8.3
Wheat Chex	11.2	Listerine	2.2
Cocoa Puffs	5.4	Macleans	2.8
Count Chocula	2.0	Pepsodent	7.9
Freakies	0.7	Sensodyne	3.1
Frosty O's	1.3	Ultra Brite Regular	6.2
Golden Grahams	6.9	Ultra Brite Mint	1.9
Granola (Pillsbury)	3.8	Others	4.9

today there are over 50 nationally advertised brands. The proliferation of brands seems to be a continuing trend. The capacity limit on the number of frequently-purchased products imposed by the number of brands that a supermarket, for example, can handle, has been increased and a typical supermarket built in the last five years has the size and capacity to deal with close to 12,000 products, compared to about 8,000 products in the 1960s and early 1970s.

The small-target market for most brands is further exemplified if one considers the 20/80 rule, i.e., 20 percent of the brand's customers probably account for 80 percent of the brand volume.

The magnitude of the problem, in terms of number of brands and their relative share, is illustrated in Exhibit 13–8, which summarizes the market share for brands with over one percent share in a number of product categories. It is interesting to note that these brands do not account for all sales in these markets, but rather, in each market, there is a set of even smaller brands competing for survival and growth. Market proliferation is a real problem! The arbitrary nature of the market definition for the products in Exhibit 13–8 does not detract from the severity of the problem. It is not very meaningful to think in terms of percentage of the total market and, for any given product a more specific definition of the served market would be helpful. Yet, most brands compete in more than a single market. Cereals, for example, compete in the breakfast, snack, dessert topping, and baking markets. Another way of looking at this is that any brand, even a major one (such as Campbell's canned soups), does not really have a very large share of the relevant use occasion (e.g., lunch market). A more useful share definition might be by a given occasion of use, as opposed to the total market.

What are the implications of the small-share position of most brands? An obvious implication is the need for much more accurate positioning and segmentation efforts. It requires a great concentration of effort on the potentially most valuable segment of the market. Furthermore, the brand does not have to appeal to everyone. Brands in categories with numerous small-share brands have the luxury of appealing to a relatively narrow market segment with unique benefits or problem solutions that would allow a clear differentiation of the brand from its competitors. Further implications of small-share include the timing and geographical distribution of the brand and the required marketing efforts.

THE OVERALL MARKETING PROGRAM

The focus so far in this chapter has been on four components of the marketing program, and (implicitly) their dependency on the product decisions of the firm. Before launching a new product marketing campaign, concern should be given to the interdependency among the various marketing mix variables, the various determinants of the marketing program, and the unique marketing program decisions. Exhibit 13–3 briefly illustrated some of the interdependencies among the various marketing mix components and the pricing decision. Similar analysis when conducted for all marketing components should reflect the idiosyncrasies of the firm, the product, its market, likely competitors, and various environments. Of particular interest in this context are the product line and market share considerations. The marketing program, not unlike other management decisions, is subject to a large number of factors (as highlighted in the Product/Marketing Planning Model discussed in Chapter 6). These variables should be considered in the selection of the most appropriate marketing mix that accompanies the new product introductory effort.

OBJECTIVES OF THE MARKETING PROGRAM

The new product objectives of the firm provide the guidelines not only for the new product development activities of the firm but also for the design of the marketing strategy for the new product (or product line).

These objectives determine the criteria for evaluating the new product performance. Of greatest importance is management's trade-off between short- and long-term performance, which affects the allocation and scheduling of the marketing resources.

The specific marketing objectives should be stated in operational terms and provide a basis for specific price, advertising, promotion, and distribution objectives.

LEVEL OF EFFORT—BUDGET

The determination of the marketing budget is conceptually no different than the budget determination of any other marketing function (such as advertising). Hence, any of the approaches to budget determination and allocation can be applied to the overall marketing budget.

The microeconomic rules for resource allocation[8] provide conceptual guidelines for determining the size and allocation of the marketing budget. Following this approach, and assuming perfect information, the optimal marketing budget is achieved when the marginal revenue from the marketing program equals

the marginal revenue generated from other programs and is equal to the marginal cost associated with the marketing activities. The allocation of the marketing budget among functions, products, programs, and markets should also follow this rule and the two processes of determining the marketing budget size *and* its allocation should be undertaken simultaneously. Given an optimal allocation, the ratio of the incremental response to incremental marketing expenditure is equal for all marketing activities. This ratio is equal to the marginal return (as measured in contribution to profits) of the last dollar of marketing expenditure. If this ratio is greater than one, additional marketing expenditures will result in a positive contribution to profits. The optimal marketing budget (if not constrained) is realized when the ratios are equal to one. If it is less than one, the level of marketing expenditures should be reduced. The incremental contribution for incremental marketing expenditures (contribution/cost) for each function, product, program, and market is simply the derivative of these functions.

When the marketing budget is constrained, the total net contribution may be *less* than that which can be expected under the unconstrained case.

The microeconomic approach to budget determination, although conceptually attractive, is based on the assumption of perfect information. In most cases, response functions for each marketing program are not known. The absence of this information constrains our ability to determine the optimal size of the marketing budget and its allocation. The major value of the microeconomic theory is thus not in providing an optimal solution, but rather in providing a *framework* within which to think about the marketing budget and allocation problem.

This "theoretical" approach ignores, however, most of the organizational considerations surrounding the *reality* of determining the size and allocation of a marketing budget. These

---

[8]See, for example, Mansfield (1970), Stonier and Hague (1957), Henderson and Quandt (1958), or any other microeconomic texts.

EXHIBIT 13–9

SOME ILLUSTRATIVE ADVERTISING SCHEDULES OF 1000 GRP IN A 10 WEEK
INTRODUCTORY CAMPAIGN

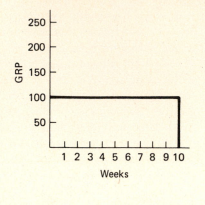
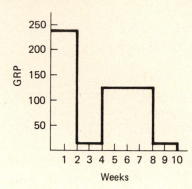
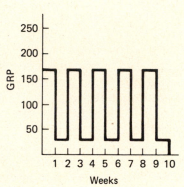
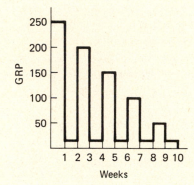

considerations include the role of marketing in the corporation (its relationship with sales, management, etc.), the characteristics (and power) of the decision-makers responsible for the marketing budget decision, the degree of centralization of the marketing function, the procedures for allocating marketing costs, etc.

Any budgeting approach, therefore, should take into consideration the following features:

- The marketing budget determination is a *process* involving a number of marketing and corporate participants.
- The processes of determining the size and

allocation of the marketing budget should be undertaken simultaneously.

- The marketing program and function managers should be involved throughout the process.
- Corporate management has a key role in the determination of the marketing budget and its allocation. They must assure an allocation of marketing effort consistent with their objectives for short- and long-term profitability and needs of current and future products.
- Management's assessment of a program's anticipated contribution to the firm's object-

ives (e.g., profits) can serve as a surrogate to the theoretical criterion for budget (or any resource) allocation.

TIMING OF EFFORT—SCHEDULING

One of the most difficult marketing decisions is the scheduling of the marketing program. The complexity of the scheduling decision is clearly evident if one considers the almost infinite number of possible scheduling patterns for any realistic set of marketing activities. Scheduling involves the order of introduction of the major components of the marketing effort and should address questions such as: Should sampling precede cents-off coupons? Should advertising precede the sampling? When should store product demonstrations take place in relation to the media advertising? In addition, scheduling requires the determination of the distribution of marketing effort (on each of these components) including the allocation of the advertising budget over media and time. Consider, for example, an advertising budget of 1,000 GRP (or another appropriate measure) and the numerous patterns one can employ for allocating it over the first ten weeks of a new product introduction. Exhibit 13–9 illustrates some of the possible patterns. Selecting the "right" pattern requires a good understanding of the nature of the response function and the nature, magnitude, and scheduling of the other marketing variables. (If, for example, 80 percent effective distribution can be gained after only eight weeks, the patterns in Exhibit 13–9 are not very sensible.)

The scheduling decision is further complicated by institutional constraints which restrict the freedom to design any conceivable pattern. In addition, since time can be traded off against monetary costs—most marketing programs can lead to faster responses if one is willing to pay the extra cost involved—an

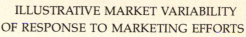

EXHIBIT 13–10

ILLUSTRATIVE MARKET VARIABILITY
OF RESPONSE TO MARKETING EFFORTS

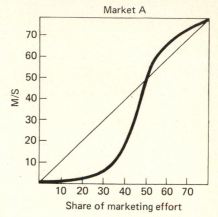

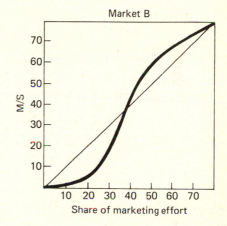

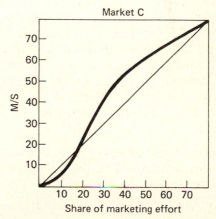

explicit time/money trade off for marketing activities should be undertaken as part of the budget determination and resource scheduling processes.

SPACE ALLOCATION OF EFFORT—GEOGRAPHICAL DIFFUSION

The scheduling of marketing activities cannot be limited to time scheduling but should also incorporate an explicit allocation of effort across space. Given the geographical dispersion of markets, a key component of any marketing program is the geographical diffusion of a new product. National introduction is not always the best way to introduce a new product. In fact, there are distinct advantages to carefully determining the order of entry into the various markets. To the extent that the marketing response functions vary from one market to another, the order of entry should take this into account. Assume, for example, an S-shaped response function. If the response function of the three sets of markets is as illustrated in the hypothetical functions in Exhibit 13–10, a firm with a given introductory budget would be better off allocating first to markets in the C cate-

gory, moving then to markets in the B category, and only then devoting resources to markets of category A. Furthermore, entry into markets in the A category would be feasible only to the extent that the company could marshall enough resources (over 30 percent share of marketing effort) to generate any positive responses.

An often-mentioned reason for national introduction is the economies of scale associated with a national advertising (and occasionally distribution) plan. Yet, the tremendous increase in media costs has changed the economics of national network time and in numerous cases a more efficient media budget is that which is based on local media (supplemented, to the extent necessary, by national network time).

Another reason for questioning the necessity of a national introduction is the geographical distribution of the target market segment. In many cases this distribution is not uniform across the country and a regional marketing plan can be more efficient.

These and other factors (such as the geographical distribution of competitive strength, and idiosyncratic regional characteristics) suggest that the geographical diffusion of a new product should be determined explicitly in each case, rejecting the notion that a *national* introduction is always the *ideal* pattern.

DESIGNING A CONTROL MECHANISM

The discussion in this chapter focused on the generation of a number of alternative marketing strategies and the evaluation of a number of their components (e.g., pricing, distribution, advertising, etc.). Following the testing of the components of the marketing mix, an overall marketing strategy can be designed which is to be further tested via test market or some of its

alternatives (as discussed in Chapter 14). The final marketing program also serves as the basis for conditional forecast of the likely performance of the new product or product line (to be discussed in Chapter 15). The final part of the development of a marketing program for the introduction of a new product involves the design of a control mechanism.

The objective of this phase is to develop a monitoring system to permit continuous evaluation of performance and adaptation to changing environmental factors. Such a monitoring system should provide guidelines for:

- Changing marketing strategy
- Product repositioning and modification
- Product deletion

The approach for the design of such a system involves four interrelated programs:

1. Design and implementation of an adaptive experimentation philosophy which allows for continuous assessment of the performance of various marketing strategies.

2. Continuous monitoring of consumers' (and other stakeholders') attitudes toward the firm and its products, their perceived positioning of the relevant products and changes in their needs, problems and other relevant attitudes and behavior. Such information can provide an "early warning" system for likely changes in product performance.

3. Design of a marketing information and control system which integrates and summarizes all relevant marketing information and provides management with an ongoing report on the current performance of its products and their associated marketing strategies. This performance evaluation can also be compared to the performance of competing products (e.g., changes in market shares, positioning, brand switching matrices, etc.) and historical performance of the brand and other similar products.

4. An ongoing economic evaluation of the product's performance.

CONCLUDING REMARKS

Having developed a new product and its associated components—the packaging, branding and various services—the job of marketing is the design and evaluation of a marketing campaign which lends itself to an adaptive experimentation philosophy and is consistent with the overall corporate objectives. As suggested in Chapter 6, the design of a marketing strategy for a new product should not result in a single strategy but rather include a number of contingency plans to deal with a number of future scenarios. The design of a marketing campaign encompasses most of the concepts, theories, methods, and substantive knowledge accumulated in the discipline of marketing over the years. Its essence, however, is the generation of a number of creative marketing strategies and their systematic evaluation. In this respect, the design of a marketing strategy for a new product is not dissimilar from the procedures followed in the design of a marketing strategy for existing products and services.

To better appreciate the scope and complexity of designing and evaluating a marketing strategy for a new product, select a product of your choice and list the marketing decisions that have to be made before it can reach the intended target market. Be as specific as possible and, for each decision, identify a number of alternative strategies (e.g., different prices, distribution outlets, etc.). Once you have identified these options decide how you would go about selecting the best integrated strategy and how you would implement it as part of an adaptive experiment.

14

Test Market and Its Alternatives

Introduction

Test Market Objectives

Performance Evaluation
Pilot Run
Test Market as a Showcase

Limitations of Test Market

Projectability of Test Markets
Transferability of Results
Competitive Retaliation
Cost Considerations

Design Considerations in Test Market

Test Market Selection
Test Market Experimental Design
Data Requirements for Test Market Analysis
Timing and Duration

Alternatives to Test Market

In-Home Use Tests
Central Location (Laboratory Simulation) Tests
Minitest Market
Regional Rollout
Adaptive Experiments

Selecting a Testing Procedure

Concluding Remarks

INTRODUCTION

Test market, the final stage in the new product development process, is often considered a necessary safeguard against the introduction of "wrong" new products. Many companies make test market a mandatory stage prior to the final approval of the national market introduction of a new product. Yet, more than any other stage in the new product development process, alternatives to test market are often sought. This search for alternative approaches is motivated by some of the more obvious limitations of test market and should be applauded as consistent with the need for continuous evaluation of research procedures and the search for new and better ones. Yet, the question whether test market can be abolished, and if yes, what alternatives can be considered, should be evaluated explicitly. This chapter is thus designed to discuss both test market—its objectives, advantages, limitations, and design considerations—and its major alternatives.

TEST MARKET OBJECTIVES

Test market is a *controlled experiment* which is conducted in a limited but carefully selected part of the marketplace. A "typical" test market of consumer grocery and drug product companies, according to a survey by Churchill (1971), involves three test market areas, lasts about ten months, relies predominantly on store audits, measures simultaneously a number of marketing variables, is conducted in a "normal" (not "controlled") market environment, and is undertaken primarily for new brands in an existing product category (only about one-quarter of all tests are conducted for new products in new categories). Test markets have two major objectives and occasionally a third. These objectives are:

1. To evaluate the performance of the new product and alternative marketing strategies. This requires the prediction of sales, profit, and other consequences (either in absolute or relative terms) of one or more marketing programs for the new product entry;

2. To serve as a pilot operation for the identifi-

cation of unanticipated problems associated with the introduction of the new product;

3. To serve as a showcase example for the "success" and appeal of the new product.

PERFORMANCE EVALUATION

The performance evaluation of the new product *often* centers around two major aspects:

a) The prediction of the sales, market share, and financial performance—profit, ROI, etc.—of a new product over time;

b) The evaluation of the feasibility and performance of alternative marketing strategies.

The test market stage is typically the first time in the new product development process that *all* the relevant marketing variables can be tested *together*. Alternative marketing strategies based on different combinations of packaging, pricing, advertising, trade, and consumer promotional and distribution mixes can be tested under realistic market conditions for a reasonable length of time.

To assess the performance of a test product and its associated marketing strategy (which can vary in terms of the type, level, and schedule of its various components), most test markets rely heavily on *store audits* which measure the product's sales volume and market share. These measures are often supplemented by a number of waves of consumer surveys, which measure the levels of and changes in consumers' awareness of and attitudes toward the test brand, the incidence of trial, the brands from which the new brand attracts its customers (the brand-switching pattern), and, most importantly, the repeat purchase pattern and volume. Assessing the repeat purchase probabilities of the new product and the expected level of purchase are critical components of the new product's performance evaluation, and require the establishment of a consumer panel in the test market areas.

Whatever the sources of the data used, the primary output of test market should be projected sales, profit, and share, conditional on the alternative marketing strategies under evaluation. These and some of the other performance measures which are often used in test market are summarized in Exhibit 14–1. To obtain such output, a prediction model has to be established to translate the actual results of the test market into projected annual national sales, profit, and market share. The design of a test market should therefore take into account the data that would be required as input to the new product forecasting model chosen by the firm.

It is difficult to translate the *absolute* levels of test market performance (with respect to sales, share, or profit) to expected performance of the total market unless historical data are available on the relation between test and national market performance for the given product type. If such data are not available, it is desirable for a test market to evaluate a number of alternative

EXHIBIT 14–1

SOME ILLUSTRATIVE PERFORMANCE MEASURES

Number and share of households aware of the product

Percent of households buying the product

Share among buying households

Number and share of households buying the product for the second, third, fourth, etc., time

Total volume sales

Share of volume

Volume per buying household

Share of volume by household

Volume per 1000 households

Total dollar sales

Dollar share

Dollar per buying household

Dollars per 1,000 households, etc.

Under a variety of marketing strategies and, if appropriate, different competitive reactions, these and similar measures can be assessed for:

Total market level

Market segments

Distribution outlet

Source of business (own products—canibalization vs. competing products), etc.

marketing plans which could suggest an effective *relative* measure of performance.

Furthermore, since the results of most test markets do not suggest a clear-cut and unequivocal "GO" (great success) or "NO GO" (a real failure) decision, it is important to set in advance the decision rules to determine which course of action to take. Some of the key options

EXHIBIT 14–2

SOME OF THE LIKELY DECISIONS FOLLOWING A MARKET
TEST

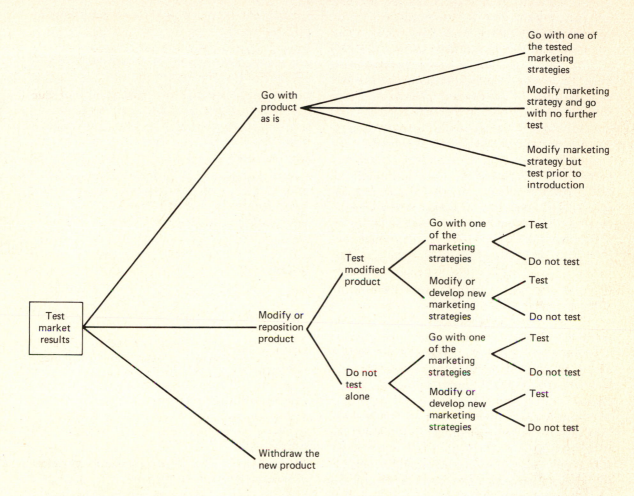

following a test market are illustrated in Exhibit 14–2.

Even with available historical data, whenever test market is used only to assess the likely performance of the new product the most one can expect is to find "if you have a loser, a medium success, or a giant success. It cannot fine tune a payout plan between a two share and a three share. It is useful, however, in telling us whether we will make our minimum" (Klompmaker, Hughes, and Haley, 1976).

Given this type of expected results, the reluctance to test alternative marketing strategies, the considerable direct and indirect costs of test market, and its other limitations, it is often used only as the last check before national introduction. In fact, it has been said that "when you go into test market, you've made the decision to go. The test market can, of course, alter your plans by giving you a no-go. But in the absence of bad results, you continue" (Light in Klompmaker, Hughes, and Haley, 1976). Yet in his survey of 54 test markets, Churchill (1971) found that 50 percent of the test markets fell short of management expectation (or the test market goals), 42 percent matched expectations, and in only 8 percent of the cases did subsequent performance exceed management expectations. Churchill suggests that this may reflect unrealistic test market sales goals, but this should be further examined in light of the evidence on the validity of test market, which is addressed in a subsequent section.

PILOT RUN

The second objective of test markets, especially for innovative new products, is to serve as a pilot operation aimed at locating unanticipated problems in the marketing of the new product as well as to provide training and experience in implementing the marketing strategy. As early as 1964 Achenbaum recognized this *managerial control function* of test market.

In stressing this function of test market Achenbaum offers the analogy of the pilot manufacturing plant which, despite its restrictive scope, can serve a very useful function by: giving management greater confidence in going ahead, permitting them to iron out unanticipated difficulties, allowing them to check out and undertake further research into specific elements of the operation, providing valuable experience while the risks are small, allowing the observation and training of the operational team, and offering some measure of the costs involved.

A test market can offer these benefits of a pilot operation with respect to all aspects of the marketing mix (and their interactions). The most critical area for such testing involves distribution—the securing and maintaining of the desired channels of distribution with effective display and promotion within them and the physical product logistics (involving shipping, stocking, breakage, etc.).

The second aspect of the marketing mix which can benefit greatly from a test market pilot operation is the advertising and promotion efforts of the firm and, in particular, the level and scheduling of these campaigns—those longitudinal and interactional elements which cannot be tested easily using non test market procedures. Yet, even the product and price decisions of the firm which most likely went through a number of pretest market research phases can benefit from a careful examination under more "natural" purchase, usage, competitive, and other environmental conditions.

TEST MARKET AS A SHOWCASE

Whenever management expects difficulties in obtaining the desired distribution for its new product, it faces the temptation to use test market as a showcase example. In this case, the real objective of the test market is not so much to help decide whether to "go" or "not go" with the new product or to test alternative marketing strategies but rather to achieve as much success as possible and use this "track record" as a major promotional tool for gaining the desired national distribution.

The desire to have a demonstrated success story is a legitimate management objective. Yet, it is quite dangerous to include it under the label of test market, since there would be pressure to select the area or areas most favorably disposed toward the product and the company. These areas are in most cases nonrepresentative, and no valid projections can be obtained from them.

LIMITATIONS OF TEST MARKET

Test market is often viewed as the last opportunity to "debug" the product and marketing plan of the firm, reduce the risk and costs of a mistake, and offer an accurate "fix" on the likely product performance. It does have, however, a number of serious limitations. These limitations should be weighed against the advantages of test market in determining the overall cost and value of undertaking this research phase.

The major limitations of test markets can be stated in terms of the following research questions:

1. Can the results of test market be projected to the national market?
2. Can the local plan be transferred to the national market?
3. What are the risks of revealing one's plans to competitors?
4. What are the costs of test market?

PROJECTABILITY OF TEST MARKETS

The major question facing the users of test market is to what extent the results are projectable to the national market. The AC Nielsen company compared the first year national and test market share performance of 50 new brands and concluded that "the odds are about 50–50 that the national performance will match test results within ±10 percent." Similarly, the (unpublished) experience of a number of companies suggests that having a "successful" test market does not guarantee in any way a national success.

The numerous reasons for the questionable projectability of test market results include:

Lack of representativeness of the test market areas No three areas of the country can be representative of the entire country. Geographical/climatic, population, economic, and legal differences among regions are often reflected in differences in consumers' attitudes and behavior, as well as differences in competitive and distribution patterns. This inherent diversity of markets was succinctly summarized by Zeltner in his commentary, "When Should You Market Test" (1977), who said, "the US is simply not a lot of Peorias added together." It is important to carefully select test market areas which are representative of the intended national market.

Questionable time projectability Even if test market results are completely accurate and projectable at the time of the test market, given that the national introduction is usually some time in the future, it is extremely difficult to accurately project the results of the national introduction from the test market results. Whereas all marketing research studies are subject to this limitation, it is especially crucial in test market if it is viewed as the most accurate test of "real" market performance. Competitive actions, for example, are rarely fully developed at the test market stage and may not be reflected in the test market results.

The representativeness of the marketing efforts of the firm and its competitors Even if the test market areas are representative with respect to consumer characteristics and their likely response to the firm's offerings, there are two other key aspects which have to be representative if the results of the test market are to be projected accurately. These factors are the nature of the marketing effort of the firm and its competitors. The marketing effort of the firm in a test market is rarely representative. Since everyone in a firm knows that "all eyes are on the test market" it is not unusual for managers to devote extra efforts to achieve and maintain a high level of effective distribution, design the best possible advertising schedule, and in general devote special attention and care to all of the marketing variables—attention that is rarely, if ever, achieved at the national level. These extra efforts tend to suggest an upward bias for all test market results, i.e., if a test market indicates a failure, it is likely that the product will not succeed at the national level (although there is no empirical evidence to test this hypothesis since no company is willing to go ahead with national introduction when the test market suggests a failure). Yet, on the other hand, if a test market indicates a "success" there is no guarantee that the product will actually achieve a market success. And, in fact, the high level of failure of new products (many of which were successful in test market) supports this contention.

TRANSFERABILITY OF RESULTS

Even if the results of test market can be projected nationally, a key question facing management is the transferability of results. Levels of spending in test market are often higher than the level that can be justified on a national basis. Given the different cost structure of operation within a limited number of test markets, it is often felt that such "extra expenses" are justified. Yet, this level of expenses (and the previously-mentioned added quality of effort under the test conditions) raises serious questions as to management's ability to transfer the results to a national scale.

The differences in the scale of operation between test markets and the national market is huge. It applies not only to the design, execution, and evaluation of the marketing strategies, but also to the actual product. Limited production for test market is usually done under tighter specification and control than possible in mass production for a national market.

COMPETITIVE RETALIATION

Introducing a product into test market announces your plans to the competitors and enables them to examine your product and marketing strategies, as well as monitor the success of your efforts. If the tested product does not have a patent protection or long technological or manufacturing lead time, the test market can lead to a loss of a valuable competitive advantage in the actual marketplace. Companies entering a test market can hardly expect to keep it a secret. A number of services and publications (such as *Advertising Age*) report on test market activities on a regular basis.

Knowing about a competitive test market allows a firm to monitor the performance of the competitor's product and develop and introduce its own similar product. Helene Curtis, for example, had a baking soda-based deodorant called Arm-in-Arm in test market. The results of the successful test market were noted not only by Helene Curtis, but also by Church and Dwight Company which introduced its own baking soda deodorant under the Arm & Hammer label, forsaking test market and beating Helene Curtis to the National introduction of the product. These and similar cases are not uncommon.

Furthermore, there is nothing to prevent a competitor from interfering with the actual test market operations, i.e., changing his marketing strategy to complicate the reading of the test market results. In fact, if a competitor is considering entering the market with a product similar to the one tested, it might be a sound competitive strategy to monitor the test market (by setting his own consumer panels). Once a conclusion as to the expected performance of the new product is reached, the competitor might engage in a number of retaliatory activities that restrict the ability of the test marketer to accurately read the response to the original test market efforts.

In a 1966 article in *The Wall Street Journal* (Stanton, 1966), for example, a number of quotes from knowledgeable competitors were presented to highlight the "spoiler" tactics employed in test markets. Consider, for example, the following:

- A supermarket executive in a frequently-used test market area:

  A competitive response and more often deliberate clearcut distortion by competitors is a far from unique accompaniment to the launching of a new product in test markets.

- A marketing manager of large household products:

  Competitors will do anything possible to muddy test market sales figures. They make special price deals on their own products with the stores, they expand their advertising heavily, and they'll even do things like yanking the number one brand off the shelves temporarily just to foul up sales comparisons.

The "jamming" or "spoiling" of a rival's testing is, according to this *Wall Street Journal* article, "a common and accepted procedure by most big marketers. Much of it is intentional, but some of it results from sheer jostling among many new products introduced at roughly the same time into a restricted number of test cities."

COST CONSIDERATIONS

An obvious drawback of test markets is their cost. The monetary cost for a year-long test in several markets (a typical design) was reported in 1967 to be in the vicinity of $500,000 (Stanton, 1967). Today, the cost of test market is often over $1 million, and in a few cases is reported to be closer to $1.5 million (Silk and Urban, 1976). These costs include the cost of a pilot plant to manufacture the product, all marketing expenses (advertising, couponing, trade allowances, etc.), the collection of marketing information, as well as the administration of the test. It is difficult to determine, however, the exact cost of a test market since it depends on the accounting procedures of the firm, particularly, the cost allocation rules. How, for example, is management time allocated to the test market? In most cases these internal costs are not calculated in the cost of test market. However, test market tends to attract more management attention than most other activities and therefore diverts management time without being accounted for. Another difficulty in accounting for the true cost of test market is the allocation of the cost of test manufacturing facilities in cases in which the test production costs are as high as those required for full mass production.

In addition to the direct monetary cost of test market, there are the lost opportunity costs which are reflected as *time costs*, i.e., the cost of both the delay in entering the national market and the loss of lead time which might be due to an early entry by a competitor who found out about the product, its marketing strategy, and performance in the test market.

Another long-term cost consideration involves *image and reputation cost*. If test market is a failure it may lead to the loss of reputation and credibility for the firm. This "psychological" cost should not be overlooked since the odds are that at least one out of two products in test markets will fail. These odds are quite consistent with the published record of test market performance. AC Nielsen, for example, reported a success ratio of 54.4 percent (of 103) and 46.6 percent (of 204) new health and beauty aids, household and grocery brands which were tested in 1961 and 1971, respectively. Similar experience was also reported for Cadbury with 60 percent success (Cadbury, 1975) and General Foods with 46 percent (*Business Week*, 1973).

The damage to the firm's reputation which a poor product can cause is especially serious if the tested brand is presented as part of a family brand. The damage of having a loser is not only among consumers but also among the trade who might be reluctant the next time around to distribute the product and promote it actively.

Another type of psychological cost is due to the effect of a test market failure on the firm's own personnel, especially the salesforce.

The real cost implications of a test market (even a successful one) on the salesforce is a major factor which often has been ignored. Any test market effort requires considerable efforts by the sales personnel. Given a limited number of hours per day, unless the company increases its salesforce (an unlikely move in most cases), salespersons are forced to devote less time to other products. In effect the test product cannibalizes the other products with respect to the salesperson's time and effort. This cost is rarely included in the direct cost of test market operations.

DESIGN CONSIDERATIONS IN TEST MARKET

Test market, whether undertaken as a pilot operation or as a vehicle to assess the market performance of a new product under alternative marketing strategies, requires careful planning and design. Exhibit 14–3 illustrates, for example, some of the steps recommended by the A.C.

EXHIBIT 14–3

A.C. NIELSEN'S RECOMMENDED STEPS TO SUCCESSFUL TEST MARKET

1. **Decide on the primary purpose of the test**   New product acceptance, promotional return, price revision, or some other basic question must be of predominant importance. The test should be designed to find an answer to a single major issue.

2. **Plan ahead**   Before entering the test market, develop a realistic, full-scale marketing strategy covering the entire area in which the product will eventually be advertised and sold. Set a price consistent with promotion and profitability needs.

3. **Set test goals based on the overall marketing plan**   If national sales of a certain level are necessary to assure success, set goals for the test at the same level.

4. **Seek the facts**   Be completely objective and realistic in evaluating the performance of your product or your advertising-merchandising plan.

5. **Benefit from comparative testing**   Since the purpose of testing is to evolve a successful marketing program, a single test permits no comparative evaluation. Whenever possible, test several products or plans in different test markets . . . so that a *selection* can be made of the *most profitable* plan.

6. **Profit from professional advice**   A call or letter to a firm dealing continuously with test marketing problems will not only provide much-to-be-desired objectivity, but will also help to avoid pitfalls.

7. **Select representative test areas**   Proper selection from the standpoint of size, geographical location,

EXHIBIT 14–3 (continued)

population characteristics, etc., permits results to be more closely duplicated on a regional or national scale. The test areas should also contain promotional facilities (i.e., television, radio, etc.) of the type contemplated for broader use later.

8. **Employ proper research procedures**   Budget adequately to permit accurate reporting of retail sales—at the point of sale where records are available and auditing techniques can be used. Allow the sample size and design to be determined by the test problem.

9. **Establish a test base**   Before the test is started, determine the individual and total sales of competitive brands. This provides a base against which subsequent changes may be compared and realistically appraised.

10. **Follow competitors' shares of market**   Some will hold established share, some will either gain or lose. Analyze those who are successful and locate their sources of strength. Ideas for improving your own strategy may evolve.

11. **Welcome exposure to competitive retaliation during the test**   This is the only way to tell how the product or plan will fare when normal competitive conditions prevail. Don't attempt to test in a vacuum.

12. **Examine retailer cooperation and support**   Are retailers carrying all package sizes . . . providing adequate inventory . . . conforming to prescribed pricing policies, etc?

13. **Wait for repeat sales after the initial purchase**   Is your share continuing upward, leveling off, or declining?

14. **Coordinate advertising and promotion**   Poor timing can result in loss of full dealer support.

15. **Avoid over-advertising or over-promotion during the test**   Don't do more in a test than you plan to do on a broader basis. This suggestion may need modification when tests are determining ultimate potential and staying power of a new product.

16. **Evaluate all possible sales-influencing factors**   (including those of competitors) such as salesforce, season, weather conditions, distribution, inventories, out-of-stock, days' supply, age of stocks, location in store, and shelf space.

17. **Avoid interference with the test once it is launched**   If the test involves television advertising, for example, maintain that media. "Changing horses" will inevitably confuse the test results.

18. **Adjust test findings to changes which occur during the test interval**   Take into consideration changes in the economy, any major change in the total market for the product, the competitive situation, retailers' reactions to the product or merchandising plan, and consumers' reactions to the product or advertising appeal.

19. **Allow the test to run its course**   Many tests require only six months for preliminary appraisal; others, as long as three years. Unusually strong positive or stong negative results permit earlier decisions, as do high-volume products with a fast use-up in the home—provided that full distribution can be obtained early in the test period. Low-volume products with a long home life usually require a longer interval for test results to become conclusive. Also, products with low distribution usually require a longer testing period.

Be sure to allow enough time for possible deterioration of product color or flavor, which might show up only after periods of two or three times normal shelf life. Allow also for merchandising and advertising to reach maximum effectiveness; many promotions need repeated impacts and the passage of time before they can be properly evaluated.

Above all, be patient—and don't be pressured into "getting into the market" before sales and market shares have stabilized . . . the test is completed . . . and its results analyzed.

Nielsen company to assure successful test market. Common to these and similar prescriptions is the focus on *planning* and five major design considerations, namely:

1. Selection of test market areas;
2. Development of an experimental design to test the effect of various strategy variables;
3. Identification of the data requirement for the analysis of test market results;
4. Determination of the timing and duration of a test market;
5. Development of a conditional new product forecasting model.

The first four of these considerations are discussed next, while the test market-based new product forecasting model, a key factor in determining the information required for the test market and its utility, is discussed in Chapter 15.

TEST MARKET SELECTION

The selection of representative and "matched" test market areas is an essential part of the design of any test market. Representativeness is crucial if the results of the test markets are to be *projected* nationally, whereas matching is a necessary condition for any reliable comparison of different treatments among test markets.

To achieve these two objectives it is desirable to avoid the arbitrary selection of a few markets (such as Syracuse, New York; Columbus, Ohio; or Sacramento, California) as test areas and to undertake instead a cluster analysis of cities (or other relevant units such as the US Standard Metropolitan Areas, the company's sales districts, TV markets, etc.).

Despite the obvious attractiveness and advantages of a clustering approach to the selection of test market areas, most companies tend to use fairly subjective decision rules. Cadbury, for example, chooses test areas based on factors such as "[their] own marketing activity, competitive activities, availability of stock, seasonality, the size of the test area in relation to the budget set for the product, the structure of the trade in the selected area, and the degree of anticipated retailer cooperation" (Cadbury, 1975). Other factors usually considered in selecting test market areas are the degree of testing activities in the given markets, the "typical" area population (avoiding nonrepresentative areas such as college towns), and the relative isolation of the test areas (no communication between them).

Using cluster analysis as the technique for the selection of test market areas involves a number of steps:

1. *Identification of the relevant units* of analysis (cities, SMAs, states, or even stores).
2. *Selection of the relevant dimensions* on which the units are to be clustered. The variables to be chosen depend on the product involved and the objectives of the test market. Exhibit 14–4 illustrates 14 variables, their measurement, and source of data which were used in one of the early applications of cluster analysis to the test market selection problem. Other variables often used in the selection of test markets include: availability of mass media for advertising, the isolation of TV markets from other markets, the availability of desired distribution outlets, and how closely the area approximates the national population mix with respect to some key demographic characteristics such as age, sex, and income.
3. *Determination of the clustering model* and algorithm and deciding on whether to standardize the data, weight the variables, decide in advance on the number of areas in

EXHIBIT 14–4

FOURTEEN SMSA CHARACTERISTICS USED IN CLUSTER ANALYSIS FOR TEST MARKET SELECTION

Reprinted by permission from P.E. Green, R.E. Frank, and P.J. Robinson, "Cluster Analysis in Test Market Selection," *Management Science*, Vol. 13, April 1967, p. B-392. Copyright 1967, The Institute of Management Sciences.

Charac-teristic number	Description of characteristics	Measurement units	Data source
1	Population	Thousands of persons	*Sales Management*
2	Number of households	Thousands of households	*Sales Management*
3	Retail sales	Thousands of dollars	*Sales Management*
4	Effective buying income	Thousands of dollars	*Sales Management*
5	Median age	Number of years	U.S. Census
6	Proportion male	Percent	U.S. Census
7	Proportion nonwhite	Percent	U.S. Census
8	Median school years completed for persons 25 years and over	Number of years	U.S. Census
9	Proportion of labor force unemployed	Percent	U.S. Census
10	Retail outlets	Thousands of outlets	U.S. Census
11	Wholesale outlets	Thousands of outlets	U.S. Census
12	Newspaper circulation of daily and Sunday papers	Thousands of papers	*Printers' Ink*
13	Television coverage	Thousands of homes reached	American Research Bureau
14	Monthly circulation of transit ads	Thousands of exposures	*Printers' Ink*

each cluster, and other clustering-related questions.[1]

4. *Selection of test market areas* based on the results of the cluster analysis. The results

can be presented in a number of forms as illustrated in Exhibits 14–5 and 14–6, and the researcher has to make three major decisions:

- How many test markets to select. For projectability, it is desirable to select at least one (and preferably two or more) test areas from each cluster.

- How many areas within each cluster to select. This decision depends on the number of alternative strategies to be

---

[1]The interested reader is referred to the clustering literature or the relevant chapters in Green and Tull (1978) and Green (1978a). For a detailed discussion of different clustering models and algorithms and related issues, see Hartigan (1975), Anderberg (1973), and Everett (1974).

EXHIBIT 14–5

RESULTS OF A CLUSTER ANALYSIS OF 88 STANDARD METROPOLITAN
STATISTICAL AREAS

Reprinted by permission from P.E. Green, R.E. Frank, and P.J. Robinson, "Cluster Analysis in Test
Market Selection," *Management Science*, Vol. 13, April 1967, p. B-396. Copyright 1967, The Institute of
Management Sciences.

Cluster number	City	Cluster number	City	Cluster number	City
1	Charlotte Nashville Omaha Oklahoma City Memphis	7	Birmingham Syracuse Tulsa Grand Rapids Youngstown	13	Peoria Davenport Richmond Fort Lauderdale Hartford
2	Bridgeport Louisville New Haven Rochester Toledo	8	Binghamton Knoxville Chattanooga Harrisburg Canton	14	Paterson Cincinnati Miami Portland New Orleans
3	Orlando Flint Shreveport Beaumont Mobile	9	St. Louis Newark Pittsburgh Cleveland Buffalo	15	Tampa Providence Jersey City York Wilkes-Barre
4	Jacksonville Wichita San Antonio Tucson Bakersfield	10	Springfield Worcester Albany Allentown Lancaster	16	Indianapolis Kansas City Baltimore Houston Washington
5	Dayton Fort Worth Columbus San Bernardino Denver	11	Dallas Seattle Atlanta Minneapolis Milwaukee	17	San Francisco Detroit Boston Philadelphia
6	Albuquerque El Paso Tacoma Salt Lake Sacramento	12	Phoenix San Jose Gary Fresno Wilmington	18	San Diego Norfolk Charleston Honolulu

Excluded from the analysis were the nation's three largest SMSAs—New York, Chicago, and Los Angeles.

EXHIBIT 14-6

HIERARCHICAL CLUSTERING OF THE 50 LARGEST SMSAS

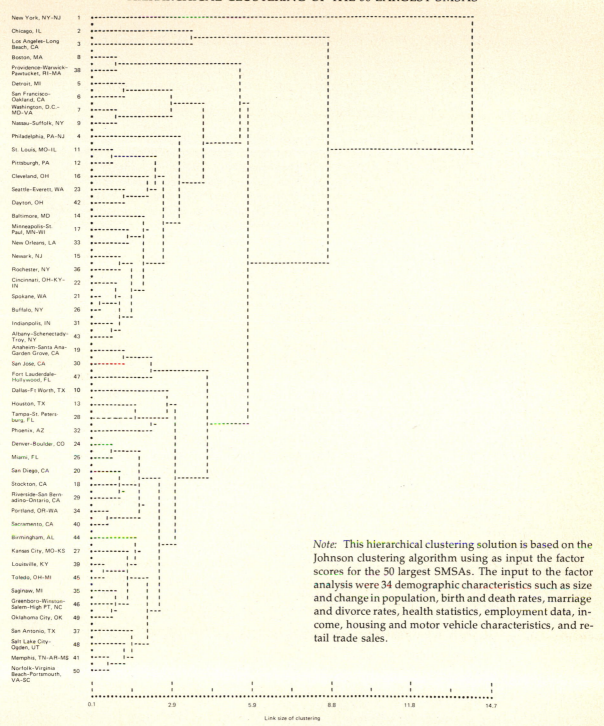

Note: This hierarchical clustering solution is based on the Johnson clustering algorithm using as input the factor scores for the 50 largest SMSAs. The input to the factor analysis were 34 demographic characteristics such as size and change in population, birth and death rates, marriage and divorce rates, health statistics, employment data, income, housing and motor vehicle characteristics, and retail trade sales.

EXHIBIT 14–7

BRIEF DESCRIPTION OF 12 MAJOR CENSUS GROUPS BASED ON ZIP CODE CLUSTERS

Source: Computer Cartography Inc., Customer Clusters: Taxonomic Relationships.

Group	Title	Number of clusters	Description
1	Educated elite suburban white family areas	4	Dramatically high levels of socioeconomic status as reflected in their college-plus educations, incomes in the top brackets and predominantly managerial and professional occupations. Suburban families with sub-teen and teenage children typify these areas. They purchase major appliances and automobiles at uniformly high levels. These clusters represent the "arrived" families at the top of the ladder of social and economic achievement.
2	Ascendant white middle class, mostly suburban	4	Middle to upper-middle class families with incomes at moderately high levels and college-plus educations. They consume major goods at a high rate, probably using debt leverage. Parents are young, in their thirties, and appear to have already risen a rung or two on the socioeconomic ladder or are about to rise.
3	Mobile middle class outlying areas	3	The only up-scale non-metropolitan areas. They are small growing satellite suburbs "beyond the beltway" or "new" towns. They bring in some of the rural non-farm populations in their areas but are, in general, fairly small communities.
4	City elite enclave with its support staff, singles areas	3	Found in the heart of the largest U.S. cities. Their residents live in high-rise rented structures and are typically small families or single primary individuals living alone. ZIPs are large in population size. Being dense, the ZIPs in Group 4 pick up some down-scale peripheral areas, but the "gold coast" aspect is obvious in high levels of top income, education, and occupational categories. College students are present in some abundance.
5	Ascendant middle class urban fringe factory areas	3	Peripheral metropolitan communities with dispersed new industrial plants accompanied by their labor pool of both skilled workers and second-echelon management.

EXHIBIT 14–7 (continued)

Group	Title	Number of clusters	Description
6	Middle class blue collar families, suburban areas	2	Predominantly suburban towns where manufacturing is the dominant activity. Typical neighborhoods have skilled operatives and craftsmen/foremen, not laborers. House values and incomes are mid-range, just below average to just above.
7	Lower middle to middle blue collar nonmetro areas	4	Manufacturing towns, but largely non-metropolitan and rural. Mining, lumbering, and various small industries support the rather down-scale families living in these areas.
8	Low income to poverty rural farm areas	6	Down-scale rural populations predominantly engaged in farming and rural industry. These vast non-metropolitan tracts of land are sparsely inhabited and, in general, contain components of migrant labor and small tenant farmers. They do not share in the general affluence of the metropolitan suburbs.
9	Suburban rural poverty areas with Spanish migrant labor	2	The "bottom of the barrel" as far as most indicators of socioeconomic status are concerned. They are the "left out" areas of the U.S., including Indian reservations, dust-bowls, and hard scrabble hill country.
10	Middle to lower middle blue collar ethnic urban areas	4	Characterized by high concentrations of foreign stock. They vary in components of skilled versus unskilled labor with concomitant variations in level of income. They are stable, older, and located in the "row-house" neighborhoods of large industrial cities.
11	Low income city and fringe blue collar areas	2	Typified by menial laboring low income and poor populations. These clusters are generally concentrated in the Northeast but range southward. They are distinguished from the ghetto clusters by the fact that they generally contain small to moderate black populations.
12	Black urban poverty areas	3	The culmination of black migration to central metropolitan areas. They are characterized by broken homes, poverty, unemployment, and the general syndrome of black urban deprivation.

tested. If two strategies are tested the researcher requires at least two areas from the same cluster (i.e., two areas "matched" on the characteristics used for clustering).

- Which areas to select from the various clusters. Here convenience, cost, and idiosyncratic considerations (such as competitive activities) can be the major determinants of the locations selected.

The procedure suggested above and the temptation of testing a number of alternative strategies would suggest a relatively large number of test areas. This appears to be in sharp contrast to current practice which, according to Churchill's (1971) review of 54 test markets, involves in most cases three or fewer test areas. The distribution of the number of test areas reported by Churchill is:

Number of test areas

1 — 21%
2 — 24%
3 — 22%
4 — 15%
5 — 7%
6 or more — 11%

A clustering approach to the selection of test market areas also can be employed at the zip code level. The Computer Cartography Corporation, for example, has clustered all US zip codes based on 71 demographic census variables into 40 clusters (each representing a type of community) which, in turn, were grouped into 12 major clusters. Exhibit 14–7 summarizes the major descriptions of these 12 groups. For test market area selection, one first has to select the desired group (or groups), then

zip codes within the selected group. The zip codes can be selected at random and are especially useful for mail testing of stimuli (e.g. products), the response to which is sensitive to demographic census characteristics.

TEST MARKET EXPERIMENTAL DESIGN

Test market is in essence a controlled experiment for testing alternative marketing plans. It should therefore be designed as an efficient experiment allowing for sufficient controls. In particular, experimental designs for test market should allow for testing the effect of *alternative* marketing strategies. If, for example, alternative advertising weights or messages are to be tested, a setting such as AdTel dual cable television in two markets, supplemented by controlled store distribution and audit and a continuing household diary panel is most desirable. Yet, whether one uses one of the available test market facilities or designs a tailor-made test market, it is essential to consider the number of alternatives to be tested, the need to read results with a certain level of statistical confidence, and costs. Test market design cannot be done, therefore, by management alone; it requires both managerial and design considerations.[2]

When approaching test market as an experiment, many of the typical shortcomings of test markets can be avoided. It is unlikely under these circumstances to go to test market only with a single marketing plan, since one can easily measure the effect of a number of alternative plans with no major increase in the required number of test market areas. Consider, for example, the case of a market test which

---

[2]For an excellent review of the experimental design literature, see Winer (1971).

measures only a single marketing strategy whereas at the same time one could use a Latin square design to measure with a small increase in the number of test areas the effect of three distinct strategies, such as three levels of advertising expenditures, three levels of a discount coupon, and three package designs. In fact, one can employ a Greco-Latin square design and with no increase in the number of test areas add another experimental variable such as the nature of advertising execution. Exhibit 14–8 illustrates these two simple designs.[3] Other designs which incorporate more variables and allow for the measurement of carry-over effects can and have been utilized (see, for example, Henderson, Hind, and Brown, 1961).

An important consideration in employing such experimental designs for test market is the fact that the experimental unit does not have to be an entire SMSA but can be a section of a city, a store, a group of respondents, etc. It is this flexibility, combined with the efficiency of experimental designs, that led the way to the development of various minitest markets and other test market alternatives.

In analyzing the test market results, ANOVA and MANOVA can serve as the primary analytical procedures. In addition, covariance analysis can be employed as a control for any market area differences not controlled by the test market selection procedure.

The availability of efficient experimental designs may increase the temptation to test a large number of variables. It is important to caution against over-testing at this stage since the addition of variables, even under the most efficient experimental design, does increase the number of required test units and, hence, the cost of the test market. This cost should, of course, be balanced against the expected value of the information gained from the test.

---

[3]Other designs are presented in Winer (1971) and Banks (1965).

EXHIBIT 14–8

ILLUSTRATIVE EXPERIMENTAL DESIGNS FOR NINE AREA TEST MARKETS

LATIN SQUARE DESIGN

A	B		
	1	2	3
1	C_1	C_2	C_3
2	C_3	C_1	C_2
3	C_2	C_3	C_1

GRECO-LATIN SQUARE DESIGN

A	B		
	1	2	3
1	$C_1 D_1$	$C_2 D_2$	$C_3 D_3$
2	$C_3 D_2$	$C_1 D_3$	$C_2 D_1$
3	$C_2 D_3$	$C_3 D_1$	$C_1 D_2$

Market area	Marketing strategy alternatives			
	A	B	C	D
1	1	1	1	1
2	1	2	2	2
3	1	3	3	3
4	2	1	3	2
5	2	2	1	3
6	2	3	2	1
7	3	1	2	3
8	3	2	3	1
9	3	3	1	2

DATA REQUIREMENTS FOR TEST MARKET ANALYSIS

To fully benefit from a test market, a "before-after" monitoring system should be designed and implemented to assess not only consumer reactions to the new products under alternative (types and levels of) marketing strategies, but also the trade reactions and likely competitive response.

The monitoring system should be designed to cover a long enough time period to enable the stable measurement of the repeat buying patterns and longer-term reactions of the trade and competitors. The typical types of data obtained from test market can include the following:

Store audits Typically 40–70 stores in a test area provide the information on product category sales before and during the test market period. The data most commonly collected include (for each package size):

• Brand sales and share
• Distribution and out-of-stock
• Inventory levels
• Type of display—wing, end aisle, stack, etc.
• Shelf position, location, level, and facing
• Point-of-purchase promotions
• Price and price deals
• Degree of cooperation and special problems, if any

Consumer purchase panels Consumer purchase panels provide the necessary input for any effort to establish the repeat purchase probability of the new brand. These panels can vary from 500 to 1,500 households who report all their purchases in the selected product categories via mail-in diaries. Data provided by this source include:

• Trial rate
• Repeat rate
• Depth of repeat
• Purchase frequency and cycle
• Source of business (cannibalization)
• Characteristics of target segments
• Response to various marketing stimuli such as sampling, coupons, etc.

Consumer attitude and usage study This study can be conducted in conjunction with the consumer panel or as an independent study. This is usually conducted as a telephone (or occasionally a personal) interview a number of months after introduction. Occasionally this can be conducted in a number of waves such as 3, 6, and 12 months after introduction and occasionally also as a preintroduction stage. Typical attitude and usage studies include information on:

• Brand awareness
• Advertising recall
• Benefits sought
• Brand trial and use pattern
• Attitude toward the brand and its competitors
• Brand likes and dislikes
• Socioeconomic, demographic, and psychographic characteristics
• Reactions (both attitudinal and behavioral) toward other marketing stimuli such as coupons, samples, etc.

Distribution check A study of stores to determine the number and type of distribution outlets which carry and promote the product. This type of study reports on:

• Share of outlet by type and size of outlet carrying the brand
• Selected store audit items

Test markets tend to use most of these data sources. In determining management's exact data requirements, it is important to give special attention to the following research issues:

1. Size and composition of sample
2. The sampling unit
3. The length of time during which data would be collected
4. The time unit involved—for example, daily, weekly, or monthly store data
5. The desired overlap among services

6. The exact information to be collected in each study
7. Design of a tailor-made series of studies or purchase of some of the available services such as AdTel's or MRCA's special test market panels, etc.
8. The operational definitions of the various performance measures (and their comparability across the various data sources).

TIMING AND DURATION

The timing of test market represents a major problem area. Ideally, test market should be conducted as the last check before a "go" decision is made, which clears the way to the necessary capital investment. Yet, because of long production lead time, it is not uncommon to find situations in which management makes the major capital commitment without the benefit of test market results. Such a decision increases management's creeping commitment to the introduction of the given product and raises serious questions as to the expected value of a test market.

The duration of test markets varies markedly. It is not uncommon to find a year-long test market especially if a number of strategy changes are undertaken during this period. The duration of test market depends on a number of factors and most importantly on:

• The purchase frequency (based on use cycle) of the product;
• The product's seasonality pattern;
• The number and nature of marketing strategy variables examined;
• The degree to which pretest market surveys to estimate the repeat purchase probabilities were used;
• The nature and impact of competitive activities;
• The results of the test market.

The longer the test market the higher management confidence in its results. Yet, longer test markets tend to increase the direct and indirect costs and the likelihood that competitors will evaluate the results and enter the national market earlier with a similar product. It is important, therefore, to design test markets that balance the two conflicting forces and avoid excessively long test periods.

The distribution of test markets by duration was reported by Churchill (1971) for 54 tests as:

Duration of test, months	Number of test markets
Less than 6	13%
6 - 8	28%
9 - 10	17%
11 - 12	22%
13 - 15	7%
16 - 24	7%
over 24	6%

The median duration of test markets in this survey was 9.6 months, but it varied markedly between controlled tests with 6.4 months and the normal (uncontrolled) tests with 11.3 months. Of interest is the fact that in only 47 percent of the cases the test duration was as planned. In 23 percent of the cases the test was suspended early (either because of exceptionally favorable or unfavorable results). In 30 percent of the cases, tests were extended beyond their originally planned duration, due to uncertainty about the nature of the results.

Analyzing consumer panel data to establish the trial rate and repeat purchase probability, and to forecast the expected sales levels is one of the major ways used to shorten the test period. Another procedure, aimed at the same objectives, is the dynamic (nonstationary stochastic) process suggested by Lipstein (1964). Lipstein measures the market's stability prior to the new product entry, the disequilibrium (in market shares) created by the introduction of the test product, and the market's return to stability. He offers an index of the stability (or volatility) of the market which provides rigorous indication of the impact of the marketing efforts (generating a high index of volatility) as well as an indication as to when the market has returned to stability. This return to stability is essential for an accurate evaluation of the brand's performance (avoiding the overstating of share which is typical if the measurement is taken too early). Applying this procedure to a number of test market situations has resulted in considerable shortening of the test period to "approximately one-half the usual length of time for test market using conventional methods of analysis" (Lipstein, 1968).

ALTERNATIVES TO TEST MARKET

The limitations of test markets have led to two major developments: (a) greater reliance on simpler and cheaper research procedures administered earlier in the product development process to answer many of the questions concerning consumer acceptance of the new product, its positioning, and other marketing variables; and (b) a number of alternative procedures for test market.

The focus of this section is on the major alternatives to test market. These include five types of procedures which vary with respect to the philosophy underlying them, the data collection procedures they involve, and their cost and time requirements. These five sets of procedures include: in-home use tests, central location tests, minitest markets, regional rollouts, and adaptive experimentation.

Whereas all five can be considered as alternatives to test market, the first three can also be used as a precursor stage to test market; i.e., given the high direct and indirect costs of test market and its other limitations, one may employ any of the first three procedures to help determine whether to "go" or "not go" with test market and then use the test market results employed to test a variety of marketing and to validate the results of the test market simulator. Yet, most test market simulators are product variables such as packaging, sampling, price, etc.

IN-HOME USE TESTS

In-home use tests were discussed in Chapter 13 as one of the major approaches to product evaluation. In a somewhat modified form this approach can and has served as one of the cheapest and fastest alternatives to test market. A number of research firms offer such tests combined with a market simulator, and a number of companies have been using them on a regular basis, either as a substitute for test market or as a precursor to one.

A prototypical in-home use test is aimed at assessing the new product's:

- Trial rate,
- Repeat purchase pattern, rate, and volume,
- Source of business for the new brand (e.g., cannibalization),
- Market segments most attracted to the new product,
- Perceived product positioning,
- Major strengths and weaknesses of the marketing plan; in particular, the effect of

the advertising, sampling, and price on the product's usage and share.

To provide input to these and similar areas of investigation, typical in-home use tests involve a before-after type design with one interview prior to using the product and one or more interviews following the product usage.

The sample   Typical in-home use tests are based on a stratified sample. Respondents are screened by telephone to determine if they meet screening criteria such as age, sex, and product usage. Those subjects who qualify and agree to participate are then interviewed personally. The sample is usually drawn from those (metropolitan) areas that were identified by the firm as their primary target market.

The first interview   Consumers who have met the screening criteria are personally interviewed. The interview begins by obtaining the respondent's purchase and usage behavior in the product class of interest. This includes questions relating to:

- Brand awareness and purchase,
- Frequency of purchase,
- Volume purchased of the brands bought in the past x weeks,
- Favorite brand(s),
- Benefits sought in product class,
- Purchase interest.

Having supplied the desired purchase and usage information, the respondent is usually shown a set of either final or rough commercials, on a TV size screen. The commercials usually include a test commercial (for the new brand in question) and a number (usually three) of competitive commercials. The order of the commercials is rotated to avoid order bias, and a number of test commercials can be shown by splitting the sample following an experimental design. If no TV advertising is planned for the product, the same procedure can be followed with magazine ads which can be presented either as a portfolio of ads or can be presented less obtrusively by tipping them into a magazine and asking the respondents to go over the magazine without directing their attention to the ads.

After exposure to the commercials, the respondent is given a sum of money, and a display of the products (with prices) is placed before her (him). The respondent is told that she (he) must buy one of the brands in the product category, but can keep the change and the product. Second choice preference is also obtained, along with reasons for brand selection. If the test brand was not selected in either of the first two choices, and if the firm is considering *sampling*, then those who did not choose the test brand get a free sample. This step of the interview usually includes a number of diagnostic questions concerning the respondent's reactions to the commercials and the advertised brands, as well as a short battery of background characteristics (demographics, socioeconomics, and attitudinal data).

The second interview   The respondent is called on the telephone and asked to answer a number of questions relating to:

- Usage of the test product (who used it, when, how),
- Reaction to the product, open-ended responses, direct comparison with brand usually bought on a number of attributes, and problems encountered in usage.

Next, the respondent is told she (he) can once again have a sum of money, and is asked to use it to buy one brand in the product category. The respondent's brand choice (the new brand, the brand usually bought, or any other brand) is the initial data for the calculation of the repeat purchase probability.

To facilitate the brand selection task, the interviewer can leave with the respondent at the conclusion of the first interview a set of photographs which simulate a supermarket shelf display. If such photographs are used, they help increase the realism of the response, since the respondent is reminded of *all* brands. Second choice preference is also obtained, and if the test product is not selected, the respondent's intention to buy the product in the future may be obtained. In all cases, reasons for brand selection are asked for.

The third (or nth) interview Subsequent interviews can also be conducted following the format of the second interview. Adding a third, fourth, or even fifth interview can increase management confidence in the accuracy of the prediction model. In these cases, the procedure is usually to predict the third choice from the first two data points. If the results are accurate, the study can stop. Alternatively, an additional number of calls is included. Each additional interview, however, requires the actual delivery of the selected product.

Data obtained from such in-home use tests are among the major inputs to a new product forecasting model aimed at predicting both trial and repeat purchase. In addition, the data from in-home use tests can be analyzed to provide diagnostic insights into consumers' acceptance of the product. These can include analysis and evaluation of brand-switching patterns, identification of the key demographic, psychographic, and purchase/usage patterns which discriminate between buyers and nonbuyers, satisfied versus dissatisfied users, etc., as well as an assessment of the perceived positioning of the brands by various segments (such as benefit or usage segments).

The major output from an in-home use test, however, is the forecasting of the trial and repeat purchase rates. A number of in-home use data-based forecasting models have been developed and implemented. The major features

of these models are quite similar and include not only the results of the study, but also a number of external inputs concerning the expected distribution, advertising, etc. An example of one of the available models is Robinson Associates' SPEEDMARK® model. The SPEEDMARK® model is a modified form of the Parfitt–Collins (1968) trial-repeat purchase model in combination with a computer simulation. The primary output of this model is a 24-month market share projection for the new product being tested. The general form of the model is:[4]

Estimated factory dollar sales = Retail sales = (Deal pricing effect × Distribution effect × Seasonality) × (Promotional trial + Advertising trial + Repeat purchasing) + "Pipeline" sales. The specific equations of the model are:

$$\text{Deal pricing} = D\left\{1 + CE\left[(P^*/\hat{P})^{1/2} - 1\right]\right\}_t,$$

$$\text{Distribution} = \frac{1}{100}\left(a - bA_t + cA_t^2 + dA_t^3\right),$$

$$\text{Seasonality} = \left[1 + G\left(\bar{S} - 1\right)\right]_t,$$

$$\text{Promotional trial} = \left[UBS^* \sum_{i=1}^{n} P_i T_i^*\right]_{t-m},$$

$$\text{Advertising trial} = \left[IUB\left(1 - S^*\right) \sum_{i=1}^{n} P_i T_i\right]_{t-q},$$

$$\text{Repeat purchasing} = \left[\sum_{j=1}^{24} {}_j R_{t-1} \cdot S_j\right]_t,$$

---

[4]The material on SPEEDMARK® is presented with the permission of Robinson Associates, Inc., Bryn Mawr, Pa.

where t = monthly time periods from 1 to 24,

i = major classes of potential consumers for the product,

j = repurchase occasions for the product among consumers who have made a "trial" first purchase, running from 1 through 24,

n = number of defined classes of potential consumers,

D = constant representing the product's factor sales price per "average" purchase unit,

C = proportion of national distribution outlets covered by consumer price-off promotional dealing of the new product,

E = coefficient of demand elasticity of the new product,

P^* = standard retail price of market leader at time of entry,

$\hat{P}$ = mean retail price of new product during consumer price-off promotional dealing,

a, b, c, d = numerical constants used to convert the effect on sales of product "availability" (i.e., its distribution level) from a linear function to an S-shaped curve,

A_t = parameter representing the mean national percentage distribution achieved by the product, through all consumer outlets,

G = sensitivity of new product to characteristic seasonal fluctuations of market category,

S = seasonal index of unit volume for market category,

U = proportion of new product's potential customer base already using one or more products in the market category;

B = parameter representing the aggregate potential consumer base for new product,

S^* = proportion of new product's potential customer base reached with promotional (sampling) activity,

I = parameter representing the "impact" or effect of the product's advertising (all media) in "priming" potential customers to "try" it under a specific projection condition,

P_i = parameter reflecting the proportion of the aggregate potential consumer base for the product represented by a single consumer class,

T_i = parameter representing the incremental "trial" inducement strength of the product among advertising "primed" potential customers,

T_i^* = parameter representing the incremental "trial" (i.e., first purchase) inducement strength of the product after having been subjected to promotional (sampling) activity,

m = subscript denoting arithmetic mean lag between application of consumer promotional activity and its impact in stimulating trial purchase,

q = subscript denoting arithmetic mean lag between application of consumer advertising and its impact in stimulating trial purchase,

$_jR_{t-1}$ = parameter representing the number of customers "qualified" (in terms of previous purchases) to make a subsequent product purchase,

S_j = parameter representing the probability of a customer making a subsequent purchase.

SPEEDMARK® via its computer simulator can further be used to assess the effects of variations in marketing plans (e.g., coupon introductions, shifts in advertising expenditures) and the effects of changes in product configuration (such as price, package size, or specific product characteristics).

This model has been applied to a variety of frequently-purchased consumer products and the reported results suggest a high predictive accuracy, not unlike the results of other in-home use-based forecasting models.[5]

CENTRAL LOCATION (LABORATORY SIMULATION) TESTS

"Laboratory" pretest market evaluation of new products is very similar in *concept* to the procedure employed in an in-home pretest market evaluation. The primary objective of such pretest market evaluation procedures is to simulate the awareness-trial-repeat purchase process using controlled laboratory and product usage tests. A number of commercial new-product laboratory tests are currently in operation. Yankelovich, Skelly, and White have offered a laboratory test market system since 1968. In its first ten years of operation, it has completed over 500 studies. Elrick and Lavidge offer a similar laboratory procedure under the name of the COMP system (Burger, 1981); Robinson Associates' SPEEDMARK® can be adjusted for central location tests; and Management Decision Systems, Inc. has developed the ASSESSOR procedure. Since this latter procedure is the best documented approach (Silk and Urban, 1978), it was selected as the illustrative approach for this class of research approaches and models.[6] In reviewing the ASSESSOR system, it is important, however, to note the great similarities among the various laboratory simulation tests. This similarity is evident if one examines the data obtained by some of the major procedures as summarized in Exhibit 14–9.

---

[5] For a comparison of SPEEDMARK and other simulated test market approaches see Robinson (1981)

[6] The discussion of the ASSESSOR model is based on Silk and Urban (1978) and the sales literature of Management Decision Systems, Inc.

ASSESSOR, as all pretest market laboratory simulators, includes two parts:

The laboratory   A simulated shopping environment in a large suburban shopping center is used to measure consumer attitudes and preferences toward specific brands in the test product's category. The packaging, advertising copy, retail price, and point of purchase strategy of the test product are all employed in a seven-step research procedure:

1. *Respondent Screening.* Potential participants are individually intercepted and screened for appropriate product category usage and desired demographics. Qualified participants are offered a modest cash reward to encourage participation.

2. *Initial Interview.* Participants complete a self-administered questionnaire measuring brand and advertising awareness and product usage, plus attitudes (measured on a seven-point bipolar satisfaction scale) and preferences (measured by a constant sum, paired comparison procedure) for their "evoked set" of brands. By asking consumers only about brands they really know, i.e., their "evoked set," more reliable measurements of consumer attitudes are obtained.

3. *Advertising Exposure.* Participants are shown advertising for the leading brands in the category and for the new product.

4. *Advertising Evaluation.* A short questionnaire measures each respondent's reaction to the advertising.

5. *Shopping.* Participants are given the opportunity to purchase a product in the category, using incentive money previously given to them. The shopping environment is similar to a section of a drug store or supermarket so that facings, shelf positions, and price can be controlled to simulate alternative strategies or duplicate the expected in-store situation.

EXHIBIT 14–9

A COMPARISON OF DATA OBTAINED BY VARIOUS LABORATORY SIMULATION
APPROACHES

		Yankelovich LTM	ASSESSOR	SPEEDMARK®
Before exposure to new brand	Proportion of consumers who buy any brand in category	Lab. store; questionnaire	Screening	Screening
	Brand and advertising awareness	—	Initial interview	Initial interview
	Product usage	Questionnaire	"	"
	Brand preference prior to exposure to advertising	Questionnaire	"	"
	Benefits sought in product class	Questionnaire	"	"
EXPOSURE TO NEW BRAND				
After exposure to new brand	Purchase of new brand	Lab. store	—	Lab.
	Reasons for buying or not buying product and new brand	FGI	—	Follow-up interview
	Reactions to product and advertising	Questionnaire and FGI	Follow-up interview	"
HOME USAGE				
After usage	Usage of test product (who, when, how)	Call back tel. interv.	Follow-up interview	Call back tel. interv.
	Reactions to product, satisfaction/ dissactifaction, evaluation on attributes	"	"	"
	Anticipated future usage	"	"	"
Other data	Size of product category and its rate of growth	Secondary Sources	—	—
	Share of existing brands	"	Initial interview	Initial interview
	Marketing activities and expenditures of existing brands	"	—	—
	Proposed marketing activities (advertising, distribution, pricing, etc.) for new brand	Management	Management	Management

6. *Home use.* Those who do not buy the new product are given a sample of it so that all respondents will have the opportunity to use it under normal in-home conditions.

7. *Follow-up.* Several weeks after the shopping center process, a telephone questionnaire, similar to the initial questionnaire, is administered focusing on: attitudes and pref-

erences for the new product, as well as the opportunity to make a mail order repurchase of the new brand, coupled with an intention-to-buy response (on a 5-point scale) for those who did not select the new product. These data provide the basis for estimating the respondents' repeat purchase probabilities and general reactions toward the new product.

The model Data compiled during the laboratory phase and in the callback interviews form the basis for the ASSESSOR model analysis. The model component comprises two independent analysis methods which, when merged, balance the final results and insure their reliability. The first of these convergent techniques predicts share as a function of consumer preferences before and after use of the product. The second bases its prediction on the trial and repeat rates under alternative marketing strategies as measured in the laboratory and in the callback interview. The primary objectives and output of ASSESSOR include:

- Long-run share estimates (based on both attitude and preference measures).
- Estimates of sources of business for the new product (including cannibalization) based on perceived similarities to existing brands.
- Diagnostic information on the positioning of the test product versus its competitors.
- A model structure for evaluating alternative marketing strategies.

The overall structure of the system developed to meet these requirements is presented in Exhibit 14–10. The critical task of predicting the brand's market share is approached through the use of two models which are similar in structure but are calibrated in different ways. Convergent results strengthen confidence in the prediction (although given that both models come from the same research design, the measurement input for both models is affected by common source of methods variance). Diver-

gent outcomes suggest the need for further analysis to identify sources of discrepancies and to provide bases for reconciliation.

The ASSESSOR estimation and calibration procedures are based on a number of steps (which are discussed in detail in Silk and Urban, 1976). The preference model is based on the earlier work of Pessemier and his colleagues (1971, 1972) (with respect to the predictive accuracy of brand purchases based on laboratory brand preference data), Luce's probability theory of choice (1969) (which provides the foundation for the link between brand preference and purchase probabilities), and McFadden's theory of population choice behavior (1970).

The expected market share for a new brand is estimated by the following ASSESSOR preference model:

$$M(t) = E(t)\frac{1}{N}\sum_{i=1}^{N} L_i(t) \, ,$$

where $M(t)$ = expected market share for the new brand t,

$E(t)$ = proportion of consumers who include brand t in their relevant set of alternatives,

$L_i(t)$ = predicted probability that consumer i chooses brand t after having tried the new brand

$$L_i(t) = \frac{[A_i(t)]^\beta}{[A_i(t)]^\beta + \sum_{k=1}^{m_i}[A_i(k)]^\beta} \, ,$$

where t = index for the new brand,

k = index for established brands, $k = 1, \ldots, m_i,$

$A_i(t)$ = estimated preference for consumer i for brand t after having tried the new brand.

Expected market share is thus a product of the evoking proportion $[E(t)]$ and the average conditional probability of purchase of the new brand $\frac{1}{N}\sum_{i=1}^{N} L_i(t)$ A similar procedure can also be followed for estimating the market share

EXHIBIT 14–10

STRUCTURE OF THE ASSESSOR SYSTEM

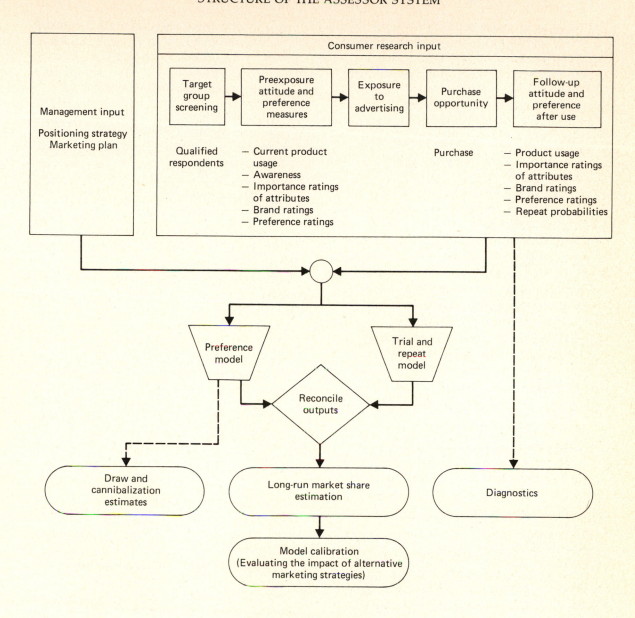

of established brands following introduction of the new brand.

ASSESSOR's trial-repeat model follows, to a large extent, the Parfitt and Collins (1968) approach—i.e., the estimation of the expected long-run market share is found by multiplying the trial and repeat estimates. *Trial* is modeled in the ASSESSOR model as:

$$T = FKD + CU - (FKD)(CU) \, ,$$

where F = long-run probability of a consumer making a first purchase of the new brand given awareness and availability of it (i.e., the percentage of respondents who purchased the new brand in the laboratory on their simulated shopping trip);

K = management judgment of the long-run probability that a consumer becomes aware of the new brand (as a function of the planned marketing action);

D = management judgment of the long-run probability that the new brand is available to a consumer (e.g., percent of retail outlets which will ultimately carry the new brand weighted by their sales volume in the product category);

C = management judgment of the probability that a consumer will receive a sample of the new brand;

U = probability that a consumer who receives a sample of the new brand will use it.

The *repeat* purchase rate is modeled as:

$$S = \frac{R(k,t)}{1 + R(k,t) - R(t,t)} ,$$

where the transition probabilities are defined as follows:

$R(k,t)$ = probability that a consumer who last purchased *any* of the established brands k will switch to the new brand t on the next buying occasion—the willingness to buy the new brand in the future by those who did not purchase it in the post-usage survey.

$R(t,t)$ = probability that a consumer who last purchased the new brand will repurchase it again on the next buying occasion—the proportion of respondents who make a mail order repurchase of the new brand.

Having estimated the market share based on both the preference-purchase probability model and the (structurally equivalent) trial and repeat purchase model, the results are compared as well as the structure of the models, i.e., the evoking proportion $E(t)$ is compared to trial T and the average conditional probability of buying the new brand $\frac{1}{N} \sum_{i=1}^{N} L_i(t)$ is compared to the share of repeat purchase S.

Lack of agreement between the evoking proportion $E(t)$ and trial T could imply that the assumptions concerning awareness K and retail availability D are not compatible with those made in estimating the evoking proportion. In comparing the conditional purchase probability and the repeat rate, it is important to note that effects of in-store promotional support are not represented in the repeat rate estimate derived from the post-usage interview. For product classes where substantial in-store promotional programs are employed, upward adjustments in these initial estimates of repeat rates are necessary and justifiable. Furthermore, an important assumption implicit in the formulation of the ASSESSOR model is that the frequency of purchase of the new brand will be the same as that for established brands. This assumption can, however, be relaxed by weighting the ultimate repeat rate S by an index that reflects the new brand's usage rate relative to that for established brands.

Overall experience to date with the ASSESSOR market share prediction model has suggested extremely high predictive accuracy as can be seen in the following six cases reported by Silk and Urban (1978):

Product	ASSESSOR's predicted market share (%)	Observed test market share (%)	Difference
Deodorant	10.6	10.4	+0.2
Antacid	9.6	10.5	−0.9
Laundry product	1.8	1.8 two 2.0 cities	0.0 −0.2
Household cleanser	12.0	12.5	−0.5
Shampoo	3.0	3.2	−0.2
Dishwashing product	9.3	8.5	+0.8

This high reported validity of a simulated test market procedure is consistent with the claims of all the commonly available services. The most extensive validation has been reported for Yankelovich, Skelly and White's LTM which has validated over 160 cases with 92 percent success—the LTM prediction closely matched results of the test market.

Pretest market laboratories have been conducted primarily for packaged consumer products—health and beauty aids, drugs, personal care products, food and beverages, and household products. Yet as early as 1966, Payne reported on a pseudo-store (simulated retail store) approach to the testing of consumer durables. The pseudo store was located in a shopping center to assess consumer response to a new TV set in circumstances resembling a purchasing decision situation; several brands of sets (the test and a number of control sets) were displayed and demonstrated to respondents recruited in the shopping center.

Such tests can easily be designed as a useful testing procedure whenever demonstration of a product is essential and the manufacturer has only a limited number of prototypes. In designing such pseudo-store tests, it is desirable, however, to place the respondent in an actual choice situation and not limit their involvement to an "expert type" evaluation of the various products.

MINITEST MARKET

Minitest markets have been conducted in a variety of ways. In their simplest form, minitests are an extension of a simulated test market. Charlton, Ehrenberg, and Pymont (1977) report on a UK minitest market based on a panel of households[7] which were visited weekly, and after exposure to a color brochure that displayed a set of available brands, were asked to place orders for brands from a variety of product categories which were immediately filled from a mobile van. This procedure allows for the assessment of the most sensitive indicator of a new product's potential success or failure—the level of repeat buying. In addition, the data provide the basis for calculating the cumulative penetration level (percentage of households who buy the brand at least once in a given time period) and average buying frequency (the average number of times the buyers buy the brand in the same time period)—the two key ingredients of the NBD model (Ehrenberg, 1972).

An analysis of minitest market data for five different product classes using Ehrenberg's (1972) NBD repeat buying model led to the conclusion that the brand choice patterns of the minitest panel for established brands "are generally like those in real life" in the sense of being consistent with models known to describe purchase behavior occuring under natural conditions.

The UK minitest market "was developed to bridge the rapidly widening gap between product testing on the one hand, with its inabil-

[7]The initial panel in 1968 consisted of 500 households; it was expanded to 1,000 in 1970 and to 1,500 in 1974.

ity to predict sales volume, and the area test market on the other, with its fast escalating cost. The aim is to expose a new product to test market evaluation, which means whether or not in a competitive environment consumers will pay real money for it, at a cost comparable with that of product testing" (Charlton Ehrenberg and Pymont, 1972).

The UK minitest market is used primarily for the evaluation of new products and measuring the effect, under controlled conditions, of alternative marketing activities. Although similar facilities are not common in the US, the concept of a minitest market is attractive and should not be ignored. In considering such tests, a number of modifications are feasible, such as the inclusion of procedures allowing for TV exposure (via portable equipment for showing either rough commercials or even final ones) or the utilization of *mail delivery* of products based on either mail or telephone orders from a special catalogue which includes the descriptions of the new test brands, with or without occasional direct mail or telephone advertising (aimed at simulating the effect of a real-world advertising campaign).

A second minitest market procedure is one involving *controlled distribution* in a set of stores with or without consumer purchase diaries. A number of such minitest markets are currently in operation in the US positioned somewhere between pretest market laboratory simulations and full-fledged test markets.

One of the better-known and most comprehensive minitest market procedures is the one offered by AdTel. AdTel City (located in the east central US), AdTel Midwest, and AdTel West offer three unique minimarkets, each with rigid controls over a real life consumer marketplace.

Specifically, the unique characteristics of the AdTel minimarket are:

• Each city utilizes a cable TV system which has been divided into two or more independent clusters of TV homes. The cluster-

ing is sufficiently dispersed throughout the AdTel market to insure population matching on demographics, life styles, and retail shopping behavior. AdTel has the ability to intercept inbound network or local commercials on time owned by its client and substitute alternative commercial treatments to each cable population. Thus, alternative copy, spending level, media scheduling, and other TV advertising plans can be tested in a single test city.

• Controlled store placement services are available for securing "instant distribution" on new products. AdTel covers 85 percent or more of the test area's all commodity volume in each AdTel market with its panel of food, drug, and mass-merchandising stores. Cooperating retail stores accept AdTel clients' new products on a guaranteed sale basis. Retailers will usually cooperate with new product placement and promotions when performance requirements are consistent with their normal trade policy. Using controlled store placements as a substitute for the company salesforce during testing has the benefit of shortening the test market duration and preventing loss of image among retailers should the product fail.

• A 2,000-family ongoing weekly consumer diary panel within each city. The panel allows the assessment of trial, frequency, and amount of repeat purchase as well as measures of brand-switching and cannibalization. Special diaries are set up whenever the regular diary format does not cover the product category of interest; and occasionally, for low-incidence brands and categories, the panel is supplemented with in-home pantry and medicine chest inventory checks.

• In addition to the real life and continuous television advertising and in-store promotions, AdTel minimarkets also measure the effect of alternative sampling, couponing, and other types of consumer promotions.

According to AdTel, their minitest markets produce tighter security against competitive measurement, controlled and accurate delivery of major marketing plan components, lower cost, and more timely and flexible testing procedure than traditional test market operations:

- The AdTel control stores are relatively few in number (25 to 50 per market), a laboratory-or pilot plant-produced product can be utilized without commitment of extensive capital expenditures often required to adequately supply larger test markets.

- The absence of syndicated sales reporting services in the AdTel markets and the tight security AdTel maintains over the location of its diary panel cable homes make it almost impossible for competitors to accurately determine what plan is being tested, or measure its effectiveness.

The AdTel minitest markets have been utilized in a large number of cases involving both packaged and nonpackaged consumer goods and services. The reported experience with AdTel minitest markets is most encouraging. As of January 1978, AdTel had reported on 73 new product tests. Of the 73 tests, 39 products were recommended to clients for national introduction, and 34 received recommendations against marketing with the plan that was tested. Of the 39 projected successes, all are currently in national distribution having achieved or exceeded the AdTel projected sales volume. Of the 34 projected failures, only one brand was introduced over AdTel recommendations to the contrary, and that product is no longer in national distribution. In a 1970–71 validation study, a comparison of the pound shares in the AdTel panel for seven new cold cereal brands with SAMI warehouse withdrawal data (as projected by Market Science Associates) showed a correlation of 0.79 between the two data sources at the national level, and 0.90 at the regional market level. The upper panels of Exhibit 14–11 compare graphically the

AdTel versus SAMI projections, whereas the bottom panel compares the results of AdTel and national panel data for a new food product for the first 32 weeks after introduction.

REGIONAL ROLLOUT

Regional rollouts have often been used as a "testing" step prior to national introduction. In this respect management intends to make the decision whether to introduce the product or service nationally based on the results of the regional introduction. In many of these cases, however, since the regional rollout does not follow any specific experimental design, it cannot offer any clearcut guidelines as to how the product or its associated marketing strategy can be improved. The results allow only the determination of whether the overall performance is above or below expectations. Even if performance in the given region exceeds the goal, the decision whether the product should move to the next region or be "killed" depends on the representativeness of the region and the ability to project the results from one region to others.

Regional rollouts, unless designed following a specific adaptive experimental plan, should not be viewed as testing, since projections from them to the national level suffer from the same problems associated with poorly designed test markets. The major advantage of a regional rollout is that it reduces to some extent the cost and risk of national introduction. Similar to test market, it does serve as a pilot operation, yet it suffers from all the limitations of test markets (competitive exposure, vulnerable trade relationships, etc.) without the benefits of a well-designed test market experiment.

Regional rollouts by themselves can offer very little information that could help improve the product, its positioning, or its marketing strategy. The major advantage of this approach is it reduces the cost and risk of entry and takes advantage of some special considerations (such as initially limited production capabilities, re-

EXHIBIT 14–11

COMPARISON OF ADTEL MINITEST MARKET RESULTS WITH REGIONAL AND NATIONAL PRODUCT PERFORMANCE

Reprinted by permission from "How to Test and Measure the Sales Effectiveness of TV Advertising," a brochure published in 1973 by AdTel, a subsidiary of Burke Marketing Services, Inc., Chicago, Ill.

AdTel. vs. regional SAMI projections: seven cereal brands

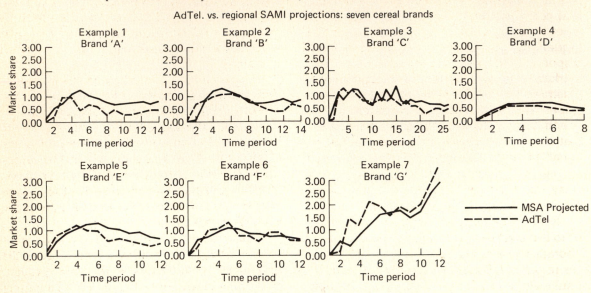

AdTel vs. national SAMI projections: four cereal brands

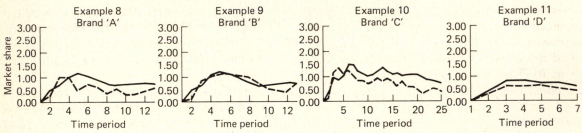

AdTel city vs. national dairy panel: New buyer development for a food product
Example 12

Four-week period after introduction	1–3	4	5	6	7	8
Cumulative Triers (% of total households)						
AdTel City	6.0	8.6	10.6	12.0	12.9	14.1
National dairy panel	6.2	8.2	9.7	11.1	12.3	13.8
Cumulative Repeaters (% of total triers)						
AdTel City	20.4	36.0	38.0	41.5	45.0	46.1
National dairy panel	N/A	31.9	37.5	40.6	42.0	42.2
Volume trial*						
AdTel City	9.9	13.8	16.4	18.8	19.7	21.3
Total U.S.	11.2	14.2	16.6	18.4	20.1	21.8

*Cumulative product class volume accounted for by cumulative triers

gional distribution, limited distribution and marketing capabilities, limited resources, or special competitive considerations). An important consideration in determining whether to enter the desired market (national or part of it) sequentially or simultaneously, is the expected response function of the various markets. If markets vary in their response functions, as illustrated in Exhibit 13–10, a firm with limited resources will be better off considering a sequential entry. In this context, one should note that many products never attempt to "go national" but rather are regional brands. For them a "regional" rollout will mean a sequential entry into their total market as opposed to a simultaneous entry into all markets.

Regional rollouts can serve a function similar to test markets if they follow some form of a laboratory test market simulation. In this case, the regional rollout can serve to validate the results of the simulated test market projections and as a testing ground for improving the marketing mix. Given the high cost and risks of national introduction, a regional rollout might serve as one useful way of reducing these costs and risks. The function of the regional rollout and its role in the overall testing procedure should be determined explicitly, however.

ADAPTIVE EXPERIMENTS

In contrast to a sequential entry (as suggested by a regional rollout), the idea underlying adaptive experimentation is to consider the entire market (whether a region or the entire country), but instead of entering it with a single strategy, which could provide few guidelines for future decisions, the adaptive experimentation approach (as discussed in Chapter 6) requires the generation of a number of alternative strategies and their simultaneous testing in a number of test areas.

Implementing an adaptive experimentation approach can be viewed as a large-scale test market operation which encompasses all or part of the target market. The advantage of such an approach is that if the entire market is included there is no lengthy delay and the product is actually introduced to the whole target market—whether a region or the entire country—but under a number of alternative marketing strategies.

Conceptually, such an approach is most attractive if previous research efforts suggest the desirability of introducing the new product (i.e., there is no doubt that a "go" decision is warranted) but have left a number of unanswered questions relating to decisions such as: what is the best level of advertising or distribution, what should be the nature and amount of premiums and consumer promotions, what is the "best" price, etc.

The major obstacles to the utilization of such an approach are often management (especially sales management) reluctance to accept the concept, and difficulties in implementing it. Direct-mail operations are especially suitable for such an approach and, in fact, it has been applied in this context as part of the new product testing and introduction efforts of a large direct mail firm.

SELECTING A TESTING PROCEDURE

Given the objectives of test market, its limitations, and the available alternative procedures, a key question facing management is whether to test market or not. In essence the question is more complex since management may decide to use both test market and one or more of the alternative procedures in some sequence. For example, one may start with a simulated test market procedure (either based on an in-home use test or a central location laboratory test), followed by a test market, followed by a regional rollout, followed by a careful strategy of adaptive experimentation.

In determining whether to use a test market, employ one of the other alternatives, or any combination of the above, it has been useful in a number of cases to formulate the problem as a decision tree. This approach was implemented, for example, by the Cadbury group (Beattie, 1969), who evaluated two options of "go to test market" or "go national" using a Bayesian decision tree. In reporting on the results of this approach, Beattie suggests, "the decision tree approach proved helpful as a rational way of relating marketing judgments to the sequential decision which had to be made."

Whether one uses the simplistic Bayesian decision tree or a more complex procedure such as risk analysis (Hertz, 1964) or a DEMON type model (Charnes et al, 1968) is immaterial. The key is that the decision to "go" or "not go" with a test market, and the specific sequence of research approaches to be employed should be determined not based on "habit" but rather on an explicit evaluation which takes into account the expected cost and value of the information to be obtained. The cost determination should include not only the direct cost of the testing procedure but also all the indirect costs such as lost opportunities due to the delay in market introduction, the cost of management involvement, the cost of introducing a poor product, etc.

The determination of the expected value of any given approach is even more complex and requires answering questions such as these:

- How projectable are the results of the simulated test market procedures? Most such tests are conducted in one or a very few locations, and the projectability of the results to the desired target market should be examined carefully.

- Does the testing procedure result in a conditional forecast? Most of the pretest market simulators such as ASSESSOR and SPEEDMARK® provide their estimated market share projections under a number of alternative marketing conditions. Mangement can, for example, change the level of advertising expenditures (which in the ASSESSOR model could result in a modified level of awareness and in the SPEEDMARK® model in a different parameter for the effect of advertising on "priming" potential customers), or the extent of its sampling program (which would, in the ASSESSOR model, effect the C and U parameters in the trial model).

Another approach to assessing the degree to which the expected results depend on changes in the marketing strategy of the firm and its competitors can be undertaken by a series of sensitivity analyses.

- How confident can management be with the results of the tests? Since confidence depends on the validity of a test, it is important to examine the historical performance of the tests. In examining the performance record, one should, however, go beyond the published, and usually excellent, validation examples and explore the experience with *all* known applications within the relevant product class.

In addition it is useful to increase the confidence in the results of the *specific* procedure under study (and not to rely on other cases). This suggests some sort of interim validation such as the one suggested for the Yankelovich Laboratory Test Market (LTM).[8] The first question in the LTM procedure is "Is the LTM producing relatively 'normal' data; i.e., does the use of

---

[8] The discussion of LTM, a business service of Yankelovich, Skelly, & White, Inc., is included with their permission.

the product category, as reported in the LTM background questionnaire, correspond to known usage data, and does the relative brand usage data, as reported in the LTM background questionnaire, correspond to known brand shares?"

- Have any adjustments been made to correct for any possible bias in the results of the various testing procedures? Most conscientious about such adjustments is the Yankelovich LTM which includes in its estimation procedures specific adjustments for novelty/salience and a judgmental corrective factor. The specific LTM estimation procedure takes the form of:

Estimated share
$$= S \cdot N_{(0.60-0.80)} \cdot C_{(0.25-0.75)} \cdot RUK,$$

where S = laboratory store sales;

N = novelty/salience factor which reduces the sales of the new product by 20 to 40 percent;

C = a clout factor which retains between 25–75 percent of $S \cdot N$ and is determined based on the proposed marketing effort (e.g., advertising, distribution, etc.) versus the advertising weights and distribution levels of existing brands in relation to their market shares;

R = repeat rate (LTM repurchase rate);

U = usage factor (calculated as the ratio of the new product usage frequency to the product category as a whole). This is based on the usage frequency for the new product versus other brands, the anticipated future frequency rate, the reported usage frequency of current brands among users, and the price differential;

K = judgmental corrective factor based on a comparison of the results of the preceding analysis with LTM

norm. This comparison is with respect to: the size and growth rate of the category, the shares of the key existing brands, and the proportion of the new product's share derived from category expansion versus conversion from existing brands.

The novelty/salience correction is designed to correct for exaggeration of laboratory results—the higher the novelty of the new product and interest in the category, the higher the laboratory effect in exaggerating sales. This correction is based on answers to the following questions:

- How does the proportion of consumers who buy anything at all in the laboratory store compare with norms?

- What is the nature of the reasons given for buying or not buying anything at all in the laboratory store?

- What are the types of reasons given for buying or not buying the new product in the laboratory store?

- Is there any evidence that the new product, after being bought and taken home, was not used at all because no function was found for it?

- Does the level of satisfaction/dissatisfaction with the new product suggest possible novelty/salience effects?

- Have the projected results been adjusted to take into account anticipated competitive activities or retaliatory activities? Some of the laboratory test market simulations allow for testing of likely impact of competitive actions. To the extent that competitive retaliation is expected, and not reflected in the results of the testing procedure, an appropriate adjustment should be made.

Guarding the results of any test market or alternative test market procedure against such possible test distortions should allow for more accurate answers to the following key questions:

- What is the expected performance of the new product in terms of market share and sales (based on estimates of trial rate, repeat purchase among the triers, the average number of units bought, the frequency of buying, and the trade acceptance and promotion commitment to the product)?

- What is the likely impact (cannibalization) of the new product on the firm's other products?
- What is the relative effectiveness of the various marketing strategy variables employed—the type, level, and schedule of advertising, distribution, promotion, etc.?
- Is the introductory marketing program operational and implementable?

CONCLUDING REMARKS

Even if the two major objectives of test market could be achieved, the decision whether to test market or not should balance the expected advantages against the costs and limitations of test market and its alternatives. In recent years considerable attention has been given to alternatives for test market procedures requiring a clearcut understanding of the decisions facing management—whether to select a product and marketing plan for national introduction, regional introduction, or alternatively, to decide whether to enter test market or not. In examining any of these and other relevant decisions, the obvious decisions of "killing" the test product or alternatively going back to the drawing board to redesign the product, its positioning, or its marketing strategy should not be overlooked.

In evaluating test market and its various alternatives, it would be helpful to remember Seymour Banks' (1964) comment regarding test marketing (which applies also to the other alternative test market procedures)—"implementation of test marketing means regarding the test market operation as a sample of geography, a sample of marketing effort, and as a sample of history. Sound decisions must be based upon a careful and detailed attempt to project those samples to the appropriate national populations. The process of making national projections requires integration of such data with all other information obtainable, both factual and conceptual."

Having considered the various testing procedures, management is often faced with another decision: whether to employ one of the currently available research services or develop an in-house procedure. The determination of this decision is not different from any other make-buy decision and requires a careful evaluation of the pros and cons of each of the procedures.

To further comprehend the various testing options and the conditions under which each of them is most appropriate, select a product or service of your choice and design for it an appropriate testing procedure specifying the information you would like to obtain and the conditions under which you would select a test market and/or alternative procedures.

New Product Forecasting Models

INTRODUCTION

A major ingredient of any new product development system is a model for forecasting the success of the new product or service. Such a model should provide management with a *set of estimates* (ranging, for example, from the most optimistic to the most pessimistic ones) of the *total volume* that would be bought by each *market segment* in each of the relevant *geographical areas* in a defined *time period,* with defined *environmental conditions,* and under a set of alternative *marketing programs.*

A variety of new product forecasting models have been developed over the years by both academicians and business firms.[1] The question facing the potential users of new product forecasting models is, Which model is the most appropriate for their needs? Answering this question requires both familiarity with the available new product forecasting models and criteria for their evaluation. The first sec-

tion of this chapter proposes a classification system of new product forecasting models. A set of criteria for their evaluation is presented in the next section, followed by a brief description of some of the more commonly-used new product forecasting models.

New product forecasting models should not be used only after completing the evaluation of the product and its corresponding marketing mix, but rather, forecasting of the potential results (sales, profits, and share) of a new product should be undertaken *at each stage* in the new product development process. In earlier stages, such as the concept testing stage, the forecast is by necessity tentative and broad. As management narrows its product and marketing options the forecasting task can and should be done more precisely, narrowing the range of likely results.

CLASSIFYING NEW PRODUCT FORECASTING MODELS

The proposed framework for the classification of new product forecasting models is presented in Exhibit 15–1 and is based on eight sets of characteristics—the purpose of the model, the type of products and services that can be studied, the unit and level of analysis, the model format, the dependent variable, the independent variables, the required data, and the analytical procedures employed.

---

[1]For reviews of some of these models, see Kotler (1971, Chap. 17) and Rao and Cox (1978). Some of the key models are reproduced in Wind, Mahajan and Cordozo 1981.

The purpose of the model   New product forecasting models vary considerably with respect to their objectives, such as the forecast of total market demand (i.e., ignoring the distinction between trial and repeat purchase) versus the forecast of first purchase (trial) (e.g., Eskin, 1973) versus the forecast of repeat purchases (e.g., Claycamp and Liddy, 1969). A second objective-related distinction among new product forecasting models is the use of the model for predictive purposes only (e.g., Ehrenberg, 1971) versus its additional utilization as a diagnostic tool that provides insight into the nature

EXHIBIT 15–1

A FRAMEWORK FOR CLASSIFICATION OF NEW PRODUCT FORECASTING MODELS

A. Purpose of model

Forecasting of aggregate market demand vs. trial or repeat purchase forecast

First purchase models vs. repeat purchase models

Prediction vs. prediction and diagnostics

Forecasting of total sales vs. weekly, monthly, quarterly, or annual sales

B. Type of products and services

Frequently purchased vs. infrequently purchased (durables, . . .)

New product vs. new brand in an established product class

Consumer vs. industrial products and services

C. Unit and Level of Analysis

Unit: Individual vs. household
        Consumers vs. units bought

Level: Market segment vs. total market

D. Format of model

Diffusion vs. adoption/behavioral models

Deterministic vs. stochastic

E. The dependent variable

Type of variables:

Brand choice (trial) vs. frequency of purchase (repeat) vs. quantity purchased

Brand sales vs. brand share

Number of variables:

Single vs. two or more

Type of scale:

Nominal-ordinal-interval-ratio-mix

F. The independent variable

Type or variables:

Time

Marketing variables—price, deals, advertising, etc.

Customer characteristics—situation specific (attitude, awareness, etc.) vs. general customer characteristics

Competitive activities

External environmental forces

Number of variables:

Single vs. two or more

Type of scale:

Nominal-ordinal-interval-ratio-mix

G. The required data

Type of data

Primary data vs. historical data on similar products (analogy)

Consumer response to actual product vs. response to concept description

Consumer responses vs. sales data

Test market vs. pretest market with an existing product (in-home use test, . . .)

Panel vs. nonpanel data

Data collection procedure—telephone, mail, personal

Number of observations required

Time and cost of data collection

Representation of sample

H. Analytical procedures

Simulation vs. analytical procedures

Parameter estimation across product classes vs. within a product class

One step vs. multiple-step approach

of the response function to various marketing variables and strategies (e.g., Claycamp and Liddy, 1969). In addition one can distinguish among forecasting models based on the forecast horizon—number of years forecasted—and the forecasting periods—weekly, monthly, quarterly, or annually.

The type of products and services covered New product forecasting models can be classified according to the frequency of purchase of the given product or service—frequently-purchased items (Claycamp and Liddy 1969) versus infrequently purchased ones such as durables (e.g., Bass, 1969; Brown et al., 1965; and Ryans, 1974). Whereas this distinction is quite arbitrary—products are bought at different frequency levels ranging all the way from every day to once in a life time—it does serve as a useful classification variable since it provides the rationale for focusing on single purchase behavior versus trial and repeat purchase forecasts.

A second aspect of the type of product involved is the *newness* of the product—whether the product presents a completely new product class or a new item in an established product class. In general, the newer the product, the greater the need to base the forecast on actual experience with, and usage of, the product. If an early reaction to a totally new product is desired (e.g., at the concept testing stage) the research design (and forecasting model used) should assure that the consumers truly understand the new product. This can be done by visual aids which "educate" the respondents. Finally, one may distinguish between consumer and industrial products and services. Given, however, that with the exception of conjoint analysis-based forecasting simulators, there has been a lopsided emphasis on forecasts of consumer products, the appropriate distinction should be the potential *applicability* of the model to the forecast of industrial products and services.

The unit and level of analysis New product forecasting models differ also with respect to the unit of analysis employed by them—whether it is the individual (e.g., Blattberg and Golanty, 1974) or the household (e.g., Lipstein, 1970).

A second distinction is between a forecast of the number of consumers (either individuals or households) and the number of units bought. This distinction is essential when consumers differ in their level of product usage. A meaningful forecast of the demand for a specific airfare for a flight across the North Atlantic, for example, is the number (and share) of *trips* and not the number (or share) of consumers preferring this fare, although the latter information can be important diagnostically.

In addition to the unit of analysis decision, it is important to determine the level of analysis—a market segment or the total market. The selection of the "right" level of analysis (including the level of segmentation) depends on the degree of homogeneity of the given market and the firm's segmentation strategy. From a diagnostic point of view, forecasts by segment are more helpful, and it is often desirable to compare the results one can obtain from a total market forecast with those derived from an aggregate of the separate segment forecasts.

Format of model New product forecasting models can be classified based on two sets of characteristics concerning their format:

The diffisuion versus adoption/behavioral nature of the model. Diffusion models are based on the forecasting of a *product's* life cycle function, whereas adoption models focus on the *individual's* adoption process of moving from a state of unawareness toward the trial of a new product. The distinction between diffusion and adoption was considered at least as early as 1962 by Rogers. Diffusion type models include a number of distinct models ranging from exponential models such as the Fourt and Woodlock model (1960), to the logistic (S-shaped) model such as the one used by Griliches (1967) and Mansfield (1961), through an epidemological diffusion model as described by Bailey (1957) and modified as a new product forecasting model by Bass (1969), to the reliability of engineering diffusion model which was utilized by Burger (1968) in his new product forecasting model.

The adoption/behavioral forecasting models, on the other hand, are based on explicating the adoption process with or without explicit inclusion of marketing variables. The DEMON model (Charnes et al., 1966, 1968) and the BBD&O NEWS model, as briefly summarized in Exhibit 15–2, are examples of forecasting models of this type.

Deterministic versus stochastic nature of the model. The stochastic nature of a new product forecasting model (see, for example, Nakanishi, 1973) can be expressed in the model's functional format, its assumptions (e.g., constant versus changing rate of repurchase), and the nature of the output—whether the output of the forecast is presented as a point estimate, as in most models, or as a probability distribution (discrete or continuous) of possible estimates.

The dependent variable New product forecasting models differ considerably in terms of the dependent variable they employ. Whereas some use brand choice (e.g., Eskin, 1974), others focus on the frequency of purchase (e.g., Herniter, 1974) or the quantity to be purchased (e.g., Hamburg and Atkins, 1967). Furthermore, while most models focus only on the forecast of a given brand's sales, a few employ a brand's market share as the dependent variable (e.g., Cima et al., 1973). Ignored here are models which do not use *purchase* (sale) mea-

sures but rather focus entirely on other consumer responses such as awareness or attitudes. Two exceptions, however, are (a) models which use a measure of consumers' *intentions* to buy a product as the sole dependent variable and (b) the more common case in which a number of purchase- and nonpurchase-based dependent variables are used. The most common (and managerially critical) of such variables are:

Awareness. The percent of consumers aware of a brand. This dependent variable measures the effectiveness of the introductory advertising and promotional campaign and often serves as the basis for calculating the percentage of triers.

Trial. The percentage of consumers who are aware of the brand and have tried it. Trial models often parallel epidomological models. Yet, in the introduction of a new brand, trial is not always a meaningful measure since the company can induce trial by heavy promotion and sampling activities. In this case, the more appropriate measure is the percent of consumers who *bought* the brand at least once. Occasionally, trial is measured by volume of sales (and not percent of consumers). Yet, this is a less desirable measure since the major objective of the trial measure is to assess the brand's penetration among the target segment. Occasionally, one might focus not only on the level of trial but on the *timing* of it, i.e., slow versus fast growth. Often this is a function of the frequency of purchase in the category and the total promotional activities (of the firm and its competitors). Yet, it is desirable to model it explicitly since it has major implications for the nature and schedule of the marketing mix associated with the new product introduction. Timing of purchase is also an important consideration in defining the respondent task in concept testing type studies. There is considerable evidence to suggest that the longer the time horizon con-

EXHIBIT 15–2

THE DEMON MODEL

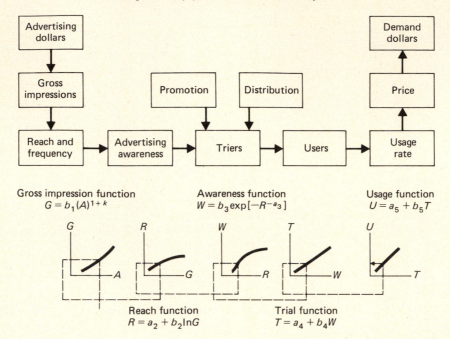

Gross impression function
$$G = b_1(A)^{1+k}$$

Awareness function
$$W = b_3 \exp[-R^{-a_3}]$$

Usage function
$$U = a_5 + b_5 T$$

Reach function
$$R = a_2 + b_2 \ln G$$

Trial function
$$T = a_4 + b_4 W$$

sidered by the respondents, the higher the stated likelihood of purchasing the product. Armstrong and Overton (1971), for example, found that on the average (across different price ranges for a given product—a minicar) the intentions to purchase the product within the next four years were 52 percent higher than those for purchasing it within the next 12 months.

Repeat. The percent of triers who bought the brand at least twice. Repeat buyers can include those who buy it on a regular basis and among this group, one can distinguish between those who satisfy most of their product class requirements with the given brand versus those who satisfy only a small portion of their total re-

quirements with it. Given this heterogeneity of the repeat phenomenon, one can often distinguish between repeat as a measure of the percent of triers who bought the product at least twice and their long run (equilibrium level) usage of the brand.

Intention to buy is commonly used as the dependent variable in concept testing studies and predictive models based on such data. It is essential, however, to validate the results of such models and establish the relationship between intentions and actual purchase behavior.

Other differences among forecasting models include the number of dependent variables employed (whether a single variable, a number of variables, or an index—such as a

EXHIBIT 15–2 (continued)

THE NEWS (NEW PRODUCT EARLY WARNING SYSTEM) MODEL

Reprinted with permission from *The Theoretical Basis of NEWS,* BBDO, Management Science
Department, 1971.

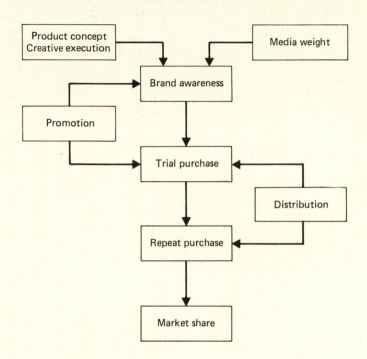

factor score—of a number of relevant variables), the operational definitions of these variables, and the measurement scales utilized in defining the dependent variable(s). (For a critical discussion of the measurement aspects, see Green and Tull, 1978.)

The independent variables   Five categories of independent variables can be employed in new product forecasting models:

Time. The simplest and most commonly used independent variable is "time." These models assume that future trends in purchases will not differ markedly from past purchases. In the new product forecasting area they extend the sales results of a test market to the future

using any one of a number of possible functional forms. Models in this category range from simple time series extrapolations to exponential smoothing and Markov chain analysis.

Marketing variables. Price, deals, advertising, in-store promotional activities, and other marketing policy variables have been incorporated in a number of new product forecasting models (Charnes et al., 1966 and 1968; Claycamp and Liddy, 1969; Massy, 1969; and Urban, 1968 and 1969a). Other models have ignored such variables and assumed some "average" marketing strategy. Some of the new product forecasting models that incorporate marketing variables are presented in Exhibit 15–3.

Customer characteristics. The adoption/behavioral forecasting models include as independent variables a number of customer characteristics. These characteristics are both situation specific (such as attitudes toward or awareness of the given brand, product category interest, occasion of use, etc.) *and* general customer characteristics (such as age, income, personality, life style, and the like).

Competitive activities. Only a few product forecasting models take explicitly into account the nature and magnitude of the competitors' likely activities and retaliation against the company's new entry. Yet, to the extent that such variables are included, as in a number of unpublished forecasting simulations, they have improved the predictive accuracy of the forecast. Information on likely competitive activities is often based on management's subjective judgment. Role playing (for a review of role playing in forecasting, see Armstrong, 1978) and analysis of competitors' past behavior can be used. In addition, conjoint analysis type concept and product tests often incorporate likely competitive actions as factors and levels allowing for a simulation of the effect of likely competitive activities.

External environmental forces. A few of the

EXHIBIT 15–3

MARKETING VARIABLES INCORPORATED IN A FEW ILLUSTRATIVE NEW
PRODUCT FORECASTING MODELS

Dependent variable	Independent variables of:			
	DEMON (Charnes et al., 1966, 1968)	NEWS (BBDO, 1971)	NW AYER (Claycamp and Liddy, 1969)	Leo Burnett Early Test Market Forecasting Model (Leo Burnett, unpublished)
Awareness of or knowledge about product	Advertising dollars Gross impressions Reach and frequency	Product concept Creative executive Media weight Promotion	Product positioning Media impressions Consumer promotion recall Category interest	Advertising weight (GRP) Past awareness level
Initial purchase	Advertising awareness Promotion Distribution	Promotion Distribution	Distribution Packaging Family brand Consumer promotion Product satisfaction Category usage	Price Awareness Past trial levels
Repeat purchase	—	—	Relative price Product satisfaction Repeat purchase frequency	Repeat rate Trial level Decay rates Trial usage rate Repeat usage rate

new product forecasting models explicitly include environmental forces such as economic conditions, cultural and social factors, or political and legal considerations. These variables are usually *assumed* under the model's stability over space and time. They are expected to be most important for any long run forecasting effort or when market conditions might change between the testing and the product introduction time. In these cases, as discussed in Chapter 7, the forecast should be undertaken under an explicit set of alternative future scenarios.

As with the dependent variables, forecasting models can and do differ, not only with respect to the type of independent variables employed but also with respect to the number of variables, their measurement (with and without time lags), and scaling properties.

The required data New product forecasting models differ considerably with respect to the data they require. A major distinction can be made based on the source of data used: whether it consists of what people say (e.g., study of buyer intentions or expert judgment), what people do (e.g., actual purchase in a test market), or what people have done (e.g., analysis of historical data). More specifically, models differ with respect to their reliance on four types of data:

1. Most new product forecasting models are based on primary research data. A few models are based on existing syndicated data such as MRCA, Nielsen, or Simmons, and a very few rely on historical data on similar products which serve as a basis for analysis by analogy.

2. Consumer response to an actual product versus response to a concept description. Whereas most forecasting models utilize data derived from consumers' response to an actual product, a few are based on consumers' response to concept descriptions. These models are further removed from the "natural" market environment, but at the same time have the advantage of being undertaken prior to actual product development and at a considerably lower cost.

3. Test market data versus pretest market data derived from in-home use tests or other consumer surveys based on actual experience with the product. The major distinctions between these two sources of data are the "realism" of the marketing stimuli, the length of time prior to introduction required for developing the forecast, and obviously the cost involved.

4. Sales response as measured for example by store sales (e.g., Greene, 1974) as opposed to consumer response data, especially purchase and simulated purchase (e.g., Blattberg and Golanty, 1974).

Other important characteristics of the data used in new product forecasting models are:

- Panel data (e.g., Ahl, 1970, or Barclay, 1963) versus nonpanel data (e.g., Bass, 1969, or Blattberg and Golanty, 1978).

- The specific data collection procedure—telephone, mail, or personal interviews.

- The number of observations required for parameter estimation. The models range from one observation per respondent in a consumer study to one-to-twelve months of sales data, or panel data on three or more observations per respondent.

- The cost and time required for data collection.

- The representativeness of the sample.

Analytical procedures Three major aspects of analytical procedures should be considered.

1. Should you use a simulation or an analytical approach? Most forecasting models are based on analytical procedures such as

time series analysis and a variety of (linear and nonlinear) multiple regression analyses. Some forecasting models involve simulations. These simulations can be used as the sole procedure or in combination with some other analytical approach. For example, some of the recent approaches for measuring consumers' evaluation of new products and services (via a conjoint analysis procedure) were coupled with a computer simulation leading to estimates of brand shares and brand switching patterns for the new products and concepts versus the established products.

2. Should the model parameters be estimated within a given product class (e.g., Ahl, 1970) or across a number of product classes (e.g., Claycamp and Liddy, 1969)?

3. And finally, should a new product forecasting model be based on a single step analysis (e.g., Herniter, 1973) or on a multiple step approach? A typical example of the latter type is the NW Ayer forecasting model (Claycamp and Liddy, 1969) which is based on three sets of submodels—a product knowledge submodel which is the input to a trial model which in turn is the input to a repeat purchase model.

CRITERIA FOR EVALUATING NEW PRODUCT FORECASTING MODELS

The importance of selecting an "appropriate" new product forecasting model is hardly debatable. The question, of course, is: What is meant by "appropriate"? Since there is no consensus as to the optimal characteristics of "appropriate" models, and new product forecasting models do differ on a variety of characteristics, it is essential to specify, based on the firm's information needs, what characteristics the selected new product forecasting models should have.

The obvious and most important criterion for evaluation of new product forecasting models is the model's actual performance, i.e., the accuracy of its forecast. Yet, this criterion often is of limited practical value in evaluating various new product forecasting models since most models are claimed (by their developers) to provide an extremely high level of accuracy. A recent survey of 151 companies conducted by the National Conference Board indicated that the median forecast error for individual product lines (not restricted, however, to new products) was around 5 percent. Assuming that two

models can predict equally well, the question is, What other criteria can management use in evaluating alternative forecasting models? Exhibit 15–4 presents proposed criteria for evaluating new product forecasting models, which include in addition to the predictive accuracy of the models the ability to develop and implement them and their diagnostic power.

The predictive accuracy To determine the predictive accuracy of a model, the user should examine not only the extent to which the forecast deviates from the actual product performance, but also:

1. The short- and long-run forecasting accuracy with respect to (a) the length of time and amount of effort required to *start* the growth stage, (b) the rate of market growth in terms of triers, repeat buyers, and volume, and (c) the level of penetration when the steady state stage is reached;

2. The ability to identify future turning points (reversals of trends);

3. The economic consequences of a forecasting error.

The major difficulty with these considerations, however, is the frequent lack of available information on the model's long-run forecasting accuracy and its performance in identifying turning points. Similarly, information on the cost of forecasting error is not always available. If it is, one can build into the model an estimation procedure that minimizes the cost of error.

A useful procedure for an initial validation of new product forecasting models is to test the model against case histories on past new product introductions. Although not a true validation, it does offer an early indication of the models' predictive ability. Such validation should be supplemented, however, with true

EXHIBIT 15–4

CRITERIA FOR EVALUATION OF NEW
PRODUCT FORECASTING MODELS

1. **Predictive accuracy**

 Short and long term
 Ability to identify turning points
 Economic vs. statistical evaluation

2. **Ability to develop and implement the model**

 Technical (mathematical, statistical, and programming) skills required
 Management acceptance
 Data required—type, timing, and cost
 Time required for model development, implementation, and maintenance
 Cost of model development, implementation, and maintenance

3. **Diagnostic power**

 Forecast for defined market segment(s)
 Forecast under defined marketing efforts
 Forecast under defined competitive and environmental conditions
 Assessment of uncertainty

validation efforts (on a set of data not used in estimating the model parameters).

Ability to develop, implement, and maintain the model In evaluating a company's ability to develop, implement, and maintain a forecasting model, concern must be given to the following factors:

1. Technical skills required for the development and implementation of the model, in particular the mathematical, statistical, and programming skills;

2. Management acceptance of (including ability and willingness to use) the model. This factor is frequently associated with the *simplicity* of the model and its "common sense" appeal;

3. The data required and ability to generate it within acceptable time and cost constraints;

4. The time and cost required for model development, implementation, and maintenance.

Diagnostic power In addition to these considerations, the diagnostic power of the model should be taken into account. Many new product forecasting models do not provide diagnostic insights into the relative impact of various marketing strategies on the anticipated product performance. Yet, it seems that a forecasting model in order to be of practical value should provide management with *conditional forecast* estimates, i.e., anticipated forecasts for each target market segment under various marketing strategies and alternative competitive and environmental conditions.

Recognition of the importance of the diagnostic power of new product forecasting models is increasing and evident, for example, in a number of attempts to modify existing models to incorporate in them a conditional forecast feature (e.g., Eskin, 1974, and Nakanishi, 1973) or take into account alternative competitive actions (Kotler, 1971). Exhibit 15–5 illustrates two types of conditional

EXHIBIT 15–5

ILLUSTRATIVE CONDITIONAL FORECASTS

Forecasts conditional on marketing effort

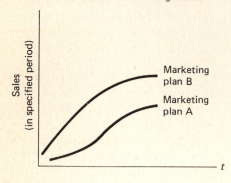

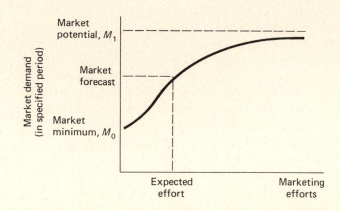

Forecasts conditional on marketing environment

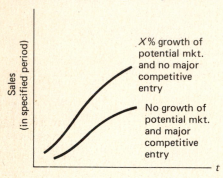

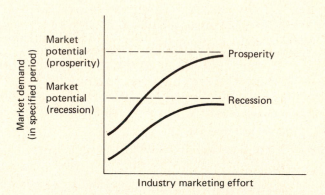

forecasts—forecasts conditional on (a) different marketing strategies (top panel of Exhibit 15–5) and (b) forecasts conditional on different assumptions concerning critical exogenous variables such as market growth, competitive reactions, and government interventions. Some of these effects are illustrated in the bottom panel of Exhibit 15–5. In all of these cases, one obviously should be concerned with the accuracy of the diagnostic power of the model.

Whereas forecasts conditional on the firm's marketing efforts are relatively straightforward and can be estimated quite accurately by conjoint analysis-based simulators and test market data, the incorporation of competitive effects and effects of other participants in the marketing system (such as retailers) is much more complex.

Competitive date of entry, type and level of marketing effort can have a major impact on the performance of a new product. The competitive effect can be treated in three major ways:

1. Separate estimation of the market demand (taking into consideration that the market demand is also a function of the marketing effort of the firm and its likely competitors) and the market share the firm is likely to obtain;

2. Incorporating in a new product forecasting model competitive interaction parameters, such as the market penetration coefficients of each likely competitor;

3. Simultaneous estimation of the likely performance of the firm's new product and the competitors' performance given various competitive reactions.

The competitive considerations should not be limited, however, to the forecasting of the likely competitive impact on the firm's new product performance and should be extended to an examination of their impact on decisions such as:

• The timing of the firm's new product introduction and its impact on the cost and timing of the new product development process;

• The positioning of the new product and its associated marketing strategy.

Many new product forecasting models either ignore the distribution variable or include it, as in the NW Ayer New Product Model, as one of the variables affecting trial. Yet, at times it might be desirable to develop a separate distribution (retail) forecasting model to assess the likely retail response to the firm's marketing variables—both those directed at the retailer (e.g., salesforce efforts, trade promotions, point-of-purchase and advertising support) as well as those directed at the consumers that can affect the ease and volume of sales (e.g., consumer advertising, price, etc.).

An important diagnostic insight new product forecasting models should provide is an assessment of the uncertainty involved in the new product introduction. The specific procedures for assessing uncertainty differ depending on the forecasting method used. For subjective judgments, for example, this can be done either by asking the respondents (experts or consumers) to assess the uncertainty of their forecast (either directly or by providing estimates for low, high, and most likely conditions) or by comparing the results of different forecasting methods. For econometric type models, regression analysis yields useful and inexpensive estimates of uncertainty. Standard errors assess the effects of error in estimating the forecast coefficients. Cross validation on a holdout sample offers an accurate way of assessing the uncertainty of the forecast. Similarly, Monte Carlo simulations can be used to assess the effects of various types of errors.[2]

Since all forecasting methods involve a fair amount of uncertainty, the focus of forecasting developers and users should be not on a point estimate but rather on the range of possible outcomes.

It is quite rare that a single model will dominate on all these criteria. As a result, it is desirable to consider the use of more than one forecasting model, i.e., apply the Campbell and Fiske philosophy (1959) to the forecasting area. Following this approach would increase the user's confidence in results which appear to be consistent across two or more models. The selected models should be continuously validated and reviewed. This continuous examination may result in the modification or even replacement of existing models depending on their performance.

---

[2]For a discussion of these and other approaches to assessing the uncertainty of various forecasting methods, see Armstrong (1978).

SOME ILLUSTRATIVE NEW PRODUCT FORECASTING MODELS

Given the large number of available new product forecasting models, no single chapter can offer a comprehensive review of all such models. The objective of this section, therefore, is to illustrate some of the major types of new product forecasting models which vary with respect to their data bases. These include:

1. Subjective estimates by management of the new product's likely performance;

2. Analogy—finding a new product with similar characteristics to those of the new product under concern and assuming that the sales pattern of the new product will be similar to that of the analogous product;

3. Consumer-based models. These new product forecasting models include two major sets of models: (a) trial or first-purchase models and (b) repeat models. These two models can be based on concept testing data, pretest market data, test market data, and early sales data.

These three types of forecasting models vary with respect to the stage in the new product development process for which they are most appropriate. Management's subjective estimates and analogies are usually used at the idea/concept screening stage, prior to the undertaking of a consumer-based concept evaluation study. If this initial evaluation suggests a *GO*, and a concept test is conducted, the next stage is a forecasting model based on the data generated in the concept testing study. Again, assuming a GO decision, a product is developed and a simulated test market (or a simplified in-home use test) can be designed, the results of which serve as the basis for a pre-test market forecasting model. If a GO decision is reached at this stage and a test market is undertaken, the data from the test market can

serve as the basis for a test market-based forecasting model. Finally, if the product is introduced to (regional or national) market, the early sales results can be utilized as the basis for an early sales-based forecasting model.

The various models, despite their close association with various stages in the new product development process, are not "pure" type models. Past experience of marketing managers and their subjective estimates can be incorporated in other forecasting models such as some of the concept testing-based models. Furthermore, a forecasting model structured for test market type data (i.e., requiring, for example, information on awareness, trial, repeat and amount used by regular users) can be used at a simulated test market stage combining actual results of the simulated test market (on trial, repeat and amount of usage, for example) with estimates from previous introductions (i.e., analogy) on the awareness level and its dependency on level of advertising, promotion, and distribution activities of the firm.

The models illustrated in the following sections incorporate a number of these components and they were selected, to a large extent, so as to encompass the key components of new product forecasting models.

SUBJECTIVE ESTIMATES OF NEW PRODUCT PERFORMANCE

Subjective estimates of the likely new product performance are often used at early stages of idea/concept screening. These estimates can be based on those of the relevant marketing managers as well as of other relevant personnel, such as the salesforce and other boundary persons.

The subjective estimates vary markedly in

their degree of formalism. They can range from some intuitive informal estimates suggested in a brainstorming-type session to formal and structured systems. These latter approaches include applications of the Delphi method (e.g., Linstone, 1975), the Analytic Hierarchy Process (Saaty, 1977; Wind and Saaty, 1980), a decision theory framework (Pengilly and Moss, 1920), conditional forecasting procedures, and the design of the chain ratio method for estimating the likely demand for a given product.

The Delphi method interrogates a panel of "experts" by a sequence of questionnaires. Although applied primarily to the probing of likely distant future events (technological developments, etc.) and their impact, it occasionally has been applied to the subjective assessment of the likely performance of a new product given a variety of environmental conditions and assumptions on the marketing effort of the firm and its competitors.

The Analytic Hierarchy Process (AHP) has been applied to the initial screening of new product concepts (Wind and Saaty, 1980). In this application, a group of managers were asked to evaluate a set of concepts according to their likely performance on a set of objectives (e.g., sales, share, profitability, etc.) under a set of alternative environmental scenarios (e.g., specific levels of inflation, changes in consumer life styles, various competitive actions, etc.).

In addition, a series of evaluations of the interrelationships among the various concepts was undertaken. The procedure resulted in the assignment of priorities for each of the concepts reflecting their perceived relative attractiveness to the judges with respect to the set of relevant criteria under alternative environmental scenarios.

The third approach to formal subjective forecasting of new concept/product performance involves the development of a *decision theory* model which can take into account likely consumer reactions to the new product and the likely competitive reactions. Pengilly and Moss

(1970), for example, reported an early application at P&G in which the sales and marketing staff provided information on the likely sales of a set of new products relative to competitive products under different prices and price reactions of the competitors. These data were then submitted to a linear programming model.

A related application of subjective judgments to the development of new product forecasts involves a procedure similar to that used in the development of *subjective conditional forecasts*. This latter approach helps decisionmakers to explicitly consider the likely effect of various variables (competitive actions, environmental conditions, etc.) on the performance of the new product. As in the case of the application of the AHP, it can lead to an open discussion of the assumptions and information held by the various participants.

A somewhat different approach to subjective forecasting is the construction of the *chain ratio method*. This procedure involves the design of a logical sequence of likely events that culminates in a forecast of the desired behavior. Consider, for example, the following hypothetical chain ratio for the demand for a new diet beer concept:

Population

× Personal discretionary income per capita

× Average percentage of discretionary income spent on beverages

× Average percentage of amount spent on beverages that is spent on beer

× Expected percentage of amount spent on beer that will be spent on diet beer

× Likely market share the new concept is likely to achieve.

Examining this hypothetical example suggests that (a) the desired results (likely amount to be spent by consumers on the new diet beer concept) can be achieved by a variety of chains (following a somewhat different sequence of links) and (b) many of the links can be estimated, based on "hard" data. Hence, this approach is quite helpful for integrating subjective judgments with "hard" data. Given the arbitrary nature of the sequence of links, it is desirable to construct more than one chain and compare the results.

ANALOGIES

Whether consumer-based information on likely new product acceptance is incorporated in a new product forecasting model or not, it is advisable to check the likely performance of the new product against the historical performance of similar products. If no new product in a given product class has ever achieved more than 40 percent trial and no more than half of the triers have ever continued buying it (repeat), it is not very likely that the new product under consideration will outperform this historical trend. Hence, the use of analogies can serve as a useful additional check on the results of any new product forecasting model.

When time or money constraints preclude the use of consumer-based studies to assess new product performance, one still can use analogies as an approximation for the likely performance of the new product. Analogies require a careful identification of the similarities between the new product(s) and the products to serve as the base for comparison. Once the comparative products are identified, analogies can be conducted to answer two key questions:

- What is the likely performance of the new product?
- What marketing efforts are required to achieve certain levels of performance?

To answer these questions, two different data sets are required. To assess the range of likely product performance, all that is needed is the historical performance of similar products. In this context, the narrower the definition of

similarity the better. In pharmaceutical products, for example, an analogy to new drugs is not as helpful as an analogy to drugs in the same therapeutic class and, even more specifically, to drugs in the same therapeutic class by a given market segment (e.g., specialty) and similar market conditions (level of satisfaction with existing drugs, etc.).

Exhibit 15–6 illustrates a series of models used as a basis for estimating the likely performance of a new product. These models should be empirically derived, but often can be related to conceptual models. The trial curve presented in Exhibit 15–6 is the conventional S-curve. Other cases can obviously be identified and it is not uncommon to find, especially when sampling and heavy promotional activities accompany the new product introduction, an exponential curve. Furthermore, the trial curve can be established for either households or volume. The Fourt-Woodlock forecasting model, for example, focuses on number of triers attracted, percent repeat and depth of repeat. Parfitt–Collins, on the other hand, relies primarily on volume trial—percent of product category purchasing accounted for by the new product. The volume trial automatically takes into consideration the heavy users. Since heavy users are probabilistically more likely to be the early triers,[3] the volume trial curve rises more rapidly in the first few months after introduction than the household trial curve. Furthermore, it also removes, to a large extent, the seasonality factor, since the volume trial is based on category volume which reflects the seasonal trend among both triers and nontriers. Diagnostically, one would therefore prefer to have information on both functions.

---

[3]A number of studies among physicians clearly indicate that the heavy drug users category is the most likely to be the first to try any new drug in the given category. This finding as it relates to consumer populations was also found by Parfitt and Collins (1968).

EXHIBIT 15–6

ILLUSTRATIVE NEW PRODUCT PERFORMANCE MODELS USED AS A BASIS FOR
FORECASTING BY ANALOGY

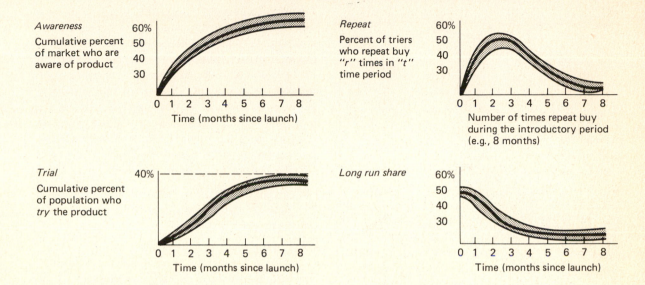

The repeat function often takes the form of the Gamma–Poisson formulation which Ehrenberg (1971) termed the *NBD* (Negative Binomial Distribution).[4] As with trial functions, the repeat can be in terms of percent of triers who repeat their purchases (as suggested, for example, in the Fourt-Woodlock model) or in terms of volume. In this latter case (which is illustrated at the bottom panel of Exhibit 15–6), the focus is on the repeat purchase rate—subsequent category purchases which are devoted to the new product—among triers who bought at least once more. The repeat purchase rate is a key component of the Parfitt-Collins model and the core of most repeat-purchase models.

Whereas functions such as the ones illustrated in Exhibit 15–6 can give an idea of the likely range of performance for any new product with similar characteristics to those of the products used to develop the specific trial and repeat functions, none of these functions offers the necessary diagnostic information to assess the required marketing efforts to achieve desired performance levels. Here again, analysis by analogy can be quite helpful. Consider, for example, the illustrative functions in Exhibit 15–7. Having such empirically-based functions for the various dependent variables can be of considerable diagnostic value. Ideally, one would like to have more detailed functions which are not limited to overall marketing expenditures, but rather separate the response functions for advertising, promotion, and dis-

---

[4]The NBD—Gamma-Poisson—formulation assumes that different repeat buyers have different long-run rates of buying and that these rates follow a Gamma distribution. The Poisson part assumes that in the short run each buyer will randomly deviate from his particular long-run rate so that his chance of any given purchase frequency follows the Poisson distribution.

EXHIBIT 15–7

ILLUSTRATIVE NEW PRODUCT MARKET
RESPONSE FUNCTIONS USED AS A BASIS FOR
FORECASTING BY ANALOGY

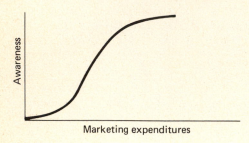

Marketing expenditures

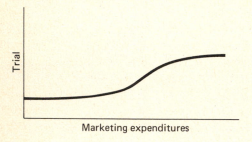

Marketing expenditures

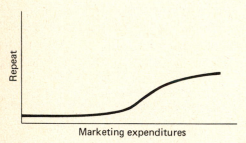

Marketing expenditures

accurate information on) interactions among the various marketing mix variables, the competitive reactions to the new product introduction, and the likely changes in relevant environmental forces.

The data requirement for forecasting by analogies can be substantial and should be reflected in the design of the firm's marketing information system. The development of such models is a critical component of the new product evaluation system and should be attempted even in those cases in which the firm relies heavily on primary research on the likely performance of each new product. The major benefits of such a system are that it provides:

• An early indication of likely performance of new concepts even prior to a formal concept testing;

• A range of likely performance against which the results of other new product forecasting models can be evaluated.

CONSUMER BASED NEW PRODUCT TRIAL (FIRST PURCHASE) FORECASTING MODELS

Concept testing studies can offer the basis for trial projections. Firms which have cumulative experience with concept testing procedures often can develop rules for translating concept testing results to percent of trial (in test market conditions). Exhibit 15-8 illustrates such a translation rule for a frequently purchased household product category.

Trial can be estimated quite accurately. The NW Ayer trial model, discussed later in this section, has been reported to have high predictive accuracy. Similarly, Eskin, in an unpublished paper, reported an extremely high trial predictive accuracy using three variables: number of people who tried the product class in the last year ($\beta = 0.92$); availability of the brand

tribution expenditures. Data availability is a serious constraint, however, on the ability to develop such functions. Unless a company is heavily involved in new product introduction, it can be helpful to include in the response functions the experience of one's competitors. Even though such data can be generated, their reliability decreases as the detailed level of analysis increases. In this context, a more serious limitation involves the control for (having

EXHIBIT 15–8

A SIMPLIFIED CONVERSION OF CONCEPT
TESTING RESULTS TO PRODUCT TRIAL

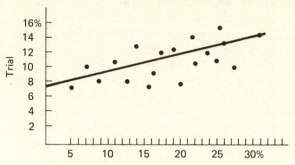

Percent of respondents who rated the concept as
"definitely would buy" and chose it as the most
preferred one.

(effective distribution) ($\beta = 0.83$); and degree of marketing support ($\beta = 0.58$). The R^2 of this model was 0.95 (with a standard error of 0.15). The R^2 can be further improved by adding concept testing scores to the model.

If a concept-testing study is based on a conjoint analysis design, the associated computer simulation can result in estimates of trial, source of trial, and likely cannibalization. The experience with conjoint analysis-based simulators has been quite favorable, especially when the simulation is incorporated with a trial forecasting model (similar to those used in pretest market forecasting models). This includes not only information on consumer choice between various new concepts and the current products, but also information on likely level of distribution, advertising, and promotion of the given brand and its competitors, and the degree of product class penetration.

The main value of the conjoint analysis-based trial simulators which are included in some of the pretest market models is their ability to estimate the market share of each new concept (product) formulation (and brand)

under any number of conditions such as:

- Introduction of a new concept with no competitive retaliation;

- Introduction of a new concept with competitive retaliation in terms of changes in their current marketing strategy or by the introduction of new or modified brands;

- Changes in consumer preferences for various product attributes (such as increased price sensitivity as a result of increased inflationary pressures).

Conjoint analysis-based simulators have been employed in forecasting the likely response to new product concepts in a variety of product categories ranging from frequently purchased consumer products for which the forecast is primarily of trial (e.g., foods, cosmetics, etc.) through consumer and industrial services (e.g., airline services, financial services, etc.) to the design of durable consumer and industrial products (e.g., cars, office reproduction equipment, etc.).[5]

Despite the recent growth in the utilization of these models, both at the concept testing and simulated test market stage, most of the first purchase (trial) forecasting models have been based on test market or early sales data.

The underlying behavioral concept of most of the trial (diffusion type) models is the adoption-imitation process, i.e., the new brand is first adopted by the "innovators" who in turn "influence" others to adopt it via word of mouth communication and demonstrated brand usage.

The basic diffusion model can be presented as:

$$\frac{dN(t)}{dt} = a\left[\bar{N} - N(t)\right] + bN(t)\left[\bar{N} - N(t)\right],$$

---

[5]For a more complete list of areas of conjoint analysis applications, see Green and Srinivasan (1978) and Wind (1978c).

where $dN(t)/dt$ = rate of diffusion at time t, i.e., slope of $N(t)$,

$N(t)$ = cumulative number of adopters at time t,

$\bar{N}(t)$ = population of potential adopters (ceiling on number of adopters at time t),

a = constant, coefficient of innovation,

b = constant, coefficient of imitation.

The various diffusion models vary in terms of their assumptions concerning the value of a and b, whether $\bar{N}(t)$—market potential—is constant or not, the degree to which the diffusion model is only a function of time or also a function of the marketing strategies of the firm, the relationships of the new brand with other products in the marketplace, and whether the model takes into consideration the spatial (geographic) diffusion pattern. Exhibit 15–9 classifies the major first-purchase diffusion models based on these variables.

Fourt and Woodlock (1960), for example, assumed that $b = 0$, that is, diffusion is a pure innovative-effect model. Mansfield (1961) and Fisher and Pry (1971), on the other hand, assume that $a = 0$, i.e., their diffusion models are pure imitation-effect models. In contrast, Bass (1969) assumes positive values for both a and b and, hence, incorporates both innovativeness and imitation effects.

The diffusion models vary also with respect to the way they treat the market potential. Most models (such as the Bass, Fourt and Woodlock, and Fisher and Pry) assume that it is constant over time (either as the total population or a fraction of it), while others, such as the Mahajan and Peterson (1980) and Dodson and Muller (1978), assume that the potential adopter population changes over time, i.e., $\bar{N}(t) = f(S(t))$, where $S(t)$ is a vector of all relevant exogenous and endogenous variables affecting $\bar{N}(t)$.

The diffusion models of Bass (1969) and Fourt and Woodlock (1960) do not include marketing strategy effects. This omission has been overcome in a number of extensions of the basic diffusion model. Robinson and Lakhani (1975) incorporate marketing variables by representing b—the imitation coefficient—as a function of marketing strategy variables such as advertising, promotion and price. In this case, b in the basic diffusion model is a function of $M(t)$, that is, $b = B(M(t))$, where $M(t)$ is a vector of marketing decision variables at time t. Horsky and Simon (1978) incorporated the marketing strategy variables, not through their effect on b, but rather through their effect on the eventual number of adopters $\bar{N}$ and innovators a. Price changes and product modifications expand the eventual number of adopters $\bar{N}$, while advertising serves as a source of information to innovators and, hence, effects the coefficient of innovation a.

Further extension of the basic diffusion model was suggested by Peterson and Mahajan (1978), who incorporated in the model the complementarity, substitutability, contingent and independent relations of the new brand with other brands in the marketplace. The substitution effect, for example, is incorporated in the basic diffusion model by adding the constant c, which represents the substitution effect—the interaction between the adopters of product j and the nonadopters of product i, which results in a decrease in the rate of diffusion for product i (i.e., potential adopters of i who buy j). This effect can be presented as:

$$\frac{dN_i(t)}{dt} = a_i\left[\bar{N} - N_i(t)\right] + b_iN_i(t)\left[\bar{N} - N_i(t)\right] - c_iN_j(t)\left[\bar{N}_i - N_i(t)\right].$$

Most of the diffusion models ignore the spatial diffusion pattern. Yet, given that the pattern of new product introduction rarely follows the regional pattern (even when national introduction is planned not all areas receive the products at the same time and with the same

EXHIBIT 15–9

FIRST-PURCHASE DIFFUSION MODELS OF NEW PRODUCT ACCEPTANCE

Reprinted from the *Journal of Marketing,* published by the American Marketing Association, Exhibit
from "Innovation Diffusion and New Product Growth Models," by V. Mahajan and E. Muller,
Volume 43, Fall 1979, pp. 55–58.

Models	Coefficient of internal influence	Coefficient of external influence	Eventual number of buyers
BASIC MODELS			
Bass (1969)	constant	constant	constant
Fourt and Woodlock (1960)	0	constant	constant
Mansfield (1961)	constant	0	constant
Hendry (1972)	constant	0	constant
Lekvall and Wahlbin (1973)	constant	constant	constant
EXTENSIONS			
Robinson and Lakhani (1975)	f (price)	constant	constant
Horsky and Simon (1978)	constant	f (advertising)	constant
Hernes (1976)	f (time)	f (time)	constant
Bass (1978)	f (demand elasticity, learning parameters, price)	f (demand elasticity, learning parameters, price)	constant
Peterson and Mahajan (1978)	f (product relationships)	constant	constant
Mahajan and Peterson (1980)	constant	constant	f (all relevant variables)
Mahajan et al. (1979)	constant	0	f (housing starts)
Dodson and Muller (1978)	0	constant	f (advertising)
Chow (1967)	constant	0	f (price)
Lackman (1978)	constant	0	f (profit/sales)

Diffusion model, $n(t) = a\Delta N(t) + bN(t)\Delta N(t)$, where a is coefficient of external influence, b is coefficient of internal influence, $\Delta N(t)$ is the difference between eventual number of adopters and current number of adopters.
$\Delta N(t) = \bar{N} - N(t)$ for all of the above except for Mahajan and Muller (1979), Chow (1967), and Lackman (1978), where $\Delta N(t) = \ln\bar{N} - \ln N(t)$. Here $N(t)$ is the cumulative number of adopters at time t and $\bar{N}$ is the eventual number of adopters.

intensity), incorporating a spatial diffusion pattern is most desirable. Mahajan and Peterson (1980), for example, offer a limited spatial extension of the basic diffusion model. In this application, they express a, b, and $\bar{N}$ as a function of distance, but limit the spatial diffusion pattern to an initial product introduction in one region.

In addition to the basic diffusion model and its various extensions and the conjoint analysis-based first-purchase forecasts, the forecast of new product trial also has been the subject of

extensive econometric modeling efforts. One of the most widely used models in this category for frequently-purchased products is the NW Ayer model (Claycamp and Liddy, 1969):[6]

$$IP = a_2 + b_{21}(AR) + b_{22}(DN \cdot PK) + b_{23}(FB) + b_{24}(CP) + b_{25}(PS)^* + b_{26}(CU) + e,$$

[6]This model and regression equation appeared in Claycamp and Liddy (1969) and are reproduced with the permission of the American Marketing Association.

where IP = initial purchase,
   AR = advertising recall which in turn is a function of product positioning (PP), media impression (AHI), copy execution (CE), consumer promotion (CP*), and category intent (CI), and takes the form of:

$$AR = a_1 + b_{11}(PP) + b_{12}\sqrt{AHI \cdot CE} + b_{13}(CP^*) + b_{14}(CI) + e,$$

   DN = distribution,
   PK = packaging,
   FB = family brand,
   CP = consumer promotion,
   PS* = product satisfaction,
   CU = category usage,
   e = error,

The specific regression equation identified for this model, based on over 100 cases, is:

Initial purchase
= −16 + 0.19 (Distribution × Packaging)
+ 9.25 (Family brand)
+ 0.09 (Consumer promotion)
+ 0.02 (Product satisfaction)
+ 0.07 (Category usage)
+ 0.37 (Predicted adv. recall)

Advertising recall
= −36 + 0.76 (Product positioning)
+ 2.12 ($\sqrt{\text{Media impressions}} \times \sqrt{\text{Copy execution}}$)
+ 0.04 (Consumer promotion recall)
+ 0.39 (Category interest)

CONSUMER BASED REPEAT PURCHASE AND SHARE FORECASTING MODELS

When the long-run performance of a product depends on repurchase (including cases such as the need for renewal of contract), a first-purchase (trial) forecasting model should be supplemented with a repeat-purchase model.

The separation of sales into trial and repeat is critical, given that the same level of sales can be reached by various combinations of trial and repeat, including the extreme disastrous case of only trial and no repeat. Furthermore, having information on the trial-repeat breakdown offers critical diagnostic insights. Consider, for example, the case of very low trial and high repeat, which suggests the need to change the introductory marketing strategy to generate higher trial levels.

Some of the various trial-repeat combinations for a given level of sales are illustrated in the following table:

Total sales in period t	=	Number of first-time buyers in period t	×	Average purchase volume per period per time t	+	Number of repeat buyers in period t	×	Average purchase volume per period per repeat customer
100	=	100		1		0		0
100	=	20		1		10		8
100	=	50		1		25		2
100	=	70		1		30		1

An examination of these four cases suggests that it is helpful to focus on the number of triers and repeaters and, to the extent that there are any differences in the average purchase volume of the two (as is often the case), these data should also be included.

The focus on repeat should not be limited, however, to the number (or proportion) of first purchasers. The Fourt and Woodlock (1960), Massy (1969), Eskin (1973) and most other repeat-purchase models recognize the need to model the *depth of repeat* (the repeat purchase of one-time buyers, two-time buyers, and so on). The repeat-purchase models vary, however, in their formulation. Exhibit 15–10 briefly classifies most of the published repeat-purchase models on a number of critical characteristics. Three of these models are briefly discussed.

The Fourt and Woodlock Model (1960) is based on the concept of repeat ratio. The first repeat

EXHIBIT 15–10

REPEAT PURCHASE MODELS

Source: V. Mahajan and E. Muller, "Innovative Behavior and Repeat Purchase Diffusion Models,"
Wharton School Working Paper, 1980; reprinted with permission.

Models	Determin- istic stochastic	Inte- grated process	Distinguishes between			Includes			
			Unaware– potential	Types of information	Depth of repeat	Word of mouth	Impulse purchase	Decay	Recycle
1 Fourt and Woodlock (1960)	D				✔				
2 Parfitt and Collins (1968)	D								
3 Claycamp and Liddy (1969): AYER	D		✔						
4 Nakanishi (1973)	S	✔			✔			✔	
5 Massy (1969): STEAM	S	✔			✔				
6 Assmus (1975): NEWPROD	D		✔					Partial	Partial
7 Urban (1970): SPRINTER	D	✔	✔		Partial	✔		Partial	✔
8 Midgley (1976)	D	✔		✔		✔			✔
9 Blattberg and Golanty (1978): TRACKER	D		✔		✔			Partial	
10 Dodson and Muller (1978)	D	✔	✔			✔		✔	✔
11 Lilien and Rao (1978)	D	✔				✔		✔	
12 Mahajan and Muller (1979)	D	✔	✔	✔	✔	✔		✔	✔
13 Kalwani and Silk (1980)	S	✔			✔				

ratio, for example, is the fraction of triers who make a second purchase. Second, third, and other repeat ratios are similarly defined and can be interpreted as the probability that a first-, second-, third-time buyer will buy again. The repeat sales equation used in this model is:

$$S_t = N_{F_t}\left[1 + \frac{N_{1t}}{N_{F_t}} + \frac{N_{1t}}{N_{F_t}}\frac{N_{2t}}{N_{1t}} \\ + \frac{N_{1t}}{N_{F_t}}\frac{N_{2t}}{N_{1t}}\frac{N_{3t}}{N_{2t}} + \dots \right],$$

where S_t = total sales in period t,

S_{F_t} = average purchase volume per period per first-time buyer,

N_{F_t} = number of first-time buyers,

N_{1t} = first-repeat ratio (fraction of triers who made a second purchase),

$\dfrac{N_{2t}}{N_{1t}}$ = second repeat ratio (the fraction of first repeaters who made a second repeat purchase).

This model is often used by NPD (National Purchase Diary Panel, Inc.) to predict first year volume. Their experience with it is not satisfactory, however, in predicting the long-run sustaining volume, for which they use the Parfitt and Collins model.

The Parfitt and Collins model (1968), as does the Fourt and Woodlock model, requires panel data. It does differ, however, in its formulation. It is not based on the number of new buyers in each period. Rather, the Parfitt and Collins model is designed for long-run share S predictions as a function of three factors:

$S = prb$,

where p = ultimate penetration rate of the brand (percent of product class buyers who try the brand),

r = ultimate repeat-purchase rate (new brand purchases as percentage of all purchases by persons who once purchased this brand),

b = buying rate index of repeat purchase of this brand (when average buyer is 1.00).

Using this formulation, if for example 34 percent of the buyers in this market ultimately try the brand ($p = 0.34$), and 25 percent of their subsequent repurchases go to this brand ($r = 0.25$) and those buying the brand buy an average quantity ($b = 1.00$), the predicted long-run equilibrium brand share would be 8.5 percent ($0.34 \cdot 0.25 \cdot 1.00$). If the brand attracts on average heavier buyers ($b = 1.20$), then the predicted share would be higher — 10.2 percent ($0.34 \cdot 0.25 \cdot 1.20$).

These ultimate share predictions can be made as soon as the penetration curve and repeat purchase curve stabilize (tend to move toward an asymptotic value). As illustrated in Exhibit 15–11, this avoids the need to wait until the stabilization of share.

The Fourt and Woodlock and the Parfitt and Collins models do not include, explicitly, any marketing strategy variables. Parfitt and Collins, for example, stated explicitly the two key assumptions of their model:

- The retail distribution of the new brand is uniformly high in the area under study or, failing that, it is not substantially worse now than it is likely to be in the foreseeable future;

- Besides the advertising and promotional activity during the brand's launch (including competitors' retaliatory measures), the circumstances of the market will remain

EXHIBIT 15–11

ILLUSTRATIVE CUMULATIVE PENETRATION AND REPEAT-PURCHASING RATE

Reprinted from the *Journal of Marketing Research*, published by the American Marketing Association. Exhibit from "Use of Consumer Panels for Brand-Share Predictions," by J.H. Parfitt and B.J.K. Collins, Volume 5, May 1968, pp. 132, 133

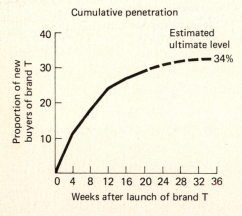
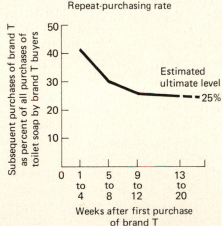

much the same in the future as they have been during the prediction measurement.

A model which develops a marketing strategy dependent repeat buying model is the NW Ayer model. According to this model, which has not been successfully validated, however, the repeat purchase is a function of four variables:

- Initial purchase prediction (which, as discussed earlier incorporates all the marketing variables except price),
- Relative price,
- Product satisfaction,
- Purchase frequency.

Most repeat-purchase models use the concept of depth of repeat. These models differ, however, in their formulation and complexity (from the relatively simple Fourt and Woodlock model, through the sophisticated and somewhat more complex Eskin (1973) model, to the most complex STEAM model (Massy, 1969)—which presumes population heterogeneity and introduces the concept of depth of trial classes and different propensities to enter them). In addition, repeat forecasting models vary in the way they are incorporated in long-run share and usage forecasts. As with first-purchase (trial) models, most models are claimed (by their developers) to be highly valid. The user of these models should, therefore, select the one which best fits his or her need or, alternatively, build a model using some of the more desirable components from the currently-available models.

INCORPORATING A FORECASTING MODEL IN AN ECONOMIC EVALUTION SYSTEM

The output of new product forecasting procedures is rarely considered in isolation from other factors involved in the "go—no go" decision. It is important therefore to consider a formal integration of the new product forecasting methods with the firm's economic evaluation system. One of the more comprehensive systems that incorporates forecasting and economic evaluation is the DEMON (DEcision Mapping via Optimum "go—no go" Networks) model developed to aid management in evaluating alternative plans for the introduction of new products and alternative marketing research studies that could help improve the product's profitability (Charnes et al., 1966 and 1968). The marketing planning framework of DEMON and its key functions were presented in Exhibit 15–2. These functions, which are determined by a least squares regression on data available on over 200 packaged goods products,

are oversimplistic since they ignore other possible determinants of the key dependent variables. Trial, for example, can be affected by advertising frequency, promotion activities, distribution, and price. These modifications can easily be incorporated, however, in the model. The unique feature of the DEMON system is its focus on the search for an optimal path through a total information network subject to management's specified constraints concerning:

- The payback period,
- The planning horizon,
- Minimum acceptable profits for a "go" and "on" decision,
- Minimum degree of confidence needed for a "go" and "on" decision,
- Total marketing research budget.

The model evaluates the various (research)

patterns to a "go" and "on" decision by calculating the estimated profit (based on the cost and demand estimates) and risk for each path. The "best" path is selected, and if an "on" decision (specific study) is recommended the next step would be an evaluation using the results of this study.

The SPRINTER (Specification of PRofits with INteractions under Trials and Error Response) model (Urban, 1970) is similar in its objective to DEMON with the added feature of considering relevant interactions of the new product with the other products of the firm.

DEMON, SPRINTER, and the more recent POSSE system (Green et al., 1981, and Appendix B) all offer formal procedures for incorporating the results of new product forecasting models in an economic evaluation system. Whether these modeling efforts or others are used is immaterial. The key to appropriate usage of new product forecasting models, however, is their incorporation in some formal economic evaluation system that can translate trial, repeat, intentions to buy, and other results of forecasting models into "go," "on," or "no go" decisions.

CONCLUDING REMARKS

No single best forecasting model has yet been identified. Each of the numerous new product forecasting models is based on specific assumptions and data requirements. Since the data availability and accuracy needs of new product forecasting models vary by the specific decision for which the forecast is needed, it is desirable to develop a *system* of forecasting models. Such a system (composition of a number of diverse forecasting methods) would ideally be based on at least four concepts:

1. *The inclusion of the most appropriate forecasting method for each stage of the new product development process.* Recognizing the cost and value of information at early stages of development, it would be desirable to have a relatively cheap and quick forecasting procedure with lower accuracy. Such a procedure should offer input to a simple "go—no go" decision by assessing the likelihood that the new product's performance would fall within some acceptable range. In contrast, at later stages of development, much greater accuracy is needed and hence different forecasting methods should be con-

sidered. This concept is not unlike the evolutionary model building proposed by Urban and Karash (1971).

2. *The inclusion of at least two forecasting methods at each stage of the new product development process.* This multiple method approach would offer cross-validation of the outcomes and would increase management's confidence in the forecasting results.

3. *An explicit make-buy decision.* In selecting new product forecasting models, one should not be constrained by the existing commercial models. A make-buy decision should be made based on an examination of the available commercial models (such as the NW Ayer trial model, the ASSESSOR pretest market simulator, and others) against the advantages of designing an idiosyncratic forecasting model for the firm which could incorporate the most attractive features of the various commercial models.

4. *Avoid overly sophisticated models.* Many of the new product forecasting models tend to err in being overly sophisticated and mathe-

matically elegant. Yet, an interesting finding of two recent evaluations of various forecasting methods (Armstrong, 1978, and Ascher, 1978) suggest that the more sophisticated model does not necessarily lead to more useful forecasts.

Forecasting the likely performance of new concepts/products is a critical step of every new product development effort. It should be incorporated as an integral part of the new product development system, and continuous attention should be given to the modification and improvement of the forecasting system so as to assure a reliable and valid forecasting methodology. This requires continuous followup and examination of the statistical and economic accuracy of the system.

Since *new product* forecasting is a complex and difficult task, improvement of this methodology and its implementation could have secondary benefits to the other forecasting tasks facing a firm (e.g., environmental forecasting, etc.).

Given the large number of new product forecasting models one can choose from, one of the most difficult tasks facing staff members responsible for developing a new product forecast and managers concerned with the approval of such forecasts is which of the various models to select. To gain a better understanding of the factors which determine the selection of a new product forecasting model, select a product or service of your choice and develop for it a new product forecasting model. In developing such a model, you can select an existing model, construct a new one using any components of any of the existing models, or alternatively, design a model from scratch.

Evaluate the resulting model giving particular attention to the confidence you would have in results suggested by the model you selected.

16

Organizing for New Products

Introduction

Building Blocks of Organizational Design

New Product Goals, Strategy, and Tasks
Organizational Structure
Technology
Organizational Resources
People
Management Style and Decision Processes
Informal Organization

Demands on Organizational Design for New Products

Overcoming Barriers to Innovation
Encouraging Creativity and Innovations
Assuring Top Mangement Involvement
Assuring Interfunctional Links
Assuring Continuity
Enabling a Mix of "Make-Buy" Activities
Achieving the Right Mix of Differentiation and Integration
Recognizing Task Heterogeneity
Allowing for Interorganizational Cooperation
Preventing Suboptimization

R&D Models for the Organization of New Product Development

R&D—Marketing Interface
R&D—Manufacturing Interface

INTRODUCTION

In their now classic article, "How to Organize for New Products," Johnson and Jones (1957) illustrate the need for new product organization by the following list of "typical" occurrences:

- Executives who want new products, but do not know or cannot agree on what kinds of products to be interested in
- Inventors who do not know what to invent
- Laboratory crowded with development projects, but with few new products coming out, and too many of these not paying off
- Downhearted idea-man whose brain child was squashed for unexplained reasons
- "Floating" product idea that has been considered for years, but has never had a decision made on it
- "Bootleg" project in the laboratory that management does not know about
- "Orphan" project that goes on and on because nobody has given it the thought or had the heart to kill it

- "Bottomless hole" product that took three times as long and cost five times as much as expected, and finally got to market behind all other competitors
- Product with "bugs" that were hidden until 10,000 came back from consumers
- "Me too" product that has no competitive reason for existence
- Product that had the sales "engineered out of it"
- Scientific triumph that turned out to have no market when someone thought to investigate it
- Salesforce that jumped the gun ahead of production
- Salesforce that was not "interested" in the added product.

These and similar events are not uncommon in most organizations. Successful management of new products requires, therefore, not only the development and implementation of a new product development procedure (as discussed in Chapters 8 through 15) but also the design of an organization structure and procedures which will enable the achievement of the new product objectives of the division, strategic business unit (SBU), and the corporation.

The primary objective of this chapter is to explore and evaluate the range of organizational designs for new product development. More specifically, the chapter focuses on five areas: the building blocks of organizational design, the demands on (and criteria for evaluation of) organizational design for new products, the R&D model for the organization of new product development, alternative approaches to the organization of new product development, and integrated approaches to the design of new product organization.

BUILDING BLOCKS OF ORGANIZATIONAL DESIGN

Designing an organization for new product development calls for the determination of the most desired alternatives concerning:

- The specific new product development strategy and tasks,
- The organizational structure including the authority, status, communication, and reward systems, as well as the degree of decentralization, division of labor, and location of activities.
- The technology required for and work flow of new product development,
- The organizational, material, and capital resources required for and dedicated to new product development efforts,
- The type of persons required for carrying out the new product development tasks,
- Management style and the decision process of the key decision makers,
- The informal organization and its impact on the characteristics and performance of the formal organization.

The seven decision areas constitute the major building blocks of an organization and, as illustrated in Exhibit 16–1, are closely interrelated. The discussion of these decisions will be brief and focused primarily on those aspects which affect directly the organizational designer's choice among these elements in the design of an efficient organization for new product development.[1] The organizational designer's freedom is constrained, however, by a number of factors such as (Khandwalla, 1977):

- The business environment
- Law
- Technology
- The culture within which the organization operates
- Size, age, and type of business
- Management ideology
- The norms and preferences of the rank and file
- The organization's traditions, precedents and current organizational design
- The available resources

---

[1] The discussion thus assumes some basic familiarity with the organizational behavior literature. The readers who are not familiar with this literature are encouraged to review one of the basic texts, such as Khandwalla (1977) or Galbraith (1977).

EXHIBIT 16–1

KEY BUILDING BLOCKS OF ORGANIZATIONAL DESIGN

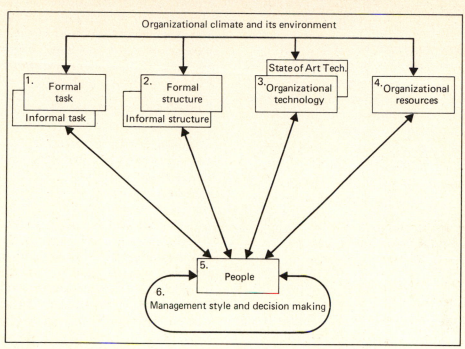

NEW PRODUCT GOALS, STRATEGY, AND TASKS

Growth, particularly via the addition of new products and services, has long been recognized as one of the essential requirements for the survival of the firm. Robert Hartley (1976), for example, after examining eleven of the major marketing mistakes of recent history, concluded: "While at first glance a low-or-no growth philosophy seems workable; upon closer inspection such a philosophy can be seen as sowing the seeds of its own destruction, unless reversed before too late."

The development and commercialization of new products are often included, therefore, among the primary operating goals of the firm.

The operating goals of any organization emerge from the organization's interaction with its stakeholders (which can take the shape of competitive, bargaining, cooperational, and co-alitional relations)[2] and the interaction among conflicting intraorganizational forces. These external and internal forces as reflected in the operating goals of the firm stress the feasibility (or lack of it) of various courses of action and provide operational guidelines for the resource allocation and strategic choices of the firm.

The specific new product related operating goals can be categorized following the framework suggested by Perrow's (1970) classi-

_____

[2]For a discussion of the nature of these relationships, see Thompson and McEwen (1958).

fication of organizational goals:

- Developing products and services which *serve social needs* and, hence, confer legitimacy on the organization;
- *Output goals* which reflect the organization's choice about the type and number of businesses to be involved in;
- *System goals* and *derived goals* which reflect the organization's choice of performance criteria and decision-making style (e.g., degree of risk-taking);
- *Product characteristic goals* which reflect the organizational positioning goals and trade offs among product features. For example, the emphasis on high quality and high price versus standard quality and low price.

The specification of new product-related operating goals provides the starting point for the corporate "goal-means" hierarchy. An illustrative new product goal-means hierarchy can start with an objective to increase the firm's profits from new products, which in turn can be translated into a specific rate of return from various classes of new product activities within a specified period of time, down to the specific new product development tasks and their associated budget and timing.

New product development *tasks* are often specified as a set of activities (such as the ones outlined in the various chapters of Part II of this book). These activities should be linked explicitly to a set of objectives/goals that provide direction, allocate responsibilities, set constraints on and motivate the behavior of the organizational members and groups and provide *criteria* for evaluating the organization's new product development activities.

In the absence of a normative theory of organizational effectiveness, the specific goals (effectiveness criteria) should be determined by the firm for all its relevant organizational levels reflecting their idiosyncratic characteristics at a given time, space, and environmental scenario. This specification of desired effectiveness criteria should encompass all relevant individuals, groups, or components of the organization which are involved in the new product development process, have control over and are held accountable for various aspects of it.

ORGANIZATIONAL STRUCTURE

Organizational structure is the set of durable and formally sanctioned relationships and arrangements designed to reduce internal and external uncertainty, permit the organization to engage in a variety of tasks, and secure for it a high degree of coordination among these tasks so that it achieves its goals efficiently (Khandwalla, 1977). The elements of structure include the way the organization members are grouped (departmentalization and levels of decentralization), the relationships among these groups and the individuals comprising them, the arrangements about who reports to whom (the hierarchical structure, delegation of authority, and division of labor), the communication network among the various organizational members and groups and between them and the external environment, the organizational system of rewards and sanctions, and the organizational measures of performance. These elements when designed into an integrated system constitute the organizational structure.

Departmentalization The grouping of organizational members is often depicted pictorially by an organization chart. Exhibit 16–2 illustrates two typical organizational charts which demonstrate the differences among the two organizations with respect to the location of the new product activities.[3]

---

[3]For a discussion of other new product organization structures see the section at the end of this chapter.

EXHIBIT 16–2

ILLUSTRATIVE NEW PRODUCT ORGANIZATIONAL CHARTS

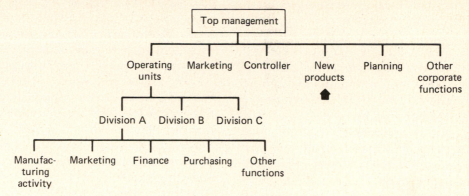

Centralized new product development

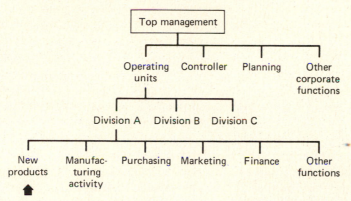

Decentralized new product activities

The strengths and weaknesses of these and other organizational structures for new product development are discussed later in this chapter. It is important, however, at this stage to understand the factors that affect the way an organization groups its members.

Minimizing the cost of coordination is suggested by Thompson (1967); his study implies initial grouping of individuals and groups which are reciprocally dependent, followed by grouping of individuals and groups which are serially or sequentially dependent (one-sided dependency) and finally grouping of individuals or groups who are only indirectly dependent on one another. While Thompson emphasizes the interdependencies of activities, other considerations are span of control and ease of supervision, the degree of specialization of the tasks to be performed, the level of diversification of the demand for the services performed, the individual and group enrichment of the tasks (that require modules for which the individual or the group has responsibility and control), and most importantly the similarity of the physical and mental tasks (decisions) that have to be performed and hence the similarity of information (and other resources) required for the performance of the various tasks.

A key decision in the determination of the type of departmentalization that is needed is the organization's degree and nature of *decentralization*. The major advantages of a decentralized structure are its motivational power (by providing autonomy, responsibility and rewards), its effect on the organizational speed of response, its impact on the time allocation of top corporate management (freedom from routine decisions allowing them to devote more time to long term strategic issues) and its serving as a training ground for future top managers. On the other hand, decentralization also has a number of weaknesses since it can lead to suboptimization, and increase the resistance to corporate-wide changes.

In general, higher levels of decentralization tend to be associated with larger organizations, organizations of professionals, organizations performing in a highly competitive environment and in those cases in which management has a more participative ideology. Yet, it is important to note that even in a decentralized organization not all operations have to be decentralized. Hence, it is not uncommon to find highly decentralized firms with centralized new product development operations.

When considering the design of an organizational structure for efficient and effective new product development activities the overall organizational level and nature of decentralization are viewed as major constraints. Hence the organization designer should focus primarily on the level of decentralization, division of labor, and location of the various activities and responsibilities of the new product development decisions and tasks.

The reward and motivational system The search for pleasure (rewards) and avoidance of pain (punishment) as dominant motivational forces have long been recognized in the behavioral sciences. Consistent with this view, monetary and nonmonetary compensation systems have been designed to motivate employees in a direction consistent with the achievement of organizational objectives. The importance of an appropriate reward system is equally important in the design of an organization structure for new product development.

The needs and wants of the key participants should be identified and a reward system designed to meet these needs while at the same time directing the participants' activities toward the desired corporate objectives. This relatively simple idea is not easy to implement, however, when considering the type of personnel required for successful new product development activities. Innovative R&D personnel, for example, often strive for approval by reference groups outside the organizational boundaries. A reward balance model (Wind, 1971) modified to the new product development area can thus be constructed to provide guidelines for the type of information required in the design of efficient reward systems. I.e., who are the relevant reference groups of each of the participants in the system? What are the criteria used by these groups to evaluate favorably the new product development activities of the relevant organizational members? Are these criteria consistent with those of the organization's own objectives, and if not, how can conflict between the two be avoided?

Following this approach requires flexible (nonstandardized) reward systems which might vary from one individual to another. Consider, for example, the case of "Dr. A," a scientist who strives for recognition by his fellow scientists and enjoys R&D activities. Promoting him, as a reward for the successful development of a new product, to the head of the new product division is dysfunctional (losing a good scientist and gaining a poor manager). He would much rather go on working on another project associated with appropriate recognition and professional reward. On the other hand, if "Dr. B," a fellow scientist, strives for managerial position and power within the organization, he would welcome the opportunity to be rewarded for the successful development of a new product by heading the new unit, and moving away from R&D activities.

TECHNOLOGY[4]

Technology is both a constraint on the organization's new product development capabilities (can a new product idea be converted into a product given the current state of technology?) and a challenge (what process and product technology developments are possible given the current level of technology?).

In designing an organization to facilitate an efficient and effective new product development activity, the current level of technology (including the state of information technology) is an important consideration. Not only should the organizational structure and personnel fit the available and needed technology but the organization should be designed in a way conducive to the stimulation of internal technological developments *and* acquisition and integration of relevant external technological developments.

The current and desired technological sophistication of the firm (and especially the gap between the two) have major implications for the required corporate resources, in particular the capital-intensive nature of the operation, and the demand on quality of personnel.

Traditionally, technology has been limited to manufacturing technology either with respect to development of new products and packaging or improvement in the manufacturing process itself (note for example the coverage of the patent laws and the range of activities of most R&D departments). Yet, when considering technology for new product development it should not be limited to manufacturing technology and should encompass service elements as well as the marketing, financial and management technology of the firm. Consider, for example, the current level of marketing technology with respect to distribution and promotion. A direct mail insurance company, for example, can develop new products within the boundaries of their distribution technology or alternatively develop a new distribution method involving telephones or computerized vending machines. If such a system is adopted it establishes new boundaries for the firm's new product activities and might lead to the development of new insurance products which previously were not feasible.

A major consideration with respect to technology is the discrepancy (if any) between the level of technology of the firm and the state of the art in both the conventional field of interest and other areas from which technology might be transferred to the given area. Consider, for example, the watch industry and the impact the semiconductor technology had on its current mode of operation—digital and quartz watches increased rapidly their share of the watch market at all price levels.

ORGANIZATIONAL RESOURCES

The capital, material, and human (in particular managerial) resources of the firm are major constraints on the firm's ability to successfully undertake new product development activities. In discussing the requirement for a successful new product development system (Chapter 8) we emphasized the need for a continuous system which has major resource implications, especially for small firms.

---

[4]Excluded from this discussion is the customer's (or potential customer's) technology which, despite its important effect on the design of new products, has only limited effect on the way the firm has to organize its new product development efforts.

Whereas capital resources can in most cases be obtained for the development and commercialization of a good new product idea, the material and human resources do place major short-run constraints on the firm's ability to develop new products.

Intangible resources such as good will (corporate image) and management expertise also have implications for the nature of the new products a firm may want to develop. The need to develop new products consistent with the corporate image may restrict the boundaries of the new product development activities of the firm.

The strengths and weaknesses of the organizational resources also affect the nature of the firm's new product development activities. Consider, for example, a firm with strong marketing expertise but weak R&D. In the short run such a firm might be better off focusing on the identification and acquisition of potentially promising new products (developed by others) and introducing them on a large scale taking advantage of its marketing expertise and resources, rather than relying on its own R&D to invent new products.

Organizational resources affect not only the nature of the new product development activities of the firm, but also the way the firm organizes for new product development. The reliance on outside resources for new product idea generation, development, and evaluation might be required if the firm does not have the necessary human resources. The development of a permanent organizational unit devoted to new product development (such as a new product department) versus a temporary unit (such as a task force) depends to a large extent on the available resources, the scope of the new product activities, and the nature of the required R&D expertise and its related scientific knowledge base.

Furthermore, since the speed of new product development depends to a large extent on the resources available, the organizational resources that can be allocated to new product development (and subsequently to the market introduction of these products) reflect management trade off between time (speed of development) and resources.

PEOPLE

Human resources are by far the most important asset of an organization. It is people who invent new products and make the various new product decisions. The design of an organization for new product development should therefore reflect the type of people required. New product development involves a variety of tasks which require quite distinct qualities. Most notable among the required tasks, and hence desired personnel traits, are creativity, political/negotiative skills, administrative skills, and strong persistence and motivation.

Creativity New product development involves a considerable amount of creativity, especially at the idea/concept/product generation and development stages. Hence, to the extent possible, recruiting creative people (based on guidelines such as those discussed in Chapter 9) would increase the likelihood of developing innovative new products and making creative decisions.

Political/negotiative skills The new product development process involves participants from various organizational functions—R&D, marketing, finance, etc. Furthermore, in many organizations new products under development compete for resources with each other and with existing products and activities. The competition for resources for new product development among various organizational units is especially severe in a strongly decentralized structure. Hence, the successful management of a new product development effort requires a considerable amount of political sensitivity and negotiative skill, as well as an organizational design with built-in rewards for cooperation.

Administrative skills The complexity of the new product development process requires strong administrative skills to coordinate the efforts of diverse individuals and groups, plan and manage the process on schedule and within the determined budget.

Persistence and motivation The frustrations and obstacles in the way of a new product development process are many. It is rare to find a new product process which goes smoothly with no setbacks, occasional failures and at least some resistance from various organizational members. One of the major requirements for a successful new product development effort is persistence and strong motivation on behalf of the new product "champion(s)".

It is unrealistic to expect a single individual to possess all these required creative, negotiative, administrative, and motivational skills. The personnel solution for new product development, therefore, is the hiring, training, and retaining of a *group* of individuals who *together* possess all these skills. Having individuals with such skills still requires an appropriate organizational design which puts these skills together, enhances them (e.g., an organizational climate and reward system which encourages creativity), and directs them toward the achievement of the organization's new product objectives, recognizing that different skills are required at different stages in the new product development process.

MANAGEMENT STYLE AND DECISION PROCESSES

An organizational climate receptive to new product ideas is often viewed as one of the determinants of a successful new product development system. The organizational climate is in turn strongly influenced by management style. Similarly, the actual new product decisions of the firm reflect the managerial style of the organization. The design of a new product organization requires, therefore, an understanding of the current management style, either accepting it as a major constraint or trying to make it more receptive to the demands of new product innovation and development.

Of the various dimensions of management style identified in the organizational behavior and marketing literature, six have major implications for the design of an organization for new product development. These six dimensions of managerial style include the beliefs about and preference for risk taking, the research and planning orientation of management, the choice rules and process employed, the belief about participative management, administrative flexibility, and the efficiency of coercion.

Risk-taking Management trade off between risk-taking and risk-aversion is often a major determinant of the nature and outcome of the firm's new product development efforts. Risk-aversion style implies conservative management which emphasizes stability, evolutionary change, and reluctance to accept radically new products which depart markedly from the current operations. Innovative new products require some degree of risk-taking. A risk-aversion management style makes the development and acceptance of innovative new products quite difficult and is often one of the major reasons for the development of "me too" products.

Some degree of risk-taking is, therefore, a necessary component of an organizational climate receptive to innovation. Khandwalla (1977) in a study of 103 Canadian firms found that high-risk-taking firms were characterized by entrepreneurial, growth-oriented decision-making, empahsis on R&D, technological leadership and innovativeness, a general proclivity to high risk, high-return investments, external financing of investments, and competitive orientation.

Research and planning orientation Management acceptance of the point of view that the solution of most problems can benefit by the right type of research-based information, as opposed to a seat-of-the-pants, intuitive managerial judgment, is a major factor in determining the nature of the firm's new product development process. Intuitive managerial judgment, although important, cannot substitute for a well-designed and executed research program embedded within a formal planning approach. Having a critical research orientation (neither avoidance of research nor a blind reliance on the research outcome) coupled with a strong planning orientation (systematic search for opportunities, systematic and rigorous assessment of alternatives, emphasis on long-term strategic consideration, etc.) is essential to the success of the firm's new product development effort.

Choice rules In making choices concerning the various decisions involved in the new product development process, management can employ a number of choice rules. The specific choice rules employed determine to a large extent the nature and outcome of the new product development process. If, for example, management insists on some optimization rules, the required information and choice process is much more complex than if management were to employ a satisficing rule (Simon, 1960). With few exceptions, most new product decisions do not lend themselves to an optimization procedure. In these cases the choice rule employed, whether disjunctive, conjunctive, or other, can result in a different outcome. A trade-off model, for example, implies that management is willing to trade off any criteria (sales growth, for example) against some other evaluative criteria (such as expected prof-

itability or market share). On the other hand, if management employs an elimination-by-aspect procedure or some threshold model, when a proposed new product is not likely to perform above a critical threshold level on some criterion (such as sales growth), the proposed product will be killed.

Participative management The two extreme orientations on this dimension are an individualistic decision-making orientation with aversion toward institutionalized participative management versus the team management orientation. No rules can be set concerning the dominance of either of these orientations. Organizations should strive for a balanced approach in which decisions able to benefit from participative management do so while decisions made more effectively and efficiently by an individual are not burdened by team decision.

Administrative flexibility A new product development process requires an organic (versus mechanistic), flexible (versus rigid) administrative orientation in which authority is vested in situational experts as opposed to a rigid bureaucratic organization.

The characteristics of organic/flexible organizations found by Khandwalla (1977) in his study of 103 Canadian firms resemble the characteristics typically associated with a creative/innovative organization. These characteristics include: open channels of communication; free flow of information throughout the organization; managers' operating style allowed to vary freely; free adaptation by the organization to changing circumstances; emphasis on getting things done rather than on following formally laid-out procedures; job behavior permitted to be shaped by the requirements of the situation and personality of the individuals doing the job.

Coercion A coercive authoritarian management orientation, although inconsistent with the creative innovative aspects of new product development, can occasionally be quite effective in the management of more routine aspects of the new product development process, if the environment is hostile and restrictive. Yet, since coercive management tends to *force* the introduction of changes, use threats to reduce noncompliance, and resolve disagreement with authoritarian rulings, it is not a stable and effective long-run orientation. Furthermore, not all managers have the personality traits required for an effective execution of an authoritative management style.

Given the complexity and multiphase nature of any new product development process, the heterogeneity of individual personality traits and organizational characteristics, no single ideal management style can be identified. Each of the six dimensions, if combined with appropriate other values, can in certain circumstances be an appropriate orientation that helps achieve the desired corporate objectives. The organizational designer should, therefore, examine these and other orientations and select the ones best suited for the various stages of the new product development process. Similarly, in examining existing new-product organization design it is important to identify the managerial orientation of the managers involved directly with new product development as well as the style of top management. Often one can find clues for the lack of

new product success in the managerial style of the firm.

INFORMAL ORGANIZATION

Understanding the informal organization—the structure of activities, norms, relationships, and patterns of communication, among individuals, groups and organization units, over and above those sanctioned by the organizational hierarchy—is essential for successful planning and implementation of the firm's new product development activities. In particular, in designing (or changing the design of) an organization for new product development the following considerations should be taken into account: Which members of the organization get along well together and which do not? How consistent are the formal and informal lines of communication? Are the formal leaders of the organization also the informal ones? (This is especially crucial in R&D operations in which expert power is often more significant than formal organizational authority power.) How consistent are the informal norms with the formal norms of the organization? How likely is it that the various discrepancies between the formal and informal organization would affect the new product development process and outcomes and in what direction is it likely to affect them?

DEMANDS ON ORGANIZATIONAL DESIGN FOR NEW PRODUCTS

A survey conducted by Booz, Allen, and Hamilton (1968) among companies which have been relatively successful with new products, identified organizational difficulties as the major hindrance to new product development. Over half of all the problems mentioned focused directly on some organizational aspect and over 80 percent of the companies were concerned with some kind of organizational problem. Those mentioned included definition of responsibilities, working and reporting relationships, communication patterns, top management support, size of organization, organizational structure, and the organizational systems and procedures. Organizational problems are even more pervasive if one considers the organizational component of some of the other problems mentioned by the respondents, such as poor control and follow-up, poor definition of objectives, inadequate business analysis, inappropriate personnel qualifications, etc.

More recently, an executive of Booz, Allen, and Hamilton (Nylen, 1978) singled out four (organizationally related) managerial problems which seriously impede new product success: lack of top management commitment, inadequate organization for new products, misunderstanding of the role of the marketplace in new product development, and management failure to accept the risk inherent in the new product process.

Effective new product development requires special attention to designing an organization which avoids these issues and is responsive to the demands of effective and efficient new product development systems. These demands include:

- Overcoming the organizational barriers to innovation

- Encouraging creativity and innovations

- Assuring top management involvement

- Assuring interfunctional coordination

- Assuring the continuity of the new product development process

- Allowing for a mix of "make-buy" activities

- Achieving the right mix of differentiation and integration

- Recognizing task heterogeneity

- Allowing for *inter* organizational cooperation

- Preventing suboptimization

A brief discussion of the nature of these demands and their implications for design of new product organization follows. These con-

siderations are especially (but not exclusively) relevant to non programmed innovation. Programmed (routine) innovation, such as routine style changes in automobiles, home appliances and fashion, although requiring creativity, are distinguished from the non programmed innovation by the well-defined routines available for generation, evaluation, and implementation of the programmed changes.[5]

OVERCOMING BARRIERS TO INNOVATION

The organizational and social change literature has long emphasized the inertia, risk-avoidance, and resistance to change which characterize many individuals and organizations. Strategies to overcome this resistance to change are typically suggested. Shepard (1967), for example, in discussing innovation resistance and innovation-producing organization offers the following prescriptions:

> It (innovation in innovation resisting organizations) requires an unusual combination of qualities: a creative but pragmatic imagination, psychological security, and an autonomous nature; an ability to trust others and to earn the trust of others; great energy and determination; a sense of timing; skill in organizing; and a willingness and ability to be Machiavellian where that is what the situation requires.

Non programmed new product innovations are potentially threatening changes which might disturb the status quo and be perceived by some organizational members as threatening and harmful (for example, by reallocating resources from established brands to a new product). Given this possibility the new product organization should allow for: (a) an orderly

---

[5]For a discussion of programmed vs. non-programmed innovation, see Knight (1967).

and open way of raising questions on the desirability of certain new product development efforts, and (b) development of an incentive system to generate the needed support for new product development.

A frequent barrier to progress in the new product development activities is not the conscious objections by "opponents" of the new product but rather the endless delays imposed by "the supporters" of the new product development. This is often the case when those involved in the new product development are also responsible for ongoing operations. In these cases, the short-term pressures of current operations tend to dominate and shift downward the priorities of new product activities.

Separate incentives for new product development activities, frequently scheduled progress reports, and organizational separation (devoting separate personnel to the new product development activities) are among the more common organizational solutions to this major obstacle.

ENCOURAGING CREATIVITY AND INNOVATIONS

One of the most difficult assignments for organizational designers is the design of a structure which encourages creativity and produces innovative products. One school of thought subscribes to the idea that the key to creativity and innovation are the *people* and that creative individuals will perform creatively and innovate in any organization, regardless of its structure and climate. Yet, there is an opposing school of thought that believes that the "right" organizational structure and procedures can encourage creativity (and conversely, the "wrong" organizational structure and procedure can impede creativity).

Studies of organizational climate and creative organizations have identified a number of characteristics that help increase creativity. These characteristics[6] include:

- Offer individual, challenging work
- Realistic and explicit goal setting
- Immediate feedback
- Reward structure and recognition of creative work
- Openness and allowance of conflict
- Mixture of specialization
- Job enlargement
- Involvement
- Porous organizational boundaries
- Less conformity

These and other characteristics have often been proposed as the determinants of innovative organizations. Yet, empirical support for these generalizations is relatively weak. Evan and Black (1967), for example, in a study of 104 staff proposals for ideas for innovation, found that successful proposals are found in organizations with:

- A higher competitive position
- A higher degree of staff professionalism
- A higher degree of formalization of rules
- A higher degree of communication between staff and line personnel
- A higher degree of quality of proposals
- A higher degree of perceived needs for the proposal
- A lower degree of management professionalism (are they more likely to rely on the judgment of the professional staff?)

---

[6]The discussion in this section is an adaptation, used with permission, of A. Gerstenfeld, *Effective Management of Research and Development,* © 1970, Addison-Wesley Publishing Company, Inc. For another view of the creative organization see the findings of Gary Steiner's 1965 study of *The Creative Organization* which were briefly discussed in Chap. 8.

EXHIBIT 16–3

ILLUSTRATIVE DIFFERENCES AMONG VARIOUS ORGANIZATIONAL FUNCTIONS

Source: From a pilot study by Lorsch and Lawrence, 1965.

Function	Degree of departmental structure	Orientation toward time	Orientation toward others	Orientation toward environment
Research	Low	Long	Permissive	Science
Sales	Medium	Short	Permissive	Market
Production	High	Short	Directive	Plant

Not significant in discriminating between successful and unsuccessful proposals were managerial receptivity to change, the organization's degree of centralization, the size of the organization, and the number of proposals per manager.

These findings are obviously limited to the organizations and proposals examined in this study, but they do suggest the need to avoid generalizations and stereotypes of innovative organizations and instead use a more empirical approach to the identification of the factors contributing to the encouragement of organizational creativity and innovation.

ASSURING TOP MANAGEMENT INVOLVEMENT

The importance of top management involvement in and commitment to the new product development process has been generally accepted. The staggering costs of most new product development efforts require allocation of resources by top management. The question however is, How can the new product development organization assure such involvement and commitment to start and bring to fruition the new product development efforts, while not curtailing the freedom and entrepreneurial spirit required for an effective "innovative" type organization?

Two common solutions are participation by some members of top management in a new product team, venture group, or task force, or alternatively, via some form of an evaluation and approval procedure.

ASSURING INTERFUNCTIONAL LINKS

Given the interfunctional nature of new product development as discussed in Chapter 1,[7] any organizational design would have to allow for effective and efficient links among the various organizational functions involved in the various states of the new product development process. The design of organizational mechanism(s) to facilitate such links is complicated not only by possible differences in task and goal perceptions and by diverse professional orientations of the various functions (as illustrated in Exhibit 16–3), but also by individual differences among the members of the various functions which could affect their behavior and attitude toward members of other functions.

---

[7]For a more detailed discussion of these interfunctional links, see Wind (1981).

These and other factors tend to encourage interfunctional conflicts. It is one of the major tasks of the organizational designer to turn this potential conflict into a constructive force and build in necessary interfunctional cooperative mechanisms and incentives.

Of special importance in this context is the development of an organizational design which encourages and assures the necessary cooperation among the key new product development functions such as R&D, marketing research, and marketing. The importance of marketing and marketing research to the new product development efforts has been emphasized throughout this book. Accepting the importance of these interactions requires, however, that they be reflected in the way the firm organizes its new product development efforts.

ASSURING CONTINUITY

As strongly emphasized in Chapter 8, one of the requirements for a successful new product development effort is the design of a *continuous* system and the avoidance of single-shot activities.

Conceptually, the continuity requirement is important to (a) allow for reexamination of rejected ideas/concepts/products, (b) benefit from the expertise gained in the process of developing a new product (learning curve effects in the new product development and not only the production stage), and (c) facilitate a system which allows for a balanced portfolio of new product activities (i.e., at any given point in time the firm should have L new products/ideas at the idea generation stage, K in the new concept evaluation stage, M in the new product development stage, N in various stages of new product evaluation, etc.).

Against these conceptual considerations stand the organizational solutions of ad hoc teams of one sort or another, and the practice of promoting the manager of a successful new product development effort to manage the new product's market introduction. These arrangements contribute to the lack of permanency required for any continuous new product development effort.

The new product organization designer should therefore evaluate the merits of organizational solutions which do not allow for continuity, and seek organizational designs which (a) take advantage of temporary units, (b) avoids counter-continuity incentive schemes, and assures continuity via other organizational solutions.

ENABLING A MIX OF "MAKE-BUY" ACTIVITIES

The decision whether to undertake an internal new product development effort ("make") or alternatively to go the merger and acquisition route ("buy") has significant implications for the desired organizational design. This decision is further complicated by the fact that it can, and should, be made at *each stage* of the new product development process. How can an organization be designed to maintain the flexibility required at *each stage* to consider either internal development (e.g., R&D effort) or purchase of the desired outcome from outside sources (e.g., buying or licensing technology)?

If all the make-buy decisions are planned in advance, an organization can be designed to accommodate it. Yet, given the sequential nature of all new product decisions it is extremely difficult to make *all* the make-buy decisions in advance. Hence, the organizational design should be flexible, guarding against the natural desire of a "make" type organization to undertake *all* activities internally and reject almost automatically any "buy" consideration.

ACHIEVING THE RIGHT MIX OF DIFFERENTIATION AND INTEGRATION

Two major dimensions of any organization are:

a) The *differentiation* of organizations into subunits to obtain task specialization (to deal effectively with their technical and market environment). This differentiation involves not only differentiation along the task dimension but also with respect to structure, norms (occupational orientations), and time.

b) *Integration* of the activities of these subunits to achieve an effective unity of effort.

The importance of understanding these dimensions and in particular the conditions under which one can achieve effective collaboration among different organizational units is especially crucial for the design of an organization for new product development which involves a large number of organizational units, requires considerable amounts of differentiation, and hence has strong needs for integrative devices.

One of the most exhaustive studies on the problems of differentiation and integration in complex organizations is the study by Lorsch (1965) of the development and transfer of new technological and scientific knowledge into new product and process applications in two large chemical companies. Summarizing previous research on the topic, Lorsch studied two hypotheses[8] on the processes of organizational differentiation and integration:

(a) "If a structural integrative device is effective in integrating basic subsystems, it will tend to be intermediate between the basic subsystems in structure and occupational orientation." (Note that this hypothesis implies that an integrative unit which is not in the middle may be more similar to one of the basic units it is linking but it will then necessarily be more differentiated from the other units that need integration and hence less effective in achieving integration.)

(b) "Within any organizational system the greater the differentiation between any two subsystems in relation to the requisite integration, the greater will be the difficulties in obtaining effective integration between them."

These hypotheses were confirmed in the Lorsch study. The effectiveness of a structural integrative device appears to be related to its intermediate position in structure and occupational orientation between the basic subsystems it is linking. Within each system integration effectiveness between subsystem pairs is a function of the degree of differentiation between them. Additional findings relating to the differentiation-integration dimension were:

- The basic subsystems in the studied organizations were differentiated around their respective tasks in both structure and occupational orientation.

- Integrative devices of both the structural and process type tend to emerge.

- The effectiveness of process integration devices appears to be related to the norms about the locus and mode of conflict resolution. When conflict was confronted and worked through within the setting of these devices, the devices seemed to be functional in integrating the activities of the several subsystems.

- Intermediate position of the structural integration devices, less systems structure, and system norms that sanction conflict resolution at the lowest level of the organization, have led to an organization with high differentiation, sound integration and better system performance.

[8]A third hypothesis was also stated: (c) "If other system characteristics are similar, the greater the degree of total differentiation within each system, the greater the problems of integration and the greater the dysfunctional consequences in system performance." Yet the study did not allow Lorsch to test this hypothesis directly, although some of his findings suggest that this is an *oversimplified* hypothesis.

RECOGNIZING TASK HETEROGENEITY

The heterogeneity of organizational tasks, especially with respect to the development, manufacturing, and marketing of new products, suggests that the structure of a complex organization should not necessarily be homogeneous (Leavitt, 1962). In fact, Lorsch (1965) found that "different subsystems should and often do have different degrees of structure depending upon the requisites of their tasks. Similarly, different occupational orientations are appropriate for different tasks."

Accepting this finding and premise suggests that different stages of new product development, manufacturing, and marketing require different organizational tasks, structure, technology, people, and organizational climate. The R&D director whose task is the stimulation and management of the creative activities of a laboratory of scientists would require a less rigid structure, more permissive interpersonal style, a research task orientation and a longer time focus than the marketing manager involved with the design and implementation of the introductory marketing program or the production manager in charge of the highly programmed activity of manufacturing.

ALLOWING FOR INTERORGANIZATIONAL COOPERATION

New product development, not unlike marketing, is one of the major boundary functions of any organization. Throughout the development process contacts are made with external organizations ranging from marketing research and law firms who work for the firm, through innovative firms which can provide the necessary technology, to government agencies (such as the FTC or FDA) whose approval may be required.

The design of an organization for new product development, therefore, should take into consideration this requirement for inter-organizational communication. These inter-organizational relationships differ markedly in their complexity and organizational design implications. Whereas relationships with a law firm or marketing research supplier are quite routine, some of the inter organizational relationships such as those with outside inventors can be complex. The gearing for adaptation and utilization of innovations developed elsewhere (especially by foreign inventors) requires special organizational design considerations by creating a climate conducive to the systematic search, evaluation, and acceptance of external innovations.

The organizational design implications of inter-organizational relations include:

- The intrinsic rewards versus extrinsic benefits of the interorganizational relations. Extrinsic benefits are detachable from the persons or organizations who supply them and hence offer external criteria for choosing between possible organizations. Intrinsic rewards offer no such criteria since the inter organizational association is to a degree an end in itself.[9]

- The reciprocal versus unilateral nature of the inter organizational association. Reciprocal relationships can lead to either mutual attraction (if the relationships are based on intrinsic rewards) or exchange (if the relationships are based on extrinsic benefits). Unilateral relationships on the other hand can lead to a one-sided attachment (if based on intrinsic rewards) or power relationships if the relationships are based on extrinsic benefits.[10]

- The expected degree of conflict versus cooperation and the type of cooperation and coalition formations one may expect.

---

[9] This distinction is based on Blau, 1964.
[10] Ibid.

EXHIBIT 16–4

ADVANTAGES AND DISADVANTAGES OF ALTERNATIVE LOCATIONS OF NEW
PRODUCT ACTIVITIES

Reprinted with permission from D.S. Hopkins, *Options in New Product Organization*, N.Y., The
Conference Board, 1974.

Location	Advantages	Disadvantages
Corporate level	Allows better coordination and control of all the company's programs for innovation.	Corresponds to the advantages of the divisional level location.
	Resources available for new-product development can be concentrated where the outcome is likely to be most fruitful.	
	New-product decisions are less likely to be colored by the more parochial, short-term considerations of divisional management.	
	New product ideas need not necessarily be tied to the kinds of products, technologies, and markets with which individual divisions are familiar.	
	Senior corporate management is kept more aware of on-going new-product activities, with the result that these will probably receive greater attention and support.	
Divisional level	New products developed at the divisional level are more likely to be attuned realistically to customer needs, market opportunities, and productive capabilities of each division.	Corresponds to the advantages of the corporate level location.
	Division-wide involvement and commitment to the new-products program may increase the chances of success.	
Corporate and divisional levels	Offers flexibility in allocating company-wide resources for new product development between corporate and operating levels.	Responsibility for new products is divided, perhaps causing problems in communication, duplication of effort, or missed opportunities.
	Policy control and perspective can be retained at the corporate level, while the divisions can continue to play an active role in new-products programs.	Difficulties may arise in making a fair and logical allocation of responsibilities between the two levels.
	Helps to engender an innovative environment throughout the company.	Unless there is an effective control system, the number of products under development may turn out to be too many — or too few.
		This arrangement is suitable only for firms of substantial size that are well-staffed at both corporate and divisional levels.

- The different environmental and inter-organizational interactions one can expect from members of various organizational roles. Parson (1960) distinguishes between the interorganizational role set, relations of technical, managerial and institutional members. In the context of new product development efforts, top management is likely to have different modes and nature of inter organizational interactions than technical or scientific members of the organization.

PREVENTING SUBOPTIMIZATION

New product development activities often lead to new technology or ideas which may not fit current organizational units. If this is the case and the new product activities are within an operating unit (a division, a business unit and the like) there is high likelihood that the idea or technology will be discarded.

Limiting new ideas and development to those most compatible with the current nature of operations of the units is especially likely in a multidivision, decentralized organization. In such cases the competition among the various divisions might restrict the free flow of ideas among the divisions and could lead to lost opportunities from the overall corporate point of view.

To avoid such suboptimization the new product organizational design should allow for mechanisms and incentives for transfer of ideas among organizational units as well as consider the advantages (versus the disadvantages) of an additional centralized corporate new product development unit which could evalute the potential of new product ideas without the restricted boundaries of the current operations, budget, and objectives of the operating units of the organization.

This solution of a corporate new product development unit (reporting to general management) offers not only a broader view of new product activities, but also enhances the clout of the new product activities. Some of the advantages and disadvantages of corporate versus divisional versus dual (corporate *and* divisional) location of new product activities are summarized in Exhibit 16–4 which is based on a study of 100 "experts"—executives involved in new product activities—conducted by Hopkins (1974) for the Conference Board.

R&D MODELS FOR THE ORGANIZATION OF NEW PRODUCT DEVELOPMENT

The R&D literature has long been concerned with the question of how best to organize the R&D function. Given the importance of the R&D component of new product development efforts, and the well-accepted view of *R&D as a process* not unlike the new product development process, the R&D organizational models can serve as useful examples for new product organizational design. Consider, for example, the description of innovation in the R&D litera-ture (Battelle, 1973):

> Innovation is a complex series of activities beginning at first conception when the original idea is conceived; proceeding through a succession of interwoven steps of research, development, engineering, design, market analysis, management decision making, etc.; and ending at first realization; when an industrially successful product which may actually be a thing, a technique, or a process, is accepted in the marketplace.

This "thought process" model is descriptive of the events which happen in R&D *or* in marketing *or* in production as individuals try to solve problems and respond to external demands. In an organizational behavior sense, innovation is *risk-taking behavior*—financial as well as social; individual as well as organizational. The spending of dollars for both technology (traditional R&D) and marketing research and development activities is an effort to reduce the risk of innovation. When not coordinated, the technical and marketing risk reduction efforts may proceed out of phase with each other.

The part of the R&D process in which we are interested is concerned with *innovation*. It confronts such problems as:

- Identifying opportunities
- Finding creative solutions
- Tracking progress
- Knowing when to quit
- Overcoming organizational inertia
- Motivating people to take risks
- Determining the optimal mix of basic research, applied research, and development.

The need to solve these and similar problems, which are not unlike the ones faced by managers of new product development efforts, coupled with the realization that a large number of R&D failures are due to nontechnical (Primarily marketing) reasons (In a 1970 study of 91 R&D projects, 32 percent were viewed as successful while 16 percent failed due to technical reasons and 52 percent due to nontechnical failures), have led to the development of and experimentation with numerous organizational designs and to a "broadening" of the R&D perspective and especially to greater focus on the R&D-marketing and R&D-manufacturing interfaces and the organizational implication of these needed interfaces.

R&D-MARKETING INTERFACE

The close interface between marketing and R&D is illustrated in Exhibit 16–5. The nature and type of the interaction and collaboration problems between the two functions have been examined in a number of studies.[11] One of these studies among 116 innovation projects (Chakrabarti and Bonoma, 1977, and Souder, 1981) clearly identified some of the common problems of R&D-marketing interaction:

1. Marketing and R&D parties often disagree on resources, plans, and responsibilities. They frequently fail to air these differences in opinions and collaborate early enough during the life cycle of the project. Thus, latent conflicts may emerge at a later date during the project and disrupt it at a critical point.

2. There are some rather natural organizational, professional, and human proclivities that tend to reinforce a cultural separateness of R&D from marketing.

3. The degree of harmony, joint involvement, and felt partnership between R&D and marketing were found to be significant determinants of the overall success of a firm in managing the innovation process. A lack of marketing inputs, guidance, commitments and interest were the major reasons found for project failures.

4. Nearly all firms appear to have some incidence of R&D-marketing coordination problems. Large firms and large projects, however, seem to have a higher incidence of R&D-marketing coordination problems.

---

[11]See for example Hanan (1965) or Berenson (1968). Berenson not only examined the boundary and interface between marketing and R&D but also proposed a general analogue model (based on mass transfer concepts) for structuring the transfer of R&D results to the marketplace.

EXHIBIT 16–5

R&D—MARKETING INTERFACE IN THE PROCESS OF TECHNOLOGICAL INNOVATION

Reprinted with permission from "Information Flow, Management Styles, and Technological Innovations," by J. Goldhar, L.K. Bragow, and J.J. Schwartz, which appeared in *IEEE Transactions on Engineering Management*, Volume EM-23, No. 1, February 1976, p. 53. Copyright © 1976 IEEE.

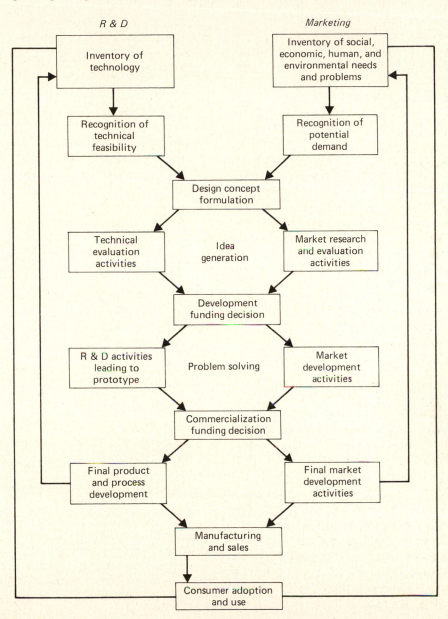

5. Centralized R&D structures were found to have a higher incidence of R&D-marketing coordination problems than divisional structures.

Because of these and other forces, some mechanisms are required to bring R&D and marketing together within the innovation process. Chakrabarti and Bonoma (1977) examined the effectiveness of ten integrative mechanisms: technical one-person show, commercial one-person show, technical project manager, commercial project manager, dyad (a strong interpersonal relationship between a marketing person and an R&D person), product manager, technical line management, commercial line management, new products development, and product committee (a standing high level committee linked to lower level ad hoc task forces and work groups). Their findings, although of questionable generalizability to all cases, do offer some interesting insight into the effectiveness of the various mechanisms. They found:

• No *one* "best" way to obtain an effective R&D-marketing interface. The choice of an "appropriate" management method depends on the nature of the technology and the market environment.

• The project manager system, the dyad mechanism, the product committee system, and new product departments appear to be appropriate mechanisms for managing undeveloped technologies, and for handling environments where the product specifications and user needs were not well understood.

• Product manager system and a commercial (marketing) one-person show appear to be appropriate for managing well-developed technologies and handling well-known market environments.

• Overall, the most *ineffective* ways found to manage the R&D marketing interface were:

the technical one-person show (R&D tries to do it all), the technical project manager system (an R&D-based project manager runs the show), and the technical line management method (the project is run by a top-down R&D line management system). Top-down management, formalized structures and paper-work systems are therefore not effective integration mechanisms.

• In general, teams, task forces, and project systems were the most effective ways found to manage the R&D-marketing interface.

• The most successful innovating firms had internal organizational climates that were promotive of R&D-marketing collaboration, and used teams, dyads, task forces and project management systems to link R&D and marketing. These mechanisms were reinforced with planned early involvements of R&D and marketing personnel in the project decision making. The emphasis was on frequent face-to-face exchanges, rather than on administrative hierarchies or paperwork systems.

• Management can directly influence the degree of R&D-marketing collaboration through two actions: (1) the careful selection and legitimization of the product or projects manager's role; (2) the implementation of joint reward systems.

R&D-MANUFACTURING INTERFACE

To facilitate transferring the results of R&D to operations, a number of organizational approaches have been employed. Quinn and Mueller (1963), for example, specified nine such approaches: task force groups; corporate development units; outside companies; staff groups at corporate levels; a top executive with

EXHIBIT 16–6

CONDITION FOR THE EMPLOYMENT OF R&D TRANSFER MODELS

Source: A. Gerstenfeld, *Effective Management of Research and Development*, ©1970, Addison-Wesley
Publishing Company, Inc., adaption of pages 43–53. Reprinted with permission.

| Conditions | R&D transfer models | | | | |
	Product specification and drawings (1)	Manufacturing participation in R&D (2)	R&D participation in manufacturing (3)	Corporate coordination (4)	Transfer team
Nature of new product	Uncomplicated	Average complexity	Complex	Moderate complexity	Complex
Production process	Flexible	Not relevant	Continuous	Infrequent new products	High quantity
Transfer time	Not critical	Critical	Not critical	Critical	Not relevant
Production cost	No need for reduction	Essential to reduce cost	Not a major factor	Not a major factor	Minimum production cost is desired
Required skills of transfer personnel	Minimal	Manufacturing engineer with required R&D skills	An R&D Engineer with manufacturing skills	A coordinator with required skills	Personnel is available
Relation between R&D & manufacturing	Independent	Manufacturing is dependent on R&D engineering	Manufacturing is dependent on R&D engineering	Can vary	Can vary
Physical proximity of R&D lab and manufacturing flexibility	Not relevant	Not relevant	Not relevant	Not relevant	Have to be located near each other

multifunctional line authority; a research group with a special budget to buy time on operating machines; individual researchers who entrepreneur their ideas through pilot facilities and into the market; multilevel committee responsibility; and an entrepreneurial group at corporate level.

Gerstenfeld (1970) synthesized these and other organizational approaches into five basic transfer models:

- Product specification and drawings,
- Manufacturing participation in R&D,
- R&D participation in manufacturing,
- Corporate coordinator,
- Transfer team.

In evaluating these models, Gerstenfeld has identified the conditions under which each of these models is most appropriate. These conditions are summarized in Exhibit 16–6.

ALTERNATIVE APPROACHES TO THE ORGANIZATION OF NEW PRODUCT DEVELOPMENT

New product committees, task forces, venture teams, or managers are a few of the numerous organizational forms employed by consumer and industrial firms to organize their new product development activities. In addition, a substantial number of firms employ outside venture groups to undertake part or all of their new product development activities.[12]

These various internal organizational forms vary with respect to three major dimensions:[13]

- *Time commitment*—Whether the unit is full or part time. This dimension is often associated with organizational separation. Full time units can, at least conceptually, be designed as organizational units separate from the operating units. Such a desirable situation is often not feasible if the new product development is carried out on a part time basis by personnel who have other operating responsibilities and, hence, cannot devote the time and priorities required for successful new product development.

- *Permanency status*—whether the unit is permanent or temporary. This dimension is also linked to organizational separation. Permanent units tend to be organization-

ally separable even though there are cases to the contrary.

- *Servicing level*—whether the unit services the entire firm (corporate), a division (business), or a product group (or line).

These three dimensions lead to 12 organizational forms of which 8 are generically distinct. Those 8 units and their characteristics are illustrated in Exhibit 16–7. These organizational forms vary not only with respect to the three primary dimensions (of time commitment, permanent status, and servicing area), but also with respect to the organizational characteristics most appropriate for them (e.g., organizational size, type of product lines, etc). The relationship, suggested by Benson and Chasin (1976), between the eight new product organizational forms and some key organizational characteristics are specified in Exhibit 16–8.

The functions assigned to and performed by the various organizational forms vary considerably from total involvement in *all* phases of the new product development by a new product division or department, to, typically, a limited involvement by a new product task force. The specific new product development functions undertaken by each organizational form in the Benson and Chasin survey is summarized in Exhibit 16–9.

An examination of the 8 organizational forms suggests some overlap among them. Hence the following discussion focuses on five major organizational forms:

- New product development department or division
- New product manager and the new product aspects of brand management
- Venture team

---

[12]Consider, for example, the new product activities discussed by Stefflre (1971) and more recently, those of Booz, Allen Venture Mangement Inc.

[13]This approach is based on a study of 267 consumer and industrial firms with sales over $50 million.Its discussion is excerpted, by permission of the publisher, from *The Structure of New Product Organizations,* An AMA Management Briefing, by G. Benson and J. Chasin, © 1976 by AMACOM, a division of American Management Associations. All rights reserved.

EXHIBIT 16–7

CLASSIFICATION OF NEW PRODUCT ORGANIZATIONAL FORMS

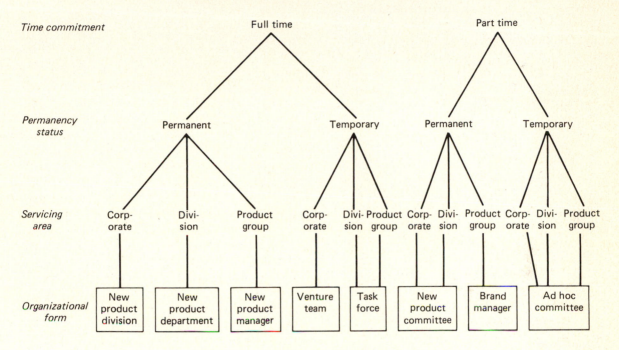

- Task force
- New product committee—both permanent and ad hoc committees

The next section discusses some of the distinguishing characteristics of these organizational forms. In examining them, it is important to note, however, that many organizations employ more than a single new product organizational form. Benson and Chasin (1976) for example, found in their survey of new product organization that 41 percent of the companies surveyed employed more than a single new product organization form.

NEW PRODUCT DEVELOPMENT DEPARTMENT OR DIVISION

Both the new product department and division are full-time permanent units. The two differ in the organizational level they serve and degree of self-sufficiency. A division tends to be more self-sufficient, and larger with full-time staff. Technically oriented firms tend to have their R&D unit organized along these lines. In this case, problems of interorganizational coordination (with marketing, finance, production, etc.) might arise.

EXHIBIT 16–8

CONDITIONS FOR SELECTING SPECIFIC NEW PRODUCT ORGANIZATIONAL FORMS

Reprinted, by permission of the publisher, from *The Structure of New Product Organizations*, An AMA Management Briefing, by G. Benson and J. Chasin, © 1976, by AMACOM, a division of American Management Associations, p. 18. All rights reserved.

General characteristics of firm/division	Div'n	Dep't	NPMgr	NPCom	BrMgr	TaskF	VentT	AdHoc
Size/Resources								
Large	X	X	—	—	—	X	X	—
Moderate	—	X	X	—	—	X	X	—
Small	—	X	—	X	X	X	—	X
Product Divisions								
Dissimilar	—	X	X	X	X	X	X	X
Similar	X	—	—	—	—	X	X	X
Not divisionalized	—	X	X	X	X	X	X	X
Product lines								
Consumer	X	X	X	X	X	X	—	X
Industrial	X	X	—	X	—	X	X	X
Service	—	X	—	X	X	X	—	X
New product demand								
Continuing	X	X	X	—	—	—	—	—
Sporadic	—	—	—	X	X	X	X	X
New product concern								
Innovative	X	X	—	—	—	X	X	X
Me-too	X	X	X	X	—	X	X	X
Line extensions	X	X	X	X	X	—	—	—

A new product department can serve either a single division or strategic business unit (in a decentralized organization) or a number of divisions or SBUs.

NEW PRODUCT MANAGER AND NEW PRODUCT ASPECTS OF BRAND MANAGEMENT

A new product manager initiates, plans, and coordinates the new product activities for a product group, line, or brand within a division or department. It is a permanent function within a decentralized organization. It is often a one-person new product department.

A similar function but on a part-time basis is often performed by brand managers where part of their responsibility involves line extensions and modification of existing products.

VENTURE TEAM

The philosophy behind venture management is to provide a group of individuals freedom and

EXHIBIT 16–9

FUNCTIONS ASSIGNED TO NEW PRODUCT ORGANIZATIONAL FORMS

Phases—tasks	Div'n (35) %	Dep't (111) %	NPMgr (40) %	NPCom (76) %	BrMgr (89) %	TaskF (45) %	VentT (22) %
Initial screening	100	97	90	71	83	27	45
Fund authorization:							
Exploratory activity	74	66	31	62	41	11	31
Market evaluation	57	65	19	58	47	13	40
Authorize R&D effort							
Make feasibility study	77	77	50	67	43	22	40
Develop prototype	71	69	35	74	47	23	45
Time schedules/budgets:							
Prepare time schedule	80	89	75	45	64	66	72
Monitor time schedule	82	90	77	59	72	60	54
Prepare budget	80	81	64	37	58	48	59
Monitor budget	80	85	60	50	57	44	50
Authorize product testing:							
Consumer testing	62	63	36	40	65	28	54
Test marketing	57	59	41	53	67	30	59
Test marketing:							
Preparation of plan	74	80	80	33	88	50	45
Control preparation	62	63	70	23	67	44	50
Responsibility for test marketing	57	56	65	20	70	32	50
Launching/commercialization:							
Participate in launching	77	74	68	40	89	52	68
Control launching	48	53	53	35	71	32	59
Task involvement average	71	73	57	49	64	36	51

flexibility in the design and development of new businesses (Jones and Wilemon, 1972). A study among 112 industrial and consumer products venture managers (Hill and Hlavacek, 1972) and a second study among 24 large consumer and industrial goods companies (Jones and Wilemon, 1972)[14] suggested the following

[14] These characteristics and the findings which follow are excerpted, by permission of the publisher, from "Emerging Patterns in New Venture Management," by K.A. Jones and D.L. Wilemon, *Research Management*, November 1972, pp. 26–27.

characteristics of venture teams:

- *Organizational separation.* Separation from the operating organization, and flexibility in role and place in the organization. Despite the desired organizational separation of venture teams, their success depends to some extent on their ability to borrow personnel and other resources from other parts of the firm. Hence the importance of the acceptance of the venture team by others.

- *Multidisciplinary.* Venture team participants are drawn from virtually all organizational functions—design and application engineering, production, market research, finance, etc. Some of the typical contributions to the venture team by various functional areas are listed in Exhibit 16–10.

- *Diffusion of authority.* Team members are free to develop their own relationship to each other in light of the overall mission to be accomplished. Team managers often appear indistinguishable from other team members.

- *Environment of entrepreneurship and freedom.* Segregation from other administrative units of the firm, absence of time pressures and freedom from the confinement of job descriptions appear to foster a free-wheeling atmosphere conducive to innovative activity. Entrepreneurial spirit and high involvement is further heightened by financial arrangements which permit members of the team to share in the profits of the venture.

- *Top management linkage.* Venture team man-

EXHIBIT 16–10

SOME TYPICAL FUNCTIONAL CONTRIBUTIONS TO VENTURE TEAMS

Reprinted, by permission of the publisher, from K.A. Jones and D.L. Wilemon, "Emerging Patterns in New Venture Management," *Research Management,* November 1972. Copyright © 1972, Industrial Research Institute.

Marketing

Marketing research assistance

Pricing

Personnel

Marketing analysis and model building

Market strategy formulation

Manufacturing

Manufacturing cost and feasibility

Consulting on product cost

Plant feasibility

Process feasibility

Legal Department

Patent procedures and advice on protection

Licenses

Product liability advice

Finance

Financial analysis, pro forma statements, cash flow analysis

Budgets

Personnel

Engineering

Design

Technical feasibility

Machine design

Consulting of engineering costs

Product testing

Research & Development

Technical feasibility and development assistance

Technical testing

New methods and materials

Cost estimates

agers usually report to the chief administrative officer of the business unit, hence ensuring both free communication with the top and top management support.

- *Broad mission*. Venture teams are a goal-directed endeavor whose efforts are intended to achieve a single result—the development of new products and businesses for the corporation. Yet, the team's mission is generally defined in a broad enough manner which permits considerable discretion in its pursuit.

- *Flexible life span*. Venture teams are usually free from pressures of strict deadlines. Even where there is a well-defined developmental sequence with check points, the completion time allowed for each is only loosely defined. The planning horizons used by venture teams vary markedly and in the Jones and Wilemon study ranged from one to ten years with about 70 percent of the studied teams indicating a venturing time frame of three to five years.

- *Flexible structure*. Teams may be composed of part-time, full-time or some combination of part- and full-time members. The number of members can vary markedly (Jones and Wilemon, for example, found teams with 0 to 250 full-time members, 0 to 50 part-time members, and a mean size of ten members.

These characteristics of venture teams have both positive and negative implications for venture managers (and participants). These implications were examined explicitly in the Jones and Wilemon (1972) study of venture managers. Their findings in this regard are:

- The foremost factor venture managers *liked* about their jobs was the challenge of working in an atmosphere of ideas, working on a multidisciplinary activity and high degree of visibility.

- The things most often *disliked* about venture management were the long time period from recommendation to feedback concerning success or failure of a venture, not being able to see a project through to completion and a general feeling of being removed from the mainstream of corporate activity.

TASK FORCE

Task forces usually group individuals from various functional areas to form a special ad hoc unit for the purpose of coordinating and managing the development of an assigned new product. In most cases the product concept is specified, but there are cases in which new product task forces are called for the generation of new product ideas, or for the performance of any or all of the activities involved in new product development. Task forces operate either full- or part-time, for a prescribed life span or until their task is completed or aborted. Several task forces can operate simultaneously within any organization.

NEW PRODUCT COMMITTEE

New product committees can be either permanent or temporary, but involve only part-time participants. As with task forces, committees are usually staffed with representatives of the various functional departments. In most cases a new product committee operates as a part-time new product department.

New product committees are distinct from new product review committees which are usually composed of top management and focus not on the development of new products, but rather on the approval of new product proposals.

New product committees often are the solution when the formal organization is too weak to manage successfully the new product development efforts.

INTEGRATED APPROACHES TO THE DESIGN OF NEW PRODUCT ORGANIZATION

Successful new product development, technological change, and innovations occur as a result of complex sets of human interactions, information flows, creativity, risk-taking and decision-making of individuals, groups and organizations under rapidly changing, complex, and uncertain environmental conditions. Designing an "optimal" organization to facilitate new product development activities is, therefore, not an easy task. Understanding the components of organizational design, the barriers to innovation, the organizational requirements for new product development, and the various possible new product organizational forms, are therefore necessary conditions for the design of an organization for new product development activities. Yet, the idiosyncratic personal, interpersonal, organizational, and environmental conditions preclude the prescription of a single "best" organizational design.

Despite this need for a "tailor-made" organizational design there are two major concepts which if integrated could help provide the

necessary guidelines for designing an organization for new product development. These concepts are that of a VP of innovation and a modular system for new product organization.

VP OF INNOVATION MODEL[15]

The *VP of Innovation* concept is based on the recognized need for a high-level focal point for new product development activities. In most organizations, today's problems and pressures drive out tomorrow's goals. Fire fighting is the major enemy of planning and in particular long-range planning. Yet, the survival and growth of most organizations depend on their ability to develop and market successfully new innovative products. It is important, therefore, to establish a top management position respon-

---

[15] The discussion in this section is based on Wind and Goldhar, 1977.

EXHIBIT 16–11

ILLUSTRATIVE ORGANIZATIONAL CHART FOR VP OF INNOVATION

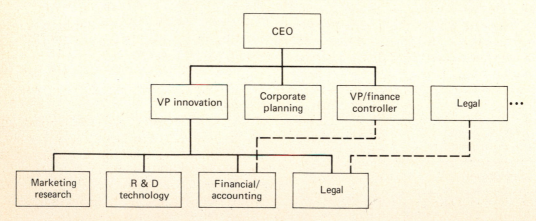

sible for the planning, organization, motivation, coordination, implementation, and control of technological, business, and marketing innovations. The hierarchical position of the VP of Innovation is illustrated in Exhibit 16–11. Organizationally, such a position should be at the same level as corporate planning, marketing and the major operating units.

The responsibilities of the VP of Innovation are envisioned as encompassing the activities of planning, coordinating, communicating, implementing, and controlling the entire new product activities of the firm. These include, for example:[16]

- Strategic planning: environmental scanning, option development, and techno-economic analysis and forcasts,
- New product-related information management,
- R&D planning,
- New product-related marketing research,
- New business venture,
- New product introductions,
- Setting and allocating the new product development priorities and budget,
- Control and monitor the new product activities of the firm,
- Provide a focal point for the new product activities of the firm and the communications related to these activities.

The VP of Innovation is the top executive in charge of *all* new product activities of the firm. This position legitimates the role of innovation and provides a highly visible focal point for a concentrated planned effort at the development of truly new and innovative products.

The personnel reporting to the VP of Innovation are drawn from a variety of other organi-

zational functions and hence should maintain some functional (dotted line) relationship with their home departments (such as marketing, finance, and legal). This, in effect, results in a matrix organization (Gailbraith 1977) with its associated advantages.

The only function which can report directly to the VP of Innovation with no other organizational affiliation is the R&D function. The advantages of this arrangement are that this would allow the development of the most appropriate organizational climate for R&D activities while at the same time enhancing the necessary interface between R&D and other relevant functions, such as marketing. Furthermore, reporting to a VP of Innovation could increase the status of R&D and help create an organizational climate in which the R&D efforts are better coordinated with markets and corporate needs.

The creation of a VP of Innovation job with associated staff does not assure by itself the success of the firm's new product activities. Such a unit may become isolated from the rest of the organization. If it does not perform in an accepted way for the operating divisions, they are likely to start their own new product activities. There is a potential for friction and conflict in the unit's relationship with the other business functions. Finally, the unit's visibility, separate status, and lack of regular sources of revenues may make it vulnerable to budget cuts in bad times.

Recognizing these and other limitations is important in determining whether to accept such an organizational solution and if yes how to design it in a way that would assure the achievement of the corporate new product objectives.

The VP of Innovation should work closely with the corporate directors (VPs) of planning, marketing, and marketing research. These functions can (with or without the chief executive officer) constitute the "future group" of the corporation, which is in charge of plotting the

---

[16]For a somewhat different formulation of required new product tasks and activities (not in the context of a VP of Innovation, however) see Murphy (1962).

future course of the firm with respect to both products (businesses) and markets.

MODULAR APPROACH

Recognizing the diversity of firms and situations, which precludes the development of a single "best" new product organization, Benson and Chasin (1976) suggested a modular system for new product management. Such a system would

> . . . possess the flexibility to efficiently fulfill the new product development needs of small and large companies and their divisions as well as those of consumer and industrial goods firms, initiate and manage short- and long-term development projects, and develop innovative as well as me-too products. The modular system provides a channel of communication between all participating departments of the firm and would coordinate the new product efforts of these units. To be effective, the system should be free of functional department biases, provided with a respectable budget to finance the initial stages of new product investigations, unhampered by the necessity for top management clearance, and permitted to exploit qualified people within the firm at every step of the development process. The system should be given full responsibility for all phases of the new product effort. Top management must create and cultivate such an environment and free it from destructive internal politics.

Such a modular system would include:[17]

I. A core component—a new product development department. The primary re-

sponsibilities of such a department (which can vary in size depending on the size of the organization and the desired level of new product activities)[18] are:

a) Developing short- and long-term product plans.
b) Generating and collecting new product ideas.
c) Screening and evaluating the feasibility of new product concepts.
d) Making screening decisions.
e) Allocating funds from predetermined budgets for marketing investigations.
f) Exploring the technical and commercial feasibility of new product concepts.
g) Recommending new product projects and development priorities.
h) Coordinating new product activities of functional departments.
i) Preparing and revising budgets and schedules.
j) Monitoring and enforcing adherence to approved budgets and schedules.
k) Performing product testing, test marketing.

II. *Executive approval and review committee,* which would include the VP of innovation and other executives from relevant functions.

III. *Ad hoc component including task forces and/or venture teams.* To assist the new product development department in its activities, add to its flexibility and take advantage of skills available in other parts of the organization, it might be advisable to plan on the

[17]The modular system proposed by Benson and Chasin includes two other components . . . a liaison committee and new brand manager. These concepts are not viewed by the author as essential for a new product organization. Yet, the readers are encouraged to consider these and other organizational forms besides the ones suggested here.

[18]Note that in small firms the department can include a single person. In such cases it might be appropriate, at least in the short run, to give such a person the title and responsibility of a new product manager.

EXHIBIT 16–12

COMMUNICATIONS FOR EFFECTIVE NEW PRODUCT EVOLUTION

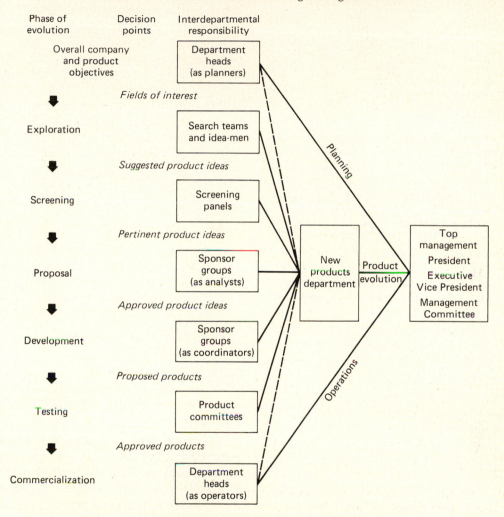

organization of ad hoc task forces (for new products related to the current product line of an existing division or business unit) or venture teams (for new products not related to any existing business unit).

The modular basis of new product organization is further illustrated in Exhibit 16–12 which presents the Johnson and Jones (1957) conceptualization of the new product development process.

CONCLUDING REMARKS

New products are rarely developed without explicit planning and an organizational arrangement. Ideas might emerge spontaneously but a successful systematic development of new products requires a "champion" and organizational support. A strong "champion", especially if located in a powerful position in the organization, might marshall the necessary resources to develop and introduce a new product. Yet, in general, the odds of successful (and especially continuous) new product development efforts are much higher if there is an organizational arrangement supportive of the complex, continuous, and resource-demanding activities of new product development.

The organizational behavior literature can provide useful guidelines for the necessary organizational design considerations, some of which were briefly discussed in this chapter.

In designing an organization for new product development one final consideration should be made explicitly—To what extent should the organizational arrangement be built around the current personnel (and organizational structure) of the firm or should the organizational design be free of such constraints and be free to hire the necessary personnel and change the current organizational structure? Conceptually, from the *organizational* point of view the latter orientation is preferred. Yet, market and environmental conditions might make it very difficult, especially in the short term.

The presence of such constraints complicates considerably the organizational design task and requires greater creativity and flexibility in the development and implementation of any necessary organizational changes aimed at the development of an efficient and effective new product development system.

Designing an organization for new product development is one of the most complex tasks involved in the management of the new product activities of a firm. Too often the temptation is to remain within the boundaries of the current organization, viewing it as a constraint on the new product development activities of the firm.

Yet, the importance of having an appropriate organizational design for new product development calls for explicit effort at designing an organization capable of meeting the varied tasks of new product development efforts.

To help your understanding of the complexities involved and the implementation problems, select a company of your choice, make any assumptions concerning its line of business, current organizational structure, objectives, technology, and personalities involved, and design for it a specific organization for new product development. Once designed, make an explicit list of the major advantages and disadvantages of this organization and consider for each disadvantage, the alternatives available to overcome it. Upon completion of this task, modify your organizational design and compare it to one of the more common organizational designs (such as a new product development department or committee). In making this comparison, assess the advantages and disadvantages of each form, and identify the conditions under which a specific organizational design seems to be most appropriate.

PART THREE

MANAGEMENT OF EXISTING PRODUCTS

Despite the importance and glamour of *new* product development activities, the financial survival and growth of all organizations depend, to a large extent, on the effective management of its current products and services. The two chapters in this part briefly encompass some of the major aspects of this important area.

Chapter 17 focuses on organization for existing products. It's built on the foundation of organization design discussed in the first part of Chapter 16, but focuses on the various organizational forms utilized in the management of existing products. The second chapter in this part is devoted to the key interrelated decisions of product modification, repositioning, and deletion. The importance of these options, their determinants, and the approaches one can utilize in making these decisions are outlined.

Excluded from this part of the book is a discussion of the marketing strategy for established products. This exclusion is due to the coverage of such material in most marketing management and strategy texts. Similarly, this part of the book does not deal explicitly with the general concepts and methods of generation, evaluation, implementation, and control of (product or other) strategies since there are no differences between the relevance of these concepts and methods to product or other management decision domains.

Organizing for Product Management

INTRODUCTION

How should a firm organize to achieve an effective and efficient management of its current products? *Product management* is widely used by both consumer and industrial product firms. Yet is this the "best" organizational design? When should it be employed? When should other organizational structures such as market management, functional organization, and hybrid designs such as product/market management, or geographical/product structure, be employed?

The objective of this chapter is to briefly examine these alternative organizational designs, identify some of the major considerations for selecting an organizational form, and outline some of the difficulties involved in changing an organizational design. This discussion is followed with two sections on the relationship between organizational design and product planning and the control and monitoring system.

BRAND MANAGEMENT

In their college recruiting brochure, P&G, the company that introduced the brand management system, describes this organizational approach this way:

> Brand Management is the mainspring and moving force behind all our marketing. Nearly fifty years ago Procter & Gamble pioneered the Brand Management concept, concentrating the marketing responsibility for each brand in the hands of a capable manager who focuses all managerial and marketing skills on just that brand. This brand independence enables us to market vigorously a number of different products, some competitive with others in our line. It assures that each brand will have behind it the kind of single-minded drive it needs to succeed.
>
> This drive is supplied by a separate Brand Group which plans, develops, and directs the marketing efforts of its product. The Brand Group usually consists of just three or four people: Brand Manager, Assistant Brand Manager, and Brand Assistant. The Brand Group is expected to know more about its product and how to increase consumer acceptance than anyone else in the Company.
>
> The Brand Manager leads the Brand Group,

assigning the Assistant Brand Manager and Brand Assistant broad areas of responsibility: developing the annual marketing plan; developing and executing the advertising copy strategy; planning and selecting media; planning sales promotions; coordinating package design; and analyzing and forecasting business results.

Whereas the responsibilities of a brand management group vary only to a limited extent from one brand group or company to another, the number of managerial levels and size of the group may vary markedly. GF, for example,[1] employs a slightly more elaborate system described below:

> *Assistant Product Manager:* This is the starting point for recent business graduates, their first position on the Product Management team.
>
> Early in his or her work at White Plains headquarters, the Assistant Product Manager assumes primary responsibility in the areas of

---

[1]The following description is quoted from the GF Product Management brochure "Career Opportunities at General Foods." Reprinted with permission of General Foods Corporation.

volume planning (market and share forecasting), financial budget control, production planning coordination, promotion execution, coordination with legal and purchasing functions, and business analysis. This work helps build a quick and intimate acquaintance with the brand and the various General Foods functional resources.

As he or she gains experience, the Assistant Product Manager often assumes responsibility for national promotional strategy, planning and execution, as well as packaging strategy and execution. The Assistant Product Manager may also begin to have contact with one of GF's five advertising agencies—just 45 minutes away in Manhattan—and thus have opportunity for early exposure to the advertising side of GF's business.

Since the marketplace itself is a crucial test of any marketing strategy, the Assistant Product Manager will typically be assigned for a brief period to one of GF's sales districts. During this time, he or she will become thoroughly familiar with the needs and views of retailer organizations, the operations of GF's sales teams, and the position of GF brands in relation to competition.

Associate Product Manager: The move to Associate Product Manager is an important step. Frequently, the Associate Product Manager is the brand's major representative in dealing with manufacturing, technical or marketing research, and also plays an important role with the advertising agency. In some cases, an Associate Product Manager will have full charge of a small brand, with responsibility for initiating, planning, and developing overall strategies for copy, media, and promotional programs for the assigned product, as well as for the execution of the programs after they have been approved.

Product Manager: The Product Manager leads all the functional resource efforts affecting a single product or several related brands. He or she directs the efforts of Associates and Assistants and has a responsibility for their training and overall development.

The Product Manager is responsible for the development of the annual marketing plan and current fiscal year objectives. This is accomplished within a five-year strategic plan that also requires the development of long-term business objectives for the product.

The Product Manager develops marketing strategies to reach objectives, and reviews and adjusts marketing plans each quarter. After objectives and marketing strategies are approved by senior marketing executives, the Product Manager is responsible for their execution and for brand performance. Typically, the Product Manager has primary responsibility for performance against franchise (volume and share) objectives.

Also, the Product Manager is the key contact for advertising agency relations and spends a major portion of his or her time planning and implementing consumer advertising and sales promotion efforts, while working with the agency and promotional development specialists.

Product Group Manager: As a senior marketing manager, the Product Group Manager's responsibilities may be of two kinds. He or she may direct the activities of three or more Product Managers and their brands, or be in charge of one of the company's largest franchises. The Product Group Manager is responsible for the strategic planning of the businesses he or she supervises, as well as for the quality of execution against shorter-term programs. A Product Group Manager will also be expected to play a large role in the financial and overall business management of his or her brands. In some divisions, the position of Product Group Manager is the highest marketing level below Marketing Manager.

Category Manager: In most divisions, the Category Manager is the top level reporting to the Marketing Manager. He or she is responsible for the success of many related products or several of the company's largest and most important franchises, and the long- and short-term marketing margin of the category. Also, the Category Manager oversees the allocation of resources within the category for the most effective performance, and recommends an overall set of objectives and strategies to maximize GF's opportunities within the category. In many cases at GF, categories account for sales volumes well in excess of $200 million.

Marketing Manager: The Marketing Manager is responsible for the direction of marketing activities across the division's entire menu segment (Coffees, Desserts, Pet Foods, etc.). The Marketing Manager is the prime mover in shaping long-term strategies and is the ultimate determinant of the quality of near-term marketing activities. As a member of the General Manager's staff, the Marketing Manager participates in developing financial strategies to improve the overall profitability of the division's franchises. At General Foods, the Marketing Manager's responsibility can cover annual net sales running as high as $1.6 billion.

Conceptually, the brand management system allows a multi product corporation to gain the benefits associated with entrepreneurial spirit and decentralization. The brand manager is often compared to the "president" of his brand who, according to one description, "must know more about his brand than anyone else, outthink the competition, come up with new product ideas, hammer out marketing budgets, get good ads out of the agency, wheedle work out of the market research department, induce his company's salesmen to put their backs into it, romance distributors and retailers, meet management's sales goals, maintain and improve his market share—and return the company a tidy profit on his brand" (*Business Week*, 1965a).

The responsibilities of brand management vary to some extent depending on whether they are in an industrial or consumer goods company. These differences are clearly illustrated in Exhibit 17–1. Such diversity is also evident within a given industrial category by type, size, and other characteristics of the firm. Despite this diversity in brand managers' activities, authority, and responsibility, most brand managers tend to focus on a common set of activities:[2]

- Establishing the product's marketing objectives
- Planning the marketing, product, and packaging activities to achieve product objectives
- Determining expense budget for each of the marketing activities
- Scheduling the marketing activities (especially type, frequency, and timing of promotions)
- Establishing (ongoing) measurements and control review procedures
- Communicating plan to assure understanding by those who will implement it (especially the salesforce)
- Creating and maintaining enthusiasm for the plan
- Monitoring progress and effectiveness of performance according to preestablished standards
- Specifying corrective action when plan and performance are at variance
- End-of-year report to management
- Post-mortem plan reevaluation for learning purposes

Brand management involvement with these decisions and activities varies markedly. Note, for example, the reported finding by Clewett and Stasch (1975) that 25 percent of the brand managers they studied indicated that "they have the freedom to make only moderate changes in their product's annual marketing plan, and another 67 percent reported that they are even more restricted in this regard."

Their reasons for the variation in the role brand management plays in various companies are:

1. The number of brands involved and their relative importance.

2. The number of management levels involved in the decision-making and plan-approval process.

---

[2] These items are based on Clewett and Stasch (1975).

EXHIBIT 17-1

RESPONSIBILITIES OF PRODUCT MANAGEMENT

Responsibility	Industrial (product manager)	Consumer (brand manager)	Governmental (product manager)
Profit	+	+	+
Coordination	+	+	+
Sales:			
Development	−	+	−
Promotion	−	+	−
Assistance	+	+	+
Direction	−	+	−
Planning	+	+	+
Consolidation	+	+	−
Customer service	−	+	−
Merchandising	+	+	−
Competition	+	+	+
Manufacturing	+	−	+
Engineering	+	−	+
Training	−	+	−
Market:			
Analysis	+	+	−
Research	+	+	−
Planning	+	+	+
Forecasting:			
Profit	+	+	+
Sales	+	+	−
Market	+	+	−
Inventory	+	+	−
Distribution	+	+	−
Advertising	−	+	−
Promotion	−	+	−
Product:			
Research contact	+	−	+
Development contact	+	+	+
Test marketing	−	+	−
Introduction	+	+	+
Planning	+	+	+
Packaging	−	+	−
Control	+	+	+
Modification/improvement	+	+	+
Pricing	+	+	+
Quality	+	+	+
Legal aspects	+	+	−
Technical service	+	+	−
Consumer research	−	+	−
Operations research	+	+	+
Purchasing	+	−	−
Systems	+	+	+
Computer applications/services	+	+	+

Key: Plus sign corresponds to major emphasis; minus sign, to minor emphasis.

3. The number and type of marketing mix elements employed and the location of their providers (inside or outside the firm).

4. The nature and magnitude of the resources and support services used in common for a number of brands.

5. The brand's stage in its product life cycle and the nature and changes in the relevant product environment.

The commonly-held view of a brand manager as a "superman" and an "ideal" organizational problem solver for the effective management of a brand ignores, however, a number of key problems associated with this organizational form. Namely:

• Brand managers, although saddled with enormous responsibility, are denied a corresponding authority. They have no authority over the salesforce; the selection of an advertising campaign involves numerous other participants among whom the brand manager is often the most junior and inexperienced executive; rarely, if ever, does a brand manager have any voice in the determination of the brand's price; and the brand manager has little control over the production and management costs of the brand.

• The wide responsibilities of the brand manager tend to lead to the development of a *generalist* with little in-depth understanding of any of the key functions. This is not bad by itself, especially if the brand manager takes advantage of the numerous service departments (such as marketing research or advertising), which can offer him or her the necessary expertise. Yet, it is in most cases up to the brand manager to seek their advice and utilize it. Furthermore, a hierarchical brand management system with a number of assistant and associate brand managers tends to create a relatively large management team composed primarily of generalists with little reward or incentive for the development of staff expertise.

• Given the pressures of daily management activities of the brand and its promotions, most brand managers don't have time for any strategic thinking and their efforts tend to be tactical and short term in nature.

• The large number of relatively routine activities which occupy the bulk of the brand manager's time lead to an overemphasis on the bureaucratic aspects of the job and an underemphasis on the entrepreneurial functions. This problem was recognized by Dietz (1973), for example, who proposed three variations of brand management: (a) *brand coordinator*, who has bureaucratic responsibilities but no entrepreneurial responsibilities, (b) *brand champion*, who has bureaucratic responsibility combined with responsibility for making entrepreneurial recommendations, and (c) *brand director*, who has bureaucratic responsibility along with responsibility for entrepreneurial action and profits.

The demands on and expectations from brand managers are significant. These are illustrated in the following list of criteria suggested by Ames (1963) for the evaluation of a product manager's effectiveness:

1. Is he on top of varying market conditions and requirements so that he is able to accurately interpret the changing needs of his product's business?

2. Does he draw together complete and imaginative plans for his product area that are acceptable to top mangement?

3. Do his plans include concrete programs for effecting required improvement in his product's business?

4. Does he follow up and, if necessary, modify approved plans to see that product objectives are achieved?

5. Is he generally regarded by other executives as the most knowledgeable about his product's requirements, and do they look to him for ideas on what they should do to meet the product's needs?

MARKET MANAGEMENT

Market-based organization is often viewed as a logical extension of the marketing concept. To best reach the firm's target market segments, each segment requires the design, implementation, and control of a separate marketing strategy. These activities can in turn be best performed by a management team devoted to the specific market segment.

A market-based organization requires, therefore, a detailed knowledge of the market and its division into homogeneous segments, each of which is served by a dedicated organizational unit. This form of organization is often recommended for firms with a single or few products, which operate in multiple markets.

Conceptually, this is an attractive basis for organization under the following conditions:

- The markets are classified based on their response to marketing variables. A common approach to the determination of the market units is some demographic characteristic such as SIC in industrial markets or geographical location for international markets. Yet, unless the market has an identifiable marketing response function, organization by market is a questionable basis for organization since its only advantage is administrative convenience.

- The market segments which constitute the basis for the market organization can be reached separately.

- The market segments differ from each other and are relatively stable over time.

- The products involved are not too numerous and complex for the market managers to understand and market effectively.

When these conditions are met, market managers are the individuals with the full-time responsibility for planning, implementing, and controlling the firm's marketing efforts in a given market segment.

PRODUCT/MARKET MANAGEMENT

Product brand management is a commonly proposed solution for a firm with multiple products marketed to a single or few markets. Conversely, market management is the solution for a firm with a single or few products aimed at multiple markets. With the added complexity of multiple products and multiple markets and the increasing number of firms confronted by such complexity, a new organizational form has been proposed—the *product/*

EXHIBIT 17–2

A PRODUCT/MARKET ORGANIZATION

		Market managers					
		Manager 1	Manager 2	Manager 3	. . .	Manager j	. . . Manager k
Product managers	Product 1 Product 2 Product 3 ⋮						
	Product *i*						
	⋮ Product *n*						

market management organization.

A simple representation of this organizational form is illustrated in Exhibit 17–2. An examination of this exhibit reveals the potential conflict associated with this type of organizational design. Assuming product and market managers of equal authority, who is going to determine the corporate strategies in cases in which there are clear-cut conflicts between product manager *i* who wants to maximize sales of his product to all market segments and market manager *j* who does not want to sell product *i* to his market, either because it requires more effort than the selling of other products or because his customers prefer an alternative product?

Charles Ames, of McKinsey and Company, who recommended the product/market management structure, recognized this likely conflict and commented on it: "Although it is inevitable, the conflict arising from the interaction of product managers and market managers should not be viewed as a negative factor. In fact, this kind of conflict is specifically what the dual management concept is designed to produce. It should be regarded as a positive force" (Ames, 1971).

This dual-management concept calls for product managers being held accountable for all aspects of product line management, including long-term profitability. Similarly, market managers are held accountable for long-term growth and profitability of their assigned markets.

Neither manager would have line authority for decisions and actions that affect his areas of concern, yet both are given full responsibility for using their knowledge and ideas about the market and product to get the best possible decisions and actions. If the two evaluate the market and product correctly, and design an appropriate plan, they will be successful in their roles. Thus *both* should be held accountable in this fashion to ensure the best planning and management job for each product/market segment.

If planning for a larger number of discrete product/market segments is believed to provide the basis for accelerating profit growth (or the achievement of other corporate objectives), the dual management approach might be appropriate. Under this approach the roles of the two types of managers would most likely include the following activities:[3]

Market managers should concentrate their efforts on:

- Developing a comprehensive understanding of customer and end-user operations and specifying ways that the existing product/service package can be promoted and improved to provide a competitive edge.

- Identifying related products and/or services that represent attractive opportunities for profitably increasing the company's participation in the market through either internal development or acquisition.

- Drawing together at regular intervals an organized summary of the most attractive opportunities in the marketplace, specifying what must be done internally to capitalize on them, and recommending a first-cut strategy for the business.

- Developing a reputation for industry expertise among key customer and end-user groups and bringing this know-how to bear on the negotiation of major orders and on the training and development of field sales personnel.

In a similar vein, *product* managers should focus on:

- Protecting the pricing integrity of their product—that is, seeing to it that the pricing policies and practices in one market do not jeopardize the company's position or profit structure in another.

- Maintaining product leadership by making certain that product design, cost, and performance characteristics not only are broadly responsive to customer needs in all markets but also are not inadvertently altered to meet the needs of one market at the expense of the company's position in another.

- Ensuring that their product is responsive to market needs while at the same time protecting the engineering and production process from getting cluttered with a proliferation of small-lot, custom, or special orders; in effect, they temper market managers' enthusiastic customer orientation with sober judgments on operating capability and economics.

- Ensuring that production scheduling and capacity are intelligently planned to profitably meet current and anticipated aggregate demand of various markets.

- Providing the in-depth technical and/or product knowledge required to support selling efforts on major and complex applications.

These broad activities are the core of the job of market and product managers. However, the makeup and importance of the company's various products and markets should determine the specifics of their job structure. Product managers invariably function on a full-time basis but may, of course, be given responsibility for more than one product. According to Ames, there is little latitude in structuring this position.

The market manager's job, however, may be structured in three different ways, depending on the number, importance, and geographic spread of the markets involved. Thus his or her role may be set up as:

---

[3] These prescriptions are based on Ames (1971).

1. *A part-time staff planner.* This role structure gives the market focus without the added cost of full-time market managers. Companies which follow this approach add market planning assignments to the responsibility of senior salespeople, sales managers, or application engineers who have some expertise in a given end-use market. This compromise approach is normally followed by companies which deal in such a large number of markets that they simply cannot afford to provide full-time market manager coverage for each one.

2. *A full-time staff planner.* Following this approach, the product/market planning job is divided into two parts—product managers and market managers—who operate in parallel.

3. *A full-time staff planner with line sales responsibility.* Giving the market manager line sales responsibility, as well as the staff planning assignment, adds direct responsibility for a group of salespeople who specialize in selling to the accounts that make up the specific served market.

This approach gives one person a combined responsibility for both planning and execution within each market area and thus makes it possible to hold him or her fairly accountable for results. It also ensures that the market manager has a firsthand feel for customer and market requirements.

Despite the conceptual attractiveness of this organizational form, practically it is limited because it is often difficult to justify the degree of sales specialization inherent in this kind of arrangement. Although most companies can point to a cluster of accounts in certain geographic areas for which they could economically justify a specialist salesperson, to get national coverage they often must turn to the general salesperson who sells all products to all markets. Accordingly, in most cases, it simply is not feasible to work out an arrangement where the salesforce can be divided neatly under several market managers.

The product/market organization form is conceptually attractive given its attention to both the products and markets. Yet, it is plagued with operational problems. These include the difficulty in defining the market units, the high likelihood of conflict between the two interests, and the lack of a clearcut responsibility for the design and execution of the needed marketing strategy.

OTHER ORGANIZATIONAL FORMS

Whereas the brand, market, and product/market management approaches have been the major approaches used to manage the marketing activities of established products, a number of other approaches also have been employed. These include the functional and geographic approaches as well as a number of hybrid approaches.

The *functional* approach to organization tends to be associated with centralized marketing operations in which there are no products or market managers. Functional organizations (when compared to *product* organizations) seem to be more appropriate (Walker and Lorsch, 1968) where:

1. The task is repetitive or routine.
2. Less differentiation in structure and time

orientation but greater differentiation in terms of goal orientation is required.

3. Integration can be achieved by plan.
4. Conflicts can be managed through the hierarchy.

Functional organizations, according to a study by the same authors, are also less psychologically demanding on the individuals involved. Individuals feel satisfied but with less feeling of stress and involvement.

Occasionally, however, a functional organization can be combined with a product or market organization as a *matrix organization*. In both of these cases the key to the establishment of effective organization is the identification of the relevant marketing functions—advertising, packaging, distribution, etc., the specification of the detailed roles associated with them, the allocation of tasks, responsibilities, authority, and activities between the functional managers and the product or market managers, and the establishment of coordination (and conflict resolution) mechanisms.

Whereas a functional organization offers the greatest incentive for specialization, it is likely to suffer from coordination problems and possibly a lack of focus for product or market planning, implementation, and control activities.

A *geographical* basis for organization is often dominant in international operations. The advantages of using a country or region as the basis for organization are obvious from an administrative convenience point of view, although to the extent that a country or a region does not represent a homogeneous market segment, this basis for organization cannot serve as a substitute for a market organization.

Geographical bases also have been employed domestically, primarily in conjunction with some other basis, forming again some type of a matrix organization.

EXHIBIT 17–3

PURE AND HYBRID ORGANIZATIONAL DESIGN

Adapted from J. Galbraith, "Matrix Organization Designs," *Business Horizons,* Feb. 1971. © 1971 by the Foundation for the School of Business at Indiana University. Reprinted by permission.

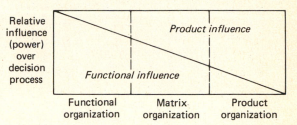

Whenever a *matrix* organization or similar *hybrid* organization form is selected, it is important to consider the advantages and disadvantages of the allocation of resources and power which are implied by the specific hybrid design.

The relative power (e.g., authority and responsibility for resources, etc.) in the decision process can vary from a predominantly resource-based structure (e.g., a functional organization) to a self-contained, program-based structure (e.g., a product or market organization). Exhibit 17–3 illustrates the two extremes and the conditions under which a matrix organization makes sense. One should consider, however, a number of other possible hybrid designs. If management in a functional organization desires a higher level of product orientation, they can adopt a number of approaches, namely, the introduction of product task forces, product teams, or product integrators (product managers). Alternatively, if the management of a product organization desires to increase the level of functional involvement in the decision process they can introduce functional task forces, functional teams, or functional managers.

SELECTING AN ORGANIZATIONAL DESIGN

Given the variety of possible organizational designs for the management of existing products, an explicit selection should be made to determine the most appropriate organizational form. The design of an organization for the management of existing products involves, in principle, the same considerations a company should utilize in the design of an organization for new product development as specified in Chapter 16.

Among the various approaches to organizational design for the management of existing products, the information-processing approach[4] seems especially appropriate. This approach requires the following steps:

• Identification of the physical and mental tasks (decisions and information requirements) that have to be undertaken. This can usually be done by modeling the decision process and the information required for each decision.

• Grouping of tasks into jobs and assigning them to groups and individuals, i.e., arrange functions and responsibilities based on the natural grouping of tasks involved. If, for example, the information required for effective management of existing products involves primarily information on various market segments, a market organization seems to be called for, etc.

• Given the natural grouping of activities (and decisions) determine: (a) information and other resources required for performing the job effectively, (b) measures of performance compatible with the organizational objectives, (c) the necessary incentive system, (d) criteria and procedures for recruiting, selecting, and training the new required personnel.

The information-processing (and other) approaches to the selection of an organizational design are of two major types: A *forward* selection in which the process centers around changes from the present system or from a prototypical system and a *backward* design which starts with the design of an *idealized system* (Ackoff, 1974 and 1976),[5] and having identified it

---

[4]For a detailed discussion of the information approach to organizational design, see Galbraith (1973 and 1977). Organizational design, according to Galbraith, is concerned with the creation of mechanisms that permit coordinated action across a large number of interdependent roles. The ability of an organization to successfully coordinate its activities by goal-setting, hierarchy, and rules depends on the frequency of exceptions and the capacity of the hierarchy to handle them. As task uncertainty—the difference between the amount of information required to coordinate cooperative action and the amount of information actually possessed by the organization—increases, the number of exceptions increases until the hierarchy is overloaded. At this stage there are two major information-processing-based design strategies that can be employed: (a) reducing the need for information processing (this can be achieved by the creation of slack resources and/or the creation of self-contained tasks) and (b) increasing the capacity to process information (by investment in vertical information systems and/or the creation of lateral relations.

[5]The major characteristics (and rationale) for idealized designs are (according to Ackoff): the conversion of planning from a retrospective to a prospective orientation; the invitation and facilitation of widespread participation of all stakeholders in the system; generation of consensus among those who would otherwise disagree on what should be done about the system; encouragement of an examination of the whole system rather than a focus on one or more parts to the exclusion of the others; inducement of more creativity in design and enlargement of the designers' concept of what is feasible.

moves backward toward the current state and design a system that has the highest likelihood of moving the organization toward the "idealized" state.

There is no single best organizational design for the management of existing products. The ideal organizational form depends on the idiosyncrasies of the organization, its products, markets, available personnel, objectives of the key decision makers, management's preference for investment, profit, or cost centers, and other organizational, environmental, and situational considerations.

Whereas all these factors call for a tailor-made approach to organizational design, it is important to note that in general, *program based organizations* (e.g., a unit which has responsibility for developing a total strategic plan for serving a particular market segment, and guiding resource effort in its execution) have been on the average more successful in developing and introducing new products than businesses without a program organization. In a survey among the 1000 largest U.S. manufacturing companies, Corey and Star (1971) found that new product successes (over 20 percent of 1967 sales accounted for by new products) were re-ported by 37 percent of the businesses which had product program managers, while only 20 percent of the businesses without product program managers made this claim.

Therefore, considering the selection of an organizational design for the management of existing products, a number of complicating factors should be taken into account including:

- The divergent objectives of various organizational actors and the likely lack of clear and explicit prioritization of objectives and activities.

- The reluctance to undertake organizational designs which lead to major departures from the current situation.

- Lack of a planning and research mechanism that can link effectively (even in a probabilistic manner) the organizational design to the anticipated performance (effectiveness and outcomes) of the organization.[6]

- The need to balance the conflicting demands of (a) designing and executing focused segmented strategies in multiple markets and (b) coordinating the activities of large resource units in serving different markets simultaneously.

ORGANIZATIONAL CHANGE

Whenever an evaluation of the firm's current organizational form suggests that it is not the most appropriate design, an important decision should be made to determine whether the discrepancy between the current and desired approach is large enough to justify undertaking a change.

Organizational changes often lead to numerous unanticipated consequences. Some of these consequences might be positive, fol-

---

[6]For an initial effort in this direction see Emshoff and Saaty (1978) who applied Saaty's Analytic Hierarchy Approach (Saaty, 1977 and Appendix A) to the long-range planning process. Conceptually, a similar approach can be utilized to address the question of the selection of an "optimal" or near optimal organizational design.

lowing a "Hawthorne effect" of some sort or another, but others might have negative impact.

In determining any organizational change, the appropriate literature[7] should be explored to identify those factors that can be used to reduce resistance to change and increase the likelihood that the planned change will be implemented successfully.

Although a detailed discussion of the organizational change literature is outside the scope of this book, some of the major hypotheses on how to reduce resistance to change might provide useful insight into the problems likely to be encountered and strategy to be considered in introducing a new organizational form. The hypotheses (based primarily on Watson, 1973) are that resistance to change will be less if the suggested change is:

- Felt by the participants as their own—not one devised and operated by outsiders,

- Clearly and wholeheartedly supported by top management,

- Seen by the participants as reducing their present burdens,

- Consistent with values and ideals that have long been acknowledged by participants,

- The kind of *new* experience that interests participants,

- Nonthreatening to the participants' autonomy and security,

- Considered as important to the participants,

- Adopted by consensual group decision,

- Introduced in a way that relieves fears and responds to objections of opponents,

- Recognized as likely to be misunderstood and misinterpreted, and provisions are made for feedback and further clarification as needed,

- Associated with high acceptance, support, trust, and confidence among the participants,

- Kept open to revision and reconsideration.

These and similar hypotheses (from the organizational change literature) suggest various strategies for enhancing the likelihood of acceptance of an organizational change. Yet, at times, resistance to change might be healthy and desirable. Not all changes are "good." Resistance may highlight legitimate problems that have to be addressed constructively by the proponents of the change.

Whereas the traditional organizational change literature was concerned primarily with resistance to change and strategies to overcome it, the more recent literature on information-processing approaches to organizational design have emphasized the conditions under which organizational change would be required. Galbraith, for example, concluded that if the organization is faced with greater uncertainty (due perhaps to technological change, higher performance standards, increased competition, or diversified product lines, etc.), the amount of required information processing is increased and hence the organization *must* adopt at least one of the four coping strategies (creation of slack resources, creation of self-contained tasks, investment in vertical information systems, or creation of lateral relations). Failure to select one of these strategies when the information uncertainty increases would distort the balance between the task information requirements and the organization's capacity to process information and hence could lead to reduced performance through budget or schedule overruns.

---

[7]See for example, Bennis, (1966); Etzioni (1966); Beer (1975); Watson (1973); Coch and French (1948); Zaltman, Duncan and Holbek (1973).

PLANNING AND ORGANIZATIONAL DESIGN

Common to all organizational forms is the responsibility the relevant personnel have for preparing an annual marketing plan. The focus and scope of the plan differs depending on the organizational design employed—a product plan by brand managers, a market plan by market managers.

The great variability of product/marketing plans is clearly evident if one examines the format used by various firms. (See, for example, the Conference Board's collection of plans, Hopkins, 1972.) These plans, despite their diversity, share a number of characteristics:

I. A large number of organizational participants are involved in the design, implementation, and control of the plans:

   a. The *corporate* mission, objective, and strategy (which provide the general guidelines for the product and marketing plans) are typically determined by top management.

   b. The product (or marketing plan) is designed by the appropriate manager (e.g., product or market manager) with inputs (and clearance) from other relevant organizational participants— production planning, sales force, corporate planning, sales planning, R&D, marketing research, advertising and advertising agency, procurement, etc.

   c. The *approval* of a plan typically involves a number of levels in the corporate hierarchy.

II. Product/market plans vary in their level of specificity, yet most of them include:

   a. A situation analysis (the market, competitive and distribution environment, product performance, etc.).

   b. Identification of current and anticipated problems and opportunities.

   c. A set of objectives which are linked to assumed future conditions, and the overall tactical and strategic objectives of the firm. These objectives, to be of value, have to be translated into explicit and realistic goals for specific products and functions.

   d. Detailed objectives, strategies, and allocation of resources for advertising and promotion, customer service, salesforce, media, and other relevant functions. Typically these objectives and strategies try to link profit planning with tactical plans.

   e. An analysis of the P&L effect of the plan. Exhibit 17–4 illustrates the structure of a P&L statement for a brand.

   f. Control and review procedures. The scope of a typical product/market plan is illustrated in Exhibit 17–5 which reproduces the topical outline of a product line plan for a home furnishing product. Since the heart of the plan is the strategy component, Exhibit 17–6 presents an illustrative format for this section of the product/market plan.

III. Most product/market plans are accompanied with a detailed schedule. Exhibit 17–7 illustrates such a schedule for an annual marketing plan of a large division of a diversified manufacturer which also identifies the key participants at each stage of the process.

The detailed scheduling of a plan could further benefit from some of the standardized planning procedures such as PERT or CPM as discussed in Chapter 6.

EXHIBIT 17–4

———————— (BRAND NAME) PROFIT AND LOSS STATEMENT 19.. BUDGET

Reprinted with permission from F.B. Ennis, *Effective Marketing Management*, New York:
Association of National Advertisers, 1973, p. 18.

	Previous year	(Percent sales)	Current year	(Percent sales)	New year	(Percent sales)
1. Total market						
Value	—		—		—	
Unit volume	—		—		—	
Percent increase/decrease	— %		— %		— %	
2. Brand share	— %		— %		— %	
3. Brand shipments						
Value	—	(100%)	—	(100%)	—	(100%)
Unit volume	—		—		—	
Percent increase/decrease	— %		— %		— %	
4. Cost of goods						
Fixed costs	—	(%)	—	(%)	—	(%)
Variable costs	—	(%)	—	(%)	—	(%)
Total costs	—	(%)	—	(%)	—	(%)
5. Gross margin	—	(%)	—	(%)	—	(%)
6. Marketing expenses						
Media/production	—	(%)	—	(%)	—	(%)
Advertising reserve	—	(%)	—	(%)	—	(%)
Sampling/couponing	—	(%)	—	(%)	—	(%)
Trade allowances	—	(%)	—	(%)	—	(%)
Other promotion	—	(%)	—	(%)	—	(%)
Total marketing expenses	—	(%)	—	(%)	—	(%)
7. Other expenses						
Marketing research	—	(%)	—	(%)	—	(%)
Salesforce cost	—	(%)	—	(%)	—	(%)
Distribution cost	—	(%)	—	(%)	—	(%)
Administration	—	(%)	—	(%)	—	(%)
Miscellaneous income and expense	—	(%)	—	(%)	—	(%)
Total other expenses	—	(%)	—	(%)	—	(%)
8. Profit contribution	—	(%)	—	(%)	—	(%)
Increase/decrease	— %		— %		— %	

EXHIBIT 17–5

TOPIC OUTLINE FOR PRODUCT-LINE MARKETING PLAN: A HOME FURNISHINGS
COMPANY

Source: D.S. Hopkins, ''The Short Term Marketing Plan,'' 1972, pp. 27–32; reprinted by
permission of the Conference Board.

I. Product policy statement

State briefly but explicitly the price range, quality
level, distribution policy and brand strategy
being used to reach the line's intended consumer
markets.

II. Marketing background

1. *Definition of consumer markets*

   Describe the consumer markets in which each
   product line has been sold.

   a) Characteristics of significant consumer
      groups
      Show population and per capita purchases
      by:
      Intended use of purchase (own use, gift,
      etc.)
      Family status and size
      Family income
      Geographic region
      Other significant consumer characteristics

   b) Known or assumed consumer preferences
      and buying habits
      Product feature preferences
      Shopping habits
      Motivation for purchases (rank by
      importance)
         Product features
         Brand awareness
         Price
         Advertising
         Promotion
         Packaging
         Display
         Sales assistance
         Other

   c) Significant consumer market trends: size,
      characteristics and buying habits
      Recent trends
      Expected changes

2. *Market size and sales statistics*

   a) Market trends (past 5 years)
      Industry sales

Product type sales
Price index

b) Distribution trends
   Industry sales by type of outlet, (i.e., retail,
   premium and institutional, and further by
   major types of outlets within each broad
   area, i.e., department store, chain store,
   specialty store, etc.)
   Product type sales by type of outlet
   Product type sales by method of
   distribution (direct or wholesale)

c) Product line sales trends
   Sales dollars
   Sales dollars by type of outlet
   Share of total market
   Share of product type market
   Share of key outlet distribution
   Sales dollars by method of distribution
   Price index

3. *Product line profit and cost history (5 years)*

   a) Profit history
      Net profit dollars
      Net profit as percent of sales
      Return on investment

   b) Manufacturing cost history
      Gross profit dollars
      Gross profit as percent of sales

   c) Marketing cost history (5 years)
      Show how marketing money has been
      spent and with what results
      Advertising cost
         Dollars by type, i.e., national,
         cooperative, and trade
         Percent of sales
         Share of advertising vs. share of market
      Promotion, display and fixturing cost
         Dollars
         Percent of sales
         Fixture placements
      Distribution cost (includes distributor
      discount, transportation, warehousing,
      inventory carrying costs, and the cost of

EXHIBIT 17–5 (continued)

distributor selling aids)
  Dollars
  Percent of sales
  Distribution coverage vs. potential
    kind of accounts
    number of accounts
    sales potential of accounts
  Field selling costs
  Dollars
  Percent of sales
  Direct account coverage vs. potential

4. *Competitive Comparison*

Highlight significant differences between this company and its competition
Product line composition and acceptance
Distribution methods and coverage
Field selling methods
Consumer marketing programs

5. *Conclusions*

Summarize the major problems and opportunities requiring action based on analysis of background information. Consider:
Consumer and trade market penetration
Distribution coverage
Product line needs
Price revisions
Cost reductions
New market and product opportunities

III. Primary marketing and profit objectives

1. *Marketing objectives*
Sales dollars
Market share by major type of outlet

2. *Profit objectives*
Gross profit dollars
Gross profit as percent of sales
Net profit dollars
Net profit as percent of sales
Return on investment

Note external qualifying assumptions such as business cycle trends, industry trends, changes in size and characteristics of consumer market segments, distribution trends, competitive activity, price levels, import quotas, and factory capacity.

IV. Overall marketing strategy

State the strategic direction to be followed in order to achieve primary product line marketing and profit objectives.

1. *Consumer and trade market emphasis*

2. *Trademark and product feature emphasis*

3. *Marketing mix emphasis*

4. *Functional objectives*

Establish the contribution needed from each functional area in order to implement the overall strategy and to achieve primary objectives.

a) Field selling
Distribution objectives expressed in number, size, quality, and type of wholesale, retail, premium and institutional accounts needed to meet sales volume objectives.

b) Product development
New product objectives expressed in numbers, types, introductory dates, sales volume and profit contributions from new products.

c) Advertising
Identify markets to be reached
Communication objectives (nature of message and retention level sought by consumers and trade customers)
Trade participation objectives in cooperative advertising programs

d) Promotion and fixturing
Sales objectives for major promotions
Fixture placement and sales volume objectives

e) Merchandising
Objectives for the number and type of new merchandising programs and for trade participation in the company's programmed merchandising

EXHIBIT 17–5 (continued)

f) Business operation
Customer delivery service objectives
Inventory turnover objectives
Product line composition and size
objectives
Pricing objectives

V. Pro forma financial statements and budgets

1. *Marketing budgets*

Field selling expense
Advertising expense
National
Cooperative
Trade
Promotion expense
Consumer
Trade
Fixturing and display expense
Product development expense
Market research expense
Distribution expense
Administrative and allocated expense

2. *Pro forma financial statements*

a) Annual profit and loss statement (expense
detail as shown above)
Next year pro forma by quarter
Current year budget by quarter
Last year actual by quarter

b) Annual revision of five-year pro forma
Profit and loss statement (expense detail
for broad categories)

VI. Action plans

1. *Product line plans*

a) New product objectives

b) New product positioning vs. identified
product needs of consumers

c) New product specifications
Style, weight, size, finish, etc.
Manufacturing cost
Selling price

d) New product budgets
Exploration and screening

Development
Market introduction

e) New product event schedule
Design releases
Designs complete
Market tests complete
Production releases
Advertising planned and scheduled
Selling aids complete
Distribution achieved
Commencement of consumer advertising,
promotion, and selling

f) Planned deletions and accompanying
phase-out programs

2. *Advertising plans*

a) National advertising (by individual
campaign)
Definition of consumers and their buying
motivations
Message theme and objectives
Reach and frequency objectives
Budgets
Preparation and execution schedules
Creative plans
Media plans

b) Cooperative advertising programs
Trade participation objectives
Budget
Relationships to other marketing programs
Preparation and execution schedule

c) Trade advertising (by individual
campaign)
Message and audience objectives
Budgets
Preparation and execution schedules
Creative plans
Media plans

d) Trademark changes

3. *Sales promotion and display plans*

a) Consumer and trade promotion objectives

b) General description of promotion
programs, budgets and calendar

c) Fixturing programs and budgets

EXHIBIT 17–5 (continued)

4. *Major packaging plans*

5. *Trade selling plans*

   a) Description of significant changes in distribution policy
      Approved outlets
      Distribution methods

   b) Distribution coverage objectives

   c) Account coverage objectives

   d) Selling expense budgets

   e) Specific new account targets

   f) Special trade merchandising programs and calendar

   g) Field selling programs and calendar

   h) New services for trade customers
      Delivery service
      Inventory backup
      Selling support, or the like

   i) Sales quotas for each salesman by product line

6. *Special market research projects*

   Include a general description of each project, its objectives, budget and timetable

7. *Pricing recommendations*

8. *Special cost reduction programs*

   Include a general description of each program, its expected dollar savings, and an assignment of responsibilities

EXHIBIT 17–6

FORMATS FOR STRATEGY DOCUMENTS

Reprinted with permission from F.B. Ennis, *Effective Marketing Management*, New York: Association of National Advertisers, 1973, pp. 153–161.

Outline	Description	Examples of possible comments
	I. MARKETING STRATEGIES	
1. Objectives	State the unit and/or dollar sales to be achieved, along with any other comments that might further define the brand's overall marketing goals.	Maintain a leadership position in the market Achieve sales/profits of $ ____ through shipments of _____ . Foster growth by increasing per capita consumption.
2. Strategy Positioning	Define exactly how the brand is to be positioned in the market relative to its competitive environment.	The only brand that can duplicate the performance of two different products. Offers a major consumer benefit that competition can't match. Highest quality at lowest price.
Spending	Describe how the marketing investment is to be spent, in relation to the objectives to be achieved.	Outspend competition 2 to 1. Spend more heavily during peak consumption periods. Spend full available dollars during first year's introduction.

EXHIBIT 17–6 (continued)

Outline	Description	Examples of possible comments
Advertising/Promotion	Refer to any key strategic elements in the advertising and promotion programs that will importantly contribute to achieving the targeted goals.	Capitalize on proven success of basic advertising theme. Use promotion to trade up consumer to more profitable size. Switch from print to TV based on test market success.
Other	Comment on any other significant aspects of the brand's basic make-up or approach that will help accomplish its goals.	Expand product into balance of U.S. Introduce two line extensions. Offer trade margin parity with competition.

II. COPY STRATEGIES

Outline	Description	Examples of possible comments
1. Objectives	State who the target audience is and the basic message to be communicated to this audience.	Convince mothers of young children that they will prefer our product because . . . Convince all teenagers that our product works twice as fast as Brand X.
2. Strategy Basic Concept	If developed, describe the basic campaign idea that will be used to convey the above message to the target audience.	For people who can't brush after every meal. Leave the driving to us. Put a tiger in your tank.
Concept Support	Depending on the campaign approach, state the supporting reasons why the basic message should be believed.	Contains GL 70. Contains a combination of fast acting ingredients. 4 out of 5 doctors recommended . . .
Tone	If appropriate, describe the environmental setting in which the advertising is to be cast.	Contemporary; sincere Masculine; humorous. Soft; feminine; reassuring. News announcement.

III. MEDIA STRATEGY

Outline	Description	Examples of possible comments
1. Objective	State who the target audience is, the media weight to be applied to this audience, and any other comments that best define the media objectives to be achieved.	Reach young mothers as often as practical. Provide added emphasis in peak consumption periods. Concentrate weight in high growth markets.

EXHIBIT 17–6 (continued)

Outline	Description	Examples of possible comments
2. Strategy	Indicate the media selected for this purpose; the reasons for its selection; and the reach and frequency it will deliver, if appropriate.	TV will continue to be brand's primary medium because . . . Daytime network TV will be used to deliver year-round reach and frequency at maximum efficiency. Nighttime spot will be used in major markets during the high consumption season. Major market newspaper ads will be used to support the summer promotions.
IV. PROMOTION STRATEGIES		
1. Objective	Outline the specific goals of the promotional effort, listing them in the order of their importance.	Stimulate impulse buying in high traffic outlets. Increase distribution. Extend brand trial. Increase frequency of purchase.
2. Strategy	State how these objectives will be achieved, describing the essential make-up of the promotions to be employed.	Offer periodic direct incentives to consumers to purchase in multiple package quantities. Offer two major display allowances to the trade. Drop a 10¢ mail coupon to _____ million homes. Conduct two national consumer-oriented promotions involving self-liquidating premiums.
V. PRICING STRATEGIES		
1. Objective	State the purposes of the recommended retail price structure.	Maintain a gross profit margin of ____ %. Maintain price parity with major competition. Offer consumers a better value on larger sizes.
2. Strategy	If appropriate, explain how these goals are to be achieved.	Increase retail price by 2¢ next June. Reduce the price on the economy size. Immediately follow competition on any price adjustments. Reduce production costs by ____ %.

EXHIBIT 17–7

MARKETING PLANNING SCHEDULE: A DIVISION OF A DIVERSIFIED
MANUFACTURER

Source: D.S. Hopkins, *The Short Term Marketing Plan*, 1972, pp. 36–37; reprinted by permission of
The Conference Board.

Date	Activity	Participants
Sept. 1	Five year economic forecast This is a broad forecast based on projections of national economic growth, and includes forecasts of growth in major end use markets for company products	Corporate economist
Sept. 10	Field forecasts Forecasts of industrial materials and contract and supply dept. sales by products	Zone managers Regional managers
Sept. 20	Marketing planning review Review of progress on current year plans, and outline of principal elements of next year's plans	Director of marketing Marketing managers
Sept. 30	Market research annual forecast Forecast based on economic forecast, and opinions of marketing and sales managers	Market research
Oct. 10	Five year market growth and division penetration Marketing analysis for the five year plan	Director of planning Director of marketing Director, commercial research & development
Oct. 15	Marketing and sales opinions of field forcasts	Marketing managers Sales managers
Oct. 20	Preliminary annual & five year plans Factory five year plan Factory annual plan Divisional administrative expense	Division Vice President VP, manufacturing Director of planning
	Five year sales objectives	Director of marketing VP, general sales VP, special industry sales

EXHIBIT 17–7 (continued)

Date	Activity	Participants
Nov. 10–12	Preliminary review of annual and five year profit plans	Division vice president
Nov. 20	Annual marketing plans completed	Director of marketing Market managers
	This includes reviews with sales managers.	
Nov. 25– Dec. 15	Revision and review Annual and five year plans Sales Manufacturing Divisional expense	Division vice president VP, general sales VP, contract & supply dept. VP, special industry sales Director of marketing
Dec. 15	Marketing plans typed	Marketing managers
Dec. 15	Dress rehearsal	Division vice president
	Annual and five year plans	
Dec. 20	Presidential review	President
Jan. 10	Marketing plans book issued	Director of marketing
	Book includes budgets, policy objectives and marketing plans	

This section is a schedule for use in devising marketing plans. It shows: 1) the responsibilities of both marketing and sales personnel in developing annual marketing plans; 2) the integration of marketing plans into the Annual Profit Plan and Five Year Plan development process; 3) the timetable of activities.

CONTROLLING AND ORGANIZATIONAL DESIGN

Effective management of a brand does not stop with the implementation of the plan. A continuous control and monitoring system is required to provide management with continuous feedback on the brand's performance. The control aspects of a brand are critical and should not be limited to after-the-fact evaluation of total sales, market share, or achieved profitability. Rather the control system should provide, on an ongoing basis, the above information by relevant market segments, should enable the firm to evaluate the effectiveness of its various marketing efforts and, ideally, should also provide early warning signals of likely changes in product performance.

To fully implement an efficient control system, an adaptive experimentation philosophy was suggested earlier in the book as the best conceptual approach. As discussed in Chapter 6, adaptive experimentation allows management to learn while doing. It provides continuous and immediate feedback on the brand's performance and the effectiveness of its marketing strategies (whether it be a new advertising campaign, a different advertising weight, a new packaging design or a change in distribution policy, new point-of-purchase display, the introduction of a coupon, etc.). There is no substitute for a well-designed and carefully-executed adaptive experiment. Such an approach does not have to be expensive. Its success depends primarily on management's recognition of the benefits associated with it. Conceptually, therefore, there is a distinct advantage to any organizational design which facilitates the design and implementation of an adaptive experimentation approach. If such an approach can be conducted separately for each brand, a decentralized (brand management type) design would be the preferred organizational form. Yet, in many multiproduct/multimarket firms, the implementation of an adaptive experimentation approach requires close coordination among various brands and markets, suggesting the advantages of a more centralized marketing organization, or a hybrid design which could facilitate such coordination.

The second component of any control system is the development of an information feedback system which provides the necessary performance measures for each brand (by all relevant sizes, forms, etc.) at the market segment level. In designing such an approach one can follow the product performance matrix approach suggested in Chapter 5. This approach

suggests the advantages of decentralized marketing organizations, in particular, brand or market management which can offer an organizational climate conducive to the generation, analysis, and dissemination of such information. Yet, to assure uniform compliance with this evaluation procedure across brands and markets, there should be some corporate guidelines and requirements.

The third component of a control and monitoring system is the need to develop an early warning system in which management can identify in advance any likely problems in product performance. Such a system requires the development not only of procedures for *timely* measures of product performance and the *prediction* of future performance, but also survey or panel data which allow the assessment of consumers' attitudes toward a given brand and, especially in longitudinal type designs, the prediction of *changes* in consumers' needs, lifestyles, and attitudes toward the brand and its competitors. Systematic analysis of consumer complaints might help in providing some early indications of likely problems, but even a comprehensive and accurate system of analysis of complaints is not a substitute for a well-designed consumer survey in which management assesses consumer reactions to the brand and its competitors, the effectiveness of the marketing efforts of the firm and its competitors, and consumers' reactions to other environmental forces and events. None of the organizational forms discussed above have any advantage in initiating and maintaining such a control mechanism. Again, it is management's recognition of the need for such a system and their subjective assessment of its value (versus its expected costs) that governs the implementation of such a control system.

The preceding discussion indicates that, to a large extent, the design of a control and monitoring system is not a function of organizational design but rather of the personalities involved. Whatever organizational design is

EXHIBIT 17–8

PRODUCT FACT BOOK—RECOMMENDED LIST OF EXHIBITS

Reprinted with permission from F.B. Ennis, *Effective Marketing Management*, New York:
Association of National Advertisers, 1973, pp. 135–136.

Shipments by volume

1. Total unit shipments by month — last five years
2. Monthly shipment trend by sales area — last fiscal year
3. Monthly shipment by package size — last fiscal year
4. Quarterly shipments of regular pack vs. promotion pack — last five years

Shipments by value

5. Total dollar sales by quarter — last five years
6. Total dollar sales by sales area — last fiscal year

Consumption trends

7. Annual industry consumption by package size — last five years
8. Annual consumption and market share of major brands — last five years
9. Bimonthly consumption by brand and size — last two years
10. Seasonal index of consumption, company vs. industry — last two years
11. Geographic index of consumption, company vs. industry — last two years
12. Consumption by type of retail outlet, company vs. industry — last two years

Brand development (consumption relative to population)

13. Total brand development by sales area, company vs. industry and major brands — last fiscal year
14. Brand development by package size and major regional sales areas — last three years
15. Trend in brand development indices, worse vs. best sales areas — last three years

Distribution profile

16. Bimonthly distribution trend by sales areas — last fiscal year
17. Brand distribution by type of outlet — last two years

18. Brand distribution by package size — last fiscal year

Competitive profile

19. List of competitive products, by size and retail price
20. Estimated media and promotion expenditures, company vs. industry and major competitive brands — last three years by semi-annual periods
21. competitive media schedule by major brands — last fiscal year
22. Competitive promotion schedule by major brands — last fiscal year

Consumer profile

23. Current consumer demographics by age, income, sex, education, family size, etc.
24. Summary of major research on consumer attitudes, product performance, usage habits, etc.

Promotion data

25. List and timing of brand's major promotions — last two years
26. Summary of results of each major promotion
27. Current fiscal year promotion strategy
28. Current fiscal year promotion plan

Media data

29. Current fiscal year media strategy
30. Summary of current fiscal year media plan
31. Media reach and frequency statistics by sales areas — current fiscal year
32. Brand media expenditures by medium — last two years

Advertising copy

33. Current brand copy strategy
34. Current copy strategies of major competitive brands
35. Major brand copy claims
36. Major competitive copy claims

EXHIBIT 17–8 (continued)

Research data	Financial data
37. Summary of product's distinguishing characteristics vs. competition	42. Brand's current price and profit structure, by package size
39. Summary of major promotion tests	43. Outline of basic P&L profile — last three years
40. Summary of major product tests	44. Outline of balance sheet statistics — last three years
40. Summary of major product tests	45. Trend in P&L operating ratios to sales — last three years
41. Summary of major advertising copy tests	

selected, it is crucial that it incorporates incentives for the design and implementation of an effective control system.

Typically in a brand management structure (and desirable in all other organizational forms as well), the control and monitoring activities are summarized in a *product fact book*.[8] The objective of this book is to provide, in an organized and easily accessible way, a summary of all the relevant marketing information about the brand's market and competitive environment, and a permanent record of the brand's marketing activities and performance. Exhibit 17–8 illustrates the topical coverage of a typical product fact book.

An examination of this exhibit suggests that many of the performance measures of a brand (and its competitors) should be obtained on a regular basis. Often a monthly or bimonthly status report is called for, which summarizes the brand's performance over the relevant period, highlights any variances from the plan, and suggests any corrective actions or changes in the plan. Such documents typically include data on brand performance (sales, market share, profits), budget status (re gross margin, advertising and promotion, etc.), any detailed sales reports (by sales district, market segment, etc.), production and inventory reports, advertising and promotion summaries (media and copy status including competitive copy), and other relevant competitive activities (e.g., new PR programs, new packaging, new products, and new promotional activities). In addition, any test results or other relevant research reports[9] completed during the report period are typically summarized in the monthly or bimonthly reports and added to the product fact book.

CONCLUDING REMARKS

The decision of how to organize for an effective and efficient management of existing products is one of the most complex organizational decisions. There are no perfect solutions nor is there any "ideal" organizational design. Any organization should be designed to fit the desired

---

[8] The product fact book is occasionally supplemented with a *daily work book* which includes a subset of the information in the fact book that is needed for daily operation of the brand.

[9] This section usually includes a summary report and analysis of the Nielson, SAMI, or MRCA data bought by the firm. Occasionally it can also include the results of specialized surveys.

organizational tasks, current personnel, organizational technology and structure. The question of personnel is critical. To some extent one can view personnel as a variable and change it to fit the desired organization. Yet, at least in the short term, the current personnel, especially the managerial personnel, constitute an important constraint on management's freedom to change the organizational design. This often leads to the selection of an organizational design that best fits the current personnel, in their current positions or newly created positions.

Occasionally companies go through a series of organizational changes—from a brand management to a market management, from a market management to a brand management, from either to a product/market management system, and so on. Change can be healthy. Yet at the same time too-frequent changes might be dysfunctional and could lead to disruptions in the smooth operations of the organization.

Organizational designs that involve organizational changes require great sensitivity for the personnel issues (their needs, object-ives, and motivations) and the complexity of organizational life. There is no exact science of organizational design, yet the area of organizational behavior provides us with some guidelines that can refine the art of organizational design and increase the likelihood of developing a successful organization. One should not expect, however, the organizational design to solve all the ills of the organization. It is not a panacea, but rather one of a number of necessary (but not sufficient) conditions for effective management of existing products.

Brand management organization is the most typically used organizational form for the management of existing products and services. Given the various advantages and limitations of this organizational form, specify the conditions under which you would consider this the most desirable form of organization. Following such a listing, think about the conditions for which such an organizational form would not be appropriate. Having identified these conditions, identify an alternative organizational design that might overcome some of the limitations of a brand management structure.

Product Modification, Repositioning, and Deletion

INTRODUCTION

The product/market activities of the firm should be directed toward the achievement of its desired product/market portfolio. This requires, as discussed in Chapters 5 and 6, an evaluation of the current (versus desired) portfolio and determination of five major decisions:

1. Should the current product portfolio be changed?

2. Should the market portfolio be changed? This decision should be made whether or not the product portfolio requires changing.

3. Should the marketing strategies be changed? This decision should be made with or without a change in the product or market portfolio.

4. If the product portfolio requires a change, should the change be via product modification, reposition, deletion, or introduction of new products?

5. If new products or markets are to be added to the product/market portfolio, should they be acquired via mergers and acquisitions or developed internally?

The focus of this chapter is on the product modification, repositioning, and deletion decisions. These decisions are interrelated. Product deletion, for example, cannot be made in isolation from consideration of other options such as changes in markets, marketing strategy, or in product specification or positioning.

The chapter examines the product modification, repositioning, and deletion decisions and centers on four key questions:

- How important are the product modification and deletion decisions?

- What are the key determinants of the product change decision?

- How can the product modification/deletion process be modeled?

- How can product change, including product deletion, be implemented?

THE IMPORTANCE OF PRODUCT MODIFICATION AND DELETION

The importance of developing an explicit approach to the product modification/deletion decision is clearly evident when considering the following:

- The pressures for new product introduction increase constantly the number of products of most firms.

- Product proliferation is also evident in most product classes in which different sizes, packages, and forms increase the range of available products.

- The increasing number of brands in many product categories has led to the proliferation of small-share brands (as illustrated in Exhibit 13–8). This trend and the added proliferation of product sizes and forms reduce the economies of scale in production; increase the complexity of production scheduling, inventory management, and logistics; and can reduce the effectiveness of the marketing and distribution strategies.

- The only unquestionable fact about product life cycle is that eventually the sale of every product decreases leading to the product's "death."

- The 20/80 rule (20 percent of the products account for 80 percent of the profits) suggests that in most multiproduct firms, a small portion of the product line accounts for most of the sales and profits of the firm.[1]

- The "dog" category in the BCG product portfolio framework and similar categories in most other portfolio models suggest the need to delete some products, divest the business, or alternatively, invest in it sufficient amounts to change its status.

- "Dogs" tend to require disproportionate management time which is especially bothersome in small firms with limited management resources.

- Changes in availability or cost of raw materials and other production or marketing components may require the undertaking of product changes.

- Changes in consumer tastes and, in particular, the size and characteristics of particular market segments may require changes in the products offered by the firm.

- Changes in competitive activities, technological developments, and environmental conditions may require corresponding changes in the product offerings of the firm.

These factors suggest the need for continuous evaluation of the performance of each product and product line to determine whether the product requires any change in features (including physical and aesthetic, product and package changes, brand name, etc.), positioning or marketing program, and whether the product line should be expanded, reduced, or its nature and positioning changed.[2]

Product and product line changes are often motivated by and designed to overcome current or anticipated *problems* which might lead to a worsening in the product's performance. Yet, given the rapid environmental changes, an equally important motivation for considering changes in product features, positioning, or marketing strategies is to capitalize on *opportunities* for improved performance. Low-growth firms are often those who ignore this important consideration. Munsingwear, for example, has watched a continuous decline of its Penguin brand golf shirts from 12 percent of the market in the early 1970s, to less than 8 percent at the end of the decade. Partly, this is due to lack of response to competitors such as the Lacoste-Izod brand and partly to ignoring major trends in the market such as the jogging craze (and its implications for jogging clothes) and other lifestyle changes (*Business Week*, 1980).

If product and marketing changes cannot sufficiently improve the expected product performance, the final consideration should be to delete the product(s) from the product mix.

[1]See, for example, *Wall Street Journal* (1962).

[2]For a slightly different formulation of the product modification decision, see Cardozo (1979, pp. 31–60), who suggested that a manager may modify an existing product line by altering individually or jointly each of seven distinct attributes of a product line: position, physical characteristics, package, brand, amount and nature of value added, expansion or reduction of the product line, and composition of the product line.

KEY DETERMINANTS OF THE PRODUCT CHANGE DECISION

Under what conditions should a product be modified, repositioned or, at the extreme, deleted? It is obvious that poor performance might trigger such changes. Yet, decisions concerning product changes should not be based on past performance but rather on expectations concerning future performance. It is thus essential that the product modification/deletion decisions be based on a set of relevant variables and their projected states. Variables which are commonly viewed as reasons for changes in product formulation and positioning as well as deletion are:

• Decline in amount or rate of sales, market share, or profitability. Information on the projected product performance on these and other relevant dimensions is an integral part of the product performance matrix and, hence, should serve as regular ongoing input to any product modification/deletion model.

• Changes in consumers' attitudes toward the product. Changes in perceptions of and preference for a product (versus its competitors) might be reflected in an immediate change in purchase and usage pattern or alternately could provide an early warning signal for likely future changes in purchase and usage patterns.

• Introduction of new competitive products or changes in current or expected competitive activities. Such changes can affect the competitive position of the product.

• The introduction of new products (by the firm) which could alter the positioning of the product line and lead to cannibalization of existing products.

• Change in government regulations with respect to the product (preventing the use of red dye #2, saccharine, etc.), its components, or its marketing program.

• Change in the distribution system or distributor characteristics, which might affect the product's availability and positioning.

• Technological changes which might affect the life expectancy of the product, its competition, or its purchase and consumption system.

• Other changes in product positioning and availability, consumer needs, competitive and environmental characteristics, etc.

• Change in the resources of the firm and its driving forces. Such changes (whether a result of internal or external conditions) can suggest the advisability of product (or even business) deletion leading toward a more efficient resource utilization within a desired business/market portfolio.

Continuous monitoring of market demand, competitive activities, and other environmental conditions, coupled with a situation analysis of the firm's performance and resources (as part of a systematic marketing audit) offers, as discussed in Chapter 6, the necessary information for assessing whether any changes are required in the product decisions of the firm. Such information can and should be supplemented, however, with another, less frequent source of insights based on the analysis of successful versus unsuccessful products.

Identifying the factors associated with unsuccessful performance and assessing the product's performance on them on a regular basis provides the necessary input for deciding whether a product change is required or not required.

The analysis of successful versus unsuccessful products can be based on data on product performance and its correlates *within* the product line (e.g., a pharmaceutical company would consider only pharmaceutical products) or *across* product lines. The analysis of product class data is typically easier and at least partially under the direct control of the firm. (In most industries, there is enough competitive information available to allow for the analysis of product performance within a category for both the products of the firm and its competitors.) Analysis across product classes has to rely, on the other hand, on published studies such as those associated with the SAPPHO (Scientific Activity Predictor from Patterns with Heuristic Origin) project (Rothwell, 1972) and NewProd (Cooper, 1979) or, alternatively, on commercially available data bases such as the PIMS (Profit Impact of Market Strategy) data[3] (Strategic Planning Institute, 1977).

The PIMS program evaluates businesses (a division, a product line, or other profit center which sells a distinct set of products or services to an identifiable group of customers with a well-defined set of competitors) and not individual products. Yet, the program and especially its specialized reports (such as the "PAR ROI Report," the "Cash Flow PAR Report," the "Strategy Sensitivity Report," and the "Optimum Strategy Report"), which examine the performance of a particular business, offer answers to key strategic questions which could

provide guidelines to whether a change is required in the firm's current strategies and operation.

These questions are:

1. What profit rate (ROI[4]) can the particular business expect (as "normal") considering its particular market, competitive position, technology, and cost structure?

2. If the business continues on its current track, what will its future operating results be?

3. What strategic changes in the business have promise of improving these results?

4. Given a specific contemplated future strategy for the business, how will profitability or cash flow change, short term and long term?

Of particular value as input to the decision whether a change in product strategy might be required or not are the PAR ROI reports for the particular business. These reports—in addition to suggesting the "PAR" ROI (an estimate of the ROI that was "normal" for businesses with similar characteristics, and the trend of actual vs. "PAR" ROI)—offer a detailed analysis of the factors which can explain the particular profit performance of the business. This analysis includes 28 factors grouped into five categories: attractiveness of the environment, competitive position, differentiation from competitors, effectiveness of investment use, and discretionary budget expenditures. These factors are listed in Exhibit 18–1, which illustrates a PAR ROI report for a particular business as reported in Gale, Heany, and Swire (1977). The PAR ROI is the sum of the five category impacts added to

[3]For a further discussion of PIMS and its various reports, see the publications of the Strategic Planning Institute, 1 Broadway, Cambridge, MA, 02142. A detailed description of the PIMS program and data are included in Abell and Hammond (1979), while a summary of the major limitations of this program is presented in Wind and Mahajan (1981b).

[4]The PIMS measure of ROI is net pretax income/ average investment when income is after deduction of corporate expenses but prior to interest charges, and investment includes both working capital and fixed capital at net book value.

EXHIBIT 18–1

PAR ROI REPORT OF THE IMPACT OF ROI-INFLUENCING FACTORS: A DIAGNOSIS OF STRATEGIC STRENGTHS AND WEAKNESSES

Source: "Illustrative PIMS Par ROI Report," © The Strategic Planning Institute, 1977, Cambridge, Mass.

	PIMS mean	This business	Impact	Sensitivity: A change of	Sensitivity: Changes impact by
Attractiveness of environment			0.6		
1 Purchase amt-immediate custs	5.2	4.0	1.8	0.20	−0.31
2 Real market growth, short run	8.2	−4.1	−0.6	2.00	0.20
3 Industry (SIC) growth, long run	9.1	6.8	−0.5	1.00	0.02
4 Selling price growth rate	6.8	0.5	−0.1	1.00	0.00
Competitive position			0.2		
5 Market position			−2.9		
Market share	23.7	15.0		5.00	3.05
Relative market share	61.7	34.8			
6 Industry concentration ratio	56.5	51.0	−0.2	5.00	0.19
7 Employees unionized (%)	48.3	0.0	2.6	5.00	−0.25
8 Immed customer fragmentation	12.2	25.0	0.2	2.00	0.04
9 Market share growth rate	3.3	8.1	0.7	2.00	0.31
10 Market share instability	4.0	1.2	−0.3	0.50	0.06
Differentiation from competitors			2.8		
11 Relative product quality	25.9	34.3	0.8	5.00	0.75
12 Price relative to competition	103.5	100.3	0.1	1.00	−0.08
13 Standard products/services		Yes	0.5		
14 Relative compensation	100.9	102.0	0.0	1.00	−0.10
15 New product sales/total sales	11.9	0.0	1.3	5.00	−0.49
Effectiveness of investment use			5.0		
16 Investment intensity index			7.3		
Investment/sales	56.1	33.0		5.00	−2.71
Investment/value added	96.7	65.6			
17 Value added per employee ($000)	30.0	23.8	−1.7	5.00	1.67
18 Vertical integration	58.8	51.9	−0.8	2.00	0.37
19 Relative integration backward		Less	−0.9		
20 Relative integration forward		Same	−0.3		
21 Fixed capital intensity	52.3	42.4	0.5	5.00	−0.36
22 Capacity utilization	79.6	76.3	−0.4	5.00	0.30
23 Investment per employee ($000)	30.4	15.6	0.4	5.00	−0.12
24 Inventory/sales	18.8	10.7	1.0	2.00	−0.34
25 FIFO valuation?		No	0.0		
26 Newness of P&E (NBV/GBV)	55.0	52.0	0.0	2.00	0.27
Discretionary budget expenditures			1.4		
27 Marketing expense/sales	10.8	7.7	1.5	2.00	−1.27
28 R&D expense/sales	2.4	2.5	−0.1	0.50	−0.23

the PIMS average ROI. The individual *impact* values are the expected amount by which the ROI of this business is helped by a favorable (or hurt by an unfavorable) position relative to the average business. In the particular example illustrated in Exhibit 18–1, the impact of the five categories was $0.6 + 0.2 + 2.8 + 5.0 + 1.4$, which when added to the average PIMS ROI of 22.1, results in a PAR ROI for the given business of 32.0 percent.

AN APPROACH TO THE PRODUCT MODIFICATION/DELETION DECISION

The proposed approach to the product modification/deletion decision is based on two phases:

Phase 1 is a general and routine evaluation of each product's performance on a set of key performance measures. The performance measures should be consistent with the firm's product portfolio dimensions. The performance review should be programmed resulting, at the minimum, with the assignment of each product to one of three categories:

1. Acceptable current and projected performance which requires no change in strategy;
2. Acceptable current and projected performance but a product which could benefit from some change in strategy;
3. Unacceptable current or projected performance.

Phase 2 is a detailed evaluation of all the products which fall into the last two categories.

Whereas the initial evaluation can be completely programmed, the second detailed evaluation calls for specific analysis of the current and projected performance of the given product, and the expected impact of a change in the current strategy (e.g., product modification, repositioning, or even deletion) on the remaining product line and the performance and strength of the firm's overall product/market portfolio.

This approach to the product change decision is illustrated in Exhibit 18–2 which presents a simplified model of the product modification/deletion decision. The model is based on four major parts.

I. Determination of the inputs to the product modification/deletion decisions. This involves determination of corporate objectives, resources, and constraints, the determination of the desired product/market portfolio and the establishment of specific and explicit product performance criteria. In addition, the product modification/deletion decision, not unlike all corporate decisions, requires inputs from the continuous monitoring of the current and anticipated environment of the firm.

II. Routine monitoring and evaluation of each product and the resulting decisions of this routine evaluation (phase 1).

III. Detailed evaluation of each product including the generation and evaluation of alternative strategies concerning product modification, repositioning, marketing strategy changes, or product deletion (phase 2).

IV. Establishment of procedures for implementation of the decisions reached in Part III.

The next two parts of this section are devoted to a discussion of some specific procedures that can be utilized in the two phases

EXHIBIT 18–2

A PRODUCT DELETION AND MODIFICATION MODEL

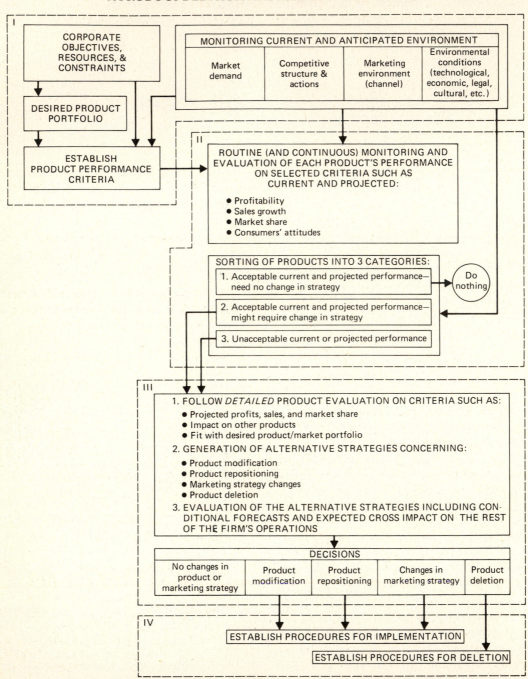

(Parts II and III) of the product change/deletion model. A discussion of implementation options (Part IV) follows, and the relevant components of Part I are incorporated in the discussion of the other parts of the model.

ROUTINE EVALUATION OF CANDIDATES FOR CHANGE

Any system for routine performance evaluation of each product should provide *a systematic and routine way for identifying any performance deviation* from the established norms on the various performance measures of the firm. These deviations can be in terms of a comparison of the current or projected performance with:

- Past performance
- Target performance
- Performance of similar (e.g. competitive) product(s)
- Performance of other products of the firm

These performance measures should be on all relevant dimensions avoiding, however, the two extremes of (a) an overall evaluation on some single performance index which (although commonly used) is not very informative and can lead to wrong conclusions, and (b) either too much information on the selected factors or information on too many factors. Both of these cases can result in information overload and excessive cost of data collection and processing.

The system should also provide *diagnostic insights* on the nature of and reasons for the deviations. Such diagnostic insights are essential for the identification of necessary corrective measures.

A number of approaches to the routine evaluation of product performance have been proposed, primarily in the context of the product deletion decision, but they can be equally valuable as input to the product change decision which includes, aside from the option of product deletion, the options of product modification and repositioning.

Two major approaches to the routine evaluation of product performance are those which attempt to develop a single overall index of product performance and those which evaluate the products on a number of dimensions, with no attempt to summarize these evaluations as a single index.

INDEX APPROACH TO PRODUCT PERFORMANCE EVALUATION

An index approach to programmed product evaluation requires three major sets of management decisions:

1. Determination of the relevant dimensions of performance, including specific operational definitions of the relevant dimensions.
2. Determination of the weight of each factor.
3. Assessing the performance of each product on these variables. These assessments can be based on "hard" accounting data (for variables such as sales and market share), and subjective managerial estimates (for variables such as projected required management time, likely introduction of superior competitive products, etc.).

Some of the variables included in such indices are illustrated in Exhibit 18–3.[5] The development of such evaluation forms is not an easy task, and it is particularly difficult to estimate the required weight of the various factors.

---

[5] For other product evaluation lists see Hurst (1959) and Kotler (1965). Hurst, for example, suggested ten criteria: profitability, scope of product line, marketing efficiency, production efficiency, cost, price, value, quantity, service, and competition.

EXHIBIT 18–3

AN ILLUSTRATIVE SCREENING FORM FOR ROUTINE PRODUCT EVALUATION

		Performance rating**				
		Actual perform-ance	Unacceptable (below target) (1)	Acceptable (on target) (2)	Good (above target) (3)	Factor weight	Total score
Product sales*	Absolute product sales						
	Sales volume as percent of firm's sales						
	Sales growth						
	Sales as percentage of projected sales						
	Expected future sales volume						
	Expected future sales growth						
Market share*	Current (absolute) share						
	Current relative share						
	Trend of market share						
	Share as percentage of projected share						
Industry sales*	Sales volume						
	Sales growth						
Competitive position*	Strength vs. major competitive products						
	Superiority vs. anticipated new products						
	Product quality (absence of complaints)						
Profit contribution*	Profits and return on investment (based on net present value of contribution flow)						
	Projected profits and ROI						
Investment requirements for:	New plant and equipment						
	Working capital						
	Management time						
	Marketing support						

EXHIBIT 18–3 (continued)

AN ILLUSTRATIVE SCREENING FORM FOR ROUTINE PRODUCT EVALUATION

		Performance rating**					
		Actual perform- ance	Unacceptable (below target) (1)	Acceptable (on target) (2)	Good (above target) (3)	Factor weight	Total score
Strategic fit— compatibility with:	Desired product portfolio						
	Planned production facilities						
	Distribution outlets						
	Marketing organization						
	Corporate image						
Environmental fit— compatibility with:	Legal requirements						
	Political climate						
	Ecological standards						
	Changing consumer tastes						
	Technological development						
Marketing efficiency*	Promotion elasticity						
	Adv elasticity						
	Price elasticity						
Production efficiency	Cost of production						
	Production flexibility						

*These data have to be collected and analyzed not only for the total market but also by all relevant market segments.

**The rating scale can vary depending on management's preference to include other numerical values (such as 2, 4, 5, 6, 7, or 10 point scale or even 100 points), other semantic labels — dimensions (such as desirability, acceptability, or degree to which the item (evaluation variable) describes the product) and complete labeling of each rating point (vs. the illustrated labeling of the extreme points only).

Conceptually, the list of factors and variables should be linked to the dimensions of the product portfolio utilized by the firm, include both indication of problems *and* opportunities, and be relatively short. Yet, the tendency has been to expand the list of variables considerably. Given that the performance index is designed for a *routine* evaluation to identify "problem products" which will be subjected to further in-depth evaluation, one might argue for a rela-

tively small number of key (and "objectively" measured) variables.

The determination of the weight of these factors should follow an empirical determination in which the relative contribution of the various factors to the product's profitability (or other high-order objective) is determined, as in the PIMS project. Alternately, management's subjective judgments can be used. In these cases, their evaluation can be assessed by a number of procedures such as conjoint analysis or the Analytic Hierarchy Process. It is desirable to avoid self-explicated approaches (such as importance ratings) since they tend to overstate the importance of less important factors.

To the extent that management's subjective evaluations are used to determine the weight of the variables and the position of the various products on them, it is desirable to collect such information from the relevant managers and to assess explicitly their degree of consensus. Lack of consensus suggests the need for further evaluation including the collection of additional (empirical) data.

One of the more structured approaches to routine product evaluation is the PRESS model proposed by Hamelman and Mazze (1972) and further modified by Armstrong (1973).

PRESS is a basic ROI model which centers around a Selection Index based on a ratio of the square of product i's percent contribution margin to its percent resource cost utilization. This formula was criticized by Armstrong (1973) who accepted the basic concept of measuring a product's performance in terms of the relations between its contributions and resources used, but suggested a simpler index which does not square the numerator.

The Hamelman–Mazze and Armstrong indices are:

Hamelman–Mazze: *Armstrong:*

$$SIN_i = \frac{(CM_i/\Sigma CM)^2}{FC_i/\Sigma FC}, \quad DIR_i = \frac{CM_i/\Sigma CM}{FC_i/\Sigma FC}$$

where SIN_i = selection index for product i,

     CM_i = contribution margin for product i,

     FC_i = facilities costs for product i,

     DIR_i = direct index.

According to Armstrong, the advantages of the direct index are that it can handle the cases of negative contribution margins (which the Hamelman-Mazze fails to account for) and avoids the bias of SIN in favor of large margin

products (versus a few smaller products whose sum contribution can be greater).

Despite the limitation of the PRESS selection index (which could be replaced with DIR_i), the PRESS model and procedure is conceptually appealing. It is based on a computer-aided model which consists of four integrated parts: PRESS I is the primary model and uses standard cost-accounting and marketing-performance data. This phase includes not only the calculation of the performance index but also the preparation of a number of other performance ratios for all products which are of significant diagnostic value. These ratios include:

- Material cost to selling price
- Labor cost to selling price
- Product labor cost as a percentage of total labor costs
- Variable overhead to selling price
- Variable overhead as a percentage of total overhead costs

Following phase I analysis, PRESS II, III, and IV perform analyses concerned with price changes, sales trends (historical and projected), and product interaction (complementarity and substitutability) and their effect on the contribution margin of selected products.

These and similar approaches to the construction of a single product performance index are subject, however, to the limitations of any index, such as:

1. A single index tends to mask important qualitative differences. Consider for example the following three products.

Product	Rating on market share	Rating on profitability	Total score (performance index)
A	9 (high)	1 (low)	10
B	1 (low)	9 (high)	10
C	5 (average)	5 (average)	10

It is obvious that the three products differ markedly in their performance. Yet, an index (assuming equal weight for the two factors) would treat the three as identical.

2. To the extent that components of the index require subjective evaluation by management, it is not clear who should be the respondents and how discrepancy in evaluation (among them) should be treated. Should concensus be sought (as in a Delphi approach) or does the lack of consensus on the evaluation of a given product suggest a need for further evaluation?

3. In most multifactor indices there is considerably high correlation among the variables. Hence a weighting system that does not take this correlation into account can provide a distorted system of weights. Similar distortion (due to correlation among the variables) is also present if no weights are given (which in fact implies an equal weight for each item). In this latter case if for example there are five measures of sales and only one for profitability, the actual weight of these factors in the index is five to one and not an equal weight.

MULTIDIMENSIONAL SCREENING OF PRODUCTS

Given the limitations of a single index, an alternative approach is to identify a small set of critical factors, and without weighing them to assume a choice model which requires further examination of every product that does not meet *all* the selected criteria. An example of this method is the first computerized phase of the Kotler (1965) procedure. According to this approach every product is subject to evaluation on five criteria:

- Has the product's *share of total company sales* declined for K_1 or more periods?

- Have *recent sales*, after adjustment for cyclical factors, shown a consecutive decline for K_2 or more periods?

- Has *market share* shown a consecutive decline for K_3 or more periods?

- Has the *gross margin* on this product declined for K_4 or more periods?

- Has the product's *coverage of its overhead* amounted to less than K_5 percent?

The five questions are linked in a series and a negative answer to *all* questions is required to avoid further investigation of the product. Such a procedure, whether based on these factors or others, is much more appropriate for a first step routine (and computerized) evaluation of product performance. As with the index approach, the design of such a system requires active management participation to determine the idiosyncratic product performance measures and their operational definitions.

IN-DEPTH EVALUATION OF CANDIDATES FOR CHANGE

Having identified "problem products," management has to evaluate each of these identified products in much greater depth. This evaluation can vary in the degree to which it is structured. At the one extreme is a totally unstructured approach in which management reviews each "problem product" separately on a number of key dimensions. Alternatively, this phase can incorporate a more structured approach based on formal evaluation forms and even the development of some overall performance index. Kotler (1965), for example, suggested a combined approach which involves three distinct phases for dealing with problem products (the dubious products he identified in the first computerized evaluation of all products). These three phases include:

- Management team fills out rating forms for all dubious products.

- A computerized evaluation of these forms to determine a product retention index for each dubious product.
- Management team review of these indices to determine which products to drop.

The specific rating form suggested by Kotler is based on seven scales (with a 0 to 1 rating) encompassing the following dimensions:

1. What is the future market potential for the product? (Low—High)
2. How much could be gained by product modification? (Nothing—A great deal)
3. How much could be gained by marketing strategy modification? (Nothing—A great deal)
4. How much useful executive time could be released by abandoning this product? (A great deal—Very little)
5. How good are the firm's alternative opportunities? (Very good—Very poor)
6. How much is the product contributing toward its direct costs? (Nothing—A great deal)
7. How much is the product contributing to the sales of the other products? (Nothing—A great deal)

As with the indices for the initial evaluation, a "retention index" (whether based on weighted or unweighted attributes, and regardless of the specific attributes used) is subject to serious limitations, suggesting that little can be gained by such formalism. Management, therefore, would be better off focusing on the detailed evaluation of all "problem products" on all relevant dimensions. Such evaluation requires considerable data especially on the projected performance of the product and its likely interactions with other products.

The need for a detailed diagnostic evaluation (instead of an oversimplified examination of some overall performance index) is especially crucial if one examines not only the option of whether to delete a product, but also the whole range of alternatives including possible product modification and repositioning. These two decisions require considerable information and have to be based on some empirical evidence on likely consumer reactions to product changes in light of other likely changes in competitive offerings and environmental conditions.

Such analysis can be enhanced by the use of computer simulations for the assessment of the likely outcomes (on a number of dimensions) of changes in the firm's actions under a variety of competitive and environmental conditions. Such simulations can and have been developed. Technically, simulations are simple to construct and their major demands are on (a) management willingness to use them and participate in their design (by providing the necessary inputs on the relevant dimensions, decision rules, and assumptions) and (b) the required marketing and accounting information.

Simulation-based approaches which rely on idiosyncratic models and analysis vary markedly from approaches such as those suggested by Berenson (1963) who called for the specification of specific courses of action for various levels of a performance index. He suggested the calculation of a weighted summary measure of performance ΣV (based on the score on five dimensions—financial security, financial opportunity, marketing strategy, social responsibility, and organized intervention) and the development of the following rules:

If ΣV is approximately X_1, take action A_1;

If ΣV is approximately X_2, take action A_2;

If ΣV is approximately X_3, take action A_3, etc.

Such an approach is unrealistic since any given total performance score can be derived from various components, each requiring different solutions.

The inability to a priori prescribe specific

courses of action is especially evident when one considers that most product changes (repositioning or deletion) can have major implications on the entire product line. This product interdependency—whether with respect to demand, marketing activities, or production—requires careful and explicit evaluation before any product change is actually implemented.

IMPLEMENTATION OF PRODUCT CHANGE DECISIONS

Changes in technology, consumer tastes, competitive offerings, legal, and other environmental factors contribute to the need for changes in the formulation or positioning of existing products. These changes require careful technical examination (can the product formulation be changed for example), the assessment of consumers' likely reaction to the changed product, and the likely reactions of the other stakeholders to these changes.

These evaluation procedures are not unlike the ones utilized during the development of a new product. The added complexity, however, is that with existing products the firm already has some market franchise and any change should be evaluated with respect to its likely impact on both the current customers (and distributors) and potential new customers.

Strategically, the maintenance of the existing customer base is not always desirable. Yet, knowing with a high level of confidence the likely reaction of the current segment(s) to any proposed change is essential input for management decisions.

Contemplated product changes can range from changes in marketing strategy involving no physical changes in the product or its formulation to changes in the product formulation, positioning, and marketing strategies. The selection of a specific change strategy should be carefully examined and its likely impact on the relevant performance dimensions assessed. In this respect changes in a product's current formulation, positioning, and marketing strategy (including its target market segment) should follow the same procedures as the ones used for the generation and evaluation of new product strategies.

If the evaluation of possible product changes suggests no likely improvement in a "problem product" the deletion decision should be considered. This involves in effect a number of specific decisions on how to implement the decision. At least four such strategies should be considered:

1. *Sell the entire product line,* its production and/or marketing facilities (this decision is occasionally known as divestment, and includes those cases in which a firm sells its product line to another firm (such as RCA's sale of its computer division; Dupont's sale of Corfam, etc.). The divestment decision can involve only production facilities, any aspect of the entire operation (e.g., patents, distribution outlets, the brand name, etc.), or the entire operation.

2. *Discontinue the product line.* In contrast to the case in which the product is sold as an ongoing concern to another firm, there are numerous cases in which a firm decides not to continue the production or marketing of the product.

3. *Prune the product line.* Instead of deleting the entire product line (as in the above two cases) often a firm can improve its overall

EXHIBIT 18–4

A.D. LITTLE'S PARTIAL GUIDELINES FOR SINGLE BUSINESS UNIT RESOURCE ALLOCATION

Reprinted by permission of Arthur D. Little, Inc., Cambridge, MA.

		Industry maturity			
		Embryonic	**Growth**	**Mature**	**Aging**
Competitive position	**Strategic thrust** / Dominant / **Investment**	All-out push for share / Hold position / Invest slightly faster than market dictates	Hold position / Hold share / Invest to sustain growth rate (and preempt new (?) competitors)	Hold position / Grow with industry / Reinvest as necessary	Hold position / Reinvest as necessary
	Strategic thrust / Strong / **Investment**	Attempt to improve position / All-out push for share / Invest as fast as market dictates	Attempt to improve position / Push for share / Invest to increase growth rate (and improve position)	Hold position / Grow with industry / Reinvest as necessary	Hold position or harvest / Minimum reinvestment or maintenance
	Strategic thrust / Favorable / **Investment**	Selective or all-out push for share / Selectively attempt to improve position / Invest selectively	Attempt to improve position / Selectively push for share / Selective investment to improve position	Custodial or maintenance / Find niche and attempt to protect / Minimum and/or selective reinvestment	Harvest or phased withdrawal / Minimum maintenance / Investment or disinvest
	Strategic thrust / Tenable / **Investment**	Selectively push for position / Invest (very) selectively	Find niche and protect it / Selective investment	Find niche and hang on or phased withdrawal / Minimum reinvestment or disinvest	Phased withdrawal or abandon / Disinvest or divest
	Strategic thrust / Weak / **Investment**	Up or out / Invest or divest	Turn around or abandon / Invest or divest	Turn around or phased withdrawal / Invest selectively or disinvest	Abandon / Divest

performance by selective deletion of products from its product line. This is probably the most common form of product deletion and among the easiest to implement.

4. *Run out the product.* This strategy was suggested by Talley (1964) as the cutting back of all support costs to a minimum level to allow for maximum profits over the remaining life of the product. Such a policy requires good information on the marketing elasticities of various market segments, and the positioning of the product in these segments. Such information is required to determine whether to reduce *all* marketing efforts or to reduce them selectivily, maintaining sufficient marketing effort against profitable market segments.

The specific deletion course of action should be linked to the recommendation derived from an analysis of the product/market portfolio of the firm. Consider, for example, the recommended deletion and other strategy and investment options offered by A.D. Little for products at various stages of their life cycle and competitive positions. Exhibit 18–4 summarizes those recommendations which should be further refined based on a more detailed analysis of the entire product portfolio of the firm which, in many cases, cannot be limited to the two dimensions suggested by the A.D. Little portfolio. Furthermore, the final deletion option should be evaluated in terms of its likely long-run impact on all the relevant dimensions of the portfolio, the other products of the firm and the stock market evaluation of the firm (in terms of P/E ratio, band rating etc.). This can best be achieved by comparing the overall performance of the firm for the projected portfolio including the candidates for deletion with a portfolio which assumes the deletion of the given products.

CONCLUDING REMARKS

In contrast to the new product development area, which has received considerable attention and resources, product modification and deletion decisions have received relatively little attention in the marketing literature.

Furthermore, product modification decisions often have been treated separately from the product deletion decisions, despite the fact that these two sets of decisions should be treated explicitly together as two among a number of alternative courses of action a firm can undertake in response to either current or projected unsatisfactory product performance.

A two-step approach to the modification/deletion decision has been suggested in which the factors which call for consideration of a new product/market strategy are not unlike those affecting the new product decisions of the firm. Similarly the research methods used to determine the likely outcome of the various strategies are the same as those utilized in the new product development process.

Explicit attention should be given to the product change/deletion decisions since the potential profit contributions of such decisions are in many cases significantly larger (especially in the short run) than the profit contribution of the new product activities of the firm.

To fully appreciate the nature of product modifications, repositioning, and deletion decisions and their interdependencies, select a number of products or services of your choice, and for each specify the conditions under which you would consider modifying the product or service, repositioning it, changing its marketing program, or deleting it. Having identified these conditions, select one of your products or services and for one condition requiring product modification, design an approach that will allow you to generate and evaluate various product modification strategies. Upon completion of this task, repeat it for conditions that might require product repositioning or deletion.

Having completed these evaluations, compare them to the approaches one would use in developing new products and note the differences between a system geared to the development of totally new (and ideally innovative) products from one aimed at product modification and repositioning.

PART FOUR

EXTENSIONS AND CONCLUSIONS

The last part of the book focuses on two critical areas. Chapter 19 extends the concepts, methods, and strategy discussed in earlier chapters to organizations other than those involved with frequently purchased consumer products—the organizations which have been the focus of most marketing courses and texts.

Since the concepts, methods, and strategy discussed throughout this book are as relevant to other organizations, Chapter 19 briefly discusses the idiosyncratic characteristics of these organizations and suggests how the material covered in the book can be applied to them.

Chapter 20 provides further extensions of the material in terms of how it can be implemented and pulled together. Obstacles to successful implementation are identified and coping strategies suggested. In addition, the chapter includes suggested directions for future research.

Extensions to Nonconsumer Products

INTRODUCTION

Most of the discussion and examples throughout this book, not unlike the rest of the marketing literature, have had an implicit focus on frequently-purchased consumer products, from the point of view of large, profit-oriented manufacturing firms doing business in domestic markets. Yet, the concepts, approaches, and methods proposed in this book are equally applicable to a variety of other organizations. It is therefore the objective of this chapter to briefly discuss some possible extensions of the material discussed so far to seven areas:

- Infrequently purchased consumer goods (versus frequently purchased ones)

- Services (versus tangible goods)

- Industrial products (versus consumer goods)

- Retail and other intermediate marketing organizations (versus manufacturers)

- Small businesses (versus large firms)

- Nonprofit and government organizations (versus profit-oriented organizations)

- International operations (versus domestic operations)

The areas in parentheses are those covered implicitly in this book so far, whereas the ones to the left are the focus of discussion in this chapter. The chapter is organized along these areas. Each section highlights some of the unique characteristics of the area (distinguishing it from the more conventional area discussed so far) and the implications of these differences to product decisions and approaches.

The basic premise underlying the discussion in this chapter is that product decisions and their associated marketing strategies should be based on an in-depth understanding of the buying process. Hence, it is the differences in the buying processes involved in these seven areas that are emphasized and that serve as guidelines for identifying the product policy implications.

INFREQUENTLY PURCHASED CONSUMER GOODS

As the name implies, the major differentiating characteristic of infrequently purchased goods (such as durables or catering services) is their frequency of purchase. This by itself has a number of major implications to various stages in the product evaluation process, namely, there is little utility in repeat-buying measures (although there are a number of exceptions to this rule). Adjustments should be made in conventional concept and product testing procedures to take into consideration less regular usage patterns, and often more complex and lengthy decision processes.

Related to the frequency of purchase question are a number of other unique characteristics of infrequently purchased products such as:

- *The cost of the item*—Typically these products are more expensive than frequently purchased products.

- Many of these products have *high social visibility,* increasing not only the perceived financial risk but also the social/psychological risk of the purchase.

- Many infrequently purchased products are *bought as gifts* rather than for personal use.

- *Multiple purchases*—As society becomes more affluent, the larger the market segment that buys a number of products within the same product category. Consider, for example, the multiple-TV homes, the large number of radios in a typical household, the two-, three-, and even four-car family.

- The *order of purchase* of products within a broader product category (such as the order of appliance purchases) varies among market segments.

- Many manufacturers of infrequently purchased goods offer a *large variety* of products (consider, for example, the product range offered by GE, GM, etc.), most of which are clearly identified as manufactured by the same firm. This *"family branding"* is less common across product categories of frequently purchased products. (It is not well known, for example, that Maxwell House, Jell-O, Post cereals, and Birds-Eye frozen foods are all products of General Foods.)

- *Complex and less familiar.* Infrequently purchased products (TVs, calculators, etc.) are often more technologically complex than frequently purchased products. In addition, innovative new infrequently purchased products often differ from existing products in such drastic ways that a considerable amount of education is needed to acquaint the consumer with the new product and its performance.

These and other characteristics of infrequently purchased goods do not reduce the value of the major marketing concepts underlying product decisions discussed throughout this book. Consider for example:

Market segmentation. The markets for such products vary not only with respect to the desired product attributes/benefits but also with respect to current inventories of products (a much more critical factor than the inventory of frequently purchased products) and intended usage occasion (gift versus personal usage, etc.). These factors alone suggest the greater complexity of and need for segmentation of markets for infrequently purchased products.

Product positioning. There is nothing in the characteristics of infrequently purchased products to suggest less need for positioning by segment. In fact the likelihood of high social risk and family branding considerations suggest the need for careful positioning.

Product/market planning. The planning concepts and approaches discussed in earlier chapters are as relevant to infrequently purchased products as they are for frequently purchased ones. Given the typically longer new product development process of infrequently purchased products (it can take, for example, three to five years to develop a new car), planning becomes even more critical.

Given that such concepts are equally relevant for this class of products, the question is whether any of the product/marketing decisions and research programs are affected by the unique characteristics of these products. Some of the research designs employed are affected. For products purchased very infrequently, it might be difficult to find qualified buyers. Screening is thus required, which increases the research cost. Stimulus designs are also more complex. Concept testing studies may require visual presentation and occasionally even an educational communication program aimed at explaining the new product concept. In addition, evaluation of the appropriateness of the concept, and its likely purchase for different occasions (such as gifts) and the frequency of occurrence of various occasions become of greater importance. In-home use tests take a different slant, aimed more at assessing product performance and utility under realistic conditions rather than as a way to assess the likely repeat purchase common to most of the in-home tests for frequently purchased products.

Similarly, introductory campaigns and test markets have quite different characteristics. Sampling is mostly impractical, and introductory coupons are not as common even though more recently, discount offers on new cars, home appliances, and electronic equipment have been quite popular. Test markets are usually longer and require careful monitoring of both consumer and retail reactions to the product. Relevant pretest market simulators have to be different. Although conceptually equally applicable to infrequently purchased products,

most of their usage has been limited to frequently purchased products. Yankelovich, Skelly, and White, who have conducted over 500 pretest market studies, reported on *no* infrequently purchased products in their LTM (Laboratory Test Market) brochure (Yankelovich, Skelly, and White, 1978).

These differences are based on a prototypical view of the category "infrequently purchased consumer goods," yet it is important to realize that this category is quite heterogeneous. This implies that for certain products and situations the research approach might be closer to that of frequently purchased products.

SERVICES

According to the Conference Board (1979), consumer services made up approximately 31 percent (580 of the 1887 billion dollars) of the 1978 GNP. It is not surprising, therefore, that service marketing has been receiving increasing attention in the marketing literature. A number of articles have appeared focusing on the unique characteristics of services (Rathmell, 1966; Judd, 1968; Besson, 1973; Bateson, 1977; Chase and Acquilano, 1977; Uhl and Upah, 1977; and Shostak, 1978) and the marketing of areas such as financial services (banking, insurance, etc.) health care, and transportation. A critical examination of this literature suggests two major conclusions:

1. There seem to be very few "pure" goods without a service component. With the exception of a few extreme cases, most goods require some supporting services, and services even when offered with no associated goods often have marketing characteristics similar to those of products. This would suggest that the marketing concepts and approaches applied to products can be applied also to services.

2. There are a few unique service characteristics which could have significant impact on some of the research designs involved in new service development. As with infrequently purchased products, these unique features tend to have little impact, however, on the viability and relevance of the major marketing and product concepts and approaches for service development and mangement.

Some of the major distinguishing characteristics of services and their impact on new service development research designs are:

Intangibility. Since in many cases no physical product has to be developed (note that in some cases services do require physical product presence; for example, the automatic bank teller which is a service involving a high-technology product), in-home use tests are not very meaningful, and it is often appropriate to move directly from concept testing to test market or its alternatives.

Difficult to patent. Services, to the extent that they are centered around ideas and not technological developments, are difficult to protect with patents. This increases the ease of competitive entry, which can change markedly the economic viability of a new service concept. It can also reduce the incentive for large investments in R&D operations and rather focus the new service development efforts on the development of "me too" services or service improvements.

Most services are *difficult to standardize.* Whenever personal service is involved (such as rent-a-car, banking, hotels, etc.) one can expect considerable quality differences. One of the keys to the success of service franchise operations is their ability to standardize the services and reduce the quality variance. Lack of standardization makes it difficult to develop accurate concept descriptions and increases the uncertainty involved in predicting market performance from concept test results.

Services tend to require *direct relationship between the client and the service provider.* This relationship can also involve the client's participation in the service "production" process itself. This characteristic has major implications for the service distribution decisions and requires the inclusion in any service study information about the client's desired interactions with the service provider (service delivery system). The required client interrelationship and lack of standardization increase the difficulty of describing a service concept in terms which are general enough to convey the concept and yet reflect the likely interpersonal context of the service delivery.

Many services have *no clear lines of demarcation between the outlet, service, and product components.* Consider, for example, banking, legal, medical, insurance, and other services which combine the outlet decision (e.g., which bank to use, which physician, which insurance agent, etc.) with the specific "product" decision, i.e., which products and services to select (e.g., from different banking "products" such as loans and different services such as investment counseling, etc.). This characteristic further increases the difficulty of concept/product testing. If, for example, a bank is concerned with new financial services, the question is not only what would be consumer reaction to these services but would the service offer enough incentives to *shift from* another bank or *add* the bank which offers the new service. Similarly, when offering a new insurance product, the key questions are how likely are consumers to add it to their current insurance inventory and would they be inclined to acquire it from a source other than their current insurance supplier, e.g., agent.

These and other characteristics of services suggest that the general product concepts and methods discussed in the context of frequently purchased products are equally applicable to services. Changes may be required, however, in the research designs involved.

INDUSTRIAL PRODUCTS AND SERVICES

The basic marketing concepts of segmentation/positioning and the need for systematic product planning are as critical for industrial as they are for consumer products and services. The development of industrial products is more complex, however, than for consumer goods. This added complexity is a result of the following unique characteristics of industrial buying situations:

- Organizational buying often involves a large number of organizational members. The composition of the relevant buying center (Wind, 1978b) tends to change from one purchase situation to another and organizational mobility makes it even more difficult to identify the relevant buying center members who should be the respondents in the new product/service studies.

• Given that most organizational buying centers are composed of a number of individuals who could vary in their perceptions and preferences, it is not clear what is the best way of capturing these differences to assess the "organizational response" to the new concept/product. Some methodological approaches have been proposed to deal with multi person buying centers but additional work is still needed and care should be given with any new industrial product/service to the selection of the correct respondents and analysis of multi-person data.

• As discussed in Chapter 9, new products are sometimes developed or their need first recognized by the using organization. In these cases new industrial product development activities should include a system for capitalizing on this behavior.

• Many industrial products and services are bought based on specifications developed by the buying center. In these cases, the specifications offer guidelines for the new product development activities. Alternatively, if the manufacturing firm designs new products not covered by the current specifications, attention should be given to the likelihood of getting the new product approved by the buying firm and its specifications accepted.

• System buying is a common practice in a number of industries. In these cases the new product development activities should take it into consideration in the design of new concepts and products, which should be designed as systems or as individual products which fit specific systems. Even

when no formal system buying is employed, any *new* product, to be accepted, should fit the current system or allow for (and justify) a system change.

• Before and after sales services are often important components of the product bundle sought by the buying firm. In these cases, the design of industrial products should take this into consideration, and concept/product testing should incorporate not only physical product features but also all the relevant service components such as financing terms, warranties, installation, delivery schedule, etc.

• Completeness of a service line (i.e., the ability of the offered products and services to meet the buyer's needs) is often an important consideration in the purchase decision of organizational buyers. The development of new products or the product modification and deletion decisions should, therefore, be carefully evaluated against the desired product line. The implication of this to the design of concept/product studies is that concepts/products should not be evaluated only as individual items but also as part of a complete product/service line.

• Many industrial products can benefit from the experience curve concept. In these cases, the product portfolio dimensions suggested by the Boston Consulting Group's share/growth matrix are much more appropriate than for products which do not have the benefit of the experience curve. This does not preclude, however, the need for specific determination of the portfolio dimensions most compatable with management's idiosyncratic needs.

• In many industrial cases, buyers possess more information, knowledge, and power than sellers. Professional buying practices (as reflected by the professional status of purchasing agents and material management departments) have to be taken into

7

consideration in designing industrial products and marketing strategies.

These and other characteristics of industrial buying suggest the importance of employing in the design of industrial products and services, most of the concepts and approaches discussed in this book. Conjoint analysis based on new product development studies, including the more recent POSSE methodology (Appendix B) has been widely used by industrial firms. Similarly, the Choffray and Lilien (1980) microsegmentation methodology has been implemented in the design of a number if industrial products,

such as smart computer terminals, copiers, and solar cooling systems.

Most of those applications have ignored, however, the problem of multiperson buying centers and its implications for data collection, analysis, and interpretation. Incorporation of these considerations (as, for example, in the Wind, Grashof, and Goldhar, 1978, study) can improve the value of industrial marketing research studies and offer management better guidelines for the design of new products and services and their accompanying marketing strategy.

RETAIL AND OTHER INTERMEDIATE MARKETING ORGANIZATIONS

Retail and other intermediate marketing organizations (IMOs) are faced with dual "product" decisions relating to the positioning of the firm, as well as its products and services. The positioning of a retail outlet itself considers the store or firm as the product, and the same concepts and approaches used in the management of new and current products can be applied to the design and management of the retail outlets.

In this respect the major differences between IMOs and manufacturers center around the difficulties in presenting new retail and IMO concepts. The use of concept testing, therefore, is quite limited. Yet, the new "product" development efforts of retail firms, as related to their own offering—design of the store, location, range of services, etc.—require three major research phases:

- Idea/concept generation
- Concept evaluation focusing on consumers' reactions to the suggested benefits (and not necessarily to specific design options)

- Test market- and/or adaptive experimentation-type rollout

A more unusual characteristic of retail firms and other IMOs is their product assortment decision. The design of a product assortment is one of their major tasks and involves *systematic* search activity to identify the "right" products for the target market segments. This systematic search involves the discovery of "new" products, their evaluation on their likely compatibility with the firm's overall positioning, and their likely acceptability by consumers. In this respect, market research studies conducted by the manufacturer can serve as useful, although limited, inputs to the retailer's own forecasting and optimization models.

Concepts and approaches developed for consumer products (and discussed throughout the book) are equally applicable to retail and other IMO decisions such as: (a) the positioning of the store and the selection of product assortments; (b) associated marketing and merchandising activities, and (c) the other product-related decisions of these firms.

SMALL BUSINESSES

One often hears the argument that the approaches (and especially the various research steps and system designs) for new product development and product management are only appropriate for large firms. Managers of small firms often believe that they cannot afford and should not engage in such expensive "extravaganzas." Their entrepreneurial skill, which helped them start their firms, is viewed by them as the needed ingredient for success.

Subscribing to this point of view can be disastrous. Systematic new product development efforts are aimed at reducing the risk of new product introduction and increasing the odds of success. It is primarily the small firm which cannot afford a high risk. There are few small firms, if any, which could sustain a fraction of the loss incurred by Ford on the Edsel, by DuPont on Corfam, or by AT&T on its Picture Phone. The premise of this book, therefore, is that the approaches and concepts presented here are as applicable for small firms as they are for large ones, and, furthermore, that small firms cannot afford *not* to use them. Investment in these approaches and systems should not be discarded because of the absolute size of the investment. Rather, it is the cost/benefit relationship that should determine the nature and size of the investment.

Furthermore, the concepts and approaches are not only appropriate for small firms but also for small-share brands. The number of small-share brands has been on a steady increase, due to brand proliferation activities (in the form of line extensions, appeal for variety, and small market segments), the entry of new domestic and foreign competitors, and a variety of facilitating conditions (such as larger retail outlets, new distribution outlets and promotional and advertising media, technological developments, etc.). In addition, management ac-

ceptance of cannibalization, the natural reluctance to delete "dying" products, and the desire to offer a full line of products also contribute to the proliferation of small-share brands. Common to small-share brands (of both large and small firms) are the following major problems:

- High consumer and trade vulnerability
- High cost of operation due to limited economies of scale and likely suboptimal use of resources
- Limited profits and cash for expansion and investment
- Inefficient market response functions

Given these and other limitations of the small-share brands, how can management improve their odds of success? The following set of prescriptions (propositions) could serve as an initial guideline for action that could lead to the desired objective:

I. Follow a selective-growth strategy; i.e., strive for large share of small, well-defined market segments.

II. Increase the *effectiveness* of marketing strategies by focusing on:

- Strategic marketing planning
- Adaptive experimentation and other approaches to assess the market response function to various marketing strategies
- Contingency plans
- Product/market portfolio analysis and decisions
- Cost/benefit analysis to decide whether to maintain, decrease, or increase share
- Creative strategies

III. Assure a unique positioning (by segment).

IV. Move toward *product line* management, encompassing product line:

- Positioning
- Pricing
- Service
- Distribution
- Promotion
- Advertising

Accepting these strategies (even on a trial basis) implies an acceptance of the basic premise of this book that the concepts and approaches used by large consumer product firms are equally relevant and applicable to small-share brands. Employing these strategies requires reliance on marketing research and modeling activities. Explicit analysis of the cost versus value of information should, therefore, be undertaken.

The major difference between small—and large—share brands or between the small (resource poor?) and large (resource rich?) firms is not in their *approach* to product decisions but rather in the number of simultaneous new product development and implementation activities they can undertake, and the level of risk they can absorb.

NONPROFIT AND GOVERNMENT ORGANIZATIONS

Government programs as well as the products and services of nonprofit organizations can be viewed as "products" that require development and marketing. Consider, for example, the energy area. The achievement of the government's energy objectives requires a developmental program not unlike the one a firm might develop if it were to embark on a new product development activity. Ideas for new programs and products have to be generated, evaluated, and developed. The surviving programs should be tested and those likely to meet the government's objectives introduced. The development of such a system requires the utilization of the concepts and methods discussed throughout the book. It is only through such systematic research-based approaches that the programs ("products") developed have a high likelihood of being compatible with consumers' values and expectations and meeting the government's objectives.

Similarly, non profit organizations such as churches, universities, and cultural institutions can benefit from the employment of concepts and approaches typically used in the development of frequently purchased consumer products. The "products" of nonprofit organizations are often intangible and their design, not unlike the design of consumer products, requires input on consumer preferences and needs. University programs (adult education, etc.), cultural events, and other nonprofit programs have to appeal to a target segment. As such, it is important that they are designed based on the results of consumer concept/product tests, and positioned in a way consistent with the overall positioning of their organization.

Some "products" of government and nonprofit organizations involve no direct benefit to certain consumer segments and do imply certain (nonmonetary) costs. Consider, for example, the 55-mile speed limit which results in time costs, and the disposable bottle laws which can involve convenience costs. In these and similar cases the design of the program itself as well as its marketing program can benefit from better understanding of consumers' needs and likely reaction to it. The government agency involved or the nonprofit organization should examine the full range of available alternatives and not accept the first "attractive" solution.

The generation and evaluation of alternative programs can thus be better achieved if the concepts and approaches suggested in this book are employed.

INTERNATIONAL OPERATIONS

The entry into foreign markets is much more complex than the entry into new market areas within one's own country. The major international product decisions facing a firm involve the same sets of decisions one has to go through in the domestic market, but instead of a focus on a single market, the international product decisions are repeated within each selected country. In addition, there are three other sets of interrelated decisions which management has to make involving (a) the country selection decision, (which of the 150 or so countries to go after), (b) the selected mode of entry (e.g., export, joint venture, direct foreign investments, etc.), and (c) the degree of international orientation and commitment. This latter set includes the decision on whether the firm would operate ethnocentrically (sell home country products to other countries), polycentrically (design separate products for each country), regiocentrically (design regional products) or geocentrically (design global products to meet the needs of specific market segments in any number of countries). Related to these is the decision on the degree of product standardization (same product including position, brand, etc.) in most or all countries within which the firm operates or the design of differentiated product strategy for different countries to take advantage of idiosyncratic country characteristics.[1]

International product decisions are closely related to the other international decisions of the firm (country selection, mode of entry, and international orientation) and require considerable input for the design and evaluation of the "best" product strategy. This input at the most detailed level requires consumer and trade studies in each country aimed at assessing the likely reactions of relevant segments within the country to various product concepts (including existing products from the home country and other countries, modification of existing products, or concepts for totally new products). Such data, although the most accurate and desirable, are likely to be quite expensive (both in terms of money and time). Hence, in a number of cases management can rely on other sources to assess the likely performance of various products in selected countries. These approaches include:

Use of expert judgment. The opinions and commitments of export agents, import agents, and international trade companies are often used as key inputs to the product decisions of the firm. Products can be sold to these intermediate marketing organizations in their original form or after some modifications. In both cases, it is the input from the relevant international IMO that dictates the product selection and strategy.

Use of product performance analogies across countries. If one examines the performance of similar products introduced in the target or

---

[1]For further discussion of the international product decisions of the firm see Wind (1977c), Wind and Perlmutter (1977), and Wind and Douglas (1981).

similar countries, following similar positioning/target segments, insights might be gained into the product's likely pattern of diffusion in the target country. Such analysis can also identify the product characteristics which are most likely to be accepted in various countries. Ideally, this type of analysis would result in a systematic understanding of the product characteristics and marketing strategies most likely to result in successful acceptance of the product under different environmental (including competitive and government) conditions. This phase implies the need for somewhat different analysis of new product opportunities and combines some of the characteristics of new product generation and evaluation procedures.

Development of an international product life cycle function. A by-product of the analogy analysis discussed above can be the development of an international product life cycle function for similar products which can provide insights into the order of entry into various countries. An international PLC can identify the likely "innovators" versus the "laggards" and the time lag in the acceptance of analogous products by the various countries.

Introduction of products from one country to another. Products can be introduced either in their existing form or in some modified version. In these cases new product development research should focus on the acceptability of the given products in the new countries. Such compatibility analysis avoids the need for the first few stages in the new product development process since a company starts with an existing physical product. The focus of such studies should be on the likely compatibility of the product with consumer and trade preferences and expectations. Such studies can be very comprehensive, encompassing an analysis of all product components—including positioning, features, packaging, name, etc.—but start with an existing product as opposed to a concept which would have to be developed.

Sophisticated international companies can *cluster world markets* (countries or sections within countries) based on their likely response to marketing variables and product offerings. In this case, international experience can be used as test markets for entry to other markets within the same cluster of countries. Such analysis can be conducted either based on actual data on the market response functions of various countries, or based on management subjective assessment of such response functions. In both cases it is important to update the information.

OTHER EXTENSIONS

Many of the product (and marketing) concepts and approaches discussed in this book, although traditionally restricted to products (or services), can be extended to other areas. To illustrate these extensions, let's consider the concepts of product positioning, which can be expanded to cover the positioning of a corporation, and market segmentation, which can be expanded to the segmentation of all the relevant stakeholders of the firm.

CORPORATE POSITIONING

Corporate positioning has been the implicit focus of public relations specialists. Some companies, especially in the retail and service industries, have long recognized the value of it and have tried to establish a unique corporate positioning. Saks Fifth Avenue, Neiman Marcus, I. Magnin, and Dunhill are a few examples of retailers who achieved a corporate positioning of high status, high prestige and high service and price operators. Similarly, the store names Korvettes, K-Mart, and Two Guys, for example, connote a lower price and service image (positioning). One of the problems with Sears and its struggle in the menswear area has been the lack of a clear identity as to the type, quality, and range of merchandise it offers. Service companies such as rental car agencies and fast food franchises have also recognized the value of positioning. "We Try Harder," has long been the hallmark of Avis' operation. Burger King tried to position its fast food franchise along the "Have It Your Way" theme. At times the name suggests a positioning. "Budget Rent-A-Car" or "Dollar-A-Day" suggest cheap rental service.

These examples suggest a corporate positioning closely identified with the product and service offerings of the firm. Manufacturing firms, on the other hand, have been less identified with unique positioning. Obviously, there are exceptions. IBM, Xerox, and other large industrial firms are often identified with a specific positioning which governs the firm's major line of operation. The positioning of the firm can restrict the firm's line of operation and the close identification of Xerox with office reproduction equipment has contributed in no small way to the difficulties it faced in trying to penetrate other markets such as the computer market.

In situations in which specific products and/or positioning are identified with the company—either the manufacturer or distributor—it is important that explicit attention be given to corporate positioning. From a market demand point of view, the corporate positioning should be consistent with and enhance the positioning the product is trying to convey. This is no easy (or even attainable) objective for many multiproduct line firms.

Corporate positioning should not be undertaken, however, only to enhance product positioning. The modern corporation is confronted with a large number of stakeholders who can affect the future performance and survival of the firm. In dealing with these stakeholders, it is essential for a firm to have an identifiable positioning. Consider the following case:

In a recent study on attributes used by security analysts in evaluating various companies in a given industry, it was found that innovativeness was one of the major determinants of the security analyst's recommendation whether to buy, hold, or sell the stock of firms within this industry. The firm which sponsored this study was perceived as noninnovative, a perception which clearly affected the security analyst's evaluation of the firm's stock. The firm decided to embark on a campaign aimed at security analysts focusing on its new product R&D activities. Within a few months the price of the firm's stock increased considerably above the average for the industry.

In considering corporate positioning, the same strategy considerations and research methods used in product positioning can be employed with the added complexity that the corporate positioning could serve as an appropriate umbrella under which the various product positionings can be developed in a way consistent with the overall corporate positioning.[2]

The corporate positioning concept has major strategic implications for the overall direction of growth and performance of the firm. In fact, it is consistent not only with the concept of corporate image but also with the concept of a corporate mission which offers guidelines for the firm's activities in new product and market development areas, mergers and acquisitions, and other marketing or product decisions.

---

[2]A unifying (umbrella) corporate positioning is not always desirable. There are cases in which a diversified company would be better off with no explicit and visible link among its various operating units' products and services. Little can be gained, for example, by linking Brown's & Williamson Tobacco, Saks Fifth Avenue and Birben to the British Assoc. Tobacco corporate identity.

STAKEHOLDER SEGMENTATION

Whereas the traditional concept of market segmentation has been applied to the segmentation of the market(s) facing the firm, the importance and heterogeneity of the various stakeholders facing the modern corporation require the development of marketing strategies aimed at various stakeholder segments. The various stakeholders of the firm, such as security analysts, suppliers, government officials, employees, environmental groups, and other groups and institutions critical to the survival of the firm, are all quite heterogeneous. Their segmentation and determination of their key characteristics should include:

- Criteria they use in making decisions relevant to the firm
- Perception of the firm and its competitors
- Attitudes and behavior toward the firm

and other relevant characteristics, all of which require the undertaking of an explicit segmentation analysis of these groups to assess their likely impact on the firm and offer guidelines for the design of appropriate marketing strategy aimed at them. Such studies can follow the same procedures used in consumer (or industrial) segmentation studies.[3]

CONCLUDING REMARKS

"But we are different" is the belief of every manager. Yet, as is quite evident from the previous discussion, once the differences are explicated, the same concepts and approaches can be employed in most cases. The difficulty is in the implementation. Care should be taken, therefore, to carefully plan and manage the implementation phase. This should be coupled with a recognition that the "product" decisions of the seven types of organizations involved in the development and marketing of products and services (other than frequently purchased consumer goods) can be based fundamentally on the same set of concepts and approaches. Any differences are likely to require even greater reliance on research, since many of these organizations are faced with a much more complex task than the one found by a typical consumer goods firm.

Having identified a number of idiosyncratic characteristics of various firms involved with other than frequently purchased consumer goods, select for each of the seven organizational types discussed in this chapter a specific firm and identify for it the major product policy concepts, methods, and strategies discussed in this book which can be applied to it.

Having completed this task, identify those concepts which might be applied with some modification and specify explicitly the needed modification for each of the selected organizations. Following this, list those concepts, methods, and strategies which are *not*, in your view, applicable to the given organization and the reasons for their lack of applicability.

Finally, for each organization, ask yourself the question, "Are there any other concepts or methods which might be required as guidelines for the product policy decisions of this organization and which are not currently included in the repertoire of concepts, methods, and strategies discussed in this book?"

---

[3]Occasionally, insightful segmentation can be gained from the analysis of secondary data or content analysis of published material (such as policy statements of government officials).

20

_____Pulling It All Together

Introduction

Obstacles to Success

Internal Obstacles
External Obstacles

Coping Strategies

Marketing-Oriented Strategic Thinking and Planning
A Future Oriented Research Perspective
Portfolio Perspective
Long-Term Integrated Marketing Plan
Organizational Design
Design and Implementation of a Marketing Audit
Offensive Competitive Strategies
Defensive Competitive Strategies
IMO Strategies
Experimentation and Focus on Productivity
Building a Cumulative Knowledge Base
Creative Strategy and Execution

Directions for Future Research

Organizational Issues
Information Management Issues
Portfolio Issues
Translation Issues

Concluding Remarks

INTRODUCTION

The first part of this book (Chapters 1–7) discussed the foundation of product (and, to a large extent, marketing) policy. The second and major part of the book (Chapters 8–16) covered the new product development process, while the third part (Chapters 17 and 18) briefly discussed some aspects of the management of established products. Chapter 19 suggested that the concepts and approaches discussed in the book are relevant not only to frequently purchased consumer products manufacturers, but also to most other types of organizations. Furthermore, the concepts and approaches presented in this book have all been field-tested by various firms. Yet, it is their *implementation and integration* which is the most difficult part of the product policy area.

The objective of this chapter is to offer some insights and guidelines for better implementation of any product-related changes. These changes range from relatively minor ones, such as small product modifications, to major changes involving product line deletions or additions. The term *product change* is used in this chapter to refer to all such changes. The chapter starts with a brief discussion of the internal and external obstacles to successful implementation of product decisions. The bulk of the chapter, however, is devoted to the discussion of 12 key coping strategies management can employ to help achieve its objectives and increase the odds of successful implementation. These 12 coping strategies, most of which were discussed previously in various sections of this book, are:

1. Marketing-oriented strategic thinking and planning.
2. A future-oriented research perspective.
3. A portfolio perspective.
4. A focus on an integrated, long-term marketing program.
5. Design of an organization supportive of the generation, evaluation, implementation, and control of the desired product/marketing strategies (and tactics) of the firm.
6. Design and implementation of a marketing audit
7. Design, evaluation, and implementation of offensive competitive strategies.
8. Design, evaluation, and implementation of defensive competitive strategies.
9. Design, evaluation, and implementation of strategies for retail (and other IMO) organizations.
10. Encouragement and undertaking of experimentation (especially adaptive experimentation) and a focus on productivity.
11. Building a cumulative knowledge base of previous experience leading to firm-wide empirical *generalization* which can serve as the foundation for the marketing theory of the firm.
12. Creative strategy and execution.

These coping strategies are not the only ones available to the firm. Yet, they constitute some of the major concepts and approaches proposed and developed in this book.

The final section of this chapter is devoted to the identification of those areas requiring additional conceptual, methodological, and empirical development. These directions for future research constitute an agenda for the sophisticated academic and industry researcher, and also suggest to the managerial reader those areas in which our current knowledge is still limited and could benefit from further research.

OBSTACLES TO SUCCESS

The implementation of product policies, especially if they involve change (in terms of the development and introduction of a new product, modification of existing products, etc.), is rarely a smooth activity. There are numerous internal and external obstacles to any organizational change, particularly to changes of potentially lasting and substantial impact. Product changes often fall in this category. It is imperative, therefore, that managers be aware of the obstacles facing the design, approval, and implementation of innovative product policies—those with high potential return but also relatively high risk.

INTERNAL OBSTACLES

Two sets of internal obstacles—attitudinal constraints and resource constraints—tend to affect a firm's ability and willingness to design and implement innovative product strategies.

Attitudinal factors, particularly top management's attitude toward risk, are among the major determinants of a firm's level of innovativeness. Risk aversion too often characterizes management's attitude toward innovative products and programs, especially those requiring a sacrifice of short-term goals in favor of longer-term goals. Such an orientation makes it extremely difficult to get new product programs initiated; and even when programs are started, the likelihood of final approval is relatively small. Similarly, innovative product changes or associated marketing strategies are often rejected in favor of "me too" and status-quo strategies. A risk-averse management style, once diffused throughout the organization, tends to hamper any creativity or entrepreneur-

ship and drives away from the firm the more creative and independent persons.

Lack of a marketing orientation is also a major obstacle to innovative product strategies. Firms which lack a marketing orientation tend to make decisions based on financial or production considerations. This rarely leads to the generation of truly innovative products and strategies.

A financial orientation tends to focus on cost savings and short-term financial goals (such as improved earnings per share) rather than longer-term investment in new products or markets.

Similarly, a production orientation tends to focus on more efficient utilization of the current production capacity rather than on acceptability of the products to consumers.

Furthermore, a nonmarketing orientation tends to limit the firm's use of and reliance on marketing research—resulting in another major obstacle to the design and implementation of innovative product strategies.

The attitudinal obstacles to success do not always stem from management resistance to the introduction of innovative (high risk) products and ideas. In many situations, the problem is an overanxious management which, in its desire to introduce new products, skips too many of the steps discussed in this book. Consider, for example, the case of the Smooth & Easy sauce and gravy bar. Standard Brands was so intrigued by the concept of a thickening agent in the form of a refrigerated gravy stock made from margarine that, according to an *Advertising Age* editorial (October 8, 1979), it

> rushed the product into the marketplace even before it resolved internal debate over the product's positioning. It compounded this error by

giving insufficient attention to cost evaluations and production requirements, oversold Smooth & Easy to the trade, over-advertised it, under-rated its inherent appeal, operated with inadequate media planning, bungled packaging, misread test market research, put too many 'cooks' in the kitchen to meddle with the product, and relied too heavily on advertising to reverse ingrained consumer resistance to commercial gravies. So Standard Brands blew more than $6,000,000.

Resource constraints present another serious obstacle to innovative product strategies, although these constraints can be overcome in the long run if management has a favorable and supportive attitude toward the proposed product strategies and is willing to invest the necessary resources to relax these constraints.

In the short term, however, if the firm lacks the capital and/or human and technological resources needed for effective development and implementation of an innovative product program, it is extremely difficult, even for innovative managers, to get the needed organizational commitment and resources.

Related to the resource constraints are the unique strengths and weaknesses of the firm and their impact on the freedom a firm has to design product strategies. The relevant strengths and weaknesses are not limited to those concerning the marketing operation of the firm, such as unique positioning, distribution strength, etc., but also its operation including financial strengths, strong supply position, manufacturing skills, technical proficiency, personnel skills, etc.

EXTERNAL OBSTACLES

The external obstacles to successful implementation of any product policy are numerous. As discussed in Chapter 7, these include:

- *Consumers*—who might be reluctant to buy the product.

- *Retailers* (and other intermediaries)—who might be reluctant to stock, promote, and distribute the product.

- *Competitors*—who might embark on a counterattack, which reduces the relative attractiveness of the firm's new offering.

- *Government (and other) regulatory agencies*—which might impose numerous restrictions on the firm's freedom to design and market its products.

The activities of these and other participants in the marketing system, coupled with environmental conditions such as high inflationary pressures, should be forecasted in advance and taken into consideration when designing an innovative product and marketing program and implementing it.

In discussing the internal and external obstacles, the focus has been on the *restrictive* nature of these forces. Overcoming the negative obstacles is a *must* if an innovative product strategy and the procedures required for its development, evaluation, and implementation are to be employed. Yet, as long as an explicit obstacle analysis is conducted, it might be helpful if management took advantage of the opportunities that analysis of the internal and external forces reveals. In this context, a useful research procedure is the explicit analysis of four forces:

- Restricting internal forces
- Restricting external forces
- Enhancing internal forces
- Enhancing external forces

This analysis should incorporate subjective management judgment and available data.

COPING STRATEGIES

Given the numerous internal and external forces which can affect the success of any product policy, how can management increase the chances of employing a successful program design and implementation? The concepts and approaches discussed throughout this book, coupled with the strategies proposed in the numerous behavioral science studies on overcoming resistance to change,[1] can help if employed effectively. Of particular value in increasing the odds of successful implementation are the 12 key concepts and approaches briefly discussed below.

MARKETING-ORIENTED STRATEGIC THINKING AND PLANNING

Product policy, whether it involves the design and introduction of new products or changes in current products and their associated strategies, has a higher chance of reaching the implementation stage if arrived at after a careful strategic analysis, evaluation, and choice process. The strategic marketing orientation discussed throughout this book should be applied to all levels of management (not only top management), and it should not be limited to the design of product strategy. It should also be employed to achieve the necessary support and approval for the introduction of the required changes. In the latter case, the initiator of the change should clearly assess the possible internal and external obstacles to the acceptance of the change and design strategies to overcome them.

In employing a strategic perspective in the design of the firm's product programs and their implementation plans, all the planning concepts and approaches discussed earlier should be considered. A detailed implementation plan should include, at the minimum, detailed key programs, their schedule, budget, required resources, organizational responsibilities, and to the extent possible, some key contingencies that might be required in response to major problems or new developments. The implementation plans should cover all relevant levels of management, operating, and staff units. The planning of an implementation plan is as critical to the success of the proposed change as the quality and innovativeness of the proposed change itself and its corresponding strategy.

A FUTURE-ORIENTED RESEARCH PERSPECTIVE

One of the central themes of this book has been the importance of marketing research inputs to the design and evaluation of product strategies. Accepting this view, particularly the need to base product decisions on a good understanding of the market and projections of expected future events, is critical if management is to increase its chances of success. Future-oriented research can uncover obstacles to the acceptance of the product change, and, if acted upon, reduce the risk of the proposed change.

PORTFOLIO PERSPECTIVE

Even when the change considered by management involves a single product, the impact of the change on the product/market portfolio of

---

[1]Chapter 2 offers a brief discussion of the resistance to change literature.

the firm should be explicitly examined. Having a clear understanding of the portfolio implications of any proposed change makes strategic sense and can also help "sell" the change internally.

An understanding of the various portfolio approaches and concepts discussed in Chapter 5 is thus an essential first step. Most of the portfolio models employed by industry are of the standardized type (primarily the ones offered by BCG, McKinsey, and A.D. Little); however, given the conceptual advantages of customizing the portfolio approach based on the idiosyncratic characteristics of the firm, it is desirable to carefully evaluate the portfolio models used and, to the extent that management feels uncomfortable making strategic decisions based only on the present criteria (dimensions), a change in a portfolio model might be called for.

should be well integrated with the entire marketing program.

Furthermore, the design of any product change and its associated marketing program should take an explicit long-term orientation. In the introduction of a new product, for example, one should not consider just the single product, but plan (at the time of introduction) the next steps both in terms of product line extensions and planned changes in any of the marketing mix variables (e.g., repositioning, price change, and the like). Such considerations are quite critical in assuring long-term performance. Consider, for example, the introduction of Radio Shack's first home computer. By emphasizing its low price, they established a positioning which might not be compatible with the positioning of the second computer model they introduced some time later aiming at the small business owner.

LONG-TERM INTEGRATED MARKETING PLAN

Product changes cannot and should not be evaluated without the inclusion of their effect on the current and expected marketing programs of the firm. The typical division of marketing decisions into discrete product, price, promotion, advertising, and distribution decisions is arbitrary and, although convenient from a pedagogical point of view, is not the way consumers respond to a marketing stimulus. Consumers respond to the totality of a marketing offering, not a separate component. Price, for example, is not perceived as too high or too low in some absolute sense, but rather in terms of the *value* the product delivers versus its costs (and often not just the purchase price, but the total usage cost). Given these and the other interdependencies among the components of the marketing program, and between them and product changes, any product change strategy

ORGANIZATIONAL DESIGN

Since some of the most serious obstacles to the acceptance and successful implementation of product-related changes are internal, an appropriate organizational design is a must. Chapters 16 and 17 focused on some of the organizational considerations, and one should never underestimate the importance of designing organizational structures and procedures which encourage innovative thinking and reduce the likelihood of "killing" ideas for change even before examining them. A proper organizational design, as discussed in Chapters 16 and 17, would offer the necessary *rewards* for performance related to the implementation of the desired strategy. Furthermore, appropriate organizational design could facilitate implementation by assuring *involvement* and procedures necessary for carrying out the planned product changes. Yet, no organizational design can eliminate all implementation problems, nor can it by itself assure creativity. An appropriate organizational design can help overcome many obstacles to product change. It can further help by identifying the necessary resources (especially personnel) and structuring procedures for their effective utilization.

DESIGN AND IMPLEMENTATION OF A MARKETING AUDIT

A strategic orientation, as specified in Chapter 6, calls for a continuous analysis and forecast of the changing environment of the firm (discussed in Chapter 7). The continuous monitoring and projection of the environment have to be supplemented, however, with a *marketing audit*. Chapter 6 briefly discussed this concept as it relates to the situation analysis that has to be undertaken as part of the input to the product/marketing strategy of the firm.

A marketing audit should cover the following areas:

1. Marketing orientation, objectives, and strategy
2. Product/market portfolio
   - Profitability analysis
   - Market segment response analysis
   - Cost/benefit analysis
3. Marketing environment
   - Market
   - Competition
   - Marketing institutions and practices (distributors, suppliers, facilitating marketing organizations)
   - Macroenvironment (demographic, economic, social/cultural, political/legal, technological, international)
4. Marketing functions
   - Product
   - New products
   - Price
   - Distribution
   - Salesforce
   - Advertising
   - Promotion
5. Marketing research, information, planning, and control system
6. Marketing organization
   - Formal structure
   - Functional efficiency
   - Interfunctional efficiency

The premise of an effective audit is that it should be designed to encompass the current situation, its projected state (ideally under a number of alternative scenarios), the assumptions made in making a projection, the needed research, if any, to further assess the situation, and finally a set of conclusions regarding each factor and combination of factors. The final evaluation of any audited area should be in terms of a specific listing of all the relevant opportunities and problems, the likelihood of their occurence, and their likely impact on the firm. Any audit framework should be modified to meet the idiosyncratic needs of the firm. Recognizing this need for tailoring, Exhibit 20–1 suggests one approach to the structuring of the product area of a marketing audit.[2]

OFFENSIVE COMPETITIVE STRATEGIES

One of the major obstacles to successful product changes is unanticipated competitive actions. The new product battlefield is strewn with casualties of strong and unexpected competitive retaliatory actions. The actions often

---

[2]Other formulations of the marketing audit can be found in Kotler, Gregor, and Rogers (1977) and Hughes (1978).

can be anticipated if an explicit competitive analysis is conducted. Any firm initiating a product change should consider explicitly before finalizing its plan the likely competitive retaliation. (Will they meet our price? Will they increase their promotional efforts? Will they try to block us from achieving the required distribution?)

Furthermore, a firm's strategy options should include product changes designed to

EXHIBIT 20–1

MARKETING AUDIT: THE PRODUCT

A. Current products	Today	Projected: Status quo	Projected: Pessimistic	Projected: Optimistic	Assumptions/ needed research	Conclusions
FOR EACH PRODUCT BY MARKET SEGMENT						
Size of segment						
Growth						
Concentration of customers						
End users						
50% of volume by ______ % users						
80% of volume by ______ % users						
Intermediate customers						
50% of volume by ______ % customers						
80% of volume by ______ % customers						
Key characteristics of segment						
Geographic						
Demographic						
Psychographic						
Benefits sought						
Purchasing and shopping						
Media						
Number of competitors serving segment						
Entry of new competitors						
FOR EACH PRODUCT						
Who buys the product?						
Who uses the product?						
How is the product used?						
Where is the product bought?						

EXHIBIT 20–1 (continued)

A. Current products	Today	Projected			Assumptions/ needed research	Conclusions
		Status quo	Pessimistic	Optimistic		
How is the product bought?						
Why is the product bought?						
What is the market segment(s)' response function to the firm and its competitive marketing strategies? Advertising Promotion Price Distribution						
Are changes needed in: Product features/benefits? Product design? Packaging? Name? Service?						
FOR EACH PRODUCT LINE						
What are the product line objectives?						
Should any products be phased out?						
Should new products be added?						
Can any products benefit from modification or repositioning?						

	Likelihood of occurrence (0–100%)	Likely impact on the firm (1–10)
OPPORTUNITIES		
_____	_____	_____
_____	_____	_____
_____	_____	_____
_____	_____	_____
PROBLEMS		
_____	_____	_____
_____	_____	_____
_____	_____	_____
_____	_____	_____

EXHIBIT 20–1 (continued)

B. New products	Today	Projected			Assumptions/ needed research	Conclusions
		Status quo	Pessimistic	Optimistic		
Number of new products introduced in past 3 years and likely to be introduced in next 3 years						
Percent of sales from products introduced in past 3 years and likely to be introduced in next 3 years						
Is there a new product development system?						
How many new ideas/concepts/products are in development?						
No. of new ideas						
No. of new concepts						
No. of new products						
How effective is the new product development system?						
Overall system						
New product generation process						
Idea/concept screening process						
Product design process						
Product testing process						
New product forecasting models						
Other components of the system						
Is adequate research and business analysis being done before the "go" decision?						
Are the new product activities well organized?						

	Likelihood of occurrence (0–100%)	Likely impact on the firm (1–10)
OPPORTUNITIES		
_____	_____	_____
_____	_____	_____
_____	_____	_____
_____	_____	_____
PROBLEMS		
_____	_____	_____
_____	_____	_____
_____	_____	_____
_____	_____	_____

attack competitors' market position and vulnerability. Market structure analysis which identifies the strengths and weaknesses of the various competitors often can suggest opportunity gaps as targets for new or modified products (and associated marketing strategies).

DEFENSIVE COMPETITIVE STRATEGIES

Product policy should not be concerned only with the introduction of new products or the modification and repositioning of existing products, but should also consider explicit strategies to defend its current products and markets against competitive action.

The professional marketing literature has devoted little attention to this topic. Yet, from a practical point of view, this is one of the most critical decision areas of any firm.

Ideally, the market and environmental monitoring activities of the firm should discover areas of dissatisfaction which could invite competitors. Southwest Airlines, for example, owes its existence to the dissatisfaction among air travelers within Texas and to the lack of sensitivity of Braniff and Texas International Airlines (the air carriers who dominated the market prior to Southwest's entry) to this situation. Similarly, monitoring competitive activities, including test market and other market and technological research activities (as can be assessed from patent applications, personnel recruiting patterns, etc.) can offer early indications of likely competitive moves. The preventive competitive analysis should not be limited to the current competitors. New competitors may enter the industry, and customers may switch their purchases from products in the given product category to new areas.

Defensive strategies can include planned cannibalization of current products and line extensions. Planned cannibalization is often em-

ployed by pharmaceutical firms before the patent expiration of one of their drugs and is aimed at switching the physician's loyalty to a new and better-protected drug. This is a sound preemptive move designed to reduce the impact of the unavoidable competition from generic products which often enter the market as soon as the patent protection of a branded drug expires. Line extensions are often aimed at attracting market segments which otherwise might be attracted to a competitor; for example, consider the case of low-tar spinoffs of established cigarette brands which are added to the line to prevent the migration of the low-tar seekers to other brands.

Response to early warning signals and preemptive moves are the best preventive strategies. Yet, unfortunately, many firms do not take full advantage of such strategies. In these cases, the burden of defensive marketing strategy falls on the firm *after* a competitor has already committed itself at least to a test market and occasionally to regional or national introduction. In these cases, there are a number of competitive strategies a defending firm might consider. These should be evaluated based on careful and explicit analysis in order to avoid emotional reactions. Among the defensive strategies a firm might consider are:

Do nothing—an especially attractive strategy if the competitive entry does not endanger the defending firm's market position.

Design strategies that might force the competitor out of business or reduce his profitability. At the extreme, especially when the defending firm is large relative to the attacker, such strategies might be illegal and subject to the penalties of predatory practices. The most visible of these strategies is price reduction. Equally effective, however, are strategies aimed at restricting the effective distribution a new product can achieve, trade and consumer promotional activities which offer added incentives to promote and buy the defending firm's products, and increased advertising and marketing expenditures which can reduce the effectiveness of the entering firm's marketing program and raise considerably the cost of entry into the market. The timing of these and similar strategies is also crucial. Two major timing strategies can be followed: (a) early response (e.g., at test market) aimed at discouraging the entering firm from staying in the market, and (b) a later response (after a full commitment of the entering firm) which, if effective, can have devastating effects on the entering firm. The line of demarcation between legal and illegal defensive strategies is thin, and management should use both legal judgment and their own ethical values as guidelines in selecting a strategy.

Design strategies that will increase the relative attractiveness of the firm's offering to the target segment. Such strategies can include repositioning, product improvements, or other changes aimed at increasing the *value* of the product to its customers. Many of the strategies used in point two above can also be employed in this context, but the distinguishing characteristic is the degree to which the strategies *increase* the perceived value of the product offering in the *long run* (not only during the introductory "war" with the entering competitor).

IMO STRATEGIES

The success of any product change strategy depends not only on the firm, but also on the response and support of the intermediate marketing organizations (IMOs), particularly, the retail outlets in the case of consumer goods. Effective strategy, therefore, takes explicitly into account the objectives and interests of the other participants in the marketing system so as to design and implement marketing strategies aimed at them.

As with the analysis of likely competitive reactions, the analysis of likely IMO reaction should be modeled explicitly either by developing separate retail response models (not unlike the development of market response models for each major competitor) or incorporating retail-related variables in the firm's overall marketing response models (not unlike the inclusion of competitors in an advertising-response model by using share of advertising as one of the independent variables).

In developing retail strategies, some of the considerations which should be taken into account are:

- Short- and long-term support the IMO is likely to offer the manufacturer,

- Cost of using specific IMOs for distribution and promotion of the product,

- Degree of control the firm has over the IMOs' activities,

- Impact the IMOs' image and activities might have on the desired positioning and performance of the product(s) under consideration,

- Desired level and type of distribution coverage.

EXPERIMENTATION AND FOCUS ON PRODUCTIVITY

The importance of adaptive experimentation was clearly emphasized in Chapter 6. Such a philosophy is critical for increasing the chances of achieving the desired long-term profitability. Furthermore, in many cases (in which the firm is reluctant or unable to undertake the necessary marketing research studies) it is the only viable way of providing guidelines for ensuing years' strategies.

Related to the adaptive experimentation approach is the needed focus on *productivity*. Strategy alone, regardless of its excellence, cannot lead to the desired results. Good opera-

EXHIBIT 20–2

THE RELATIONSHIP BETWEEN STRATEGY AND OPERATIONS

		Operations	
		Poor	Excellent
Strategy	Poor	I	II
	Excellent	III	IV

tions are also required. The relationship between stratey and operations is illustrated in Exhibit 20–2. The ideal, of course, is to be in cell IV. Yet, firms often find themselves in cells I or III—the poor operations cells. Adaptive experimentation can help improve the quality of the firm's long range strategy; however, it must be supplemented with approaches to improve operations. This focus on productivity requires a careful monitoring system coupled with plans of action designed to improve low productivity areas. Unfortunately, focusing on productivity is frequently used by firms as a cost-cutting procedure which might even involve major cuts in long-term investments (such as the investment in the development of truly innovative new products). This should not be the case, and management should not look at productivity as the *alternative* to innovative strategy. Both are required to increase the odds of successful implementation of product changes.

BUILDING A CUMULATIVE KNOWLEDGE BASE

Most companies lack a corporate memory. Studies are often conducted with little regard for the findings of previous studies (especially when not conducted on the same product). Improvements in the quality of management decisions require a corporate memory. A centralized data bank that allows for easy anal-

ysis of findings (across a wide range of products and situations) and their convenient retrieval is a must. The results of previous studies and the firm's relevant experience should serve as the foundation for a series of generalizations about the firm's products, markets, and marketing effectiveness. Generalizations such as: "The range of trial for products in product category X, market Y, and market expenditure level Z has been 10–40% with an average of 26%" or "Repeat purchase *ranged* from 10–50% of trial with an average of 30%" can serve as major input to the strategic plans of the firm. If these are the findings, it is quite unlikely that the firm can expect (without drastic changes in its mode of operation) a trial higher than 40%, or a repeat higher than 50% of trial. Furthermore, conservative planning will call for a trial closer to 26% and a repeat of 30% of trial.

An important component of any cumulative data base is information on the firm's marketing effectiveness. Market response functions should be developed and updated regularly. Having a series of valid response functions can help improve the marketing activities of the firm, as well as provide guidelines for the allocation of resources among the various marketing activities.

Developing a set of empirical generalizations is critical not only for improving the long-term quality of the firm's decisions, but also as one of the first steps toward the development of relevant marketing theory rules.

CREATIVE STRATEGY AND EXECUTION

William Rothschild, of the GE corporate planning and developing staff, in the preface to his book, *Strategic Alternatives*, states:

> . . . I have spent hundreds of hours consulting with general managers, strategic planners, and even chief executive officers of small, medium,

and large corporations. As a result of these personal experiences, and on the basis of discussing these topics with other practitioners, I have become concerned about the *lack of creativity* and of true strategic alternatives in management. Management have been willing to analyze their environments, competition, and resources, and have committed considerable organizational time, money, and personnel only to come up with the same old answers or with slight modification of their existing strategy" (Rothschild, 1979).

The need for *creative* strategy is critical. Yet, successful programs (cell IV of Exhibit 20–2) require both efficiency and creativity, not only in strategy but also in execution. Product changes (and their associated marketing strategies) require a *translation* from consumer preference or R&D ideas into specific product formulation and its associated marketing and promotional material. This translation, as alluded to in numerous places throughout this book, is the most difficult task facing any firm.

The creative quality of the execution, whether in terms of product design or promotional material, has considerable impact on the likelihood of successful implementation of any product change. Creative execution can improve the effectiveness of the marketing investment. It is not uncommon, for example in direct mail operations, for a *creative* execution to pull two or three times better than a controlled mailing. Similarly, an especially creative advertisement can multiply the effectiveness of every dollar invested in advertising.

DIRECTIONS FOR FUTURE RESEARCH

The major premise of this book is that an explicit research-based approach to the planning of a firm's product/marketing decisions is a must and increases the likelihood of making the "right" decisions (i.e., decisions which are at least consistent with management's objectives and are responsive to changing consumer behavior, competitive actions, and other environmental conditions). Whether one adopts the models and approaches suggested here or others is immaterial as long as an effort is made to formalize the product decision process in accordance with the idiosyncrasies of the firm. Short-term implementation and long-term improvement of the concepts and approaches discussed in this book, however, require answers to a number of key questions. Specifying these questions could help identify some of the more critical areas for future research in the product policy area as well as identify, for the managerially-oriented readers, some of those areas in which our current concepts and approaches might be a bit weak. No attempt is made to develop an exhaustive research agenda. Rather, the selected research areas are those seen as addressing both needed practical management questions *and* offering a conceptual or methodological challenge to the basic researchers in the field. The specific research areas identified are grouped into four categories relating to issues of organizational design, information management, portfolio management, and the translation of marketing inputs into strategy, and strategy into response.

ORGANIZATIONAL ISSUES

How does a firm organize its product-planning function? Current organizational design schemes (such as brand, market, product-market, functional, or other hybrid organizations) offer few guidelines. New organizational concepts should be developed and the effectiveness of alternative organizational designs for new product development and management of existing products tested.

How are corporate objectives and criteria determined? The identification of the relevant objectives and criteria at all levels of management (e.g., corporate, strategic business unit, product line, and individual brand levels) is essential for the determination of *boundaries* for the product/market decisions of the firm as well as the criteria for evaluating alternative strategies. Yet, there are a number of unanswered questions concerning how to relate the findings of empirical product/market boundaries to management's concerns and organizational structure, and how to identify and resolve conflicting objectives among the relevant management team. These and similar questions suggest the need to study corporate management's perceptions and preferences. In fact, most of the recent procedures utilized in consumer behavior can be employed in the study of corporate executives.

Related to the above is the question: How explicit should management objectives and criteria be? Although a number of approaches, such as conjoint analysis and the Analytic Hierarchy Process have been utilized successfully to explicate the relative importance of various criteria, the political/negotiative environment of many firms gives rise to many situations in which it might be preferable not to know the explicit criteria. What are these conditions, and how would lack of explicit criteria affect the "quality" of management decisions?

How does management encourage the generation of truly innovative and creative alternatives? The generation of *new product ideas* has received considerable attention in the marketing and R&D literature. Yet, little attention has been given to the systematic encouragement of generating creative new product and marketing strategies.

How can the marketing decisions (and orienta- tion) be best integrated with the other business functions—finance, R&D, production, personnel, procurement, legal, and top management? What are the implications—for the design of product-related research procedures—of the need for such integration?

INFORMATION MANAGEMENT ISSUES

How to design and implement a monitoring system and forecasting models of changes in the environmental conditions and the firm's performance? Many current marketing information systems tend to offer too much disjointed environmental data. Little effort is given to the development of systematic scanning of the entire environment (consumers, competition, technology, legal, economic conditions, etc.). Similarly, too little attention has been given to the ongoing monitoring of the firm's performance. Furthermore, most of the monitoring systems do not include *projections* of trends. User-oriented MIS should be designed, incorporating advances in information-dissemination technology (e.g., on-line information systems) and forecasting (especially environmental forecasting techniques). In addition, greater attention should be given to (a) the development of new data collection analysis and dissemination methods and (b) the implementation and modification of *existing methods*, adjusting them to the needs of continuous monitoring of *changes* in the relevant environmental forces and the firm's performance.

In designing marketing studies (for the generation and evaluation of alternatives), *how often should these studies be conducted to assure accurate capturing of changes in consumer attitudes and behavior and market and environmental conditions?*

How does management assess operationally the "cost versus value" of the various concepts (such as adaptive experimentation, contingency plans, etc.) and research and management science tools (such as environmental monitoring programs, forecasting models, etc.), and how are possible conflicts between the desired approaches and the political reality of the firm reconciled?

Given the diversity of research approaches to the generation and evaluation of alternatives, *which mix of approaches is most appropriate and under what conditions?*

How are models for new product development, product modification, repositioning, and deletion designed and implemented to incorporate forecasts of likely consumer (and other relevant stakeholder) responses under alternative marketing strategies and environmental conditions with feasibility and cost data?

Given that all product decisions should be based on likely future behavior, *how can the various research approaches (which tend to be static in nature) be adopted and refocused on the dynamic nature of the market and offer the type of forecasts management requires at an acceptable confidence and cost level?*

To what extent do the major analytical approaches (such as conjoint analysis) used in consumer studies relating to concept screening and product testing, for example, apply to situations involving low consumer involvement (versus the more traditional case of high involvement) and imagery attributes (versus physical product attributes)?

How can changes in consumer and organizational buying behavior be accounted for by the research approaches utilized within the boundaries of the product-related research efforts of the firm? Consider, for example, the change in many consumer and organizational situations toward "system buying," or changes toward routine computer-based buying, or consumer buying for inventory (hoarding behavior), and their implications for the required research design and analysis. Similarly, given that most products are used by a number of people (e.g.,

members of the buying center and not just a single individual) under a variety of usage situations, how can the product research approaches reflect this complexity which, if considered explicitly, require an analysis of n-way matrices of consumers' (multiple respondents per family) evaluation (perception and preference of a variety of products and relevant product categories) on a set of attributes, under a relevant set of usage occasions. Given this complexity, the tendency is often to focus only on a subset of these matrices. Yet, advances in analytical procedures of three-way matrices and innovative designs enable the explicit treatment of a larger number of matrices being more responsive to management information needs.

PORTFOLIO ISSUES

How does management operationalize and implement the product portfolio concept? The portfolio concept is relevant at all levels of management (e.g., the strategic business or the corporate level), and its boundaries (the product categories and market segments involved and the evaluative criteria employed) should reflect management's strategic and visionary orientation. The major difficulties in implementing the portfolio concept, however, are operational and require a considerable amount of basic research efforts. These efforts might center around the seven steps required in the development of a portfolio management approach, which include:

1. Management determination of the level and units of portfolio analysis. The level decision ranges from the corporate through the SBU to a single product line. The unit of analysis can range from the typical product to the more desirable product positioning by segment. The unanswered question is:

what are the interrelationships among the various levels and units of analysis?

2. Identification of the relevant dimensions, including single variable dimensions and composite dimensions. What *should* be the relevant dimensions, and how do they relate to those used by the standardized portfolio models?

3. Determination of the relative importance of the various dimensions.

4. Construction of a matrix based on the chosen dimensions (to the extent that two or more dimensions are viewed as the dominant ones).

5. Identification of the present position of the firm's products (businesses or other unit(s) of analysis) on the relevant portfolio dimensions.

6. Projection of the likely position of each product on the relevant dimensions if (a) no changes are expected in environmental conditions, competitive activities, or the firm's own strategies and (b) specific changes *are* expected in these forces.

7. Determination of the desired portfolio of products including the position of each (existing and new) product—as a basis for the development of alternative strategies that would close the gap between the current and desired portfolio—and desired allocation of resources among these products.

How can resource allocation models be designed and implemented to help allocate the firm's resources among products, markets, and marketing programs; and what are the implications of such models to the desired research approaches in terms of required data collection and analysis?

How can management determine the desired mix of internal versus external development activities?

How does the firm schedule (and allocate resources over time to) the various product/marketing activities; and how should the allocation vary by scenario (e.g., recession versus economic boom, etc.)?

How are product lines for various market segments designed (and evaluated)? In particular, which of the following strategies is most desirable?

• Each product is aimed at a single segment.
• Each product is aimed at a number of segments.
• A product line is aimed at a single segment.
• A product line is aimed at a number of segments (ideally a product per segment).
• Some hybrid of the above.

TRANSLATION ISSUES

What procedures can be developed for the translation of:

• Research findings (such as consumer perceptions of and preference for various product attributes) into physical (and imagery) product attributes?
• Strategy alternatives into product attributes and associated marketing strategy?
• Information from market response models into the design of product and marketing related strategies?

Since a number of research procedures have been developed for these and other needed transformations, the focus on future development efforts should be on the validation of these procedures and on modifications aimed at simplifying the data requirements and increasing the relevance of the information collected.

CONCLUDING REMARKS

Recent years have witnessed a tremendous growth in the utilization of analytical approaches to product marketing planning in general, and new product development in particular. New product forecasting models based on concept testing, simulated test market, or test market data are all widely used. Marketing practitioners should not be concerned with whether analytical approaches work or not, but rather with which of the many available approaches is best suited for their firm and the specific product/market situation involved. Academic and industry researchers, at the same time, face the challenging task of developing new analytical approaches which not only offer a more elegant solution, but also address the implementation problems discussed earlier, and others relating to the reliability and validity of the data obtained. A good example of this developmental direction is the POSSE model and algorithm (Green et al., 1981) which offers an operational approach to product design optimization. In addition, given new technological developments such as video terminals and other information systems capable of two-way communication (which are expected to reach 25 percent of US households by the end of the decade), new research procedures should be developed to capitalize on these developments and offer product (and marketing) decision makers better and more timely information on which to base their decisions.

The necessary conceptual and methodological developments in the product planning area, in today's environment and even more so in the changing environment of the future, make it an exciting and challenging area for basic and applied research. Progress in this area, however, requires close collaboration between the academic basic researcher and industry practitioner who can provide the real world (and laboratory) data for developing, testing, and implementing new analytical approaches for product/marketing planning.

APPENDIXES

Appendix A

Research Methods For Product Policy

INTRODUCTION

Product decisions, not unlike most management decisions, require a considerable amount of information. The last two decades have witnessed major advances in marketing research, particularly in the areas of choice modeling and measurement and data analysis procedures. Many of these methods were briefly discussed throughout the book. The objective of this series of appendixes is to provide the reader (who is unfamiliar with these approaches) with a better intuitive understanding of the purpose, input, and output of some of the major procedures.

This appendix includes a brief description of most of the analytical approaches referred to in the text:

1. Multiple regression
2. Multiple discriminant analysis
3. AID
4. Analysis of variance
5. Factor analysis
6. Clustering
7. Multidimensional scaling (MDS)
8. Conjoint analysis
9. Analytic hierarchy process

The discussion of these approaches is very brief since comprehensive expositions are widely available. Most advanced marketing research texts describe the first eight methods and their applications to marketing problems (including various product decisions). In addition, specialized texts on these procedures abound offering the interested reader an in-depth understanding of the methods and their implementation.

The discussion of all approaches is divided into seven parts:

- Objectives
- Output
- Algorithmic logic
- Critical assumptions
- Input data
- Available computer programs
- Extensions (where applicable)
- References

These appendixes are not designed as a *how-to-do-it* guideline for researchers interested in the actual implementation of the procedures, but rather as a brief managerial overview aimed at familiarizing the reader with the various approaches. Those who are interested in utilizing these procedures are encouraged to study the additional readings suggested and experiment with the specific approaches.

REGRESSION ANALYSIS

OBJECTIVES

Regression analysis is the most common approach to establish statistical association between a set of independent variables and a single dependent variable. The simple bivariate case of a single independent variable X and a dependent variable Y is presented graphically in Exhibit A–1.

The case of $Y = a + bX_i$ can be extended to include additional independent variables. A multiple regression equation with three independent variables is:

$$Y = a + b_1X_1 + b_2X_2 + b_3X_3 + e.$$

The objectives of regression analysis are:

1. To establish a function that relates the independent variables to a dependent variable.
2. To examine the strength of the relationship between the independent and dependent variables (e.g., prediction values of the dependent variable).
3. To assess the statistical significance of the relationship between the independent and dependent variables.
4. To determine the relative importance of each of the independent variables.

OUTPUT

The typical output of multiple regression programs (such as BMD 03R) includes the following:

- Regression equation
  $Y = a + b_1X_1 + b_2X_2 + \cdots + b_nX_n$.
- Coefficient of multiple determination (R^2) which offers a measure of the percent of variation in the dependent variable accounted for by the independent variables (for the sample and adjusted for the population).
- Overall measure of the statistical significance of the regression (F test).
- Relative importance of each independent variable as determined by the regression coefficient, the partial regression coefficient, and the accounted-for variance contributed by each independent variable.
- Statistical significance of the contribution of each independent variable as measured by standard errors and the t test.

ALGORITHMIC LOGIC

The most commonly used regression algorithm is *least squares*. This method finds the line that

EXHIBIT A-1

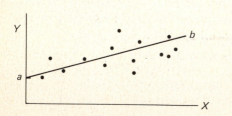

minimizes the sum of squared deviations of the observed values of Y_i from their estimated counterparts $\hat{Y}_i$.

CRITICAL ASSUMPTIONS

The major assumptions of multiple regression analysis are:

- The relation between the independent variables and the dependent variable is presumed (in the simple case) to be linear.
- There is no correlation (multicollinearity) between the independent variables themselves. (This is a critical assumption if correct interpretation of the regression coefficients is desired; it is not as critical for forecasting purposes.)
- A series of distributional assumptions.

INPUT DATA

A data matrix for the dependent variable and the independent variables. Data can include both continuous scales (e.g., income, age) or categorical variables (e.g., sex, occupation). The latter are coded as dummy variables (0, 1).

AVAILABLE COMPUTER PROGRAMS

Most of the statistical computer packages include a number of regression programs. BMD offers all variable regression programs (BMD–03R) and a stepwise program (BMD–02R).

EXTENSIONS

The single linear case can be extended to various nonlinear equations. In addition, nonlinear probability models, such as logit, can be employed.

REFERENCES

Brief overview: Green and Tull, 1978 (Chapter 10); Brown, 1980 (Chapters 12 and 13).

Advanced treatment: Draper and Smith, 1966; Johnston, 1972.

MULTIPLE DISCRIMINANT ANALYSIS

OBJECTIVES

Discriminant analysis is one of the major approaches used to examine the differences among two or more a priori defined groups in terms of a set of independent variables. The objectives of discriminant analysis are:

1. To find linear combinations of the independent variables that separate the groups.

2. To test whether significant differences exist among the mean independent-variable based profiles of the groups.

3. To determine which independent variables account most for intergroup differences in mean profiles.

4. To classify new subjects whose characteristics, but not group identity, are known and assumed to be from one of the a priori defined groups.

The typical output of discriminant analysis programs (such as BMD–04M) includes:

- Overall measure of the statistical significance of discriminant analysis (*F* test).
- Eigenvalues to determine the number of significant discriminant functions and the discriminatory power that can be attributed to each discriminant function.
- Standardized and original discriminant weights.
- Classification matrix that compares actual and predicted group membership.

ALGORITHMIC LOGIC

The linear combinations of the independent variables are obtained by maximizing among-groups to within-groups variation. This procedure yields a number of discriminant functions equal to the number of groups minus one.

CRITICAL ASSUMPTIONS

The major assumptions of multiple discriminant analysis are:

- The combinations of the independent

variables are presumed to be linear.
- There is no correlation (multicollinearity) among the independent variables.
- A series of distributional assumptions.

INPUT DATA

A data matrix of subjects by the dependent variable (group identification) and independent variables. Data for the independent variables can include continuous scales (e.g., income, age) or categorical variables (e.g., sex). The latter are coded as dummy variables.

AVAILABLE COMPUTER PROGRAMS

Most of the statistical packages include a number of discriminant analysis programs. BMD offers all variable discriminant analysis program (BMD–04M) and a stepwise program (BMD–07M).

REFERENCES

Brief overview: Green and Tull, 1978 (Chapter 12); Brown, 1980.

Advanced treatment: Green, 1978a; Tatsuoka, 1970.

AUTOMATIC INTERACTION DETECTION (AID)

OBJECTIVES

In exploratory analyses of observational and survey data, one does not ordinarily know the interactive relationships between the indepen-

dent variables and their effect on the dependent variable. Automatic Interaction Detection (AID) developed by Sonquist and Morgan is a multivariate technique designed to consider simultaneously the interaction (as opposed to correlation) effects among a large number of independent variables.

The objective of AID is to split the sample into a series of nonoverlapping subgroups that best explain the dependent variable. The process produces a tree that shows which independent variables are most important, how they interact, the size of subgroups, and the explained variance in the dependent variable.

OUTPUT

The typical output of an AID program includes a tree structure that shows, at each stage:

- The independent variable leading to the best binary split and how that variable is split.
- The number of individuals assigned to each of the two groups.
- The mean dependent-variable score on each of the two subgroups.
- Other summary statistics (e.g., error sums of squares).

ALGORITHMIC LOGIC

Basically, AID performs a series of one-way analyses of variance type computations. It performs a sequence of binary splits of the sample, choosing for each independent variable the split that separates the sample into two subgroups that account for most variance in the dependent variable. It then chooses from all of these "best splits" the specific independent variable which offers the overall best split. This split forms the new groups, and the same procedure continues to establish the best split for each group.

CRITICAL ASSUMPTIONS

- It is generally designed for large samples of the order of 1000 or more.
- Being a sequential search procedure, it does not specify an explicit nodel in the way, for example, ANOVA does.

INPUT DATA

A data matrix for the dependent and independent variables. The dependent variable is either interval scaled or dichotomous. The independent variables can be nominal, ordinal, or interval scaled, but they have to be recoded into nominal variables.

AVAILABLE COMPUTER PROGRAMS

Most of the computer centers have this package. The program, however, can be easily obtained from its developers.

EXTENSIONS

For the case in which the dependent variable is nominal, THAID is a preferred procedure (Morgan and Messenger, 1973). Another more recent extension is to the case of multiple dependent variables. This extension calls for the use of MAID (MacLachlan and Johansson, 1981).

REFERENCES

Brief overview: Green and Tull (1978); Brown (1980).

Advanced treatment: Sonquist and Morgan, 1964; Sonquist, Baker, and Morgan, 1974.

ANALYSIS OF VARIANCE

OBJECTIVES

Analysis of variance (ANOVA) is the most common approach to analyze the results of experiments. Univariate analysis of variance (ANOVA) involves a single response variable and a design matrix consisting of one or more treatment variables. Multivariate analysis of variance (MANOVA), on the other hand, involves more than one response variable and a design matrix that can consist of two or more treatment variables (Wind and Denny, 1974). The objectives of analysis of variance are:

1. To test the statistical significance of differences among average responses across levels of each of the various treatment variables.
2. To identify treatment levels that contribute most to significant variation across the response-variable means.
3. In case of two or more treatment variables, to find significant interactions among the treatment-level responses.

OUTPUT

The typical output of analysis of variance programs includes:

- Sources of variation in the response variable(s) (the various treatment levels and their interactions).
- Sum of squares attributed to the various sources of variation.
- Statistical significance of the various sources of variation (F-test).

ALGORITHMIC LOGIC

The basic idea of ANOVA is to partition the total sum of squares among the treatments and within the treatments, adjust the sum of squares by the appropriate degrees of freedom, and establish the statistical significance by calculating F-ratios.

CRITICAL ASSUMPTIONS

The major assumptions of analysis of variance are:

- The relation between the response variable and the treatments is presumed to be linear (in single-factor ANOVA).
- The effects of treatments are additive (in single-factor ANOVA).
- A series of distributional assumptions.

INPUT DATA

A data matrix for the dependent variable(s) and independent variables (treatments). Data on dependent variable(s) are interval scaled (e.g., ratings on advertising copy themes). Independent variables (treatments) are coded as dummy variables.

AVAILABLE COMPUTER PROGRAMS

Most of the statistical computer packages include a number of analysis of variance programs. BMD, for example, offers programs for single-factor analysis (BMD–01V), factorial designs (BMD–02V), and multivariate analysis of variance (BMD–12V).

REFERENCES

Brief overview: Green and Tull, 1978 (Chap. 11).

Advanced treatment: Snedecor and Cochran, 1967; Hays and Winkler, 1971.

FACTOR ANALYSIS

OBJECTIVES

Factor analysis is a major set of data reduction and summarization techniques[1] for a nonpartitioned data matrix.[2] The objectives of factor analysis are:

1. To reduce a large number of variables to a smaller set of underlying dimensions, called factors, by using linear combinations of the variables.

2. To examine the nature and strength of relationships among the variables (factor loadings).

3. To assess the amount of variability in the data set accounted for by each factor.

4. To determine the position of each object (e.g., respondent) in the factor space (factor scores).

OUTPUT

The typical output of factor analysis programs (such as BMD–8M) includes:

- Factor loadings matrix (k variables by l factors) in components and transformed (e.g., varimax) factor space.

- Factor scores matrix for the subjects (n subjects by l factors).

- Proportion of total variance accounted for by each factor.

---

[1] A less frequently used factor analysis for testing hypotheses, the confirmatory factor analysis, is not discussed here.
[2] A nonpartitioned data matrix is one in which no variable(s) is (are) singled out as a dependent variable(s).

ALGORITHMIC LOGIC

Factors are identified as linear combinations of the original variables. The weights of the extracted factors, when applied to the original data variables, yield (unstandardized) factor scores for each subject. The factor loadings are like regression coefficients that estimate the value of each variable on the resulting factor. Principal-components analysis is one of the major techniques for extracting factors (components). It reduces a set of associated variables to a set of mutually uncorrelated and unique linear combinations of these variables.

CRITICAL ASSUMPTIONS

The major assumptions of factor analysis are:

- The models used to reduce the data structure are primarily based on linear relationships among the original variables.

- The decision on how many factors to retain is judgmental, and so is the interpretation of the factors.

INPUT DATA

A nonpartitioned data matrix of subjects (or objects) by variables. Data are typically interval scaled, although nominal and ordinal scaled data can also be handled.

AVAILABLE COMPUTER PROGRAMS

Most of the statistical computer packages include programs for factor analysis. BMD, for example, offers a very comprehensive program which can handle up to 198 variables and a virtually unlimited number of objects (BMD–08M).

EXTENSIONS

A number of variations and extensions to factor analysis have been employed. Oblique or oblimin factor analysis, for example, relaxes the requirement of varimax rotation for no correlation among the factors. When these algorithms are used, a higher order factor analysis can also be employed in which the factors are in turn factor analyzed to form higher-order factors (Wind, Green, and Jain, 1973).

Other extensions relate to a variety of factor matching (congruence) procedures which allow the matching of two or more factor loading solutions. (See, for example, the description of the C-MATCH program in Green and Wind, 1973.)

REFERENCES

Brief overview: Green and Tull, 1978 (Chapter 13); Brown, 1980.

Advanced treatment: Harman, 1960; Rummel, 1970.

CLUSTER ANALYSIS

OBJECTIVES

Cluster analysis includes a large number of techniques aimed at separating (classifying) objects into groups (clusters). Groups are formed in a way that any member of a group is more similar to other members of the group than to members of other groups. Cluster analysis can be conducted on (a) subjects (clustering them on their scores on the various variables), as done in many segmentation studies, or (b) variables (their similarity across respondents), as done in many positioning studies.

Clustering (grouping) can be conducted in a variety of ways. It can be based on various proximity or similarity measures. Individual objects can be progressively combined to build up clusters (referred to as hierarchical clustering methods). Or the process can be performed in a nonhierarchical fashion by grouping objects, within a prespecified threshold value, around a cluster center.

OUTPUT

The typical output of clustering programs (such as BMD–P1M or the Johnson hierarchical clustering algorithm) includes:

- Full clustering sequence (a tree diagram, or dendogram).
- Object classification into the prespecified number of groups.
- Group average profile scores on the variables chosen as the basis for clustering.
- Some measure of the cluster's variability (such as average interpoint distance of all members of the cluster from their centroid).

ALGORITHMIC LOGIC

Although each clustering program has its own individual algorithmic logic for grouping, the general objective is to minimize the within-cluster variability (e.g., distance) and maximize the between-cluster variability.

CRITICAL ASSUMPTIONS

Some of the major assumptions of cluster analysis are:

- Each object can be assigned to one and only one group.
- The researcher has a major role in the analysis by being required to select the weights of the measure, procedure for clustering (e.g., hierarchical vs. nonhierarchical), and number of clusters.

INPUT DATA

A nonpartitioned data matrix of n objects (subjects) by k variables. Data can include both continuous scales (e.g., income, age) or categorical variables (e.g., sex). The latter are coded as dummy variables.

AVAILABLE COMPUTER PROGRAMS

A large variety of computer programs exists and can be easily obtained from their developers. BMD offers a hierarchical program (BMD–P1M).

EXTENSIONS

The restriction of assigning each subject to one and only one cluster can be relaxed by the use of an overlapping clustering approach. (See, for example, Arabie, Carroll, DeSarbo, and Wind, 1981.)

REFERENCES

Brief overview: Green and Tull, 1978.

Advanced treatment: Hartigan, 1975.

MULTIDIMENSIONAL SCALING

OBJECTIVES

Multidimensional scaling (MDS) refers to a large set of algorithms which spatially portray the pattern of relationship among various items (brands, attributes) as points in n (two or more) dimensions. The distance between the points (which serves as a measure of their similarity) is determined to best match the input data. The most typical input are perceptions of items and/or preference among them.

As discussed in Chapter 4, MDS has been widely used in product positioning in which consumers' perceptions of and preferences among brands are used as the input data to any number of MDS programs. In the broader context of new-product development, a number of researchers (Pessemier and Root, 1973; Shocker and Srinivasan, 1974; and Urban, 1975) have developed MDS based procedures for new-product development which involve:

- Developing a perceptual map based on

consumers' ratings of prespecified attributes.

- Assuming homogeneity of perceptions across consumers, fitting of preference data into the previously constructed perceptual maps, and representing the preference by ideal points or vector model.

- Incorporating some function for relating the distance of a (current or new) brand from an ideal point to a probability of purchase.

OUTPUT

The scaling of perceptions (dissimilarity data) typically results in single space configurations (perceptual maps). Such maps (as presented in Chapter 4) identify the number of dimensions required for portraying the data and the configuration (pattern) of relationship among the scaled items (brands, etc.) as points in that space. When scaling perceptions and other data that involve more than a single data set (such as brands and their perceived attributes), a joint space analysis is typically the output. In this case, the output includes also ideal points or vectors (as illustrated in Chapter 4). This output offers insights into the relationship (a) among the items (brands), (b) between any vector or ideal point and the points representing the stimuli (brands), and (c) among the various ideal points or vectors.

In addition, most programs print the history of computation, the final configuration in the specified dimensionality, and a graphical plot of the final configuration.

ALGORITHMIC LOGIC

Although each MDS program has its individual algorithmic logic, most programs search for the specific pattern of points in n dimensions, so that the computed interpoint distances will most closely match the input data (metric MDS) or that the *ranks* of the computed interpoint distances will most closely match the ranks of the input data (nonmetric MDS).

Similarly, in joint space programs, the ideal point fitting algorithm, for example, attempts to find a point (ideal point) in the original sample space, so that the respondents' original preference ranking (from most to least liked) can be reproduced by identifying the distance of each stimulus point from the ideal point.

For a brief technical discussion of the major MDS programs (such as MDSCAL, TORSCA, PARAMAP, INDSCAL, MDPREF, PREFMAP), see the appendix in Green and Wind, 1973.

CRITICAL ASSUMPTIONS

Some of the critical assumptions of multidimensional scaling are:

- The final solution depends on the stimuli selection and definition.

- Dimension interpretation is subjective and is particularly troublesome in relating changes in marketing strategy (including physical product changes) to psychological changes in perceptual space.

- All the nonmetric MDS algorithms are subject to the possibility of "local optimum."

INPUT DATA

MDS algorithms can handle any number of data matrices. Typically they include brand-by-brand similarity or brand-by-attribute rating or ranking. Many of the algorithms can use either a full matrix or half matrix.

AVAILABLE COMPUTER PROGRAMS

A large number of MDS programs are available as special packages or as part of more general ones.

REFERENCES

Brief overview: Green and Tull, 1978.

Advanced treatment: Green and Carmone, 1970; Green and Rao, 1972b.

CONJOINT ANALYSIS

OBJECTIVES

Conjoint analysis is concerned with the measurement of preferences. It is based on a "trade-off" type (decompositional) choice model and involves the determination of weights or part-worths of a set of independent variables. Typically, the independent variables or the choice attributes are presented as "full profile" descriptors of hypothetical product offerings,[1] each described as having different "levels" on the preselected set of factors. The specific combinations are selected by following an experimental design (typically, an orthogonal array), and the stimuli are presented as verbal, pictorial, or actual product representations. A simple additive main-effects model is commonly used to establish the relationship between ordinal dependent variables and the independent variables.

The objectives of conjoint analysis are:

1. To establish a function which relates the independent variables to the dependent variable.

2. To examine the strength of the relationship between the dependent and independent variables (e.g., prediction of choice alternatives reflecting the respondent's trade-off among the various alternatives).

3. To determine the part-worths or utility scores associated with each attribute level.

4. To determine the relative importance of each of the independent variables (factors).

OUTPUT

The typical output of conjoint analysis programs (such as MONANOVA and LINMAP) includes:

- Part-worths (utilities) for the various attribute levels.

- Relative importance weights for the attributes (factors).

- A measure of badness of fit that reflects how well the predicted rankings of choice alternatives match the rankings provided by the respondent.

ALGORITHMIC LOGIC

Two of the most commonly used conjoint-analysis algorithms are MONANOVA and

---

[1]An alternative data collection approach is the "two factor at a time" method (Johnson, 1974). Yet, all the conjoint analysis studies described in the book followed the "full profile" approach. For a discussion of the two approaches, see Green and Wind (1975b) and Green and Srinivasan (1978).

LINMAP. MONANOVA utilizes gradient-type search techniques to minimize iteratively a measure of badness of fit, such that the predicted rankings of the choice alternatives reproduce, as closely as possible, the rankings provided by the respondent. LINMAP uses mathematical programming methods (linear programming) to minimize the number of violations in terms of the recovery of respondent preferences. Compared with MONANOVA, LINMAP permits constraints on part-worths.

CRITICAL ASSUMPTIONS

The major assumptions of conjoint analysis are:

- An additive main effects model can typically describe the relationship between the ordinally scaled dependent variable and the independent variables.
- The set of independent variables is assumed to be the relevant set (no independent variables are omitted), and the levels of each factor are not too narrow or too broad.

INPUT DATA

A data matrix for the dependent variable (rankings) and levels of the independent variables for each stimulus combination. The independent variables are coded as dummy variables.

AVAILABLE COMPUTER PROGRAMS

The packages can be obtained easily from their developers. In addition, multiple regression analysis can be used.

EXTENSIONS

The main-effects model can be extended to include nonlinear and interaction terms. The conjoint analysis results can be incorporated in simulators to develop market share estimates and test various choice alternatives. The most extensive extension, to date, is the POSSE system which is based on a conjoint analysis design and is described in Appendix B.

REFERENCES

Brief overview: Green and Tull, 1978 (Chapter 14).

Advanced treatment: Green and Wind, 1973.

ANALYTIC HIERARCHY PROCESS

OBJECTIVES

The analytic hierarchy modeling and measurement process is a recent addition to the various approaches used to determine the relative importance of a set of criteria. The novel aspect and major distinction of this approach is that it structures any complex, multiperson, and multiperiod problem hierarchically and assists in determining the relative priority of the identifiable courses of action (typically presented as entities at the lowest level of the hierarchy). Consider, for example, the simple three-level hierarchy of environmental scenarios, objec-

EXHIBIT A–2

AN ILLUSTRATIVE BASIC DECISION HIERARCHY

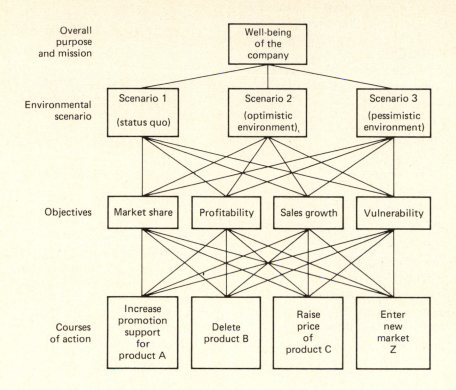

tives, and courses of action presented in Exhibit A–2. Such a hierarchy can aid management in identifying their relevant objectives, forces them to explicate the environmental scenarios most likely to affect their business decisions, stimulates their creativity in generating specific courses of action, and facilitates the evaluation of the generated courses of action on the various criteria by taking into consideration the effect of the environmental scenarios.

The objectives of the AHP are:

1. To decompose a complex problem into a hierarchy; each level consists of a few manageable elements and each element is, in turn, decomposed into another set of elements. The process continues down to the most specific elements of the problem, typically the specific courses of action considered, which are represented at the lowest level of the hierarchy.

2. To establish priorities among the elements within each stratum of the hierarchy with respect to an element (e.g., criterion) of the next higher level.

3. To establish a single composite vector of priorities for the entire hierarchy by yielding the relative priority of all entities at the lowest level that enables the accomplishment of the highest objective of the hierarchy.

These objectives are achieved while allowing for a group interaction among the relevant managers and the incorporation of any available data with the participants' subjective judgments. The AHP offers a procedure for conflict resolution among the participants and offers total flexibility for the participants, both in defining the hierarchy and judging its components.

OUTPUT

The typical output of the AHP includes:

- Importance weights, or relative priorities, for all elements within each level of the hierarchy with respect to each of the criteria in the next higher level.

- A composite priority vector for the lowest level of the hierarchy.

- Consistency ratio that measures the consistency in the respondents' evaluations with respect to random evaluations.

- The results of a series of sensitivity analyses of different hierarchical formulations and judgments.

ALGORITHMIC LOGIC

The measurement problem is formulated into a largest eigenvalue problem, and the principal eigenvector with appropriate hierarchical weighting and composition leads to a uni-dimensional scale of the priorities of the elements in any level of the hierarchy.

CRITICAL ASSUMPTIONS

1. The problem can be decomposed into a complete hierarchy.
2. There are no interdependencies among elements within the same level.

INPUT DATA

The hierarchy and a series of matrices of pairwise comparisons which indicate the strengths with which the elements in the hierarchy are perceived by a group of judges to dominate each other with respect to a given criterion (item in the higher level of the hierarchy). The relative strength is typically measured on a nine-point scale.

AVAILABLE COMPUTER PROGRAMS

The computer package can be easily developed or obtained from the developer of this technique.

REFERENCES

Brief overview: Wind and Saaty, 1980.

Advanced treatment: Saaty, 1977 and 1980.

Appendix B

Posse: A General Approach To Product Design Optimization Via Conjoint Analysis[1]

INTRODUCTION

Product design optimization procedures should address questions such as:

- What is the most profitable new/modified product to make, consistent with one's current product line, and what is the best target market for this new product?

- What market segments will optimize profits for the current product line and, given a specifically defined segment, what is the most profitable product for it?

- Given the competitive introduction of a new product, what is one's best retaliatory strategy from a product/market standpoint?

These problems are extremely complex and can be approached in a number of ways. The objectives of this appendix are: (a) to describe briefly the early contributions to the development of product optimizing models; (b) to describe the POSSE approach; (c) to present a short example of the POSSE system; and (d) to discuss briefly some of the problems still to be solved.

PREVIOUS RESEARCH ON PRODUCT OPTIMIZATION

The discussion of previous research on the topic will be brief, since excellent critical reviews have already been prepared (May, Shocker, and Sudharshan, 1980; Shocker and Srinivasan, 1979). Previous research on the problem has emphasized either an MDS scaling approach or a conjoint analysis framework. In all cases a major focus of this research has been to relate brand preferences to choice, where the latter is viewed as a necessary precursor to the development of objective functions that are revenue or profit based.

The MDS Joint Space Approach For several years now, marketing researchers have been

---

[1]This appendix was prepared by Paul E. Green, of the Wharton School, J. Douglas Carroll, of Bell Laboratories, and Stephen M. Goldberg, of the Wharton School, and is based on their earlier published article "A General Approach to Product Design Optimization Via Conjoint Analysis," *Journal of Marketing*, 45 (Summer 1981), pp. 17–37.

using algorithms, such as PREFMAP (Carroll, 1972) or LINMAP (Srinivasan and Shocker, 1973; Shocker and Srinivasan, 1977), to portray consumer preferences as a set of brand and person-derived (ideal point) locations in a common space of attribute dimensions. The PERCEPTOR model (Urban, 1975) is illustrative of approaches which are primarily based on the MDS joint-space model, and many industrial applications of this model have been made since its development.

In the simplest version of the joint-space model, brand preferences for a particular consumer are assumed to be inversely related to increasing distance of the brands from the consumer's ideal point. Conversion of this information to brand choice appears straightforward enough—a respondent simply chooses that brand which is closest to his/her ideal point. Alternatively, one might postulate a probability function (Pessemier et al., 1971; Shocker and Srinivasan, 1974) in which the probability that a consumer chooses some brand from a competing set of brands varies as a decreasing function of the distance of the brand from the consumer's ideal point.

Thus, on a descriptive (rather than normative) level one could use the joint-space model to predict the share of choices that a new brand (point location) would obtain if it were placed in the joint space while all other points (existing brand points and ideal points) were to remain unchanged by its entry. As noted above, its share of choices could be estimated either deterministically or probabilistically.

Discussion of the descriptive linkage between perceptual/preference measurements and brand choice has a long and varied history. One could argue that virtually all of the marketing-oriented MDS studies—for example, those by Stefflre (1969), Morgan and Purnell (1969), Green and Carmone (1970), Johnson (1971), Green and Wind (1973), Pessemier and Root (1973), Shocker and Srinivasan (1974), Urban (1975), and Hauser and Urban (1977)—have dealt, directly or indirectly, with the relevance of perception/preference measurement to product choice, either deterministically or probabilistically.

However, from a marketing management standpoint one is interested in the *normative* problem, namely, in finding the point location that optimizes some objective function. Depending upon the availability of appropriate cost and pricing data, one might want to maximize total profits for the firm's product line (including any effects due to cannibalization of the firm's existing brands), sales revenue, or share of choices received by the product line. In cases where the firm has no existing brands, one might want to maximize any of these objective functions for the new brand only.

The optimal product design problem requires not only procedures for estimating the value of the objective function for each point location of interest (the prediction problem) but also a way to search the space systematically to find the specific location that results in the highest profits, revenue, share of choices, or whatever is being optimized. As might be surmised, unless rigid (and probably unrealistic) conditions are placed on the nature of the objective function, one will generally *not* find a global optimum (the very best point in the whole space). Even if a global optimum can be found, it need not be unique, that is, some other location(s) may yield an objective function value that is tied with it (or "effectively tied," in the sense of being so close as to be pragmatically indistinguishable).

It was Shocker and Srinivasan (1974) who first formalized the problem of *optimal* product design in the context of an MDS-derived joint space of current brands and consumers' ideal points. While Shocker and Srinivasan suggested some possible solution strategies, including gradient search,[2] search through coarse and fine grids, and sequential, unidimensional search, their discussion was primarily programmatic, that is, no specific algorithm was presented. Still, it is important to note that Shocker and Srinivasan proposed models that consider the objective function of incremental profit (as well as the special case of market share) and described both deterministic and probabilistic choice formulations. The primary thrust of their discussion emphasized continuously varying attributes (in the context of locating a product that maximizes incremental profit). However, they also considered the possible inclusion of categorical variables under the assumption that the solution technique utilized grid search rather than the method of gradient search. (Gradient search assumes continuous variation in the coordinates of the brand attribute space.)

Subsequently, Albers (1979), Albers and Brockhoff (1977, 1979), Gavish, Horsky, and Srikanth (1979), and Zufryden (1979) proposed

explicit-solution techniques for a deterministic choice version of Shocker and Srinivasan's MDS joint-space model, in which one tries to find a new-product location in the space that maximizes the number of consumers for whom it is closest to their ideal point.[3] Related work has also been reported by Pessemier (1975). Many of these models have incorporated various types of mixed integer programming to find solutions.

Bachem and Simon (1977) and, more recently, Hauser and Simmie (1981) have also proposed joint space models for optimal product design. Both of these models are characterized by probabilistic choice functions and explicit consideration of costs and prices. However, neither paper discusses the difficult problem of actually *measuring* costs as a function of product positioning. To date, cost measurement difficulties plague all of the optimal product design approaches (including the one to be described by the present authors).

The joint-space model assumes that all consumers perceive current brands similarly but are permitted idiosyncratic ideal point locations and idiosyncratic dimension weights.[4] The algorithms do not deal with technological constraints on the variables' ranges. Nor do they include a provision for fitting vector (as well as ideal point) models (Carroll, 1980). Insofar as computational demands are concerned, research by Gavish, Horsky, and Srikanth (1979) suggests that computation time may become prohibitive for all but relatively small problems.

---

[2]By gradient search we mean an optimization procedure that uses the "hill-climbing" approach, i.e., finding a direction of steepest ascent and moving in that direction until (it is hoped) a global maximum of the objective function (that lies within the product attribute range constraints) is found. In grid search the product space is systematically divided into regions and the function evaluated at the center of each region. The search proceeds sequentially by constructing finer regions in the most promising areas of earlier searches, until an optimum is reached. In sequential, unidimensional search, we increment (decrement) the values of one variable at a time, holding all others fixed. A round is completed when each variable has been incremented through a predetermined number of levels once. The method consists of the execution of several complete rounds in succession, each time moving from the best previously computed point; the size of the increment is reduced in successive rounds as one approaches the optimum. In general, none of the above procedures guarantees that an optimum will be found.

---

[3]More formally, given a joint space of existing product locations and ideal points, one tries to find a new product location that maximizes the number of intersecting indifference hyperellipsoids. In general, the solution is not unique since one would ordinarily obtain a region rather than a single point.

[4]In this case we refer to the more recent work of Albers (1979) in which the assumption of equal dimension weights is relaxed.

However, these same authors have provided a set of efficient heuristics which can solve very large problems. While the heuristics do not produce optimal solutions, neither do the mixed integer programming methods or grid search procedures guarantee a global optimum. (Henceforth, we shall use the term "optimum" advisedly, pointing out particular algorithms and sets of conditions that guarantee a global optimum, if such cases exist.)

More recently, May, Shocker, and Sudharshan (1980) have proposed an interesting non-linear programming algorithm called QRMNEW (May, 1979). QRMNEW can incorporate technological range constraints on the (assumed continuous) product attributes, as well as more general linear constraints. May, Shocker, and Sudharshan's approach can also accommodate probabilistic choice models. In short, QRMNEW seems to satisfy the objectives Shocker and Srinivasan had in mind, at least insofar as continuous product attributes are concerned. However, like all general gradient procedures QRMNEW does not guarantee a global optimum.

With all of the effort devoted to the development of joint-space optimizing models, it is of interest to note that few commercial applications of the optimal product design models described above have been reported as yet. Thus far it would seem that the contributions to this area have been primarily methodological rather than empirical. One of the major reasons for the lack of commercial applications is the difficulty of collecting suitable data for joint-space representations, as compared to the conjoint approach, to be described next.

The Conjoint-Analysis Approach Adaptation of conjoint-analysis based methods to optimal-product design started shortly after Shocker and Srinivasan's formulation of the problem in joint-space MDS-based terms. Ironically, in contrast to the MDS descriptive techniques developed earlier, real-world applica-

tion of traditional (not optimum-based) conjoint analysis have been extensive. According to a recent survey (Cattin and Wittink, 1981); over a thousand applications of conjoint analysis have been made over the decade since its introduction to marketing research (Green and Rao, 1971; Johnson, 1974). Some firms, such as AT&T, Bell Canada, Xerox, General Motors, Ford, Smith Kline, Squibb, Pfizer, General Electric, and General Foods have each conducted several conjoint studies, spanning a wide variety of product classes.

However, with virtually no exceptions these commercial applications did not go so far as to attempt to find *optimal* attribute combinations. Rather, a typical commercial application of conjoint analysis, as discussed in various places in the book, entails the following steps:

1. By using one of a variety of data collection procedures (Green and Srinivasan, 1978), sufficient data are obtained at the individual respondent level to estimate the parameters of each person's utility function.

2. In problems of realistic size only simple main-effects additive models are fitted, so as to keep the data demands from becoming so burdensome as to jeopardize respondent cooperation.

3. The matrix of respondent-by-attribute utilities may then be related to other subject background data in an effort to identify possible market segments based on similarities in partworth functions.

4. The researcher's client then proposes a set of product configurations that represent feasible competitive offerings. These product profiles are entered into a consumer-choice simulator along with the earlier computed individual utility functions.

5. While choice simulators differ, in the simplest case each respondent's individual partworth function is used to compute the

utility for each of the competing profiles. The respondent is then assumed to choose that profile with the highest utility (i.e., the choice process is deterministic).

6. Shares of choices are obtained, by market segment if appropriate, and for the total sample through aggregation across individuals.

Hence, what most current appliers of conjoint analysis do is to test a limited number of a *priori* designed new product profiles in order to see what share each achieves in a simulated choice environment.

The first approach to adapting conjoint-analysis methods to product design optimization was proposed by Zufryden (1977). Zufryden formulated the problem as a zero-one integer programming model in which one maximizes the weighted number of first choices going to the new product. His model assumed that the consumer compares the utility of the test product with that of one's current brand favorite and chooses (deterministically) the one with the higher utility. Each consumer can also be weighted by his/her relative size of product class expenditures or some other appropriate criterion.

Zufryden pointed out how mixtures of continuous and categorical variables could be handled by means of mixed integer linear programming. He also described the inclusion of interaction terms in the subset of categorical variables (based on a procedure due to Glover and Woolsey, 1974). Moreover, Zufryden illustrated how the model could be adapted to consider cannibalization costs, as long as the overall objective function was still linear. He also considered the incorporation of additional constraints on various product attribute combinations.

Zufryden did not present any numerical examples of his approach, nor did he explain how the model itself could be implemented in terms of a *specific-solution* algorithm (although

he did cite some recent work devoted to the solution of large-scale integer programs). While no algorithmic details were provided by Zufryden, it seems pretty clear from the model's formulation that some type of implicit enumeration procedure (Balas, 1965; Taha, 1972a, 1972b; Hammer and Rudeanu, 1969) would be needed to reduce the extremely large number of evaluations that would otherwise be required to solve this model.[5]

Despite this spate of methodologically oriented papers, little in the way of actual applications of optimal product design models (either MDS or conjoint analysis based) has appeared so far. A notable exception is the study by Parker and Srinivasan (1976), reporting an extensive application of preference modeling to the design of rural health-care facilities. Preference measurements (obtained from conjoint analysis) represented an important input to the model; a heuristic search routine was used to find a solution to the problem of maximizing total net benefit, subject to a cost constraint. The heuristic could not guarantee an optimal solution but, presumably, performed well in practice. Interestingly enough, this heuristic is not based on any of the solution procedures mentioned earlier.

THE POSSE METHODOLOGY

The POSSE methodology, like Zufryden's model (1977), is based on a conjoint-analysis approach. POSSE's principal novelty is its use of response surface methods (Box, Hunter, and Hunter, 1978) to model the output of various choice simulators, either deterministically or probabilistically. For example, in industrial applications of response surface methods the

---

[5]Since each respondent can have a different utility function and cutoff level (represented by the utility of his/her current favorite), even an implicit enumeration procedure can become quite cumbersome.

yield of unknown chemical processes is often modeled through a series of designed experiments in which the control variables (temperature, pressure, reagent concentration, etc.) are systematically varied. For each such combination of control variables the researcher also records the associated yield. A simple function (often a low-order polynomial, such as a quadratic) is used to approximate the unknown function; it is this approximating function that is then optimized.

In POSSE the simulator itself becomes the process to be modeled; in effect, we develop a function that relates the control variables (product attributes) to the simulator's output—market share, sales dollars, profits, or whatever objective function is chosen. POSSE is a comprehensive system of models and programs, consisting of procedures for carrying out the following steps:

- Experimental design and stimulus construction
- Utility function estimation
- Choice simulators—deterministic and probabilistic
- Objective function estimation
- Optimization—categorical, continuous, mixed variable
- Sensitivity analysis
- Time-path forecasting

The methodology has been under development since late 1976; some 28 special-purpose computer programs are currently employed to implement the preceding steps. Research on system enhancements is still going on.

Rationale for the POSSE System   In devising the POSSE system we wished to develop an approach that:

- Could be used in cases involving either individual utility functions or, where necessary, various levels of aggregated data;

- Could be adapted to a wide variety of objective-function formulations, including those derived from deterministic or probabilistic choice processes;
- Could handle an objective function consisting of mixtures of categorical and continuous attributes, including curvilinear and interaction terms;
- Would lend itself to carrying out various kinds of sensitivity analyses;
- Would be compatible with industry's current use of conjoint analysis.

While no claim is made that POSSE is unique in terms of these objectives, some justification for their consideration is appropriate.

Objective Functions and Data Aggregation   In very many marketing situations the subject's response task precludes the opportunity to develop individual utility functions. For example, in taste testing studies involving real products, a single subject is usually limited to comparing two to four test alternatives, taken one at a time, versus a common control. While the full set of test items may be constructed according to some rather elaborate fractional factorial design, any single subject receives only a small number. In this case, values of the objective function consist simply of the proportion of persons choosing each test item over the (common) control (an empirically estimated choice probability for each test item profile) for which an approximating function is then constructed.

Similar considerations apply to test market simulations in which any single respondent is limited to evaluating one (or perhaps two) actual new-product formulations, versus the respondent's current brand favorite. In this case also, the researcher may wish to build a model that relates the probability of trying, the probability of repeat purchase, etc., to the design variables directly, rather than through the preference-derived utility functions. However, additional respondent background variables can be included in the model to accommodate respondent group differences (Green and DeSarbo, 1979; Moore, 1980).

A Variety of Objective Functions In other instances sufficient data can be collected to estimate individual utilities, but the researcher still desires the flexibility to incorporate a variety of objective functions, such as:

- Total number of test-brand first choices, each weighted by the frequency of product purchase;

- Average probability of choosing the test brand as determined by some type of probability model, such as the one described by Shocker and Srinivasan (1974);

- Total expected profits or total expected cash flow, in which both (subjective) purchase probability and conditional pay-off are measured;

- Total number of respondents *not* choosing some competitive product, conditioned on the test product;

- Number of first choices received by the test product *or* any other of the firm's current products;

- Total number of choosers of the test product that are drawn from any one of a set of *a priori* defined market segments;

- An equilibrium share of choices received by the test product, as determined from a Markov-type switching model.

Still other kinds of objective functions could be used. Suffice it to say that maximizing share of first choices (as computed from a simple deterministic choice model) is only one of a large number of possible objective functions that could be employed for specific problems.

Mixtures of Categorical and Continuous Variables In many product design studies the analyst must contend with a mixture of categorical and continuous variables. Although the continuous variables may be discretized in the course of constructing factorially designed stimuli, the researcher may still wish to have the option of fitting continuous functions (e.g., a quadratic) to a subset of the variables (Pekelman and Sen, 1979).

Moreover, in many applications (particularly those involving sensory or esthetic products) interactions between categorical or continuous variables can be important. Hence, it is useful to be able to accommodate cross-product terms and other nonlinearities in the objective function, leading to a type of mixed integer nonlinear programming model.

Sensitivity Analyses In most practical problems the researcher's client desires to know not only what the "optimal" product is but, also, what flexibility exists for departing from the optimum without unduly reducing the measure of effectiveness. In short, interest frequently centers on the development of a range of new product possibilities, all of which have objective-function values that are within some specified tolerance interval of the optimum. The optimization model should be readily adaptable to carrying out such sensitivity analyses, either for a single variable at a time or for two or more variables at a time.

Compatibility with the Status Quo Since conjoint analysis is already in use by industry researchers and since POSSE incorporates conjoint-data inputs, it seemed desirable to provide a subset of computer programs that could be applied to conventional conjoint problems. In this way, the potential system user could apply only that part of the system which best suited his/her purposes. Moreover, the additional features of POSSE could be represented as logical extensions of procedures already in use in traditional conjoint studies.

As indicated earlier, POSSE would appear to exhibit two principal distinctions compared to previous approaches. First, it utilizes the basic concepts of response surface methods in which the output of a complex process (a choice simulator, a set of taste-test results, etc.) is modeled by a simpler, approximating function. This function should be tractable enough to be optimized—globally (in the case of implicit enumeration) or, in general, locally (in the case of gradient, grid, random, or direct search). Interestingly enough, the basic idea for considering conjoint analysis in this way was mentioned shortly after the technique was introduced to marketing (Green, 1973, p. 151).

Second, POSSE has been designed as a complete system, one that includes computer programs for stimulus design, utility estimation, choice simulation, objective function formulation, optimization, sensitivity analysis, and time-path forecasting. We next turn to a brief description of the overall system and then illustrate some of its features in an empirical application.

COMPONENTS OF THE POSSE SYSTEM

Exhibit B–1 shows a listing of the principal computer programs that currently make up the POSSE system. We provide only enough expository material to cover the general functions of each subset of programs. (More technical

EXHIBIT B–1

COMPUTER PROGRAMS USED IN THE POSSE SYSTEM

Experimental design and stimulus preparation	Categorical variable optimization
DESIGN	QUALO
ORTHOTEST	QUALIN
LABEL	QUALO M
Utility function estimation	**Continuous variable optimization**
STEPWISE	QUADMO
HYBRID	MOGUL
MONREG	INDEF
THRESH	BOX
TWOWAY	HILL
	RANDO
Choice simulators	**Sensitivity analysis**
CHOSIM	TOLCO Q
BTLSIM	RIDGE
DUESIM	TOLCO 1
TABSIM	TOLCO K
Response surface and objective function estimation	**Time path forecasting**
DUEALL	SWITCH
STEPWISE	

details will be described in a methodological paper, now in preparation.)

Experimental Design Because of our interest in the measurement of selected two-factor interactions (as well as all main effects), POSSE applications utilize large experimental designs compared to the ones utilized in traditional conjoint studies. DESIGN is used to prepare various kinds of fractional factorials, ranging from a low of 32 attribute-level combinations to a high of 256 combinations, although any single respondent receives only a small set of these—typically from three to nine in the case of hybrid conjoint models (Green, Goldberg, and Montemayor, 1981; Green and Goldberg, 1981).

ORTHOTEST is used to test all designs for orthogonality and to print out those factor pairs that are not orthogonal. LABEL is employed to print the actual stimulus card descriptions. In short, the programs in this set are used collectively to prepare stimulus materials for POSSE applications.

Utility Function Estimation Since POSSE is based on a conjoint analysis approach, several programs have been developed to estimate partworth functions. STEPWISE and HYBRID are regression-based procedures used to estimate metric utility functions. MONREG is a monotonic regression program for nonmetric utility measurement, and THRESH is an alternating least-squares program used to estimate utilities in cases where respondents may use threshold-type models. All of the foregoing programs employ some type of full-profile approach. The TWOWAY program utilizes a metric procedure for fitting the two-factor-at-a-time model (Johnson, 1974).

Choice Simulators CHOSIM is a deterministic/probabilistic choice simulator, whereas BTLSIM utilizes a Bradley–Terry–Luce probabilistic choice model (Luce, Bush, and Galan-

ter, 1965). The third program, DUESIM, incorporates partworths based on hybrid conjoint models. TABSIM is a deterministic choice simulator that prints out cross tabulations of brand choice versus selected respondent background characteristics. Each of these programs is designed to handle up to 40 nine-level attributes, 10 competitive products, and a virtually unlimited number of respondents.

Objective Function Estimation DUEALL is the program that performs the "response surface modeling" feature of POSSE. The objective here is to enter a set of test products, constructed according to a prespecified experimental design, capable of fitting either continuous functions (e.g., quadratic or higher-order polynomials) or of representing the process by a discrete model involving main effects and selected two-way interactions.

DUEALL contains a choice simulator in which each test product is entered, one at a time, along with individual utility functions and existing competitive brands. Flexibility is provided for handling deterministic or probabilistic choice processes. Price or cost inputs are handled by separate subroutines. For each test product entered, DUEALL computes the objective function value, e.g., share of choices received by the test product, expected sales revenue, net sales for the firm's product line (including existing brands), and so on. STEPWISE is then used to fit the function—with either continuous, categorical (ANOVA-type), or mixed variables.

Hence the purpose of the DUEALL/STEPWISE is to develop the approximating objective function, as related to the experimental design variables representing the new product. It is this approximating function that is optimized by other programs in the POSSE system.

Categorical Variable Optimization QUALO and QUALIN are enumeration procedures used to optimize a single objective function whose arguments include all main effects and selected two-way interactions of a set of categorical variables. QUALO is the program that is used to optimize the approximating function of POSSE (as computed from DUEALL/ STEPWISE), when all product design variables are expressed categorically. QUALIN is an enumeration algorithm based on Zufryden's zero–one integer programming model; while not an integral part of the POSSE system, QUALIN provides an explicit enumeration procedure for implementing Zufryden's approach in the case where all attributes are categorical. Both QUALO and QUALIN provide globally optimal solutions. QUALO M is a multiple objective function version of QUALO that can accommodate up to five different objective functions (e.g., market share, cash flow, etc.). Goal programming is used to find the solution that minimizes the weighted sum of relative deviations from each separate goal level (as obtained by optimizing each objective function separately).

Continuous Variable Optimization If all product design attributes are continuous, a variety of algorithms are available for optimization. In the continuous variable case, DUEALL utilizes appropriate experimental designs (Box and Behnken, 1960) for fitting low-order response surfaces, such as a quadratic function. That is, once DUEALL provides objective function values for the test product design arguments, STEPWISE is used to fit a general quadratic (or possibly higher polynomial) rather than an ANOVA-type model. (In general, a quadratic function should be flexible enough to cover most cases of practical interest.)

However, if continuous functions are fitted, the appropriate optimizing programs (unlike QUALO and QUALIN) cannot guarantee a global optimum; in general, the programs achieve a local optimum. QUADMO, MOGUL, and INDEF (Bunch and Kaufman, 1977) are

all gradient-based optimal-seeking methods, while BOX (Box, 1965) and HILL utilize direct search.[6] RANDO employs systematic grid search as well as function evaluation via randomly selected grid points.[7]

In the case where the arguments of the (approximating) objective function are mixed (continuous and categorical), a combination of QUALO and one of the routines from the continuous-variable optimizing set is used to find conditional optima for each appropriate categorical-variable level for those terms carrying categorical- and continuous-variable interactions.

Sensitivity Analysis TOLCO Q is employed when the arguments of the objective function are all categorical. This program computes the effect on the objective function of varying the levels of each product attribute one at a time when all other attributes are fixed at their optimal levels.

RIDGE, TOLCO 1, and TOLCO K are used for the case of continuous variables, in which the objective function is quadratic. RIDGE explores the general nature of the quadratic surface by using the technique of ridge analysis (Hoerl, 1964).

TOLCO 1 computes values of the objective function as each argument of the function is varied from its optimal setting, while all others are held at their optimal levels. TOLCO K extends this basic approach to the case of varying

---

[6]Direct search methods (Box, 1965) do not compute derivatives in seeking the optimum; rather, they employ direct function evaluations and various kinds of schemes for using the best value obtained from earlier evaluations to select new directions in the space for further evaluation.

[7]In general, grid search and random-function evaluation are highly inefficient compared to gradient and direct search. As such, the primary value of grid search or random methods is to serve as a check on more efficient methods, particularly when multimodal functions are suspected.

$2, 3, \ldots, K$ arguments at a time, all others being held at their optimal levels.

Time-Path Forecasting SWITCH is a program for time-path projections of market share that is based on a first-order Markov brand switching process (Urban, 1975). SWITCH incorporates a number of features in which share projections are computed before and after the introduction of a new product. Four different procedures for estimating repeat purchase probabilities for the new product are incorporated and gain–loss matrices are computed as part of the program's standard output.

In summary, it should be noted that the POSSE sequence subsumes traditional procedures for carrying out conjoint analysis. That is, one could use the experimental design module and one of POSSE's simulators to carry out a conventional conjoint analysis. In other instances programs in the Design, Response Surface Fitting, Optimization, and Sensitivity Analysis modules can be used directly for setting up and analyzing taste test experiments in which intermediate choice simulators are not used. In other cases programs like SWITCH can be used in conventional research studies where brand switching data are obtained.

Thus, POSSE is really a set of computer programs that can be applied to various kinds of product optimal design problems, rather than a specific model and computer program sequence. The relatively loose couplings among the programs also provide flexibility for adding new algorithms in response to new kinds of applications, as they may arise.

A PILOT APPLICATION OF POSSE

Some 15 applications have now been made of the POSSE methodology. Consumer durables, telecommunications, foods, office equipment, and ethical drugs are the major product classes to which POSSE has been applied so far. Since all of these applications have entailed proprietary products, it is not possible to discuss any of the specific studies, but for illustrative purposes we can describe a hypothetical case which, nonetheless, is drawn from actual commercial studies. It should be mentioned, however, that all numerical values described in the case are fictitious.

In this case study only a relatively small portion of the POSSE program series will be employed. This is not unusual since the methodology has been developed to serve as a general set of program modules which can be drawn upon to cope with a variety of problem situations.

Study Background The illustrative case entails the design of a pickup truck for U.S. consumers interested in a truck for personal (as opposed to commercial) use. The design attributes under consideration are shown in Exhibit B–2. In this case management was interested in eight attributes, each expressed in terms of three levels. Note that some of the attributes (e.g., Shoulder Width; Box Length) are inherently continuous while others (e.g., Type of Radio/Price; Engine Type/Price/MPG) are categorical. However, management interest was confined to the specific levels shown in Exhibit B–2; hence, the study design was to be restricted to categorical variable optimization.

Other constraints were placed on the problem by management. First, accurate cost data for the possible designs represented by the attribute levels in Exhibit 2–2 were not readily available; it was decided to use estimated sales revenue as the objective function to be optimized. Second, in past studies, the firm had typically employed an 11-point, intentions-to-purchase scale, ranging from "absolutely no chance" (scale value zero) to "absolutely certain" (scale value 10). The firm wished to continue to employ this type of evaluative scale.

Respondents for the survey were prospective pickup truck purchasers—those respon-

EXHIBIT B–2

ATTRIBUTES AND LEVELS—PICKUP TRUCKS

A. Shoulder width
1. 62 inches
2. 64 inches
3. 66 inches

B. Box length
1. 6½ feet
2. 7 feet
3. 7½ feet

C. Width between wheel houses
1. 46 inches
2. 48 inches
3. 50 inches

D. Trailer towing capacity
1. 5000 pounds
2. 7000 pounds
3. 10000 pounds

E. Payload Capacity
1. 1100 pounds
2. 2100 pounds
3. 3600 pounds

F. Type of radio/price
1. AM/standard
2. AM/FM/$80 more than standard
3. AM/FM/CB/$120 more than standard

G. Engine type/price/MPG
1. 6-cyl gasoline/standard/22 MPG
2. V-8 gasoline/$185 more than standard/17 MPG
3. V-8 diesel/$750 more than standard/25 MPG

**H. Base price of standard truck
(without options)**
1. $4300
2. $4600
3. $4900

dents who indicated, during a screening interview, that they planned to purchase a pickup truck for personal reasons sometime during the next 12 months. All data were collected via personal interview in three central-facilities locations.

The POSSE study was part of a larger "truck clinic" survey in which respondents saw and evaluated all of the major new truck models being introduced in the 1979-model year. However, the POSSE findings were to be used for pickup truck engineering designs in future model years.

There were 486 respondents in the total sample. The personal interview consisting of:

- The POSSE tasks
- Background data on vehicle ownership and usage
- Psychographics and demographics

took less than a half hour, on average, to complete. Except for the POSSE tasks, all other questions were self-administered.

Stimulus Design In view of the large 3^8 design (with 6561 possible combinations) of Exhibit B–2, a fractional factorial was developed to reduce the number of master design combinations to only 81. The experimental design module, consisting of DESIGN, ORTHOTEST, and LABEL, was used for this series of steps. DESIGN was employed to construct the master fractional factorial design, ORTHOTEST was applied to check that all effects of interest were orthogonal, and LABEL was used to prepare the prop card descriptions.

Exhibit B–3 shows a portion of the sample output from DESIGN. The attribute levels of Exhibit B–3, along with the descriptions of each attribute level in Exhibit B–2, served as input to LABEL which, in turn, prepared a computer printout in the form of stimulus prop descriptions. Exhibit B–4 illustrates this output by

EXHIBIT B–3

A PORTION OF THE MASTER DESIGN OUTPUT FROM DESIGN

Stimulus combination	A	B	C	D	E	F	G	H
1	1	1	1	1	1	1	1	1
2	1	1	1	2	1	1	1	2
3	1	1	1	3	1	1	1	3
4	1	1	2	1	3	2	3	2
5	1	1	2	2	3	2	3	3
6	1	1	2	3	3	2	3	1
7	1	1	3	1	2	3	2	3
8	1	1	3	2	2	3	2	1
9	1	1	3	3	2	3	2	2
10	1	2	1	1	2	3	3	2
11	1	2	1	2	2	3	3	3
12	1	2	1	3	2	3	3	1
13	1	2	2	1	1	1	2	3
14	1	2	2	2	1	1	2	1
15	1	2	2	3	1	1	2	2
16	1	2	3	1	3	2	1	1
17	1	2	3	2	3	2	1	2
18	1	2	3	3	3	2	1	3
.	.	.	.	.	.	.	.	.
.	.	.	.	.	.	.	.	.
.	.	.	.	.	.	.	.	.
81	3	3	3	3	3	3	2	3

Cell entries are attribute levels (see Exhibit B–2 for descriptions).

EXHIBIT B–4

A SAMPLE STIMULUS DESCRIPTION OBTAINED FROM LABEL

Future pickup truck description

Shoulder width
62 inches

Box length
6½ feet

Width between wheel houses
46 inches

Trailor towing capacity
5000 pounds

Payload capacity
1100 pounds

Type of radio/price
AM/std

Engine type/price /MPG
6-cyl gas/std/21 mpg

Base price of truck (without options)
$4300

showing a description of the first row of the master design of Exhibit B–3.

The complete master design (part of which appears in Exhibit B–3) consists of 81 stimulus descriptions in total. All main-effect utilities for the eight attributes are orthogonally estimable as well as all two-attribute interactions for all pairs of the first five attributes; these were the attributes which management believed were most likely to interact.

DESIGN also contains a feature for respondent "blocking," that is, finding which of the 81 stimulus cards a particular respondent should receive. In this case it was decided to give each respondent nine of the 81 stimuli. For example, the first respondent received stimulus cards 1, 15, 27, 36, 38, 49, 59, 70, and 75. The cards were assigned so that each of the levels for each attribute appeared an equal number of times (three times each) *within* each respondent. A full replication of the master design was completed for every set of nine respondents.

Data Collection   Stimulus evaluations were obtained by means of a hybrid-model data collection procedure (Green, Goldberg, and Montemayor, 1981; Green and Goldberg, 1981). In the first phase of this method (the self-explicated phase), a respondent is shown each set of attribute levels, one at a time, and asked to circle his/her most preferred and second most preferred levels, assuming the pickup trucks were the same in all other respects. Following this, the respondent is asked to allocate 100 points across the eight attributes (Shoulder width, Box length, . . ., Price) so as to reflect their relative importance. Exhibit B–5 illustrates the kind of instructions that are used in the first phase of hybrid-model data collection. Scale drawings were used to show the dimensional attribute levels more clearly.

In the second phase of the data collection procedure, the respondent is shown the specific set of nine stimulus cards (assigned by the blocking design) and asked to sort the cards into two piles: more preferred versus less preferred (four in the first and five in the second pile). Then for the more-preferred set of four, the cards are ranked in terms of preference and, in sequentially preferred order, rated on the 11-point intentions-to-purchase scale that management had used in previous studies. Following this, each of the five less-preferred items is rated (without prior ranking within the set) on the same 11-point scale. Respondents are reminded that any rating assigned to items of the second set should not exceed the lowest rating assigned to items of the more preferred set. The net result is a set of nine intentions-to-purchase ratings.

Although we do not pursue the topic here, it should be noted that the blocking procedure (in which the levels of each attribute are balanced within respondent) permits the analyst to measure individual response "bias" (actually, average purchase intentions) and to relate this measure to respondent background data, if desired.

Fitting the Hybrid Utility Model   As the name suggests, the hybrid model (Green, Goldberg, and Montemayor, 1981; Green and Goldberg, 1981) contains elements of both compositional and decompositional models. Three classes of hybrid models have been proposed to date:

* A metric model in which numerically scaled ratings are obtained for both desirabilities and importances (e.g., constant sum ratings);

* A nonmetric model in which desirabilities and importances are described only in terms of ordered categories;

* A semimetric model in which desirabilities are described in terms of ordered categories and importances are obtained metrically (by means of constant-sum ratings).

In all three of these cases the motivation is the same—to combine the speed and simplicity

EXHIBIT B–5

INTERVIEWING PROCEDURE FOR SELF-EXPLICATED PORTION OF THE HYBRID UTILITY MODEL

In this part of the interview we'd like to obtain your preferences for various features of pickup trucks for personal use. Here are the eight attributes we'll be considering:

- Shoulder width
- Box length
- Width between wheel houses
- Trailer towing capacity
- Payload capacity
- Type of radio/price
- Engine/Price/MPG
- Base price of standard truck

SHOULDER WIDTH

Let's take the first attribute "Shoulder width." Here are three scale drawings of various pickup truck cabs. If the pickups were alike in all other respects, including price, which shoulder width would you most prefer? Second most prefer?

Shoulder width	First preference	Second preference
62 inches	☐	☐
64 inches	☐	☐
66 inches	☐	☐

(Repeat for remaining seven characteristics.)

CONSTANT SUM

Now that you have seen all eight sets of attribute descriptions, one at a time, we'd like to know how important the attributes themselves are to you. Assume you have 100 points which you can assign in any way you wish to the following attributes:

Shoulder width	_____	Payload capacity	_____
Box length	_____	Type of radio/price	_____
Width between wheel houses	_____	Engine type/price/MPG	_____
Trailer towing capacity	_____	Base price	_____
		TOTAL	100

You can assign zero points if you wish to one or more attributes. We only ask that you make sure that the total point count equals 100. Please assign the 100 points so as to reflect the relative importance of each of the attributes to your purchase decision.

of compositional methods (see Exhibit B–5) with the greater generality of decompositional methods (conjoint analysis) that are capable of measuring interactions and modifying initial importances/desirabilities to best predict a respondent's evaluations of complete multiattribute profiles.

In this example, a semimetric hybrid model is fitted. Our objective will be to estimate the numerical-scale value of each ordered category that, along with attribute importances (and additional parameters for group-level interactions), best predicts intentions-to-purchase ratings. Starting with the compositional (first phase) part of the model, any respondent's vector of responses can be represented by a set of cross products involving the attribute importances (normalized to total 1.0) and the dummy-coded values of the ranking categories, applied to each of the eight sets of attribute level.

To illustrate, assume that the first respondent provides responses to the first phase of the data collection task that appear in Exhibit B–6. Next, assume that in the second phase the same respondent received the first profile shown in the master design of Exhibit B–3:

A–1; B–1; C–1; D–1; E–1; F–1; G–1; H–1.

Now assume that the respondent's first-ranked preference is assigned the dummy-valued coding 1, 0; the second-ranked preference receives the coding 0, 1; and the third-ranked preference receives the coding 0, 0. The dummy variables are then multiplied by the appropriate importance weights from the constant sum task of the first phase. By applying this procedure to all eight attributes, we can set up the first row of predictor variables for the hybrid utility model as shown in Exhibit B–7.

To illustrate, level A–1 in Exhibit B–6 is ranked third and, hence, receives a dummy-valued coding of 0, 0 on X_1 and X_2, respectively. When the cross products are computed, the importance weight (0.15 in Exhibit B–6) as-

EXHIBIT B–6

ILLUSTRATIVE RESPONSES TO PHASE I OF THE HYBRID MODEL DATA COLLECTION

Rankings within attribute (1 = best)			
Attribute	Rank	Attribute	Rank
A–1	3	E–1	1
2	2	2	2
3	1	3	3
B–1	2	F–1	3
2	1	2	2
3	3	3	1
C–1	1	G–1	1
2	2	2	3
3	3	3	2
D–1	3	H–1	1
2	1	2	2
3	2	3	3

Attribute	Normalized attribute importances
A	0.15
B	0.18
C	0.06
D	0.09
E	0.05
F	0.11
G	0.22
H	0.14
	1.00

sociated with attribute A multiplies 0 in each case; hence the first two entries are zero. However, in the case of the second attribute, level B–1 is ranked second (coded 0, 1 on X_3 and X_4, respectively). In this case the importance weight (0.18) associated with attribute B multiplies 1 on variable X_4, leading to the cross product of 0.18, shown above. Similarly, we can encode the remaining eight stimulus profiles (received by the first respondent in the second phase) in terms of the first-phase results, and so on, for

EXHIBIT B–7

Attribute	Dummy variable	Value	Attribute	Dummy variable	Value
A	X_1	0	E	X_9	0.05
	X_2	0		X_{10}	0
B	X_3	0	F	X_{11}	0
	X_4	0.18		X_{12}	0
C	X_5	0.06	G	X_{13}	0.22
	X_6	0		X_{14}	0
D	X_7	0	H	X_{15}	0.14
	X_8	0		X_{16}	0

all subjects. All such encodings retain individual differences in both ranking-category components and importance weights.[8]

Then, if the sample were homogeneous and we assumed a main-effects model, denoted by the superscript (1), we could set up the regression equation:

$$Y_i^{(1)} \approx b_0 + \sum_{j=1}^{16} b_j X_{ij} , \qquad \text{(B–1)}$$

where $Y_i^{(1)}$ denotes the rating supplied by a combination of respondent and stimulus (hence i ranges from 1 to $9 \cdot 486 = 4374$ observations), b_0 is the intercept term, the b_j's are regression coefficients (in this case, implied rank category scale values), and $\approx$ denotes least-squares approximation. The intercept term measures the contribution to $Y_i^{(1)}$ when the profile contains all lowest-ranked attribute levels, while each b_j measures the contribution when some category level other than the lowest

ranked level appears (and where the level itself is weighted by the attribute's self-explicated importance).

Still assuming sample homogeneity, the model of equation (B–1) can be extended to include group-measured main effects and selected two-way interactions simply by encoding the attribute levels of any stimulus (independent of respondent and its category rank) in terms of dummy variables and cross products of dummy variables. In this extended version, denoted by the superscript (2), the model is:

$$Y_i^{(2)} \approx b_0 + \sum_{j=1}^{16} b_i X_{ij} + \sum_{k=1}^{16} c_k Z_{ik} + \sum_{l=1}^{40} d_l W_{il} , \quad \text{(B–2)}$$

where the Z_{ik} represents a dummy-valued variable, denoting some main effect for one of the eight attributes, and W_{il} represents a dummy-valued variable, denoting some two-attribute interaction effect.[9] Since all two-way interactions are estimable for all pairs (10) of the first

---

[8]This particular version of the hybrid model simply utilizes the interaction of a continuous variable (the importance weight) with a discrete variable (rank position on desirability, expressed as dummy variables). The net result is that the derived regression weight of equation (B–1) estimates a numerical score for desirability from the given rank position.

[9]It should be emphasized that these dummy-variable codings are *not* related to the encoding scheme used to characterize ranked category position in the first phase. For example, level A–1 would be encoded 1, 0 (on predictors Z_1 and Z_2 of *this* set) every time it appears as part of the stimulus description in the second phase.

five attributes and since four cross-product dummies are needed to denote each interaction, l ranges from 1 to 40. The c_k's and d_l's are regression coefficients, analogous to the b_j's.

Of course, not all of the c_k's and d_l's need be estimated or, if they are, need turn out to be significant. Generally, the Z_{ik}'s and W_{il}'s are entered in a hierarchical manner, after allowing for variance accounted for by the first-stage X_{ij}'s. *In the present example, all main effects are assumed to be carried by the X_{ij}'s; hence all Z_{ik} dummy variable terms are omitted from equation (B–2).* That is, main effects are all based on self-explicated utilities, and the selected two-way interactions are all based on the profile codings, employed in the second phase of the data collection procedure.

While equations (B–1) and (B–2) assume total-sample homogeneity in estimating the b's, c's, and d's, this is not a requirement of the model. That is, the 486×48 matrix of self-explicated attribute level rankings (dummy coded) times importance weights can be clustered first,[10] so that *separately* estimated equations for each cluster can be computed and then subjected to model comparison tests (Green and Goldberg, 1981) to see if the parameters are significantly different across clusters.

The main point of interest, however, is that part of the hybrid model contains individually varying arguments (the X_{ij}'s), while the other part contains arguments that depend only on the stimulus definition, within a given subgroup. In this way the analyst can retain individual differences while still estimating selected interaction effects and maintaining a relatively easy task for the respondent to carry out.

---

[10]There are 48 columns in this matrix since the rank position of each level is encoded by two dummies, leading to six dummy variables for each of the eight attributes. If clustering procedures are to be used, a preferable coding technique would be to substitute -1, -1 for the dummy coding 0, 0. In this way, cross-product distinctions, as based on different sets of importance weights, would be maintained.

At this point we assume that sets of b's and d's have been estimated for the (self-explicated) main effects and the selected 10 pairs of two-way interactions. We shall also assume that all of these effects are significant and that attempts to locate clusters with different hybrid utilities were not successful; that is, we assume that the total sample is homogeneous with respect to the b's and d's.

Estimating the Objective Function Having found a hybrid estimating equation that retains individual differences, the researcher can then set up a choice simulation by using DUEALL. If this approach is implemented, a set of experimentally designed new-product profiles and a set of common control-product profiles would be entered into DUEALL. The simulator would then be used to generate the sales revenue (price times estimated number of units per person times number of first choices) received by each experimental item when compared to the control items. Then, given the objective function values and the (dummy-coded) variables denoting each test product, STEPWISE would be used to find the appropriate ANOVA-type function for subsequent optimization (via QUALO).

In the present example, however, the results were to be used for future model years, in which the competitive array (control items) of trucks would not be precisely known. Moreover, on the basis of past surveys, management wished to assume that *any* predicted intentions-to-purchase rating of 9.0 or more (the top three scale positions) would be considered a purchase; predicted ratings below this level would not be considered a purchase.

Hence, DUEALL was modified to accept management's decision rule. Next, the DESIGN Program was used to generate 243 new-product profiles that provided orthogonal estimates for all main effects and the 10 two-way interactions that had been estimated during the utility-function computational step.

Then, each of the 243 products was entered into DUEALL along with each individual's utility function, as estimated from the aforementioned modification of equation (B–2). Since the price of each test vehicle (including any extra-cost options) could be computed and since it was assumed that each respondent would purchase only one truck (given that he/she purchased at all), it was a simple matter to compute the sales revenue generated for each of the 243 test profiles both at the individual level and for the aggregate.[11]

At the individual level, the application of DUEALL results in a 486×243 matrix in which a given row of the matrix represents the sales revenue generated for that respondent for each of the 243 test trucks; of course, many of the entries in a given respondent's row will be zeros, reflecting the fact that those particular attribute profiles were not sufficiently attractive to lead to an estimated intentions-to-purchase score of 9.0 or greater.

The point of interest is that the 486×243 matrix can also be used as input to a clustering program in order to see if various respondents are behaving differently insofar as their reactions to the test products are concerned. If such is the case, STEPWISE can be applied to each cluster's aggregated data separately and model comparison tests can be carried out there as well as in the utility-function estimation step.

In the present example, we shall assume a homogeneous sample, so that the total-sample sales revenue is appropriate for function fitting. In this case, the function, denoted by the superscript (3), is of the form:

$$Y_h^{(3)} \approx a + \sum_{k=1}^{16} e_k R_{hk} + \sum_{l=1}^{40} f_l S_{hl} \,, \qquad \text{(B–3)}$$

where $Y_h^{(3)}$ now represents the *aggregate* sales

revenue, a denotes the intercept term, the R_{hk}'s are dummy-coded variables for main effects, and the S_{hl}'s are dummy-coded variables for two-way interactions. The subscript h indexes the test product description so that $h = 1, 2, \ldots, 243$. Since each three-level attribute can be coded into two dummy variables, we have $8 \times 2 = 16$ dummy variables for main effects. Since the design permits all 10 two-attribute interactions (for the first five attributes) to be estimated, and there are four dummy variables for each interaction, the number of possible interaction dummies is 40.

Of course not all of the parameters in equation (B–3) need be significant. A hierarchical estimation procedure is employed, so that main effects are first fitted, followed by the selected two-attribute interactions, considered in a stepwise manner.

Exhibit B–8 shows the parameter values estimated by STEPWISE for the illustrative problem. As noted, only five out of 10 estimable two-way interaction tables are significant. It should also be noted that within each main effect and across rows and columns of each two-way table, the effects sum to zero; that is, effects-type coding (Cohen, 1968) was used in this instance.

Judging by the relative size of the main effects, Engine type/Price/MPG, Base price, and Box length are the most important attributes. The two-way interaction tables generally show positive effects due to "compatibility" (e.g., a large value of Box length associated with a large value of Payload capacity) and negative effects due to "incompatibility." The adjusted (for shrinkage) value of R^2 is 0.86, indicating a good fit of model to data.

Optimizing the Objective Function The objective function whose coefficients appear in Exhibit B–8 was then optimized by the QUALO program. The top portion of Exhibit B–9 shows a partial printout of the first-run results. The dependent variable represents the firm's

---

[11]It should be noted that the price factor (see Exhibit B–2) is treated just like any other attribute, that is, the intentions-to-purchase rating is assumed to be related to the dealer price and option prices in the same manner as any other attribute.

EXHIBIT B–8

PARAMETER VALUES ESTIMATED BY STEPWISE FOR THE GENERAL MODEL OF EQUATION (B–3)

(Adjusted $R^2 = 0.86$)

Attribute level	Main-effect coefficient
A–1	−0.47
2	0.05
3	0.42
B–1	−0.09
2	0.53
3	−0.44
C–1	0.15
2	0.02
3	−0.17
D–1	−0.12
2	0.17
3	−0.05
E–1	0.09
2	0.01
3	−0.10
F–1	−0.21
2	0.09
3	0.12
G–1	0.63
2	−0.94
3	0.31
H–1	0.41
2	0.28
3	−0.69

Two-way interaction coefficients

	B–1	B–2	B–3
A–1	0.22	−0.07	−0.15
2	−0.17	0.20	−0.03
3	−0.05	−0.13	0.18
	C–1	**C–2**	**C–3**
A–1	0.12	−0.01	−0.11
2	−0.13	0.16	−0.03
3	0.01	−0.15	0.14
	D–1	**D–2**	**D–3**
B–1	0.07	0.02	−0.09
2	−0.14	0.12	0.02
3	0.07	−0.14	0.07
	E–1	**E–2**	**E–3**
B–1	0.06	0.18	−0.24
2	−0.03	0.05	−0.02
3	−0.03	−0.23	0.26
	E–1	**E–2**	**E–3**
D–1	0.28	0	−0.28
2	−0.28	0	0.28
3	0	0	0

Intercept: 5.19

(coded) new-product sales revenue, estimated from the sample data. As can be noted, we obtain the following optimum profile:

A–3; B–2; C–1; D–2; E–3; F–3; G–1; H–1.

Interestingly enough, the interaction effects were not so strong as to swamp the main effects; with the exception of attribute E, the optimal profile is also the one that would be selected by a main-effects-only model.

In this same (unconstrained) run, the top five profiles were requested; these appear in descending order with respect to the objective function. Finally, the implicit enumeration procedure evaluated only two percent (151 out of 6561 possible combinations) to find the optimal profile. Since the algorithm evaluates (either explicitly or implicitly) all possible attribute combi-

EXHIBIT B-9

PARTIAL PRINTOUTS OF TWO RUNS OF QUALO

RUN 1—UNCONSTRAINED OPTIMUM

No. of attributes:	8
No. of two-way tables:	5
No. of top profiles printed:	5
Total No. of nodes evaluated:	151
No. of potential nodes:	6561

Y-value	Levels of attributes							
	A	B	C	D	E	F	G	H
7.780	3	2	1	2	3	3	1	1
7.760	2	2	2	2	3	3	1	1
7.750	3	2	1	2	3	2	1	1
7.730	2	2	2	2	3	2	1	1
7.680	3	2	1	2	2	3	1	1

RUN 2—CONSTRAINED OPTIMUM

No. of attributes fixed: 2

Attributes fixed:	Attribute	Level
	1	1
	2	1

Y-value	Levels of attributes							
	A	B	C	D	E	F	G	H
6.660	1	1	1	1	1	3	1	1
6.660	1	1	1	2	2	3	1	1
6.630	1	1	1	1	1	2	1	1
6.630	1	1	1	2	2	2	1	1
6.530	1	1	1	2	2	3	1	2

nations, the profile found by QUALO is globally optimal. In this specific run it is also unique.

Subsequent to the first run of QUALO, management wished to find out what would happen if Shoulder width were fixed at 62 inches and Box length were fixed at 6½ feet. Accordingly, a constrained run of QUALO was made, with results appearing in the lower portion of Exhibit B-9. The best profile, given the constraints on attributes A and B, is now:

A-1; B-1; C-1; D-1; E-1; F-3; G-1; H-1.

with an objective function value of only 6.66; this is a decrease of 14 percent from the unconstrained optimum. Moreover, because of interaction effects, the best levels of attributes D and E *also* change; again, the top five profiles (as requested by the researcher) are printed out.

EXHIBIT B–10

PARTIAL PRINTOUT OF THE TOLCO Q SENSITIVITY ANALYSIS

No. of attributes:	8							
No. of two-way tables:	5							
No. of levels in each factor:	3	3	3	3	3	3	3	3

Optimal profile and the optimal objective function value:

Objective function value		Profile levels						
7.780	3	2	1	2	3	3	1	1

Sensitivity analysis of attribute A while other attributes are kept fixed at their level in the optimal profile:

Level	Objective function value
1	7.060
2	7.600

Sensitivity analysis of attribute B while other attributes are kept fixed at their level in the optimal profile:

Level	Objective function value
1	6.920
3	7.140

Sensitivity analysis of attribute C while other attributes are kept fixed at their level in the optimal profile:

Level	Objective function value
2	7.490
3	7.590

Sensitivity Analysis Returning to the unconstrained optimal profile shown in the top portion of Exhibit B–9, management next wished to know how sensitive the objective function would be to departures from the optimal levels of each attribute, assuming that all other attributes remained at their optimal levels. For this purpose, TOLCO Q, one of the programs in the Sensitivity Analysis module, was used.

Exhibit B–10 illustrates the results for the first three attributes: Shoulder width, Box length, and Width between wheel houses. Within this set, the value of the objective function decreases most (from 7.78 to 6.92) when Box length decreases from its optimal level of 7 feet to its worst level of 6½ feet.

Over the whole set of eight attributes, Engine type/Price/MPG, Trailor towing capacity,

and Price (in that order) displayed the greatest effect on the objective function as their levels changed from best to worst.[12]

Although not illustrated here, it should be mentioned that TOLCO Q (like TOLCO K for continuous variables) is easily modified to handle simultaneous variation in more than one attribute at a time. However, if there are an appreciable number of levels per attribute, the output becomes too voluminous to be useful; single-attribute sensitivity analysis appears to

---

[12]Both the QUALO and TOLCO Q runs each took less than 10 seconds of CPU time on a DEC 10 computer. (A technical paper, now in preparation, will report computing times for various optimization and sensitivity analysis programs in the POSSE series.)

be the most helpful to management in large-scale studies.

Identifying the Best Target Segment Having found the globally optimal product profile, it is a simple matter to return to the DUEALL program and enter this product description for individual evaluation. If the approximating function is accurate, then QUALO's optimal product should, of course, do better than any of the 243 test products or any other test profile, randomly or systematically generated. Accordingly, a different set of 243 profiles were generated (by DESIGN) and tested by RANDO. The QUALO-derived optimum outperformed all of these contenders, thus supporting the goodness of fit already noted in Exhibit B–8. Finally, RANDO was used to generate 300 additional profiles at random; the QUALO-derived optimum outperformed all of these, as well.

The next step in the analysis was to find the background characteristics of those respondents who "chose" the optimal product. In this case we elected to use a stringent cutoff measure, namely an estimated intentions-to-purchase score of 10.0 or higher; 92 out of 486 respondents met this criterion. Their selected background characteristics, as obtained from a two-group discriminant analysis, appear in Exhibit B–11.

As observed from Exhibit B–11, the target market segment for the optimal product is younger, with a greater incidence of unmarrieds, females, of managerial, professional, or technical occupations, and suburban dwellers. This segment is also higher in education and annual household income. Psychographically, the target segment appears to take a functional view toward pickup trucks (with high interest in good gas mileage), but considers itself free spirited and favorably disposed toward imported vehicles. In short, the target segment

EXHIBIT B–11

SELECTED BACKGROUND CHARACTERISTICS OF THOSE MOST ATTRACTED TO
THE OPTIMAL NEW PRODUCT

Background variables	Those most attracted to optimal new product (N = 92)	Others (N = 394)
DEMOGRAPHICS		
Percent male	88%	97%
Percent married	66%	83%
Age	32.8	41.9
Occupation:		
Managerial, professional, technical	34%	16%
Education	13.9 years	11.8 years
Annual household income	$26020	$24504
Suburban area dweller	24%	11%
PSYCHOGRAPHICS		
Factor 1	Functional/economic	Top-of-the-liner
2	Trendy/free spirited	Conservative
3	Import lover	Detroit lover

appears to be "upscale" and receptive to innovation. Assuming that the cost of reaching this segment is similar to other possible target segments, this would appear to be the most attractive initial segment to promote.

Recapitulation In reviewing the computer steps that were followed in the preceding example, it is of interest to note that one or more programs were used from the Experimental design, Utility function estimation, Response surface and Objective function estimation, Categorical variable optimization, and Sensitivity analysis modules of Exhibit B–1. Since purchase likelihoods were used directly, the Choice simulator module was not relevant. Since all variables were categorical, the Continuous variable optimization module was not needed (except for the RANDO program). Finally, since management was interested only in first purchase, the Time path forecasting module was not needed either.

This limited use of the POSSE system is quite typical. Any specific application of POSSE generally entails only a small portion of the available programs, although some modules, such as Experimental design, are used in virtually all applications.

A second point of interest is that since POSSE utilizes response surface techniques as an initial step toward fitting a tractable approximating function of the choice system under study, it is essential that this function fit the data well (which was the case here) and that various cross-checks be introduced to see that the function is representative.[13] At the very least, the function should exhibit a high (adjusted for shrinkage) R^2 and should hold up well upon cross-validation.

However, other safeguards are important to consider as well. First, the response data in

DUEALL can be clustered, and separate functions fitted by STEPWISE if model comparison tests suggest a multimodal response surface. Second, two or more different sets of experimental designs can be used to cross-validate the parameters of the objective function. Third, ancillary programs, such as RANDO, can be employed to check on the superiority of the optimal profile generated by QUALO (or one of the other optimizing techniques). Fourth, stepwise fitting methods (that add variables hierarchically) should always be applied with the usual caution associated with this class of procedures (Weisberg, 1980, pp. 190–196).

In our judgment, the flexibility and general tractability of response-surface methodology more than compensates for the time required to test the adequacy with which the objective function represents the process. Moreover, through the use of clustering procedures and model comparison tests, the researcher is not forced to rely on the fitting of a single objective function except, of course, in cases where only aggregate data can be obtained. In all other cases, hybrid models or componential segmentation methodology can be employed.

In any case, by approximating the behavior of a choice process by a relatively simple mathematical function, one gets a clearer understanding of the essentials of the system (including its sensitivity to changes in the manipulable variables). As a matter of fact, such simplifications are routine in the construction of the original partworth functions, the formulation of consumer choice rules, and similar attempts to reduce the complexity of the real evaluation/choice process.

CURRENT PROBLEMS AND FUTURE PROSPECTS

The field of optimal product market design is just starting to pique the attention of researchers in marketing. It is expected that future de-

---

[13]The cross-checks, in this example, consisted of additional systematic and randomly generated runs by RANDO.

velopments will continue to expand the power of these methods. Still, there are many problems to be researched, both from a conceptual–methodological standpoint and from an empirical view as well.

Data Collection Problems MDS and conjoint-derived methods make extensive use of respondent-supplied data on perceptions, preferences, and choice. In general, these data will come from surveys or simulated test markets, depending upon whether verbal product descriptions or real products are used. As the costs of data collection continue to mount, it is becoming increasingly important to collect simpler kinds and smaller amounts of respondent data.

Hybrid models, of the type illustrated here, offer one approach to the problem by estimating some parameters at the individual level and others at the subgroup level. Clearly, other kinds of task simplifications need to be developed and tested for reliability and validity.

The data collection problem is particularly acute in the case of MDS-derived methods where one might have to obtain perceptual judgments as well as preference judgments for a large set of existing and hypothetical products. In our opinion, the data collection problems of MDS-derived product optimizers may well restrict their application to either small-scale product descriptions or academically based studies, where the costs and time constraints of data collection are much less severe.

Optimization and Sensitivity Analysis Problems Despite the large number of nonlinear algorithms and heuristics that are available from the mathematical programming literature, relatively little is known about their relative efficiency and stability. In the case of categorical attributes—the situation illustrated in this paper—one can find (via implicit enumeration) a global optimum, although it may not be unique. However, in general, nonlinear pro-

gramming algorithms for continuous variables can find only local optima. This may present major problems in the case of multimodal functions.

Nonsequential search strategies, such as factorial search, grid search, and simple and stratified random search, offer ways to cope with multimodal functions but, in turn, are extremely inefficient compared to gradient-based procedures (Brooks, 1958). Quite possibly, a combination of algorithms may be most appropriate for the case of continuous (or mixed) variables, but little is known about the relative efficiency, accuracy, and stability of these approaches.

Heuristics, of the type already applied by Parker and Srinivasan (1976) and Gavish, Horsky, and Skrikanth (1979) also represent areas for further research. Although this class of methods does not produce an optimum, the results might be fully satisfactory in cases of practical interest.

Greater application of sensitivity analysis can also be anticipated in future research on product–market optimization. In most commercial problems, management is interested in the availability of a spectrum of new product possibilities, rather than a single best product—particularly if each item in the array is within some allowable tolerance interval of the best product. Programs such as TOLCO Q, TOLCO 1, and TOLCO K are illustrative of the kinds of procedures needed to round out researchers' current interest in the optimization step.

Other kinds of problem formulations are needed as well. In the case of POSSE, for example, virtually all of the applications have involved the simpler case of introducing (or modifying) a single new product. Extensions of the approach to handle the introduction (either concurrently or sequentially) of two or more products would be useful in a variety of applied contexts. In this case, the response measure might be the contribution to overhead and profits (or some other suitable criterion) achieved by the firm's total product line, as a function of the attribute levels of the various products making up that line. Little experience has been assembled as yet on this extension. However, in a recent industrial electronics study an experimental design was set up that permitted the researcher to solve for the pricing of four different (but related) new products that maximized total-line contribution to the firm's overhead and profits.[14]

Another possible extension of product design optimization involves the utilization of *multiple* objective functions, such as expected market share, extent of cannibalization of existing products, and degree of draw from the industry's major competitor. In this case the researcher might wish to apply goal programming techniques (e.g., QUALO M) or similar procedures for handling multiple objectives.

Time Path Forecasting As indicated by Shocker and Srinivasan (1974), product design optimizers are essentially static, that is, they make no allowance for market learning, switching away from the new product in the future, and the impact of the firm's marketing tools (promotion, direct-sales effort, distribution coverage) on the development of sales for the new product over time. What appears to be needed is an expanded version of POSSE-like systems to incorporate other controllable variables and to appraise the likely effects of competitive retaliation to the firm's actions.

The SWITCH program represents a start in this direction but much more work is needed. One of the more promising possibilities involves recent developments in stochastic brand-choice models (McFadden, 1980; Jones and Zufryden, 1980; Zufryden, 1980). These

newer models include the incorporation of additional explanatory variables (e.g., product attributes, price, promotion), so that the entries of a brand switching matrix can be made conditional on a set of control variables (and other exogenous variables as well).

Assuming that this type of purchase-behavior model is also applicable to the response-surface approach, it may be possible to extend POSSE (or similar procedures) to optimize share, profits, etc., over a specified planning horizon where the choice process is modeled dynamically.

Reliability and Validity Testing Perhaps the most important area of all for future research is the problem of measurement reliability and validity. After all, POSSE and other product optimizers generally utilize consumer data from surveys or other kinds of artificial-choice environments. To date, little is known about the reliability and validity of either MDS-based or conjoint-based methods, although Green and Srinivasan (1978) summarize the main findings (as of early 1978) in the case of conjoint procedures. So far, the evidence suggests that the reliability of conjoint tasks appears acceptable, by survey standards, as long as the stimulus descriptions are relatively simple and the number of separate evaluations is not excessive. Moreover, the internal validity (i.e., estimating judgments for holdout stimuli during the survey) of conjoint procedures also compares favorably with survey-based techniques in general.

The major problem, however, concerns external (predictive) validity—the ability of conjoint procedures to predict actual market choice behavior or, at least, judgments made after the survey or experiment (Wittink and Montgomery, 1979). The jury is still out on this question.

For example, Parker and Srinivasan (1976) report favorable predictive validity scores in choices involving primary health care centers;

[14]The researcher may also wish to model the situation in which a competitor introduces a new product, so that a suitable modification of one's own product must be found to minimize the competitive impact.

other encouraging studies are those of Fiedler
(1972) on condominiums and Davidson (1973)
on air transportation. However, poor predictive
validity was found by Bither and Wright (1977).

Clearly, product optimization procedures
are only as good as the quality of the basic data
that underlie them. Much more research has to
be carried out on the external-validity question.
At best, external validation is a difficult and
costly undertaking—one that management is
not always interested in doing, particularly
since the validation itself may turn out to be
ambiguous. Nonetheless, some opportunities
exist for at least reasonably controlled conditions, such as in-store or in-home experiments
in which optimally designed products are
placed in real competitive situations, while controlling for many of the extraneous influences
on consumer evaluation. And, however difficult the task, this research is vital to the longer
term value of current-product optimizers and
the many enhancements that are planned for
the future.[15]

---

[15]It is interesting to note that three recently prepared
books (Pessemier, 1977; Urban and Hauser, 1980; and
Wind, 1981) all have sections on product design
optimization.

Bibliography

Bibliography

Aaker, D.A. (1975), "ADMOD: An Advertising Decision Model," *Journal of Marketing Research*, 12 (February), 37–45.

——— and J.G. Myers (1975), *Advertising Management*, Englewood Cliffs, N.J.: Prentice-Hall.

Abell, D.F. and J.S. Hammond (1979), *Strategic Market Planning*, Englewood Cliffs, N.J.: Prentice-Hall.

Abrams, G.J. (1974), "Why New Products Fail," *Advertising Age* (April 22), 51–52.

Abrams, J. (1969), "Reducing the Risk of New Product Marketing Strategies Testing," *Journal of Marketing Research*, 6 (May), 216–220.

Achenbaum, A. (1964), "The Purpose of Market Testing," in *AMA Proceedings, 47th National Conference*, Chicago: American Marketing Association, 575–587.

Ackoff, R.L. (1962), *Scientific Method: Optimizing Applied Research Decisions*, New York: John Wiley.

——— (1970), *A Concept of Corporate Planning*, New York: Wiley-Interscience.

——— (1974), *Redesigning the Future*, New York: John Wiley & Son.

——— (1976), *Designing a National Scientific and Technological Communication System*, Philadelphia: University of Pennsylvania Press.

——— and F.E. Emergy (1972), *On Purposeful Systems*, Chicago: Aldin–Atherton.

——— and J.R. Emshoff, "Advertising Research and Anheuser-Busch, Inc.—1963–68 and 1968–1974," *Sloan Management Review*, 16 (Winter 1975), 1–15 and (Spring 1976), 1–15.

Adams, J.L. (1974), *Conceptual Blockbusting: A Guide to Better Ideas*, San Francisco: Wilt. Freeman & Co.

Addelman, S. (1962), "Orthogonal Main-Effect Plans for Asymmetrical Factorial Experiments," *Technometrics*, 4 (February), 21–46.

AdTel Brochure (1973), "How to Test and Measure the Sales Effectiveness of TV Advertising," Chicago: AdTel.

Advertising Age (1976), Tylenol Product Announcement (April 26).

——— (1978), "FTC Reveals Intentions to Challenge Trademarks" (May 15), 115.

——— (1979), "Editorial Viewpoint" (October 8), 16.

Ahl, D.H. (1970), "New Product Forecasting Using Consumer Panels," *Journal of Marketing Research*, 7 (May), 159.

Albach, H. (1965), "Zur Theorie des Wachsenden Untermehmens," *Schriften des Vereins fur Socialpolitik*, 34NS, Berlin: Duncker and Mumblot.

Albers, S. (1979), "An Extended Algorithm for Optimal Product Positioning," *European Journal of Operations Research,* 3, 222–231.

———— and K. Brockhoff (1977), "A Procedure for New Product Positioning in an Attribute Space," *European Journal of Operations Research,* 1, 230–238.

———— and ———— (1979), "A Comparison of Two Approaches to the Optimal Positioning of a New Product in an Attribute Space," *Jeitschrift fur Operations Research,* Band 23, 127–142.

Alderson, W. (1957), *Marketing Behavior and Executive Action,* Homewood, Il.: Richard D. Irwin, Inc.

————and P.E. Green (1964), *Planning and Problem Solving in Marketing,* Homewood, Il.: Richard D. Irwin.

Alexander, R.S. (1964), "The Death and Burial of 'Sick' Products," *Journal of Marketing,* 28 (April), 1–7.

Alford, C.L. and J.B. Mason (1975), "Generating New Product Ideas," *Journal of Advertising Research,* 15 (December), 27–34.

Allen, M.G. (1979), "Diagnosing GE's Planning for What's Watt," in *Corporate Planning: Techniques and Applications,* R.J. Allio and M.W. Pennington (eds.), New York: AMACOM.

Allen, M.S. (1962) *Morphological Creativity,* Englewood Cliffs, N.J.: Prentice-Hall

Allio, R.J. and M.W. Pennington (eds.) (1979), *Corporate Planning: Techniques and Applications,* New York: AMACOM.

American Management Association (1963), *Corporate Growth through Merger and Acquisition,* New York: American Management Association.

American Marketing Association Definitions Committee (1948), "Report of the Definitions Committee," *Journal of Marketing,* 13 (October).

Ames, B.C. (1963), "Payoff from Product Management," *Harvard Business Review,* 43 (November–December), 141–152.

———— (1971), "Dilemma of Product/Market Management," *Harvard Business Review,* 49 (May–April).

Amstutz, A.E. (1967), *Computer Simulation of Competitive Market Response,* Cambridge, Mass.: MIT Press, 97.

Anderberg, M.R. (1973), *Cluster Analysis for Applications,* New York: Academic Press, Inc.

Andrews, B. (1975), *Creative Product Development: A Marketing Approach to New Product Innovation and Revitalization,* New York: Longman Group Limited.

Angelus, T.L. (1969), "Why Must New Products Fail," *Advertising Age* (March 24), 85–86.

Ansoff, H.I. (1965), *Corporate Strategy,* New York: McGraw-Hill.

———— (1977), "The State of Practice in Planning Systems," *Sloan Management Review,* 18 (Winter).

Arabie, P., J.D. Carroll, W. DeSarbo, and Y. Wind (1981), "Overlapping Clustering: A New Methodology for Product Positioning," *Journal of Marketing Research,* 18 (August).

Armstrong, G.M. (1973), "Comments on the Hamelman-Mazze Model for Product Abandonment Decisions," *Journal of Marketing,* 7 (October), 75–77.

Armstrong, S.J. (1978), *Long-Range Forecasting: From Crystal Ball to Computer,* New York: Wiley-Interscience.

———— and T. Overton (1971), "Brief vs. Comprehensive Descriptions in Measuring Intentions to Purchase," *Journal of Marketing Research,* 8 (February), 114–117.

Ascher, W. (1978), *Forecasting: An Appraisal for Policy Makers and Planners,* Baltimore: Johns Hopkins Press.

Aspinwall, L.V. (1962), "The Characteristics of Good Theory," in *Managerial Marketing: Perspectives and Viewpoints,* W. Lazer and E.J. Kelley (eds.), Homewood, Ill.: Richard D. Irwin, 633–643.

Assmus, G. (1975), "NEWPROD: The Design and Implementation of a New Product Model," *Journal of Marketing Research,* 12 (January), 16–23.

Bachem, A. and H. Simon (1977), "Optimal Product Positioning in an Attribute Space," University of Bonn working paper, Bonn, Germany.

Bailey, N.T.J. (1957), *The Mathematical Theory of Epidemics*, New York: Hafner Publishing Co.

Baker, M.J. (1975), *Marketing New Industrial Products*, London: The MacMillan Press.

Balanchandran, V. and S. Jain (1972), "A Predictive Model for Monitoring PLC," in *Relevance in Marketing/Marketing in Motion*, F. Allvine (ed.), Chicago, Il.: American Marketing Association, 543–546.

Balas, E. (1965), "An Additive Algorithm for Solving Linear Programs with Zero-One Variables," *Operations Research*, 13, 517–546.

Balderson, F.E. and A.C. Hoggatt (1962), *Simulation of Market Processes*, Berkeley, Ca.: Institute of Business and Economic Research, University of California.

Banks, S. (1964), "Implementation of Test Marketing," in *AMA Proceedings, 47th National Conference*, Chicago: American Marketing Association, 597–604.

————— (1965), *Experimentation in Marketing*, New York: McGraw-Hill Book Co.

Banting, P.M. (1978), "Unsuccessful Innovation in the Industrial Market," *Journal of Marketing*, 42 (January), 99–100.

Barclay, W.D. (1968), "Probability Model for Early Prediction of New Product Market Success," *Journal of Marketing*, 27 (January), 63–68.

Barnett, N.L. (1968), "Developing Effective Advertising for New Products," *Journal of Advertising Research*, 8 December, 13–20.

————— (1969), "Beyond Market Segmentation," *Harvard Business Review*, 27 (January–February), 152–166.

Bass, F.M. (1969), "A New Product Growth Model for Consumer Durables," *Management Science*, 15 (January), 215–277.

————— (1978), "An Integration of the New Product Growth Model with the Experience Cost Function and Optimal Pricing," presented at the TIMS/ORSA National Meeting in New York City (May).

————— and Wittink (1975), "Pooling Issues and Methods in Regression Analysis with Examples of Marketing Research," *Journal of Marketing Research*, 12 (November), 414–425.

Bateson, J. (1977), "Do We Need Service Marketing?" *Marketing Consumer Services: New Insights*, Report 77–115, Boston: Marketing Science Institute.

Batsell, R.R. and Y. Wind (1980), "Product Testing: Current Methods and Needed Developments," *The Journal of the Market Research Society*, 22, 2.

Battele Columbus Laboratories (1973), *Science Technology and Innovation*, Washington, D.C.: National Science Foundation.

BBDO, Management Science Department (1971), *The Theoretical Basis of NEWS*, unpublished.

Beattie, D.W. (1969), "Marketing a New Product," *Operations Research Quarterly*, 20, 429–435.

Beckwith, N.E. (1972), "Multivariate Analysis of Sales Responses of Competitive Brands to Advertising," *Journal of Marketing Research*, 9 (May), 168–176.

Beer, S. (1975), *Platform for Change*, New York: John Wiley & Son.

Belville, H. (1966), Unpublished MBA Thesis, New York University.

Bennis, W. (1966), *Changing Organizations*, New York: McGraw-Hill.

Benson, G. and J. Chasin (1976), *The Structure of New Product Organizations*, New York: AMACOM.

Benson, P.H. (1965), "Distribution of Consumer Choices for Qualitative Food Characteristics," *Food Technology*, 19 (July), 116–119.

Berelson, B. and G. Steiner (1964), *Human Behavior: An Inventory of Scientific Findings*, New York: Harcourt, Brace & World.

Berenson, C. (1963), "Pruning the Product Line," *Business Horizons*, 6 (Summer), 62–72.

————— (1968), "The R&D Marketing Interface—A General Analogue Model for Technology Diffusion," *Journal of Marketing*, 32 (April), 8–15.

Berlyne, D.E. (1963), "Motivational Problems Raised by Exploratory and Epistomic Behavior," in *Psy-*

chology: *The Study of a Science*, S. Koch (ed.), New York: McGraw-Hill.

Bernhardt, L. and K.E. MacKenzie (1972), "Some Problems in Using Diffusion Models for New Products," *Management Science*, 18 (October), 187–200.

Besson, R.M. (1973), "Unique Aspects of Marketing Sources," *Arizona Business*, 20 (November), 875

Bierman Jr., H. (1980), *Strategic Financial Planning*, New York: The Free Press.

———— and S. Smidt (1980), *The Capital Budgeting Decision*, 5th edition, New York: The MacMillan Company.

Bither, S.W. and P. Wright (1977), "Preferences between Product Consultants: Choices vs. Preference," *Journal of Consumer Research*, 4 (June), 39–47.

Blackman, A.W. (1973), "New Venture Planning: The Role of Technological Forecasting," *Technological Forecasting and Social Change*, 5, 25–49.

———— (1974), "The Market Dynamics of Technological Substitutions," *Technological Forecasting and Social Change*, 6, 41–63.

Blattberg, R.C. and J. Golanty (1978), "Tracker: An Early Test Market Forecasting Model for New Product Planning," *Journal of Marketing Research*, 15 (May), 192–202.

Blau, P.M. (1964), *Exchange and Power in Social Life*, New York: John Wiley.

Booz, Allen, and Hamilton (1968), *Management of New Products*, New York, brochure.

Boston Consulting Group (1970), *The Product Portfolio*, Boston.

Bourne, F.S. (1957), "Group Influences in Marketing and Public Relations," in *Some Applications of Behavioral Science Research*, R. Likert and S.P. Hayes Jr. (eds.), Paris: UNESCO.

Bowman, B.F. (1963), "Coordinating Technical & Marketing Research," in *Product Strategy and Management*, Berg and Shuchman (eds.), New York: Holt, Rinehart, and Winston, 446–447.

Bowman, E.H. (1976), "Strategy and Weather," *Sloan Management Review*, 17 (Winter), 49–62.

Box, G.E.P. and D.W. Behnken (1960), "Some New Three Level Designs for the Study of Quantitative Variables," *Technometrics* (November), 455–475.

————, W.G. Hunter, and J.S. Hunter (1978), *Statistics for Experimenters*, New York: John Wiley & Sons.

Box, M.J. (1965), "A New Method of Constrained Optimization and a Comparison with Other Methods," *Computer Journal*, 8, 42–52.

Boyd, H.W. and W.F. Massy (1972), *Marketing Management*, San Francisco, Harcourt Brace Jovanovich.

Brady, D. and F.G. Adams (1962), *The Diffusion of New Products and Their Impact on Consumer Expenditures*, Philadelphia: Economics Research Unit, University of Pennsylvania.

Brantel, C. (1963), "American Motors Corporation, An Empirical Study of the Firm," unpublished Ph.D. dissertation, Fordham University.

Brooks, S.H. (1959), "A Comparison of Maximum Seeking Methods," *Operations Research*, 7, 431–457.

Brown, D.A., S.F. Buck, and F.G. Pyatt (1965), "Improving the Sales Forecast for Consumer Durables," *Journal of Marketing Research*, 11 (August), 229–231.

Brown. F.E. (1980), *Marketing Research: A Structure for Decision Making*, Reading, Mass.: Addison-Wesley.

Brown, L.A. (1978), "Diffusion Research in Geography: A Thematic Account," *Studies in Diffusion of Innovation*, Discussion Paper No. 53, Columbus: Department of Geography, The Ohio State University.

Brown, R.G. (1963), *Smoothing, Forecasting, and Prediction of Discrete Time Series*, Englewood Cliffs, N.J.: Prentice-Hall Inc.

Bucklin, L.P. (1963), "Retail Strategy and the Classification of Consumer Goods," *Journal of Marketing*, 27 (January), 50–55.

Bunch, J.R. and L. Kaufman (1977), "Indefinite Quadratic Programming," Computing Science Technical Report #61, Murray Hill, N.J.: Bell Laboratories.

Burger, P.C. (1968), "Developing Forecasting Models for New Product Introduction," *AMA Proceedings* (Fall), Chicago: American Marketing Association, 112–118.

———— (1972), "COMP: A New Product Forecasting System," Working Paper 123–72, Evanston: Northwestern University.

———— (1978), "New Product Management," in *Review of Marketing—1978*, G. Zaltman and T.V. Bonoma (eds.), Chicago: American Marketing Association.

Burns, T. and G. Statler (eds.) (1961), *The Management of Innovation*, London: Tavistock Publications.

Business Week (1965a), "The Man with Too Many Hats" (May 22).

———— (1965b), "The Power of Proper Packaging," Special Report (February 20), 90–114.

———— (1973), "The Rebuilding Job at GF" (August 25).

———— (1974a), "Two-Way Squeeze in New Products" (August 10), 130–132.

———— (1974b), "Vanishing Innovation" (August 10).

———— (1975), "Marketing when the Growth Slows" (April 14), 44–50.

———— (1976), "How GM Manages Its Billion Dollar R&D Program" (June 28), 54–58.

———— (1979), "The Devils in the Product Liability Laws" (February 12), 72–78.

———— (1980a), "The Shrinking Standard of Living" (January 28), 72.

———— (1980b), "Corporate Strategies: Munsingwear, A Belated Quest for Innovation and Marketing Pizzazz" (May 12), 100–102.

Butler, D.H. (1976), "Development of Stochastic Marketing Models," in *Speaking of Hendry* (1976), The Hendry Corporation.

————, "Evaluating New Product Opportunity," ibid.

Butler, B.F., Jr., "The Next Brand into the Market," ibid.

Buzzell, R.D. (1966), "Competitive Behavior and Product Life Cycle," *AMA Proceedings*, Chicago: American Marketing Association, 46–68.

———— and V. Cook (1969), *Product Life Cycles*, Cambridge, Mass.: Marketing Science Institute, 29–35.

————, T.G. Bradley, and R.G. Sutton (1975), "Market Share—A Key to Profitability," *Harvard Business Review*, 53 (January–February), 97–106.

————, J. Matthews, T. Levitt, and R. Nourse (1972), *Marketing: A Contemporary Analysis*, 2nd edition, New York: McGraw-Hill.

Cacchione Jr., F.J., D. Gross, and Y. Wind (1977), "Consumer Attitudes as Guidelines for a New Distribution System," in *Moving A Head with Attitude Research*, Y. Wind and M. Greenberg (eds.), Chicago: American Marketing Association, 139–143.

Cadbury, N. (1975), "When, Where, and How to Test Market," *Harvard Business Review*, 54 (May–June), 96–101.

Campbell, D.T. and D.W. Fiske (1959), "Convergent and Discriminant Validation by Multitrait, Multimethod Matrix," *Psychological Bulletin*, 56 (March).

Cardozo, R. (1979), *Product Policy: Cases and Concepts*, Reading, Mass.: Addison-Wesley.

———— and Y. Wind (1980), "Portfolio Analysis for Strategic Product-Market Planning," Wharton School Working Paper, University of Pennsylvania, Philadelphia.

Carman, J.M. (1977), "Theories to Describe Some Competitive Conditions in which the Firm Operates," in *Behavioral Models for Market Analysis: Foundations for Marketing Action*. F. Nicosia and Y. Wind (eds.), Hinsdale, Il.: Dryden Press.

Carroll, J. (1976), "A Note on Departmental Autonomy and Innovation in Medical Schools," *Journal of Business*, 49, 4, 531–534.

Carroll, J.D. (1969), "Categorical Conjoint Measurement," presented at the Mathematical Psychology Meeting, Ann Arbor, Michigan (August).

———— (1972), "Individual Differences and Multidimensional Scaling," in *Multidimensional Scaling: Theory and Applications in the Behavioral Sciences*, Vol. I, R. Shepard, A. Romney, and S. Nerlove (eds.), New York: Seminar Press.

———— (1980), "Models and Methods for Multidimensional Analysis of Preferential (or Other Dominance) Data," in *Proceedings of Aachen Symposia on Decision Making and Multidimensional Scaling*, E.D. Lanterman and H. Feger (eds.), Berlin: Springer-Verlag.

———— and J.J. Chang (1967), "Relating Preference Scaling Solutions Via a Generalization of Data to Multidimensional Coombs' Unfolding Model," Murray Hill, N.J.: Bell Telephone Laboratories, Mimeographed.

———— and ———— (1969), "How to Use INDSCAL, A Computer Program for Canonical Decomposition of N-Way Tables and Individual Differences in Multidimensional Scaling," Bell Laboratories, Murray Hill, N.J.

———— and ———— (1970), "Analysis of Individual Differences in Multidimensional Scaling Via an N-Way Generalization of Eckart-Young Decomposition," *Psychometrika*, 35, 283-319.

————, P.E. Green, and W.S. DeSarbo (1979), "Optimizing the Allocation of a Fixed Resource: A Simple Model and Its Experimental Test," *Journal of Marketing*, 43 (January), 51–58.

Catry, B. and M. Chevalier (1974), "Market Share Strategy and the Product Life Cycle," *Journal of Marketing*, 38 (October), 29–34.

Cattin, P. and D.R. Wittink (1981), "Commercial Use of Conjoint Analysis: A Survey," research paper, Graduate School of Business, Stanford University.

Chakrabarti, A.K. and T.V. Bonoma (1977), *Art Exploratory Study of the Coordinating Mechanisms between R&D and Marketing as an Influence on the Innovation Process*, Pittsburgh, PA: Technology Management Studies Group, University of Pittsburgh (August).

Chakravarti, A., A. Mitchell, and R. Staelin (1979), "Judgment Based Marketing Decision Models: An Experimental Investigation of the Decision Calculus Approach," *Management Science*, 25 (March), 251–263.

Chambers, J.C. (1974), *An Executive Guide to Forecasting*, New York: John Wiley and Sons.

———— S. Mullick, and D. Smith (1971), "How to Choose the Right Forecasting Technique," *Harvard Business Review*, 49 (July–August), 45–74.

Channon, D.F. and M. Jalland (1978), *Multinational Strategic Planning*, New York: AMACOM.

Charlton, P., A.S.C. Ehrenberg, and B. Pymont (1972), "Buyer Behavior Under Mini Test Conditions," *Journal of the Market Research Society*, 14 (July), 171–183.

Charnes, A., W.W. Cooper, J.K. DeVoe, and D.B. Learner (1966), "DEMON: Decision Making Via Optimum Go-No Go Networks—A Model for Marketing New Products," *Management Science*, 12 (July), 865–887.

———— et al. (1968), "DEMON Mark II: External Equations Solution and Approximation," Management Science, 14 (July), 682–691.

Chase, R. and N. Acquilano (1977), *Production and Operations Management*, Revised edition, Homewood, Il.: Richard D. Irwin, Inc.

Child, I.L. (1968), "Esthetics," in *Handbook of Social Psychology*, Vol. III, Lindzey and Aronson (eds.), Reading, Mass.: Addison-Wesley, 853–916.

Choffray, J.M. and G.L. Lilien (1980), *Market Planning for New Industrial Products*, New York: John Wiley.

Churchill, Jr., V.B. (1971), "New Product Test Marketing—An Overview of the Current Scene," an address to the Midwest Conference on Successful New Marketing Research Techniques, Market Facts, Inc.

Churchman, C.W., R.L. Ackoff, and E.L. Arnott (1957), *Introduction to Operations Research*, New York: John Wiley & Sons.

Cima, F., G. Campioni, and P. Giani (1973), "A Forecasting Model for the Market of Competitive Products," *Technological Forecasting and Social Change*, 5, 51–65.

Clarke, D.G. (1973), "Sales-Advertising Cross Elasticities and Advertising Competition," *Journal of Marketing Research*, 10 (August), 250–261.

Claycamp, H.J. (1974), "Rescue Investment Analysis Program" (mimeographed, July 30).

———— (1977), "New Product Investment Decisions and Management Science Techniques: Why the Gap," mimeographed.

———— and L.E. Liddy (1969), "Prediction of New Product Performance: An Analytical Approach," *Journal of Marketing Research*, 6 (November), 414–420.

Clewett, R.M. and S.F. Stasch (1975), "Shifting Role of the Product Manager," *Harvard Business Review*, 54 (January–February), 65–73.

Cliff, N. (1966), "Orthogonal Rotation to Congruence," *Psychometrika*, 31.

Clifford, Jr., D.K. (1964), "Leverage in the Product Life Cycle," *Dun's Review* (May).

Coch, L. and J.R.P. French, Jr. (1948), "Overcoming Resistance to Change, *Human Relations*, 1, 512–532.

Cohen, J. (1968), "Multiple Regression as a General Data-Analytic System," *Psychological Bulletin*, 70, 426–443.

Computer Cartography Inc. (1979), *Customer Clusters: Taxonomic Relationships*.

The Conference Board (1979), "Gross National Product," *Economic Road Maps*.

Constandse, W. (1971), "Why New Product Management Fails," *Business Management* (June), 163–165.

Cook, V.J. and T.F. Schutte (1967), *Brand Policy Determination*, Boston: Allyn & Bacon.

Cooke, E. and B. Edmondson (1973), "Computer Aided Product Life Cycle Forecasts for New Product Investment Decisions," in *Increasing Marketing Productivity and Conceptual and Methodological Foundations of Marketing*, T. Green (ed.),

Chicago: American Marketing Association, 373–377.

Coombs, C.M. (1964), *A Theory of Data*, New York: John Wiley & Sons.

Cooper, R.G. (1975), "Why New Industrial Products Fail," *Industrial Marketing Management*, 4 (December), 315–326.

———— (1976), *Winning the New Product Game*, Montreal: McGill University.

———— (1979), "The Dimensions of Industrial New Product Success and Failure," *Journal of Marketing*, 43 (Summer), 93–103.

———— (1980), *Project NEWPROD: What Makes a New Product a Winner*, Montreal: Quebec Industrial Innovation Centre.

Copeland, M.T. (1923), "Relation of Consumers' Buying Habits to Marketing Methods," *Harvard Business Review*, 1 (April), 282–289.

———— (1925), *Principles of Merchandising*, Chicago: A.W. Shaw Company.

Corey, E.R. (1975), "Key Options for Market Selection and Product Planning," *Harvard Business Review*, 53 (September–October), 119–128.

———— and S. Star (1971), *Organization Strategy—A Marketing Approach*, Boston: Division of Research, Graduate School of Business, Harvard University.

Cox, Jr., W. (1967), "Product Life Cycles as Market Models," *Journal of Business*, 40 (October), 375–384.

Crawford, C.M. (1972), "Strategies for New Product Development," *Business Horizons*, 15 (December), 49–58.

———— (1977), "Marketing Research and the New Product Failure Rate," *Journal of Marketing*, 41 (April), 51–61.

Cunningham, M.T. (1969), "The Application of Product Life Cycles to Corporate Strategy: Some Research Findings," *British Journal of Marketing* (Spring), 32–44.

Cyert, R.M. and J.G. March (1963), *A Behavioral Theory of the Firm*, Englewood Cliffs, N.J.: Prentice-Hall, Inc.

————, J.G. March, and E. Feigenbaum (1959), "Models in a Behavioral Theory of the Firm," *Behavioral Science,* 4, 81–95.

Davidson, J.D. (1973), "Forecasting Traffic on STOL," *Operations Research Quarterly,* 24, 561–569.

Davidson, J.H. (1976), "Why Most Consumer Brands Fail," *Harvard Business Review,* 54 (March-April), 119.

Day, G.S. (1977), "Diagnosing the Product Portfolio," *Journal of Marketing,* 41 (April), 34.

Deese, J. (1965), *The Structure of Association in Language and Thought,* Baltimore: The Johns Hopkins Press.

Dhalla, N.K. and S. Yuspeh (1976), "Forget the Product Life Cycle Concept!" *Harvard Business Review,* 54 (January-February), 104.

Diamond, S.A. (1973), *Trademark Problems and How to Avoid Them,* Chicago: Crain Communication, Inc.

Dichter, E. (1964), *Handbook of Consumer Motivations,* New York: McGraw-Hill.

Diehl, R.W. (1972), "Achieving Successful Innovation," *Michigan Business Review* (March), 6–10.

Dietz, S. (1973), "Get More Out of Your Brand Management," *Harvard Business Review,* 51 (July-August).

Dodds, W. (1973), "An Application of the Bass Model in Long Term New Product Forecasting," *Journal of Marketing Research,* 10 (August), 308–311.

Dodson, J.A. and E. Muller (1978), "Models of New Product Diffusion through Advertising and Word-of-Mouth," *Management Science,* 15 (November), 1568–1578.

Dominguez, G.S. (1976), *How To Be a Successful Product Manager,* New York: American Management Association Extension Institute.

Dominguez, L. and F. Nicosia (1977), "Some Practical Problems in Building Substantive Marketing Models," in *Behavioral Models for Market Analysis: Foundations for Marketing Action,* F. Nicosia and Y. Wind (eds.), Hinsdale, Il.: Dryden Press.

Draper, N.R. and H. Smith (1966), *Applied Regression Analysis,* New York: John Wiley.

Drucker, P.F. (1963), "Managing for Business Effectiveness," *Harvard Business Review,* 41 (May–June), 59–60.

———— (1973), *Management: Tasks, Responsibilities, Practices,* New York: Harper and Row.

Dun's Review and Modern Industry (1963), "The ABCs of Operations Research," 82 (September).

Dusenbury, (1965), "Applying Advanced Science to Marketing and Advertising Planning," *Printer's Ink* (September 24), 20–21.

Eastlack Jr., J.O. (1964), "Consumer Flavor Preference Factors in Food Product Design," *Journal of Marketing Research,* 2 (February), 38–42.

Ehrenberg, A.S.C. (1965), "An Appraisal of Market-Brand-Switching Models," *Journal of Marketing Research,* 2 (November), 347–362.

———— (1971), "Predicting the Performance of New Brands," *Journal of Advertising Research,* 11 (December), 3–10.

———— (1972), *Repeat-Buying,* Amsterdam: North-Holland.

Einhorn, M.J. (1970), "The Use of Nonlinear, Non-compensatory Models in Decision Making," *Psychological Bulletin,* 73, 221–230.

Emshoff, J.R. and T.L. Saaty (1978), "Applications of Analytical Hierarchies for Long Range Planning Processes," Working Paper, Wharton Applied Research Center, University of Pennsylvania (May).

Engel, J.F., D.T. Kollat, and R.D. Blackwell (1978), *Consumer Behavior,* 3rd edition, New York: Holt, Rinehart, and Winston, Inc.

Ennis, F.B. (1973), *Effective Marketing Management,* New York: Association of National Advertisers, Inc.

Eskin, G.J. (1973), "Dynamic Forecasts of New Product Demand Using a Depth of Repeat Model," *Journal of Marketing Research,* 10 (May), 115–129.

———— (1974), "Causal Structures in Dynamic Trial-Repeat Forecasting Models," talk presented at the 57th International Marketing Conference, Montreal (April 15–18).

Etzioni, A. (1966), *Studies in Social Change*, New York: Holt, Rinehart and Winston.

Evan, W.M. and G. Black (1967), "Innovation in Business Organizations: Some Factors Associated with Success or Failure of Staff Proposals," *Journal of Business*, 40 (October), 519–530.

Everett, B. (1974), *Cluster Analyses*, London: Heinemann Educational Books, Ltd. (Social Science Research Council.)

Feigenbaum, E. and J. Feldman (eds.) (1963), *Computers and Thought*, New York: McGraw-Hill.

Fiedler, J.A. (1972), "Condominium Design and Pricing: A Case Study in Consumer Trade-off Analysis," in *Proceedings, Third Annual Conference*, V. Venkatesan (ed.), Chicago: Association for Consumer Research, 279–293.

Fisher, J.C. and R.H. Pry (1971), "A Simple Substitution Model for Technological Change," *Technological Forecasting and Social Change*, 2, 75–88.

FitzRoy, P.T. (1976), *Analytical Methods of Marketing Management*, Great Britain: McGraw-Hill.

Fogg, C.D. (1976), "New Business Planning—The Resource Allocation Process," *Industrial Marketing Management*, 5 (March), 3–11.

Forbes (1978), "Second Chance for Pennwalt" (February 20), 63.

Forrester, J.N. (1961), *Industrial Dynamics*, Cambridge, Mass.: MIT Press.

Fortune (1979), "Business Triumphs of the Seventies (December)."

Fourt, L.A. and J.W. Woodlock (1960), "Early Prediction of Market Success for New Grocery Products," *Journal of Marketing*, 25 (October), 31–38.

Frank, R.E., W.F. Massy, and D.G. Morrison (1964), "The Determinants of Innovative Behavior with Respect to a Branded Frequently Purchased Food Product," in *AMA Proceedings, 47th National Conference*, Chicago: American Marketing Association.

————, ————, and Y. Wind (1972), *Market Segmentation*, Englewood Cliffs, N.J.: Prentice-Hall.

Frawley, S.G. and T. Saaty (1978), "Political Behavioral and Analytical Hierarchies: Implications for Group Decision Making," Working Paper, University of Pennsylvania (November).

Frederixon, M. (1969), "An Investigation of the Product Life Cycle Concept and Its Application to New Product Proposal Evaluation within the Chemical Industry," unpublished doctoral dissertation, Michigan State University.

Freimer, M. and L.S. Simon (1967), "The Evaluation of Potential New Product Alternatives," *Management Science*, 13 (February), 279–292.

Galbraith, J. (1973), *Designing Complex Organizations*, Reading, Mass.: Addison-Wesley.

———— (1977), *Organizational Design: An Information Processing View*, Reading, Mass. Addison-Wesley.

Gale, B.T. (1979), "Planning for Profit," in *Corporate Planning: Techniques and Applications*, R.J. Allio and M.W. Pennington (eds.), New York: AMACOM, 160–171.

————, D.F. Heany, and D.J. Swire (1977), *The PAR ROI Report: Explanation and Commentary on Report*, Cambridge, Mass.: The Strategic Planning Institute.

Gavish, B., D. Horsky, and K. Srikanth (1979), "Optimal Positioning of a New Product," working paper MERC 79–05, Graduate School of Management, University of Rochester.

Gensch, D.H. (1970), "Different Approaches to Advertising Media Selection," *Operations Research Quarterly*, 21 (June), 193–217.

———— (1973), "Advertising Planning, Mathematical Models," in *Advertising Media Planning*, Amsterdam: American Elsevier Scientific Publishing Co.

Gerbner, G., O.R. Holsti, K. Krippendorff, W.J. Paisley, and P. Stone (1969), *The Analysis of Communication Content–Developments in Scientific Theories and Computer Techniques*, New York: John Wiley & Sons.

Gerlach, J.T. and C.A. Wainwright (1968), *Successful Management of New Products*, New York: Hastings House.

Gerstenfeld, A. (1970), *Effective Management of Research and Development*, Reading, Mass.: Addison-Wesley.

Ginzburg, E. and E. Reilly (1957), *Effective Change in Large Organizations*, New York: Columbia University Press.

Glover, F. and R.E. Woolsey (1974), "Converting the Zero/One Polynomial Programming Problem to a Zero/One Linear Program," *Operations Research*, 22 (January–February), 180–182.

Golabi, I., C.W. Kirkwood, and A. Sichermann (1978), *Selecting a Portfolio of Projects Using Decision Analysis*, San Francisco: Woodward-Clyde Consultants.

Goldhar, J., L.K. Bragow, and J.J. Schwartz (1976), "Information Flow, Management Styles, and Technological Innovations," *IEEE Transactions on Engineering Management*, Vol. EM-23, No. 1 (February), 53.

Green, P.E. (1962), "Bayesian Statistics and Product Decision," *Business Horizons*, 5 (Fall), 101–109.

———— (1973), "Measurement of Judgmental Responses to Multiattribute Marketing Stimuli," Technical Publication 545, American Society for Testing and Materials, Philadelphia, Pa.

———— (1974), "On the Design of Choice Experiments Involving Multifactor Alternatives," *Journal of Consumer Research*, 1 (September), 61–68.

———— (1978a), *Analyzing Multivariate Data*, Hinsdale, Il.: The Dryden Press.

———— (1978b), "Consumer Choice Models in Consumer Behavior," Paul D. Converse Lecture, University of Illinois (May).

———— and F.J. Carmone (1968), "The Performance Structure of the Computer Market: A Multivariate Approach," *Economics and Business Bulletin* (Fall), 1–11.

———— and ———— (1970), *Multidimensional Scaling and Related Techniques in Marketing Analysis*, Boston: Allyn & Bacon.

———— and ———— (1974), "Evaluation of Multi-attribute Alternatives: Additive Versus Configural Utility Measurement," *Decision Sciences* (April).

————, ———— and D.P. Wachspress (1976), "Consumer Segmentation Via Latent Class Analysis," *Journal of Consumer Research* (December).

————, J.D. Carroll, and S.M. Goldberg (1981), "A General Approach to Product Design Optimization via Conjoint Analysis," *Journal of Marketing*, 45 (Summer).

———— and W.S. DeSarbo (1978), "POSSE (Product Optimization and Selected Segment Evaluation)—A New Approach to Product Design and Market Segmentation," private memo (August).

———— and ———— (1979), "Componential Segmentation in the Analysis of Consumer Behavior," *Journal of Marketing*, 43 (October), 83.

————, R.E. Frank, and P.J. Robinson (1967), "Cluster Analysis in Test Market Selection," *Management Science*, 13 (April), B-392.

———— and S.M. Goldberg (1981), "A Nonmetric Version of the Hybrid Conjoint Analysis Model," paper presented at the Third ORSA/TIMS Market Measurement Conference, New York University, March.

————, ————, and Mila Montemayor (1981), "A Hybrid Utility Estimation Model for Conjoint Analysis," *Journal of Marketing*, 45 (Winter), 33–41.

———— and J. McMennamin (1973), "Marketing Position Analysis," in *Marketing Managers' Handbook*, S.H. Britt (ed.), Chicago: The Dartnell Corporation.

———— and V. Rao (1971), "Conjoint Measurement for Quantifying Judgmental Data," *Journal of Marketing Research*, 8 (August), 353–363.

———— and ———— (1972a), "Configuration Synthesis in Multidimensional Scaling," *Journal of Marketing Research*, (February).

———— and ———— (1972b), *Applied Multidimensional Scaling: A Comparison of Approaches and Algorithms*, New York: Holt, Rinehart, and Winston.

———— and V. Srinivasan (1978), "Conjoint Analysis in Consumer Research: Status and Outlook," *Journal of Consumer Research*, 5 (September), 103.

———— and D.S. Tull (1978), *Research for Marketing Decisions*, 4th ed. Englewood, N.J. Prentice-Hall.

_____ and Y. Wind (1973), *Multi-Attribute Decisions in Marketing: A Multiattribute Approach,* Hinsdale, Il.: The Dryden Press.

_____ and _____ (1975a), "Recent Approaches to the Modeling of Individuals' Subjective Evaluations," in *Attitude Research Bridges the Atlantic,* Philip Levine (ed.), Chicago: American Marketing Association, 123–153.

_____ and _____ (1975b), "New Way to Measure Consumers' Judgment," *Harvard Business Review,* 53 (July-August), 107–117.

_____ , _____ , and H.J. Claycamp (1975), "Brand-Features Congruence Mapping," *Journal of Marketing Research,* 12 (August), 306-313.

_____ , _____ and A.K. Jain (1972), "Benefit Bundle Analysis," *Journal of Marketing Research* (April).

_____ , _____ , and _____ (1973), "Analyzing Free Response Data in Marketing Research," *Journal of Marketing Research,* 10 (February).

Greene, J.D. (1974), "Application of Management Science to Test Market Forecasting," AMA International Conference in Montreal.

Griliches, Z. (1967), "Hybrid Corn—An Exploration in the Economics of Technical Change," *Econometrics* (October), 501–522.

Gross, I. (1968), "Toward a General Theory of Product Evolution: A Rejection of the 'Product Life Cycle' Concept," MSI Working Paper P43-10 (September).

Gunn, W.N. (1972), "Packages and the Environmental Challenge," *Harvard Business Review,* 50 (July-August), 103–111.

Gussow, D. (1978), *The New Merger Game,* New York: AMACOM.

Guzzardi Jr., W. (1979), "The Mindless Pursuit of Safety," *Fortune* (April 9), 54–64.

Haber, R.N. (ed.) (1969), *Information Processing Approaches to Visual Perception,* New York: Holt, Rinehart, and Winston.

Haley, R.I. (1968), "Benefit Segmentation: A Decision-Oriented Research Tool," *Journal of Marketing,* 32 (July), 30–35.

_____ (1971), "Beyond Benefit Segmentation," *Journal of Advertising Research,* 11 (August), 3–8.

_____ and P. Case (1979), "Testing 13 Attitude Scales for Agreement and Brand Discrimination," *Journal of Marketing,* 43 (Fall), 20–32.

_____ and R. Gatty (1968), "The Trouble with Concept Testing," *Journal of Advertising,* 8.

Hamburg, M. and R.J. Atkins (1967), "Computer Model for New Product Demand," *Harvard Business Review,* 45 (March-April).

Hamelman, P.W. and E.M. Mazze (1972), "Improving Product Abandonment Decisions," *Journal of Marketing,* 36 (April), 20–26.

Hammer, P.L. and S. Rudeanu (1969), "Pseudo-Boolean Programming," *Operations Research,* 17, 437–454.

Hanan, M. (1965), *The Market Orientation of R&D,* New York: American Management Association.

Hansen, F. (1972), *Consumer Choice Behavior: A Cognitive Theory,* The Free Press.

Hardin, D. (1966), "A New Approach to Test Marketing," *Journal of Marketing,* 30 (October), 28–31.

Harman, H.H. (1960), *Modern Factor Analysis,* 2nd revision, Chicago: The University of Chicago Press.

Harper Jr., P.C. (1976), "New Product Marketing: The Cutting Edge of Corporate Policy," *Journal of Marketing,* 40 (April), 76–79.

Harris, S. (1968), "CPM for New Product Introduction," in *Successful Management of New Products,* J.T. Gerlach and C.A. Wainwright (eds.), New York: Hastings House, 79–83.

Hart, A. (1966), "A Chart for Evaluating Product Research and Development Projects," *Operations Research Quarterly,* 17 (December), 374–378.

Hartigan, J. (1975), *Clustering Algorithms,* New York: John Wiley.

Hartley, R.F. (1976), *Marketing Mistakes,* Columbus, Ohio: Grid, Inc.

Hauser, J.R. and P. Simmie (1981), "Profit Maximizing Perceptual Positions: An Integrated Theory for the Selection of Product Features and Price," *Management Science,* 27 (January), 33–56.

_____ and G.L. Urban (1977), "A Normative Methodology for Modeling Consumer Responses to Innovation," *Operations Research*, 25, 579–619.

Henderson, J.M. and R.E. Quandt (1958), *Microeconomic Theory: A Mathematical Approach*, New York: McGraw-Hill.

Hays, W.L. and R.L. Winkler (1971), *Statistics: Probability, Inference, and Decision*, New York: Holt, Rinehart, and Winston, Inc.

Henderson, P.L., J.F. Hind, and S.E. Brown (1961), "Sales Effects of Two Campaign Themes," *Journal of Advertising Research*, 6 (December), 2–11.

Hendry, I. (1972), "The Three Parameter Approach to Long Run Forecasting," *Long Range Planning*, 5 (March), 40–45.

Hernes, F. (1976), "Diffusion and Growth—The Non-Homogeneous Case," *Scandinavian Journal of Economics*, 78, 427–36.

Herniter, J.D. (1973), "An Entropy Model of Brand Purchase Behavior," *Journal of Marketing Research*, 10 (November), 361–375.

_____ (1974), "A Comparison of the Entropy Model and the Hendry Model," *Journal of Marketing Research*, 11 (February), 21–29.

_____ and V. Cook (1978), "A Multidimensional Stochastic Model of Consumer Purchase Behavior," in *Behavioral and Management Science in Marketing*, A.J. Silk and H. Davis (eds.), New York: John Wiley, 237–268.

Hertz, D.B. (1964), "Risk Analysis in Capital Investment," *Harvard Business Review*, 42 (January-February), 95–106.

Heyvaert, H. (1977), "Strategic Management Performance," quoted in Montgomery and Weinberg, "Strategic Intelligence System", Stanford University Working Paper, Graduate School of Business.

Hilgard, E. and G. Bower (1966), *Theories of Learning*, New York: Meredith Publishing.

Hill, R. (1973), *Marketing Technological Products to Industry*, Oxford: Pergamon Press.

_____, R. Alexander, and J. Cross (1975), *Industrial Marketing*, 4th edition, Homewood, Il.: Richard D. Irwin.

Hill, R.M. and J.D. Hlavecek (1972), "The Venture Team: A New Concept in Modeling Organizations," *Journal of Marketing*, 36 (July), 44–50.

Hinkle, J.R. (1966), *Life Cycles*, A.C. Nielsen Co. (September 27).

Hise, R.T. (1977), *Product Service Strategy*, New York: Petrocelli/Charter.

Hlavecek, J.D. (1974), "Toward More Successful Venture Management," *Journal of Marketing*, 38 (October), 56–60.

Holbrook, M.B. and J.A. Howard (1976), "Frequently Purchased Nondurable Goods and Services," in *Selected Aspects of Consumer Behavior*, a summary from *The Perspective of Different Disciplines*, prepared for the National Science Foundation, U.S. Government Printing Office.

Holsti, O.R. (1969), *Content Analysis for the Social Sciences and Humanities*, Reading, Mass.: Addison-Wesley.

Holton, R.H. (1958), "The Distinction between Convenience Goods, Shopping Goods, and Specialty Goods," *Journal of Marketing*, 23 (July).

Hopkins, D.S. (1972), *The Short Term Marketing Plan*, New York: The Conference Board.

_____ (1974), *Options in New Product Organization*, New York: The Conference Board.

_____ (1980), *New Product Winners and Losers*, New York: The Conference Board.

_____ and E. Bailey (1971), *New Product Pressures*, New York: The Conference Board.

Horngren, C.T. (1972), *Cost Accounting: A Managerial Emphasis*, 3rd edition, Englewood Cliffs, N.J.: Prentice-Hall, 403.

Horsky, D. and L.S. Simon (1978), "Advertising in a Model of New Product Diffusion," presented at the TIMS/ORSA National Meeting in New York City (May).

Howard, J.A. and J.N. Sheth (1969), *The Theory of Buyer Behavior*, New York: Wiley.

Hughes, G.D. (1978), *Marketing Management: A Planning Approach*, Reading, Mass., Addison-Wesley.

Hurst, D. (1959), "Criteria for Evaluating Existing Products and Product Lines," in *Analyzing and Improving Marketing Performance*, A. Newgarden (ed.), New York: AMA Report #32.

Hurter, A.P. and A.H. Rubenstein (1978), Market Penetration by New Innovations: The Technological Literature," *Technological Forecasting and Social Change*, 11, 197–221.

Hussey, D.E. (1978), "Portfolio Analysis: Practical Experience with the Directional Policy Matrix," *Long Range Planning*, 11 (August), 2–8.

Hyett, G.P. and J.R. McKenzie (1976), "Effect of Underreporting by Consumer Panels on Level of Trial and Repeat Purchasing of New Products," *Journal of Marketing Research*, 13 (February), 80–86.

Hoerl, A.E. (1964), "Ridge Analysis," *Chemical Engineering News*, 60, No. 50, 67-71.

Isenson, R. (1969), "Project Hindsight: An Empirical Study of the Sources of Ideas Utilized in Operational Weapon Systems," in *Factors in the Transfer of Technology*, Cambridge, Mass.: MIT Press, 157.

Iuso, B. (1975), "Concept Testing: An Appropriate Approach," *Journal of Marketing Research*, 12 (May), 228–31.

Johnson, R.M. (1971), "Market Segmentation: A Strategic Management Tool," *Journal of Marketing Research*, 8 (February), 13–18.

———— (1974), "Trade-off Analysis of Consumer Values," *Journal of Marketing Research*, 11, 121–127.

Johnson, S.C. and C. Jones (1957), "How to Organize for New Products," *Harvard Business Review*, 35 (May-June), 49–67.

Johnston, J. (1972), *Econometric Models*, 2nd edition, New York: McGraw-Hill.

Jones, J.M. and F.S. Zufryden (1980), "Adding Explanatory Variables to a Consumer Purchase Behavior Model: An Exploratory Study," *Journal of Marketing Research*, 17 (August), 323–334.

Jones, K.A. and D.L. Wilemon (1972), "Emerging Patterns in New Venture Management," *Research Management* (November).

Judd, R.C. (1968), "Similarities or Differences in Product and Service Retailing," *Journal of Marketing*, 32 (Winter).

Kahn, H. and B. Bruce–Briggs (1972), *Things to Come: Thinking about the 70s and 80s*, New York: The Macmillan Company.

———— and A.J. Wiener (1967), *The Year 2000: A Framework for Speculation on the Next Thirty-Three Years*, New York: The Macmillan Company.

Kalwani, M.U. and D.G. Morrison (1977), "A Parsimonious Description of the Hendry System," *Management Science*, 23 (January), 467–477.

Karger, D.W. and Z.A. Malick (1975), "Long Range Planning and Organizational Performance," *Long Range Planning* (December).

———— and R.G. Murdock (1972), *New Product Venture Management*, New York: Gordon and Breach.

Katz, R.L. (1976), *Management of the Total Enterprise*, Englewood Cliffs, N.J.: Prentice-Hall.

Khandwalla, P.N. (1977), *The Design of Organization*, New York: Harcourt Brace Jovanowich, 266.

Kitching, J. (1967), "Why Do Mergers Miscarry," *Harvard Business Review*, 45 (November-December).

———— (1973), *Acquisitions in Europe: Causes of Corporate Successes and Failures*, Geneva: Business International.

Klein, D. (1967), "Some Notes on the Dynamics of Resistance to Change: The Defender Role," in *Concepts for Social Change*, G. Watson (ed.), Washington, D.C.: National Institute for Applied Behavioral Science.

Kline, C.H. (1955), "The Strategy of Product Policy," *Harvard Business Review*, 33 (July-Aug.), 91–100.

Klompmaker, J., D. Hughes, and R. Haley (1976), "Test Marketing in New Product Development," *Harvard Business Review*, 54 (May-June).

Knight, K.E. (1967), "A Descriptive Model of the Intra-Firm Innovation Process," *Journal of Business*, 40 (October), 478–496.

Koestler, A. (1967), *The Act of Creation*, 2nd edition, New York: Macmillan.

Kollat, D.T., R. Blackwell, and J. Robeson (1972), *Strategic Marketing*, New York: Holt, Rinehart & Winston.

Konopa, L.J. (1966), "New Products: Assessing Commercial Potential," *Management Bulletin #88*, New York: American Management Association.

Kotler, P. (1965), "Phasing Out Weak Products," *Harvard Business Review*, 43 (March-April), 107–118.

———— (1971), *Marketing Decision Making: A Model Building Approach*, New York: Rinehart & Winston.

———— (1980), *Marketing Management: Analysis, Planning, and Control*, 4th edition, Englewood Cliffs, N.J.: Prentice-Hall.

————, W. Gregor, and W. Rogers (1977), "The Marketing Audit Comes of Age," *Sloan Management Review*, 18 (Winter), 25–43.

———— and G. Zaltman (1976), "Targeting Prospects for a New Product," *Journal of Advertising Research*, 16 (February), 7–20.

Kovac, F.J. and M.F. Dague (1972), "Forecasting by Product Life Cycle Analysis," *Research Management* (July).

Kruskal, J.B. (1965), "Analysis of Factorial Experiments by Estimating Monotone Transformations of the Data," *Journal of the Royal Statistical Society*, Series B, 27, 251–263.

Kuehn, A.A. (1962), "Consumer Brand Choice—A Learning Process?" in *Quantitative Techniques in Marketing Analysis*, R.E. Frank, A.A. Kuehn, and W.F. Massy (eds.), Homewood, Il.: Richard D. Irwin, Inc.

———— and R.L. Day (1962), "Strategy of Product Quality," *Harvard Business Review*, 40 (November-December), 100–110.

Lackman, C.L. (1978), "Gompertz Curve Forecasting: A New Product Application," *Journal of the Market Research Society*, 20 (January), 45–47.

Laczniak, G.R., R.F. Lusch, and J.G. Udell (1977), "Marketing in 1985: A View from the Ivory Tower," *Journal of Marketing*, 41 (October), 47–56.

Lambin, J.J. (1970), "Optimal Allocation of Competitive Marketing Efforts: An Empirical Study," *Journal of Business*, 43 (October), 468–484.

Larréché, J. and D.B. Montgomery (1977), "A Framework for the Comparison of Marketing Models: A Delphi Method," *Journal of Marketing Research*, 14 (November), 487–498.

Lasswell, H.D. (1942), *Analyzing the Content of Mass Communication: A Brief Introduction*, Washington, D.C.: Library of Congress, Experimental Division for Study of War-Time Communications, Document No. 11.

Lazo, H. (1965), "Finding a Key to Success in New Product Failures," *Industrial Marketing* (November), 74–77.

Learner, D.B. (1968), "Profit Maximization through New Product Planning and Control," in *Applications of the Sciences in Marketing Management*, Frank Bass et al. (eds.), New York: John Wiley & Sons, 151–167.

Leavitt, H.J. (1962), "Management According to Task: Organizational Differentiation," *Management International*, I, 13–23.

Lekvall, P. and C. Wahlbin (1973), "A Study of Some Assumptions Underlying Innovation Diffusion Functions," *Swedish Journal of Economics*, 75, 362–77.

Lemont, F.L. (1971), "New Products: How They Differ; Why They Fail; How to Help Them Do Better," *Advertising Age* (April 15), 43–45.

Lerviks, A. (1976), "A Diffusion Model for New Consumer Durables," *Scandinavian Journal of Economics*, 78, 571–86.

Levitt, T. (1962), *Innovation in Marketing: New Perspectives for Profit and Growth*, New York: McGraw-Hill.

———— (1965), "Exploit the PLC," *Harvard Business Review*, 43 (November-December), 81–94.

———— (1966), "Innovative Imitation," *Harvard Business Review*, 44 (September-October), 63.

———— (1975), "Marketing Myopia," *Harvard Business Review*, 53 (September-October), 26.

Levy, S.J. (1959), "Symbols for Sale," *Harvard Business Review,* 37 (July-August), 117–124.

Light, L. and C. Pringle (1970), "New Product Forecasting Using Recursive Regression," in *Research in Consumer Behavior,* D. Kollat, R. Blackwell, and J. Engel (eds.), New York: Holt, Rinehart and Winston.

Lilien, G.L. and A.G. Rao (1978), "A Marketing Promotion Model with Word-of-Mouth Effects," Working Paper 976–78, Sloan School of Management, Massachusetts Institute of Technology, Boston (February).

Linstone, H. (1975), *The Delphi Method: Techniques and Applications,* Reading, Mass.: Addison-Wesley.

———— and D. Sahal (1976), *Technological Substitution,* New York: American Elsevier Publishing Company.

Lippincott, J.G. and W.P. Margulies (1956), "Packaging in Top Level Planning," *Harvard Business Review,* 34 (September-October), 46–54.

Lipstein, B. (1964), "The Design of Test Marketing Experiments," *AMA Proceedings, 47th National Conference,* Dallas, Texas, 588–596.

———— (1968), "Test Marketing: A Perturbation in the Market Place," *Management Science,* 14, B437–448.

———— (1970), "Modelling and New Product Birth," *Journal of Advertising Research,* 10 (October).

Arthur D. Little Company (undated), "Resource Allocation for Multi-Industry Corporations," internal report.

———— (1961), "The 5 "Ms" of Packaging," *Consumer Packaging* (November).

Little, J.D.C. (1966), "A Model of Adaptive Control of Promotional Spending," *Operations Research* (November), 1075–1097.

———— (1970), "Models and Managers: The Concept of a Decision Calculus," *Management Science* (April), B466–485.

———— (1975a), "BRANDAID: A Marketing Mix Model, Part I: Structure," *Operations Research,* 23 (July-August), 628–655.

———— (1975b), "BRANDAID: A Marketing Mix Model, Part 2: Implementation, Calibration, and Case Study," *Operations Research,* 23 (July-August), 656.

———— and L.M. Lodish (1969), "A Media Planning Calculus," *Operations Research,* (January-February), 1–35.

Locander, W.B. and R.D. Scamell (1976), "Screening New Product Ideas—A Two Phase Approach," *Research Management,* 19 (March), 14–18.

Longman, K.A. (1971), *Advertising,* New York: Harcourt Brace Jovanovich, Inc.

Lorsch, J.W. (1965), *Product Innovation and Organization,* New York: The Macmillan Co.

———— and P.R. Lawrence (1965), "Organizing for Product Innovation," *Harvard Business Review,* 43 (January-February), 109–123.

Lotka, A.J. (1956), *Elements of Mathematical Biology,* New York: Dover.

Louis, A.M. (1978), "Polaroid's One Step Is Stopping Kodak Cold," *Fortune* (February 13), 77–78.

Luce, R.D. (1969), *Individual Choice Behavior,* New York: Wiley.

————, R.R. Bush, and E. Galanter (eds.) (1965), *Handbook of Mathematical Psychology,* Volume III, New York: John Wiley and Sons, 249–410.

MacDonald Jr., M.B. (1969), *Appraising the Market for Industrial Products,* New York: National Industrial Conference Board, 112.

MacKinnon, D.W. (1965), "Personality and Realization of Creative Potential," *American Psychologist,* 20, 273–281.

Mackworth, J.F. (1963), "The Relation between the Visual Image and Post-Perceptual Immediate Memory," *Journal of Verbal Learning and Verbal Behavior,* 2, 75–85.

MacLachlan, D.L. (1972), "A Model of Intermediate Market Response," *Journal of Marketing Research,* 9 (November), 378–384.

———— and J.K. Johansson (1981), "Market Segmentation with Multivariate AID," *Journal of Marketing,* 45 (Winter), 74–84.

Mahajan, V. (1978), "Innovation Diffusion in a Dynamic Potential Adopter Population," *Management Science*, 24, 1589–1597.

———— (1979), "A New Product Growth Model with a Dynamic Market Potential," *Long Range Planning*, 12 (August), 51–58.

———— and E. Muller (1979), "Innovation Diffusion and New Product Growth Models," *Journal of Marketing*, 43 (Fall), 55–58.

———— and ———— (1980), "Innovative Behavior and Repeat Purchase Diffusion Models," Wharton School Working Paper, University of Pennsylvania, Philadelphia, PA.

———— and R.A. Peterson (1979), "First Purchase Diffusion Models of New Product Acceptance," *Technological Forecasting and Social Change*, 15 (November).

———— and ———— (1980), "Integrating Time and Space in Technological Substitution Models," *Technological Forecasting and Social Change*, 14 (August).

————, ————, and N. Malhotra (1979), "A New Product Growth Model with a Dynamic Market Potential," *Long Range Planning*, 12 (August), 51–58.

Makridakis, S. and S.C. Wheelwright (1977), "Forecasting: Issues and Challenges for Marketing Management," *Journal of Marketing*, 41 (October), 24–38.

Mansfield, E. (1961), "Technical Change and the Rate of Imitation," *Econometrica* (October), 741–766.

———— (1970), *Microeconomics: Theory and Applications*, New York: Norton.

———— et al. (1971), *Research and Innovation in the Modern Corporation*, New York: Norton.

———— and J. Rappoport (1975), "The Cost of Industrial Product Innovations," *Management Science*, 21 (August), 1380–1386.

Martino, J.P. (1972), *Technological Forecasting for Decision Making*, New York: American Elsevier Publishing Co.

Massy, W.F. (1969), "Forecasting the Demand for New Convenience Products," *Journal of Marketing Research*, 6 (November), 405–412.

————, D.B. Montgomery, and D.D. Morrison (1970), *Stochastic Choice Models of Buying Behavior*. Cambridge, Mass.: The MIT Press.

———— and D.G. Morrison (1964), "The Determinants of Innovative Behavior with Respect to Branded, Frequently Purchased Food Products," in *Reflections on Progress in Marketing*, G. Smith (ed.), Chicago: American Marketing Association.

Maxmen, J. (1976), *The Post-Physician Era: Medicine in the 21st Century*, New York: Wiley-Interscience.

May, J.H. (1979), "Solving Nonlinear Programs without Using Analytic Derivatives," *Operations Research*, 3 (May-June), 457–484.

————, A.D. Shocker, and D. Sudharshan (1980), "On Optimal New Product Location, with a Simulation Comparison of Methods," working paper, University of Pittsburgh.

Mayer, E. (1964), *Systematics and the Origin of Species*, New York: Dover Publishing, Inc., 297 (first published by Columbia University Press).

McCann, J.M. (1974), "Study of Market Segment Response to the Marketing Decision Variables," *Journal of Marketing Research*, 11 (November), 399–412.

McCarthy, E.J. (1975), *Basic Marketing: A Managerial Approach*, Homewood, Il.: Richard D. Irwin.

McFadden, D. (1970), "Conditional Logit Analysis of Qualitative Choice Behavior," in *Frontiers in Econometrics*, P. Zaremka, ed., New York: Academic Press, 105–142.

———— (1980), "Econometric Models for Probabalistic Choice Among Products," *Journal of Business*, 53 (July), 513–19.

McGuire, E.P. (1972), *Generating New Product Ideas*, New York: The Conference Board.

———— (1973), *Evaluating New Product Proposals*, Report No. 604, New York: The Conference Board.

McGuire, W. (1977), "Psychological Factors Influencing Consumer Choice," in *Selected Aspects of Consumer Behavior*, Robert Ferber (ed.), a publication of the National Science Foundation, Washington, D.C.

Mickwitz, G. (1959), *Marketing and Competition*, Helsingfors, Finland: Centraltryckeriet.

Midgley, D.F. (1976), "A Simple Mathematical Theory of Innovative Behavior," *Journal of Consumer Research*, 3 (June) 31–41.

———— (1977), *Innovation and New Product Marketing*, New York: Halsted Press.

———— and G.R. Dowling (1978), "Innovativeness: The Concept and Its Measurement," *Journal of Consumer Research*, 4 (March), 229–242.

Miller, S.J., M.B. Mazis, and P.L. Wright (1971), "the influence of Brand Ambiguity on Brand Attitude Development," *Journal of Marketing Research*, 8 (November), 455–459.

Mills, V. (1974), "Avoid These Errors in New Product Research," *Advertising Age* (July 15), 26.

Miracle, G.E. (1965), "Product Characteristics and Marketing Strategy," *Journal of Marketing*, 29 (January), 18–24.

Modern Textiles Magazine (1964), article by Jordan P. Yale (February), 33.

Monroe, K.B. (1979), *Pricing: Making Profitable Decisions*, New York: McGraw Hill.

Montgomery, D.B. and C.B. Weinberg (1979), "Strategic Intelligence Systems," *Journal of Marketing*, 43 (Fall), 41–52.

Moore, C.L. and R.K. Jaedicke (1976), *Management Accounting*, 4th edition, Cincinnati, Ohio: Southwestern Publishers.

Moore, W.L. (1980), "Levels of Aggregation in Conjoint Analysis: An Empirical Comparison," *Journal of Marketing Research*, 17 (November), 516–523.

Morgan, J.N. and R.C. Messenger (1973), *THAID: A Sequential Analysis Program for the Analysis of Nominal Scale Dependent Variables*, Ann Arbor, Mich: Institute for Social Research, University of Michigan.

Morgan, N. and J. Purnell (1969), "Isolating Openings for New Products in a Multidimensional Space," *Journal of the Market Research Society*, 11 (July), 245–266.

Morrison, D. (1979), "Purchase Intention and Purchase Behavior," *Journal of Marketing*, 43 (Spring), 65–74.

Moskowitz, H.R. (1978), "Sensory Analysis: A New Technology for Product Development," paper presented before the Association of National Advertisers, New York (February).

————, D.W. Stanley, and J.W. Chandler (1977), "The Eclipse Method: Optimizing Product Formulation through a Consumer Generated Ideal Sensory Profile," *Canadian Institute Food Science Technology Journal*, 10 (July), 161–168.

Muller, E. (1978), "A Dynamic Model of Informative and Persuasive Advertising in Relation to Entry Deterrence," Working Paper, Department of Economics, University of Pennsylvania, Philadelphia.

Murphy, J.H. (1962), "New Products Need Special Management," *Journal of Marketing*, 26 (October), 46–49.

Myers, J.H. and W.R. Reynolds (1967), *Consumer Behavior and Marketing Management*, Boston: Houghton Mifflin Company.

Naert, P. and P. Leeflang (1978), *Building Implementable Marketing Models*, Boston: Martinus Division, Leider.

Nakanishi, M. (1973), "Advertising and Promotion Efforts on Consumer Response to New Products," *Journal of Marketing Research* (August), 242–249.

National Science Foundation (1978), *National Patterns of R&D Resources: Funds and Personnel in the U.S., 1953-1978/9*, Washington, D.C., NSF 78–313.

Naylor, T.H. (1979), *Corporate Planning Models*, Reading, Mass.: Addison-Wesley.

Nelson, P. (1970), "Information and Consumer Behavior," *Journal of Political Economy*, 78 (March-April), 311–29.

Nerlove, M. and K. Arrow (1962), "Optimal Advertising Policy under Dynamic Conditions," *Econometrica*, 29 (May), 129–142.

Neuhaus, C.F. and J.R. Taylor (1972), "Variables Affecting Sales of Family Branded Products," *Journal of Marketing Research*, 9 (November), 419–422.

Nevers, J.V. (1972), "Extensions of a New Product Growth Model," *Sloan Management Review*, 13 (Winter), 78–79.

Nicolleti, B. (1975), "First-Time Buyers of a Repurchasable New Product," *European Journal of Marketing*, 9, 109–116.

Nicosia, F.M. (1966a), *Consumer Decision Processes*, Englewood-Cliffs, N.J.: Prentice-Hall.

———— (1966b), "Brand Choice: Toward Behavioristic-Behavioral Models," in *Management and Behavioral Sciences in Marketing*, New York: Ronald Press.

Nielsen, A.C. (1960), "Twenty Steps to Successful Marketing," brochure.

The Nielsen Researcher (1968), "The 'Life Cycle' of Grocery Brands," A.C. Nielsen Company.

———— (1978), "New Items Revisited," A.C. Nielsen Company.

———— (1979), "New Product Success Ratio," A.C. Nielsen Company.

North, H. and D. Pyke (1969), "Probes of the Technological Future," *Harvard Business Review*, 47 (May-June), 68–82.

O'Meara Jr., J.T. (1961), "Selecting Profitable Products," *Harvard Business Review*, 39 (January-February), 83–89.

Osborn, A.F. (1953), *Applied Imagination: Principles and Procedures of Creative Thinking*, 3rd edition, New York: Charles Scribner and Sons.

Oxenfeldt, A. (1966), *Executive Action in Marketing*, Belmont, Calif.: Wadsworth.

Ozga, S. (1960), "Imperfect Markets through Lack of Knowledge," *Quarterly Journal of Economics*, 74 (February), 29–52.

Palda, K.S. (1971), *Pricing Decisions and Marketing Policy*, Foundations of Marketing Series, Englewood Cliffs, N.J.: Prentice-Hall.

Parfitt, J.H. and B.J.K. Collins (1968), "Use of Consumer Panels for Brand-Share Predictions," *Journal of Marketing Research*, 5 (May), 131–145.

Parker, B.R. and V. Srinivasan (1976), "A Consumer Preference Approach to the Planning of Rural Primary Health-Care Facilities," *Operations Research*, 24 (September-October), 991–1025.

Parsons, L.J. (1975), "The Product Life Cycle and Time-Varying Advertising Elasticities," *Journal of Marketing Research*, 12 (November), 476.

———— and R.L. Schultz (1976), *Marketing Models and Econometric Research*, New York: Elsevier North Holland.

Parsons, T. (1960), *Structure and Process in Modern Societies*, New York: The Free Press.

Patton, A. (1959), "Top Management's Stake in the Product Life Cycle," *Management Review* (June).

Payne, D. (1966), "Jet-Set, Pseudo-Store and New Product Testing," *Journal of Marketing Research*, 3 (November), 372–376.

Pearl, R. (1925), *Studies in Human Biology*, Baltimore: Wilkins and Wilkins.

Pekelman, D. and S. Sen (1974), "Mathematical Programming Models for *Determining* Determination of Attribute Weights," *Management Science*, 29 (April), 1217–1229.

———— and ———— (1979), "Measurement and Estimation of Conjoint Utility Functions," *Journal of Consumer Research*, 5 (March), 263–271.

———— and E. Tse (1980), "Experimentation and Control in Advertising: An Adaptive Control Approach," *Operations Research*, 28 (March-April).

Pellou, E.C. (1969), *An Introduction to Mathematical Ecology*, New York: Wiley-Interscience.

Pengilly, P.J. and A.J. Moss (1969), "Choice of a New Product, Its Selling Pattern and Price," *Operations Research Quarterly*, 20 (June) 179–185.

Perrow, C. (1970), *Organizational Analysis: A Sociological View*, Belmont, Calif.: Wadsworth.

Pessemier, E.A. (1966), *New Product Decisions: An Analytical Approach*, New York: McGraw-Hill, 141–158.

———— (1975), "Market Structure Analysis of New Product and Market Opportunities," *Journal of Contemporary Business* (Spring), 35–67.

———— (1977), *Product Management: Strategy and Organization*, New York: John Wiley and Sons.

————, P. Burger, R. Teach, and D.J. Tigert (1971), "Using Laboratory Brand Preference Scales to Predict Consumer Brand Purchases," *Management Science*, 17 (February), B371–385.

———, ———, and D.J. Tigert (1967), "Can New Product Buyers Be Identified?" *Journal of Marketing Research,* 4 (November), 349–54.

——— and P. Root (1973), "The Dimensions of New Product Planning," *Journal of Marketing,* 37 (January), 10–18.

Peterson, I. (1978), "Bulb Snatching in Supermarkets," *The New York Times,* Section 3 (May 14), 1, 11.

Peterson, R.A. and V. Mahajan (1978), "Multi-Product Growth Models," in *Research in Marketing,* J. Sheth (ed.), Greenwich, Conn.: JAI Press, 201–231.

Polli, R. and V. Cook (1967), "Product Life Cycle Models: A Review Paper," MSI Working Paper No. P-43-2 (November).

——— and ——— (1969), "Validity of the Product Life Cycle," *The Journal of Business,* 42 (October), 390.

Prince, G.M. (1970), *The Practice of Creativity,* New York: Harper and Row.

Printers' Ink (1965), "The New Power of Packaging: Management Takes Control," (June 11), 13–18.

Quinn, J.B. and J.A. Mueller (1963), "Transferring Research Results to Operation," *Harvard Business Review,* 41 (January-February), 49–66.

Raiffa, M. and R. Schlaifer (1961), *Applied Statistical Decision Theory,* Cambridge, Mass.: MIT Press.

Ramond, C. (1974), *The Art of Using Science in Marketing,* New York: Harper & Row.

Rao, V. and K. Cox (1978), *Sales Forecasting Methods: A Survey of Recent Developments,* Cambridge, Mass.: Marketing Science Institute, 167.

Rathmell, J. (1966), "What Is Meant by Services?" *Journal of Marketing,* 32 (October), 32–36.

Reed, S.F. (1972), "The Fit-Chart Approach to Corporate Diversification," *Mergers and Acquisition* (Summer), 17–32.

Richman, B.M. (1962), "A Rating Scale for Product Innovation," *Business Horizons,* 5 (Summer), 37–44.

Rink, D.R. (undated), "An Empirical Investigation of the Use of the PLC," Northern Illinois University Working Paper.

Robertson, T.S. (1971), *Innovative Behavior and Communication,* New York: Holt, Rinehart and Winston, 16–20.

Robicheck, A.A. and S.C. Myers (1965), *Optimal Financing Decisions,* Englewood Cliffs, N.J.: Prentice-Hall.

Robinson, P.J. (1981), "A Comparison of Pretest Market New Product Forecasting Models," in *New Product Forecasting: Models and Applications,* Y. Wind, V. Mahajan, and R.N. Cardozo (eds.), Lexington, Mass.: Lexington Books.

———, P. Farris, and Y. Wind (1967), *Industrial Buying and Creative Marketing,* Boston, Allyn and Bacon.

Robinson Associates, Inc. (1973), *The Future of Retailing,* Bryn Mawr, Pa.

Robinson, S.J.Q., R.E. Hickens, and D. Wade (1978), "The Directional Policy Tool for Strategic Planning," *Long Range Planning,* 11 (January), 2–8.

Robinson, V. and C. Lackhani (1975), "Dynamic Price Models for New Product Planning," *Management Science,* 21 (June), 1113–1132.

Rockwell Jr., W.F. (1968), "How to Acquire a Company," *Harvard Business Review,* 46 (September-October).

Rogers, E.M. (1962), *Diffusions and Innovations,* New York: The Free Press.

——— (1976), "New Product Adoption and Diffusion," *Journal of Consumer Research,* 2 (March), 290–230.

——— and F.F. Shoemaker (1971), *Communication of Innovations: A Cross-Cultural Approach,* New York: Collier McMillan Ltd.

——— and J. Stanfield (1968), "Adoption and Diffusion of New Products: Emerging Generalizations and Hypotheses," in *Applications of the Sciences in Marketing Management,* F. Bass et al. (eds.), New York: John Wiley, 227–50.

——— and P.C. Thomas (1975), *Bibliography on the Diffusion of Innovations,* Ann Arbor: University of Michigan, Department of Population Planning.

Roman, K. and J. Maas (1976), *How to Advertise,* New York: St. Martin's Press.

Rothberg, R.R. (1976), *Corporate Strategy and Product Innovation,* New York: The Free Press.

Rothschild, W.E. (1976), *Putting It All Together: A Guide to Strategic Thinking*, New York: AMACOM.

———— (1979), *Strategic Alternatives: Selection, Development, and Implementation*, New York, AMACOM.

Rothwell, R. (1972), "Factors for Success in Industrial Innovations," from *Project SAPPHO—A Comparative Study of Success and Failure in Industrial Innovation*, Brighton, Sussex: SPRU.

Royal Dutch Shell Company (1975), *The Directional-Policy Matrix: A New Aid to Corporate Planning*, U.K.

Rummel, R.J. (1970), *Applied Factor Analysis*, Evanston, Il.: Northwestern University Press.

Ryans, A.F. (1974), "Estimating Consumer Preferences for a New Durable Brand in an Established Product Class," *Journal of Marketing Research*, 11 (November), 434–443.

Saaty, T.L. (1977), "A Scaling Method for Priorities in Hierarchical Structures," *Journal of Mathematical Psychology*, 15 (June), 234–281.

———— (1980), *The Analytic Hierarchy Process: Planning, Priority Setting, and Resource Allocation*, New York: McGraw-Hill.

———— and J.P. Bennett (1977), "A Theory of Analytical Hierarchies Applied to Political Candidacy," *Behavioral Science*, 2 (July), 237–245.

———— and ———— (1980), "Theoretical Aspects of Negotiating with Terrorism," in Arms Control and Disarmament Agency, Dr. R. Kupperman (ed.).

———— and R.S. Mariano (1979), "Rationing Energy to Industries: Priorities and Input-Output Dependence," *Energy Systems and Policy* (Winter).

Savage, C.W. (1970), The Measurement of Sensation: A Critique of Perceptual Psychophysics, Berkeley: University of California Press.

Scharf, C.A. (1971), *Acquisitions, Mergers, Sales, and Takeovers: A Handbook with Forms*, Englewood Cliffs, N.J.: Prentice-Hall, 84–113.

Schewing, E.E. (1974), *New Product Management*, Hinsdale, Il.: Dryden.

Schlaifer, R. (1959), *Probability and Statistics for Business Decisions*, New York: McGraw-Hill.

Schoeffler, S. (undated), "Nine Basic Findings on Business Strategy, the PIMS Letter on Business Strategy, No. 1"

————, R. Buzzell, and D. Heany (1974), "Impact of Strategic Planning on Profit Performance," *Harvard Business Review*, 52 (March-April), 137–145.

Schon, D. (1967), *Technology and Change*, New York: Dell.

Schotter, A. and G. Schwödiauer (1980), "Economics and the Theory of Games: A Survey," *Journal of Economic Literature*, 18 (June), 479–527.

Schramm, W. (1954), "How Communication Works," in *The Process and Effects of Mass Communication*, Urbana, Il.: University of Illinois Press.

Schultz, R.L. and J.A. Dodson Jr. (1978), "An Empirical Simulation Approach to Competition," in *Research in Marketing I*, J. Sheth (ed.), Greenwich, Conn.: JAI Press, 269–302.

———— and M.D. Henry (1979), "Implementing Decision Models," in *Marketing Decision Models*, R.L. Schultz and A.A. Zoltners (eds.), New York: Elsevier North Holland.

———— and D.P. Slevin (1975), "A Program of Research on Implementation," in *Implementing OR/MS*, New York: American Elsevier.

Schumpeter, J.G. (1961), *The Theory of Economic Development*, Harvard Economic Studies Volume 46, Cambridge, Mass.: Harvard University Press.

Selltiz, C. et al. (1959), *Research Methods in Social Relations*, New York: Holt, Rinehart & Winston.

Sharpe, W.F. (1970), *Portfolio Theory and Capital Markets*, New York: McGraw-Hill.

Shepard, H. (1967), "Innovation Resisting and Innovation Producing Organizations," in *Organization and Managerial Innovation*, L.W. Rowe and W.B. Boise (eds.), Pacific Palisades, Calif.: Goodyear.

Shephard, R.N. and P. Arabie (1979), "Additive

Clustering: Representation of Similarities as Combinations of Discrete Overlapping Properties," *Psychological Review*, 86, 87–123.

Sherif, C.N. and M. Sherif (1967), *Attitude, Ego-Involvement, and Change*, New York: John Wiley and Sons.

Shocker, A.D., D. Gensch, and L.S. Simon (1969), "Toward the Improvement of New Product Search and Screening," *Proceedings of the Fall Conference*, Chicago: American Marketing Association.

———— and V. Srinivasan (1974), "A Consumer-Based Methodology for the Identification of New Product Ideas," *Management Science*, 20 (February), 921–937.

———— and ———— (1977), "LINMAP (Version II): A FORTRAN IV Computer Program for Analyzing Ordinal Preference (Dominance) Judgments via Linear Programming Techniques and for Conjoint Measurement," *Journal of Marketing Research*, 14 (February), 101–103.

———— and ———— (1979), "Multiattribute Approaches for Product Concept Evaluation and Generation: A Critical Review," *Journal of Marketing Research*, 16 (May) 159–180.

Shoemaker, R. and R. Staelin (1976), "The Effects of Sampling Variation on Sales Forecasts for New Consumer Products," *Journal of Marketing Research*, 13 (May), 138–143.

Shostack, L.G. (1978), "The Service Marketing Frontier," in *Review of Marketing*, G. Zaltman and T. Bonoma (eds.), Pittsburgh: Graduate School of Business, University of Pittsburgh and the American Marketing Association.

Silk, A.J. (1969), "Preference and Perception Measures in New Product Development: An Exposition and Review," *Industrial Management Review*, 11 (Fall), 21–37.

———— and G.L. Urban (1978), "Pre-Test Market Evaluation of New Packaged Goods: A Model and Measurement Methodology," *Journal of Marketing Research*, 15 (May).

Simon, W. (1960), *The New Science of Management Decision*, New York: Harper & Row.

Smallwood, J.E. (1973), "The Product Life Cycle: A Key to Strategic Marketing Planning," *MSU Business Topics* (Winter), 29–35.

Smith, W.R. (1956), "Product Differentiation and Market Segmentation as Alternative Marketing Strategies," *Journal of Marketing*, 21 (July), 3–8.

Snedecor, G.W. and W.G. Cochran (1967), *Statistical Methods*, 6th edition, Ames, Iowa: Iowa State University Press.

Sonquist, J.A. and J.N. Morgan (1964), *The Detection of Interaction Effects*, Monograph No. 35, Ann Arbor, Michican: University of Michigan, Survey Research Center, Institute for Social Research.

————, E.L. Baker, and J.N. Morgan (1974), *Searching for Structure*, revised edition, Ann Arbor: Institute for Social Research, University of Michigan.

Souder, W.E. (1977), Executive Summary to *An Exploratory Study of the Coordinating Mechanisms between R&D and Marketing As An Influence on the Innovation Process*, study funded by the National Science Foundation, undertaken by the Technology Management Studies Group, School of Engineering, University of Pittsburgh.

———— (1981), "Disharmony between R&D and Marketing," *Industrial Marketing Management*, 10, 67–73.

Spencer, M., C. Clark, and P. Hoguet (1961), Business and Economic Forecasting: An Econometric Approach, Homewood, Il: Richard D. Irwin Inc.

Srinivasan, V. and A.D. Shocker (1973), "Linear Programming Techniques for Multidimensional Analysis of Preferences," *Psychometrika*, 38 (September), 337–370.

Stanton, F. (1967), "What Is Wrong with Test Marketing?" *Journal of Marketing*, 31 (April), 43–47.

Stanton, T. (1966), "Test Market Results Are Clouded by 'Spoiler' Tactics of Competitors," *The Wall Street Journal* (May 24).

Staudt, T. and D. Taylor (1970), *A Managerial Introduction to Marketing*, 2nd edition, Englewood Cliffs, N.J.: Prentice-Hall.

Steele, L.W. (1975), *Innovation in Big Business*, New York: Elsevier.

Stefflre, V. (1969), "Market Structure Studies: New Products for Old Markets and New Markets (Foreign) for Old Products," in *Applications of the Sciences in Marketing*, Bass, King, and Pessemier, eds., New York: John Wiley and Sons, 251–268.

―――――― (1971), *New Products and New Enterprises: A Report on an Experiment in Applied Social Science*, Irvine, Calif.: University of California.

Steiner, G. (1965), *The Creative Organization*, Chicago: The University of Chicago Press.

―――――― (1969), *Top Management Planning*, London: MacMillan.

Stern, L.W. (1967), "Acquisitions: Another Viewpoint," *Journal of Marketing*, 31 (July), 39–46.

Stevens, S.S. (1975), *Psychophysics: An Introduction to Its Perceptual, Neural, and Social Prospects*, New York: John Wiley.

Stewart, M. (1957), "Resistance to Technological Change in Industry," *Human Organization*, 16 (Fall), 36–39.

Stibal, M.E. (1977), "Disco—Birth of a New Marketing System," *Journal of Marketing*, 41 (October), 82–88.

Stigler, S.P. (1961), "The Economics of Information," *Journal of Political Economy*, 69 (June), 213–225.

Stone, G.P. (1954), "City Shoppers and Urban Identification: Observations on the Social Psychology of City Life," *American Journal of Sociology*, 60, 36-45.

Stonier, A.W. and D.C. Hague (1957), *A Textbook of Economic Theory*, New York: Wiley.

Strategic Planning Institute (1977), *The PIMS Program: Selected Findings*, Cambridge, Mass., brochure.

Sumner, M. and D. Marquis (1969), *Successful Industrial Innovations*, Washington, D.C.: NSF 69–17, U.S. Government Printing Office.

Swalm, R.O. (1966), "Utility Theory—Insight into Risk Taking," *Harvard Business Review*, 44 (November-December), 123–138.

Taha, H.A. (1972a), "A Balasian-Based Algorithm for Zero-One Polynomial Programming," *Management Science*, 18 (February), B–328–343.

―――――― (1972b), "Further Improvements in the Polynomial Zero-One Algorithm," *Management Science*, 18 (October), 226–227.

Talley Jr., W.J. (1964), "Profiting from the Declining Product," *Business Horizons* (Spring), 77–84.

Tarde, G. (1962), *The Laws of Imitation*, Clousestor.

Tatsuoka, M.M. (1970), *Discriminant Analysis: The Study of Group Differences*, Champain, Il.: Institute for Personality and Ability Testing.

Tauber, E.M. (1972a), "What is Measured by Concept Testing?" *Journal of Advertising Research*, 12.

―――――― (1972b), "HIT: Heuristic Ideation Technique—A Systematic Procedure for New Product Search," *Journal of Marketing*, 36 (January), 58–70.

―――――― (1975), "Discovering New Product Opportunities with Problem Inventory Analysis," *Journal of Marketing*, 39 (January), 67–70.

―――――― (1977), "Forecasting Sales Prior to Test Market," *Journal of Marketing*, 41 (January), 80-84.

―――――― (1981), "The Utilization of Concept Testing for New Product Forecasting: Traditional vs. Multiattribute Approaches," in Wind, Mahajan, and Cardozo (1981).

Taylor, D., P. Berry, and G. Block (1958), "Does Group Participation When Using Brainstorming Facilitate or Inhibit Creative Thinking," *Administrative Science Quarterly*, 3, 23–47.

Taylor, V.W. (1977), "A Striking Characteristic of Innovators," *Journal of Marketing Research*, 14 (February), 104–107.

Technology Assessment & Forecast (1979), Ninth report of the Patent and Trademark Office, U.S. Department of Commerce (March).

Telchrowe, D., A.A. Robicheck, and M. Montalbano (1965), "An Analysis of Criteria for Investment Financing Decisions under Certainty," *Management Science* (November).

Thompson, J.D. (1967), *Organizations in Action*, New York: McGraw-Hill.

―――――― and W.J. McEwen (1958), "Organizational Goals and Environment: Goal Setting as an Interaction Process," *American Sociological Review*, 23, 23–31.

Thurston, L.L. (1959), *The Measurement of Values*, Chicago: University of Chicago Press.

Toffler, A. (1970), *Future Shock*, New York: Random House.

Trout and Ries (1972), "The Positioning Era Cometh," *Advertising Age*.

Tversky, A. (1972), "Choice by Elimination," *Journal of Mathematical Psychology* (November), 341–367.

Tull, D.S. (1967), "Relationships of Actual and Predicted Sales and Profits in New Product Introductions," *Journal of Business*, 40 (July), 233–250.

Twedt, D.W. (1973), *A Survey of Marketing Research*, Chicago: American Marketing Association.

Udell, G.G. and K.G. Baker (1977), "A Systematic Approach to New Product Evaluation," Working Paper, Innovation Center, University of Oregon.

Uhl, K. and G. Upah (1977), "The Marketing of Services: A Set of Propositions," paper presented at the Macromarketing Theory Seminar, University of Colorado, Boulder.

Urban, G.L. (1967), "SPRINTER: A Tool for New Product Decision Makers," *Industrial Management Review*, 8 (Spring), 43–55.

_____ (1968), "A New Product Analysis and Decision Model," *Management Science*, 14 (April), 490–517.

_____ (1969a), "New Product Growth Model for Consumer Durables," *Management Science*, (January), 215–227.

_____ (1969b), "SPRINTER MOD I: A Basic New Product Analysis Model," reprinted from a Sloan School of Management Working Paper, MIT, Cambridge, Mass. Paper presented at the 1969 AMA Businessman's Meeting in Atlanta (June 17).

_____ (1970), "SPRINTER MOD III: A Model for the Analysis of New Frequently Purchased Consumer Products," *Operations Research*, 18 (September), 805–855.

_____ (1975), "PERCEPTOR: A Model for Product Positioning," *Management Science*, (April), 858–871.

_____ and J.R. Hauser (1980), *Design and Marketing of New Products*. Englewood Cliffs, N.J.: Prentice-Hall.

_____ and R. Karash (1971), "Evolutionary Model Building," *Journal of Marketing* Research, (February), 62–66.

Utterback, J. (1971), "The Process of Innovation: A Study of the Origination and Development of Ideas for New Scientific Instruments, *IEEE Transactions on Engineering Management* (November).

Vanderwicken, P. (1974), "P&G's Secret Ingredient," *Fortune* (July), 75–79, 164, 166.

VanHorne, J.C. (1977), *Financial Management and Policy*, 4th edition, Englewood Cliffs, N.J.: Prentice-Hall.

Vidale, M.L. and H.B. Wolfe (1957), "An OR Study of Sales Response to Advertising," *Operations Research*, 5 (June), 370–381.

von Hippel, E. (1977), "Transferring Process Equipment Innovations from User-Innovators to Equipment Manufacturing Firms," *R&D Management* (October).

_____ (1978), "Successful Industrial Products from Customer Ideas," *Journal of Marketing*, 42 (January), 39–49.

Vroom, V.H., L.D. Grant, and T.S. Cotton (1969), "The Consequences of Social Interaction in Group Problem Solving," *Organizational Behavior and Human Performance*, 4, 77–95.

Wakefield, B.R. (1965), "Mergers and Acquisitions," *Harvard Business Review*, 43 (September-October).

Walker, A.H. and J.W. Lorsch (1968), "Organizational Choice: Product vs. Function," *Harvard Business Review*, 46 (November-December), 129–138.

The Wall Street Journal (1962), "More Companies Drop Slower—Moving Goods to Improve Earnings (August 9).

_____ (1973), "An Untimely End: How a New Product Was Brought to Market Only to Flop Miserably" (January 5), 6.

Wang, Y. (1964), "Critical Path Analysis for New Product Planning," *Journal of Marketing,* 28 (October), 53–59.

Watson, G. (1973), "Resistance to Change," in *Processes and Phenomena of Social Change,* G. Zaltman (ed.), New York: Wiley-Interscience.

Webb, E.J., D.T. Campbell, R.D. Schwartz, and L. Sechrest (1966), *Unobtrusive Measures: Nonreactive Research in the Social Sciences,* Chicago: Rand-McNally & Co.

Weber, J.A. (1976), *Growth Opportunity Analysis,* Reston, Va.: Reston Publishing Company.

Weisberg, S. (1980), *Applied Regression,* New York: John Wiley & Sons.

Weston, J.F. (1973), "Investment Decisions Using the Capital Asset Pricing Model," *Financial Management,* 2 (Spring), 25–33.

Wilson, A. (1969), "Industrial Marketing Research in Britain," *Journal of Marketing Research,* 6 (February), 15–28.

Williams, D.J. (1969), "A Study of a Decision Model for R&D Project Selection," *Operations Research Quarterly,* 20 (September), 361–373.

Wind, Y. (1971), "A Reward-Balance Model of Buying Behavior in Organizations," in *New Essays in Marketing Theory,* G. Fisk (ed.), Boston: Allyn and Bacon, 206–217.

———— (1973), "A New Procedure for Concept Evaluation," *Journal of Marketing,* 37 (October), 2–11.

———— (1975), "Product Portfolio: A New Approach to the Product Mix Decision," in *Combined Proceedings,* Ronald C. Curhan (ed.), Chicago: American Marketing Association.

———— (1977a), "Brand Choice," in *Selected Aspects of Consumer Behavior,* R. Ferber (ed.), Washington, D.C.: U.S. Government Printing Office, 235–258.

———— (1977b), "Brand Loyalty and Vulnerability," in *Consumer and Industrial Buying Behavior,* A.G. Woodside, J.N. Sheth, and P.D. Bennett (eds.), New York: Elsevier North Holland, 313–319.

———— (1977c) "The Perception of the Firm's Competitive Position," in *Behavioral Models for Market Analysis: Foundations for Marketing Action,* F. Nicosia and Y. Wind (eds.), Hinsdale, Il.: The Dryden Press.

———— (1977d), "Research for Multinational Product Policy," in *Multinational Product Management,* W.J. Keegan and C.S. Mayer (eds.), Chicago: American Marketing Association, 165–184.

———— (1978a), "Issues and Advances in Segmentation Research," *Journal of Marketing Research,* 15 (August), 317–337.

———— (1978b), "Organizational Buying Behavior," *Review of Marketing* Volume I, 160–193.

———— (1978c), "New Developments in Conjoint Analysis," paper presented at the 25th Annual Midwest Conference of the American Statistical Association (March).

———— (1978d), "Organizational Buying Center: A Research Agenda," in *Organizational Buying Behavior,* T.l Bonoma and G. Zaltman (eds.), Chicago: American Marketing Association, 67–76.

———— (1979a), "A Research Program for a Marketing Guided Approach to Mergers and Acquisitions," *Proceedings,* Chicago: American Marketing Association.

———— (1979b), "Product-Market Planning Models: Concepts, Techniques, and Needed Development," in *Analytic Approaches to Product and Marketing Planning,* A. Shocker (ed.), Cambridge, Mass.: Marketing Science Institute, 39–66.

———— (1980), "Going to Market: Some New Twists," *The Wharton Magazine* (Spring), 34–39.

———— (1981), "Marketing and Other Business Functions," in *Research in Marketing,* Volume 5, Sheth (ed.), Greenwich, Conn.: JAI Press, pp. 237–264.

———— and R.N. Cardozo (1974), "Industrial Marketing Segmentation," *Industrial Marketing Management,* 3 (March), 153–165.

———— and H.J. Claycamp (1976), "Planning Product Line Strategy: A Matrix Approach," *Journal of Marketing,* 40 (January), 2–9.

———— and J. Denny (1974), "Multivariate Analysis of Variance in Research on the Effectiveness of TV Commercials," *Journal of Marketing Research,* 11 (May), 136–142.

———— and S.P. Douglas (1981), "International Portfolio Analysis and Strategy: The Challenge of the 80s," *Journal of International Business Studies* (Spring).

———— and J. Goldhar (1977), "Innovation and the R&D-Marketing Interface," paper presented at the TIMS/ORSA Conference.

————, J.F. Grashof, and J.D. Goldhar (1978), "Market Based Guidelines for Design of Industrial Products," *Journal of Marketing,* 24 (July).

————, P.E. Green, and A.K. Jain (1973), "Higher Order Factor Analysis in Classification of Psychographic Variables," *Journal of the Market Research Society,* 15, 224–232.

———— and D. Gross (1979), "An Analytical Hierarchy Approach to the Allocation of Resources within a Target Product/Market/ Distribution Portfolio," paper presented at the ORSA/TIMS Workshop on Market Measurement and Analysis, Stanford University (March 26–28).

————, S. Jolly, and A. O'Connor (1975), "Concept Testing as Input to Strategic Marketing Simulations," in *Proceedings of the 58th International AMA Conference,* E. Mazzie (ed.), Chicago: American Marketing Association, 120–124.

———— and D. Learner (1979), "A Note on the Measurement of Purchase Data: Surveys vs. Purchase Diaries," *Journal of Marketing Research,* 16 (February), 39–47.

———— and V. Mahajan (1981a), "Designing Product and Business Portfolios," *Harvard Business Review,* 59 (January-February), 155–165.

———— and ———— (1981b), "Market Share: Concepts, Findings, and Directions for Future Research," *Review of Marketing,* Volume 2.

———— (1982), *Portfolio Analysis and Strategy,* Reading, Mass.: Addison-Wesley, forthcoming.

————, V. Mahajan, and R. Cardozo (eds.) (1981), *New Product Forecasting: Models and Applications,* Lexington, Mass.: Lexington Books.

———— and H. Perlmutter (1977), "On the Identification of Frontier Issues in Multinational Marketing," *Columbia Journal of World Business,* 12 (Winter) 131–139.

———— and P.J. Robinson (1972), "Product Positioning: An Application of Multidimensional Scaling," in *Attitude Research in Transition,* R.I. Haley (ed.), Chicago: American Marketing Association, 155–175.

———— and T. Saaty (1980), "Marketing Applications of the Analytic Hierarchy Process," *Management Science* 26 (July), 641–658.

———— and R. Thomas (eds.) (1979), *Advances in Organizational Buying Research: The Case of Acquisition of Scientific and Technical Information,* Washington, D.C.: National Science Foundation.

———— and ———— (1980), "Conceptual and Methodological Issues in Organizational Buying Behavior," *European Journal of Marketing,* 14, 239–263.

———— and T. Tyebjee (1977), "On the Use of Attitude Research in Product Policy," in *Moving A Head with Attitude Research,* Y. Wind (ed.), Chicago: American Marketing Association, 147–156.

Winer, B.J. (1971), *Statistical Principals in Experimental Design,* 2nd edition, New York: McGraw-Hill.

Wittink, D.R. and D. Montgomery (1979), "Predictive Validity of Tradeoff Analysis for Alternative Segmentation Schemes," *Proceedings of the American Marketing Association Educators' Conference,* Minneapolis (August).

Wong, Y. (1964), "Critical Path Analysis for New Product Planning," *Journal of Marketing,* 28 (October), 53–59.

Wright, R.V.L. (1978), "A System for Managing Diversity," in *Marketing Management and Administrative Action,* S.H. Britt and H.W. Boyd Jr. (eds.), New York: McGraw-Hill.

Wylen, D.W. (1978), "New Product Failure—Maybe It's Not Just a Marketing Problem," Booz, Allen & Hamilton, Inc., brochure.

Yankelovich, Skelly and White (1978), *Laboratory Test Market: History of Performance—1968-1978,* New York, in-house publication.

Young, F.W. and W.S. Torgenson (1967), "TORSCA, A Fortran IV Program for Shephard-Kruska Multidimensional Scaling Analysis," *Behavioral Science*, 12, 498.

Zaltman, G. (1967), *Marketing: Contributions from the Behavioral Sciences*, New York: Harcourt, Brace & World.

————, R. Duncan, and J. Holbek (1973), *Innovations and Organizations*, New York: John Wiley & Sons.

Zarecor, William D. (1975), "High Technology Product Planning," *Harvard Business Review*, 53 (January-February), 108–115.

Zeltner, H. (1977), "When Should You Market Test? Five Guides Help You Decide," *Advertising Age* (January 17).

Zufryden, F.S. (1977), "A Conjoint Measurement-Based Approach for Optimal New Product Design and Market Segmentation," in *Analytic Approaches to Product and Market Planning*, A.D. Shocker (ed.), *Proceedings of the AMA/MSI Workshop at the University of Pittsburgh*, Cambridge, MA: Marketing Science Institute, 100–114, November).

———— (1978), "An Empirical Evaluation of a Composite Heterogeneous Model of Brand Choice and Purchasing Time Behavior," *Management Science*, 24 (March), 761–773.

———— (1979), "ZIPMAP—A Zero-One Integer Programming Model for Market Segmentation and Product Positioning," *Journal of Operational Research Society*, 30, 63–70.

———— (1980), "A Multivariate Stochastic Model of Brand Choice and Market Behavior," in *Research in Marketing*, Vol. 3, J.N. Sheth (ed.), Greenwich: CT: JAI Press, pp. 273–303.

Index

Index

Galbraith, 493, 512
Gale, 117, 531
Game theory, 39
Gamma–Poisson formulation, 451
Gap analysis, 258–260
Generalizability, 24
Gerbner, G., 281
Gerlach, J.T., 218
Gerstenfeld, A., 272, 485
Gestalt concept, 10, 26, 78
Global environment, 179
GNP, 186
Golabi, I., 334
Goldhar, J., 553
Gompertz curve, 50
Good Housekeeping seal of approval, 356, 370
Good will, 470
Government attitudes, 31
Government organizations, 555–556
Greco-Latin square, 361, 362, 415
Green, P.E., 20, 22, 33, 39, 74, 83, 91, 101, 103, 139, 158, 162, 163, 215, 283, 291, 352, 370, 371, 441, 460, 577
Greene, J.D., 443
Griliches, Z., 439
Grocery Manufacturers Association, 208
Gross, I., 64
Group ideation, 273
Group vs. individual creativity, 252–253
Growth function, 50
Growth maturity, 46
Growth opportunity analysis, 267, 268
Growth/share matrix, 110, 119–121, 552
Growth stage of product life cycle, 47–49, 53
Guarantees, 369
Guzzardi, W., Jr., 185

Haber, R.N., 368
Haley, R.I., 283, 294, 401, 402
Hamburg, M., 439
Hamelman, P.W., 538
Handbook of Consumer Motivation, 253
Hartley, R., 465
Hawthorne effect, 512
Hazardous Substances Labeling Act, 183
Helmer, O., 195
Henderson, P.L., 415
Hendry model, 76, 77
Herniter, J.D., 38, 439, 444

Hertz, D.B., 41, 318, 320, 432
Heuristic ideation technique (HIT), 265, 266
Hierarchical clustering analysis, 84, 85, 89, 99
Hierarchy of objectives, 156
Hilgard, E., 79
Hill, R., 489
Hinkle, J.R., 51
HIT, *see* Heuristic ideation technique
Hlavacek, J.D., 489
Holbrook, M.B., 70
Holton, R.H., 70, 73
Home computers, 190
Hopkins, D.S., 208, 481, 513
Horngren, C.T., 12
Housing and Urban Development (HUD), 185
Howard, J.A., 33, 70
HUD, *see* Housing and Urban Development
Hudson Institute, 193, 194, 199
Hughes, G.D., 401, 402
Hurdle rates, 315, 317

Idiosyncratic models, 540
Image, 78, 227, 230, 304, 371, 405, 470, 575
    see also Consumers, perceptions of
IMO, *see* Intermediate marketing organizations
Income tax, 316
Independent inventors, 264
Individual vs. group creativity, 252–253
INDSCAL model, 162, 345, 346
Industrial products, 548, 551–553
    classification of, 68–70
Informal organization, 473
Information component of packaging, 356
Information management, 574–575
Infrequently purchased consumer goods, 548–550
In-home tests, 342, 418–422
Innovation, 11
Innovation Center, University of Oregon, 305
Innovations, 269
Innovative maturity, 46
Innovative new products, 240–242
Innovator characteristics, 28–29
Input/output analysis, 68, 70, 189
Institute for Motivational Research, 253
Intellectual blocks to creativity, 250
Intellectual characteristics of creative persons, 250–251
Intention to buy (ITB) scores, 279, 298, 299
Interactive decision models, 41–43